Morphology
and Its Relation to Phonology and Syntax

Morphology
and Its Relation to
Phonology
and
Syntax

edited by
Steven G. Lapointe
Diane K. Brentari
Patrick M. Farrell

CSLI Publications
Center for the Study of Language and Information
Stanford, California

Copyright © 1998
CSLI Publications
Center for the Study of Language and Information
Leland Stanford Junior University
Printed in the United States
02 01 00 99 98   5 4 3 2 1

Library of Congress Cataloging-in-Publication Data

Morphology and its relation to phonology and syntax / edited by Steven G. Lapointe,
Diane K. Brentari, and Patrick M. Farrell.

p.   cm.

Papers presented at a workshop held May 5–7, 1995, University of California, Davis.
Includes bibliographical references and index.

Contents: The suffix *-ize* in English / Rochelle Lieber—Deriving passive without theta
roles / Hagit Borer—The functions of voice markers in the Philippine languages / Peter
Sells—On the autonomy of compounding morphology / Jerrold M. Sadock—Identity
avoidance in phonology and morphology / Moira Yip—Impoverishment theory and
morphosyntactic markedness / Rolf Noyer—Interfaces : explanation of allomorphy
and the architecture of grammars / David M. Perlmutter—Level (non)ordering in
recursive morphology : evidence from Turkish / Sharon Inkelas and C. Orhan
Orgun—Isomorphism and monotonicity / Mark Aronoff.

ISBN 1-57586-113-5 (alk. paper).
ISBN 1-57586-112-7 (pbk. : alk. paper)

1. Grammar, Comparative and general—Morphology—Congresses. 2. Grammar,
Comparative and general—Phonology—Congresses. 3. Grammar, Comparative and
general—Syntax—Congresses. I. Lapointe, Steven, 1952–   . II. Brentari, Diane.
III. Farrell, Patrick, 1953–   .
P241.M65   1998
415—dc21   97-39330
CIP

∞ The acid-free paper used in this book meets the minimum requirements of the
American National Standard for Information Sciences—Permanence of Paper for
Printed Library Materials, ANSI Z39.48-1984.

CSLI was founded early in 1983 by researchers from Stanford University, SRI International, and
Xerox PARC to further research and development of integrated theories of language, information,
and computation. CSLI headquarters and CSLI Publications are located on the campus of
Stanford University.

CSLI Publications reports new developments in the study of language, information, and
computation. In addition to lecture notes, our publications include monographs, working papers,
revised dissertations, and conference proceedings. Our aim is to make new results, ideas, and
approaches available as quickly as possible. Please visit our web site at
http://csli-www.stanford.edu/publications/
for comments on this and other titles, as well as for changes and corrections by the author and
publisher.

Contents

Authors and Discussion Participants

MARK ARONOFF, Professor, Department of Linguistics, State University of New York, Stony Brook.

MARK C. BAKER, Associate Professor, Department of Linguistics, McGill University.

HAGIT BORER, Professor, Department of Linguistics, University of Massachusetts, Amherst and Department of Linguistics, University of Southern California.

DIANE BRENTARI, Associate Professor, Department of Audiology and Speech Sciences, Purdue University.

ANDREW CARSTAIRS-MCCARTHY, Associate Professor, Department of Linguistics, University of Canterbury, New Zealand.

PATRICK FARRELL, Associate Professor, Linguistics Program, University of California, Davis.

DONKA FARKAS, Associate Professor, Board of Studies in Linguistics, University of California, Santa Cruz.

SHARON INKELAS, Associate Professor, Department of Linguistics, University of California, Berkeley.

RICHARD D. JANDA, Assistant Professor, Department of Linguistics, University of Chicago.

STEVEN G. LAPOINTE, Associate Professor, Linguistics Program, University of California, Davis.

WILL LEBEN, Professor, Department of Linguistics, Stanford, University.

ROCHELLE LIEBER, Professor, Department of English, University of New Hampshire.

ROLF NOYER, Assistant Professor, Department of Linguistics, University of Pennsylvania.

C. ORHAN ORGUN, Lecturer, Linguistics Program, University of California, Davis.

DAVID M. PERLMUTTER, Professor, Department of Linguistics, University of California, San Diego.

JERROLD M. SADOCK, Professor, Department of Linguistics, University of Chicago.

PETER SELLS, Associate Professor, Department of Linguistics, Stanford University.

MARGARET SPEAS, Associate Professor, Department of Linguistics, University of Massachusetts, Amherst.

ANDREW SPENCER, Senior Lecturer , Department of Language and Linguistics, University of Essex, UK.

GREGORY STUMP, Associate Professor of English and Linguistics, Department of English, University of Kentucky.

MOIRA YIP, Professor, Department of Linguistics, University of California, Irvine.

Introduction

STEVEN G. LAPOINTE, DIANE K. BRENTARI, AND PATRICK M. FARRELL

Over the past twenty years, numerous proposals have been made concerning the role of morphology in the grammar and its interactions with syntax and phonology. These proposals have offered a range of answers to such fundamental questions as the following:

- How are morphological rules and representations like or unlike those in the syntax?
- How are they like or unlike those in the phonology?
- To the extent that morphological rules and representations are distinct from those in the other components, what *are* they like, and how do they interact with information in the syntax and the phonology?

Given the centrality of morphology to the study of grammar, the answers that we ultimately provide for such questions will have a profound effect on how we view the various parts of a grammar and their interactions.

It is against this background that the Linguistics Program at the University of California, Davis, hosted a workshop-style conference on May 5 – 7, 1995. The purpose of the conference was to bring together a number of researchers who have been working on these topics in different theoretical frameworks, to address some of the issues concerning the role of morphology in the grammar and to determine where at least partial agreement on these issues might be reached. The meeting was organized so as to try to maximize discussion and interaction among the participants. The first day was devoted to morphology-syntax issues and the second day to topics on the morphology-phonology interface. Only two formal paper presentations were scheduled in each morning or afternoon session on the first two days, in order to allow participants time to concentrate on the particular issues being examined in each case. Each paper presentation was followed by a formal commentary and an informal discussion period. The morning of the third day was devoted to a broader discussion of some of the topics raised during the earlier sessions. By including discussion periods after each formal paper and commentary, and by including a longer discussion period on the third day, we hoped to create an opportunity for the participants to engage in a stimulating and thoughtful dialogue on the topics we were examining.

The present volume represents the results of the Davis conference. We have arranged the papers and commentaries in the order in which they were presented at the meeting; in addition, we have included transcripts of portions of the discussion sessions. The rationale for this organization is to try to capture for the reader both the content and the tone of the interchanges which occurred during the meeting. By doing this, we hope to present to the reader a reasonably faithful record of the events that transpired and the ways in which ideas mentioned at one point in the meeting triggered ideas and discussion at later points. Few proceedings volumes aim at providing the reader with an appreciation of what actually occurred during a conference, and so we are hoping that the present collection will prove to be a unique document along these lines.

Shelly Lieber leads off with a study of the English causative morpheme *-ize*. She argues that the four meanings which she identifies with this suffix involve overlapping Lexical Conceptual Structures (LCSs) in the sense of Jackendoff 1990 and much subsequent work. She concludes from this that part of the meaning of this morpheme is fixed and determinate, while the remainder is indeterminate and subject to pragmatic inference. She goes on to argue against several alternative approaches to the meaning of *-ize*, including (a) a strictly syntactic analysis like the one which she proposed in her 1992 book (Lieber 1992), (b) a purely argument structure based account like that of Williams 1981, and (c) a multi-level movement approach involving the Uniform Thematic Assignment Hypothesis (UTAH; Baker 1988) of the sort proposed by Hale and Keyser 1993. Instead, Lieber argues that her analysis of *-ize* supports a linking account like that of Bresnan and Kanerva 1989 and Jackendoff 1990. In his commentary on Lieber's paper, Patrick Farrell argues that a UTAH-plus-incorporation approach to *-ize* affixation of the sort proposed by Hale and Keyser (as well as a similar approach to N —> V conversion and N incorporation) does not suffer from some of the problems raised by Lieber, since the D-structures required by such an account are well within the range of expected underlying structures on this approach. Instead, Farrell suggests that the problem with this general view is that it leads us to expect a range of possible D-structures which are unattested, and hence this approach leads to incorrect predictions in other kinds of cases.

In the next formal paper, Hagit Borer argues for a novel view of argument structure changing rules within the general Principles and Parameters framework (P&P; Chomsky 1981, 1986). The basic idea of her approach is that grammatical function changes are not a matter of the direct manipulation of argument structure or the mapping between argument structure and syntactic structure. Rather, arguments are listed in an unordered set in the lexical representations of Vs, functional categories in syntactic structures encode aspectual notions of various sorts—in particular, a result state—and the various possibilities for Case assignment and interpretation of NPs (or DPs) result from movement of those phrases to the SPEC positions governed by the aspectual functional categories. Borer shows how unaccusative/unergative differences and properties of verbal vs. adjectival passives can be treated within this approach. Andrew Spencer counters in his commentary that there are at least four potential problems with Borer's general approach to relation-changes via movement through the SPECs of aspectual phrases. First, the analogy that she draws between

English bare plural objects and Finnish partitive-marked objects is only partial, as there are cases of non-eventive predicates in Finnish which can take either accusative or partitive objects, a situation that is not expected on Borer's account. Second, Spencer points out problems for the aspect phrase account of passives posed by Russian imperfective -*sja* passives. Third, he notes problems raised by the antipassive construction in Chukchee, where the demoted object in the antipassive must pass through the appropriate aspectual SPEC position, even though it is supposed to be as "trapped" inside the VP as the demoted subject NP in English passives is. Finally, he observes a number of features of the V agreement system of Koryak, which involve overlapping nominative/accusative (NOM/ACC) and ergative/absolutive (ERG/ABS) features in both the prefixal and suffixal V agreement markers, a type of split ergativity that cannot be handled in an obvious way on the movement-through-SPEC approach.

Continuing on the topic of the representation of arguments and their morphological reflexes, Peter Sells reanalyzes voice markers and the linked nominal prefixes in Tagalog and other Philippine languages. He considers several recent approaches to these elements, especially Guilfoyle, Hung, and Travis' 1992 P&P approach involving multiple functional categories, SPEC positions, and movement, and Kroeger's 1993 lexical mapping account. After discussing numerous problems with these earlier analyses, Sells proposes a novel account in which (a) the subject is not an overt NP or DP, but rather is a null *pro*, (b) the NP marked with a NOM prefix is actually an adjunct phrase linked to the *pro*, and (c) voice marking on the V determines which of its arguments bears the NOM prefix and so gets linked to the *pro* subject. Sells shows how a wide range of the split subject and topic properties in the Philippine languages follow from this account. On the other hand, Peggy Speas takes a rather different tack. Sells begins his paper by suggesting that because the Philippine languages lack true NOM/ACC or ERG/ABS properties, the voice systems of these languages form a third distinct type of system. Speas argues instead that standard views of the NOM/ACC and ERG/ABS systems are wrong. In particular, she argues that the notion that arguments are linked to specific syntactic positions with voice markers mediating those links is incorrect and that an approach like Borer's should be adopted. Once we adopt this view, Speas contends, the voice marking systems in the Philippine languages begin to look a lot less like a separate type of system.

In the final paper on morphology-syntax interactions, Jerry Sadock argues that compounding is a process that is independent from mechanisms of any other component of a grammar. After discussing the failure of various nonmorphological criteria that have previously been proposed for determining the properties of compounds, Sadock turns to a closer examination of compounding in Welsh and Hebrew. These historically unrelated languages show many typological similarities, which Sadock enumerates, but he goes on to argue that they exhibit distinct constructions for combining nominals, with Welsh employing a syntactic construction and Hebrew using morphological compounding. He ends by sketching an analysis of the two types, in the process offering an account of some of the puzzling differences in the details of the nominal-combining constructions of the two languages. In his commentary, Mark Baker takes exception to Sadock's general claim concerning the autonomy of compounding. Baker gives a number of reasons for being more optimistic about a syntactic movement analysis of English compounds along the lines of Sproat 1985 and Lieber 1992. He shows that under a functional categories-plus-movement approach the differences exhibited by the syntactic structures of Welsh and Hebrew can be exploited to account for the differences found in the nominal combining constructions of the two languages. He concludes by showing that the seven languages which obey his "Polysynthesis Parameter" (Baker 1996) exhibit substantially the same range of possible compounding types, underscoring along yet another dimension the grammatical commonalities of these languages.

In the first paper devoted to morphology-phonology interactions, Moira Yip discusses a wide range of cases involving avoidance of formally identical adjacent morphemes and function words and analyzes them in terms of Optimality Theory (OT; Prince and Smolensky 1993; McCarthy and Prince 1993). Her general approach to identity avoidance is to assume that the Obligatory Contour Principle (OCP; Leben 1973, McCarthy 1986, Yip 1988, Odden 1988, among others), viewed as a violable constraint, outranks MORPHDIS, a constraint proposed by McCarthy and Prince 1995 to disallow a single form from doing double duty as the realization of two distinct morphemes. Yip shows how well-known cases of haplology involving English plural + possessive (* -s + 's) and Mandarin perfective + current relevant state (* -le + -le) can be handled using this assumption. She goes on to apply this method in several cases involving interactions between the syntax and the morphology, including Mandarin double pronouns, classical Greek articles, the English double -ing constraint, and Hindi double object markers. Yip concludes by demonstrating how this approach to identity avoidance can shed light on cases of echo-word formation exhibited in Javanese habitual-repetitive reduplication. In her commentary, Diane Brentari offers two more cases of haplology from Choctaw, based on earlier work by Stemberger 1981, in support of Yip's OT approach to identity avoidance. Brentari observes that the constraint that seems to be at work in the cases at issue is probably not the OCP in general but rather a constraint corresponding to just that part of the OCP which regulates output contour representations. Such a constraint, which she dubs *REPEAT, needs to be parametrized for the prosodic or grammatical constituents affected and the relevant morpheme realization. Brentari notes that there is a heterogeneous group of strategies employed by individual languages to avoid haplology, and she closes by raising the issue of how to integrate constraints on phonological form with constraints on the occurrence of specific morphemes with specific shapes.

In the next formal paper, Rolf Noyer argues that the theory of Impoverishment rules—feature-deletion rules that apply before other spell-out rules in the theory of Distributed Morphology (Bonet 1991, Halle and Marantz 1993)—as originally formulated cannot account for the full range of possible morphological syncretisms. However, when it is augmented with a class of markedness-reducing feature-changing rules, the resulting extended theory of Impoverishment rules holds advantages over the alternative Referral Rule approach of Zwicky 1985 and Stump 1993. Noyer supports this contention through an extensive reanalysis of morphological neutralization in Nimboran, treated recently by Inkelas 1993. He ends by noting cases that may remain a problem for the extended theory of Impoverishment. Andrew Carstairs-McCarthy suggests to the contrary that Noyer's extended Impoverishment approach is less restrictive than it may at first seem, as it allows several kinds of syncretism which appear not to exist. Carstairs-McCarthy suggests a set of constraints on the lexical semantics of inflectional features which disallow the nonexistent kinds of syncretism which he raises, while also handling the first case of neutralization in Nimboran which Noyer analyzes. Carstairs-McCarthy also argues that this set of constraints correctly handles the pattern of syncretism found in definite vs. indefinite V paradigms in Hungarian and correctly excludes various nonexistent syncretisms in these paradigms, while again such cases pose problems for the extended Impoverishment approach. He ends by suggesting that the last two cases of neutralization in Nimboran may still require the use of Referral Rules, Noyer's arguments notwithstanding.

David Perlmutter argues in the next paper that OT can be used to provide insights into a set of well-known alternations in French involving a clash between grammatical gender and phonological requirements in the realization of prenominal modifiers (e.g., *ce* [sə] *choix* 'this choice,M' ~ *cette* [sɛt] *voix* 'this voice,F' ~ *cet* [sɛt] *été* 'this summer,M' ~ *ce été). The analysis hinges on the assumption that the syllable structure constraint ONSET (= "syllables have onsets") outranks the syntactic constraint requiring gender agreement in such forms. Perlmutter discusses problems with the traditional formulation of the restrictions at work here, motivating the need for a phonological constraint to dominate a syntactic one in the OT constraint hierarchy for French. He extends the analysis to show how the account fits in with a broader set of facts concerning liaison and elision involving French nominal modifiers. Perlmutter argues against several possible counteranalyses of the French facts involving lexical underspecification of features and the use of Lexical Blocking, and he closes by arguing that the proposed account leads to the conclusion that grammatical components are not as strictly modular as they have generally been assumed to be in generative work. In his comments, Rich Janda argues on the basis of an extensive array of dialectal and historical facts that the prenominal modifiers in French do not form a single class which consistently avoid hiatus with a following vowel-initial word and that a host of morphological, morphosyntactic, and syntactic factors seem to determine which of the suppletive forms is chosen in any given case. From this study, he concludes that an OT analysis like the one offered by Perlmutter (and the closely related account developed independently by Tranel 1994) fails primarily because it claims that a general phonological constraint (ONSET) is the single factor determining which suppletive forms are selected across the range of prenominal modifiers.

In the last formal paper, Sharon Inkelas and Orhan Orgun point to a number of problems that arise on the standard view of Lexical Phonology (Kiparsky 1982). They propose instead that each morphological construction is associated with its own distinct phonological effects, which they dub a COPHONOLOGY. Inkelas and Orhan show how the two main problems with Lexical Phonology that they identify—lexical economy, in which not all levels in the phonology are activated in the phonological derivation of a word, and looping, where forms are submitted to a level out of order—disappear on the cophonology approach. They then illustrate the utility of this approach by examining the complex interactions in Turkish of Sezer stems (an open class of mostly place names) with compounding, stress, and other phonological processes, and they demonstrate the problems faced by a standard Lexical Phonology analysis in accounting for these forms. While endorsing Inkelas and Orgun's general conclusions, Greg Stump argues that a realizational approach to morphological form that includes a device of metageneralization (Zwicky 1994, Stump 1995) is to be preferred. He contends in particular that the cophonology and metageneralization approaches differ along several dimensions, in particular, that a metageneralization can be posited only when there is a common feature of the outputs of more than one morphological rule, whereas the cophonology approach allows a cophonology to be associated with only a single morphological construction. Stump argues that the metageneralization approach is to be favored in terms of this difference, both in the specific case of the analysis of the Turkish Sezer stem forms analyzed by Inkelas and Orhan and more generally in cases involving generalizations about stem choice.

Mark Aronoff begins his general commentary on the morphology-phonology interface with some animated and entertaining remarks about methodology and the relations of grammatical components to one another. He then proposes that morphology should be viewed as a kind of grammatical "disease", because it typically involves the breaking of expected isomorphisms in the mapping across grammatical components, and hence it generally leads to unnatural and pathological interfacing. To illustrate this point, he works through an example concerning juncture strength in Tamil. He observes that a "healthy" system would exhibit a strictly monotonic increase in boundary strength when elements are combined, from the weakest (involving lexicalized, bound, derivational forms) to the strongest (involving phrase-level combinations), but that's not quite what we find in Tamil. Compounds in this language work in the expected way: those involving bound forms show weak juncture, while those involving free forms show strong juncture. Derivational affixes also come in two types, one with weak juncture and the other with strong juncture. However, inflectional suffixes take weak juncture exclusively, despite the fact that we would expect them to show strong juncture because of their interactions with word-external, phrasal elements. Aronoff draws the moral here that the "disease" of morphology is what leads to this nonmonotonic and unnatural mapping between components, and that this is a general property of morphology across languages.

Finally, Steven Lapointe uses his general commentary on the morphology-syntax boundary to tie the discussion back to issues raised in the earlier part of the conference by focusing on two broad questions about the interface between morphology and syntax: (a) Is head movement really needed in accounting for the morphosyntactic properties of phrases? and (b) Are the structural properties of compounds sufficiently like those of syntactic phrases that we can analyze compounds strictly in terms of syntactic mechanisms? In suggesting that the answers to both of these questions is "no", Lapointe observes for (a) that work by Borer 1991 and Speas 1991a,b eliminates much of the initial motivation behind positing head movement to account for inflectional properties of words. In the case of (b), he notes (echoing remarks made earlier by Sadock) that the initial N elements in English synthetic compounds have decidedly different properties from the direct object NPs of the corresponding Vs, suggesting that a different mechanism is involved in assigning theta roles in compounds. Further, he notes that the distributional properties of modifier phrases in English NPs are markedly distinct from those of the nonhead elements in N-N root compounds. Lapointe argues that such considerations indicate that the properties of compounds are not obviously derivable solely by syntactic means.

As is evident from this brief overview of the papers that follow, the conference participants did not come to a "grand synthesis" which everyone agreed was the correct way to view the interactions of morphology with the other grammatical components. In light of the range of theoretical perspectives that the participants brought to the discussions, it is not at all surprising that this should be the case. Nonetheless, several topics and themes tended to thread their way through the talks and discussion sessions over the course of the meeting. Perhaps most dramatically, Aronoff's comments on nonisomorphism between morphology and the other components of a grammar led in the general discussion session to a vigorous debate over the issue of what it means to say that some large percentage of the facts that are typically labeled as "morphology" can be accounted for by another component (phonology, syntax, semantics, or pragmatics) and that the remaining percentage of the facts cannot. During this extended interchange, some of the participants emphasized the large percentage of facts that can be accounted for by other components and so suggested that there is a great deal less for morphology to do than one might otherwise expect. Others focused on the remaining percentage as proof that a separate component of morphology really is needed. A third and smaller group voiced the opinion that redundancy across components is not necessarily a bad thing, and the fact that there is a large overlap between morphology and various other components does not automatically mean that there is no morphology. As this topic is a crucial one for all cross-component interactions in a grammar, it is not surprising that it occupied a great deal of the general discussion period.

A number of further points wound their way through the various discussion sessions. Thus, some of the questions raised in the general discussion about how much of morphology can be accounted for in other components echoed issues about the use of pragmatics in determining the meanings of derived forms in the discussion of the Lieber and Farrell papers at the beginning of the conference; issues about the extent to which syntax can account for the properties of compounds were addressed explicitly not only in Sadock's and Baker's papers and in the ensuing discussion, but also in Lapointe's commentary toward the end; the issue of where to draw the boundary between phonology and morphology came up in the discussions of both the Yip and Brentari papers and the Inkelas-Orgun and Stump talks. Numerous analytic problems were also explored in the discussions: How should we handle cases in which none of the potential output forms for a morpheme in a particular context are acceptable? What is the range of possible case marking systems, if we recognize the type represented by the Philippine languages is one distinct from, and not simply a variation on, the two standard types of NOM/ACC and ERG/ABS? What are the appropriate ways to handle the linearization of constituents? What are we to say about cases where the only evidence for positing a particular syntactic structure is the morpheme order, but the morphemes turn out to potentially appear in either order? Might distinctions between affixal and nonaffixal morphology still need to be maintained, even on a thoroughly realizational approach to morphological rules? And several broader issues about theory and methodology were touched on, including (a) What are some of the learnability issues in morphology (raised in the discussion after the Inkelas-Orgun and Stump papers and in the general discussion)? and (b) How do we know when we are dealing with phenomena in separate linguistic domains, whether we are distinguishing gender classes (as in the discussion about Romanian NEUTER N forms after the Noyer and Carstairs-McCarthy talks), or distinguishing grammatical components (as in the discussion about binding theories in the general discussion)? While general agreement was not reached on any of these topics at the conference, the participants certainly succeeded in their attempts to talk past their theoretical differences in order to engage in a frank, open, and remarkably collegial dialogue about these potentially quite contentious issues.

A few brief words need to be said about how the Discussion chapters were produced. We tape recorded nearly the entire conference. From those recordings, the first editor prepared reasonably faithful transcripts of the discussion sessions and then edited out the hems and haws, smoothed over the false starts and hesitations, and deleted portions which were either addressed directly in the formal papers and commentaries or were clearly off on a tangent. These changes led to the final versions presented here. At the end of the process, there were only six rather than the anticipated eight Discussion chapters. Because of a technical problem which was discovered only some time after the conference, there was no recording of the discussion of the Borer and Spencer papers, and at that point there was no way to reconstruct which of the participants had said what during that session. We very much regret the absence of that recording and the discussion chapter that would have appeared for those talks. In the case of the discussion after the Perlmutter and Janda papers, a clean recording does exist, but on inspection it turned out that all of the points that were raised and examined during that session were explicitly addressed in the final versions of the papers, and so a separate Discussion chapter in this case would have been redundant.

Finally, we wish to acknowledge our enormous debt of gratitude to all the people without whom the conference and this volume would not have been possible. First, we wish to thank the participants in the conference for their insights and good humor which resulted in a gathering that truly was, in Mark Aronoff's words, "a weekend in morphological paradise." We also wish to thank the participants for their cooperation and patience during each stage in this long process of organizing and hosting the conference and editing the proceedings volume. Thanks also to the people who served as moderators during the various sessions and did a wonderful job keeping the papers and the discussion sessions within the allotted time periods: Diane Brentari, Patrick Farrell, Larry Hyman, Almerindo Ojeda, Mary Schleppegrell, Lenora Timm, and Moira Yip. A number of linguistics students at UC Davis were an enormous help in the organization of the conference, both before and during the meeting, including Suporn Chenhansa, Ulrike Christofori, Mary DiDomenico, Paul Dilgard, Jeff Hobbs, Angela Foin, Gitti Lindner, Dave Lupien, Sarah Nielsen, Naoko Ogawa, Sharon Peter, and Lorri Lovett-Gill. We especially want to thank Catalin Kaser and Justin Spence for their help with the tape recordings and Alison Rukeyser for organizing the student volunteers and for managing the logistics at the conference site. Debra Dalke and Jeanne Hart provided able and efficient administrative support for the conference. Dikran Karagueuzian and Tony Gee at CSLI Publications deserve a special note of thanks for their support and editorial assistance in getting this volume published.

Finally, we wish to thank the College of Letters and Science at UC Davis, and in particular former Executive Associate Dean Al Harrison, for supporting our efforts by providing the funds that made the conference possible.

References

Baker, M. 1988. *Incorporation*. Chicago: University of Chicago Press.

Baker, M. 1996. *The Polysynthesis Parameter*. New York: Oxford University Press.

Bonet, E. 1991. *Morphology after Syntax: Pronominal Clitics in Romance*. Doctoral dissertation, MIT.

Borer, H. 1991. The Causative-Inchoative Alternation: A Case Study in Parallel Morphology. *The Linguistic Review* 8, 119-158.

Bresnan, J. and J. Kanerva. 1989. Locative Inversion in Chicewa: A Case Study of Factorization in Grammar. *Linguistic Inquiry* 20, 1-50.

Chomsky, N. 1981. *Lectures on Government and Binding*. Dordrecht: Foris Publications.

Chomsky, N. 1986. *Barriers*. Cambridge, MA: MIT Press.

Guilfoyle, E., H. Hung, and L. Travis. 1992. Spec of IP and Spec of VP: Two Subjects in Malayo-Polynesian Languages. *Natural Language and Linguistic Theory* 10, 375-414.

Hale, K. and S.J. Keyser. 1993. On Argument Structure and the Lexical Expression of Syntactic Relations. In K. Hale and S.J. Keyser, eds., *The View from Building 20: Essays in Honor of Sylvain Bromberger*, 53-110. Cambridge, MA: MIT Press.

Halle, M. and A. Marantz. 1993. Distributed Morphology and the Pieces of Inflection. In K. Hale and S.J. Keyser, eds., *The View from Building 20: Essays in Honor of Sylvain Bromberger*, 111-176. Cambridge, MA: MIT Press.

Halle, M. and A. Marantz. 1993. Distribute

Inkelas, S. 1993. Nimboran Position Class Morphology. *Natural Language and Linguistic Theory* 11, 559-624.

Jackendoff, R. 1990. *Semantic Structures*. Cambridge, MA: MIT Press.

Kiparsky, P. 1982. Lexical Morphology and Phonology. In I.S.-Yang, ed., *Linguistics in the Morning Calm*, 3-91. Seoul: Hanshin.

Kroeger, P. 1993. *Phrase Structure and Grammatical Relations in Tagalog*. Stanford, CA: CSLI Publications.

Leben, W. 1973. *Suprasegmental Phonology*. Doctoral dissertation, MIT.

Lieber, R. 1992. *Deconstructing Morphology: Word-Formation in Syntactic Theory*. Chicago: University of Chicago Press.

McCarthy, J. 1986. OCP Effects: Gemination and Antigemination. *Linguistic Inquiry* 17, 207-263.

McCarthy, J. and A. Prince. 1993. Prosodic Morphology I: Constraint Interaction and Satisfaction. Technical Report-3, Rutgers University Center for Cognitive Science.

McCarthy, J. and A. Prince. 1995. Faithfulness and Reduplicative Identity. In J. Beckman, L.W. Dickey, and S. Urbancyk, eds., *Papers in Optimality Theory*. *University of Massachusetts Occasional Papers* 18, 249-384. Amherst, MA: GLSA

Odden, D. 1988. AntiAntigemination and the OCP. *Linguistic Inquiry* 19, 451-475.

Prince, A. and P. Smolensky. 1993. Optimality Theory: Constraint Interaction in Generative Grammar. Technical Report-2, Rutgers University Center for Cognitive Science.

Speas, M. 1991a. Functional Heads and the Mirror Principle. *Lingua* 84, 181-214.

Speas, M. 1991b. Functional Heads and Inflectional Morphemes. *The Linguistics Review* 8, 389-417.

Sproat, R. 1985. *On Deriving the Lexicon*. Doctoral Dissertation, MIT.

Stemberger, J. 1981. Morphological Haplology. *Language* 57, 791-817.

Stump, G. 1993. On Rules of Referral. *Language* 69, 449-479.

Stump, G. 1995

Tranel, B. 1994. French Liaison and Elision Revisited: A Unified Account within Optimality Theory. *Linguistic Symposium on Romance Linguistics* 24.

Williams, E. 1981. Argument Structure and Morphology. *The Linguistic Review* 1, 81-114.

Yip, M. 1988. The Obligatory Contour Principle and Phonological Rules: A Loss of Identity. *Linguistic Inquiry* 19, 65-100.

Zwicky, A. 1985. How to Describe Inflection. *Proceedings of the Berkeley Linguistic Society*, 372-386. Berkeley, CA: Berkeley Linguistic Society.

Zwicky, A. 1994. Morphological Metageneralizations: Morphology, Phonology, and Morphonology. Paper presented at the Kentucky Foreign Language Conference, University of Kentucky, April, 1994.

The Suffix *-ize* in English: Implications for Morphology

ROCHELLE LIEBER

Causatives have long been of interest to both syntactic and morphological theory. There exists a vast literature (see especially Comrie 1976, Shibatani 1976, and Levin 1993 and references cited therein) exploring both *syntactic* (periphrastic) causatives like *make* and *let* in English and *faire* in French, and so-called *morphological* causatives like those that appear in many languages of the world, in which a morpheme attaches regularly to a verb stem to make a causative verb denoting the same action as the verbal base (Marantz 1984, Baker 1988, Hoffman 1991). There is also some attention paid to what some have called *lexical* causatives, that is, pairs like *kill* and *die* or the inherent causative/inchoative alternation in verbs like *break* or *open* in English. Most attention has been paid, in other words, to processes of causativization having to do with verbs, either free or bound, and not to derivational affixes creating causatives that attach to categories of base other than verb.[1] Such suffixes, among them *-ize*, and *-ify* in English, are both less productive and less regular in the meaning change that they effect than the causatives typically discussed in the literature, yet they are still in some measure regular and productive. Some of their irregularity clearly comes from the fact that they are category-changing. In this paper I will focus on one of these category-changing causative affixes, the suffix *-ize* in English. Surprisingly, a study of the affix *-ize* can tell us a number of things about current morphological theory, ranging from the role of lexical semantics in the grammar, too long neglected by generative morphologists, to the nature of the morphology-syntax interface. So while this paper will start out narrowly focussed on a single suffix in English, it will end by ranging quite widely over some of the major debates in current morphology.

What I propose to do in this paper is first to look closely at the suffix *-ize*, which henceforth I will refer to for lack of a better term as a *category-changing causative*, exploring its meaning in terms of Lexical Conceptual Structures (Jackendoff 1990, Pinker 1989). I will look at the LCS of *-ize* in relation to that of other verb-forming affixes in English and Dutch, considering the relationship between LCS and productivity. Later I will consider what category-changing

---

[1] An interesting example is the article by Nedyalkov and Silnitsky (1973) which gives quite a thorough typology of causatives without mentioning category-changing affixes like *-ize*. One recent article which does not neglect category-changing causative affixes is Levin and Rappaport Hovav 1994.

causatives like -*ize* tell us about larger issues in morphological theory, specifically about the linking between LCS and argument structure, about incorporation models of morphology like that in Hale and Keyser 1993 and about theories of morphology that adhere to the Separation Hypothesis of Beard (1987, 1988).

Since the discussion will begin with a study in lexical semantics, I must set out here some of my assumptions about semantic representation. I will be assuming roughly the framework of semantic decomposition of verbs developed by Jackendoff in a series of works (1983, 1987, 1990), in which verbal meanings are represented as a hierarchically organized frame of basic verbal semantic primitives (Events like CAUSE, GO, and INCH—i.e., "become"—and States like BE) and their arguments. Arguments can be specified as Things, Paths, Places, or Properties. In this theory traditional thematic relations such as Agent, Theme, and Goal are not considered to be primitives; rather they are convenient labels for the arguments of semantic functions like CAUSE, BE, and GO. For example, Agent is the first argument of CAUSE, Theme the first argument of BE or GO, and Goal the argument of the Path function TO. Theories of verbal meaning such as those of Talmy (1985), Pustejovsky (1991), Tenny (1987), Dowty (1991), and others make it clear to me that there is more to the meanings of verbs than what can be represented using Jackendovian-style LCSs, and I will need to resort to a few modifications of Jackendoff's system below. Nevertheless I will continue to couch the discussion in terms of this formalism, as it for the most part illustrates the points that I wish to make well enough, and hope that nothing in the end hinges seriously on this choice.

1. The Data: A Preliminary Look at -*ize*

According to Marchand (1969:318), -*ize* is a suffix which originates in OGreek as -*izō*, is borrowed through Ecclesiastical Greek into Latin as -*izare*, and thence into Old French and Middle English. Marchand finds it especially productive between 1580 and 1700, and again quite productive in the nineteenth century and afterwards, where the growth of science and technology clearly contribute to its utility. Its continued productivity in the twentieth century is corroborated by the calculations that Harald Baayen and I report in our (1991) study of English derivation. There we found -*ize* to be the only productive affix forming verbs from adjectives (other affixes tested were -*ify*, *en*-, and *be*-), and to be the second most productive affix forming verbs from nouns (*de*- was quite a bit more productive than -*ize*, an observation to which I will return below).[2]

---

[2]A recent recalculation of P for *de*- and -*ize* yields the following figures: denominal *de*-, P=0.0465; denominal -*ize* P=0.0072; deadjectival -*ize*, P= 0.0138. The figure for P, as explained in detail in Baayen and Lieber 1991, is obtained by dividing the number of hapaxes, i.e., words with frequency of 1 (n_1) by the number of tokens (N).

Let us first consider what sort of semantic work this suffix does; the examples in (1) are representative:

(1) a. unionize
      civilianize
      epitomize
      velarize
   b. anesthetize
      oxidize
      texturize
      apologize
   c. summarize
      hospitalize
   d. cannibalize
      economize

The examples in (1a) illustrate by far the largest class of -*ize* words. They are typically either causative or inchoative in meaning (often both, in fact), and can be paraphrased informally as "cause to become x", where x is a nominal or adjectival stem or in the inchoative reading simply "become x". The forms in (1b) can also be either causative or inchoative typically, but they encode a more motional meaning; to *anesthetize* someone is to cause anesthetic to go into or to pervade someone, and to *apologize* is to cause an apology to go to someone. We might therefore characterize the meaning of the forms in (1b) as "cause x to go to/in/on y", where x again must be a noun. Inchoative readings are also possible for some forms of type (1b); for example, *oxidize* can be used to mean simply become impregnated with oxide with no overt agent specified (*With exposure to air, the organic matter oxidized*). On this interpretation we would informally represent the -*ize* form to mean "x go to/in y", where x is again the base noun. Forms in (1c) are always causative, and like those in (1b) they involve a motion component; they differ from the items in (1b) in that the base noun is typically construed as a goal, rather than as a theme. So they might be characterized as meaning "cause to go to/in x", where x is the base noun. Finally, the items in (1d) strike me as being rather different in meaning from the preceding classes. Unlike them, forms like *cannibalize* and *economize* seem not to be causatives. Instead, they might be interpreted as meaning "act/do/make in a manner like x" or "act/do/make in x manner"; this is the class that Marchand (1969:320) characterizes as meaning "subject to a special (technical) process connected with". Note finally that a particular -*ize* word may actually be open to more than one of these possible meanings, that is, may belong simultaneously to more than one class. For example, *capitalize* may be used to mean "cause to become capital", or "cause capital to go to something, supply with capital", according to the *American Heritage Dictionary*.

2. The Lexical Semantics of -*ize*

To begin to formalize the semantics of the suffix -*ize* in English let us look first at a typology of word formation that is tentatively sketched out in Lieber and Baayen 1993:69. According to Lieber and Baayen, forms of word formation can fall into the following categories:

(2)   a. Semantically determinate (e.g., -*er*, -*able*)
        b. Semantically indeterminate
            i. No fixed LCS (e.g., N to V conversion)
            ii. Partially fixed LCS (e.g., *ver-, be-, ont-*)

Semantically determinate affixes have lexical conceptual structures which are entirely fixed. Examples might be the adjective forming -*able* in English, which (in terms of argument structure) externalizes an internal argument. Two or more semantically determinate affixes may be homophonous. That is, they may be phonologically identical in shape, yet share no aspect of their lexical semantics; their semantic representations are entirely disjoint. Here Lieber and Baayen (1993) give as examples the comparative -*er* and the agentive -*er* in English, clearly a pair that show no more than accidental identity of shape.

In contrast, semantically indeterminate methods of word formation have Lexical Conceptual Structures which are in some way unfixed. The most extreme case might be a method of word formation like noun to verb conversion, which Lieber and Baayen (1993) argue is entirely open. In that work and in Baayen and Lieber in press, we analyze the various semantic possibilities for N to V conversion in English and Dutch on the basis of the CELEX lexical database of English. We argue that there is no stable LCS that is added to the meaning of the noun to form the verb. Hence some noun to verb conversions are causative (*to cork*) or causative/inchoative (*to compost*) and others neither (*to boss*); some involve a motion component (*to air*) and others do not (*to clock, to ape*). What seems to be going on in conversion is that there is no fixed LCS that accompanies the category shift of noun to verb. Rather, when a noun is shifted in category to a verb it is only pragmatic inference which determines what the resulting LCS of the verb will be.

Less extreme than N to V conversion are affixes like the Dutch verb-forming prefixes discussed in Lieber and Baayen 1993. There we argue that a prefix like Dutch *ver-* has a partially fixed LCS, as illustrated in (3):

(3) LCS for Dutch *ver-*
    [$_{Event}$**CAUSE (**[$_{Thing}$],[$_{Event}$GO [$_{Thing}$], [$_{Path}$FROM
    ([$_{Thing, Place, Event}$]) TO ([$_{Thing, Property, Place}$])])])]

Like many verbs with causative components, Dutch *ver-* verbs can optionally be inchoative; I will represent this here by using boldface for elements of the

LCS which are optional.[3] Individual verbs vary from one another in the category of stem to which *ver-* attaches (noun, adjective, or verb), and in the position that the stem occupies in the resulting LCS. For example, the verbs *verhuizen* 'to move house', *verarmen* 'to make/become poor', and *verzetten* 'to move, reposition' are formed from nominal, adjectival, and verbal bases, respectively. *Verhuizen* means roughly "x cause y to move from house to house" where the noun stem *huis* occupies both the FROM and TO argument positions in (3) above. *Verarmen*, similarly, means "x cause y to go from some unspecified state to poor (or poorer)", and *verzetten* "x cause y to go from the act of moving to an unspecified place, i.e., away". Among the denominal *ver-* verbs, the nominal stem sometimes occupies the source or goal argument positions (or both) as in *verhuizen*, sometimes the theme position (*verharen* 'to shed hair') and sometimes even the agent position (*verwormen* 'to be eaten by worms'). The reader is referred to Lieber and Baayen 1993 for further illustration and explanation.

Returning to the various cases of *-ize* set out in (1), it is fairly clear that *-ize* does not constitute four homophonous affixes. At least the first three categories have causative meaning, and the first two alternate causative with inchoative. Although they seem to differ to some extent in the nature of the Event which is caused or which happens, the differences are not radical enough to my mind to suggest homophony. On the other hand, it is also fairly clear that *-ize* is not completely semantically determinate; if it were we would not be able to distinguish the four categories that we have. This means that *-ize* must fall somewhere in category (2b), the affixes which are semantically indeterminate in some way. Our first task, then, is to determine exactly in what ways the LCSs of *-ize* forms are indeterminate. I will begin to do this by first formalizing the informal semantic glosses given above for each category in (1a-d) using Jackendovian-style LCSs:

(4) a. $[_{Event}$ **CAUSE** $([_{Thing} \quad], [_{Event}$ INCH $[_{State}$BE $([_{Thing} \quad], [_{Place}$AT $([_{Thing,} \quad _{Property}$base N,A$])])])]$
   (unionize, civilianize, epitomize, velarize)

b. $[_{Event}$**CAUSE** $([_{Thing} \quad], [_{Event}GO([_{Thing}$base N$], [_{Path}$TO/ON/IN $([_{Thing} \quad])])])]$
   (anesthetize, oxidize, texturize, apologize)

c. $[_{Event}$CAUSE $([_{Thing} \quad], [_{Event}$GO $([_{Thing} \quad], [_{Path}$TO $([_{Thing}$base N$])])])]$
   (summarize, hospitalize)

---

[3]See Levin and Rappaport Hovav 1994 for an insightful discussion of the causative/inchoative alternation.

d. $[_{Event}ACT ([_{Thing}], [_{Manner}LIKE ([_{Thing, Property}base N])])]$
   (cannibalize, economize)

(4a-d) constitutes a rough first pass through the lexical semantics of -ize forms. Again, the parts of the LCS represented in boldface in (4a,b) are meant to be treated as optional. The absence of the CAUSE function in either of these LCSs gives rise to the purely inchoative reading that these verb forms may have. The LCSs in (4a,b, and c) are relatively straightforward. The sequence of functions INCH - BE in Jackendoff's notation indicates the meaning "become"; see Jackendoff 1990 for justification of this notational choice. (4b) and (4c) both have the motional function GO inside the CAUSE function and differ only in the argument position that the noun stem occupies. In (4b), it is the argument of GO, that is, the Theme argument, whereas in (4c), the stem is the argument of the Path function, that is, the Goal. The LCS in (4d) is much rougher and less carefully formalized than the previous three, as it appears to deal with a class of verbs that Jackendoff has had relatively little to say about, those which denote action without motion or change of state (e.g., verbs like *yawn, kiss, dance, boss*); I therefore take some liberties in the representation. What seems crucial to represent here is first that although these verbs are Event verbs, since they do not have either a motional meaning (usually represented by GO), or an inchoative meaning (represented here by INCH-BE), they require yet another primitive, which I will call ACT here following Pinker (1989), for reasons which will become clear shortly. ACT will take the place of the primitive AFF (affect, do) from Jackendoff 1990 which Harald Baayen and I make use of in our 1993 paper.

If this rough characterization of the semantic classes of -ize is correct, it appears that verbs formed with the suffix -ize are similar in some ways to verbs formed by N to V conversion and in others to verbs formed by prefixation of *ver-, be-,* or *ont-* in Dutch. They are like N to V conversion in that at least part of the Event that is created is fixed by pragmatic inference; whereas the Event inside the Cause function is fixed for the Dutch verbal prefixes (GO for *ver-*, INCH-BE for *be-* and *ont-*), this seems not to be the case for -ize. On the other hand, at least one subtype of -ize is like *ver-* in that variations of meaning stem from the different argument positions that the base noun may occupy in the LCS. Further, forms in -ize do not exhibit the wide variations in LCS that Baayen and I have shown to exist in N to V conversion cases, and branding -ize as identical to conversion seems incorrect to me. In fact, I would like to argue that the LCS of -ize is even less free than it first appears, and in order to do this, I must first digress and examine the semantic function CAUSE.

The LCSs I have made use of thus far have not fully displayed Jackendoff's formalism. Jackendoff (1990) in fact distinguishes two separate tiers in LCSs to encode nuances in verbal meanings concerning causation and agentivity. On the "thematic tier"—the only one we have been representing—is represented

Agent, the first argument of CAUSE. Alongside this tier, Jackendoff postulates a second "action tier" to represent the notion of Actor, which in his notation is the first argument of another primitive AFF (affect). In a LCS with a CAUSE function on the thematic tier, the first argument of CAUSE may or may not be linked to the first argument of AFF. If it is not, a resulting sentence will express what Jackendoff calls "extrinsic agency" (*The wind rolled the ball down the hill*). If the first argument of CAUSE is linked to the first argument of AFF, the agent may be interpreted as a volitional actor (*Chloe deliberately rolled the ball down the hill*) if it is annotated as [+volitional] or as an involuntary actor (*Chloe rolled the ball down the hill accidentally*) if it is annotated as [-volitional]. Jackendoff also allows the action tier to accompany LCSs in which there is no CAUSE function on the thematic tier. If the first argument of AFF is [+volitional], and it is linked with the first argument of GO on the thematic tier the result is a sentence like *Chloe deliberately rolled down the hill*. If the first argument of AFF is [-volitional], we might have *Chloe accidentally/unintentionally rolled down the hill*. Jackendoff further argues that both tiers are necessary in order to tease apart distinctions between Theme, the argument of GO or BE on the thematic tier (i.e., that which moves) and Patient, the second argument of AFF (i.e., that which undergoes the action) on the Action tier.

It is beyond the scope of this paper to propose a complete semantic analysis of causation; I will make two brief comments on Jackendoff's choice of formalism, however. First, as mentioned briefly above, Jackendoff pays little attention to those verbs which denote pure action without motion or change of state, an omission that is problematic for me, as one group of -*ize* verbs clearly falls into this class. Second, the use of two tiers to tease apart aspects of causation strikes me as introducing some redundancy in the system.   In particular, it seems superfluous to me to distinguish those CAUSE arguments which express only extrinsic agency and hence are not paired with the argument of AFF from those that express unintentional agency (e.g. *Chloe unintentionally rolled the ball down the hill*) and therefore are paired with a [-volitional] first argument of AFF. The two cases can be distinguished purely on the basis of animacy of the argument. Let us assume that we need a feature [±animate] in any case, and that it may be paired with the feature [±volitional]. If arguments can be annotated with a combination of these features, we will be able to make all the distinctions that we need: extrinsic agents are [-animate, -volitional], involuntary actors [+animate, -volitional], volitional agents [+animate, +volitional]. Presumably, the feature combination [-animate, +volitional] is ruled out on logical grounds, at least in nonscience-fiction contexts. I therefore propose to express the nuances of causation and agency without the addition of a second tier of LCS.

Rather, I will make use of some of the notation developed in Pinker 1989 which seems both to express the nuances that are necessary for describing -*ize* verbs and to sidestep the problems discussed above with Jackendoff's notation. Pinker (1989) decomposes verbs in much the same way that Jackendoff does, but he pays more attention to what I have called pure action verbs, that is, those like *boss* and *clock* which do not denote either motion or change of state. Pinker represents verbs such as these using the function ACT. ACT verbs can take either one argument or two and in addition often contain a "manner" component that encodes the particular nature of the action involved, as illustrated by Pinker's (1989:193) own examples *yawn* and *kiss*:[4]

(5) a. *yawn* $[_{Event}ACT ([_{Thing}\ ][_{Manner}$ 'yawning'])]
    b. *kiss* $[_{Event}ACT ([_{Thing}\ ], [_{Thing}\ ], [_{Manner}$'kissing'])]

Significantly, for our purposes, the predicate ACT can also be used in Pinker's system to subordinate another Event, in which case the subordinated Event is interpreted as an Effect; the ACT function in effect takes the place of both Jackendoff's CAUSE and his AFF by conflating them. For example, Pinker represents the causative verb *break* with the LCS in (6) (1989:198).[5]

(6) *break* $[_{Event}ACT ([_{Thing}\ ], [_{Thing}\ Y\ ], [_{Event}\ GO ([_{Thing}\ Y\ ],$
    $[_{Property}$ 'broken'   ])])]

The inchoative interpretation of *break* simply lacks the ACT function. Pinker does not explicitly discuss cases like *The wind rolled the ball down the hill*, that is, those that Jackendoff considers as exhibiting "extrinsic agency" but not voluntary action, but annotating Pinker's ACT function with the features [±animate, ±volitional] should allow us to cover the range that we need. The adaptation of Pinker's notation not only seems to streamline the representation of causation that Jackendoff develops, but also, as we will see below, gives a further clue to what the four classes of -*ize* verbs have in common.

In (7), I recast the rough LCSs of (4) in terms of our revised notation:

(7) a. $[_{Event}$ **ACT (**$[_{Thing}\ ], [_{Event}\ INCH\ [_{State}BE ([_{Thing}\ ], [_{Place}AT$
    $([_{Thing, Property}$base   N,A])])])]
    (unionize, civilianize, epitomize, velarize)
    b. $[_{Event}$ **ACT (**$[_{Thing}\ ], [_{Event}GO([_{Thing}base\ N], [_{Path}TO/ON/IN ([_{Thing}\ ])])])]$
    (carbonize, texturize, apologize)

---

[4]Pinker (1989) represents his lexical semantic structures in the form of trees rather than labeled bracketings. Although I adopt his use and interpretation of the primitive ACT here, I will continue to use it in labeled bracketings.
[5]Again, I take the liberty of substituting labeled bracketings for Pinker's trees.

    c. [$_{Event}$ ACT ([$_{Thing}$],[$_{Event}$GO ([$_{Thing}$], [$_{Path}$TO ([$_{Thing}$base N])])])]
       (summarize, hospitalize)

    d. [$_{Event}$ACT ([$_{Thing}$], [$_{Manner}$LIKE ([$_{Thing, Property}$base N])])]
       (cannibalize, economize)

What the revised LCSs in (7) suggest is that the contribution of -ize is somewhat more uniform than it at first appeared; all forms in -ize share the first semantic function ACT. All -ize verbs are action verbs of some sort. What follows the ACT function may be either a Manner function, in which case we get purely actional verbs like *cannibalize* or *economize*, or another Event function, in which case we derive causative or causative/inchoative verbs.[6] In the case of the latter, the nature of the second Event function must be fixed for each individual verb. To some extent it is the category of the base which influences this choice. With adjectival stems, the Event must be INCH-BE: since adjectives typically denote properties, the event corresponding to a property is the coming into being of that property. Noun stems typically denote Things and therefore have the freedom to appear with a wider range of Event functions. They may also occupy a range of argument positions within these functions—the Goal position as in (7a) or (7c), the Theme position, as in (7b), or the Manner position as in (7d). The interpretation of denominal -ize verbs is therefore left much more to pragmatic inference than is the case with deadjectival -ize verbs. This may account then for the fact that deadjectival -ize verbs are much more uniform and predictable in meaning than denominal -ize verbs.

    If the analysis presented here is on the right track, the suffix -ize falls somewhere between N to V conversion and the Dutch verbal prefixes in terms of its level of indeterminacy. It is more determinate than N to V conversion, in that at least one of its semantic functions is fixed, and others are partially driven by the category of the base, but it is less determinate than *ver-*, *be-*, and *ont-* in that not all semantic functions are fixed. The less determinate the LCS of the affix, the more the semantic interpretation of its derivatives is left to pragmatic inference. This fact helps to shed light on the estimation of productivity for -ize mentioned briefly above. As noted above, denominal -ize is far less productive than denominal verbs in *de-* (*debug, deflea, dethrone*). If English *de-* has a

---

[6] Note that we would not expect a causative/inchoative alternation in verbs with the LCS in (7d), as there is only one argument that can be syntactically filled. More of a question arises in the case of LCS (7c), which has two arguments that may be syntactically filled, yet never exhibits the causative/inchoative alternation. The answer here probably lies in the observation of Levin and Rappaport Hovav (1994: 61) that only verbs that do not require an external cause— that is, ones that denote an event that can come about spontaneously–can appear in the inchoative form. This same observation accounts for the fact that not every verb in class (7a) or (7b) (in fact rather few in (7b)) can appear in the inchoative.

relatively fixed LCS much like that of Dutch *ont-*[7] (that is, [$_{Event}$CAUSE ([$_{Thing}$], [$_{Event}$INCH[$_{State}$BE ([$_{Thing}$ base N], [$_{Place}$AT-END-OF[$_{Path}$FROM[$_{Place}$ON ([$_{Thing}$])]])]])]), then this finding follows: the more fixed the LCS, the more transparent and less pragmatically determined the meaning of the resulting derivation. And the more transparent the meaning, the more productive the pattern of word formation.

3. Ramifications for Morphology

We now have some idea how to characterize what -*ize* means. Our next step must be to see what light, if any, a narrow study in lexical semantics can shed on larger issues of morphology and the morphology-syntax interface. Here I mean to raise two questions. One concerns the issue of linking and the organization of the grammar; it is an issue of major importance in current morphology how best to represent the relationship between argument structure and lexical semantics on the one hand and argument structure and syntactic representation on the other. Is the linking best represented as a question of mapping (with or without the intervention of a Thematic Hierarchy), for example, as in Bresnan and Kannerva 1989/1992, or is it better expressed in terms of syntactic hierarchical relationships and movement rules as in Baker 1988, or models like Hale and Keyser 1993 or Halle and Marantz 1993? A second issue goes even further to the heart of morphology: what does the lexical semantics of a single affix like -*ize* tell us about the nature of morphemes? Are morphemes best represented as things with lexical entries, as in the theory that I have been developing over the last fifteen years (or even as rules or processes as in Anderson's (1992) A-Morphous model), or is a scholar like Robert Beard more on the right track with his Lexeme-Morpheme based model of morphology (1987, 1988)? Perhaps surprisingly, I believe that a study of -*ize* can tell us something about both these questions.

3.1 Linking

I assume that any adequate grammar must account, among other things, for at least three different sorts of facts about language. First, there are purely semantic facts such as that a verb like *open* represents either an inchoative or a causative event in which a theme and in the latter case an agent participate. Second, there are facts concerning predicate argument structure—whether the theme argument of *open* corresponds to the external or the internal argument. Finally, there are syntactic facts—what word order the sentence exhibits, for example, and how functions such as subject/external argument and ob-

---

[7]The Dutch prefix *ont-* can take either nominal, adjectival, or verbal bases. English *de-* can take verbal bases in addition to nominal ones (*declassify, deoxygenate, decarbonize*), but the comparison here is between denominal *ont-* and denominal *de-* forms.

ject/internal argument are realized. I assume as well that these three "levels of description" are pertinent whether we are talking about sub-word level objects (i.e., items classically consigned to morphology) or supra-word level objects (i.e., those belonging to phrase-level syntax). The question that I now raise is what our study of -*ize* reveals about the relationships between and organization of these "levels".

The first thing that I believe is revealed quite clearly is that a purely syntactic analysis of -*ize* like that in Lieber 1992 is thoroughly inadequate. In Lieber 1992 I briefly analyzed -*ize* using principles of syntax, with no appeal to lexical semantics or principles of argument structure. In the attempt to explain why English was predominantly right-headed in morphology, but still exhibited certain sorts of left-headed morphology, I argued that the positioning of affixes was governed by the word order parameters of English: heads are initial with respect to complements, but final with respect to specifiers and modifiers (1992:54). As verbs assign their theta-roles rightwards, any verb-forming affix which took a noun stem as its "theme"—i.e. assigned the theme role to its base—would have to be a prefix; this prediction was borne out in English by the prefix *de-* (*dethrone, defuzz*). I argued that the verb-forming suffix -*ize* conformed to the prediction as well, in that the noun stems to which -*ize* attached were not themes, but predicates: *to unionize* was 'to cause x to become a union' with x, the theme, being realized outside the word, to its right. The prediction was true, in other words, if we looked only at -*ize* forms that fell into category (1a), which is, after all, the largest group of -*ize* words. But the prediction fares far less well with -*ize* words of class (1b), where the noun stem is interpreted as theme, and is entirely unclear with respect to the other two classes of -*ize* words. In other words, as soon as we take a closer look at what -*ize* words actually do, a purely syntactic analysis becomes far less plausible.

Also inadequate are analyses which might treat -*ize* purely in terms of argument structure (e.g., Williams 1981), in other words in terms of the addition, deletion and/or binding of an internal or external argument. In such an analysis -*ize* would be treated as an affix which adds an external argument to its nominal or adjectival base, simultaneously internalizing the original external argument: thus 'x is standard' becomes 'y standardizes x'. This characterization is true enough as far as it goes, but not sensitive enough to distinguish the different classes of -*ize* words or even to recognize the causative/inchoative alternation. It in effect treats the category-changing causative as identical to regular morphological causatives, as we will see further below.

It seems clear, then, that any adequate treatment of -*ize* cannot neglect lexical semantics in favor of pure syntax or argument structure. The question then is how best to represent these levels and the linkings among them. I will concentrate here on the representation of lexical semantics and on the linking between lexical semantics (LCS) and argument structure. In the last decade two possible positions have begun to crystallize around the choice of whether or not to adhere to the Uniformity of Theta Assignment Hypothesis (UTAH) of Baker (1988:46):

(8) The UNIFORMITY OF THETA ASSIGNMENT HYPOTHESIS (UTAH)
     Identical thematic relationships between items are represented by identical structural relationships between those items at the level of D-structure.

Adherence to UTAH commits one to the position that, for example, the semantic relationship of Theme is always mapped to the internal argument position and thence to the syntactic [NP,V'] position in English D-structures. Themes that appear anywhere else—for example, as subjects with inchoative verbs—must have been moved to that position via Move α. The attraction of a theory adhering to UTAH is that inherent limits are placed on the sorts of words which might be formed; as all movement rules are subject to conditions such as ECP, movement rules affecting morphemes are no exception. A treatment of morphology that maintains a strong attachment to UTAH is that developed by Hale and Keyser (1993). Presumably, Halle and Marantz's Distributed Morphology (1993) is committed to this hypothesis as well.

The opposing position is represented by the work of Bresnan and her collaborators (Bresnan and Kannerva 1989/1992, Bresnan 1994) and by that of Jackendoff (1990). In these theories, the grammar contains three distinct levels—lexical semantics (called "thematic structure" in the work of Bresnan), predicate argument structure ("functional structure" for Bresnan), and syntax ("phrase structure" for Bresnan); these levels do not necessarily share such formal properties as hierarchical structure. Mappings from one level to another are mediated by a Thematic Hierarchy principle, but not by UTAH. A particular thematic role is not always required to appear in the same syntactic position in every D-structure. Rather, positions in lexical semantics (LCSs, as we have been calling them) are mapped to predicate argument structures in conformance to a hierarchy like that in (9) (Bresnan and Kannerva 1989/1992:75):

(9) Thematic Hierarchy
     ag > ben > recip/exp > inst > th/pt > loc

In the theory of Bresnan and Kannerva 1989/1992 and Bresnan 1994, mapping principles ensure that an agent is never mapped to an object in functional structure, that a theme/patient is unrestricted—that is, may be mapped to either subject or object, depending on the array of thematic roles in a given lexical semantic structure—and that locative expressions may not be mapped to objects. Given a theme in lexical semantics but no agent, as happens with inchoative verbs, the theme is realized as subject. No movement is involved. Jackendoff encodes argument structure directly onto LCSs; as in Bresnan's theory, no movement is involved in the analysis of inchoative verbs, for example.

Let us consider first how an analysis of *-ize* would fare in a theory committed to UTAH at all levels; for the sake of concreteness I will model my analysis on that of Hale and Keyser (1993). In order to conform to UTAH, in that theory lexical semantic relationships are represented hierarchically as in syntactic structure. Verb-forming affixes hold the position of lexical verbs in these syntactic hierarchical structures, their stems hold canonical NP positions (e.g., the theme is always [NP, V']), and word formation is effected by incorporation. A potential derivation for a word like *oxidize* is illustrated in (10):

(10)

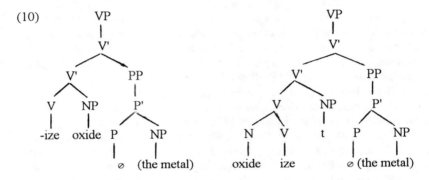

The theme noun *oxide* adjoins to the affixal verb leaving a trace. In this case the derivation is unproblematic, as the resulting verb c-commands the trace in accordance with the ECP.

Difficulties appear, however, in the derivation of *-ize* forms in which the base is not the theme, that is, in the derivation of classes (1a, c, d). Here, assuming structures like those in (10), we run afoul of the ECP. Consider, for example, the derivation of *hospitalize*, where the noun stem is goal, rather than theme:

(11)

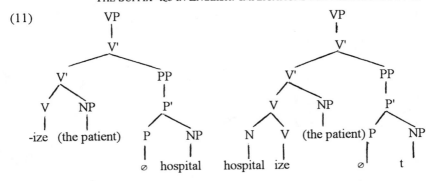

It is clear that the trace of *hospital* in (11) is not properly governed.

Hale and Keyser (1993) are faced with a similar problem in their analysis of the denominal verb *shelve*, which they derive by incorporation of the noun into a null verb. They solve the ECP problem by adopting a Larsonian (1988) analysis of double complement constructions, as illustrated in (12):

(12)

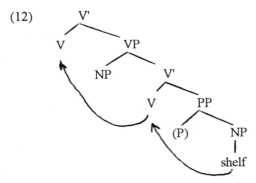

In this analysis, the noun *shelf* is first adjoined to the empty lower verb and then to the upper verb, each step in turn conforming to the ECP. Hale and Keyser note that on this analysis we should not expect to find verbs like *house* with an argument structure like that in **They housed a coat of paint*, meaning 'They gave the house a coat of paint'. A verb *house* with such an argument structure would have to be derived as in (13) (Hale and Keyser 1993:62):

(13)

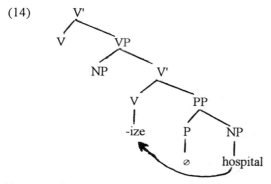

(a coat of paint)

As *house* would have to lower to the V position, its trace would not be properly governed.[8]

The Larsonian double object structure is of course available to us as well. Given this sort of analysis, we could derive *hospitalize* and similar forms as in (14):

(14)

But now, forms like *oxidize* become problematic, as their derivation matches that of the "impossible" meaning for *house* in (13).[9] The conclusion that I draw is that an analysis of *-ize* forms in which lexical semantics shares a syntax isomorphic with that of D-structure and is subject to UTAH cannot cover the

---

[8]Note that this analysis causes problems for any N to V conversion in which the N stem is potentially interpreted as theme. Hale and Keyser are forced to interpret the verb *saddle* as 'provide x with a saddle' rather than as 'put a saddle on x' to avoid exactly the sort of derivation in (13).
[9]Presumably either sort of *-ize* form could be derived without ECP violation if we assume the Larsonian structure and position the *-ize* in the upper V position. But I take such an analysis to be generally contrary to the spirit of Larson's proposal. Presumably a verb in the upper position cannot license a structure in which there is an empty lower verb position which itself licenses a prepositional complement.

full range of *-ize* formations.

What this suggests is that in some way lexical semantics is not subject to a constraint such as ECP, that hierarchical structures and isomorphism to syntax do not serve our purposes well, and rather that lexical semantics requires an independent formalism. A similar conclusion is suggested by the analysis of *ver-* in Lieber and Baayen 1993, where even a noun stem occupying the "agent" position can be incorporated (e.g., *verwormen* 'to be eaten by worms', see above), the sort of ECP violation that no amount of structural wizardry could eliminate.

In contrast, a theory like Bresnan's which distinguishes the formalism of lexical semantics from that of phrase structure has no problem with the *-ize* data. Since such a theory is not committed to an isomorphism between semantic arguments and syntactic arguments, only open arguments—that is, those not occupied in lexical semantic structure by a nominal or adjectival base—are mapped onto syntactic positions. The argument of ACT is mapped to the external argument, the argument of GO or INCH-BE to the internal argument if ACT is present, to the external argument if it is not. If the Path argument (the argument of TO/IN/ON in class (1b)) is open, it will be mapped to the internal argument. [10]

The analysis of *-ize* presented here argues strongly against a syntactic treatment of category-changing morphology like that of Hale and Keyser (1993), and it is at least consistent with theories eschewing UTAH and espousing some form of Thematic Hierarchy. But does it commit us strongly to the latter sort of theory? If so, we would also be forced to treat phenomena such as passives or unaccusatives in a nonmovement analysis. That is, where Hale and Keyser tried to treat clearly lexical phenomena in a syntactic mold, are we in effect forced in the opposite direction, to treat all syntactic phenomena in the lexical mold? I am led to wonder whether category-changing morphology like *-ize* is not in fact consistent with a coherent middle position as well, a position in which not all noninflectional morphology is alike.

Let us start with LCSs and make clear a distinction that has been implicit in the discussion thus far between open positions and closed positions in LCSs. Closed positions are ones which come to be occupied by a nominal, adjectival, or verbal base form as a result of productive category-changing word formation. Open positions are ones unoccupied in LCS. [11] In (15), for example, the

---

[10] While this sort of mapping works for the vast majority of forms in *-ize* of all classes, there are a small number of unusual structures allowed by *-ize* forms that are not predicted by the usual mapping procedures (e.g. *I sympathize with you; We characterized him as unstable*). These tend to be high frequency items in the CELEX data base, and therefore might plausibly be treated as lexicalized forms.

[11] Booij (1992) makes use of a similar distinction between closed an open positions in LCS in his analysis of the transitivity alternation in verbs like *eat*.

argument of GO is closed, those of ACT and TO/ON/IN open:

(15) *anesthetize* [$_{Event}$**ACT**([$_{Thing}$],[$_{Event}$GO([$_{Thing}$ *anesthetic*], [$_{Path}$TO/ON/IN
    ([$_{Thing}$])])])]

Let us suppose next that derivational morphology sometimes, but not always, involves the closing or filling of argument positions in LCS. In fact, it is precisely category-changing affixes like *-ize* that create an LCS in which some argument position is closed. In contrast, the sort of regular causative that is frequently discussed in the literature does not result in the closing of any argument positions in LCS; this kind of causative affix merely adds an ACT function and an open external argument to the already formed LCS of another verb. This is why regular causative morphemes lend themselves so well to treatment purely as valency-changing operations, that is, operations on argument structure: although they inevitably affect LCS, they do so in a way that only adds arguments and does not close them. What I would suggest then is that we distinguish two distinct kinds of derivational morphology. Some derivation, like category-changing *-ize*, fills, closes, or otherwise fixes argument positions of LCS. Other derivation, like the pure morphological causatives, adds or deletes argument positions. The former can only be fruitfully discussed as operations on LCS, whereas the latter can receive a reasonable analysis at the level of predicate argument structure.[12]

Turning now to linking, suppose that only open positions are mapped to argument structure, subject to UTAH or not as one wishes. In a UTAH theory the Path argument of the inchoative version of *oxidize* would be mapped to an internal argument and moved to subject position by Move α. In a nonUTAH position this argument, as the highest open argument on the Thematic Hierarchy, would be mapped directly to the subject position. All that is crucial is that the closed argument in LCS—the position of the derivational base—be out of play, and therefore irrelevant to either argument structure or phrase structure. In other words, if UTAH holds, it holds somewhere beyond lexical semantics. Morphological causatives (as opposed to category-changing causatives) can be worked out in theories committed to UTAH precisely because all argument positions involved in the word formation process are open, that is, in play as far as syntax is concerned.

The conclusion that a study of *-ize* draws me to is that lexical semantics requires a representation formally distinct from that of X' syntax. Further, category-changing word formation is not subject to certain sorts of syntactic principles. Essentially this is the same conclusion that resulted from the debate

---

[12]This distinction suggests a typology of derivation that deserves further attention. Something like this distinction is also hinted at in Rappaport Hovav and Levin (to appear).

over Generative Semantics two decades ago, albeit in a more sophisticated guise. Note that this does not signal a return to strict lexicalism; what happens to arguments that are open in LCS, we have not settled. They may well be subject to UTAH, but this is not a debate that can be settled on the basis of category-changing derivational morphology alone.

3.2 The Nature of Morphemes

A study of -ize sheds light on another fundamental issue in current morphology: whether or not affixes are signs in the Saussurian sense. Theories of generative morphology like my own (1980, 1992), and like that of Selkirk 1982, DiSciullo and Williams 1987, etc., have tended to assume that they are. In such theories, affixes have lexical entries as free morphemes do, with indication of phonological, semantic, and syntactic information. Even generative theories that consider affixes to be processes rather than things (e.g., Aronoff 1976, Anderson 1992) assume that affixes qualify as signs in the sense that they constitute a pairing of phonological and semantic information. In contrast to these theories is that of Robert Beard (1987, 1988), who denies that affixes should be given the status of Saussurian signs.

For Beard, only lexemes—that is free items—can be Saussurian signs. New signs are created from lexemes via derivation, essentially a process which effects some semantic change to a lexeme without any phonological change. Affixes are phonological pieces that may be added to derived lexemes; for example, if agentives (or subject forms) are derived from the lexemes *write* and *type*, the affixal morphemes -er and -ist will be added respectively. But -er does not mean "agentive". It is a phonological piece of material that can be added to comparatives (*lighter*) or other derivations (*New Yorker*) as well. Beard thus argues for a separation between derivation, which creates new lexemes, and affixation. Derivation can occur without affixation (e.g. an agentive like *cook*), and affixation without derivation (resulting in so-called "empty morphs"). See Carstairs-McCarthy 1992:181ff for an excellent summary and analysis of Beard's theory.

Beard's Separation Hypothesis depends on a particular characteristic that some sorts of derivation show, namely that they are semantically rather generic. That is, many languages have derivational means to create agentives or nominalizations, as well as a number of affixes which signal these general meanings. As long as the semantics of word formation sticks to these rather generic themes, the separation between derivation and affixation is tenable. Beard (1988) in fact provides a list of thirty-two sorts of derivations that are instantiated in Indo-European languages, among them *Subject* forms (English *writer, typist*), *Object* forms (English *advisee*), *Possessivity* forms (English *blue-eyed*), and *Material* forms (English *wooden*). Beard's list, however, is confined to nominal and adjectival derivations; he does not consider derivation of verbs.

It is precisely the derivation of verbs, though, that poses the stiffest challenge to the Separation Hypothesis.[13] Under this hypothesis, we would have to be able to characterize verbal derivations in the same generic manner that Beard has done for nominal and adjectival derivation. Presumably the generic category under which -ize would fall would be *Causative* or perhaps *Causative/Inchoative*. It may seem at first blush that this is the right way to characterize a suffix like -ize. After all, I have argued that the semantics of -ize is in fact only partially determinate. The only stable piece that -ize adds to the LCS of its base is the function ACT.

There are two reasons to believe that in spite of its semantic indeterminacy an affix like -ize cannot be treated merely as an instantiation of a generic class such as Causative. First, we have seen that this is far too coarse a semantic characterization for what -ize does. Not all -ize forms are causative or causative/inchoative (recall class (1d)), although all have the semantic function ACT; some -ize verbs are pure action verbs. Further, although the affix -ize shares with another verb-forming affix like *de-* a causative (or better ACT) component, they differ semantically in the Path component of the LCS; *de-* always involves motion away from, -ize sometimes, but not always, motion towards. It is not clear how the Separation Hypothesis would distinguish these affixes. The Separation Hypothesis depends first on the lack of a one-to-one relationship between an affix and a meaning, and second on the generic nature of affixal semantics. The more specific the link between a detailed semantic representation and a particular affix, the more we have something which looks like a Saussurian sign. I believe that -ize, de- and other category-changing verbal morphology such as the verb-forming prefixes in Dutch studied in Lieber and Baayen 1993 show both that affixal semantics need not be generic—in fact may sometimes be quite specific—and that the pairing can be one to one. Affixes, in other words, can have the criterial marks of Saussurian signs.

4. Conclusions

I have tried to show here that the detailed analysis of a single derivational affix can tell us a surprising amount about morphological theory. First, the semantic analysis of -ize provided above shows how affixal meaning can be quite specific, yet only partially determinate. I have argued that -ize provides an ACT function which may or may not be followed by another Event function. The latter must be fixed item by item by pragmatic inference. Second, lexical semantics does not conform to a syntactic hierarchical representation and is not subject to syntactic principles such as UTAH and ECP. If UTAH holds, it holds beyond the level of lexical semantics, contra Hale and Keyser 1993. Finally, the lexical semantics of derivational affixes, in spite of being indeterminate in

---

[13]See Carstairs-McCarthy 1992 for discussion of other cases which are problematic for Beard.

certain ways, is sufficiently specific to warrant treating affixes as Saussurian signs.

There is a subtext to this paper as well, namely that morphologists, myself included, have in recent years given too short shrift to looking at quantities of data on a particular affix. It is only possible to see what an affix like -ize does if we look at a rather large sample of words formed with -ize. This means going beyond single examples or even fairly complete descriptive studies such as Marchand (1969) to larger lexical data bases such as that available from CELEX, for these data bases help to reveal to us the richness and systematic variation in the semantic texture of an affix.

References

Anderson, Stephen. 1992. *A-Morphous Morphology*. Cambridge: Cambridge University Press

Aronoff, Mark. 1976. *Word Formation in Generative Grammar*. Cambridge: MIT Press.

Baayen, Harald and Rochelle Lieber. In press. Word Frequency Distributions and Lexical Semantics. In Michael Neuman, ed., *Research in Humanities Computing 5*. Oxford: Oxford University Press.

Baayen, Harald and Rochelle Lieber. 1991. Productivity and English Derivation: A Corpus-Based study. *Linguistics* 29, 801–843.

Baker, Mark. 1988. *Incorporation*. Chicago: University of Chicago Press.

Beard, Robert. 1987. Morpheme Order in a Lexeme/Morpheme Based Morphology. *Lingua* 72, 1–44.

Beard, Robert. 1988. On the Separation of Derivation from Morphology: Toward a Lexeme/Morpheme Based Morphology. *Quaderni di Semantica* 9, 3–59.

Booij, Geert. 1992. Morphology, Semantics and Argument Structure. In Iggy Rocca ed., *Thematic Structure. Its Role in Grammar*, 47–64. Berlin, New York: Foris Publications.

Bresnan, Joan. 1994. Locative Inversion and the Architecture of Universal Grammar. *Language* 70, 72–131.

Bresnan, Joan and Jonni Kannerva. 1989/1992. Locative Inversion in Chicewa: A Case Study of Factorization in Grammar. In Tim Stowell and Eric Wehrli, eds., *Syntax and Semantics 26, Syntax and the Lexicon*, 53–101. New York: Academic Press [reprinted from *Linguistic Inquiry* 20].

Carstairs-McCarthy, Andrew. 1992. *Current Morphology*. London: Routledge.

Comrie, Bernard. 1976. The Syntax of Causative Constructions: Cross-Language Similarities and Divergences. In Masayoshi Shibatani, ed., *Syntax and Semantics 6: The Grammar of Causative Constructions*, 261–312. New York: Academic Press.

DiSciullo, Anne-Marie and Edwin Williams. 1987 *On the Definition of Word*. Cambridge: MIT Press.

Dowty, David. 1991. Thematic Proto-roles and Argument Selection. *Language* 67, 547–619.

Hale, Kenneth and Samuel J. Keyser. 1993. On Argument Structure and the Lexical

Expression of Syntactic Relations. In Kenneth Hale and Samuel J. Keyser, eds., *The View from Building 20: Essays in Honor of Sylvain Bromberger*, 53–110. Cambridge: MIT Press.

Halle, Morris and Alec Marantz. 1993. Distributed Morphology and the Pieces of Inflection. In Kenneth Hale and Samuel J. Keyser, eds., *The View from Building 20: Essays in Honor of Sylvain Bromberger*, 111–176. Cambridge: MIT Press.

Hoffman, Mika. 1991. *The Syntax of Argument-Structure-Changing Morphology*. Doctoral dissertation, MIT. [Distributed by MIT Working Papers in Linguistics, Cambridge, Mass.]

Jackendoff, Ray. 1983. *Semantics and Cognition*. Cambridge, MIT Press.

Jackendoff, Ray. 1987. *Consciousness and the Computational Mind*. Cambridge: MIT Press.

Jackendoff, Ray. 1990 *Semantic Structures*. Cambridge: MIT Press.

Larson, Richard. 1988. On the Double Object Construction. *Linguistic Inquiry* 19, 335–392.

Levin, Beth. 1993 *English Verb Classes and Alternations*. Chicago: University of Chicago Press.

Levin, Beth and Malka Rappaport Hovav. 1994. A Preliminary Analysis of Causative Verbs in English. In Lila Gleitman and Barbara Landau, eds., *The Acquisition of the Lexicon*, 35–77. Cambridge: MIT Press.

Lieber, Rochelle. 1980. *On the Organization of the Lexicon*. Doctoral dissertation, MIT. [Distributed 1981 by Indiana University Club, 1990 by Garland Publications].

Lieber, Rochelle and Harald Baayen. 1993. Verbal Prefixes in Dutch: A Study in Lexical Conceptual Structure. In Geert Booij and Jaap van Marle, eds., *Yearbook of Morphology 1993*, 51–78. Dordrecht: Kluwer.

Lieber, Rochelle. 1992. *Deconstructing Morphology*. Chicago: University of Chicago Press.

Marantz, Alec. 1984. *On the Nature of Grammatical Relations*. Cambridge: MIT Press.

Marchand, Hans. 1969. *English Word Formation*. Munich: C.H. Beck'sche Verlagsbuchhandlung.

Nedyalkov, V. and P. Silnitsky 1973. The Typology of Morphological and Lexical Causatives. In Ferenc Kiefer, ed., *Trends in Soviet Theoretical Linguistics*, 1–32. Dordrecht: Reidel.

Pinker, Steven. 1989. *Learnability and Cognition*. Cambridge: MIT Press.

Pustejovsky, James. 1991. The Syntax of Event Structure. *Cognition* 41, 47–81.

Rappaport Hovav, Malka and Beth Levin. To appear. Morphology and Lexical Semantics. in Arnold Zwicky and Andrew Spencer, eds., *Handbook of Morphology*. Oxford: Blackwell.

Selkirk, Elizabeth. 1982. *The Syntax of Words*. Cambridge: MIT Press.

Shibatani, Masayoshi. 1976. A Grammar of Causative Constructions: A Conspectus. In Masayoshi Shibatani, ed., *Syntax and Semantics 6: The Grammar of Causative Constructions*, 1–40. New York: Academic Press.

Talmy, Leonard. 1985. Lexicalization Patterns: Semantic Structure in Lexical Forms. In Timothy Shopen, ed., *Language Typology and Syntactic Description 3: Grammatical Categories and the Lexicon*. 57–149. Cambridge: Cambridge University Press.

Tenny, Carol. 1987. *Grammaticalizing Aspect and Affectedness*. Doctoral dissertation, MIT. Distributed by MIT Working Papers in Linguistics, Cambridge.

Williams, Edwin. 1981. Argument Structure and Morphology. *The Linguistic Review* 1, 81–114.

Comments on the Paper by Lieber

PATRICK FARRELL

1. Introduction

Rochelle Lieber's study of the English suffix *-ize* distinguishes and begins to compare two potentially competing theoretical approaches to the kinds of verb formation illustrated in (1)–(4).[1]

(1)   X→V conversion
    a.   The cashier put the groceries in the [N bag].
    b.   The cashier [V bagged] the groceries.

(2)   Category-changing affixation
    a.   We put him in the [N hospital].
    b.   We [V hospitalized] him.

(3)   Incorporation (Southern Tiwa; Allen, Frantz, and Gardiner 1984)
    a.   [N *seuan-ide*]   *timū-ban*
        man-SUFFIX   AGR-see-PST

        'I saw the/a man.'

    b.   [V *ti-seuan-mū-ban*]
        AGR-man-see-PST

        'I saw the/a man.'

(4)   Morphological verb causativization (Berber; Alalou and Farrell 1993)
    a.   *y-gn*   *wrba*
        AGR-sleep boy

        'The boy is sleeping.'

    b.   *y-ss-gn*   *wryaz   arba*
        AGR-CAUSE-sleep man   boy

        'The man put the boy to sleep.'

Building on the success of Baker (1988) and others in accounting for the properties of morphological verb causativization and noun incorporation in terms of a movement transformation involving syntactic categories in a phrase-marker (i.e., head-to-head movement), the general syntactic incorporation approach to verb formation illustrated in Figure 1 for *bag* as used in (1b) has been extended in one way or another not only to X→V conversion

---

[1] I gratefully acknowledge helpful comments on an earlier draft of this paper from Mark Aronoff and Beth Levin.

(H&K=Hale and Keyser 1993) but also to certain kinds of category-changing affixation (Borer 1991).[2] Under this general approach, the meanings of the elements concerned are factored out of the process. H&K suggest that the elementary meanings of lexical items are derivable from the syntactic configuration in conjunction with some version of a principle of uniform thematic role association (UTAH), as in Perlmutter and Postal 1984 and Baker 1988.

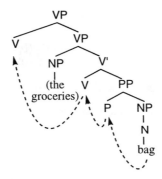

Figure 1. Syntactic incorporation approach to verb formation

Building on important developments in the articulation of theories of lexical conceptual structure (LCS) and demonstrations of their importance for understanding grammatical phenomena of various kinds (for example, Rappaport and Levin 1988, Pinker 1989, Jackendoff 1990), the possibility of treating word formation fundamentally in terms of relations between LCSs has begun to be explored not only for category-changing affixation (as in Lieber's paper on -*ize* and Lieber and Baayen 1993), but also for $X \rightarrow V$ conversion (Lieber and Baayen 1993, Rappaport Hovav and Levin to appear) and morphological verb causativization (Alalou and Farrell 1993, Farrell 1995a, 1995b). Under this approach, category-changing affixation, for example, would be characterized as filling a specified slot in the LCS of an affix with the semantic content of the base to which it attaches, as schematized in Figure 2 (following Lieber, in essence, but keeping

---

2 It should be noted, however, that Borer argues specifically against the syntactic incorporation approach to causativizing -*ize*. Hale and Keyser tentatively suggest that the syntactic process illustrated in Figure 1 occurs at a distinct level of representation known as argument structure or lexical-syntactic structure. It is far from clear, as they note, that a distinction between lexical-syntactic structure and syntax proper is motivated, since the two levels are assumed to share the same representations and governing principles. H&K's assumptions about how incorporation is supposed to work diverge in certain important ways from those of Baker 1988.

Jackendoff's formalism). Under this approach, the derived verb is associated with an (initial) syntactic frame and/or syntactic argument structure according to the same linking principles that apply to underived verbs (for example, Jackendoff 1990, Carrier and Randall 1993).

-ize:
[$_{Event}$ CAUSE ([$_{Thing}$], [$_{Event}$ GO ([$_{Thing}$],
       [$_{Path}$ TO ([$_{Thing}$ base N])])])]
+ *hospital*
$\Downarrow$

hospitalize:
[$_{Event}$ CAUSE ([$_{Thing}$], [$_{Event}$ GO ([$_{Thing}$],
       [$_{Path}$ TO ([$_{Thing}$ HOSPITAL])])])]

Figure 2. Lexical semantic approach to verb formation

The two approaches can be summarized as follows:

Syntactic incorporation approach:
- Verbs are formed via head-to-head movement in a syntactic tree.
- In conjunction with the UTAH and certain other principles for associating syntactic and semantic structures, the elementary meanings of verbs can be derived from syntactic configurations.

Lexical semantic approach:
- Verbs are formed by merging LCSs of component elements.
- In conjunction with linking principles and certain other principles for associating syntactic and semantic structures, the (initial) syntactic frames of verbs can be derived from LCSs.

Lieber argues that the properties of English *-ize* and one variety of Dutch *ver-* are such that the syntactic incorporation approach to category-changing affixation is not viable. In response, I would like to show first, that the structures needed for these affixes appear to fall squarely within the range of structures that would be needed more generally under the syntactic incorporation approach for $X{\rightarrow}V$ conversion and incorporation proper, for which reason it is unclear that *-ize* and *ver-* present any special problems for this approach; and second, that nevertheless the syntactic incorporation approach is of questionable value (at least for $X{\rightarrow}V$ conversion and *-ize* affixation), since it utilizes syntactic structure and operations that are superfluous and unmotivated.

2. A Survey of Verb Formation Processes

In this section I consider a fairly broad range of elements (characterized semantically) that can be targeted for $X{\rightarrow}V$ conversion in English and incorporation or morphological causativization cross-linguistically, in an effort to pave the way for an assessment of the two approaches to verb formation and to show that the English *-ize* and Dutch *ver-* cases, being on the same basic map as other processes, do not present any special obstacles to the syntactic incorporation approach.

A→V conversion focused on the result argument in a change of state is quite common in English. Examples include *clear, open, dry, thin,* and *empty.* The LCS of *dry* as used in *The cook dried the floor* is shown in (5).[3]

(5) *dry:* [Event CAUSE ([Thing   ], [Event INCH
        [State BE ([Thing   ], [Place AT ([Property DRY])])])])]

The analogous *-ize* case is Lieber's type (a), exemplified by verbs such as *civilianize, sterilize, unionize* and *velarize. Sterilize,* for example, would have an LCS identical to (5), except that DRY would be replaced by STERILE. N→V conversion of the same kind is exemplified by cases such as *knight* (as in *The queen knighted him*)—more generally, see Levin's (1993:184) *orphan* verbs. The following Greenlandic Eskimo example from Sadock 1986 illustrates a case of resultative noun incorporation that is roughly analogous to the case of *unionize,* as in *The workers unionized.*

(6) a. *Joorut palasi-nngor-poq   tusaamasoq*
         Joorut priest-become-INDIC famous

     'Jørgen became a famous priest.'

It is also apparently quite common for languages with morphological verb causativization to allow property-denoting stative predicates (corresponding semantically to English adjectives) to undergo causativization (Comrie 1985), as illustrated by the following example from Aleut (Golovko 1993).

(7) a. *igluqar qaka-ku-r*
         hide   dry-NONFUT-AGR

     'The hide is dry.'

     b. *ayagar igluqar qaka-t-i-ku-r*
         woman   hide   dry-CAUSE-[i]-NONFUT-AGR

     'The woman dried the hide.'

The LCS of *t-,* which may also be used with eventive verbs, must be something like:

(8) [Event CAUSE ([Thing   ], [Event INCH [State, Event   base V]])]

The differences between *t-* and *-ize* are relatively trivial: with *t-* the inchoative part of the LCS is optional rather than the causative part and the LCS of the base supplies somewhat more detail.

---

[3] Shadow type is used here to show optional portions of LCSs.

Incorporation of the theme argument in a change of state or location is very common, as is well known (Mithun 1984, Baker 1988). The approximate LCS of the Koryak verb *pčai-tɪvái* as used in (9a) (from Mithun 1984) is shown in (9b).

(9) a. *pčai-tɪvái*
boot-take off

'He took off his boots.'

b. *pčai-tɪvái*: [$_{Event}$ CAUSE ([$_{Thing}$]^{α}, [$_{Event}$ GO
([$_{Thing}$ BOOTS], [$_{Path}$ FROM ([$_{Thing}$ FEET OF α])])])]

English N→V conversion focuses on the theme argument for verbs such as *butter, saddle, muzzle, core, milk,* and *scale,* among many others (see, in particular, Levin's 1993 *butter* verbs and *pit* verbs). The LCSs of *butter* and *milk* as used in *I buttered my toast* and *The farmer milked the cow* are shown in (10).

(10) a. *butter:* [$_{Event}$ CAUSE ([$_{Thing}$], [$_{Event}$ GO ([$_{Thing}$ BUTTER],
[$_{Path}$ ON ([$_{Thing}$])])])]
b. *milk:* [$_{Event}$ CAUSE ([$_{Thing}$], [$_{Event}$ GO ([$_{Thing}$ MILK],
[$_{Path}$ FROM ([$_{Thing}$])])])]

The similar *-ize* case is Lieber's type (b), exemplified by verbs such as *oxidize, terrorize,* and *texturize.*[4]

Goal-centered N→V conversion is quite common; examples include *shelve, package, corral,* and *bag.* Lieber's type (c) *-ize,* as with *hospitalize* is semantically parallel. The LCSs of *bag* as used in (1b) is as in (11); the LCS of *hospitalize* is shown in Figure 2.

(11)   *bag:* [$_{Event}$ CAUSE ([$_{Thing}$], [$_{Event}$ GO ([$_{Thing}$],
[$_{Path}$ IN ([$_{Thing}$ BAG])])])]

The following examples illustrate goal incorporation.

(12) a. *ŋu-wu-nu-ŋiliwaṉṯə-rakulṯə-nʉa*
I-NONPAST-LOC-dead wallaby-shoulder-carry

'I throw it (the wallaby) over my shoulder.' (Twi; Mithun 1984)

b. *kotāw-akamik-ī=w*
sink-ground-ABSTRACT FINAL=AGR

'He sank into the ground.' (Cree; Denny 1989)

---

[4] The precise interpretation of the path varies with the *-ize* forms (*oxide* goes ON, whereas *terror* goes TO, for example), as it does with the N→V conversion cases. I know of no *-ize* forms, however, that are completely analogous to *milk, core,* and *scale,* i.e. where the specified path is of the FROM type.

In (12a) both the goal and theme arguments are incorporated. As (12b) involves a motion verb without an external causer, it is somewhat different from the *-ize* and N→V conversion cases—but not in a way that seems to matter. Given that verbs with incorporated Ns can typically be causativized (Baker 1988:376–381), a causative affix could presumably be added to the verb, making the cases completely parallel.

The manner argument is targeted in N→V conversion of the sort exemplified by the verbs *police, boss, coach,* and *mother*, as illustrated in (13a). The LCS of *mother* is shown in (13b).

(13) a.   She is always mothering me.

    b.   *mother:* [$_{Event}$ ACT ([$_{Thing}$]$^\alpha$, [$_{Thing}$]$,

        [$_{Manner}$ BE LIKE ([$_{Thing}$ α], [$_{Thing}$ MOTHER])])]

I have not encountered an example of incorporation that is exactly like this sort of N→V conversion. However, another variety of manner incorporation is illustrated by the following example from Nez Perce (Talmy 1985:110).

(14)   *hi-ququ̓:-láhsa-e*
       AGR-galloping-go up-PAST
       'He/she ascended galloping.'

The roughly analogous case with *-ize* is Lieber's type (d), exemplified by *cannibalize* and *economize*.

I know of no cases of English N→V conversion focusing on the agent, something which H&K claim is not possible. Although it seems to be quite rare, agent incorporation is possible cross-linguistically. In Southern Tiwa, it only occurs with passivized verbs, as shown in (15a). (15b) shows a nonpassive example from Turkish in which an agent is incorporated, under the analyses motivated in Knecht 1985 and Barker, Hankamer, and Moore 1990.

(15) a.   *khwien-ide*   *kan-edeure-ban*
       dog-SUFFIX   horse-kick/PASSIVE-PAST
       'The dog was kicked by the horse.' (Baker 1988:337)

    b.   *kız-ın*   *bacağ-ın-ı*   *arı sok-tu*
       girl-GEN   leg-POSS-ACC   bee-sting-PAST
       'A bee/some bees stung the girl's leg.'
       (Barker, Hankamer, and Moore 1990:26)

Agent incorporation is also claimed to be possible in Indonesian (Myhill 1988). Although *-ize* does not allow the agent slot to be lexically filled, Lieber claims that Dutch *ver-* does. The relevant example is given in (16) (based on Lieber and Baayen 1993).

(16) *verwormen* 'to be eaten by worms'
[$_{Event}$ CAUSE ([$_{Thing}$ WORM], [$_{Event}$ GO ([$_{Thing}$], [$_{Path}$ FROM
([$_{Thing}$]) TO ([$_{Thing}$ RUIN])])])]

The verbs *shovel, iron, funnel, rake,* and *mop* are examples of instrument-centered N→V conversion.[5] An approximation of the LCS of *shovel* as used in (17a) is shown in (17b).

(17) a. Chris shoveled the snow from the sidewalk
      b. *shovel*: [$_{Event}$ CAUSE ([$_{Thing}$]$^{\alpha}$, [$_{Event}$ GO ([$_{Thing}$],
           [$_{Path}$ TO/FROM ([$_{Thing}$])])], [$_{Means}$ USE ([$_{Thing}$ α],
           [$_{Thing}$ SHOVEL])])]

(18) is an example of instrument incorporation in Nahuatl (from Mithun 1984).

(18)   *ya? ki-kočillo-tete?ki panci*
         he AGR-knife-cut   bread
         'He cut the bread with the knife.'

As far as I know, an instrument slot cannot be filled in the LCS of *-ize.*

It does not appear to be possible to form a verb designating a transfer of possession, such as *give, send, sell, buy,* and *obtain,* wherein either the recipient or the source is targeted by any of the processes under consideration here.[6] Thus, the following hypothetical LCSs and associated verbs do not occur in English (following Jackendoff, the predicate GO$_{poss}$ is used here to indicate a transfer of possession).

(19) a. * Chris churched a lot of money.
          'Chris gave the church a lot of money.'
      b. * Chris senatorized the letter.
          'Chris sent the letter to a senator.'
      c. * [$_{Event}$ CAUSE ([$_{Thing}$]$^{\alpha}$, [$_{Event}$ GO$_{poss}$ ([$_{Thing}$],
               [$_{Path}$ FROM ([$_{Thing}$ α]) TO ([$_{Thing}$ base N])])])]
(20) a. * Chris brothered a jacket.
          'Chris got a jacket from his brother.'
      b. * Chris teacherized an A.
          'Chris obtained an A from a teacher.'

---

[5] See, for example, Levin's (1993) *funnel* verbs and *tape* verbs. Verbs that are vehicle names, such as *bicycle, boat, jet,* etc. (Levin 1993: 267), are similar in that they specify a means of motion.

[6] Some examples of transfer-of-possession verbs formed on the theme argument are *profit, credit, bankroll,* and *award.*

c. $*$ [$_{Event}$ CAUSE ([$_{Thing}$]$^\alpha$, [$_{Event}$ GO$_{poss}$ ([$_{Thing}$],
[$_{Path}$ FROM ([$_{Thing}$ base N]) TO ([$_{Thing}$ α])])])]

Moreover, I know of no cases of incorporation involving recipients or sources. Baker (1988:389) explicitly claims that recipients do not incorporate.

The picture of these word formation processes that emerges is summarized in Table 1, which shows for each process which type of semantic role it targets. It would seem that if the syntactic incorporation approach is viable for incorporation and $X \rightarrow V$ conversion, it should extend straightforwardly to English *-ize*, as well as the Dutch *ver-* case that Lieber claims is problematic.

Table 1. Semantic role targets of verb formation processes

semantic role	incorporation/ causativization	$X \rightarrow V$ conversion	*-ize* or *ver-*
result	YES	YES	YES
theme	YES	YES	YES
goal	YES	YES	YES
manner	YES	YES	YES
agent	YES	YES	YES
instrument	YES	YES	NO
recipient/source	?	NO	NO

3. The Syntactic Incorporation Approach

H&K propose the analysis shown in Figure 3a for $A \rightarrow V$ conversion of the sort exemplified by *dry* as used in *The cook dried the floor*.[7] The basic idea is that the argument structure or lexical-syntactic representation (LSR) of the verb *dry* has essentially the same structure as the underlying VP (without the subject) of the corresponding sentence with a resultative adjective (i.e., *make the floor dry*), following a version of the approach to VPs presented in Larson 1988. The only filled slot, however, is that of the adjective, which undergoes incorporation (head-to-head movement) in such a way as to occupy an appropriate verb slot in an LSR that can be inserted into (or that matches) a legitimate syntactic D-structure.[8] It should be clear

---

[7] The words in parentheses in this and other LSR representations in this paper are not part of the representation. They are provided only to assist us in associating the structures with a meaning by giving examples of the kind of words that might be inserted at a later stage of the derivation in order to give a complete phrase.

[8] Technically the process of incorporation involves adjunction to each of the heads to which there is movement, creating a structurally complex verb. I omit the details here, for the sake of graphic convenience. H&K do not fully commit to the suggested distinction between lexical-syntactic and ordinary syntactic representations.

that Lieber's type (a) *-ize* can be given the same analysis, as illustrated in Figure 3b for *sterilize*.

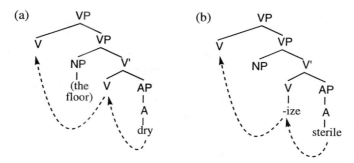

Figure 3. Incorporation analysis of A→V conversion

There are two main kinds of constraints on LSRs and the incorporation process. One constraint is imposed by the Empty Category Principle (ECP) of Chomsky 1981, which does not allow a movement to leave a trace that is not properly governed. Each of the traces left by the movements depicted in Figure 3 are properly governed, since incorporation is always into a governing head. Principles of Unambiguous Projection and Full Interpretation are claimed to yield a set of constraints on trees whose effects can be summarized as follows: all branching is binary, there can be at most one V' in a VP, and there can be at most one embedded VP in a VP. In a nutshell, the VP type found in Figure 3 is the maximum size of a verbal LSR; there can be at most two "internal" argument slots.

Under the assumption that the syntactic structures appropriate for VPs of the type *provide/fill with* THEME or *deplete of* THEME are always available for theme-centered verb formation,[9] the analyses shown in Figure 4 can be given to N→V conversion cases of the *saddle/butter/milk* variety (as suggested by H&K), as well as Lieber's type (b) *-ize* (as with *oxidize, texturize,* and *terrorize*). The idea is that the theme is in a PP (as it would be in a V NP *with/of* THEME syntactic structure such as *cover the toast with butter* or *fill the people with terror*). The noun incorporates into the empty

---

[9] This is an assumption that seems potentially problematic in that a verb like *salt* as used in *I already salted the water*, for example, certainly seems to mean "put salt in something" rather than "fill with salt" or "provide with salt". Thus, I essentially agree with Lieber that the analyses required under an incorporation approach are rather counterintuitive. This does not keep them from being technically viable, however. In allowing Ns from objects of prepositions to incorporate, H&K's approach to incorporation differs considerably from that of Baker 1988. For Baker, themes are the best incorporees precisely by virtue of the fact that they are NOT objects of prepositions and are in canonical direct object position.

P and then into the higher Vs in the familiar head-to-head movement pattern.

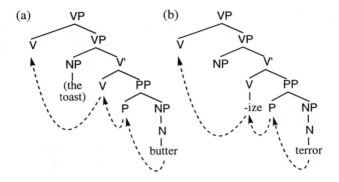

Figure 4. Incorporation analysis of theme-centered verb formation

Goal-centered verb formation is handled in a similar way in this framework, as illustrated in Figure 5 for *bag* and *hospitalize*.

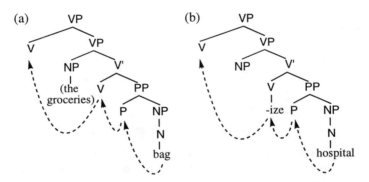

Figure 5. Goal-centered verb formation

Manner-centered verb formation of the sort considered above can presumably be handled in the same way as H&K handle verbs such as *smear* and *splash*. They suggest that the manner/means component of the verb meaning is represented as a "tag" on the verb node as shown in Figure 6. This tag may be either coindexed with an element in the LSR with which it is construed or may be construed with the external argument if there is one.

It is technically not introduced by incorporation.[10] Although H&K do not make clear how the V node in the LSR representation is ultimately filled by the manner element, let us suppose that by general convention a tag on a node automatically occupies a node that it is associated with if it needs to in order to satisfy some need, such as the need for an element with phonetic substance under some node in an LSR. This provisional analysis extends unproblematically to the *mother* type of N→V conversion and the *cannibalize* type of *-ize* affixation, as shown in Figure 7.

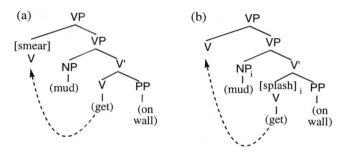

Figure 6. LSRs of *smear* and *splash*

Figure 7. Manner-centered verb formation

This same analysis appears to be appropriate and necessary for the type of instrument N→V conversion exemplified by verbs such as *shovel* and *funnel*. Since the two argument slots available in an LSR are taken by the theme and locative arguments (one shovels/funnels something into/out

---

[10] The fact that two separate devices (incorporation and "tags") are used to handle what seems to be a single phenomenon renders this whole approach suspicious. Moreover, the possibility of using tags seriously undermines any attempt to provide an explanation for non-occurring kinds of N→V conversion in terms of general syntactic constraints on incorporation, as it is unclear that tags could not be used to circumvent the supposed constraints. At the same time, it is not clear that very much depends on the tag analysis. The only motive for it appears to be that it allows the claim that recursion is highly limited in LSRs to be maintained. If one more NP/PP position is allowed in LSR VPs, the manner/means elements could be put into the same place they would occupy in an ordinary syntactic structure and a uniform incorporation analysis could be given to all cases of N→V conversion.

of/onto something), the instrument must be analyzed as an element in the manner/means component and treated as a tag on the verb node. Now, it seems that some kind of agent demotion or adjunctification (as in the passive structure of Southern Tiwa illustrated by (15a)) is what generally makes agent incorporation possible. A plausible way of analyzing this demotion is that it involves interpreting the agent as a kind of "means" adjunct, which would explain the widespread use of instrumental case and prepositions of the *by* type with demoted agents cross-linguistically. From this perspective, it seems reasonable to suggest that the agent in Dutch *verwormen* 'to be eaten by worms' and Turkish *arı sok-* 'bee sting' be treated as part of the manner/means component of the verb. Thus, *shovel* and *verwormen* might be analyzed as shown in Figure 8.

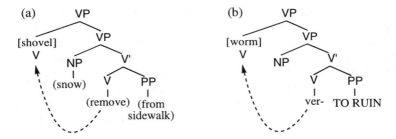

Figure 8. Agent/instrument-centered verb formation

In sum, it seems possible to give a relatively reasonable syntactic incorporation analysis of the various cases of verb formation considered here, without deviating from the basic framework outlined by H&K. The question that needs to be asked is whether there is sufficient motivation for positing so much abstract syntactic structure to handle what seem to be such formally simple word formation processes.

4. The Problem with the Syntactic Approach

H&K's only empirical justification for an incorporation approach to X→V conversion is that it appears to yield explanations for the non-occurrence of certain logically possible types of verb formation. For example, the impossibility of recipient-centered N→V conversion might be attributed to the fact that the recipient is the first object in the double-object construction. As such, it occupies the specifier slot in a maximally projected LSR, a position from which incorporation is ruled out by the ECP, as shown in Figure 9. Under this approach, the fact that the recipient argument cannot be targeted for *-ize* affixation might actually be taken as motivation for an incorporation analysis of affixal category-changing verb formation as well.

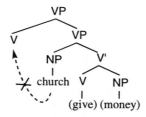

Figure 9. Illicit recipient incorporation

However, this would be an interesting explanation for the restriction in question only if there were a principled reason for restricting the recipient argument to the specifier position of the LSR VP. If position in sentence structure is what motivates assumptions about what positions arguments of a predicate occupy in LSRs—and this is the only motivation that H&K appeal to—it is unclear what would prevent incorporation of a recipient from the complement position, which would seem to be a possibility due to the existence of the alternative structure exemplified by *give money to the church* (see Figure 10a). More seriously, this analysis fails to explain the similar systematic exclusion of source-centered N→V conversion (and *-ize* affixation). Since the source in a transfer of possession can never occur as the first object, one would expect only a well-formed LSR like that shown in Figure 10b.

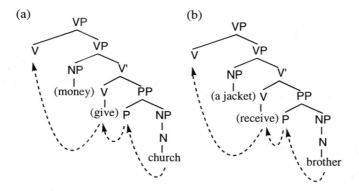

Figure 10. Seemingly viable recipient/source incorporation structures

It would of course be possible to simply stipulate that recipients and sources are necessarily in the specifier position at the level of LSR, in order to engage the ECP in an account of the fact that they cannot be targeted by N→V conversion. But in the absence of independent motivation for such a move, this could not be considered a principled explanation and would be no better than simply stipulating that recipients and sources cannot incorporate.

Following in essence the general approach of Aronoff 1980, I wish to consider an alternative explanation for this and other restrictions on N→V conversion in English that works independently of how the process is characterized theoretically. The basic idea is that the function of N→V conversion is to name a routine process metonymically: a salient constant in the routine stands for the entire process. For example, the routines PUT THINGS IN BAGS and ACT ON SOMEONE LIKE A MOTHER are named by the salient constants BAG and MOTHER. In general, "a well-chosen metonymic expression lets us mention one entity that is salient and easily coded, and thereby evoke—essentially automatically—a target that is either of lesser interest or harder to name" (Langacker 1995). An appropriate metonym for a process would be the name of a thing that by virtue of how it is conceptualized readily evokes that process.[11] A fairly specific set of constraints on N→V conversion can be formulated as follows:

(21) *Constraints on N→V conversion*

A verb of the form [$_V$ [N]] is appropriately named if

a. a characteristic behavior of the thing designated by N is the type of behavior that the verb designates, or

b. a central property of the thing designated by N is involvement in the type of event that the verb designates.

By way of illustration, one highly characteristic behavior of members of the category "mother" is taking care of children in a highly protective or nurturing way. In conformance with (21a), the verb *mother* designates the activity of taking care of someone in a highly protective way. This is an optimal case of N→V conversion, because the meaning of the noun *mother* evokes the concept of the activity that the verb names. The manner-centered cases of N→V conversion (*nurse, coach, police*, etc.) all seem to have this same character.

Along similar lines, the verb *bag* is appropriately named for the routine of putting things in bags because the noun *bag* designates a certain kind of thing that is used for putting things in. The verb *shovel* is appropriately named for the routine of moving things to or from a place with a

---

[11] This idea about the most basic limitations on the semantics of denominal verbs was expressed in Aronoff 1980 as follows: "the verb must denote something which has to do with the noun" (747). Aronoff's study and Clark and Clark 1979, which it is a response to, provide a wealth of information about N→V conversion and illuminating accounts of the potential variability and context-sensitivity of the meanings of denominal verbs—a state of affairs that is not surprising for me, given the fact that nouns are typically polysemous, but about which I have nothing to say here.

shovel because the noun *shovel* designates a certain kind of thing that is used for moving things from one place to another. The verb *butter* is appropriately named for the routine of spreading butter on things because the noun *butter* designates a certain kind of thing that one characteristically spreads on foods.

Consider in this light the nonexistence of the hypothetical transfer-of-possession verb *church* meaning "cause church to have X" or "give church X".[12] Since the noun *church* designates primarily a place that people go to worship, the verb *church* would not be appropriately named if it designated an event involving a transfer of possession with a church as recipient. Although people give things to churches (conceived of as the organizations that support the places of worship), especially money, the giving activity is not something in terms of which the noun *church* is centrally understood. If *church* were to be converted into a verb, it would presumably designate the routine of going to church. By the same token, *brother* would be a poorly named verb for the routine of obtaining things from a brother. Although we surely obtain things from brothers, the central sense of the noun *brother* is not anything like "someone from whom things are obtained". More generally, recipients and sources are characteristically animate entities or organizations—things with which we interact in various complex ways. There does not seem to be an abundance of nouns in English designating animate entities or organizations whose defining property is being a certain kind of thing to which something is given or from which something is obtained. The paucity of such nouns is, I suggest, what accounts for the apparent absence of recipient/source-centered N→V conversion in English.

This line of explanation extends to other kinds of apparently systematic gaps in the N→V conversion process. Consider, for example, the lack of agent-centered N→V conversion. Given that lexical agent suppression ordinarily results in a syntactic construction with a theme subject (as in the case of the causative/inchoative alternation: *I dried the clothes/The clothes dried*), if the agent slot in an LCS were filled by a thing whose name is that of the verb, the result would be the construction illustrated by the following hypothetical examples.

---

[12] H&K discuss the example *to house a coat of paint*, meaning "to give a house a coat of paint", in connection with what they consider a restriction on "double-object" structures. That their ECP explanation is not on the right track is indicated by the fact that the structure appropriate for "put a coat of paint on a house" would yield *house a coat of paint* without any ECP violation. The problem in this case is that *house* is not understood as designating a kind of thing on which things are put or to which things are given, which it would have to be in order to be a good name for a verb meaning "put something on a house" or "give a house something".

(22) a. * The floor maided clean.
        'The floor became clean by a maid.'
      * *maid:* [$_{Event}$ CAUSE ([$_{Thing}$ MAID], [$_{Event}$ INCH [$_{State}$ BE
           ([$_{Thing}$], [$_{Place}$ AT ([$_{Property}$])])])]

    b. * The ball boyed to the fence.
        'The ball went to the fence by a boy.'
      * *boy:* [$_{Event}$ CAUSE ([$_{Thing}$ BOY], [$_{Event}$ GO ([$_{Thing}$],
         [$_{Path}$ TO ([$_{Thing}$])])])]

The verbs *maid* and *boy*, used in this way, would be appropriately named if the noun *maid* designated a certain kind of person that causes things to undergo a change of state and the noun *boy* designated a kind of person that causes things to move to places. Although maids certainly cause things to undergo changes of state and boys move things around, these are hardly central or defining properties. The systematicity of the agent N→V conversion gap is presumably due to the fact that nouns of the relevant sort are at best quite rare.

H&K attribute to the ECP another systematic gap, illustrated by the hypothetical verbs in the following examples.[13]

(23) a. * She metaled flat.
        'She flattened some metal.'
    b. * He speared straight.
        'He straightened a spear.'
    c. * *spear:* [$_{Event}$ CAUSE ([$_{Thing}$], [$_{Event}$ INCH [$_{State}$ BE
         ([$_{Thing}$ SPEAR], [$_{Place}$ AT ([$_{Property}$])])])]

In this case again, the kind of event concept associated with the hypothetical verbs would not be something that noun meanings would readily evoke. Neither *metal* nor *spear*, for example, is understood as being a certain kind of thing that is caused to come to have some property. There do not seem to be nouns of this type.

Importantly, the constraints on N→V conversion that I am proposing are motivated quite independently of the need to account for these sorts of missing patterns. Consider, for example, the fact that *mother* means "behave in a highly protective (motherly) way toward someone" and not "put something on a mother", *bag* means "put something in a bag" and not "take something out of a bag", *shovel* means "move something to or from some-

---

[13] H&K also note that there are no denominal verbs like *shelve* used in a construction with a stranded preposition, as in *We shelved the books on. As the phrase *shelve the books* means "put the books on a shelf", the semantic content of *on* is included in the verb *shelve*. As the preposition does not contribute anything semantically and is not needed to license an NP, it is superfluous. Presumably, *shelve the books on* is excluded by the Principle of Contrast (Clark 1987).

where with a shovel" and not "take a shovel out of something", *shelve* means "put something on a shelf" and not "remove something from a shelf", and so forth. Surely, the meanings of verbs converted from nouns are not randomly related to the meanings of the nouns. Rather, the meaning of the verb *shelve* is predictable from the fact that a shelf is more appropriately characterized as "something which things are placed on" than "something from which things are removed", just like the meaning of the verb *shovel* is predictable from the fact that although we do take shovels out of garages and sheds, we don't primarily think of shovels as things we take out of places but rather as instruments for digging and moving certain kinds of substances around.

One might claim that with verbs designating changes of location, N→V conversion can target only the theme or goal argument and not the origin of movement, possibly because of an arbitrarily stipulated difference in the way the origin argument is positioned in a syntactic structure. It would then be possible to at least account for the fact that *shelve, bag, corral, pocket*, etc. cannot mean "remove from shelf/bag/corral/pocket". However, it turns out that there is a small class of origin-centered denominal verbs in English consisting of at least *mine* and *quarry* (see Talmy 1985:76, Levin 1993:131). The LCS of *mine* as used in (24a) is as in (24b).

(24) a. We mined a lot of silver.
   b. *mine*: [$_{Event}$ CAUSE ([$_{Thing}$], [$_{Event}$ GO ([$_{Thing}$],
      [$_{Path}$ FROM ([$_{Thing}$ MINE])])])]

It is surely not accidental that the nouns *mine* and *quarry* designate precisely certain kinds of places from which material is removed (and NOT into which material is placed). The way these words are interpreted as verbs is exactly as expected, given the constraints in (21). The small size of this class of verbs follows from the scarcity of nouns with the appropriate meanings, which in turn must follow from a preference for conceptualizing the locative action as being prototypically one of placing in or on.[14]

In sum, the ECP does not provide a principled explanation for the fact that there is no recipient/source-centered N→V conversion in English. Moreover, there are cognitive constraints on this word formation process that explain not only this and other missing patterns but also certain far-reaching limits on the possible interpretation of denominal verbs, concerning which the syntactic incorporation analysis and the ECP have nothing to say. It seems reasonable to suggest that the same constraints hold in general for word formation involving *-ize* and similar category-changing affixes,

---

[14] That is to say, from a certain perspective, pockets, bags, corrals, and the like are symmetrical in their locative function: we put things in them and take things out of them. For whatever reason, they are nevertheless primarily conceptualized as goals.

although, as Lieber has shown, the contribution of the affix itself to the meaning serves to impose further and different kinds of constraints. In any case, there seems to be no good reason to extend a syntactic incorporation analysis to either $X \rightarrow V$ conversion in English or category-changing affixation of the -*ize* type. Whether a syntactic incorporation analysis—possibly in the actual syntax rather than at a lexical level—is appropriate for any or all cases of the more complicated phenomenon of noun incorporation proper is a question that I necessarily leave open here.

5. Conclusion

The quasi-semantic LSRs of the syntactic incorporation approach, as presented by H&K and in this paper, do not contain sufficient semantic information to usefully characterize the core meaning of verbs. For example, there are several classes of verbs with two internal arguments and an NP PP LSR subcategorization that would have the same basic representation. Without further elaboration, there is no distinction between the structures of *mine* (in whose LSR the second complement would be a PP interpreted as an origin in a change of location), *butter* (in whose LSR the second complement is a PP interpreted as a theme in a change of location), and *bag* (in whose LSR the second complement is a PP interpreted as a goal in a change of location). More elaborate representations could certainly be developed to remedy this and other inadequacies. But it is hard to see how one could approximate the relative richness of LCSs without creating a notational variant of them. As a representation of meaning, LCSs are surely to be preferred to LSRs. But if they are not a useful schematic representation of the meanings of verbs, it is unclear what use LSRs of the kind considered here might have in a theory of grammar.

All in all, it seems preferable to dispense with LSRs and the device of syntactic incorporation for characterizing ordinary verb formation processes. $N \rightarrow V$ conversion and -*ize* affixation are adequately characterized as involving direct manipulations of LCSs. In the case of $N \rightarrow V$ conversion, an argument slot in an LCS is filled by an element of type "Thing" which names the resulting verb. In the case of -*ize* affixation, a specified argument slot in one of a small range of related LCSs is filled by an element of type "Thing" which names the base for -*ize*, as proposed by Lieber. In terms of the syntactic structure associated with the phenomena, there seems to be no reason to posit anything more than what is shown in Figure 11.

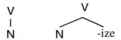

Figure 11. The syntax of $N \rightarrow V$ conversion and -*ize* affixation

References

Alalou, Ali, and Patrick Farrell. 1993. Argument Structure and Causativization in Tamazight Berber. *Journal of African Languages and Linguistics* 14, 155–186.

Allen, Barbara J., Donald G. Frantz, and Donna B. Gardiner. 1984. Noun Incorporation in Southern Tiwa. *International Journal of American Linguistics* 50, 292–311.

Aronoff, Mark. 1980. Contextuals. *Language* 56, 744–758.

Baker, Mark C. 1988. *Incorporation: A Theory of Grammatical Function Changing*. Chicago: University of Chicago Press.

Barker, Chris, Jorge Hankamer, and John Moore. 1990. Wa and Ga in Turkish. In Katarzyna Dziwirek, Patrick Farrell, and Errapel Mejías-Bikandi, eds., *Grammatical Relations: A Cross-Theoretical Perspective*, 21–43. Stanford: CSLI.

Borer, Hagit. 1991. The Causative-Inchoative Alternation: A Case Study in Parallel Morphology. *The Linguistic Review* 8, 119–158.

Carrier, Jill, and Janet Randall. 1993. Lexical Mapping. In Eric Reuland and Werner Abraham, eds., *Knowledge and Language, Volume II: Lexical and Conceptual Structure*, 119–142. Dordrecht: Kluwer.

Chomsky, Noam. 1981. *Lectures on Government and Binding*. Dordrecht: Foris.

Clark, Eve V. 1987. The Principle of Contrast: A Constraint on Language Acquisition. In Brian MacWhinney, ed., *Mechanisms of Language Acquisition*, 1–33. Hillsdale, N.J.: Lawrence Erlbaum.

Clark, Eve V., and Herbert H. Clark. 1979. When Nouns Surface as Verbs. *Language* 55, 767–811.

Comrie, Bernard. 1985. Causative Verb Formation and Other Verb-Deriving Morphology. In Timothy Shopen, ed., *Language Typology and Syntactic Description, Vol. 3*, 309–348. Cambridge and New York: Cambridge University Press.

Denny, J. Peter. 1989. The Nature of Polysynthesis in Algonquian and Eskimo. In Donna B. Gerdts and Karen Michelson, eds., *Theoretical Perspectives on Native American Languages*, 230–258. Albany: State University of New York Press.

Farrell, Patrick. 1995a. Causative Binding and the Minimal Distance Principle. In Raul Aranovich, William Byrne, Susanna Preuss, and Martha Senturia, eds., *Proceedings of the Thirteenth West Coast Conference on Formal Linguistics*, 237–252. Stanford: CSLI.

Farrell, Patrick. 1995b. Lexical Binding. *Linguistics* 33, 939–980.

Golovko, Evgeniy V. 1993. On Non-Causative Effects of Causativity in Aleut. In Bernard Comrie and Maria Polinsky, eds., *Causatives and Transitivity*, 385–396. Amsterdam and Philadelphia: John Benjamins.

Hale, Kenneth, and Samuel Jay Keyser. 1993. On Argument Structure and the Lexical Expression of Syntactic Relations. In Kenneth Hale and Samuel Jay Keyser, eds., *The View from Building 20: Essays in Honor of Sylvain Bromberger*, 53–109. Cambridge, Mass.: MIT Press.

Jackendoff, Ray S. 1990. *Semantic Structures*. Cambridge, Mass.: MIT Press.

Knecht, Laura. 1985. *Subject and Object in Turkish*. Doctoral dissertation, MIT.

Langacker, Ronald W. 1995. Raising and Transparency. *Language* 71, 1–62.

Larson, Richard K. 1988. On the Double Object Construction. *Linguistic Inquiry* 19, 335–391.

Levin, Beth. 1993. *English Verb Classes and Alternations: A Preliminary Investigation*. Chicago: University of Chicago Press.

Lieber, Rochelle, and Harald Baayen. 1993. Verbal Prefixes in Dutch: A Study in Lexical Conceptual Structure. *Yearbook of Morphology* , 51–78.

Mithun, Marianne. 1984. The Evolution of Noun Incorporation. *Language* 60, 847–95.

Myhill, John. 1988. Nominal Agent Incorporation in Indonesian. *Journal of Linguistics* 24, 111–136.

Perlmutter, David M., and Paul M. Postal. 1984. The 1-Advancement Exclusiveness Law. In David M. Perlmutter and Carol Rosen, eds., *Studies in Relational Grammar 2*, 81–125. Chicago: University of Chicago Press.

Pinker, Stephen. 1989. *Learnability and Cognition: The Acquisition of Argument Structure*. Cambridge, Mass.: MIT Press.

Rappaport Hovav, Malka, and Beth Levin. to appear. Morphology and Lexical Semantics. In Arnold Zwicky and Andrew Spencer, eds., *Handbook of Morphology*. Oxford: Blackwell.

Rappaport, Malka, and Beth Levin. 1988. What to Do with θ-Roles. In Wendy Wilkins, ed., *Syntax and Semantics 21: Thematic Relations*, 7–36. San Diego: Academic Press.

Sadock, Jerrold M. 1986. Some Notes on Noun Incorporation. *Language* 62, 19–31.

Talmy, Leonard. 1985. Lexicalization Patterns: Semantic Structure in Lexical Forms. In Timothy Shopen, ed., *Language Typology and Syntactic Description, Vol. III: Grammatical Categories and the Lexicon*, 57–149. Cambridge and New York: Cambridge University Press.

Discussion of the Papers by Lieber and Farrell

Carstairs-McCarthy: I've got a comment on what Patrick Farrell just said … the pragmatic approach, or the pragmatic element in interpreting these verb forms, I applaud very much. And a point in its support that I think one could make is this. We're all used to the idea that we have to invoke pragmatic factors in interpreting root compounds, or noun-noun compounds. I mean, a *butterfly net* is something for catching butterflies; a *mosquito net* is something for keeping mosquitoes away. Now we don't cudgel our brains trying to think out some kind of syntactic reason for this having to do with argument structure, or whatever; it's just the pragmatics. Well now, it's rather odd if you think about it that pragmatic factors should withdraw entirely and defer to syntactic-cum-argument or thematic role principles when anything *verbal* comes into play. Why? That seems to be a supporting point.

Sadock: Well, responding to that I also applaud the use of pragmatics, but I don't think that necessarily a pragmatic account is going to *eliminate* other accounts. So for example, while * *to mother* meaning "to cause something to go to mother" is pretty bad, I think equally bad is * *to addressee something*, so * *to addressee a letter* sounds just as bad as **to mother one's money*, even though an addressee is clearly the person to whom one sends something … What I'm suggesting is that there might be *some* kind of argument structure constraint in addition of course to the pragmatic constraints—which maybe reflects the grammaticalization to some extent of an originally pragmatic constraint.

Lieber: Can I break in on this, because I think that what I'm saying about this is perfectly compatible with both what Patrick is saying and what

---

Note that in this and the subsequent Discussion chapters, ellipsis dots '…' are used to indicate material that has been omitted from the transcripts of the discussion session; a dash '—' is used at the end of an utterance to indicate that the utterance was broken off in midstream, as when one speaker interrupts another or when several speakers are talking at once.

Jerry is trying to bring in, which is that there is a certain amount of the meaning of these forms that's fixed, that's determinate, and the rest is determined by pragmatic inference ... So, it's fairly easy to predict which of the items in -*ize* are going to be interpreted as Themes, as opposed to Goals. Although you'd be surprised if you look at a list that's generated in a lexical database where you get several hundred of these, there are some where you haven't the foggiest notion how they were construed when they were coined. Which is to say somebody coined them on the spur of the moment, and given some context, you might be able to figure it out, but without the context, you don't know. So, there's a determinate part to the meaning, and there's a certain amount that's, just on the fly, by virtue of your world knowledge.

Baker: I'm going to change the topic a little bit. I have a remark about the whole parallel with incorporation and a question for Shelly. The first is a sort of informational thing, about the comparisons between incorporation and what Hale and Keyser were doing. There are two kinds of incorporation you might look at, one is the incorporation of Themes or direct objects, whichever way you want to look at it, the other is the incorporation of these oblique or prepositional phrase things. Superficially, if you look at the data, you seem to see both. Hale and Keyser for technical reasons get into assuming that everything is incorporation from the prepositional phrase kind, stretching Patrick and Shelly's intuitions in the way that was talked about. Further looking at the real incorporation cases, where you have morphological complexity, I've become convinced that you really only have incorporation of the Theme kinds, and incorporation from noun into preposition into verb—I don't know of any good examples where you actually see the preposition there, which should be expected. There are a few examples where you sort of have the semantics but don't have the preposition, but I don't know of anywhere where it's very productive, or you have tests of syntactic transparency of the kind that have been talked about in the literature ...

But my question for Shelly, then, which I promised, is, how do we know that you have these lexical-conceptual representations at all? In particular, I want to quibble about your representation for (4b), the *anaesthetize, oxidize, texturize, apologize* examples. Take *texturize* in particular. You analyze that as, "to cause texture to go into a thing", but what's "texture"? I mean, "texture" is a property, it's not a thing. We can sort of say, "I give texture to something", but it really seems to me that things like *texture* and *oxidization* and so on, they're really words for properties, and if you look at them that way, class B will look a lot more like your class A.

Lieber: Sure, I think that that's a legitimate gripe about this, that it's not clear, first of all, that there is a real distinction between the change of state and the motional ones. I think that's a problem which is endemic in this particular theory of semantic decomposition. So I think that that's a larger problem for lexical semantics, and I think that I have some ideas about that which I can bore you with, in detail, some time. I think that having borrowed this formalization from Jackendoff, I've also borrowed some of the problems with it, that are endemic. So, how do you know exactly which of these categories a particular item goes into? Well sometimes items apparently go into more than one of these categories. If you look at a word like *capitalize* in the *American Heritage Dictionary*, I think that it can fall into any one of A through C meanings. So "to put capital in something" or "to cause capital to go to something", and "to turn something into capital", and so on, well that's fine, because *capital* is a sort of noun which lends itself to any one of these sorts of meanings pragmatically, so you can end up with more than one meaning given an item. I think that you don't need to take terribly seriously which items I've put in which classes. Those were what I thought were fairly good examples, but I think that you could probably make an argument for at least a few of them they might be reconstrued.

Baker: But it could turn into a deeper point if all the examples in B can be reconstrued as A. But if A is the biggest and most productive class, we could say then that A really is the meaning—putting aside C and D as small, unproductive categories. Then one can give a much richer meaning for *-ize* than you give.

Aronoff: A few points. First some references. Miller and Johnson-Laird, of course, said that nouns have conceptual structure—seven hundred pages of conceptual structure. Then there's the Clark and Clark paper in *Language* 1979. One of the things that's very important about the Clark and Clark paper is that they deal with derivations from proper nouns. In those cases, I think it's just silly to believe that there's any type of structure that makes any sense. An example is *boycott*, which is "to do what Boycott did" ... and they all work like that ... Then, they give nonce forms like *to houdini somebody*, which is "to punch somebody in the stomach, so that they subsequently die", which is, of course, what happened to Houdini, right? These are funny examples, but the larger point of this is that none of these Jackendovian, thematic things are going to be of any real value in that.

...

Noyer: I want to interject some phonology ... *-ize* is famously both Level I and Level II ... There's *métaphorize* and *metáphorize*, and I was trying to think of others on the plane. They're all kind of peculiar. But I'm kind of curious; it occurred to me that the ACT, DO, MAKE, and BASE MANNER, the type D, seem to be more correlated with the Level I, stress-shifting type of *-ize*. And this is probably more relevant to what Sharon and Orhan will say about co-phonologies, but I'm curious—is there really just one *-ize* from a phonological perspective? And does that correlate at all with any of the categories that you've suggested?

Lieber: To tell you the truth, I hadn't thought about that.

Noyer: That was my first point. My second point is that at the very end of your paper, you make this methodological point about using corpora, and I'm kind of nervous about the point of view of generative grammar, because although it may be the case that there is a corpus of words used, aren't we really concerned with what speakers individually have in their knowledge about *-ize*? Wouldn't it be more interesting to construct novel forms, or to ask people what they think about such-and-such meaning, rather than considering a corpus. I mean, I can see how the corpus would direct you into new ideas, but—you see my concern?

Lieber: No, I don't think so—

Noyer: OK ... but the question is, are we concerned with the sum knowledge of the community, or are we concerned, you know—

Lieber: No, I think that the methodological point is just this. There's a tendency in talking about an affix like *-ize* or in noun-to-verb conversion to think of the first six examples that you come up with off the top of your head, which often are the ones that come from the most productive category, or they may be the ones that are most lexicalized, one or the other. The point of using a corpus is not to make any claims about knowledge, not to exclude the sort of knowledge that we have that generates new forms, but simply to give you an idea of what sorts of forms are generated and with what frequency, so that you can get some handle on what you need to talk about in toto if you're looking at an affix. So that's the sole methodological point.

Baker: Maybe to just take up Rolf's point a little bit, you mentioned before, it's an interesting fact that a fair percentage of the ones you find, you have no idea what they mean. But maybe by that token those should be thrown out, in computing representations.

Lieber: No, I don't see why.

Noyer: ... We're modeling somebody's knowledge of it, so the question is, Who's knowledge of *-ize* are we modeling here? ... but that's just my concern, I mean, it's not really a major point, but supposing that there are a bunch of words in this corpus that have *-ize* and have really bizarre meanings, so, OK then what do we say? What does generative grammar say about that?

Aronoff: I think that Rolf is just barking up the absolute wrong tree here. I mean one would be hard pressed to defend using data other than the type that Shelly has collected. I think that going and trying to find out from a speaker what a word means is such a formidable task that we're really much better off taking advantage of the tools that we do have that can control this stuff.

Lieber: The optimal thing would be to use this sort of corpus data so you know what's out there, but also have contexts, which is something that Baayen and I are working on. This is very, very hard to get hold of, and we think we might be able to get hold of these things in contexts, so you can have some idea of the ones that you don't know off the top of your head what they might mean, what they did mean when somebody created them as nonce forms. I think that would be very useful information.

Janda: ... I wonder what the correlation is between people's judgments and how recently they were around children. If you are around children for any length of time, you hear and use a lot of these things—you tell stories, you're creative. I'm surprised at the lack of imagination of a lot of you when you say, "I can't imagine saying this." [Laughter]
    ... George Lakoff thought *agress* was impossible in the '60's, but it very quickly came into existence. And, for example, *to deep-six something* indeed indicates where something goes. With *jump*, I'm not sure what the original was. But let's take *bag*, I think that supports the pragmatics idea, at least in *bag your face*. We don't usually pick people up and stick them in bags. So with that one you have the person and take the bag to him or her, and put it over the head—with another orientation ... Lots of children create *broom*, instead of *sweep*, as in "Could you broom the doll house?" and so forth. Now there must be a stage, I would predict, where some children

could use *broom* before they have the syntactic structure in "Could you sweep this with a broom?" ...

The last thing to mention then is this pragmatics of association. How much weaker a connection could we ever have than "it has something to do with *x* "? Otherwise, you just make up a word and say "Oh it doesn't have anything to do with *x*, but I stuck *-ize* on *x* because I wanted to make a word that's a verb."

Sadock: There's such an example—*to audibilize* in football.

[*Several speakers:* "What??"]

Sadock: *To audibilize.* Actually, it means, "for a quarterback to give audible signals in the middle of a game". It should be *to audible*, but you can't say * *He's audibiling*, and so there's an irrelevant *-ize* in the example.

Janda: ... Eve Clark (following Barbara Partee) once reported that among people who are on boards of directors, there are constraints on how many boards they can be on. So *John's board* can mean "the board that John *can't* be on", because that would be too many boards. *John's board* here is the one he's *not* associated with, in any direct way. So the pragmatics win, but I don't see how the syntactic structures really come into the picture. I guess I agree with Patrick Farrell on this.

Lieber: This is what I was saying when I made the point that there are certain sorts of word formation that are semantically indeterminate completely. So I don't think you can provide any sort of basic LCS for noun-to-verb conversion; you can get anything, and you do get anything.

Deriving Passive without Theta Roles*

HAGIT BORER

1. Introduction

1.1 Lexical-Entry-Driven Approaches

Within models of argument projection assumed explicitly or implicitly in the past 15 years, a central role is played by the "bottom-up" view of grammar. Specifically, it is assumed that a lexical entry contains some syntactic information concerning the projection of its arguments, and that this information determines, by and large, the properties of D-structure. This view of grammar, labeled at times following Chomsky (1981, 1986) "D-structure as GF-θ", has been extremely influential in modeling the relationship between the lexicon and the syntax, and ultimately, between lexical semantics and syntactic representation. Much research during the '80s and the early '90s is motivated by the attempt to understand how lexical entries determine the projection of specific arguments, this attempt being a common denominator between approaches such as Baker's (1988) Uniformity of Theta Assignment Hypothesis, Pesetsky's (1990, 1995) formulation of the Universal Alignment Hypothesis, Chomsky's (1986) Canonical Structure Realization, and likewise, approaches assuming Lexical Conceptual Structure (e.g., Levin and Rappaport Hovav 1994 and previous work; Carrier and Randall 1992, 1993; and many others); approaches assuming various thematic hierarchies (e.g., Larson 1988; Grimshaw 1990, among others), etc. All these approaches, differ as they may on other matters, share an effort to deterministically project a grammatical level of representation based on the properties of individual lexical entries.

1.2 Variable Behavior Verbs

The lexical-entry-driven approach received one of its major boosts from the investigation of intransitive verbs and their division into the unaccusative and unergative classes. The systematic syntactic patterning of arguments of unaccusative verbs with direct objects, alongside the systematic syntactic patterning of arguments of unergative verbs with subjects of transitives strongly supported the view that syntactic projection

---

*The material in this paper is part of a larger body of research presented and taught in a number of places in the past two years. I am particularly grateful to audiences at Utrecht, UMass, Girona, and Tel-Aviv University for many comments. Of special benefit were insights of David Adger, Laura Benua, Jonathan Bobaljik, Angelika Kratzer, Bill McClure, Barbara Partee and Jochen Zeller. Special thanks to the participants of the Morphological Interfaces Workshop at UC Davis, and in particular to Andrew Spencer for comments on the earlier version of this paper.

information is specified in verbal lexical entries, plausibly deriving from the verb's lexical semantics.[1]

However, as has been observed in numerous studies, the unaccusative/unergative alternation is not as stable and lexical-entry dependent as it is occasionally presented. Thus consider the following examples:

(1) a. *Jan heeft gesprongen*
       Jan has jumped
    b. *Jan is in de sloot gesprongen*
       Jan is in the ditch jumped

(2) a. *Gianni ha corso*
       Gianni has run
    b. *Gianni e corso a casa*
       Gianni is run to home

(3) a. **Ne hanno corso/i due*
       of-them have run two
    b. *Ne sono corsi due a casa*
       of-them are run+agr two to home   (Hoekstra and Mulder 1990)

(4) *In het tweede bedrijf werd er door de nieuwe acteur op het juiste ogenblik gevallen*
    In the second act was there by the new actor on cue fallen
    (Perlmutter 1978)

(5) a. *ha-praxim navlu li*
       the-flowers wilted to me
       'My flowers wilted'
    b. *ha-praxim₁ navlu lahem₁*
       the-flowers wilted to-them
       'The flowers were wilting'
       (implies volition or self-directed
       motion)

(6) a. *ha-kir hitporer li*
       the-wall crumbled to-me
       'My wall crumbled'
    b. *ha-kir₁ hitporer lo₁ (le-'ito)*
       the-wall crumbled to-it
       (slowly)
       'The wall was crumbling
       (slowly)'

The paradigm in (1)-(3) shows that typical unergative verbs such as *springen* 'jump' in Dutch and *correre* 'run' in Italian, which take an unergative auxiliary (*hebben* and *avere* respectively) and which do not allow *ne*-cliticization, exhibit the full range of UNACCUSATIVE characteristics, selecting *zijn* and *essere* and allowing *ne* cliticization if a PP specifying a terminal point to the motion is added. (4) shows that Dutch impersonal passive, typically restricted to unergatives, can occur with the unaccusative verb *vallen* 'fall', provided an intention is ascribed to the argument (*fall on purpose*). Finally, (5)-(6) show that in Hebrew the argument of verbs such

---

[1] A notational clarification: The term UNACCUSATIVE here refers to verbs selecting a single argument associated with "internal" diagnostics (and not to all verbs with non-thematic subjects).

as *naval* 'wilt' and *hitporer* 'crumble' (among many others) can be internal, allowing a possessor dative, or external, allowing a reflexive dative.[2]

It has been further observed (see especially Van Valin 1990) that the unaccusative/unergative diagnostics associated with variable-behavior verbs are linked to interpretation correlations: syntactic unaccusative diagnostics are associated with telic and non-agentive characteristics. Syntactic unergative diagnostics, on the other hand, are typically associated with atelicity, and with agentive interpretation. This correlation is stated by Dowty (1991) in (7):

(7) Agentive, Atelic: definitely unergative
    Non-Agentive, Telic: definitely unaccusative

As an illustration, (5a), where *naval* 'wilt' is associated with a possessor dative, and is hence an unaccusative, clearly means that the flowers have died (an ACCOMPLISHMENT), rendering (8a) anomalous. On the other hand, (5b), associated with a reflexive dative, and hence unergative, implies that the flowers were engaged in a wilting ACTIVITY/PROCESS, and no termination is implied, making (8b) perfectly felicitous:

(8) a. *%ha-praxim navlu li kol ha-boker ve-'az yarad geSem ve-hem hit'oSeSu*
       the-flowers wilted to-me all morning and then it rained and-they recovered
    b. *ha-praxim navlu lahem kol ha-boker ve-'az yarad geSem ve-hem hit'oSeSu*
       the-flowers wilted to-them all morning and then it rained and-they recovered

If, indeed, the distinction between unaccusative intransitives and unergative intransitives is not fixed, and the same verb may appear in both classes, and if, indeed, the correlation in (7) is a robust one, then one is tempted to argue, (and see especially Van Valin 1990), that the unaccusative/unergative distinction is altogether *not* a syntactic one, but rather, an aspectual/semantic one. It is not the property of a particular lexical entry, but rather, the property of the entire predicate, of which the meaning of the verb is just one part. Such a predicate may be agentive/atelic or non-agentive/telic, and if auxiliary selection or *ne*-cliticization are dependent on aspectual distinctions, there remains little

---

[2]The possessor dative binds the determiner of the possessed NP (D-structure). The reflexive dative is coindexed with the external argument (Borer and Grodzinsky 1986).

motivation for projecting arguments of unaccusatives and unergatives in different syntactic positions. Further, within such an approach, the need for a PP defining terminal point in (1)-(3) above receives a natural account: the predicate, in the presence of such a PP, is telic, and hence we expect "unaccusative" diagnostics. In the absence of such a terminal point, atelicity results, and "unergative" diagnostics are attested.

In addressing this issue, and seeking to defend a lexical-entry-driven approach, Levin and Rappaport Hovav (1994) argue that there exist lexical rules which give rise to multiple semantic classifications of verbs, and which, in turn, license the appearance of these verbs in more than one construction. Dowty (1991), in turn, points out that the hypothesis that a large semantically coherent group of verbs has a duplicate categorization in unaccusative and unergative syntactic classes (and with corresponding different semantics in the two frames) seems to miss the point. Rather, it would appear that the distinction between unaccusative and unergative constructions, while real enough, is a distinction between different verb/argument complexes, rather than different verbs alone.

1.3   Evidence for Syntactic Representation for Variable Behavior Verbs

Within a semantic approach, a characterization of the unaccusative/ unergative distinction and its diagnostics seems readily available in exclusive AKTIONSART, non-syntactic terms. Are there, then, any reasons to assume that the syntax of unaccusative and unergative constructions is, in fact, distinct, or can their properties be attributed in their entirety to the compositional meaning of the predicates within which these intransitive verbs are embedded? Note, now, that this is a distinct question from whether the correct syntax for unaccusative and unergative constructions is lexical-entry driven. What is being asked here is whether an unaccusative PREDICATE, telic and non-agentive, is syntactically identical to an unergative predicate which is atelic and agentive, or whether the distinction between them is *syntactically* encoded. If the distinction *is* syntactically encoded, it may turn out that the distinct aspectual interpretation can be derived from the syntactic distinction.

Levin and Rappaport-Hovav (1994) give arguments that the distinction between unaccusatives and unergatives is syntactic. In addition to the arguments cited by them, consider the following argument from Hebrew.

Borer and Grodzinsky (1986) argue that possessor datives (PDs) in Hebrew exhibit, in essence, binding-like characteristics with respect to the determiner of the possessed DP. Assuming the PD to be in a c-commanding position of all (traditional) VP-internal material, excluding only the "external" argument, it can bind the determiner of a complement, either a direct object DP or a DP complement of a selected preposition, as in (9). It can further bind not just the determiner of an argument, but also determiners of DPs in adjuncts, as in (10). In fact, the only excluded local binding relation is between the PD and the determiner of an "external" argument, as illustrated by (9a) and (10b):[3]

(9) a. *ha_1-yeladim   zarku li$_{\{*1,2\}}$ 'et ha_2-kadur*
         the-boys   threw to-me   acc the-ball
         'the boys threw my ball'/*My boys threw the ball'
    b. *$Rina_1$ histaxsexa   li$_{\{*1,2\}}$ 'im ha-$mazkira_2$*
         Rina fought   to-me   with the-secretary
         'Rina fought with my secretary'

(10) a.
ha_1-yeladim   zarku   li$_{\{3,4\}}$ 'et ha_2-kadur la_3-gina leyad ha_4-mitbax
the-boys   threw   to-me   acc the-ball into-the-garden by the-kitchen
'the boys threw the ball into my garden next to the kitchen'
'the boys threw the ball into the garden next to my kitchen'
    b.
ha_1-xatulim yilelu   li$_{\{*1,2,3\}}$ bi-zman ha_2-Sena   mi-taxat la_3-xalon
the-cats   whined to-me d   uring the-nap   under to-the-window
'*My cats whined during the nap under the window'
'the cats whined during my nap under the window'
'the cats whined during the nap under my window'

Consider now the relationship between PDs and subjects of intransitive verbs. (10b) illustrates that subjects of unergative intransitives (with an activity/ process interpretation) cannot be "possessed" by PDs. However, this is not the case with subjects of unaccusative intransitives (with an accomplishment/ achievement interpretation), where the relationship is possible, with the subject post- or pre-verbal (see Borer and Grodzinsky 1986 for discussion):

(11) a. *ha_2-mitriya   nafla li_2*
          the-umbrella fell   to-me
          'my umbrella fell'
    b. *nafla li_2 ha_2-mitriya*
          fell   to-me   the-umbrella
          'my umbrella fell'

---

[3]In (9a), coincidental reference between the determiner of 'boys' and 'me' is possible, resulting in the interpretation 'my boys (= my sons)'. However, this coindexation cannot alone satisfy the condition on the occurrence of the PD, as in such a case *the ball,* as well, must be mine.

c. *ha$_2$-mitriya   nafla   li$_{\{2,3,4\}}$ al ha$_3$-Svil,   le-yad ha$_4$-mitbax*
   the-umbrella fell   to me   on the path   next-to the-kitchen
   'My umbrella fell on the path, next to the kitchen'
   'The umbrella fell on my path, next to the kitchen'
   'The umbrella fell on the path, next to my kitchen'

As is evident from (9)-(11), a possessor dative can bind the determiner of an unaccusative subject, as well as a direct object and an adjunct. On the other hand, it cannot bind the determiner of an unergative subject or a transitive subject. It is hard to see how this state of affairs can be reduced to an aspectual distinction, given the fact that adjuncts are altogether outside the argument structure complex here, and are aspectually neutral. Even more strikingly, note that possessor datives are blind to aspectual distinctions. Thus (10b) is clearly an activity/process, while (9) and (10a) are accomplishments, but the range of binding relationships possible in all is identical, without any effect on the resulting AKTIONSART. Rather, the relationship which allows possession by the possessor dative is purely structural, arguing for a distinct syntactic positioning of the unaccusative subject and the unergative subject. While the former must be "internal" to the c-command domain of the possessor dative, the latter must be "external" to that c-command domain. It is thus evident that at some level of representation the subject of (5a), an ACCOMPLISHMENT, is projected lower than the subject of (5b), a PROCESS.

2.   Towards   a Syntactic Predicate-Based   Account

We concluded that the unaccusative/unergative distinction and its aktionsart correlate, the process/eventive distinction is syntactically represented, and that the attempt to reduce its structural diagnostics to aktionsart semantics alone cannot succeed. Assuming, however, that the structural/interpretational correlation is not accidental, suppose we attempt to derive the aktionsart properties of these predicates from their syntax, and precisely from the position and the properties of the single argument in each of these predicates. In other words, suppose we attempt to link the "lower" argument position with an eventive interpretation, and the "higher" one with a process interpretation.

How can such a system be constructed? If the unaccusative/ unergative distinctions do not come from the lexical entry itself then we can no longer rely on the lexical entry to provide us with the information concerning the syntactic linking of particular arguments with particular positions. In other words, if we wish to provide, e.g., Hebrew *naval* with a unique lexical entry, but the sentences in (5a)-(5b) with distinct syntactic representations, we must abandon the assumption that *naval* assigns an "external" θ-role (or alternatively, an "internal" one), and allow the lexical entry for *naval* to specify only that it *has* an argument, which may find itself syntactically in more than one position, resulting in distinct aspectual properties.

Consider, then, the following possibility. Suppose the single argument of verbs such as *run, wilt, disappear* is not specified as EXTERNAL, INTERNAL. Suppose, in fact, that in general, arguments in lexical entries are not specified as EXTERNAL, INTERNAL, nor are there any syntactic linking conventions in lexical entries associated with the projection of arguments. It thus follows that arguments in lexical entries are not hierarchically ordered. Further, if the phrase structure of lexical projections is constructed on the basis of argument-projection information in lexical entries, it follows that beyond projecting a lexical head, lexical maximal phrases cannot have an internal hierarchical structure. Thus lexical phrases, while plausibly having a head and a maximal projection, do not otherwise project any internal structure. Instead, a lexical entry for, say, *derive* specifies the existence of two nominal arguments, and is projected as in (12a), while the lexical entry for, say, *wilt* is specified as taking a single argument and is projected as in (12b).[4]

(12) a. V^{max} b. V^{max}
          | |
     [*derive*, DP,DP]   [*wilt*, DP]

Suppose now that the hierarchical representation of arguments, clearly minimally required for c-command purposes, is achieved through the movement of arguments to the specifiers of functional projections. Specifically, the unordered arguments of the verbs in (12) are licensed in a functional specifier, e.g., by Case assignment. Thus at least DPs would have to move out of the VP, thereby being integrated into a hierarchical structure.[5] Suppose, now, that accusative Case is available, optionally, in

---

[4]In Borer 1995 it is further suggested that arguments are only specified as <x,y>, and that they become DPs or PPs as a result of either the movement to a functional specifier, or the licensing through a preposition. For some more discussion see subsection 4.2.1.

A formal question concerns the difference, if there is one, between having unattached DPs, as the diagram in (12) implies, and a flat structure. However, as no structural relationship of any meaning are stated on the structures in (12), the resolution of this issue is moot.

[5]An alternative is to base-generate the DP in the specifier of the functional category. It will become clear that in certain cases, the DPs in (12) remain in the VP (licensed either in situ or by P-insertion). Thus a unified representation

the specifier of a functional projection labeled Asp''_E (E for EVENTIVE in the AKTIONSART sense), and that the projection of Asp''_E itself is optional as well. (13) is the structure associated with an eventive interpretation:[6,7]

(13) a. $[_{Asp''E}$ Spec$_2$ Asp_{E2} $[_{V''}$ $[V, t_{DP}]]]$
                DP/t_{DP} ←——————⌐
                (ACC)

In (13), the configuration $<[_{Spec,Asp}DP_2][Asp_2]>$ is necessary (but not sufficient) for the realization of the aspectual properties of Asp_E. Neither the aspectual head, nor the DP in its specifier may be interpreted alone. Asp_E is well formed iff it is interpreted as a RESULT STATE and iff a DP in $[Spec,Asp_E]$ is predicated of that RESULT STATE (henceforth SUBJECT OF RESULT, or SOR).[8]

Suppose we adopt the view that the PROCESS/EVENT aktionsart distinction could be viewed as equivalent to the mass/count distinction in the nominal system. More specifically, and using terminology introduced by Link (1983), let us follow Bach (1986) in assuming that like mass nouns and bare plural nouns, processes are non-atomic, or CUMULATIVE, in the sense of Krifka (1991) and that like count nouns and definite nouns, eventives are atomic, or QUANTIZED, in Krifka's sense. Finally, let us adopt the assumption that for a language such as English, when the DP object is marked as QUANTIZED or CUMULATIVE, but the verb remains unmarked, the QUANTIZED/CUMULATIVE properties of the DP are inherited by the entire predicate. The syntactic structure in (13) could now be viewed as the structural means by which these "inheritance" relationship are instantiated: it is precisely the coindexation between the DP in $[Spec,Asp_E]$ and the head Asp_E which provides for the sharing of the QUANTIZED feature, and the eventive interpretation of the predicate. Note that in the absence of any inherent marking for Asp_E in a language such as English,

---

for V favors a VP-internal projection, rather than an optional generation of arguments in a wide variety of VP-internal and VP-external positions.

[6]Asp''_E is the structural equivalent of Chomsky's Agr-o", and its existence can be motivated by similar structural argumentation. For a recent review, see Runner 1995.

[7]For an independently developed account of AKTIONSART based on movement to functional specifiers see van Hout 1992, 1996 and McClure 1995.

[8]The term RESULT STATE is modified from Parsons 1990. See Kratzer 1994 for discussion.

the obligatoriness of a QUANTIZED DP in [Spec,Asp$_E$] follows. A fuller representation of (13a) is thus as in (13b):[9]

(13) b.

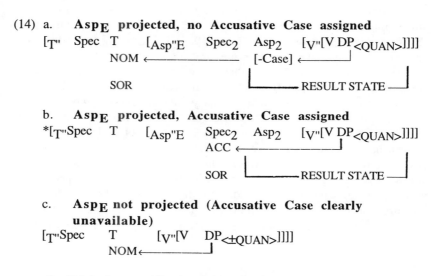

This said, let us now return to the derivation of sentences with intransitive verbs. Recall that two optionalities are associated with Asp"$_E$: it may or may not project (but when projected its specifier must be filled by an appropriate <QUAN> nominal) and when projected, its specifier may or may not be an (accusative) Case position. Consider now the resulting three derivations:

(14) a. **Asp$_E$ projected, no Accusative Case assigned**

$[_{T''}$ Spec T $[_{Asp''E}$ Spec$_2$ Asp$_2$ $[_{V''}[V$ DP$_{<QUAN>}$]]]]
NOM ⟵―――――――― [-Case] ⟵―――⏌
SOR ⌊―――― RESULT STATE ―⏌

b. **Asp$_E$ projected, Accusative Case assigned**

*$[_{T''}$Spec T $[_{Asp''E}$ Spec$_2$ Asp$_2$ $[_{V''}[V$ DP$_{<QUAN>}$]]]]
ACC ⟵―――――――⏌
SOR ⌊―――― RESULT STATE ―⏌

c. **Asp$_E$ not projected (Accusative Case clearly unavailable)**

$[_{T''}$Spec T $[_{V''}[V$ DP$_{<\pm QUAN>}$]]]]
NOM⟵―――――⏌

In (14a), the specifier is projected and hence must be filled. A DP$_{<QUAN>}$ moving into that position enters the coindexation relations with the E aspectual head giving rise to an eventive interpretation and is itself interpreted as SOR. The DP then moves to [Spec,TP] and is assigned nominative Case. This derivation is the eventive one, corresponding to

---

[9]An important question concerns the relationship between transmitting the quantized feature, rendering the DP obligatory, and the RESULT/SOR interpretation, making the DP obligatory as well, apparently redundantly. For arguments that both are, in fact, needed, see Borer 1996.)

ACCOMPLISHMENT or ACHIEVEMENT. This, I propose, is the syntactic derivation associated with the unaccusative diagnostics.

The derivation in (14b) is ruled out for familiar reasons, be it the obligatoriness of Nominative Case or Burzio's generalization which is violated here.[10] Finally, consider (14c). Here, Asp"$_E$ has not been projected, and so a DP in need of Case must travel directly to [Spec,TP], where it receives nominative. In this derivation the aspectual properties of Asp$_E$ remain inactivated, and an eventive interpretation is an impossibility. Plausibly, this is the structure of unergative non-eventive predicates.[11]

Consider now the representation of eventive transitives:

(15)

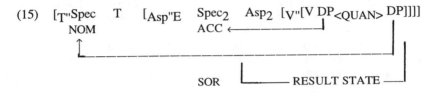

In (15) Asp$_E$ must project, or a Case position is missing. Consequently, one DP is in [Spec,Asp"$_E$], triggering the eventive reading and functioning as SOR, while another DP moves to [Spec,TP] and receives nominative Case. The argument predicated of the RESULT STATE is interpreted on a par with "internal" arguments, as "patients". The second argument, moving to [Spec,TP], receives a default "other argument" interpretation, to be matched in LF against the lexical semantics of the verb and the entire predicate. As syntactically required, this argument c-commands the "internal" argument.

As is well-known, however, not all transitive verbs are eventive, and Case is available to a direct DP complement even when transitives have a process reading. Touching briefly on the structure of such clauses, it may be useful to consider grammatical distinctions which remain unexpressed in English, but are realized in a language such as Finnish. Accusative Case in

---

[10]Obligatory nominative is trivially derived from Chomsky's EPP, or similar principles. Note that Burzio's generalization is easily statable in the structure in (14b) without any reference to the external/internal distinction, e.g., as a condition barring a derivation whose sole (aspectually active) argument is accusative (i.e., *[acc/argument; nom/expletive]).

[11]For presentational reasons, I assume that (14c) is the structure of unergative predicates, thereby equating the absence of aspectual nodes with a process interpretation. In Borer 1994 and Benua and Borer 1996, it is argued that in unergatives as well as in non-eventive transitives, a second aspectual node, Asp$_P$ (Asp-process) is projected. The process aspectual node, largely orthogonal to the discussion of passive, is not discussed in detail here.

Finnish is reserved for direct objects in eventive predicates. In non-eventive predicates, direct objects receive partitive Case. This contrast is illustrated by (16)-(18):

(16) a. *Anne rakensi taloa* (17) a. *Anne rakensi talon*
     Anne built house-PRT   Anne built house-ACC
     'Anne was building a/the house'   'Anne built a/the house'
  b. *Han luki kirjaa*   b. *Han luki kirjan*
     he read book-PRT   he read book-ACC
     'He was reading a/the book'   'He read a/the book'
  c. *Tiina heitti keihasta*   c. *Tiina heitti keihaan metsaan*
     Tiina threw javelin-PRT   Tiina threw javelin-ACC
     'Tiina threw the javelin'   into-the-forest
(18)   *Presidentti ampui kaikkia lintuja*
    president shot all-PRT birds-PRT   (also *most*-PRT)
    'The president was shooting at all the birds'
(examples from Vainikka and Maling 1993 and from de Hoop 1992)

Clearly, partitive DPs, regardless of their quantized or cumulative properties, cannot transmit their properties to Asp_E to result in an eventive interpretation. It follows that Asp''_E is not well-formed, and hence cannot be projected, in the presence of a partitive DP. I will assume that in the absence of such an aspectual structure, a functional shell, capable of assigning Case, but devoid of any interpretational value, is projected, and that partitive Case is licensed in that structure, schematized in (19):[12]

(19) $[_{T''}$ Spec   T $[_{F''}$ Spec$_2$ F$_2$ $[_{V''}[_V$ DP$_{<\pm QUAN>}$,DP]]]]
        NOM   PRT ←———┘

Finally, consider the well-known aspectual contrast between (20) and (21):

(20) a. John painted the pictures   (21) a. John painted pictures
   b. Mary refinished the furniture   b. Mary refinished furniture

(19a-b) receive an accomplishment interpretation, while (21a-b) receive a process one. The contrast between (20)-(21) follows clearly

---

[12]The causal relationship here can go either way. Within a checking model, Partitive Case would be base-generated on N, preventing the transfer of the quantized feature to Asp_E. In turn, recall that the projection of Asp_E is altogether optional. If not projected, accusative Case is not available and eventive interpretation is blocked.

within the system presented here. Recall that (13b) is well-formed iff DP is quantized. However, bare plurals (with non-generic interpretation) and mass nouns are cumulative. It thus follows that they cannot license an Asp_E node, or a RESULT interpretation. In turn, however, the nominals *furniture/pictures* do need Case, as do the subject DPs. It thus follows that while the representation for (21a-b) may not contain Asp_E, it must contain a FP shell structure, on a par with that assigned to transitive activities in Finnish, in which one of the DPs is assigned partitive Case, resulting in a non-eventive interpretation:[13]

(22)

a.

$*[_{T''}NOM\ T\ [_{Asp''}E$ $ACC\ Asp_2\ [_{V''}[V\left\{\begin{array}{l} bare\text{-}plural_{<\text{-}QUAN>} \\ mass\ noun_{<\text{-}QUAN>} \end{array}\right\}DP]]]]$

                              SOR $\longleftarrow$

b.

$*[_{T''}NOM\ T\ ([_{Asp''}E$ $Spec_2\ Asp_2)\ [_{V''}[V\left\{\begin{array}{l} bare\text{-}plural_{<\text{-}QUAN>} \\ mass\ noun_{<\text{-}QUAN>} \end{array}\right\}DP]]]]$

                            [-Case] $\longleftarrow$

                            SOR

---

[13] An interesting question concerns the correct characterization of the distribution of Possessor Datives, given the structures in (15)-(22). Given the non-hierarchical nature of the VP, it is not possible to leave the PD in the VP, or c-command of both subject and non-subject traces would result. On the other hand, outside the VP, it appears, the PD would c-command traces of both subject and object inside the VP as well.

Viewed differently, however, it is clear that the source of the problem here is not the absence of hierarchy inside the VP, but the assumption that the subject originates in the VP. There are independent reasons to assume that PD is outside the VP, at least sometimes, moving up with the verb. Even within standard VP structures, a distinction between its relationship with the subject and non-subjects would be hard to state in a straightforward way in such constructions. On the other hand, if the proposal made by Borer (1995) is true, and arguments do not receive their phrasal status until they are licensed, it could be suggested that binding between the PD and the determiner of the possessed cannot be instantiated until such phrasal status is realized. If this is on the right track, note that for "internal" arguments, such realization is in [Spec,Asp_E], while for "external" arguments it is in the higher [Spec,Asp_p] or [Spec,TP]. Assuming that PD is attached in a position c-commanding the former but c-commanded by the latter, the desirable result may be achieved. I leave the detailed execution to future research. Note that what is crucial is for there to exist a level of representation in which the subject c-commands non-subjects, clearly a property of the structures proposed here.

c. $[_{T''}$NOM T $[_{F''}$ PRT F $[_V$ [V $\begin{cases} bare\text{-}plural_{<\text{-}QUAN>} \\ mass\ noun_{<\text{-}QUAN>} \end{cases}$ DP]]]]

3. Passive Without Theta Grids

In most accounts of verbal passive, a crucial role is played by syntactic information contained in lexical entries. Considering, specifically, two influential approaches: the LGB approach (Baker, Johnson and Roberts 1989), and the LFG approach (e.g. Bresnan and Kanerva 1989), both crucially refer to the notion of EXTERNAL ARGUMENT or its equivalent. In these accounts, lexical or syntactic factors result in the effective suppression of that EXTERNAL ARGUMENT, and the subsequent "promotion" of the INTERNAL one.[14]

The role played by the external argument in adjectival passives is even more crucial. Thus in most accounts, it is assumed that a lexical rule derives adjectives from passive participles by externalizing the internal argument. Before proceeding, then, it is worthwhile to review evidence suggesting that syntactically the argument of an adjectival passive behaves like the argument of an unergative intransitive, rather than an unaccusative intransitive.[15]

Recall that in Hebrew, reflexive datives occur in unergative constructions, while possessor datives may not be associated with underived subjects. Consider in this view the following contrasts, illustrating that verbal passives act, syntactically, as unaccusative predicates, while adjectival passives (which are morphologically distinct, but related) act as unergative ones:[16]

(23) a. *ha-uga*   *hunxa*   *li*   *al Sulxan*
    the-cake   placed(V-Pass)   to-me   on table
    'My cake was placed on the table'
  b. *ha-xeder*   *kuSat*   *li*   *be-praxim*
    the-room decorated(V-Pass)   to-me   with flowers

---

[14]In LFG the notion EXTERNAL ARGUMENT is not used, and in its stead, the equivalent concept is expressed through a feature matrix specifying the relevant argument as [-r,-o].

[15]For the Baker, Johnson and Roberts 1989 account, the lexical existence of a passive participle serving as an input to the formation of adjectival passive is, to begin with, problematic, as their account involves *syntactic*, rather than lexical derivation of the V+en combination.

[16]Similar evidence for the unergativity of adjectival passives is available from Italian *ne*-cliticization (Belletti and Rizzi 1981), and from Russian genitive-of-negation (Pesetsky 1982).

'My room was decorated with flowers'

(24) a. *ha-uga₂*   *hunxa*   *la₂*   *'al Sulxan*
the-cake   placed(V-Pass)   to-it   on a table

   b. *ha-xeder₂*   *kusat*   *lo₂*   *be-praxim*
the-room   decorated(V-Pass) to-it   with flowers

(25) a. *ha-uga*   *hayta*   *munaxat*   *li*   *'al Sulxan*
the-cake   was   placed-Adj   to-me   on table

   b. *ha-xeder*   *haya*   *mekuSat*   *li*   *be-praxim*
the-room   was   decorated-Adj to-me   with flowers

(26) a. *ha-uga₂*   *hayta*   *munaxat*   *la₂*   *'al Sulxan*
The-cake   was   placed-A   to-it   on table
'The cake was on the table'

   b. *ha-xeder₂*   *haya*   *mekuSat*   *lo₂*   *be-praxim*
the-room   was   decorated   to-it   in-flowers
'The room was decorated with flowers'

Within a model linking unaccusativity and unergativity with the [±eventive] distinction, the unergative properties of adjectival passives are not surprising: since adjectives are non-eventive, we do not expect a realized Asp$_E$ node with its accompanied filled specifier, nor do we expect the argument of adjectival passives to behave as the DP occupying that specifier or displaying the diagnostics of an unaccusative subject. In turn, in a model that does not allow reference to the terms external/internal, 'externalization' clearly cannot exist. How, then, can the properties of adjectival passives be accounted for, without compromising the morphological relatedness between it and verbal passives?

A non-thematic perspective on these matters is offered in Kratzer 1994, 1995. Kratzer proposes that the assignment of external arguments is external to the VP, accomplished by an active Voice Phrase. In passive, both verbal and adjectival, the internal argument of the source verb is generated (as are all "internal" arguments") in [Spec,VP] (where the verb is a participial form). In adjectival passives, the participle is further embedded under an AP (headed by a Ø-affix). In verbal passive, the participle is embedded under an active Voice Phrase whose "external" role is saturated by a clitic, thereby rendering the phrase passive. (27a-d) are the structures Kratzer assigns to adjectival passive, verbal passive, unaccusatives and unergatives respectively:

(27) a. **Verbal Passive**
[$_{Voice"}$ Spec Voice⁰ [$_{V"}$ Spec   V]]
            CL
            "external"   "internal"   PARTICIPLE

b. **Adjectival passive**

$([_{Copula''} \quad Spec \; Copula^0) \; [_{A''}(Spec) \quad A^0 \; [_{V''} \quad Spec \qquad V]]]$

$\qquad\qquad\qquad\qquad\qquad\qquad\qquad \emptyset \qquad$ "internal"PARTICIPLE

c. **Unaccusative**

$[_{Voice''}non\text{-}active \qquad Spec \qquad Voice^0 \; [_{V''} \quad Spec \qquad V]]$

$\qquad\qquad\qquad\qquad\qquad\qquad\qquad\qquad\qquad\qquad\qquad$ "internal"

d. **Unergative**

$[_{Voice''}active \qquad Spec \qquad Voice^0[_{V''} \quad Spec \qquad V]]$

$\qquad\qquad\qquad\qquad\qquad\qquad\qquad\qquad\qquad\qquad\qquad$ "external"

Importantly, and contrary to most analyses of adjectival passives, Kratzer's structures amount to claiming that the argument of an adjectival passive is internal. Kratzer further suggests that adjectives may be either raising or control structures, depending on whether they are stage-level predicates or individual-level predicates (following Diesing 1990). For stage-level predicates, the raising structure is essentially as in (28a). For individual-level predicates, the control structure is essentially as in (28b), where the argument in the specifier of the copula controls PRO, which is "internal" in the relevant sense:

(28) a. **Stage level Adjectives**

$[_{Copula''} Spec \quad Copula^0 \quad [_{A''} \quad Spec \qquad A^0 \qquad XP]]$

$\qquad \uparrow \text{———————} \quad$ "internal"

b. **Individual level Adjectives**

$[_{Copula''} Spec \qquad Copula^0 \; [_{A''} \quad PRO \qquad A^0 \qquad XP]]$

$\qquad\qquad\quad$ "external" $\qquad\qquad\qquad\qquad$ "internal"

A full comparison of the system proposed in this paper and Kratzer's system is outside the scope of this paper.[17] Note, however, that while the structures in (27)-(28) clearly capture the fact that in both adjectival and verbal passives the subject is understood as being in a result state emerging from some event, and related to the direct argument of the verb, structurally, (27b) and (28a-b) predict that the argument of adjectival passive will always behave as an "internal" argument, or put differently, will always pattern

---

[17]A crucial difference between these models involves the different treatment of the unaccusative/unergative distinction. Here, the argument of both types is an argument of the verb, thereby allowing a unified lexical entry for variable behavior verbs. On the other hand, Kratzer assumes that the unaccusative "subject" is an argument of the verb, but the unergative "subject" is an argument of VoiceP, making the existence of a unified entry problematic.

with the argument of verbal passives and unaccusative verbs. In turn, when it is an individual-level predicate it would behave as both "internal" and "external" simultaneously. The facts in (23)-(26), as well as other tests proposed in the literature do not bear out this prediction. (25) excludes a possessor dative, showing that the argument of adjectival passive cannot be VP internal. In turn, it patterns like the subject of unergative verbs in (26a-b), clearly stage-level predicates, contrary to the prediction of the structure in (28a).

In turn, if the derivation of passive participles already involves reference to the external-internal linking convention, and as the formation of adjectival passives requires externalization, contra Kratzer (1994), clearly within a model which assumes no external-internal distinctions and per force no externalization, another account for the formation of passive participles, both in their verbal and adjectival projections, is necessary.

4. Verbal Passive without Lexical Syntactic Linking
4.1 Deriving the Participle
Before moving on, consider again the (eventive) transitive in (29):

(29) [$_{T''}$ NOM T   [$_{Asp''}$E ACC Asp^0 [$_{V''}$[V DP$_2$ DP$_1$]]]]
                                              eat   cake   Kim

In (29), DP$_2$ moves to [Spec,Asp], acquiring the SOR interpretation. DP$_1$, *Kim*, in turn, receives the default, *eater* interpretation. However, the system would allow *Kim* to move to [Spec,Asp], thereby becoming interpreted as SOR, resulting in *the cake* being assigned the default *eater* interpretation, as in (30). While (29) would give rise to (31a), (30) would give rise to (31b):

(30) [$_{T''}$ NOM T   [$_{Asp''}$E ACC Asp^0 [$_{V''}$[V DP$_2$ DP$_1$]]]]
                                SOR   eat   cake   Kim

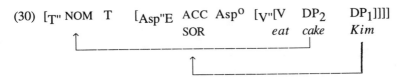

(31) a. Kim ate the cake
     b. The cake ate Kim

Although (31b) is anomalous, it is clearly syntactically well-formed: *the cake* is interpreted as the eater, and *Kim* as the eaten, in accordance with the structure. An interpretation of (31b) as synonymous with (31a) is correctly excluded. In turn, the oddity of (31b) is due to world knowledge, and not to syntactic factors, as there is a possible world in which it is not anomalous.[18]

Now consider briefly the active/passive contrast, and its discourse function. Clearly, there is a sense in which the logical subject in the active is being "demoted" in the terminology of Relational Grammar, and another argument is "promoted". In most accounts, the demotion and consequent promotion are treated as properties of the arguments involved. E.g., the subject becomes a chomeur (RG); becomes specified as [+r] (LFG), becomes an adjunct (GB), or becomes associated with a morpheme, rather than an argument (Jaeggli 1986; Baker, Johnson and Roberts 1989). Suppose, however, that "passivization" is the result of a reversal in the relationship between functional projections in the clause, rather than a change in the projection information associated with particular DPs. Specifically, suppose that in the unmarked case, T and the EVENT argument are linked with the aspectual PROCESS node, or alternatively, with nothing at all.[19] The formal operation of passivization involves the linking of T and the EVENT argument in it with Asp_E.[20] Suppose further that Nominative Case is assigned to a specifier coindexed with T. Thus the structure of an "active" clause is as in (32a), while the structure of a "passive" clause is as in (32b) (see footnotes 11, 22, 38 for a brief discussion of Asp_P):

(32) a.
$([_{Asp''P}Spec_2\ Asp_{P2})\ [_{T''}Spec_2\ T_2\ ([_{Asp''E}Spec\ Asp_E)[_{V''}[V\ DP\ (DP)]]]]]$
(NOM)   (NOM) <e>

b. $[_{T''}\ Spec_2\ \ T_2\ \ \ \ ([_{Asp''E}\ Spec_2\ \ \ Asp_{E2})\ [_{V''}[V\ DP\ (DP)]]]]$
     (NOM) <e>   (NOM)

---

[18] As the landing site of the DP determines its interpretation, we may dispense with Chomsky's 1992 EQUIDISTANCE, designed to force the external argument to land higher than the internal one.

[19] Recall that Borer 1994 argues that an additional aspectual node, Asp_P (P = process) is responsible for activity/process interpretation.

[20] The converse situation holds in ergative languages, where in the unmarked situation T is associated with Asp_E (or with nothing at all) and "antipassive" involves the association of T with Asp_P. See Benua and Borer 1996, for further discussion.

The configurational reversal in passive constructions is achieved, formally, through the mediation of the passive morpheme. Suppose, then, that the properties of such a morpheme are as in (33):[21]

(33) a. *-en*, projected as Asp_E, is coindexed with T.

　　b. *-en* is distinct from [-N].

(32)-(33) suffice to turn predicates containing passive participles to creatures syntactically akin (but not identical) to unaccusative predicates. The reason for this is clear: by assumption, Asp_E must be projected in passive constructions. In turn, once Asp_E is projected, its specifier must be filled, resulting in an eventive predicate and in an SOR argument. If we add to this the fact that in passive constructions Asp_E is coindexed with T, it follows that SOR must be nominative, and that no accusative Case is available.[22] The derivation (for a dyadic predicate) is given in (34):[23]

$$(34) \quad [_{T''} \; Spec_2 \quad T^o{}_2 \; [_{AspE} \quad Spec_2 \quad Asp^o{}_{E2} \quad [_{V''}[_V \; DP_2 \; DP_1]]]]$$
$$\qquad\qquad (NOM) \quad <e> \qquad\qquad SOR \qquad \textit{-en}$$

---

[21] See Freidin 1978. I assume that distinctness from -N prevents the participle from raising to T, thereby necessitating the presence of an auxiliary as a Tense carrier. While, by assumption, (33a) is the "essential" property of passive, (33b) is a property of the passive morpheme in languages which have participial passives. Thus in Semitic, (33b) does not hold, and passive constructions contain a fully inflected verb. This inter-language variation is not discussed further here. For discussion of passive morphemes as functional heads distinct from (grammatical) aspect heads see Ouhalla 1990.

[22] If Asp_P is not projected and T and Asp_E are not coindexed, as in an active (unaccusative) derivation, it is still possible for SOR to move to [Spec,TP] and be assigned nominative.

[23] An interesting case is verbal passivization of dative constructions, as in (i):

　　(i)　John was given a book

In (i), the argument assigned nominative is not the SOR, nor is the ability to assign accusative Case lost. On the other hand, the suppressed argument is the "agent", and the argument functioning as SOR is plausibly in [Spec,Asp_E]. Suppose that in (i) the coindexation between Asp_P and T is lost, but it is not replaced by a coindexation between Asp_E and T, but by a coindexation between T and a functional projection licensing dative. As a result, accusative Case is retained and the SOR interpretation is associated with the accusative argument. If this is the correct approach to dative constructions, it suggests that (32a) should be stated in terms of linking T with a functional projection distinct from Asp_P, and that the linking of T with Asp_E is the special case of dyadic predicates, in which the only available relevant functional projection is Asp_E.

DP_2 is moved to [Spec,Asp$_E$], where it is interpreted as SOR, but DP_1 is trapped in the VP, and I will turn shortly to its fate. Note that although the system allows either argument to move out of the VP, it also forces the moved argument to be interpreted as SOR, or in the case of a verb such as *eat,* the eaten. The derivation in (34), note, does not give rise to a particular type of query: why it is the "internal" argument that moves. Because the movement passes through [Spec,Asp$_E$], the "internal" interpretation results.[24]

The derivation in (34) further predicts that passives cannot be non-eventive (in the aktionsart sense). Given the syntactic representation for eventive predicates suggested here, it is further predicted that mass nouns and bare plurals could not function as the subjects of passive. This claim receives a striking confirmation in languages such as Italian and Spanish, where the range of interpretations associated with bare plurals and mass nouns is considerably more limited than that allowed in English. Thus Van

---

[24]A number of interesting issues arise here. First, consider the distribution of temporal aspectual modifications especially when they occur in the passive variants of process transitives, such as *"the cart was pushed for five minutes"* or *"in five minutes"*, or *"the film was seen for five minutes"* or *"in five minutes"*. Without modification, the interpretation of *the film was seen* entails an accomplishment (the film seen to its end), while the interpretation of *the cart was pushed* without modification is roughly synonymous to that of *the cart was dislocated*, again an accomplishment. However, the fact that process modification is possible for these passives appears problematic for the claim that all passives are eventive. On the other hand, it turns out that such adverbial modification is possible for clearly eventive predicates, where the eventive interpretation is preempted by adverbial modification, or for that matter, by negation or by a progressive marking:

(i)   The plane fell for a full five minutes before the pilot regained control
(ii)   The plane did not fall
(iii) The plane was falling

Classical syntactic diagnostics of the, e.g., unaccusative/unergative distinction such as auxiliary selection and *ne*-cliticization in Italian, or resultative formation in English, are not sensitive to the presence of adverbial modification, negation, or progressive, but only to the basic aspectual properties of the verb-argument complex. I suggest, then, that the relations between the aspectual force of the verb-argument complex and that of adverbial modification is somewhat akin to that which holds between the A-system and the A-bar system. The verb-argument complex forms the basic unit of aspectual meaning, in accordance with the system sketched here. Further modification functions as an operator, changing the aspectual value as a whole, but leaving unchanged the aspectual value assigned to the sub-unit composed of the verb and its arguments, which in turn determines the syntactic diagnostics of the constructions.

Valin (1991) observes the following contrasts in Italian (see also Spanish in (36)):

(35) a. *Gli spaghetti sono stati mangiati da Anna (in cinque minuti)*
          the spaghetti was eaten by Anna (in five minutes)
      b. **Spaghetti sono stati mangiati da Anna (in/per cinque minuti*
          Spaghetti was eaten by Anna (in/for five minutes)
      c. **Sono stati mangiati spaghetti da Anna (in/per cinque minuti)*
          was eaten spaghetti by Anna (in/for five minutes)

(36) a. *Estas playas han sido visitadas por mis estudiantes*
          these beaches were visited by many students
      b. **Playas han sido visitadas por mis estudiantes*
          beaches were visited by many students
      c. **(XP) Han sido visitadas playas por mis estudiantes*
          were visited beaches by many students

Bare plurals and mass nouns are independently barred in pre-verbal subject positions in Italian and Spanish. However, the ungrammaticality of (35b-c)-(36b-c) is independent of this: in (35c) and (36c) the subject is post-verbal, a position normally allowing bare plurals, but not in passive constructions:[25]

(37) *Estas playas las ha visitado touristas de todo tipo*
      these beaches them has visited tourists of every kind

4.2 The Implicit "External" Argument

Let us now turn to the argument remaining in the VP in (34). In the absence of any hierarchy in the VP, there is no prima facie information on the syntactic properties of such an argument. On the other hand, its interpretation as an "external" argument does follow. As the moved argument must be SOR, the unmoved one, by default, is the "other" argument, i.e., the "external" one.

I suggested that an argument may remain in the VP if its movement to a Case position is not independently necessary. There are two ways to render such movement unnecessary. First, the argument could be licensed if associated with an (inherent) preposition assigning it Case. Second, if the VP-internal argument does not need Case, its movement is not forced. Let

---

[25] A similar effect is attested in English. Although bare plurals and mass nouns are allowed in subject position, when they are subjects of passive, a process interpretation is not available:

(i). a. Furniture was refinished (by Mary)
      b. Pictures were painted (by John)

us now consider these two possibilities with respect to the "external" argument in (34).

4.2.1 Projecting the "External" Argument as a PP

The unmoved argument could be realized as a PP. Suppose, then, that this is so when a *by*-phrase is projected. Assuming *by* is a dummy Case marker, the properties of the "external" argument follow. The resulting structure is (38) (since everything but the *by*-phrase is outside the VP, the unordered attachment of the *by*-phrase to VP does not presents any word-order problems):

(38)
$[_{T''}$ Spec$_2$ T$_2$ $[_{V''}$ *be* $[_{Asp''}$E   Spec   Asp$_{E2}[_{V''}$[V DP$_2$ DP$_1$]]]]]
NOM   <e>   SOR ⟵————————⌟ ⇓
↑————————————————— *the cake*$_2$ -en   eat t_2 *by* DP$_1$

PP-licensing the "external" argument in a passive derivation such as (34) contrasts with its non-availability in "active" derivations:

(39) *$[_{T''}$Spec   T $[_{Asp''}$E   Spec Asp$_E$ $[_{V''}$[V   DP$_2$ DP$_1$]]]]
NOM <e>   SOR ⟵————⌟ ⇓
the cake$_2$ ⟵———— t_2 ate t_2 *by* DP$_1$

PP-licensing of "external" arguments is further impossible when it is free with respect to other arguments, as the derivation of *spray/load* illustrates:

(40) a.

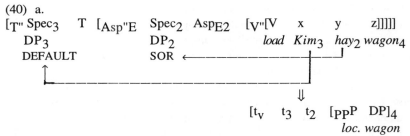

Kim loaded the hay on the wagon

b.

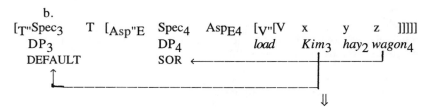

$$[t_v \quad t_3 \quad [_{PP}P \quad DP]_2 \quad t_4]$$
$$with \quad hay$$

Kim loaded the wagon with hay

c.

$$*[_{T''} \; Spec_3 \; T \; [_{Asp''}E \quad Spec_4 \quad Asp_{E4} \; [_{V''}[V \quad x \quad y \quad z \quad]]]]]$$
$$DP_3 \qquad\qquad\quad DP_4 \qquad\qquad\qquad load \quad Kim_3 \; hay_2 \; wagon_4$$
$$DEFAULT \qquad\quad SOR$$

$$[t_v \quad [_{PP}P \quad DP]_3 \quad t_2 \quad t_4]$$
$$by \quad Kim$$

*The hay was loaded the wagon by Kim
*The wagon was loaded the hay by Kim

It thus appears that the "external" argument may be PP-licensed VP-internally only in passive sentences, but not in active ones. Viewed differently, however, this is what we expect when we consider the proposal in (32)-(33). In the unmarked case, T is linked with PROCESS and subject of process, thereby barring the licensing of a subject-of-process as a VP internal PP. Once the situation is reversed, and the primary link is between T and Asp_E, the PP realization of the "agent" becomes possible, comparable to the assignment of Ergative Case to the "agent" in ergative/absolutive languages, where the primary link is between the event argument and the EVENTIVE node.

4.2.2 A Non-overt (Implicit) "External" Argument

When a dyadic predicate is passivized, recall, only one structural Case position is available, and hence only one argument may move out of the VP. In turn, that argument is interpreted as SOR. Consider, however, an argument which need not be assigned Case, because it is phonologically unrealized. The representation of such a situation is given in (41):[26]

$$(41) \; [_{T''} \; Spec \; T^O_2 \; [_{V''} \quad V^O \; [_{AspE''} \; Spec \; Asp^O_{E2} \; [_{V''}[V \; DP_2 \; DP_1]]]]]$$
$$NOM \; <e> \qquad be \qquad\qquad\qquad\qquad\qquad\qquad pro$$

Some manipulations of the structure in (41) are already ruled out: if *pro* in (41) moves to [Spec,Asp$_E$] to become SOR, DP_2, by assumption phonologically realized, could not be assigned Case, and the derivation would be ruled out. Alternatively, of course, DP_2 could be associated with

---

[26] I follow here Borer 1989, where it is argued that *pro* need not be Case marked.

an inherent P, resulting in a derivation identical to that sketched in (36), but with a null pronominal subject. Such a null pronominal subject, note, would have to have a COUNT interpretation in the relevant sense, thereby making it a definite pronominal (e.g., *she*), or a generic pronominal (e.g. *one*). In turn, DP_2 may move to [Spec,Asp$_E$], becoming SOR and leaving *pro* in the VP. Unlike DP_2, however, *pro* need not be licensed, in such a situation, by a preposition. Thus, for (41), it appears, the following range of outputs emerges:

(42) a. *$[_{Asp"E}$ *pro*[-count]$_3$ [V-*en* [$_{V"}$ t$_V$ DP_2 t$_3$]]]
    b. $[_{Asp"E}$ *pro*[+count]$_3$ [V-*en* [$_{V"}$ t$_V$ *by* DP_2 t$_3$]]]
    c. $[_{Asp"E}$ DP_2 [V-*en* [$_{V"}$ t$_V$ *pro*[-count] *t*$_2$]]]

5. On the Properties of VP-internal *pro*
5.1 Impersonal Null Subjects

Two important queries emerge immediately in the trail of the account in the previous subsection. First, the reader is no doubt wondering what licenses the occurrence of *pro* in the VP in a language such as English, where *pro* is normally not attested. Second, note that the interpretation of *pro* in passive constructions does not correspond to that of a definite pronominal or a generic pronominal. Thus *the cat was fed* does not mean that some specific person fed it, or alternatively, that it is a generic feeder who did so. Rather, *pro* in passive constructions receives an indefinite, non-specific interpretation, very much on a par with that associated with bare plurals (or mass nouns) in sentences such as *the cat was fed by (some) children*. Attempting to relate these two queries, I will suggest that the *pro* stranded in the VP in passive constructions is, indeed, an indefinite, non-specific *pro*, in essence, a null bare-plural, and further, that the following is correct:

(43) *Bare plural pro* is licensed WITHOUT IDENTIFICATION.

If a *bare plural pro* need not be identified, but licensing conditions hold of a definite *pro*, the free occurrence of such a *pro* in the VP in English is not predicted to result in ungrammaticality. On the other hand, (43) is clearly a very strong claim. Can this claim be independently motivated?

It turns out that the existence of a *bare plural pro*, as well as (43), *can* be independently supported. Consider a null subject construction discussed in Jaeggli (1987), and Cinque (1988):

(44) a. *dafku*   *ba-delet*
      knocked-pl-m   on-the-door
      'Someone knocked on the door'

b. *hifcicu*   *'et levanon*   *ha-boker*
bombed-pl-m   acc. Lebanon   this-morning
'Lebanon was bombed this morning'   (Hebrew)

(45) a. *Aseguran que van a venir a arreglar la heladera mañana de mañana.*
assure-pl that go-pl to come to fix the refrigerator tomorrow morning
'I am assured that someone will come to fix the fridge tomorrow morning'

     b. *Llaman a la porta*
call-pl at the door
'Someone is calling at the door'   (Spanish, Jaeggli 1987)

(46) a. *Prima, hanno telefonato: mi pareva tua sorella*
earlier, have-pl telephoned   : me seems your sister
'There was a phone call earlier. I think it was your sister'

     b. *Hanno comprato i giudici. Pare sia stato l'avvocato*
have-pl bought the judge. It seems it was the lawyer
'The judge was bought. Apparently by the lawyer' (Cinque 1988)

The interpretation of (44)-(46) is very similar to that of passive sentences. Further, the null subjects in (44)-(46) are interpreted as indefinite and non-specific. It is thus plausible that these subjects are indefinite *pro*'s, as are the implicit subjects in passives. If this is the case, a closer scrutiny of these null subjects may shed light on the properties of the implicit argument in passives.

First, note that in Hebrew, Italian and Spanish, the *pro* subject in (44)-(46) is plural, making the comparison with bare plurals at least suggestive.[27] Second, at least in Hebrew, this *pro* is subject to much laxer identification conditions than a definite, referential *pro*. Hebrew, as is well-known, does not allow for referential, definite *pro* subjects in present tense, as illustrated by the ungrammaticality of (47a-b). However, *bare plural pro* subjects *are* possible in the present tense (cf. (48)):[28]

(47) *'oxlim gvina*
eat-pl cheese

---

[27]A singular variant is discussed by Cinque 1988. Crucially, however, it only co-occurs with *si*, suggesting that unlike the unlicensed indefinite non-specific, "bare plural" *pro* discussed here, the singular variant is identified/licensed by *si*. A separate question, clearly beyond our scope, concerns the reason for this plurality

[28]In 3rd person past and future, definite *pro* is possible, but only with a clause-internal antecedent. In present tense, however, such an antecedent does not suffice to license a null pronominal subject, making the grammaticality of (48) even more striking.

(cf. hem 'oxlim gvina
     they eat   cheese)

(48) a. *dofkim*   *ba-delet*
    knock-pl-m   on-the-door
    'Someone knocks on the door'

    b. *mafcicim*   *'et levanon*   *ha-boker*
      bomb-pl-m acc. Lebanon   this-morning
      'Lebanon is bombed this morning'

The licensing/identification requirements for *bare plural pro* are clearly more relaxed than those needed for definite ones, raising the possibility that *bare plural pro* is licensed even in a language such as English, in which definite *pro* is barred. Further support for the indefinite, non-specific nature of *bare plural pro* comes from its inability to take an antecedent, even when the antecedent itself is a *bare plural pro*. This situation is illustrated by (49):

(49) *'omrim*   *Se-mafcicim*   *'et levanon*
    say-pl-m   that-bomb-pl-m   acc Lebanon
    'It is said (by x) that Lebanon is being bombed (by y/*x)'

On the other hand, a *bare plural pro* can serve as an antecedent for another element (providing it is not itself a *bare plural pro*), again, as expected, and parallel to the established availability of implicit argument control in passive:

(50) a. *hexlitu*   *le-hafcic*   *'et levanon*
    decided-pl-m ("PRO")   to bomb   acc Lebanon
    'It was decided (by x) to bomb Lebanon'

    b. It was decided (*pro*$_2$) "PRO"$_2$ to bomb Lebanon

So far, we have uncovered the existence of a *pro* which is interpreted as an indefinite non-specific, which need not be identified/licensed, which is plural, and which may not take an antecedent but may serve as one. As further support for the claim that such a *pro* is a *bare plural pro*, note that it can have a generic, or a universal, interpretation in both Italian and Hebrew. As is clear from the Hebrew examples, equally lax identification conditions apply to the *bare plural pro* in its generic/universal interpretation.:

(51) a. *Li, odiano*   *gli sranieri*
    there, hate-pl-m   strangers
    'They hate strangers there'

    b. *Qui,*   *lavorano anche di sabato*
    'Here,   they work even on Saturday'   (Cinque 1988)

(52) *be-Savu'ot   'oxlim   gvina*
in-Pentecost   eat-pl-m   cheese
'One eats cheese in Pentecost

Consider now a property of this construction pointed out by Jaeggli (1987), and Cinque (1988). Both observe that when interpreted existentially, our *pro* may not occur as the subject of passive or as the subject of unaccusative constructions ((53) further illustrates the phenomena in Hebrew):[29]

(53) a. **naflu   /noflim   ba-xacer   ha-boke*
    fell-pl-m/fall-pl-m in-the-yard this-morning
    'Someone fell/is falling in the yard this morning'
  b. **putru   me-ha-avoda ('al yedey ha-hanhala)   ha-boker*
    fired-pass-pl from-work   (by the management)   this-morning
    'Someone was fired from their job (by the management) this morning'

(54) a. **Fueron   arrestados por la policia*
    were-pl   arrested   by the-police (passive)
    '*Someone was arrested by the police'
  b. **Llegan   cansados despues de un viaje   tan largo*
    arrive-pl   tired   after   of a trip   so long
    'Someone arrives tired after such a long trip'   (Jaeggli 1987)

(55) a. **Sono venuti a   vedere: era   una signora anziana.*
    are   come-pl to see: it was   an elderly woman
    'Someone came to see. It was an old woman (the "comer")'
  b. **Sono   stati   catturati: era   un ragazzo*
    are   been-pl arrested-pl: it was   a boy (passive)
    'Someone was arrested. It was a boy'   (Cinque 1988)

(53)-(55) contrast with (56)-(57), where *bare-plural pro* has a generic interpretation, and its occurrence in passives and unaccusatives is grammatical:

---

[29]Pesetsky 1995 suggests that the null pronoun in constructions such as (44)-(46) must be agentive, thereby accounting for its exclusion in unaccusatives and passives. As (i) from Hebrew illustrates, however, this is clearly not the case:

(i) Sam'u   'oto   torek   'et   ha-delet
    heard-pl him   slam   acc   the door
    'He was heard to slam the door'

(56) a.
'im mafginim   bli   riSayon   ne'esarim   'al yedey ha-miStara
if demonstrate   without license   arrested-pass-pl-m   by the police
'For all x, if x demonstrates without a license, x is arrested by the police'

    b. *[kSe-kofcim   me-ha-gag]   noflim   le-mata*
      [when-jump-pl-m   from the roof] fall-m-pl   down
      'For all x, when x jumps from the roof, x falls down'   (Hebrew)

(57) a. *Qui, sono educati in un'atmosfera   protestante molto rigida*
       here, are-pl educate in an atmosphere protestant   very rigid
       'Here, one is educated in a very strict Protestant atmosphere'

    b. *Qui, vanno a scuola   gia   a quattro anni*
      here, go-pl   to-school   when   four years
      'Here, one goes to school at age four'   (Cinque 1988)

Consider how such a contrast can be accounted for. Recall that (non-generic) bare plurals and mass nouns, being [-COUNT], cannot license an eventive interpretation, and hence can never function as SOR. Recall further that by definition, passives must have a COUNT argument in [Spec,Asp$_E$], and that (in dyadic predicates) this argument ends up as the subject of the passive construction (i.e., marked nominative). It follows that just as mass nouns and bare plurals cannot function as subjects of passive (see (20)-(22) and related discussion), so *bare plural pro* cannot function as such a subject.[30]

The unavailability of non-generic *bare plural pro* subject in unaccusatives follows as well. Recall that unaccusatives are monadic VPs and a COUNT DP is essential for the formation of eventive interpretation (cf. (58)). As *bare plural pro* is [-COUNT], an unaccusative/eventive predicate cannot be formed.[31]

(58) $[_{\text{Asp"E}}$ Spec   Asp$^{o}_{E}$ $[_{V"}[V \text{ DP}]]]$
           [-ACC] ←————————⌋
           SOR

---

[30]Interestingly, it is predicted that in dative constructions, the passivized dative argument (but not the accusative SOR) could be a *bare plural pro*. As Hebrew, Spanish and Italian do not have dative shift, this prediction is, unfortunately, untestable.

[31]An interesting prediction: the ungrammaticality of unaccusatives with bare-plural subjects in languages such as Hebrew and Italian is predicted. See Borer 1995, where this point is argued, and where it is shown that the apparent grammaticality of some unaccusative constructions with post-verbal bare plural subjects is due to the existence of a licensing locative expression.

The contrast between the ungrammatical passives and unaccusatives with a non-generic *bare-plural pro*, and the grammaticality of the ones with the generic *pro*, is likewise explained. Generic expressions, interpreted on a par with definite expressions, and hence, by definition QUANTIZED in the relevant sense, can license an eventive interpretation for Asp$_E$, and function as SOR, resulting in their availability as subjects of both unaccusatives and passives.

5.2   English Null Subjects

The absence of *bare-plural pro* subjects in English must now be addressed. Specifically, why are (59a-b), on a par with (48),(52a), ungrammatical:

(59) a.   *(*pro*) knock on the door
      b.   *In Pentecost (*pro*) eat cheese

The grammaticality of (59), I suggest, is not related to the properties of *bare plural pro*, but rather, to the properties of [Spec,TP] in English. Adopting (a slightly modified) insight of Speas 1994, suppose the licensing of null pronominals is not an independent module, but rather, an extension of the licensing of functional projections. Specifically, I will assume (60):[32]

(60) XP(functional) is licensed iff XP(functional) has phonological content.

Crucially, note, as the licensing of XP(functional) is phonological in nature, it must be met by S-structure, or spellout. As is commonly assumed (cf. Emonds 1978, Pollock 1989), the verb in English does not occupy the highest functional head below CP by S-structure. Assuming, as in Chomsky 1995, that tense morphology is base-generated on the verb, TP is not phonologically licensed through phonological material in T. It thus follows that [Spec,TP] must be filled by spellout, forcing the existence of an overt pronominal in English. Hebrew, Spanish, and Italian have all been argued to allow the V to reach the highest functional head by spellout. As such, TP is phonologically licensed, and an overt material in Spec is not necessary. The grammaticality of null pronominal subjects in Hebrew, Spanish and Italian, vs. its ungrammaticality in English thus follows, without barring the occurrence of *bare plural pro* VP internally in English in passive constructions.

---

[32]Speas suggests that XP(functional) can be licensed by semantic content as well, an extension not assumed here. For a fuller discussion, see Borer 1996.

5.3 Passives of Intransitives

An interesting issue concerns the properties of passives of intransitives. As is well known, unaccusative verbs do not passivize, but in some languages, notably Dutch and German, unergative verbs do.

Consider first the modification needed to allow a grammar to have a passive of an intransitive. Recall that we took the discourse function of passive to be the "demotion" of an argument, achieved through the reversal of the primary Asp/T relationship, and the subsequent stranding of the "demoted" argument in the VP. For an intransitive, such a demotion would involve the stranding in the VP of its sole argument, having the structure in (61):

$$(61) \quad [_{T''} \text{ Spec} \quad ([_{Asp''} \text{ Asp}^{0)} \, [_{V''}[_V \quad DP]]]]$$

$$\text{NOM} \qquad\qquad \textit{-en} \qquad \left\{ \begin{array}{l} \textit{pro} \\ \text{PP} \end{array} \right\}$$

(61) cannot give rise to a licensed Asp_E, and a subsequent eventive interpretation. However, as the only distinguishing characteristic of so-called unaccusative intransitives and so-called unergative intransitives is the existence of Asp_E, it follows that passivized intransitives can never be "unaccusative". It further follows that any passive of intransitive predicate cannot have an eventive interpretation, and must have a process interpretation. This prediction is correct. (62) has a process, rather than eventive, interpretation:

(62) *Er werd gefloten*
     There was whistled   (German)

In turn, however, the structure in (61) already is in violation of (33a), requiring the passive morpheme to project as the head of Asp_E. We must, therefore, consider the possibility that in some grammars a variant of passive is available, in which the passive morpheme occupies a functional head distinct from Asp_E (possibly Asp_P). Unaccusatives would still be incompatible with passive, as the unaccusative syntax and interpretation are linked to a realized Asp_E. However, if the functional head dominating the passive morpheme does not require a filled Spec to be realized, the existence of passives of intransitives, albeit with a non-eventive interpretation, is predicted to exist.[33]

---

[33] An interesting question concerns the possibility of leaving the overt passive or unaccusative argument in situ (where it is nevertheless assigned nominative):

6. Adjectival Passives

Recall that in most accounts, adjectival passive is derived from the passive participle by externalization. In Borer 1984, however, I suggest that adjectival passive participles and passive verbal participles are derived directly from the same verbal source by -*en* affixation, and that their distinct properties result from their different syntax. Descriptively, the derivation of adjectival passives clearly involves "externalization", a process that within a model which does not make reference to such notions must be otherwise accounted for. As a first step towards an answer, consider the following claim (and see Evers, 1992, for a similar idea):

(63) a. Lexical categories must be fully specified.
     b. Functional categories are categorially underspecified.

The claim in (63) is linked to a more complete claim on the nature of lexical vs. functional projections. Suppose, adopting in essence Grimshaw's (1991) notion of Extended Projections, but modifying it slightly, we assume that every lexical projection must be dominated by (at least) one functional projection. Suppose further that functional projections are underspecified (or possibly even unspecified) categorially, and only possess some semantic value. Thus, for instance, considering the T/V complex, we may assume that T is marked as <e>, for the EVENT argument, and that it acquires categorial features (presumably, [+V,-N]) from its lexical extended-chain mate, the verb, by percolation, as depicted in (64):[34]

(64)

$$\text{PERCOLATION} \quad \uparrow \quad \begin{array}{l} T_{<e>} \\ V_{[+V,-N]} \end{array}$$

(i)   a. *nafal pagaz*   b. *neherag   yeled*
           fell bomb   was-killed boy

Assuming that *yeled*, 'boy' in (i) remains in situ, what licenses the Asp$_E$ node required for passive and for unaccusative interpretation? For discussion, see Borer 1995.

[34]I assume that the head of bare lexical projections which are not dominated by functional projections must incorporate to be licensed, while lexical projections embedded within functional projections are barred from incorporation. Therefore if adjectival passives contain a fully-projected VP, that VP must be a bare lexical projection, and no aspectual categories may dominate it.

Consider in view of this the status of the claim made above, according to which the (verbal) passive *-en* is specified as distinct from [-N]. Recall that it is assumed that (usually) *-en* is dominated by the functional aspectual projection Asp_E. Suppose, then, that *-en* is marked as eventive and as incompatible with a [-N] feature. These features in turn percolate to the aspectual head dominating *-en*, while the rest of the categorial features associated with that aspectual head are acquired via percolation from its lexical Extended-Chain mate, the V. The resulting configuration is as in (65):

(65)

$$\text{Asp} \quad \Rightarrow \quad \text{Asp}_{E,+V}$$

$$\textit{-en}_E <\neq [\text{-N}]>$$

PERCOLATION $\quad\uparrow\quad V_{[+V\ (\text{-N})]}$

In (65) the feature [-N] is barred from percolation because it is incompatible with the feature specification associated with *-en*. As a (positive) [+N] feature is not available for percolation, the participle remains underspecified categorially.

(63) embodies yet one more claim: we expect there to exist pairs of morphemes, one instantiation of which is functional, and hence underdetermined categorially, while the other is lexical, in which categorial features are provided by default lexical principles. Such pairs, note, are at least prima facie attested. Thus we have a functional *-ing* (progressive, active participle, probably distinct from [-N]) alongside lexical *-ing* (adjectival), which is [+N]; functional gerundive *-ing,* possibly distinct from [+V], alongside nominal lexical *-ing* which is [-V], giving rise to derived nominals; functional Romance *se/si*, anaphoric/middle in nature, alongside lexical *se/si* (sometimes called inherent *se/si*), etc.

From this perspective, consider a lexical, rather than functional, projection of the passive morpheme *-en*. In accordance with (63), it must be categorially fully specified. Assuming that its <distinct from [-N]> feature is a constant, a full specification, provided by default lexical principles, would render it [+N]. As in the case of verbal participles, the additional [+V] feature is provided by the morphological complement, V, by (secondary) percolation.[35]

---

[35]In turn, if the feature [±V] must be provided, we may assume that *-en* is provided with a [+V] feature which is lexically realized, but functionally suspended (or at least redundant). Another possibility would be to say that *-en* is specified as <consistent with [+V]>. Such a specification, note, would exclude the affixation of *-en,* when functional, to a [-V] element, a desirable result.

(66) $-en$ $[+N]$ $\Rightarrow$ $[+N,+V]$

         $\uparrow$

PERCOLATION $\Big\lfloor$ $V_{[+V\ (-N)]}$

When discussing the properties of verbal passive, I suggested that
$-en$, is (mostly) an eventive node, projecting as the head of Asp_E, resulting
in the argument in its specifier interpreted as SOR. Suppose that this
property as well is constant across the functional and the lexical occurrences
of $-en$. We thus expect adjectival participles to share with verbal ones the
following properties:

(67) a. [+V]
     b. <distinct from [-N]>
     c. Having a result interpretation
     d. Being coindexed with SOR
     e. Being eventive

Properties (67a-d) present no problem. The categorial nature of
adjectival passives is predicted, as well as their interpretation as denoting a
result with their subject interpreted as SOR. However, property (67e)
appears problematic. How can adjectival passive, clearly stative in nature,
be eventive?

Viewed differently, however, it is clear that property (67e) need not,
and in fact cannot, be associated with adjectival passives. Recall that the
interpretation associated with Asp_E consists of two elements. First,
[Spec,Asp_E] hosts SOR, and Asp_E in its entirety denotes a RESULT.
Secondly, Asp_E is eventive, entailing the existence of an event that
culminated in the RESULT. Suppose now that while the RESULT
interpretation is an inherent property of the E node, the interpretation of an
event leading to that result stems from embedding Asp_E under T with its
event argument. We can distinguish formally between the AKTIONSART of
adjectival passives, RESULT STATE, and that of verbal passives, EVENT
+RESULT. Verbal passive $-en$ heads an underspecified functional projection
which is a member of the Extended Projection including TP. Adjectival
passive $-en$, on the other hand heads an AP. It is not in the same Extended
Projection with TP, and hence it cannot be associated with the event
argument in it. Thus, although it denotes RESULT, an EVENTIVE
interpretation is unavailable. Consider more specifically the structure of
adjectival passives as it follows from all assumptions made thus far:[36]

---

[36]In (68) the AP dominates a fully projected VP, and V incorporates into A,
as the head of a bare lexical projection. For some arguments that adjectival
passives contain a fully projected VP, rather than just V, see Kratzer 1994.

(68) $[_{A''E}$ *-en* $[_{V''}$ [V DP (y)]]]

     ↑_____|

By assumption, in (68) *-en* projects as a lexical, rather than functional, element, which, in turn, selects a VP complement. The result is the projection of an adjective, as in (66). The selected VP, again by assumption, is not dominated by any functional projections, thereby forcing the incorporation of V onto A (cf. fn. 34). If *-en* were to select a functional structure as its complement, incorporation would have been blocked, and ungrammaticality would have resulted. Consider now the structure in (68) from the point of view of Extended Projections. Clearly, AP must either be dominated by some functional projection, or the A head must incorporate. In the absence of a target for such incorporation, let us assume that AP is dominated by a functional projection (possibly DegP, see Corver 1992 for discussion). Under plausible assumptions, the E property associated with the AP percolates up to the dominating functional structure. In turn, a DP argument of V moving to [Spec,FP] in (69) is interpreted as SUBJECT OF RESULT, resulting in (69):

(69) $[_{FPE2}$ Spec F^o $[_{A''E}$ DP_2 A^o $[_{V''}[V$ t_2 (y)]]]]

                               SOR   *-en* ←_____|

   ↑_____| ↑_____|

In (69), there must be a DP in [Spec,FP$_E$], to meet the structural well-formedness condition requiring all E heads to be coindexed with a DP in their specifier. Such a DP, in turn, is interpreted as SOR. FP, however, being part of the functional structure associated with AP, is clearly not an aspectual node.

It might be worthwhile to digress briefly and consider why FP in (69) may not be an aspectual node. I suggested that the interpretation of Asp$_E$ as eventive is dependent on licensing by T and the EVENT ARGUMENT which it dominates. If this is indeed so, then a T node which does not dominate an event argument may not license Asp$_E$. Assuming now that T in adjectival constructions, or for that matter, in all STATE predicates, does not dominate an event argument, it is clear that the functional projection dominating AP may not be aspectual in nature. It thus follows that while DP$_2$ in (69) is interpreted as SUBJECT OF RESULT, F$_E$ in (69) does not result in an aspectual eventive interpretation. We thus derive the existence of a RESULT STATE argument without an actual event: a STATE predicate.[37]

Consider now (69) from the perspective of the unaccusative/unergative diagnostics and the distribution of datives in Modern Hebrew. If, indeed, diagnostics associated with unaccusative subjects are linked with [Spec,Asp$_E$], their absence in adjectival passives is expected. If, on the other hand, unergative diagnostics are exclusionary of DPs in such a position, the availability of unergative diagnostics for subjects of adjectival passives follows as well. Note that some unergative diagnostics are expected to be excluded in APs as well, e.g., the presence of impersonal passives. As these plausibly require an event argument, they are incompatible with state, and hence unattested with APs in general.

Finally, consider two additional facets of the analysis of adjectival passives proposed here. First, as is well known, unaccusative 'verbs' *do* give rise to adjectival passives, while unergatives do not. This fact now follows directly from the structure in (69). Consider the interpretation of adjectival passives corresponding to unaccusative 'verbs', e.g., *the arrived train*, *the fallen tree*, etc. Given the structure in (69), their derivation would be as in (70):

(70) [$_{FPE2}$ Spec F^0 [$_{A''E}$ A^0 [$_{V''}$[V DP]]]]
        -*en*   *arrive*   *train*

In (70), the moved argument *train* is interpreted as SUBJECT OF RESULT, precisely the interpretation typically associated with the derived subjects in unaccusative constructions. In turn, as the argument of the V in (70) would always be interpreted as SUBJECT OF RESULT, it is clear why unergatives do not give rise to adjectival passives. As, by definition, unergative subjects never denote SUBJECTS OF RESULT STATE, clearly no adjectival passive can be compatible with the meaning of unergative constructions.

Recall that the unavailability of a RESULT STATE interpretation for "unaccusative" in verbal passives derived from the fact that verbal passives involved the direct linking of T and the event argument with Asp$_E$. As in

---

[37]Assuming the absence of an event argument in stative predicates is following Kratzer 1989. In a departure from Kratzer 1989, Kratzer 1995 suggests that the event argument is not missing in stative predicates, but rather, is of a different kind. Translated to that, the text discussion entails that the relevant event argument in stative predicates is not the appropriate one to license an Asp$_E$ node.

(70) there is no Asp_E, there is no corresponding reversal of linking relationship. Suppose, then, that when T does not dominate an event argument, and it is linked with an Aspp of sorts, such linking gives rise to a STATE interpretation.[38] In the absence of demotion, we do not anticipate a subject-of-process *bare plural pro* to be licensed V" internally. The absence of such a *bare plural pro* in adjectival passives is well documented. Adjectival passives do not have an implicit argument interpretation, nor do they allow implicit argument control, in contrast with verbal passives.

In turn, however, as is well known, an overt DP stranded in the embedded VP may, at times, be licensed by a preposition, as (71) illustrates:

(71) a.   The code remains unbroken by the Russians
      b.   The island remains inhabited by monkeys alone
      c.   The vase remains untouched by human hands

The grammaticality of (71) may appear problematic for our system, which predicts the exclusion of subject-of-process from the VP in the absence of a direct link between T and Asp_E. On the other hand, as is well known, *by*-phrases in adjectival passives have markedly different properties from those attested by *by*-phrases in verbal passives. First, they are restricted to generic interpretation, as the contrast between (71) and (72) shows:

(72) a.   *The code remains unbroken by Kim
      b.   *The island remains inhabited by Robin alone
      c.   *The vase remains untouched by Pat

The grammaticality of (71), when contrasted with the ungrammaticality of (72), suggests an independent licensing device for the argument stranded in the VP in (71), a strategy, perhaps, linked to the STATE interpretation. Note further that unlike *by*-phrases in verbal passives, *by*-phrases in adjectival passives do not allow extraction:

---

[38]Clearly, if the aspectual node involved in STATE and PROCESS interpretation is one and the same, Aspp is a misnomer. Intuitively, however, the account is attractive. Recall that we adopted here a view of AKTIONSART according to which EVENTIVE AKTIONSART is quantized, or COUNT in the relevant sense, but PROCESS AKTIONSART is cumulative, or MASS in the relevant sense. Translated to the language of Asp_E and Aspp, this would mean that while E is quantized, P is cumulative. Viewed from this perspective, the affinity of PROCESS and STATE is natural, and attributing their difference to the existence of an actual event, in the sense of the EVENT argument, is natural.

(73) a. By whom was this code broken?
     b. By whom was this vase touched?
     c. Who was this code broken by?
     d. Who was this vase touched by?

(74) a. *By whom does this code remain unbroken?
     b. *By whom does this vase remain untouched?
     c. *Who does this code remain unbroken by?
     d. *Who does this vase remain untouched by?

Interestingly, the ungrammaticality of (74a-d) contrasts with the extractability of direct arguments of APs:

(75) a. To whom does this fact remain unknown?
     b. Who does this fact remain unknown to?

The structure in (69) may provide a solution for this contrast. Plausibly, adjectival complements are attached higher than *by*-phrases, which remain internal to the VP, yielding the configuration in (70). The ungrammaticality of (74), when contrasted with the grammaticality of (73) may derive from the fact that VP is a barrier, combined with the fact that if the extracted WH element is adjoined to VP, such adjunction may, plausibly, block the incorporation of V into A:[39]

(76)
$$[_{FPE2} \; DP_2 \quad F \quad [_{A''}[-en \quad [_{V''}[V \quad t_2 \quad \underline{BY \; DP}]] \; [_{PP}(\underline{TO \; DP})\,]]]]$$

In the absence of a P-licensing strategy for the "external" argument of the embedded verb in adjectival passives, that argument cannot be syntactically realized and thus has no syntactic properties. To the extent that adjectival passives do seem, at times, to imply the existence of an agentive party, such interpretation, syntactically inert, may be due precisely to the semantic, but non-syntactic, presence of an argument.

7. Conclusion

This paper was devoted to showing that a model containing impoverished lexical entries without any information relevant to syntactic linking is still capable of deriving well-known effects typically associated with argument structure modifications, such as the suppression of the

---

[39]Such an account for the ungrammaticality of (67), note, crucially rejects Baker's 1988 Government Transparency Corollary.

external θ-role and externalization. Rather than utilize operations on lexical entries, it was shown that the appropriate combination of aspectual nodes and lexical nodes, together with a typology of projections and their types, can derive the correct configurations and the correct interpretation without any lexical convention for the linking of roles with syntactic positions.

Currently, syntactic structures duplicate much of the labor already accomplished by an enriched lexicon. The leading idea in this work is that such syntactic information should be restricted to the functional component of the grammar as much as possible, leaving lexical entries to specify, syntactically, only the number of arguments associated with each entry. To the extent that such a system is successful, it sharpens the division of labor in the grammar, making each of its components specialized and better defined.

References

Bach, Emmon. 1986. The Algebra of Events. *Linguistic and Philosophy* 9:5–16.

Baker, Mark. 1988. *Incorporation*. Chicago: University of Chicago Press.

Baker, Mark, Kyle Johnson, and Ian Roberts. 1989. Passive Arguments Raised. *Linguistic Inquiry* 20:219-252.

Belletti, Adriana and Luigi Rizzi. 1981. The Syntax of *ne*: Some Theoretical Implications. *The Linguistic Review* 1:117–154.

Benua, Laura and Hagit Borer. 1996. The Passive/Anti-Passive Alternation. Paper presented at GLOW 1996, Athens, Greece.

Borer, Hagit. 1984. The Projection Principle and Rules of Morphology. *Proceedings from the 14th meeting of the North Eastern Linguistic Society,* University of Massachusetts, Amherst.

Borer, Hagit. 1989. Anaphoric Agreement. In Osvaldo Jaeggli and Ken Safir, eds., *The Null Subject Parameter*, 69–109 Dordrecht: Kluwer.

Borer, Hagit. 1994. The Projection of Arguments. In Elena Benedicto and Jeff Runner, eds., *University of Massachusetts Occasional Papers* 17, GLSA, University of Massachusetts, Amherst.

Borer, Hagit. 1995. Class Lectures, Fall 1995, University of Massachusetts, Amherst.

Borer, Hagit. 1996. Passive without Theta Grids. Ms. University of Massachusetts, Amherst.

Borer, Hagit and Yosef Grodzinsky. 1986. Syntactic Cliticization and Lexical Cliticization: The Case of Hebrew Dative Clitics. In H. Borer, ed., *The Syntax of Pronominal Clitics. Syntax and Semantics 19.* San Diego: Academic Press.

Bresnan, Joan, and Jonni M. Kanerva. 1989. Locative Inversion in Chichewa: A Case Study of Factorization in Grammar. *Linguistic Inquiry* 20:1–50.

Carrier Jill, and Janet Randall. 1992. The Argument Structure and Syntactic Structure of Resultatives. *Linguistic Inquiry* 23:173–234.

Carrier, Jill, and Janet Randall. 1993. Lexical Mapping. In Eric Reuland and Werner Abraham, eds., *Knowledge and Language, Vol. II.* Dordrecht: Kluwer Academic Publishers.

Chomsky, Noam. 1981. *Lectures on Government and Binding.* Dordrecht: Foris.

Chomsky, Noam. 1986. *Knowledge of Language, Its Nature, Origin, and Use.* New York: Praeger Press.

Chomsky, Noam. 1995. *The Minimalist Program.* Cambridge, MA: MIT Press.

Cinque, Guglielmo. 1988. On *si* Constructions and the Theory of ARB. *Linguistic Inquiry* 19:521–582.

Corver, Norbert. 1991. Functional Heads and the Internal Syntax of Adjective Phrases. Paper presented at the GLOW conference, Leiden.

Diesing, Molly. 1990. *The Syntactic Roots of Semantic Partition.* Doctoral dissertation, University of Massachusetts, Amherst.

Dowty, David, R. 1991. Thematic Proto-Roles and Argument Selection. *Language* 67:547–619.

Emonds, Joseph. 1978. The Verbal Complex V'-V in French. *Linguistic Inquiry* 9:49–77.

Evers, Avery. 1992. West Germanic V-to-V Raising and the Incorporation Trigger. OTS Manuscript, Utrecht.

Filip, Hana. 1993. *Aspect, Situation Types, and Nominal Reference,* Doctoral dissertation, University of California, Berkeley

Freidin, Robert. 1978. Cyclicity and the Theory of Grammar. *Linguistic Inquiry* 9.4.

Grimshaw, Jane. 1990. *Argument Structure.* Cambridge, MA: MIT Press.

Grimshaw, Jane. 1991. Extended Projections. Ms., Brandeis University, Waltham.

Hoekstra, Teun and Jan Mulder. 1990. Unergatives as Copular Verbs. *The Linguistic Review* 7:1–79.

Hoop, Helen de. 1992. *Case Configuration and Noun Phrase Interpretation.* Doctoral dissertation, Rijksuniversiteit Groningen.

Hout, Angeliek van. 1992. Linking and Projection based on Event Structure. Ms., Tilburg University.

Hout, Angeliek van. 1996. *Event Semantics of Verb Frame Alternations,* TILDIL Dissertation Series, 1996–1.

McClure, William. 1995. *Syntactic Projections of the Semantics of Aspect.* Ph.D. dissertation, Cornell University.

Jaeggli, Osvaldo. 1986. Passive. *Linguistic Inquiry* 17:587–622.

Jaeggli, Osvaldo. 1987. Arbitrary *pro* and Pronominals. *Natural Language and Linguistic Theory* 4:43–76.

Kratzer, Angelika. 1989. (published 1994). Stage Level and Individual Level Predicates. In Gregory Carlson and Jeff Pelletier, eds., *The Generic Book.* Chicago: University of Chicago.

Kratzer, Angelika. 1994. *The Event Argument.* Ms., University of Massachusetts, Amherst.

Kratzer, Angelika. 1995. Class lectures, Fall 1995, University of Massachusetts, Amherst.

Krifka, Manfred. 1991. Thematic Relations as Links between Nominal Reference and Temporal Constitution. In Ivan Sag and Anna Szabolsci, eds., *Lexical Matters.* Stanford, CA: CSLI Publications.

Larson, Richard. 1988. On the Double Object Construction. *Linguistic Inquiry* 19:335–391.

Levin, Beth. and Malka. Rappaport Hovav 1994., *Unaccusativity: At the Syntax-Lexical Semantics Interface.* Cambridge, MA: MIT Press.

Link, Godehard. 1983. The Logical Analysis of Plurals and Mass Terms. In Rainer Bauerle, Christoph Schwarze, and Arnim von Stechow, eds., *Meaning, Use, and Interpretation of Language,* 302–323. Berlin: Walter de Gruyter.

Ouhalla, Jamal. 1990. *The Syntax of Head Movement: A Study of Berber.* Doctoral dissertation, University College of London.

Parsons, Terry. 1990. *Events in the Semantics of English: A Study of Subatomic Semantics.* Cambridge, MA: MIT Press.

Perlmutter, David. 1978. Impersonal Passives and the Unaccusative Hypothesis. *Berkeley Linguistic Society* 4:157–189.

Pesetsky, David. 1982. *Paths and Categories.* Doctoral dissertation, MIT.

Pesetsky, David. 1990. Experiencer Predicates and Universal Alignment Principles. Ms., MIT.

Pesetsky, David. 1995. *Zero Syntax.* Cambridge, MA: MIT Press.

Pollock, Jean-Yves. 1989. Verb Movement, UG and the Structure of IP. *Linguistic Inquiry* 20:365–424.

Runner, Jeff. 1995. *Noun Phrase Licensing and Interpretation.* Doctoral dissertation, University of Massachusetts, Amherst.

Speas, Margaret. 1994. Null Argument in a Theory of Economy of Projections. In Elena Benedicto and Jeff Runner, eds., *University of Massachusetts Occasional Papers* 17, GLSA, University of Massachusetts, Amherst.

Van Valin, Robert D. 1990. Semantic Parameters of Split Intransitivity. *Language* 66:221–260.

Vainikka, Anne, and Joan Maling. 1993. Is Partitive Case Inherent or Structural? Ms., University of Massachusetts, Amherst and Brandeis University.

Comments on the Paper by Borer

ANDREW SPENCER

Introduction

Borer argues for a model of argument projection which is syntactic but predicate-driven. This means that the surface exponents of argument structure associated with a verb will not be given in the lexical entry, but will be computed compositionally as a function of the predicate structure and the syntactic structure. The arguments of the verb in all cases comprise an unordered list. Borer's overall goal is to restrict syntactic information to the functional component of the grammar, cashing in on the redundancy inherent in current views of lexical entries and syntactic structure. I applaud this viewpoint, and, indeed, have argued that one radical conclusion that can be drawn is that there is absolutely no need in the grammar for lexical syntactic categories (N, V, A, P) (Spencer 1996a). In this commentary I shall first present a number of minor problems for this version of her system, and then some more general conceptual problems.

1. The Role of Aspect and Aspectuality

One feature of Borer's abandonment of lexical entry representations of argument structure is that she is not able to appeal to notions such as external/internal argument. This means that she has to represent the distinction between, say, unergative and unaccusatives verbs in terms of syntactic structures. Included in this will be reference to aspectual semantics in the form of a syntactic Aspect node. Borer assumes that non-agentive telic verbs are unaccusative and agentive atelic verbs are unergative. She therefore assumes that unaccusatives are associated with an eventive Aspect Phrase in the syntax, which is lacking in unergatives. In transitive eventive constructions, this Aspect Phrase is responsible for assigning Accusative case to a direct object. In *John built a house*, [a house] will land in [Spec,AspP][1] position and receive Accusative, while [John] will move to [Spec,TP] to get Nominative. (Of course, it could have happened the other way around in which case we would have got the anomalous, but

---

[1] Borer vacillates between the notation XP and X" for maximal projections. I try to follow her usage where I can.

grammatical, sentence *A house built John*.) By landing in [Spec,AspP], [a house] receives the interpretation of an incremental theme.

(1) $[_{T''}$ Spec(+Nom) $[_{Asp''_E}$ Spec(+Acc) $Asp_E°$ $[_{V''}$]]

In unaccusatives we find the same structure but the [Spec, AspP] is not able to assign case (2):

(2) $[_{T''}$ Spec(+Nom) $[_{Asp''_E}$ Spec $Asp_E°$ $[_{V''}$]]]

In a sentence such as *A man arrived*, the sole argument of the verb passes through the [Spec,AspP] position and hence receives an eventive (telic) interpretation. This means that the predicate as a whole is interpreted (preferentially?) in the absence of other adjuncts, modifiers, quantifiers and so on, as an accomplishment or achievement (change of state). The Asp''_E node effectively fulfils the syntactic function of the AgrOP node in earlier Principles and Parameters based theories. However, since the Asp''_E node is not associated with Accusative, it cannot assign case. The DP therefore has to move on to [Spec,TP] position to receive Nominative case. If, on the other hand, the Asp''_E node were to be associated with Accusative (as in a transitive construction), then the derivation would crash because of a stipulation to the effect that Nominative must be assigned.

In unergatives, there is no such Asp_E and case is assigned to the subject from TP:

(3) $[_{T''}$ Spec(+Nom) $[_{V''}$ ...]]]

Hence, *John ran* is given an agentive, atelic interpretation (as an activity). (There will also be a caseless $Asp_P°$ head to pass through, giving this interpretation.)

In the case of transitive activities with bare plural objects, Borer adopts an analysis reminiscent of that of Verkuyl (1993) (though, curiously, doesn't explicitly refer to his work). In Verkuyl's treatment a telic verb (which for Borer presumably means a verb requiring Asp_E) is given an atelic interpretation if its object bears the feature [−Specified Quantity of A]. Borer re-christens this feature [QUAN]. A [−QUAN] object cannot license Asp_E and so such a DP has to be assigned Partitive case (by analogy with Finnish) from a special functional node. Thus, (4) would be derived from a structure (5):

(4)   a.   John built houses
        b.   John drank wine

(5) $[_{T''}$ Spec(+Nom) [*John*] $[_{F''}$ Spec(+Prt)+ F°] $[_{VP}$]]

On this account the property of the bare plural alters the basic, core or inner aspect of the VP, while sentential aspect or adverbial modification (including negation) simply serves as an "operator" over the peripheral or outer aspect. Note that the functional projection which is responsible for Partitive case in (5) must be triggered by the absence of Asp_E, and not, say, by the need for an argument to receive case. This is because such a projection must not be permitted in the passive, otherwise the agent would be assigned Partitive.

The distribution of the Finnish Partitive case is a rather complex matter. Kiparsky (1995) argues that it is assigned to a DP which is marked [+H(omogeneous)] or is governed by a verb so marked. Predicates marked [+H] are those which are divisive and cumulative, i.e. those which have a [−QUAN] DP or a non-eventive verb. Subjects, too, can be marked Partitive in Finnish, but only if they are homogeneous (atelic) and only if they have 'presentational' semantics. On Kiparsky's account the assignment of Partitive isn't tied to the existence or otherwise of Asp_E nodes, so it is not difficult for him to capture this distribution. For Borer, however, it is unclear why Finnish should have any Partitive subjects, since there will always be Nominative case for them.

In connection with the Finnish analogy note that Kiparsky (1995) shows that Finnish Partitive case assignment cannot always be derived solely from the properties of a lattice-theoretic model of event semantics of the sort underpinning Borer's argumentation, but must sometimes be stipulated as part of the lexical entry. Thus, in (6) we have a non-eventive (stative) transitive predicate which nonetheless can take either Accusative or Partitive objects:

(6)   a.   Omistat nämä talo-t
                you.own these.ACC house.ACC.PL

                'You own these houses'

       b.   Omistat talo-j-a
                you.own house-PL-PART

                'You own houses'

In other words, Finnish Partitive case is not a reflex of 'inner aspectuality' after all, but of 'outer aspectuality', much like Imperfective aspect in Slavic (or indeed English). But this is not a conclusion Borer would welcome.

Applied to English, covert Partitive case assignment smacks of a (somewhat indirect) description of the original problem rather than a solution to it. Why, for instance, doesn't the DP receive genuine Partitive case marking, i.e. with *of* (cf *pint of milk, partake of this wine*)? More generally, though, appeal to a covert case has to be handled with caution, for fear of falling into the trap of older grammars of English which told us that the Vocative case of *table* was 'O table!'. This type of analogizing over surface morphosyntax is empty without strong independent motivation. For instance, given the well-studied links between Finnish Partitive and Slavic imperfective aspect, we could just as well say that we were dealing with a covert imperfective category. Thus we may assume that English bare plurals are realizations of covert Partitive case, while Finnish Partitive case is a realization of covert imperfective aspect. In Borer's original analysis the bare plural was assumed to undergo incorporation, so perhaps the Russian imperfective is a realization of covert ('abstract') incorporation, while incorporation in Chukchee is a realization of covert indefiniteness marking on DP's.

The verbal passive is derived by linking the T and its EVENT argument with Asp_E, which means that the DP in its Specifier will be assigned Nominative case. This linking accounts for why passives are eventive: *The cart was pushed* is said to have an accomplishment reading, not that of a process (unless it receives additional modification to 'trigger', or 'coerce' an atelic reading).

In Russian an interesting situation obtains. Russian has grammaticalized aspect ("viewpoint" aspect in the terminology of Smith 1991). In the perfective with most verbs it is only possible to form a passive by means of an auxiliary + passive participle construction, (7):

(7)   *Doma (byli) postroeny*
        houses (were) built

        'The houses were/have been/(had been) built'

However, a verb in the imperfective form may only be passivized using morphology originally derived from a reflexive form, REFL (*-sja* after a consonant, *-s'* after a vowel):

(8)   *Zdes' stroili-s' doma*
        here build.PAST-REFL houses

        'Houses were (being) built here'

There is no article in Russian and so it is difficult to distinguish definite from specific from generic from bare non-specific plurals. However, in (8) the most natural interpretation would be that of a non-specific plural. The same construction is equally possible with definite plurals or singular DP's:

(9)   a.   *Zdes' stroili-s' nashi novye doma*
               here build.PAST-REFL our new houses

               'Our new houses were being built here'

    b.   *Zdes' stroil-sja odin/nash bol'shoj dom*
                here build.PAST-REFL one/our large house

                'One/our large house was being built here'

There is every reason to consider the -SJA form a passive. For instance it may take an optional agentive phrase (in the instrumental case) just like the participial passive:

(10)   *Eti doma stroili-s' innostrancami*
        These houses build.PAST-REFL by.foreigners

        'These houses were being built by foreigners'

    Now, the interpretation of the participial passive in Russian is generally held to be that which Borer gives for the English passive, that is, having an eventive reading only. The problem for Borer's analysis lies in the reflexive passive. Because this is the only form which can be used with the imperfective aspect, we find that it gives an activity, non-eventive reading even in the past tense. One can think of this as a reflex of the fact that the imperfective in Russian is neutral in interpretation between English translation equivalents such as *houses were being built* or *houses used to be built*, as well as *houses were built*. In other words, any tendency which a past tense marking might have to force a perfective reading in English is wiped out by the grammatical imperfective aspect. For Borer this is presumably a reflex of 'peripheral' or 'outer' aspectuality. But what permits such a passive in the first place? Presumably, -SJA has to be projected as Asp_E and coindexed with T, in order to obtain the effects of 'subject demotion' and 'object promotion'. Then, the verb has to move through some other Aspect node marked [Imperfective] to erase the effects of the Asp_E node, while retaining its syntactic consequences (i.e. passive voice). This would make the Russian derivation parallel to that of the English *Houses were being built* in which, presumably, the eventive reading is erased by an aspectual auxiliary. The difference is that the aspectual marking is a property of the verb stem, not of an auxiliary. But in this case, why must we assume that *John built houses* is inherently non-eventive? Why shouldn't we assume that it is an aspectual modification of the telic [$_{VP}$build house] by virtue of the quantificational properties of the object?

3. Marking Grammatical Relations

    I conclude with a few brief comments about a more general phenomenon, which raises problems for many frameworks, including Borer's, namely, ergativity. Simplifying somewhat, one can identify three main types of grammatical relation: subject of intransitive clause (S), subject of transitive clause (A) and direct object (O) (cf. Dixon (1994), for whom these are grammatical primitives). In accusative languages, S/A are grouped together for the purposes of case assignment, agreement and linearization of grammatical functions. This is reflected in the partitioning of cases assigned from various specifier positions, nominative and accusative. However, in ergative languages the grouping is S/O (absolutive case) and A (ergative case). I shall consider two specific phenomena associated with the ergative type, which, it seems to me, are likely to prove problematic however the surface morphosyntactic facts are handled.

3.1 Antipassives

The first of these is the antipassive construction, in which a transitive construction is detransitivized to an unergative thereby creating an activity from an eventive predicate. Borer (footnote 20) assumes that in ergative languages T is associated with Asp_E and that in the antipassive T gets associated with Asp_P. The basic idea, then, is that canonical linkings are reversed in ergative languages (essentially the analysis proposed by Marantz 1984).

If antipassives had a unitary, non eventive interpretation this would be a very attractive solution. However, as Dixon 1994 has reminded us, antipassivization is associated with a variety of aspectual properties and alternations. In particular, the non-eventive reading is not universally found with antipassives. In a language such as Dyirbal antipassive has the principal function of putting DP's into the absolutive so as to trigger syntactic processes sensitive to S/O pivots. Here we will get antipassives with obliquely marked "chômeur" objects and absolutive-marked subjects. These constructions may have essentially the same Aktionsart properties as the corresponding actives. In particular, the initial object can still function to measure out the event (though its realization is now optional, just as the realization of the ergative-marked subject is optional in many ergative languages). In Chukchee, antipassive has a number of functions, of which the most important seems to involve the pragmatic force of absolutive case marking. A DP in the absolutive is interpreted as "affected", while an ergative or oblique DP has no necessary interpretation as affected (cf. Polinskaja and Nedjalkov 1987). Thus, antipassive is often used to prevent absolutive from being assigned to an argument. In addition, an absolutive DP tends to be interpreted as old information, while an overt obliquely marked object DP in the antipassive construction is typically used when that DP bears focus (Polinskaja and Nedjalkov 1987: 247)[2]:

---

[2] I use the following abbreviations: I 'Instrumental' AP 'antipassive', S 'subject', SG 'singular'.

(11)   a.   *ətlon kupre-te ena-ntəwat-gʔe*

           he   net-I   AP-set-3SG.S

           'It was a/the net that he set'

    b.   *ətlon kupre-te ena-ntəwat-gʔe, wanewan giŋgiŋ-e*

           he   net- I   AP -set-3SG.S,   not   throw-basket- I

           'It was the net that he set, not the throw-basket'

As in Dyirbal, this means that an antipassive can still have an eventive reading. From this we conclude that the antipassive will require the Asp$_E$ node, but for the chômeur, not for the subject. But the chômeur (whether of passive or antipassive) is supposed to be "trapped" inside the VP in a model such as Borer's.

3.2 Split Ergativity

I close with a few remarks about a wider problem posed by ergative languages for the current conventional wisdom on abstract Case assignment. Baker (1988) has argued that dependent marking, i.e. morphological case marking on DP's, head marking, i.e. agreement or cross-referencing by pronominal affixes (whatever they are), compounding (in the form of morphological or abstract incorporation) and linearization are all instantiations of abstract Case or PF Identification. This view has its attractions, and Baker skilfully manipulates the idea to account for patterns of surface transitivity alternation in the context of valency alternations. However, it is equally clear that these matters have to be kept separate. First, morphological incorporation can either be in complementary distribution with agreement or can occur in tandem with agreement. According to Baker, even if a language imposes agreement between the incorporating verb and its incorporated object, this agreement can be detached if necessary and assigned to another DP, such as a raised possessor or an initial dative and so on. However, it is at the morphological level in ergative languages where we see the greatest need to distinguish head and dependent marking. All ergative languages exhibit some kind of split in their ergativity. This is sometimes motivated by the so-called Animacy Hierarchy (or Dixon's 1994 Nominal Hierarchy), sometimes by tense/aspect, sometimes by other factors.

In Chukotko-Kamchatkan languages (Chukchee, Koryak, Aljutor) we see an interesting interplay. The general picture is this: with only very marginal exceptions there is exactly one absolutive DP in each clause (unaccusatives with incorporated subject, which show "dummy" subject agreement and in which there is no overt DP, are the chief exception). All transitive subject nominals are marked with ergative case, irrespective of their place on the Nominal Hierarchy and irrespective of tense/aspect, subordination and so on. In transitive clauses the verb always cross-references or agrees with both subject and object in person/number.[3] The ergativity split comes when we look at the pattern of agreement affixes. Ignoring the special tense/aspect forms (which are adjectival in morphology and hence essentially monovalent) we find that subjects are cross-referenced by prefixes and objects by suffixes. One prefix picks out just A functions (transitive subject) and is thus irrelevant to the question of ergativity splits. All the other prefixes pick out S/A functions, i.e., work along an accusative axis. In the suffixes we find some rather complex patterning, but a number of suffixes are clearly ergative, cross-referencing S/O, while others are neutral, picking out just O. There tends to be separate marking for number in the suffixes, which is particularly obvious in the case of Koryak, where a suffix -la- is added to (object) dual forms to form object plural forms. This also cross-references S as well as O functions and hence works ergatively. This pattern is shown in Tables 1, 2 overleaf.

As far as I can tell, no system which tries to derive PF Identification from a single set of syntactic configurations has any hope of coping with morphology of this type. This is likely to be all the more so in a system which doesn't even have notions such as "argument" to appeal to.

There is a further intriguing wrinkle here. There is evidence of a kind of animacy-inspired "inverse" system, in that the forms for 2nd or 3rd sg person acting on 1st person object are actually take-overs from the antipassive voice. I have argued that this can only be handled sensibly in a theory of agreement morphology which derives these forms by means of the formal equivalent of realizational morphology (Spencer 1995, 1996b). Then we can simply allow the forms to be accounted for by means of a rule of referral. As is well-known, syncretisms of the "take-over" type are particularly difficult to deal with in a morpheme-based system, in which inflectional pieces are stored as lexical entries with their own properties. Indeed, this type of take-over provides the strongest argument in favour of the deployment of rules of referral. It is very hard to see how a structurally based theory such as Borer's could ever account for such data, and

---

[3] There are certain exceptions here, for instance, two recently developed tenses in Chukchee and a cognate evidential tense in Koryak.

Table 1 Koryak transitive conjugation (Aorist)

subject	object			subject	object		
1sg	1sg			1pl	1sg		
	1du				1du		
	1pl				1pl		
	2sg	t-	-gi		2sg	mət-	-gi
	2du	t-	-tək		2du	mət-	-tək
	2pl	t-	la-tək		2pl	mət-	-la-tək
	3sg	t-	-n		3sg	mət-	-n
	3du	t-	-net		3du	mət-	-net
	3pl	t-	-new		3pl	mət-	-new
2sg	1sg	[ine-	-i]	2pl	1sg	[ine-	-tək]
	1du	ne-	-mək		1du	ne-	-mək
	1pl	na-	-la-mək		1pl	na-	-la-mək
	2sg				2sg		
	2du				2du		
	2pl				2pl		
	3sg	Ø-	-n		3sg	Ø-	-(la)-tkə
	3du	Ø-	-net		3du	Ø-	-(la)-tkə
	3pl	Ø-	-new		3pl	Ø-	-la-tkə
3sg	1sg	[ine-	-i]	3pl	1sg	ne-	-gəm
	1du	ne-	-mək		1du	ne-	-mək
	1pl	na-	-la-mək		1pl	na-	-la-mək
	2sg	ne-	-i-gi		2sg	ne-	-gi
	2du	ne-	-tək		2du	ne-	-tək
	2pl	na-	-la-tək		2pl	na-	-la-tək
	3sg	Ø-	-nin		3sg	ne-	-n
	3du	Ø-	-nin		3du	ne-	-net
	3pl	Ø-	-nin		3pl	ne-	-new

able 2 Koryak intransitive conjugation (Aorist)

	intransitive verbs		adjectives (in *in/kin*)
bject			
g	t-	-k	-i-gəm
lu	mət-	-mək	-muji
▮l	mət-	-la-mək	-muju
g	Ø-	-i	-i-gi
lu	Ø-	-tək	-tuji
▮l	Ø-	-la-tək	-tuju
g	Ø-	-i	-Ø/n
lu	Ø-	-gəhi	-t
▮l	Ø-	-la-i	-w

rticularly, syncretic synonymy between an transitive verb form and an antipassive. This is
the more acute given that the agreement system cuts across aktionsart classes, so that a
ansitive eventive and a transitive non-eventive will each show the antipassive syncretism.
us, these data will prove a serious problem no matter what we say about the derivation of
al antipassives.

eferences

ker, Mark 1988. *Incorporation*. Chicago: University of Chicago Press.

rer, Hagit 1994. The Projection of Arguments. In: Benedicto, Elena and Runner, Jeff
(eds.) *UMOP 17*, GLSA, University of Massachusetts, Amherst.

xon, Robert M. W. 1994. *Ergativity*. Cambridge: Cambridge University Press.

parsky, Paul 1995. Partitive case and aspect. Talk given to the *Workshop on Lexical
Structures*, Wuppertal.

arantz, Alec 1984. *On the Nature of Grammatical Relations*. Cambridge, MA: MIT Press.

linskaja, Maria, S. and Vladimir, P. Nedjalkov 1987. Contrasting the Absolutive in
Chukchee. *Lingua* 71, 239–69.

nith, Carlota, S. 1991. *The Parameter of Aspect*. Studies in Linguistics and Philosophy 43.
Dordrecht: Kluwer Academic Publishers.

encer, Andrew J. 1995. Agreement morphology is morphology. Talk presented at the
Linguistics Association of Great Britain, University of Essex, 19 September.

encer, Andrew J. 1996a. Inflection vs. derivation: or 'do we need nouns and verbs?' Talk
presented to the Workshop on Inflection, 7th International Morphology Meeting,
Vienna, 15 February.

Spencer, Andrew J. 1996b. Agreement morphology in Chukotkan. *Essex Research Reports in Linguistics* 10: 1-34.

Verkuyl, Henk 1993. *A Theory of Aspectuality: the Interaction of Temporal and Atemporal Structure*. Cambridge: Cambridge University Press.

The Functions of Voice Markers in the Philippine Languages

PETER SELLS

The Issue: Voice Marking and Non-Configurationality

Probably the most striking typological difference between a language like English and a Philippine language such as Tagalog is the latter's morphological system of voice markers on its predicates. In this type of voice marking system, one of a variety of arguments of the predicate appears in the nominative case. Consider for instance the data in (1)–(5) below. The verb stem in the examples in (1) is *bilih*.[1]

(1) *b-um-ili **ang**=**lalake** ng=isda sa=tindahan*
    bought NOM=man GEN=fish DAT=store
    'The man bought (a) fish in the store.' (Actor-nom.)

(2) *b-in-ili-∅ ng=lalake **ang**=**isda** sa=tindahan*
    bought   GEN=man NOM=fish DAT=store
    'The man bought the fish in the store.' (Patient-nom.)

(3) *b-in-ilh-an ng=lalake ng=isda **ang**=**tindahan***
    bought   GEN=man GEN=fish NOM=store
    'The man bought (a) fish in the store.' (Locative-nom.)

(4) *ipinam-bili ng=lalake ng=isda **ang**=**pera***
    bought   GEN=man GEN=fish NOM=money
    'The man bought (a) fish with the money.' (Instr.-nom.)

(5) *i-b-in-ili ng=lalake ng=isda **ang**=**bata***
    bought   GEN=man GEN=fish NOM=child
    'The man bought (a) fish for the child.' (Benefact.-nom.)

---

[1] I am grateful to Joan Bresnan, Resty M. Cena, Patrick Farrell, Chris Manning, María-Eugenia Niño and Christine Poulin for comments and suggestions on this work.

Morphology and Its Relation to Phonology and Syntax
Stephen G. Lapointe, Diane K. Brentari, Patrick M. Farrell
Copyright © 1997, CSLI Publications

Each argument has a default case marker or preposition indicating its function in the clause, which is supplanted by the nominative *ang* when that argument is cross-referenced by the voice marker morphology, which is underlined. The verbal morphology actually indicates both the aspect of the verb and the role of the nominative argument with respect to that verb. In the rest of the paper, I will indicate the role of the nominative NP in the gloss of the voice marking verb, but will not indicate the aspect, as that is not crucial to my concerns here.

For these Tagalog examples, the linear position of the nominative NP, given in bold, has no significance. Each of the NPs is preceded by a clitic that can be thought of either as a case marker or a preposition. The "=" in the examples indicates a clitic juncture between the case marker and its host. Pronouns have suppletive case forms. The linkers (LNK) in the examples below (such as (14)) are also pro-clitics, but these are not represented as such, for simplicity. As the reader will notice, there is an interaction of voice and the specificity of the Patient argument, again of no special importance here. Roughly speaking, the Actor is specific by default, while the Patient is specific only when it appears as the nominative.

Example (1) shows the Active voice, where the marker -*um*- indicates that the Actor is the nominative NP.[2] In Tagalog, reduplication is used to indicate an incomplete action. As there is no reduplication here, the action is understood as complete. In (2), the -*in*- is an aspectual infix that indicates that the action has begun, and the lack of reduplication indicates that the action is also complete; hence this is essentially a perfective interpretation. The infix -*in*- also appears in the examples (3)–(5). The voice marker in (2) is actually null, but marks the Patient or Object voice, indicating that the Patient is the nominative NP. The examples in (3)–(5) show other voices.

As is well-known, the nominative NP shows some properties which make it seem quite topic-like, and there has been some controversy as to whether it is best characterized as a subject, a topic, both, or neither (see e.g., Schachter 1976). As this paper is about linking of arguments to syntactic functions, I will look at different approaches which treat the nominative primarily as a subject, and the nature of such analyses. Kroeger (1993) presents a battery of tests for the subjecthood of the nominative; although some of these have been scrutinized and found to be not so straightforward (see Cena 1995, Schachter 1995), I believe that there is some utility in positing the subject relation and relating the nominative to it (in my own analysis, developed below, this link is not in fact as direct as in Kroeger's analysis).

Languages such as Tagalog are non-configurational: Kroeger shows (pp. 113–118) that Tagalog passes the tests of non-configurationality given by

---

[2] Throughout this paper, I will use the Philippine term "Actor" to denote the highest argument of a predicate, usually an Agent or Experiencer.

Speas (1990). More generally, the whole family of Philippine languages are non-configurational languages. Even those related Austronesian languages that have more clause-internal structure, such as Malagasy, have quite unusual configurational properties—such as the verb and Actor forming a clause-initial constituent (see Keenan 1995).

At some fundamental level, it seems clear that it is precisely because Tagalog has the system of voice markers that it is free to show non-configurational properties in the syntax. Thus, there must be some sense in which the mapping from argument structure to syntax is mediated through the morphology, and the morphology itself may determine or constrain facets of the syntax. I would like to argue here that the voice markers in a Philippine language ignore the hierarchical arrangement of argument structure, picking up instead on certain (as yet somewhat elusive) semantic concepts; this is in contrast to a language like English, where the hierarchy of argument structure plays a direct role in the morpho-syntactic linking.

I will be concentrating, then, on the following questions:

(6) a. How does the voice marking system work?

  b. What does the morphology tell us about the linking of arguments, and how does it do that?

  c. Does the fact that there is a voice marking system have syntactic consequences?

The paper is organized as follows. In the first section, I present the brief idea of the different kinds of morpho-syntactic linking I would like to consider. In the second section, I present the basic facts of the Philippine languages that need to be accounted for, and look at the fact that the voice markers do not have a purely inflectional (relation-changing) function, but also that they have an irreduceable derivational component. In the third section, I discuss various different approaches to the Philippine data, showing that by its very nature, each analysis fails to account for anything approaching the full range of facts. This should not be cause for alarm, for in fact, this is as it should be: the Philippine languages have no properties that a linking theory should explain. Finally, in section 4, I present my own analysis of the voice markers, and look at what syntactic features we should thereby expect in a Philippine language.

1   A Typology of Voice Systems

The key problem that I have identified is that of locating the sense in which the voice markers are a typological feature of Philippine languages. In this section I will briefly explore the consequences of the idea mentioned above that the hierarchy in argument structure is not projected into the syntax, and neither does it interact with the morpho-syntactic linking.[3]

Supposing for a moment that the Philippine languages do indeed constitute a distinct system, we can isolate 3 types of mapping system, which I will call: Accusative, Ergative, and P-Voice (for "Philippine voice"). For the first two types, the basic observation is that there is an argument which is the default or unmarked subject, and deviations from this mapping between arguments and functions require demotion of the status of that argument (or perhaps suppression of it) with concomitant morpho-syntactic marking.

In terms of the mapping processes, the Accusative languages function with a regular active voice, and passive as the marked voice which demotes the Actor. The morphologically Ergative languages function in essentially the opposite direction, with regular ergative voice, with Patient as the subject; for Actor subjects, antipassive demotes the Patient. Both types of language pay regard to the hierarchy in argument structure, making reference to relative position of arguments, and having a morphologically unmarked "default" linking of one particular argument as subject. Deviations from this pattern require demotion or suppression of that argument. Below, I group these two types together as "M-Voice" (Mapping-Voice) systems.

On the other hand, in the Philippine languages, there is a multi-valent voice system. More importantly, for any given voice, no non-subject argument need demote to oblique, or be suppressed. There is no basic or default instance from which the other voices are derived, and there are essentially no interactions among potential "relation-changing" processes. While I believe that this is a typological feature, it should not be viewed as a a pure "parametric" property; for instance, some Philippine languages have Passive, such as Sama (Walton 1983), Northern Kankanay (Porter 1979) and Umiray Dumaget (MacLeod 1972).

My position here is not new; Mulder and Schwartz (1981), Shibatani (1988), and de Wolf (1988) all argue that the Philippine languages are neither of the Accusative nor Ergative type, in contrast to the majority of the literature which seeks to put them into one category or the other.[4] There are certain important respects in which the Philippine languages do show ergative properties or strong similarities with ergative languages, but these do not pertain to the functioning of the morpho-syntactic component. Rather, these are generally to do with the common, but not overwhelming, morphologically unmarked status of Patient voice in many Philippine languages (e.g., in

---

[3] This is not to deny a crucial role for argument structure in, say, binding and control relations (e.g., Andrews 1985, Manning 1994).

[4] Farrell (1994) proposes an account of Cebuano which he classes as "Ergative", though it involves no mapping processes, and is similar in its mechanisms to the approach I advocate here.

(2) the voice marker is ∅), and the high frequency of Patient voice sentences.[5] However, as Kroeger (1993) shows (ch. 3), this does not mean that the Patient argument usually carries continuity of discourse reference; rather, the Actor does.

In contrast to what happens in an M-Voice system, I will argue below that the function of the voice markers in the Philippine languages is two-fold: to directly select one argument of the predicate as being the subject, and to associate a null pronominal with that subject. I will claim that the overt nominative NP is linked to that null subject, but is not the actual subject itself. I will refer to this as the NNP. As the NNP is not a true subject, it will follow that this overt argument cannot be in SpecIP, if that is the "subject position". As shown by Kroeger (1993), at least for Tagalog, SpecIP is not a subject position, but rather is a preverbal position associated with the discourse functions of either topic or focus (see (18) below).

Summarizing these claims:

(7)   Philippine voice markers:
   a.   each voice marker links a particular argument directly as the subject
   b.   the subject is itself a null pronominal
   c.   there is no subject position in the clausal syntax

Such properties have far-reaching consequences. From (7)a, it follows that the part of linguistic theory that deals with the interface between morphology and syntax must countenance direct reference to grammatical functions, in that one argument is directly picked out as the subject. Property (c) follows from (b), and if the subject is not represented directly in the phrase structure, as I will argue below, it follows that subject-properties cannot be configurationally defined. Thus, these are languages in which there are subject properties but no subject position.

2   Voice Markers and their Derivational Properties

Any analysis of Philippine morpho-syntax must account for the basic patterns of linking, such as in the data in (1)–(5) above, and for the subject-like properties of the NNP. Most of the previous literature has adopted an analysis based on the assumption that the Philippine system is an M-Voice system. I believe that all such attempts are destined to fail, as I discuss in section 3. In the present section I will look at the fact that the Philippine voice markers seem to have, in addition to any inflectional properties, some strongly derivational properties. Few, if any, voice markers have pure inflectional properties,

---

[5] This feature is often referred to as "patient primacy" (see Cena 1977, de Guzman 1992). I do not mean to suggest here that this feature is to be directly identified with ergativity.

and therefore do not function merely to realign arguments as in regular cases of linking alternations.

Here I will just focus on one aspect of the derivational properties of the voice markers, namely the fact that the semantic information that they refer to is nothing as simple as a list of thematic roles.

Consider the following Isnag data, from Barlaan (1986). The two Goal voice affixes -*an* and *i*- both involve the idea of there being separate Actor and Goal roles, but differ in that the latter includes the notion of "conveyance", something passing from Actor to Goal. Here the meaning is that the reading is to be out loud.

(8) a. *basa:-an   mu ma:n ya:n*
         read-GoalV you please that.NOM
         'Would you please read that.'

     b. *i-ba:sa   mu ma:n ya:n*
         read-GoalV you please that.NOM
         'Would you please read that aloud.' (indicates something passes from speaker to hearer)

In the next examples, the Goal voice marker -*an* transitivizes the predicate, and alters (generalizes) its meaning.

(9) a. *pisu-an*
         GoalV-verb 'to put X (onto Y)'

     b. *mag-pisu-q*
         ActV-verb 'to jump into (water)'

That is, *pisu* with the *mag*- prefix means to jump into something (usually water), while *pisu-an* has a broader meaning. What is important here is the notion of the Goal (the Y argument) being an expressible argument of the predicate, in contrast to the (b) example where the Goal is implicit, and cannot be overtly expressed. It is this property of -*an* that allows it to cooccur with 'read', as in (8)a, and it can add that dimension of meaning to whatever *pisu* means in (9)a. We see this dimension again in (10)b, where the Goal voice marking again indicates that the action passes to a distinct Goal.

(10) a. *mag-amoman tada*
         ActV-talk   3pl 'We will talk (reciprocally).'

     b. *amoman-an takayu*
         GoalV-talk   1sg-2sg 'I will talk to you.'

If the voice markers have inflectional (relation-changing) effects, these are not their only effects. As has been frequently noted in the literature (Miller 1988, Barlaan 1986, de Guzman 1991, Voskuil 1993), one must acknowledge a derivational component; sometimes meaning is added, and sometimes the meanings just are compatible.

Similar conclusions can be drawn from simple examples in Tagalog, where different Actor voice markers can give the verb different senses; for some verbs, the infix *-um-* indicates an action directed towards the Actor, while *mag-* indicates an action in the other direction. This shows up in the pairs of examples in (11).

(11)　*b-um-ilih*　　buy　　　　　　*mag-bilih*　　sell
　　　　um-abot　　reach for　　　*mag-ʔabot*　　hand to

However, note the form *mag-bigay* ('give'), where the meaning that *mag-* carries merely reaffirms the directional component that 'give' contains. There is no form **b-um-igay*, meaning 'receive'; the actual form is *t-um-anggap*, again with the voice marking reaffirming, but not contributing the meaning of, direction.

Another striking instance of the contribution that voice markers can make is seen in the following Ivatan data, from Reid (1967–68).

(12)　a.　　*omasngen*　　　*o=tao*　　　*do=takey*
　　　　　　ActV-draw near NOM=man LOC=field
　　　　　　'The man is drawing near to the field.'

　　　b.　　*iasngen*　　　　*no=tao*　　*do=takey o=libro*
　　　　　　AssocV-draw near GEN=man LOC=field NOM=book
　　　　　　'The man is drawing near to the field with a book.'

　　　c.　　*asngenen*　　　*no=tao*　　*o=takey*
　　　　　　LocV-draw near GEN=man NOM=field
　　　　　　'The man is drawing near to the field.'

Reid observes that the (a) and (c) examples do not allow the expression of the concomitant phrase 'book', "unless it is focussed on specifically", which is what happens when the verb is in the Associative voice, in the (b) example. So, in this case, it is not a matter of realigning an argument of the predicate, but rather, an adjunct has been added directly as the subject.

These simple examples show some of the ways in which voice markers have a derivational function (or at least, not a purely inflectional function). The following section looks at other ways in which the voice markers fail to show the properties of an inflectional voice system.

3　Mapping Theories

In this section I will review previous analyses of the Philippine voice system, and show how such approaches, which are intended to account for M-Voice systems, fail.

For syntactic approaches, there are two aspects to the overall picture: the analysis of the syntax (phrase structure), where the grammatical functions are defined, and then the analysis of the voice markers that feeds into that. For lexicalist mapping theories, the phrase structure part is essentially independent, and thus the (brief) discussion of lexicalist theories below will just focus on the mapping of arguments. I also discuss the kinds of approaches to Philippine voice systems that have been proposed within Relational Grammar.

3.1 Syntactic Approaches: GB

3.1.1 Guilfoyle, Hung and Travis (1992)

In an important study of the basic properties of Philippine languages, Guilfoyle et al. (1992) (hereafter: GHT) provide an account of the relation between voice marker morphology (or more strictly, the syntactically relevant effects of the morphology) and the syntax. They look at certain grammatical phenomena, and the constraints on them, and recognize the apparent non-configurational properties in a language such as Tagalog; yet they adopt a view based on a fully configurational phrase structure, founded on their assumption that "... nevertheless it seems that it [Tagalog] must be configurational at some level if we are to explain the constraints ..." (p. 394).

In its barest outline, the GHT analysis makes the following presuppositions about Philippine clause structure, as shown in the tree (13)d.[6]

(13)   a.   the underlying structure is S-V-O, with the Actor generated in SpecVP and the Patient as complement to V, for a simple transitive verb

      b.   above VP is IP, with I on the left and SpecIP on the right; SpecIP is a position in which Case is assigned (an A-position)

      c.   in all clauses, there is V-movement to I, to give a V-initial surface structure, and some NP moves to SpecIP to function as the NNP

---

[6] The GHT analysis is prefigured by Hoekstra (1986) and Weston (1989).

d.

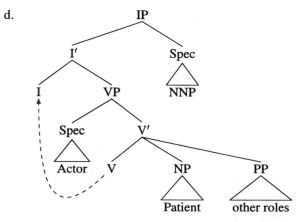

Assumptions (a) and (c) here are related, for if underlying S-V-O were not posited, V-movement would not necessarily be required. Below, I will show that all of these assumptions are flawed: there are cases where V demonstrably does not move to I, but nevertheless V precedes all other elements of the clause; and SpecIP is an $\overline{A}$-position which is to the left of I.

In the GHT analysis, the key fundamental difference between a language like English and one like Tagalog is located in the effects of the "passive" morphology; in English, passive suppresses the direct expression of the Actor, while the comparable situation in Tagalog allows the Actor to be expressed (apparently as a kind of object). While this is broadly correct, as noted above, it is also misguided in its detail: the difference does not reduce to a fact about "passive", as most Philippine languages do not have passive, but rather, the difference lies in the more general voice marker system of the Philippine languages, of which instances corresponding functionally to an English passive form a small subset.

More specifically, GHT propose that each voice marker licenses Case on a non-subject argument; for example, an active voice example like (1) above would have the marker -um- assigning Case to the Patient argument; therefore the Actor would be left without a Case-assigner, and would move to SpecIP to get Case from INFL, in the position above indicated by NNP.[7] In (2), the marker ∅ would assign Case to the Actor, leaving the Patient with no option other than to move to SpecIP.

However, this does not readily extend to the more clearly oblique or prepositional cases such as those in (3)–(5), where it must be assumed that each voice marker licenses both Actor and Patient, but then there is no prediction about which other argument is the subject, and why (GHT must assume

---

[7] This does not guarantee the correct linear position of that phrase.

that one other argument is generated without its prepositional case marker, or that that case marker incorporates into V; see p. 382, fn. 7).

3.1.2 Kroeger 1990

As noted in Kroeger (1990), Maclachlan (1989), and Sityar (1995), the GHT analysis cannot account for the full range of voice markers that the Philippine languages show. Sityar observes that the GHT view would lead one to suspect that intransitive verbs have no voice marker, as the single argument would get Case from INFL. However, intransitives typically do have voice markers, as seen in (14), and the function of such markers is not vacuous.[8]

(14) a.   *ni-burut   ang=[iya   ng   nawung]*
           R.A.-swell NOM=[3sg.GEN LNK face]
           'His face swelled.' (Ceb., Sityar (1994))

     b.   *gi-gutum   aku*
           R.P.-hungry 1sg.NOM
           'I am hungry.'

Keeping the same structural account, one could suppose that the voice markers signal the suppression of a case marker or preposition, thereby forcing one argument to move to SpecIP. Kroeger (1990) presents a general account in this vein, treating each underlying phrase as a KP, with K being one of Case clitics or prepositions, as shown in (15).

There is a puzzle here with Actors, base generated in SpecVP. If we move to the K-incorporation idea, there appears to be a paradox. If INFL is taken to be the default case marker for the subject, then Actor voice will be the reflection of K-incorporation of INFL; if so, then movement of the Actor from SpecVP to SpecIP will have no beneficial effect—by hypothesis, INFL is no longer available as a case assigner. Thus, we must assume that INFL is an extra case assigner, in addition to the K generated in each thematic phrase, and that K_{Act} is a marker of inherent case, or a preposition. The same property has appeared in Minimalist accounts—there needs to be one extra case assigner in the clause, for nominative. For instance, Richards (1995) proposes an extra case checking position, SpecΠP, at the top of the clause, for checking nominative Case (at LF).

---

[8] In the glosses, 'R.A.' stands for Realis and Actor voice, and 'R.P.' for Realis and Patient (Object) voice.

(15)

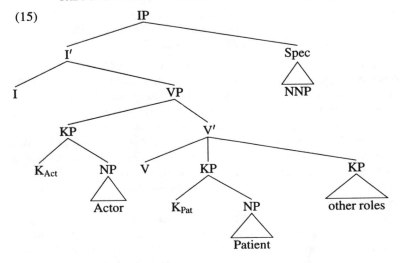

3.1.3 Clause Structure

Can it be that each voice marker licenses all of the other arguments in situ, as proposed by GHT?—This really cannot work for any language, even the most straightforward case that they consider, namely Malagasy (see Keenan 1995). Some problems were noted above. Additionally, constructions without voice markers show clearly that such assumptions are flawed. When there are no voice markers, all arguments are licensed in situ, as in the Tagalog recent past (Miller 1988, McGinn 1988). The same is true in Kapampangan (see also Gonzalez 1985, 77).[9]

(16) a.   *ka-bibili lang ng=Pedro   ng=tela*   (Tag., GHT 411)
RP-buy   just   GEN=Pedro GEN=cloth
'Pedro just bought some cloth.'

b.   *ka-raratang na   ning=mestra* (Kap., Miritikani 65)
RP-come   3sg.Act GEN=teacher
'The teacher just came.'

This is also the case in Cebuano *pag*-nominals; see (17). The order here is still head-initial; in all cases, the argument-taking head must be initial, even if there is no INFL (licensing a NOM) present, and all arguments can be licensed in situ, without the argument-taking head having any special marker. This directly contradicts the GHT idea that the bare heads license no arguments on their own—clearly, in fact, they license all of their arguments, in principle.

---

[9] The recent past involves the prefix *ka-* plus reduplication in the following stem.

(17)   ... *sa=pagkapot   sa/*ang=kawatan sa/*ang=manok*
        ... OBL=grabbing GEN/*NOM=thief   GEN/*NOM=chicken
        '... upon the thief's grabbing the chicken' (Ceb.)

Further, the assumption that the Philippine languages have a clause-internal configurational structure is quite problematic, and GHT acknowledge that a certain amount of abstract movement or other abstract relations will be necessary under their account to provide something approaching a descriptively adequate account of the observed constituent orders.[10] It seems unlikely that there is any convincing account that can be developed in this structural approach, for, as I noted above, Kroeger (1993) shows that Tagalog passes many of the tests of non-configurationality given by Speas (1990), and the ordering facts discussed in the next subsection really do not lend themselves to a hierarchical account.

Kroeger (1993) shows that IP is really a structure that forms a higher constituent above the basic clause, which he labels S, with a prepredicate head and specifier position, as shown in (18). SpecIP is a position for topic and focus phrases, and not part of the basic clausal structure.

(18)

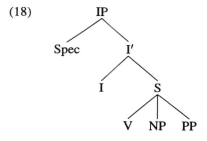

Other evidence confirms that the V-initial order cannot be derived by verb movement to INFL. In clauses with auxiliaries, an underlying Actor-V-Patient structure (see (13)d) would lead one to expect Aux-Actor-V-Patient (as in the Celtic languages—see e.g., Sproat 1985). Similarly, in nominalizations and other clauses without INFL—domains in which nominative case cannot appear—the S-V-O order would also be expected. Both of these predictions of any analysis based on the GHT-type structure are false. V-initial order is not only possible, but necessary, in every case. The facts concerning nominalizations were discussed with regard to (17) above.

To illustrate the facts with auxiliaries, let us look first at (19), which is a true biclausal structure, as can be seen from the fact that the second position clitic pronoun *siya* appears in the final position, second within in its own clause, but not in the sentence as a whole.

---

[10] For instance, when the NNP is non-final, they consider the possibility that it is coindexed with a null pronominal in SpecIP, and that the NNP moves to SpecIP at LF.

(19)   *hindi kaya ni=Pedro   ng [utus-an   siya]*
      not   able GEN=Pedro LNK [order-DatV 3sg.NOM]
      'Pedro cannot order her around.' (Tag., Kroeger 183)

In contrast, with true auxiliary examples, the pronoun positioning shows that there is just one clause. In the next two examples ((20)–(21)), the main verbs have voice markers but no aspect.[11] Here *kaya* is an auxiliary, presumably in INFL. Kroeger argues that the negator *hindi* is in SpecIP, as it counts for the computation of second position just like other more obvious phrases in SpecIP. The notional object of the verb 'order' appears in second position in the entire clause.

(20)   *hindi siya   kaya ng utus-an   ni=Pedro*
      not   3sg.NOM able LNK order-DatV GEN=Pedro
      'Pedro cannot order her around.'

(21)   *hindi siya   kaya ng bigy-an   ni=Pedro   ng=pera*
      not   3sg.NOM able LNK give-DatV GEN=Pedro GEN=money
      'Pedro cannot give her money.' (Kroeger 189)

(21)' shows the structure of (21).

(21)'

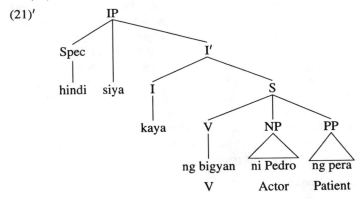

Note crucially that in these examples the Actors follow the main verbs, showing that the surface position of the verb is higher than SpecVP (see (13)d). Nevertheless, the verb cannot be in INFL, as the auxiliary is there, and these are not biclausal structures.

3.1.4 Constituent Order

With regard to ordering within S, languages vary. Tagalog does not seem to be prototypical in its ordering patterns. By far the most common (and of-

---

[11] In bi-clausal examples like (19), the lower predicate may but need not be marked for aspect (see Schachter and Otanes 1972, 257ff.). However, the mono-clausal examples only have aspect on the higher predicate.

ten rigid) requirements for the ordering of constituents within the clause put the subject effectively in **third** position. For instance, Mulder and Schwartz (1981) give the following orders for Pangasinan, where the boldface argument is the subject (p. 244).

(22)　　　Pangasinan, V - (Actor) - Subject orders:
　　a.　　V **Act** Pat Rec Ben Instr Loc
　　b.　　V Act **Pat** Rec Ben Instr Loc
　　c.　　V Act **Rec** Pat Ben Instr Loc
　　d.　　V Act **Ben** Pat Rec Instr Loc
　　e.　　V Act **Instr** Pat Rec Ben Loc
　　f.　　V Act **Loc** Pat Rec Ben Instr

Besides Pangasinan, such "nominative-third" (N3) order is also the fundamental order in Cebuano (Bell 1979), Kalagan (Collins 1970), Dibabawon (Forster 1964), Isnag (Barlaan 1986), Balangao (Shelter 1976), and Limos Kalinga (Ferreirinho 1993). In the Philippine languages, the subject is usually in a somewhat "non-canonical" position, if it has a fixed or unmarked position at all. I will take up these issues in more detail in section 4, but simply note here that N3 is a real problem for any hierarchical view of Philippine phrase structure. Travis (1991) suggests an approach to such ordering facts that distinguishes the N3 position as a kind of object position or SpecAspP, but then why subject properties should accrue to it is unclear. See also GHT, p.412, where coindexing between an empty position in SpecIP and an NP object is suggested, for such cases in Kalagan. Related accounts are developed in Sityar (1995) and Richards (1995). All of these approaches seem to me to put the NNP too low in the structure for its subject- and/or topic-properties to be explained. The ordering facts shown above in (22) instead suggest that there is no clause-internal Spec position that is actually the surface position of nominatives, as I claim in this paper.

3.2　Lexical Approaches

In Lexical Mapping Theory (LMT) and related approaches (Bresnan and Kanerva 1989, Bresnan and Moshi 1990, Alsina 1992, Arnold 1994), there are two main problems that arise. One is that there is no way to specify multiple non-core roles as subject without direct linking; that is, how does one specify that an Instrument or Benefactive becomes the subject, according to the voice marker, without directly marking the argument that way? This would void any predictive effects of the LMT system. Related to this is the second problem, which is that the system revolves around the idea of there being alternations of argument realization. The primary alternation discussed in recent work is that of (the two) Proto-Agent and Proto-Patient arguments, using terminology inspired by (but not used in) the work of Dowty (1990), although there are many other well-documented cases of argument-function alternations.

In an M-Voice system, the various processes underlying the relation-changing behavior interact (e.g., dative shift and passivization in English). Evidence for advancements from oblique usually come with such interactions. For example, in the Bantu languages, one can find evidence of obliques becoming applicative objects, which can then advance to subject under passive. These are the classic types of cases that, under lexical assumptions, motivate the kind of analysis that LMT provides. However, there are no such interactions in the Philippine languages, and there are no relation-changing processes which interact with any others (though there are derivational processes such as causative).[12] There are direct advancements of obliques to subjects, if one wants to think of it that way, but there are no other alternations or interactions. For example, all of the languages which have passive use passive to demote the Actor and make either the Patient or the Recipient the NNP; none allow passive to apply to a Patient- or Recipient-NNP form to thereby demote that argument. And the Ivatan example (12)b shows a case where an adjunct can appear as subject, or cannot appear at all (if expressed in a non-periphrastic way, of course).

The whole pattern of underspecification in LMT is intended to give four possibilities for argument realization, using two binary-valued features, or an equivalent system, as shown in (23). In M-Voice languages, arguments typically have (at least) two realizations, subject and object, subject and oblique, object and second object, and so on. Moreover, either the Actor or the Patient must be the "unmarked" subject, with marked alternatives.

(23)   LMT features: r(estricted) and o(bjective)

$\quad$ [−r]:$\qquad$ SUBJ, OBJ
$\quad$ [+r]:$\qquad$ OBJ_θ, OBL_θ
$\quad$ [−o]:$\qquad$ SUBJ, OBL_θ
$\quad$ [+o]:$\qquad$ OBJ, OBJ_θ

However, this is precisely where P-Voice languages differ; there are no function alternations. Each argument may appear in its non-nominative form (as in the nominalization above in (17)), or as an NNP, and that is all. The key to the P-Voice system is that there is no demotion of arguments based on an unmarked mapping, for there is no underlying mapping to grammatical relations (see Mulder and Schwartz 1981). The voice markers can be viewed as picking out some argument in argument structure as the subject, and the case markers can be viewed as allowing realization of any non-subject, in

---

[12] This claim is perhaps a little overstated, as some Philippine languages, such as Ilocano (Gerdts 1988) do appear to show dative shift.

the general case. Thus, the kind of alternations shown in (23) are simply irrelevant for a P-Voice language.

3.3 Relational Grammar

Within the Relational Grammar literature, there are two main approaches which have tried to view the Philippine system as some kind of M-Voice system. Bell (1979) proposed a Passive analysis of Cebuano, taking the Actor voice as unmarked, mapping the Actor to 1 (final subject); for all non-Actor voices this has the consequence that some kind of passive has applied, rendering the Actor as an oblique (a chômeur). This is problematic, as there is positive evidence that the Actor is still a term.

The alternative is an Ergative analysis, proposed by Gerdts (1988) for Ilocano, which distinguishes final relations from surface case marking. In Gerdts' proposal, the unmarked form for a two-place verb is the Patient voice, with the Actor as a final 1 and the Patient as a final 2. However, the case marking assigns Absolutive (=nominative) to the final 2, and Ergative (=genitive) to the final 1, and rules which have been taken to refer to "subjecthood" refer instead to the absolutive argument (e.g., relativization).[13] This last step is necessary as Absolutives of transitives are final 2s, while Absolutives of intransitives are final 1s, and thus it is case and not grammatical relation that generalizes across these types. The Actor voice is taken as a reflex of Antipassive, which has the effect of making the Patient a 2-chômeur. In the resulting intransitive clause (the Actor being the only term argument), the Actor is assigned Absolutive case and the Patient an Oblique case, due to its chômeur status.

In the Ergative analysis, (2) above in "Patient voice" is the underived form. The Actor is a final 1, the Patient a final 2, and by the case marking rules it is the 2 which is Absolutive; the final 1 is Ergative. (1) above is taken to be the Antipassive, and is formally intransitive: the Actor is the final 1, the Patient is a 2-chômeur, and the Locative is an oblique. The Actor is therefore the Absolutive, being the only (final) term argument.

de Guzman (1988) basically endorses the Ergative analysis, suggesting some theory-internal revisions (observing for example that in Gerdts' analysis, the final grammatical relations are somewhat unnecessary, for all surface-related phenomena trigger off of the case marking); Rowsell (1983) adopts the ergative approach for Kapampangan, and Wimbish (1987) does for Ilocano.

Both types of approach are criticized in Mulder and Schwartz (1981), who observe that the relational derivation becomes basically meaningless – all that is important is the initial semantic relations (what is Actor, what is

---

[13] It seems to remain unexplained in an Ergative analysis why it is that the absolutive takes on the function of subject in other languages.

Patient, and so on), and the surface relations or cases, depending on the particular account. They suggest that each voice marker designates a given argument as the 1 (the subject), and that such a designation is simultaneously the initial and final mapping. My proposal for the function of the voice markers follows this idea quite closely, as in my terms it does not classify the languages as having an M-Voice system.

Farrell (1994) proposes a similar account for Cebuano, except that it is built around an Ergative approach in which the key term is the final 2, which is the Absolutive in a transitive clause. Farrell proposes that the different voice markers indicate different initializations (to 2) of thematic roles relative to grammatical relations, observing too that there are no interactions of relation-changing processes.

A necessary consequence of the Ergative analysis is that the Patient is a chômeur or oblique when it is not the final Absolutive. However, Kroeger (1993:47) argues that non-nominative Patients in Tagalog are terms, rather than obliques.[14] These issues need to be explored further, as do the predictions of the Ergative analysis for the voices where neither Actor nor Patient is the absolutive (i.e., data beyond the simple Passive/Anti-Passive realm).

4   Linking from Morphology to Syntax

4.1   The Morpho-Syntax of the Voice Markers

Having argued that any M-Voice type of analysis is inappropriate for the Philippine languages, my proposal is that for each predicate, there is: (i) default linking for each argument, and (ii) linking of one argument to subject. (See also Carrier-Duncan 1985, 10ff..) The voice markers have no purely inflectional effects, but are intimately tied into derivational processes, as described above.

The subject is picked out directly in the lexical form, so there are no interesting aspects to morpho-syntactic linking, and no distinct morphological or syntactic derivations from any underlying structure.

As I will discuss below, nothing licenses or assigns nominative case; rather, it is the default case for any $\overline{A}$ position. Each voice marker indicates that some participant role in the eventuality denoted by the predicate is the subject, expressed as a null pronominal, which can then be linked to the nominative $\overline{A}$ position, much like popular treatments of the passive treat a *by*-phrase in English as an adjunct linked to a pronominal Agent argument (see, for example, Grimshaw 1990).

The basic structure of the analysis is shown in (24), for a schematic form in which the lowest argument is linked as the subject.

---

[14] There are perhaps some cases of oblique Patients in Tagalog, but Patients marked with the term marker *ng* (see (25)) are prevalent. It is possible that non-nominative Patients are oblique in Ilocano (Cena, p.c.).

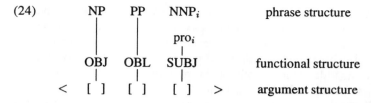

(24)　　　NP　　PP　　NNP_i　　　　　　phrase structure

　　　　　　　　　　　　pro_i

　　　　　OBJ　OBL　SUBJ　　　　　　functional structure

　　　< 　[ ] 　[ ] 　[ ] 　> 　　　　　argument structure

If the lowest level of structure here represents arguments that can be linked, the voice markers will designate one argument as the SUBJ, and associate a null pronominal with it. The other arguments will have default linkings to grammatical functions. In turn, such grammatical functions will have default realizations in the syntax as NPs or PPs; the subject will not have any realization as such, as it is a null pronominal. However, an NNP in the syntax may be coindexed with the SUBJ, as indicated schematically in (24).

Following the ideas presented in Carrier-Duncan (1985), we can say to a first approximation that case markers align with thematic relations in the way shown in (25) for Tagalog (Carrier-Duncan, p. 7). Each clitic takes a different form according to whether the host is a common noun or a proper name.

(25)　　Thematic　　　　Case-Clitic　　　　(NOM = ang/si)
　　　　Hierarchy　　　　Hierarchy

　　　　Actor　　　　　　ng/ni
　　　　Patient　　　　　ng/ni
　　　　Goal　　　　　　 sa/kay
　　　　Source　　　　　 sa/kay
　　　　Location　　　　 sa/kay

We can think of this as helping to predict a lexical entry like that in (26), again from Carrier-Duncan.

(26)　　　　　　-um-　　　-in　　　-an
　　　　bilih　(Actor　 Theme　 Source)
　　　　'buy'
　　　　　　　　ng　　　 ng　　　 sa

This indicates which voice marker makes a given role the subject, and which case marker that role gets if it is not the subject. Hence, b-um-ilih will make the Actor the subject, and the Theme will be marked with ng and the Source with sa (giving just one form of each clitic).

The Philippine languages are famous for their "split" properties of what appears to be the subject. Roughly speaking, there are "actor" properties, and there are "subject" properties. In the GHT analysis, these are taken to be properties of SpecVP and SpecIP, respectively. Here, the actor properties are taken to be properties of the highest argument in argument structure, regardless of the phrase structure realization of that argument. The remaining properties can then be viewed as true "subject" properties, as argued by Kroeger (1993). Such a split may in fact be much more widespread than has been traditionally assumed, as argued by Manning (1994). The Actor-related properties of Equi-control and Imperative formation are clearly not structurally sensitive—throughout the Philippine languages the surface position of the Actor may vary, yet the Actor-related properties remain constant.

4.2 Properties of Nominative Phrases and Subjects

My claim here is that the NNP is not the subject itself, but, rather is an $\overline{\text{A}}$-phrase. Nominative is in fact not just the case of NNPs: many pre-verbal NPs bear nominative, such as those in what I will call the focus position. This is true even in cases where the NP would not have had nominative clause-internally. The following Kapampangan data, from Rowsell (1983), is quite typical of the fronting patterns that Philippine languages show.

(27) a. *tatagalan na$_j$ ya$_i$ ning=asu$_j$ ing=pusa$_i$ king=mula*
       chase   3sg.A$_j$ 3sg.N$_i$ GEN=dog$_j$ NOM=cat$_i$ OBL=yard
       'The dog is chasing the cat in the yard.'

   b. *ing=asu$_j$ tatagalan na$_j$ ya$_i$ ing=pusa$_i$ king=mula*
       NOM=dog$_j$ chase   3sg.A$_j$ 3sg.N$_i$ NOM=cat$_i$ OBL=yard
       'The dog, it is chasing the cat in the yard.'

   c. *ing=pusa$_i$ tatagalan na$_j$ ya$_i$ ning=asu$_j$ king=mula*
       NOM=cat chase   3sg.A$_j$ 3sg.N GEN=dog$_j$ OBL=yard
       'The cat, the dog is chasing it in the yard.'

We can see that nominative case marks an $\overline{\text{A}}$-position in (27)b. The displaced NP is always nominative, even if the position it is related to in the lower clause is not.

From facts such as these, there emerges a clear generalization about what nominative marks: it marks an $\overline{\text{A}}$-position (this argument is made in more detail with other kinds of data in Sells 1995).[15] From this it follows that overt NNPs are not in fact the subjects of their clauses, as they are $\overline{\text{A}}$ phrases. In turn, it follows that there is no clause-internal subject position in the Philippine languages, as there is no phrase that could occupy it.

Now, if the NNP is not the subject of the clause, what is? I would suggest that the true subject of the clause is a null pronominal, determined by the voice marking on the main predicate. The overt NNP is linked to this pronominal in an $\overline{\text{A}}$-type relationship. Clause-types which do not have voice markers

---

[15] This is not the only function of nominative case: Cena (1995) discusses several instances of nominative-marked predicates.

cannot determine such a null pronominal, and therefore all arguments must be overtly expressed by the default case marking mechanisms.

This analysis predicts the following about Philippine "subjects" (many based on the "subject" properties in Kroeger).

(28)   Philippine "subjects":

Property 1: As the nominative NNP is in a (backwards-) anaphoric relationship to a null pronominal, there will be general definiteness/specificity effects.

Property 2: Overt NNPs will be marked like other $\overline{\text{A}}$-phrases in the language.

Property 3: The NNP will show "$\overline{\text{A}}$-properties" without necessarily being a topic or focus.

Property 4: Null anaphora (dropping the NNP) will be available, as there is always a null pronominal subject.

Property 5: All clause-external processes involving missing constituents will target this empty argument (relativization, raising, conjunction reduction).[16]

Property 6: So-called "floated quantifiers", and secondary predicates, will be predicated of the null argument, showing "subject" orientation.

Property 7: Certain cases of subject obviation will arise, as the subject is a null pronominal.

Property 8: Possessor ascension might be thought of as multiple $\overline{\text{A}}$-binding of the pronominal subject; it happens only out of "subjects", and the ascended possessor must be in a pre-predicate $\overline{\text{A}}$-position (see Bell 1979 and Sells 1995).

Property 9: The clause-internal position of the NNP will be essentially the position of an adjunct; in particular, it may appear in no fixed position, or it may appear in positions that are difficult to justify in a hierarchical structure (e.g., third).

---

[16] This is stipulative as it stands. To be explanatory, an account needs to be given as to why clause-external processes would target the null pronominal subject in preference to other potentially null positions. However, I suspect the key here is related to economy of morphological expression (the missing position is already "marked" by the verbal morphology) rather than to economy of movement or dependency links (for such an account, see Nakamura 1994).

Property 10: There are also odd apparent constituents, such as V + Actor, created by the need to license certain arguments positionally.

4.3 Clause Structure in Philippine Languages

As there is no overt subject in the clause, the NNP will not be in the canonical subject position, namely SpecIP, and the projections of IP and CP will be available for other functions. We can take it that the fact that SpecIP is essentially irrelevant for the notion of "subject" correlates with the fact that the clause is of category S, and therefore at least allows non-configurational properties, and, as noted, the NNP will have to be essentially an adjunct generated within that S, coindexed with the null pronominal in the verb. Exactly where the NNP falls with respect to the other phrases under S may be determined, as we have seen, by various quite surfacy linearization principles or preferences, if it is determined at all. S may be non-configurational, or it may have a structured but unusual configuration, as argued for Malagasy by Keenan (1995).

I will take NP preposing (see (27) above) to be movement to a focus position, in SpecCP. This position is relatively external to the clause, as it does not attract second-position clitics.

(29)

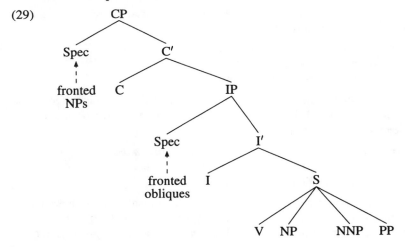

The fact that fronted NPs occupy SpecCP can be seen in the contrast with fronted obliques.[17] In the Kapampangan example in (30)a, the fronted oblique attracts the second-position copy pronoun to it. Kroeger (1993) argues that such phrases occupy SpecIP, and that the domain of clitic placement is (maximally) IP. The unacceptability of (30)b shows that the pronoun must be second in IP, not just S.

---

[17] As predicted by (29), complementizers also do not attract second-position clitics.

(30) a.   *king=tindahan ya$_i$ sinali ng=mangga ing=lalaki$_i$*
            OBL=store   3sg.N$_i$ bought GEN=mango NOM=man$_i$
            'At the store the man bought a mango.'

     b.   **king=tindahan sinali ya$_i$ ng=mangga ing=lalaki$_i$*
            OBL=store   bought 3sg.N$_i$ GEN=mango NOM=man$_i$
            'At the store the man bought a mango.'

However, if an NP is fronted, the copy pronouns are not attracted forward. For example in (31)a the pronoun must be in third position in the whole sentence. Under an analysis in which the fronted NP is in SpecCP, the pronoun is in fact in its regular second position in IP, following the verb (compare (30)a with (31)a).

(31) a.   *ing=lalaki$_i$ mena   ya$_i$ king=anak*
            NOM=man$_i$ wait-for 3sg.N$_i$ OBL=child
            'The man waited for the child.' (Kap., Richards 170)

     b.   **ing=lalaki$_i$ ya$_i$ mena   king=anak*
            NOM=man$_i$ 3sg.N$_i$ wait-for OBL=child
            'The man waited for the child.'

(32) shows the example of a fronted non-subject Actor, which again does not attract the pronouns forward.

(32)   *ing=lalaki$_j$ seli   na$_j$ ya$_i$ ing=mangga$_i$*
           NOM=man$_j$ bought 3sg.A$_j$ 3sg.N$_i$ NOM=mango$_i$
           'The man bought the mango.'

If negation is present, the pronouns are attracted to it. This suggests that negation is generated either in the I position in the tree above, or in SpecIP as Kroeger claims for Tagalog *hindi*.

(33)   *ing=lalaki$_j$ e   na$_j$ ya$_i$ seli   ing=mangga$_i$*
           NOM=man$_j$ not 3sg.A$_j$ 3sg.N$_i$ bought NOM=mango$_i$
           'The man did not buy the mango.'

These observations provide some basic arguments for the hierarchical structure in (29) that I adopt. Within the S node, the flat structure requires some ordering principles. For an N3 language, these can be given as in (34).

(34) a.   Head < X
     b.   Actor < XP
     c.   NNP < XP[−Actor]

For Tagalog, the last two may be just preferences; for Kapampangan, the order of Actor and NNP is somewhat free, but these precede all other phrasal elements (according to Mulder and Schwartz 1981).

In addition to the phrase structures based on (29), shown here in (36), I will adopt an analysis here in terms of LFG (Bresnan 1982) in which there are parallel c-structures and f-structures. Alongside the familiar grammatical functions of PRED, SUBJ, and OBJ, there will also be discourse functions. For my purposes here, the important discourse functions are FOCUS, for phrases in SpecCP, and the discourse function of the NNP, which I will call "NADJ", for "Nominative Adjunct". In the basic cases, this NADJ will be coindexed with the null pronominal subject, as shown in (35). In LFG, a null pronominal has no phrasal position in the c-structure, but only "exists" in the f-structure.

In LFG, the grammatical functions must be licensed by being selected by the predicate. The discourse functions must be linked into the rest of the structure either by being associated with other discourse functions or with other grammatical functions, and this association may be full unification (that is, structure-sharing) or coindexing as in this example.

(35)

$$
\begin{bmatrix}
\text{SUBJ} & \begin{bmatrix} \text{PRED} & \text{'pro'} \\ \text{INDEX} & i \end{bmatrix} \\\\
\text{OBJ} & \begin{bmatrix} \text{CASE} & \text{GEN} \\ \text{PRED} & \text{'man'} \\ \text{INDEX} & j \end{bmatrix} \\\\
\text{PRED} & \text{'buy'} \\\\
\text{NADJ} & \begin{bmatrix} \text{CASE} & \text{NOM} \\ \text{PRED} & \text{'fish'} \\ \text{INDEX} & i \end{bmatrix} \\\\
\text{OBL} & \begin{bmatrix} \text{CASE} & \text{LOC} \\ \text{PRED} & \text{'store'} \\ \text{INDEX} & k \end{bmatrix}
\end{bmatrix}
$$

(36)

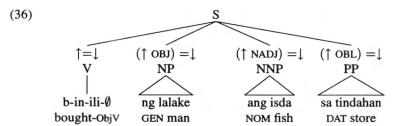

'The man bought the fish in the store.'

The main arguments for the two aspects of the nominative—its c-structure category NNP and its f-structure correlate NADJ—can be found in raising constructions (see Sells 1995).

5 Conclusion

I have argued here, following the lead of Mulder and Schwartz (1981), Shibatani (1988) and de Wolf (1988), that the system of "voice markers" in the Philippine languages does not really concern voice in the usual sense at all (that is, in the sense of an M-Voice system). Each voice marker forms a complex semantic structure with the predicate, and assigns a null pronominal to a particular argument in the resulting argument structure. This null pronominal is the real subject, and all remaining arguments are mapped directly from the result into their default functions and cases. The broadly non-configurational syntax that we see in the Philippine languages is essentially a consequence of the way the verbal morphology works, in that there can be no structural subject position in the phrase structure (for the subject is always determined directly by the verbal morphology).

Within the clause, the NNP is coindexed with the pronominal subject, and behaves itself as an Ā-category. I have motivated this by showing quite general Ā-properties of NNPs, regardless of their relation to the subject of the clause, and shown how this accounts for the syntactic behavior of the NNP.

References

Alsina, A. 1992. On the argument structure of causatives. *Linguistic Inquiry* 23, 517–555.

Andrews, A. 1985. The major functions of the noun phrase. In T. Shopen (Ed.), *Language Typology and Syntactic Description: Volume I, Clause Structure*, 62–154. Cambridge, Cambridge University Press.

Arnold, J. 1994. Inverse voice marking in Mapudungun. In S. G. et al. (Ed.), *Proceedings of BLS*, Vol. 20, 28–41. Berkeley, Berkeley Linguistics Society.

Barlaan, R. 1986. *Some Major Aspects of the Focus System in Isnag*. Doctoral dissertation, University of Texas at Arlington.

Bell, S. 1979. *Cebuano Subjects in Two Frameworks*. Doctoral dissertation, MIT, distributed by the Indiana University Linguistics Club.

Bresnan, J. (Ed.). 1982. *The Mental Representation of Grammatical Relations.* Cambridge, Mass., MIT Press.

Bresnan, J., and J. Kanerva. 1989. Locative inversion in Chicheŵa: A case study of factorization in grammar. *Linguistic Inquiry* 20, 1–50.

Bresnan, J., and L. Moshi. 1990. Object asymmetries in comparative Bantu syntax. *Linguistic Inquiry* 21, 147–185.

Carrier-Duncan, J. 1985. Linking of thematic roles in derivational word formation. *Linguistic Inquiry* 16, 1–34.

Cena, R. 1977. Patient primacy in Tagalog. Paper read at the Annual Meeting of the Linguistic Society of America, Chicago.

Cena, R. 1995. Surviving without relations. Ms. Edmonton, Alberta.

Collins, G. 1970. *Two View of Kalagan Grammar.* Doctoral dissertation, Indiana University.

de Guzman, V. 1988. Ergative analysis for Philippine languages: An analysis. In R. McGinn (Ed.), *Studies in Austronesian Linguistics,* 323–345. Athens, Ohio, Ohio University Press.

de Guzman, V. 1991. Inflectional morphology in the lexicon: Evidence from Tagalog. *Oceanic Linguistics* 30, 33–48.

de Guzman, V. 1992. Morphological evidence for primacy of patient as subject in Tagalog. In M. D. Ross (Ed.), *Papers in Austronesian Linguistics No. 2,* 87–96. Canberra, Pacific Linguistics Series A No. 82, The Australian National University.

de Wolf, C. 1988. Voice in Austronesian languages of Philippine type: Passive, ergative, or neither? In M. Shibatani (Ed.), *Passive and Voice,* 143–193. Amsterdam, John Benjamins.

Dowty, D. 1990. Thematic proto-roles and argument selection. *Language* 67, 547–619.

Farrell, P. 1994. *Thematic Relations and Relational Grammar.* New York, Garland Publishing.

Ferreirinho, N. 1993. *Selected Topics in the Grammar of Limos Kalinga, the Philippines.* Canberra, Pacific Linguistics Series B No. 109, The Australian National University.

Forster, J. 1964. Dual structure of Dibabawon verbal clauses. *Oceanic Linguistics* 3, 26–48.

Gerdts, D. 1988. Antipassives and causatives in Ilokano: Evidence for an ergative analysis. In R. McGinn (Ed.), *Studies in Austronesian Linguistics,* 295–321. Athens, Ohio, Ohio University Press.

Grimshaw, J. 1990. *Argument Structure.* Cambridge, MIT Press.

Guilfoyle, E., H. Hung, and L. Travis. 1992. Spec of IP and Spec of VP: Two subjects in Malayo-Polynesian languages. *Natural Language and Linguistic Theory* 10, 375–414.

Hoekstra, E. 1986. On the structural subject position in Tagalog. *Lingua* 70, 41–56.

Keenan, E. 1995. Morphology is structure: A Malagasy test case. Ms. UCLA. Presented at the 2nd annual meeting of the Austronesian Formal Linguistics Association, McGill University, March 1995.

Kroeger, P. 1990. Case incorporation in Philippine languages. Ms. Stanford University.

Kroeger, P. 1993. *Phrase Structure and Grammatical Relations in Tagalog*. Stanford, Dissertations in Linguistics, CSLI Publications.

Maclachlan, A. 1989. The morphosyntax of Tagalog verbs: The inflectional system and its interaction with derivational morphology. *McGill Working Papers in Linguistics* 6, 65–84.

MacLeod, T. 1972. Verb stem classification in Umiray Dumaget. *Philippine Journal of Linguistics* 3, 43–74.

Manning, C. 1994. *Ergativity: Argument Structure and Grammatical Relations*. Doctoral dissertation, Stanford University.

McGinn, R. 1988. Government and case in Tagalog. In R. McGinn (Ed.), *Studies in Austronesian Linguistics*, 275–293. Athens, Ohio, Ohio University Press.

Miller, B. 1988. *Non-Configurationality in Tagalog*. Doctoral dissertation, University of Michigan.

Mulder, J., and A. Schwartz. 1981. On the subject of advancements in the Philippine languages. *Studies in Language* 5, 227–268.

Nakamura, M. 1994. An economy account of *wh*-extraction in Tagalog. In E. D. et al. (Ed.), *Proceedings of WCCFL*, Vol. 12, 405–420. Stanford, CSLI/Stanford Linguistics Association.

Porter, D. 1979. Northern Kankanay morphology. *Studies in Philippine Linguistics* 3, 20–62.

Reid, L. 1967–68. On redefining transitivity for Philippine languages. *Philippine Journal for Language Teaching* 5, 15–28.

Richards, N. 1995. Another look at Tagalog subjects. Ms. MIT. Presented at the 2nd annual meeting of the Austronesian Formal Linguistics Association, McGill University, March 1995.

Rowsell, L. 1983. An ergative analysis of Kapampangan. Master's thesis, University of Calgary.

Schachter, P. 1976. The subject in Philippine languages: Actor, topic, actor-topic, or none of the above. In C. Li (Ed.), *Subject and Topic*, 491–518. New York, Academic Press.

Schachter, P. 1995. The subject in Tagalog: Still none of the above. Ms. UCLA.

Schachter, P., and F. Otanes. 1972. *Tagalog Reference Grammar*. Berkeley and Los Angeles, University of California Press.

Sells, P. 1995. Raising and the order of clausal constituents in the Philippine languages. Ms. Stanford University. Presented at the 2nd annual meeting of the Austronesian Formal Linguistics Association, McGill University, March 1995.

Shelter, J. 1976. *Notes on Balangao Grammar*. Huntington Beach, Calif., Asian-Pacific Series No. 9, Summer Institute of Linguistics.

Shibatani, M. 1988. Voice in Philippine languages. In M. Shibatani (Ed.), *Passive and Voice*, 85–142. Amsterdam, John Benjamins.

Sityar, E. 1995. Voice and the licensing of subjects in Cebuano. In R. Eckardt and V. van Geenhoven (Eds.), *Proceedings of ConSole II*, 239–252. The Hague, Holland Academic Graphics.

Speas, M. 1990. *Phrase Structure in Natural Language*. Dordrecht, Kluwer.

Sproat, R. 1985. Welsh syntax and VSO structure. *Natural Language and Linguistic Theory* 3, 173–216.

Travis, L. 1991. Derived objects, inner aspect, and the structure of VP. Ms. McGill University.

Voskuil, J. 1993. Verbal affixation in Tagalog (and Malay). Ms. Rijksuniversiteit Leiden.

Walton, C. 1983. Sama verbal semantics: Classification, derivation and inflection. Master's thesis, Temple University.

Weston, D. 1989. Three parallel structures in Malagasy. In P. F. et al. (Ed.), *Linguistic Notes from La Jolla, Number 15*, 62–96. Dept. of Linguistics, UCSD.

Wimbish, J. 1987. A relational grammar of Ilocano. Master's thesis, University of Texas at Arlington.

Comments on the Paper by Sells

MARGARET SPEAS

1. On Configurationality and the Assignment of Theta Roles

Sells has argued convincingly that previous attempts to extend standard analyses of case and voice to the Philippine languages have failed.[1] It doesn't work to treat the system as a nominative-accusative system, nor does it work to treat it as an absolutive-ergative system. This raises problems for both mapping theories, such as Relational Grammar and Lexical Functional Grammar, and Minimalist theories. Sells claims that the Philippine languages are neither NOM-ACC nor ERG-ABS; rather they instantiate a third type, in which voice markers are not purely inflectional, as they are in both NOM-ACC type languages and ABS-ERG languages. Rather, Philippine voice markers have derivational properties. The reason that standard analyses can't be extended to Philippine languages is that in standard analyses, both NOM-ACC systems and ERG-ABS systems involve morphosyntactic linking of thematic roles to particular syntactic positions and voice marking in such languages operates on this linking. Sells shows that in Philippine languages, it is not possible to assume some underlying linking of thematic roles to syntactic positions. Instead, the Philippine voice marker forms "a complex semantic structure with the predicate, and assigns a null pronominal to a particular argument in the resulting argument structure."

In my comments, I would like to argue that rather than calling for a new typological category, the Philippine facts provide evidence that the standard views of NOM and ERG type languages are wrong. Specifically, the idea that thematic roles are morphosyntactically linked to specific positions, and that voice morphology manipulates these linkings should be abandoned in favor of the sort of approach that Borer has outlined in her paper in this volume.

Borer's approach bears several intriguing similarities to the basic approach to Philippine languages that Sells outlines. Specifically, in her

---

[1] I am grateful to the participants in the Morphology conference for useful comments, and to Peter Sells and Hagit Borer for the interesting proposal that has inspired these comments. They should not be held responsible for any misconstruals I may have made in trying to adapt their proposals to one another.

analysis, the arguments of a predicate are not hierarchically arranged at D-Structure, just as in Sells' analysis of Philippine languages the arguments of a predicate are in a flat structure along with the predicate. In both Borer's and Sells' analyses, the association of thematic roles with structural positions is mediated by the morphology. And in both analyses, this morphology has what Sells terms "derivational properties".

The central components of Borer's theory are given in (1), and those of Sells' theory are given in (2), for comparison.

(1) The essence of Borer's theory:
     VP is unordered projection of V and arguments
     The specifier of an aspectual head with a certain event feature (ASP_{+E}) is interpreted as endstate
     NOM must be assigned
     NPs must either raise out of VP or incorporate into V

(2) The essence of Sells' theory of Philippine languages:
     VP is unordered projection of V and arguments
     Voice markers have derivational properties
     NOM must be assigned when there is a voice marker
     NOM licenses pro; NNP is in A' position with A' case

In Borer's theory, all NPs start out unordered within a projection of V. They are not assigned thematic roles within this projection. Rather, they raise to get case, and the result of these raising operations is then interpreted thematically at Logical Form. In an active sentence, one NP moves directly to the specifier of TP, and the other moves to the specifier of $ASP_{+E}P$. The specifier of $ASP_{+E}P$ is interpreted as the endstate of the action, i.e., theme, and the specifier of TP receives the remaining thematic role. In a passive sentence, -en is an overt head of $ASP_{+E}P$ which cannot assign ACC case. One NP moves through the spec,-en, and on to spec,TP, where it receives NOM case. Since it has passed through spec,$ASP_{+E}P$, leaving a trace, it receives the endstate/theme interpretation. Interestingly, the agent is not "demoted" in Borer's theory. The only sense in which the agent is oblique is that it can't get ACC case. The agent can either incorporate, if it's null, or be marked with P(by) if it's overt.

The correctness of treating the passivized NP as an endstate is illustrated by sentences like those in (3), in which it has been noted since the beginning of transformational grammar that there seem to be subtle thematic differences depending upon which NP is passivized. In (3a), the lesson extends only through whatever French material is being covered, and it is not necessarily the case that the children *learn* the French. In (3b), on the other hand, the lesson extends through the children learning French. In other words, we may consider "French" to be the endstate in (3a) and "the children" to be the endstate in (3b).

(3)   a. French was taught to the children.   *French* = endstate
      b. The children were taught French.   *children* = endstate

Thus, in Borer's theory, the VP is underlyingly unordered, and the functional (inflectional) heads have what we might think of as derivational content, as they mediate the thematic interpretation. Sells' and Borer's theories converge in that in both the VP is unordered, there is a requirement for NOM assignment, and voice markers have derivational/aspectual properties.

Sells gives a schematic structure like the following for Tagalog, in which focussed phrases may be fronted to specifiers in IP (and higher), and the arguments within VP are essentially unordered, with V coming initial in VP.

(4)

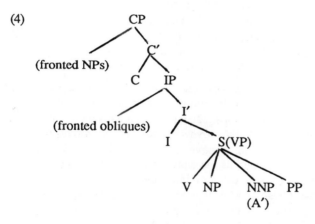

In Tagalog, there are three basic cases. All NPs bear some case marker or other.

(5)   NOMINATIVE: the NP corresponding to the VM on the verb
      GENITIVE: possessors, actors, instruments, indefinite objects
      DATIVE: goals, recipients, locations, definite objects
                              (Kroeger 1991:17)

In Sells' theory, these cases are assigned as follows:

(6) NOMINATIVE: Default case for NP in an A' position
     OTHERS: Case markers are aligned with thematic relations by convention.

The sentences in (7) are selected from Sells' paper to illustrate the voices, as well as a sentence which is in an aspect that has no voice marker. When there is no voice marker, actor and patient need not be distinguished in terms of case: both get genitive if the patient is nonspecific, and the patient gets dative if it is specific.

(7) a. Patient voice:

     B-in-ili   *ng*   *lalake*   *ang*   *isda*   *sa*   *tindahan*
     bought.PV GEN man   NOM fish DAT store

     'The man bought the fish in the store.'

   b. Dative/locative voice:

     B-in-ilh-an *ng-lalake* *ng-isda* *ang-tindaha*
     bought.DV GEN-man GEN-fish NOM-store

     'The man bought fish at the store.'

   c. No voice markers:

     Kapangunguha *pa* *lamang* *ng-bata*   *ng-mga-mangga*
     REC.PRF-gather yet only   GEN-child GEN-PL-mango

     'The child has just gathered some/the mangos.'

                                  (Kroeger 1991:61)

Given the similarities between the proposals of Sells and Borer, it will be useful to take a look at which parts of the relevant proposals might be universal, and the ways in which Philippine languages differ parametrically from English. As a starting point, I suggest the following universal Principles, and parameters of crosslinguistic variation:

(8) *Principles:*

Verb and its arguments are projected in a flat structure, with hierarchically-arranged functional categories dominating VP.

Spec of V/A (voice/aspect) is interpreted as endstate.

One case is obligatorily assigned outside of VP.

Parameters:
Obligatory case is associated/not associated with V/A

"Endstate" =   end of event
                (front end of event)
                (end location of thing in event)

Spec of V/A is/is not a null pronoun.

In both English and the Philippine languages, the VP, which includes the verb plus all of its arguments, is flat. Both languages also have functional projections which dominate VP, and in both languages these projections include a voice/aspect head, which assigns a case. The languages differ in three basic ways:

First, in English the obligatory case is not associated with the V/A marker. Rather, it is associated with a higher functional head, which in most current theories is assumed to be TP. Thus, in English, an NP must always occupy spec,TP, while in Philippine languages an NP must always occupy spec,V/AP.[2]

Second, in English, the V/A morpheme has no semantic content of its own, and so the interpretation of its specifier is purely as an endstate. In the Philippine languages, the V/A morpheme does have additional semantic content, which modifies the endstate interpretation. This will be discussed more in the following section, where I will also address the issue of whether the actor argument in the actor voice is interpreted as some kind of endstate. For now I will just note that in a sentence like *French was taught to the children*, (parallel to patient voice in Philippine languages) *French* is an endstate in the sense that the teaching ended when the relevant French teaching materials had been covered, while in *The children were taught French* (parallel to goal voice in Philippine languages), *the children* is an endstate in the sense that the teaching event ended when the French knowledge was located at/in the children. The notion of endstate is slightly different in the two cases, and Philippine languages mark this difference morphologically.

Third, Sells has shown that the overt NP associated with the V/A morpheme is in an A' position, and proposes that the actual argument associated with the V/A morpheme is a null pronoun.

I illustrate how this system works with a schematic analysis of a Philippine sentence with a patient voice marker:

---

[2]There are aspects in which an overt V/A marker does not appear. These will be discussed below.

(9)

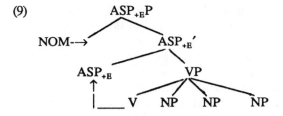

> *B-in-ilh-an   ng-lalake   ng-isda   ang-tindahan*
> bought.DV   GEN-man   GEN-fish   NOM-store

'The man bought fish at the store'

Here, one NP is associated with the spec,ASPP and hence is marked NOM. Either this NP moves overtly to spec,ASPP, and then the verb moves to a higher functional head, or the NP moves at LF. I will discuss these two options further below, when I discuss the NP order.

The NP with NOM will be interpreted as endstate, plus whatever additional content the specific morpheme provides. In this case, the patient marker is the semantically unmarked one, and so the interpretation is that of a pure endstate.

The NPs which are not marked NOM can either get case from a preposition, or default GEN. Their thematic role is then either determined by content of P, or is whatever role the verb has to assign which is not associated with the endstate. I am assuming that the Theta Criterion is another universal principle, and so any sentence will be ill-formed if all theta roles are not assigned.

Applying a Borer-style analysis to Philippine voice obviates what has been considered to be the central problem: that the construction cannot be parallel to a passive, because it does not seem to involve demotion of the initial subject. In Borer's theory, voice alternations *never* involve manipulation of grammatical relations or argument structure, and so there can be no such thing as demotion; thus, agents in a passive in English are not demoted; they just can't get accusative or nominative case. Under such a view, the core differences between English and Philippine languages have to do with whether the case assigned by the voice/aspect morpheme is obligatory, and whether the voice/aspect morpheme has semantic content. The actor in a passive (non-actor voice) is a "term" in both types of languages.

2. Voice Markers and Aspect

Now I would like to examine a bit more closely the claim that Philippine voice markers are associated with some aspect whose specifier is interpreted as an endstate. Although Sells' treatment of the voice and case morphemes involves linking of these morphemes to thematic roles, it is clear from his discussion that the semantic properties of voice morphemes which he terms "derivational" are related to thematic relations in ways that involve something other than linking.

For example, he discusses data from Isnag in which the goal voice marker indicates that the action passes to a *distinct* goal. This fact is not captured by just linking the goal argument to the NOM NP. Rather, it seems that in the goal voice, the goal is interpreted as the endstate of the action, distinct from the actor.

(10) a. *mag-amoman tada*
          ActV-talk-ASP 3pl

          'We will talk (reciprocally).'

      b. *amoman-an   takayu*
          GoalV-talk-ASP 1sg2sg

          'I will talk to you.'

                                    (Sells' example (10))

Another similar example comes from Tagalog, where actor voice has different forms, and sometimes these two forms distinguish the relationship between the actor and the endstate of the action. This suggests some sort of agreement between the actor and this voice marker, in a position designated for endstates. Thus, even actor voice is apparently associated with the endstate.

(11) *b-um-ilih*   'buy'   *mag-bilih*   'sell'
      um-abot   'reach for' *mag-?abot*   'hand to'
                        (Sells example (11))

Further, there is some evidence in Philippine languages that theta roles are associated with aspect and that case is not directly associated with theta roles.

First, we observe that the non-nominative cases are not restricted to specific theta roles. Sells hints at this when he proposes that the non-nominative NPs have default linkings to grammatical functions. Kroeger (1991) summarizes the cases of Tagalog as in (5), repeated here for convenience:

(12) NOMINATIVE: the NP corresponding to the VM on the verb
     GENITIVE: possessors, actors, instruments, indefinite objects
     DATIVE: goals, recipients, locations, definite objects
                                    (Kroeger 1991:17)

COMMENTS ON THE PAPER BY SELLS / 145

Most noteworthy in this list is the fact that non-nominative objects (patients, in Sells' terminology) are marked genitive if they are indefinite and dative if they are definite. This suggests that the cases are not best characterized in terms of lexical linking between case morphemes and particular thematic roles.

Second, it is instructive to examine constructions in the Philippine languages which do not have a nominative NP associated with the voice/aspect marker. Sityar (1995) points out that the following types of constructions have no nominative NP.[3]

(13) Constructions with no NNP:
     a. existential sentences
     b. weather predicates
     c. exclamatory sentences
     d. recent-perfective aspect
     e. experiencer predicates with indefinite objects

Under the Borer-type approach to Philippine languages that I am suggesting here, we would expect that these would all be constructions in which there was no endstate. Intuitively, this conclusion seems to be quite clearly right for existential sentences and weather predicates, and it seems plausible as well for exclamatory sentences, which assert something about the speaker's attitude rather than something about an event.

It would seem that sentences in the recent-perfective aspect would pose a challenge for my prediction, since intuitively we might think that it is impossible for an action to be completed (perfective) without having an endstate. But examination of such sentences indicates that this is precisely their interpretation:

(14) a. *Kaaalis   pa lamang ni-Pedro nang dumating*
       REC.PRF-leave yet only   GEN-P   ADV   AV.PRF-arrive
       ako
       I(NOM)

       'Pedro had just left when I arrived.'

    b. *Kakakain ko   pa lamang sa-karne*
       REC.PRF I(GEN) yet only   DAT-meat
       'I have just eaten the meat.'

---

[3]Sityar accounts for these constructions in terms of Diesing's (1992) Mapping Hypothesis. All NPs which are left within VP are mapped into the nuclear scope of the sentence. The NOM NP, she claims, is outside of the nuclear scope. This accounts for the fact that the NNP is always specific, and GEN patients are always nonspecific.

c. *Kapangunguha pa lamang ng-bata ng-mga-mangga*
REC.PRF-gather yet only GEN-child GEN-PL-mango

'The child has just gathered some/the mangos.'

(Kroeger 1991:61)

In this aspect, it seems that the endstate is de-emphasized. Perfective indicates that the action is completed, but in the recent perfective, we are just barely at the endstate. Thus, this construction is striking evidence for our hypothesis that the NOM NP is interpreted as an endstate: the absence of a NOM NP is interpreted as the absence of an endstate.

Experiencer predicates obligatorily assign GEN to the experiencer. When the other argument is indefinite, it cannot be NOM, due to the fact that the NOM argument is generally definite. Experiencer predicates do not denote events, and so we would expect them to be predicates that are not compatible with a voice/aspect marker whose spec denotes the endstate of the event.

(15) a. *Gusto namin ng-turon*
like we-GEN GEN-fritters

'We like turon.'

b. *Ayaw ng-mga-babae ng-komiks*
not.like GEN-PL-female GEN-comics

'The girls don't like comics.'

(Kroeger 1991:62)

Thus, all of the types of sentences which lack voice markers are sentences in which there no NP which is interpreted as marking the endstate of the event. Philippine languages differ from English in that the V/A marker has additional content, and this content allows the various thematic roles to be associated with the endstate.

3. Functional Projections and (Non)configurationality

In the preceding sections, I have drawn attention to the similarities between Sells' and Borer's proposals. In this section, I will look at the major differences, and discuss how the differences might be resolved. In some cases, we may want to say that the differences have to do with crosslinguistic variation, and in other cases the differences have to do with distinct, and presumably testable, disagreements on theoretical issues.

Sells' proposal includes three relevant claims about the Philippine languages:

(16) a. The argument associated with the voice/aspect marker is a null pronoun.
  b. The NP with nom case is in an A′ position.
  c. The null pronoun is a subject, although its subjecthood is not defined configurationally.

I consider Sells' arguments for the first two claims to be convincing. In principle, these claims are compatible with a Borer-style theory: she is working within a theory that admits null pronouns, and if an argument position is filled by a pronoun, presumably any overt NP associate must be in a non-argument position. Granting these claims, we must then address the question of the relationship of overt word order to the abstract structure suggested above.

3.1 The Null Pronominal Argument

Sells claims that the NP associated with the V/A marker is a pronoun. He points out that in some of the Philippine languages, the pronoun is overt rather than null, and that constructions with NNPs have properties of constructions with some overt NP coindexed with a pronoun. In the framework he adopts, the pronoun shows up as the subject in F-structure, but does not (if null) occupy a position in C-structure. This claim is not incompatible with the Borer-style analysis that I have suggested above; the analysis could be amended so that spec,ASPP is occupied by pro. This could be achieved by saying that the V/A marker assigns some case which is only appropriate for pronouns. The main problem with such an analysis will be to explain how the relationship between this pro and the NNP associate avoids violations of the binding principles.

Under either Sells' analysis, or a Borer-style amendment, the issue that remains unresolved is why (or whether) the argument associated with the V/A marker is obligatorily a pronoun rather than a full NP. One possibility is that the V/A marker is itself some kind of pronoun, which incorporates into the verb. Sells gives some reasons why such an analysis is problematic, including the fact that the pronoun can be overt in some languages. Having drawn attention to this problem, I will leave it unresolved in these brief comments.

3.2 The NNP in an A′ Position

Sells makes a convincing case that the NNP is in an A′ position. This could pose a challenge for the Borer-style account that I've suggested if we assume that A′ positions are peripheral to A positions. As we shall see below, it is not clear that the NNP is in a peripheral position.

The arguments that Sells gives for the A′ status of the NNP are summarized in (17).

(17) a. There is no evidence that licensing of NOM is associated with any specific head or position.

b. NOM case can be found on NPs other than the one associated with the V/A marker, specifically left-dislocated NPs.

According to Sells, word order varies among the Philippine languages. Looking first at Tagalog, we find that it follows the following descriptive generalizations, according to Kroeger (1991:137):

(18) (i) The actor tends to precede all other arguments.

(ii) The NP which bears nominative case tends to follow all other arguments.

(iii) "Heavier" NPs tend to follow "lighter" NPs.

(19) When (18i) and (18ii) conflict, that is, when actor is NOM, word order is free:

a. NOM actor   GEN patient

b. GEN patient   NOM actor

Also, when there is potential ambiguity, the actor must precede other arguments.

In order to get this word order, we have two options. The first is that the overt NPs could be in their underlying position. Under this assumption, there would be no overt movement, only movement at LF (or some equivalent non-movement indexing mechanism). Since we are considering the VP to be flat, in this case there is no obvious syntactic way to ensure that the first among the arguments is the one that will move at LF to the position in which it will receive the actor interpretation, since within the flat VP, all NPs will be equidistant from any potential landing sites. There could be some sort of linearization rules, but in Borer's theory there ought not be rules that refer specifically to thematic roles. If there are linearization rules, they must refer instead to the relationship between linear order and the specifier in which the NP is to be interpreted at LF. As for the NNP, even if VP is in principle flat, the NNP could be adjoined to VP in a language like Tagalog where it follows other arguments.

The second possibility is that there could be more structure than I have drawn so far: the actor could have moved to the specifier of some functional projection, and the verb could then have moved to some head above it.

Sells specifically argues against an account of the V-initial order which involves movement to INFL. Let us consider his argument in light of the fact that the Borer-style theory allows multiple functional projections. Sells points out that a V-movement account is problematic because the verb does not wind up in the second position. We can see this in sentences like those in (20), where the pronoun is a clitic that must be in second position.[4] If the verb had moved to INFL, we would expect it to precede the auxiliary *kaya*.

(20) a. *hindi siya   kaya   ng   utusan   ni   Pedro*
        not   3sg.NOM   able   LNK   order-DV   GEN   Pedro

   'Pedro cannot order her around.'

   b. *hindi siya   kaya   ng   bigy-an   ni   Pedro ng   pera*
       not   3sg.NOM   able   LNK   give-DV   GEN   Pedro GEN   money

   'Pedro cannot give her money.'

In a theory that allows multiple functional projections, this argument is not fatal, however. Suppose that the actor and other arguments are arranged in a structure like the following:

(21)

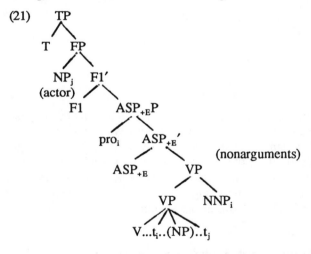

One possibility is that *kaya*, like English modals, occupies T, and the verb moves and right-adjoins to it. Then the only functional projection above TP will be NEGP, with the clitic either in or adjoined to its head. Alternatively, *kaya* might take a TP complement, and the verb would move to T. It is beyond the scope of this paper to explain why the verb does not move

---

[4]Sells also gives examples which demonstrate that these sentences do not have biclausal structures. One might also suggest that the clitic plus neg have moved to C, but Kroeger (1991) shows quite clearly that this can't be right.

farther, but at least these comments show that the auxiliary facts are not
fatal to our suggested account. In the structure above, the NNP, which is
adjoined to VP, follows all other arguments, and the actor precedes all other
arguments.

Another challenge is posed by languages like Pangasinan, where the
NNP follows the actor but precedes other arguments. One possibility for
these languages is that the NNP is adjoined to VP, but is adjoined on the left
rather than on the right:

(22)

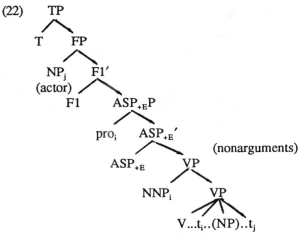

In this Section, I have looked at the major differences that distinguish
Philippine languages from English, under the Borer-style analysis sketched
out in Section 1. Both languages have an underlyingly flat VP, with arguments moving to the specifiers of functional projections, where they receive
their interpretation based upon the content of the functional head. The major
differences are that in the Philippine languages, the content of the head ASP
is richer than it is in English, and it licenses a null pronoun in its specifier
position.

4. On Subjecthood and Configurationality

Throughout this discussion, I have not addressed the issue of whether
the NNP (or some other NP) is the subject of the sentence. The is because the
question of defining a unique subject position does not arise as such in
theories such as Borer's (and other Minimalist theories) in which Grammatical Functions are defined configurationally. As Travis and Williams (1984)
and Speas (1990) point out, such theories predict that "subject" properties
may accrue to different positions, because these properties are never properties of "subjects" per se, but are rather properties of configurationally

defined positions, such as "NP which c-commands other NPs", "NP which gets NOM case", "specifier of highest functional projection", etc. These definitions in principle need not converge on one NP in a sentence.

Sells argued quite convincingly that the properties of the NNP in Philippine languages which have been taken to be subject properties follow if we consider the NNP to be in an A′ position, coindexed with a null pronoun. The NNP is more prominent than other NPs in the sentence, because being adjoined to VP, it c-commands all arguments in underlying structure. Being in an A′ position, it also can be picked out by principles of grammar that target non-argument NPs.

As for the more general issue of configurationality, although both Sells and Kroeger argue that Philippine languages are nonconfigurational, they both assign hierarchical structure to the functional projections, and Sells distinguishes the NNP from other NPs by positing a distinction between A positions and A′ positions. As Borer has shown, in theories like hers, and that of Chomsky (1992), in which all NPs move out of VP to specs of functional projections by LF, the issue of crosslinguistic variation in configurationality becomes very murky, because most of the traditional tests for configurationality for English have to be rethought. If English has a flat VP, then the tests must test something about the structure of the functional projections, not of the internal structure of the verbal projection.

Sells cites evidence that Philippine languages differ from English in the hierarchical arrangement of arguments other than that associated with the NNP. Let us take a look at this evidence, to see whether it conflicts with my claim that following Borer, at the level of VP English is also nonconfigurational.

First, actor and patient are both marked genitive in sentences like (23), in which the NNP is a dative or a locative. This suggests that their case is not licensed or checked by any particular functional category, but is rather a default case.

(23) *b-in-ilh-an   ng   lalake ng   isda ang   tindahan*
     bought.LOCV GEN man   GEN fish NOM   store

'The man bought fish at the store.'

Actually, the terminology for the case markers is somewhat misleading. As Sells shows, the case called NOM is assigned to NPs in A′ positions, and the NNP is one sub-case of this. We can characterize DAT and LOC case, when they are marked on overt NPs, to be realizations of inherent case, since they are always directly related to specific thematic roles. This makes GEN the general structural case, assigned to any argumental NP which does not have an inherent case. If we assume this, then the case facts above don't give us any evidence one way or the other about whether the actor and patient are in specifiers of functional heads.[5]

Additional evidence for a flat structure in Philippine languages comes from the diagnostics adapted from Speas 1990.

(24)   Predictions for a non-configurational language:
     a. no evidence for VP constituent
     b. no pleonastics
     c. non-subject controllees
     d. nominative reflexives
     e. no weak crossover effects
     f. no ECP effects for subjects
     g. no binding asymmetries

Actually, in that work I was arguing that the "diagnostic properties" do not necessarily pattern together. For example, Japanese shows no direct evidence for a VP constituent but has been argued extensively to have a range of configurational properties. Lack of evidence for a surface VP does not mean that there can't be a VP whose presence is masked by syntactic movement. Further, there are many languages like Italian, which are clearly configurational but which lack overt pleonastics and ECP effects for subjects. Let us focus attention on the properties which haven't been found in better studied languages, setting aside predictions a, b, and f.

As for non-subject controllees, the claim that Philippine languages can have controllees that are non-subjects is based on the contention that the NNP is a subject. According to Kroeger, controllees are generally actors. Thus, in a sentence in which the NNP is not the actor, a controlled actor will count as a "non-subject controllee". However, since in the structure I have posited above the actor winds up in the highest functional projection, these facts do not provide any argument against configurationality.

In examining the nominative reflexives, we must again be careful not to be misled by the terminology. Nominative is the case on the adjoined NNP, which is coindexed with a null pronoun. In the structure I have suggested, the null pronoun and the NNP are both lower than the actor at some level, either SS or LF. Thus, we would expect sentences in which the NNP is the patient to contain nominative reflexives. This is precisely the sort of sentence that Kroeger gives:

---

[5] I am admittedly shirking the question of why they are not distinguished morphologically.

(25)   *Pinupuri*   *lahat* *ng-mga-kandidato* *ang-kanila-ng*
        IMPERF-praise-OV all   GEN-PL-candidate NOM-3.PL-LNK
        sarili
        self

        'All the candidates praised themselves.'

(26)

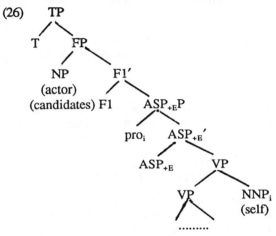

Weak crossover reveals a subject-object asymmetry, so we would predict that a language with a flat structure should not show asymmetries in weak-crossover type contexts. Kroeger shows that Tagalog lacks both agent/nonagent asymmetries and NOM/non-NOM asymmetries:

(27) a. *Sino$_i$* *ang*   *yumayapos*   *sa-anak* *niya$_i$*
       who NOM IMPERF.AV-hug DAT-child 3.SG.GEN

       'Who$_i$ hugs her$_i$ daughter?'

     b. *Sino$_i$* *ang*   *yinayapos*   *ng-nanay* *niya$_i$*
       who NOM IMPERF-hug-OV GEN-mother 3.SG.GEN

       'Who$_i$ does her$_i$ mother hug?'

(28) a. *Sino$_i$* *ang*   *binigyan*   *ng-tatay* *niya$_i$*   *ng-kotse*
       who NOM PERF-give-DV GEN-father 3.SG.GEN GEN-car

       'Who$_i$ was given a car by his$_i$ father?'

     b. *Kanino$_i$* *nabigay*   *ang-tatay* *niya$_i$*   *ng-kotse*
       whom PERF.AV-give NOM-father 3.SG.GEN GEN-car

       'Whom$_i$ did his$_i$ father give a car?'
                                 (Kroeger 1991:140-141)

When a NOM is being extracted, as in (27a-b) and (28a), the NOM is coindexed with a pro in an argument position. This pro can be the immediate antecedent of the coindexed pronoun, and so a weak crossover configuration does not arise. The crucial example is (28b). In this case, the NP which is left behind is the NNP. Here is the structure that I would assign to this sentence, given that I have suggested that the NNP is adjoined to VP (right-adjoined in Tagalog):

(29)   [$_{CP}$ *Kanino$_i$*..[$_{IP}$ *nabigay*...[$_{VP}$ [$_{VP}$ t$_v$ t$_i$]   *ang-tatay*   *niya$_i$*
        whom   PERF.AV-give   NOM-father   3.SG.GEN
        ng-kotse]]]
        GEN-car

Since the NNP is right-adjoined, the trace of the WH-phrase is to its left. Suppose the condition ruling out weak crossover violations is as stated in Chomsky 1976.

(30)   The Leftness Condition (Chomsky 1976)
      A variable cannot be the antecedent of a pronoun on its left.

Under this condition, we would expect sentence (28b) to be grammatical: since the NNP is left-adjoined, the pronoun is not to the left of the variable (trace). Thus, as long as we posit an adjoined NNP, the weak crossover facts don't tell us anything about the internal structure of the VP to which it is adjoined.

Finally, Kroeger argues that the principle governing pronominal coreference in Tagalog is that in (31), and that we can use this to determine that all NPs within VP mutually c-command.

(31) A (non-reflexive) pronoun must not take as its antecedent a phrase
      which neither precedes nor c-commands it. (1991:142)

The crucial examples are shown in (32):

(32) a. *Nagmamahal*   *ang-nanay*   *niya$_i$* *kay-Juan$_i$*
        AV-MPERF-love NOM-mother his   DAT-Juan
        'His$_i$ mother loves Juan$_i$.'

     b. *Minamahal*   *ang-anak*   *niya$_i$* *ni-Juan$_i$*
        IMPERF-love-OV NOM-child his   GEN-Juan
        'His$_i$ child is loved by Juan$_i$.'
                             (Kroeger 1991:144)

Now, since I have proposed that the NNP is left-adjoined to VP, the important question is what is the position of the dative or genitive NP in these examples? It was Kroeger who said that in Tagalog the NNP generally follows all other arguments. Yet here we find other arguments following the NNP. Suppose the argument after the NNP is postposed. Then this argument will c-command a pronoun within the NNP. Thus, we do not have conclusive evidence for nonconfigurationality.

5. Conclusion

I have suggested that Sells is correct to claim that in Philippine languages, it is not possible to assume some underlying linking of thematic roles to syntactic positions. Instead, the Philippine voice markers "ignore the hierarchical arrangement of argument structure, picking up instead on certain (as yet somewhat elusive) semantic concepts." However, I have also argued that a Sells-type analysis should be extended to languages like English. I have drawn attention to the similarities between Sells' theory for the Philippine languages and Borer's proposal for English and have suggested that the differences between the two types of languages lie in the content of the voice/aspect morpheme, and particular case which is obligatory, and the availability, proposed by Sells, of a null pronoun occupying the argument position associated with the voice/aspect marker.

References

Chomsky, Noam. 1992. A Minimalist Program for Linguistic Theory. *MIT Working Papers in Linguistics*. Cambridge, Mass: MIT.

Chomsky, Noam. 1976. Conditions on Rules of Grammar. In *Essays on Form and Interpretation*, 163–210. New York: North Holland.

Diesing, Molly. 1992. *Indefinites*. Cambridge, Mass: MIT Press.

Kroeger, Paul. 1991. *Phrase Structure and Grammatical Relations in Tagalog*. Doctoral Dissertation, Stanford.

Sityar, Emily. 1995. Voice and Existential Closure. Presented at Austronesian Formal Linguistics Association, McGill University.

Sityar, Emily. 1994. Voice and Licensing of Subjects in Cebuano. Ms. University of Arizona. To appear in CONSOLE X.

Schachter, Paul. 1976. The Subject in Philippine Languages: Topic, Actor, Actor-Topic or None of the Above. In Charles N. Li, ed. *Subject and Topic*, 491–518. New York: Academic Press.

Speas, Margaret. 1990. *Phrase Structure in Natural Language* Dordrecht: Kluwer Academic Publishers.

Travis, Lisa and Edwin Williams. 1984. Externalization of Arguments in Malayo-Polynesian Languages. *The Linguistic Review* 2, 57–77.

Discussion of the Papers by Sells and Speas

Janda: Could you comment on the label GEN? I mean, is this [used] because the marker is homophonous with the genitive? Could it be an accusative marker that just happens to be homophonous? Or a default?

Sells: Many people think that the things that are now verbs in the Philippine languages and in fact in Austronesian in general, have a nominal source. And it's called 'genitive' because it is homophonous with the genitive that you get in core genitive positions, but it's stable again throughout the Philippine languages. Well, kind of stable. In some Philippine languages, the thing that marks the Actor when it's not the subject is different from the thing that marks the Patient when it's not the subject. They're both GEN in Tagalog, but in some languages, they're different, and I think in some languages it's the one that marks the Patient that looks like the GEN, and in some languages it's the one that looks like the one that marks the Actor that's the GEN.

Spencer: Can I float a wild speculation in front of the speakers? Suppose we accept that we have to have "surfacy" ordering constraints—you don't have these complex trees or something of that sort to get the ordering—the question arises how you actually formalize the ordering, how you formally rewrite [(34)] for example in Peter's [paper]. And it strikes me that there's a reference to nominative phrase, nominative phrase comes before everything except an Actor ...   The question arises how you really formalize this. It strikes me that it might turn out to be quite difficult to do this in a pretty way, unless you adopt an Optimality Theoretic framework, where of course it's trivial more or less. You just have three constraints, and you order them in that order and it comes out very simply. So, it might be there's a sort of covert argument for introducing OT into syntax here.

Speas: The only thing is that if you adopt Peter's theory where you have a null pronoun, and then the nominative NP is associated with that, that NP could be adjoined to VP. So that could automatically get the position, I mean, the nominative NP is like after all the other arguments and before everything that's not an argument. No?

Sells: No. It's really third. This is meant to capture the things in (22) ... One of the both nice and worrying things about Optimality Theory and syntax is that it seems as though it can solve any problem, although not many people have solved many problems with it yet. I don't have the problem that you do with thinking about how to state these things anyway. It's actually not clear to me what Optimality Theory would add. So, let me say that a bit more. If you take a theory like LFG, you simultaneously have access to the constituent structure representation like that in [(35)], the functional representation in [(36)], and the argument structure representation all at the same time. And in fact I would take the claim that you need things like [(34)] to be a claim that you need a theory in which you can make reference across different grammatical levels at the same time. One of the things that's interesting about this is that you could formulate [(34c)] as something that says that the nominative NP, which is something in the c-structure, precedes anything which is not an Actor, which is a fact about the argument structure. Or you could state it as the NADJ in the f-structure has its c-structure correlate preceding everything else that's not an Actor. But on the basis of work I've done on raising in the Philippine languages, I think that actually you have to state it this way referring to the c-structure rather than to f-structure. So, one thing that's interestingly left out here is the functional information, and I don't know if there might be other reasons for wanting to refer to the grammatical functions directly. So for the Optimality Theory solution you would still have to refer to argument structure to say "the Actor precedes everything else," and to some other level of representation to say "the nominative precedes everything else." So you can maybe simplify things, but I don't think you sort of gain the number of theoretical hands you need to have.

Borer: I want to follow up on Andy's point. I share your distress about theories that can do too much, but worrying about that, I also worry about [(34)], because I'm looking at some of your criticisms of previous attempts, and one of the reasons that I think your criticism of these previous attempts was really quite successful is because you showed that there's basically no way to account for what is a very obvious word order correlation, and in fact you get all the completely wrong predictions. But suppose one were to say, as people have said, including people like Marantz, that things like word order are in fact phonological effects, and they have nothing to do with the kind of configuration that you may be getting in the syntax. And so then you can take any of the structures which you have rejected, in my opinion correctly because they couldn't get any word order effects, and have some linearization conventions, which as far as I can see from [(34)] are pretty free. One of these things is a head, another one is an Actor which comes from the realm of thematic theory, and another one is some kind of a NP but in the context of it being assigned a particular kind of case. And you're ordering them in a way that appears pretty arbitrary at any rate. Any other kind of ordering presumably would also be possible ...

Sells: I'm not sure if I share exactly the same concerns as you. I guess I always thought it would be nice to have the syntax get the order right.

Borer: That's what I said. Right, I agree—

Sells: If you think about the properties of the theory you just outlined, I mean essentially the kind of theory that you outlined is like the Minimalist theory that Richards proposed, that had the ΠP in it, where you just take the VP to be unordered, or ordered in these linear ways. The thing is then that all of the superstructure above the VP is there to capture abstract properties that we have to capture, but has no relation to the surface form of the language. That's what the idea that these things move in LF or are checked in LF—

Borer: Right, but how is it different from what you are proposing? That's what I'm asking. Because you're not getting the word order. [(29)] is not the word order. I mean everything you've said so far I agree with, but I don't necessarily see that the way that you get the word order is different.

Speas: Well, don't you have an implicit restriction on these linearization principles that says, let's say, any linearization principle has to only apply to mutually c-commanding phrases?

Sells: Sure.

Borer: Yeah, but why this linearization and not any other?

Sells: Because these are what the facts are. OK— [Laughter]
I am not somebody who believes that languages choose how to do things from maybe two or three little options. I think there are probably six or seven. [More laughter]
If you look at enough Philippine languages, these kinds of ordering restrictions seem to make sense, in some way. I agree in some sense they're not beautiful, but I think that's the way it works. For the structure in [(29)], what I would assume is that some languages have functional categories and some languages don't. Functional categories or functional projections are always configurational in this way, and there's at least one

view that says that S is always nonconfigurational. So then under S there would be an unordered structure, and then these would be the ordering principles, if there are any, and presumably in languages which do have fairly free word order, then you would have principles that are a bit like this that are maybe only preference principles that you know can be overridden by other things, and so on.

Aronoff: About these ordering principles, I mean, it seems to me they they're perfectly reasonable ordering principles of a purely pragmatic sort. And if there's nothing else operating, they're just going to kind of float up to the surface. So it seems to me they *do* go along very well with your analysis of the nonconfigurational S. If S is nonconfigurational, then you would expect this kind of otherwise perhaps invisible type of stuff to become visible.

Speas: Actually, I think it could even be compatible with your kind of theory Hagit, because what you have is an interpretive theory that interprets structures. So here's a case where you have a V and a bunch of arguments and they stay behind, and what Peter's got is, first, something that says, V is head initial, which isn't particularly controversial, and then one that says, "Interpret the first NP as the Actor," which isn't particularly different from, "Interpret Spec of a certain Aspect-phrase as the Actor."

Borer: No, I think it's very different.

Speas: Well, I mean, it specifies a particular position, and it gives an interpretation for it.

Borer: Well, OK I think it's a difference between a theory where the word order follows from the structure and a theory where the word order doesn't follow from the structure.

Speas: Well, it depends on whether you think that linear adjacency is some sort of structural property.

Borer: Well, I don't know—I really do think the word order as much as possible should come from the structure and it should be the kind of structure that we pronounce and not the LF kind. That's my opinion. And I think that to the extent that things like the analyses that you criticized could only get the word order by either having very substantial LF movement component, or alternatively the kind of linearization principles that you have too, that could operate presumably on any string, right? There is no reason in principle why they couldn't in fact reorder any string according to whatever principles, pragmatic or otherwise.

Sells: So, I guess that was one thing that was implicit in what I said. I was assuming an analysis here based on GPSG such that these are only ordering relations that hold among sisters.

Borer: Yeah, but the problem is, it seems to me a big pity that one would have to resort to various reordering principles that don't seem to follow from anything except ...

Speas: But it's not reordering, it's just the structures...

Sells: Yeah, they're not reordering. They're ordering. I don't think there is reordering.

Borer: Ordering; OK, fine ... I think if it had any structure to it, that I could tell OK, this is why this is first and this is second, then I would know why. But if it's just you know, head after a nominative in some random order as it happens to be out there, then I really don't know what it follows from.

On the Autonomy of Compounding Morphology

JERROLD M. SADOCK

1 Introduction

There is such a thing as morphology. It is a part of linguistic competence that allows for the construction of expressions that are not (necessarily) described by the combinatoric system we call syntax, not (necessarily) described by the combinatoric system we call semantics, and not (simply) special phonological interpretations of expressions that are independently given by other combinatoric linguistic abilities. Perhaps I don't need to convince anyone here of the existence of morphology. It seems to me, though, that a great deal of up-to-date grammatical research gives very short shrift to independent principles of morphology, tending asymptotically toward its elimination. Instead of independent principles of morphology working to structure independent morphological constituents, words tend, in ultra-modern theories, to be constructed according to parameterized principles of syntax. The result, it seems to me, is at best artificial, and at worst, an importation into syntax of linguistic principles that do not belong there with attendant complications that are artifacts of the failure to recognize the independence of morphology.

I want to restrict my attention to one particular aspect of morphology, namely compounding. There are several reasons for this, not the least of which is that it keeps me from dwelling, as is my wont, on West Greenlandic, since that otherwise informative language presents virtually nothing of interest in the way of stem composition, which is, of course, an interesting fact in and of itself. Another advantage of studying compounding is that this aspect of word construction is not subject to the item-process debate that complicates much of the literature on morphology. Even the staunchest advocates of non-item morphology (e.g., Anderson 1992) seem to agree that compounds are composed of pieces and are put together by means of rules of combination that in some ways resemble those found in other domains of grammar.

The lesson I wish to draw from the very hasty cross-linguistic study that is to come is that compounding as a formal technique is not connected intimately with any other aspects of the grammatical organization of a language, neither its lexicon, its syntax, its phonology, its semantics or the rest of what we might colloquially call its morphology. In this respect, we must recognize the independence of a subdivision of grammar to which compounding is specific. One of the things I want to show is that there is no direct connection between the morphosyntactic style of a language and the kind of compounding, if any, that the language presents. Languages of very different type can be similar with respect to compounding power, and those of extremely similar build, can differ strikingly. I also want to make it clear that compounding cannot be defined by referring to properties that are essentially outside the morphology. Though such properties as syntactic inviolability, semantic noncompositionality, and phonological unity are frequent correlates of compound morphology, they are in no way criterial.

I want to make the point concerning the autonomy of compounding in a third way as well. I will show that once a language has compounding as a weapon in its morphological arsenal, that device can, and usually does have a variety of different properties with regard to other parts of the grammar. Compounding in a given language (and a fortiori cross-linguistically) therefore cannot be defined precisely by reference to any single non-morphological property, be it phonological, syntactic lexical, or whatever. Nor can any group of such criteria isolate the essentially morphological phenomenon of compounding. Composition of stems is a unified phenomenon only with regard to that one component of the grammar we ordinarily call morphology.

Much of what I will have to say here was anticipated by linguists of two or three generations ago. The discussions in Bloomfield 1933 and Sapir 1921 are as informative and cogent today as they were sixty and seventy years ago. Here I am merely amplifying on their observations and relating them to current views.

2 The Autonomy of Compounding
2.1 Failure of Typological Correlations

There are probably some correlations between the presence of compounding, its productivity, and other features of grammar that are of some statistical significance. I might make use of them if I had to make bets, but these correlations, I believe, are adequately explained by considerations of history, handiness, salience, and so on—in short, on completely extragrammatical grounds.

For example, languages with little in the way of derivational and inflectional morphology will often make good use of compounding because, lacking derivational processes, they have no abbreviated way of coining new terms of art, and lacking inflection, there is little distinction between the juxtaposition that occurs in compounding and the juxtaposition that occurs in syntax. In such languages it is a very short step from a phrase consisting of two morphologically simple words to a compound.

On the other hand, languages with a great deal of power invested in derivational morphology can do without compounding altogether, and some do. They can coin all the new terms they might need by invoking derivational processes alone, as is done in Eskimo languages. Languages with an easy-to-form genitive case may eschew composition in favor of what is formally (though not necessarily functionally) possession, as is nearly the case in Icelandic.

But these correlations are not predictive. On the one hand there are languages like Chukchee (see Bogoras 1922) that are almost as derivationally efflorescent as Eskimo yet make remarkable use of compounding, and on the other, there are those like Coos (see Frachtenberg 1922, 319) that are relatively poor in morphology of any kind, yet completely lack compounding. I do not know for sure of a hard-core isolating language that lacks compounding. Pawley's (1980) description of the Papuan language Kalam suggests that it might fill the bill. Kalam is a language with an incredibly small word-stock. Pawley states that there are only about 95 verb stems in Kalam and that of these, 25 are heavily relied on. The lexicalization patterns used to expand the vocabulary that Pawley describes involve the lexicalization and specialization of entire, connected syntactic structures. However I do not know for sure if this is the only lexicalization technique that the language makes use of.

Admittedly it is the case that numerous languages of East Asia are both extremely poorly endowed with inflectional and derivational morphology, and rather hypertrophied in the area of compounding. But we might suspect the working of areal pressures here rather than typological forces. As witness to this possibility, note that many unrelated or very distantly related languages of the Far East share the same "elaborate compound" type consisting of four syllables, with partial repetition in the form of rhyme or chime: Thai: *tìm taa tìm cay* 'wake eye wake heart', i.e., 'to be full of wonder and excitement' (Hudak 1990:768); Vietnamese *dûng-da dûng-dïn* 'slowly taking one's time' (Nguyen 1990:793); Burmese *kəbyàun+kəbyan* 'in an illogical, backwards way' (Wheatley 1990:850).

In any case, in the vast middle ground of languages, those with a modicum of derivational and inflectional morphology, there does not seem to be any way of predicting whether compounding will be present or not.

2.2 Disunity of Compounding vis-à-vis Other Aspects of Grammar

The question of how to define compounds has vexed many a student of morphology (e.g., Matthews 1974 and Spencer 1991). To a large extent the attempt at a definition is traditionally made by invoking non-morphological criteria of various sorts. Ordinarily, these suggestions are accompanied by copious caveats, provisos, and apologies, the necessity for which is, as we shall see, that the extramorphological criteria all fail.

2.3 Referentiality, Specificity

It is sometimes claimed that the parts of a compound have to be non-specific or even nonreferential. (E.g., Spencer, 1991:312, Sapir 1911) However, there are well-known examples of referential, even definite components of compounds.

In English, proper names are frequently part of compounds, especially the kind called synthetic compounds in Bloomfield 1933. These may be definite enough to act as antecedents for subsequent pronominal reference:

(1)   Gingrich supporters think he is brilliant.
(2)   Volvo-owners tend to like them.

There is even anaphoric compounding in *self denial, self fulfillment* and the like, which behave referentially in much the same way as anaphora in general:

(3)   Bill tried to seek self-fulfillment
(4)   Bill convinced Mary to seek self-fulfillment.
(5)   Bill promised Mary to seek self-fulfillment.

As a matter of fact, from a morphological point of view, the English reflexive pronouns themselves look like a species of compounds in that they involve otherwise independently used stems (cf. *myself ~ my same old self ~ my goddamn self*, etc.)

In any case, no one would want to claim that the correlation between lack of referentiality/specificity and morphological boundedness works in both directions, since there are clearly non-specific, and/or non-referential elements that are not parts of words at all, let alone parts of compounds. Both in the compound *truck driver* and in one reading of *He drives a truck*, there's not necessarily any specific truck.

2.4 Lexicalization

It is not the case that compounds are, as is frequently claimed, always or even typically lexicalized: The following examples occurred in just the headlines of the main section of the Chicago Tribune, March 3, 1995:

(6) alibi witness, anti-nukes movement, balanced-budget amendment, budget loss, custody struggle, Duvalier plotters, environment rules, hunger strike, Iran buildup, knee-jerk reaction, Medicaid abortions, "motor-voter" denial, no- smoking sign, Rev. King tours, rookie officer, "St. Elsewhere" star, Simpson trial, skinhead brothers, "superward" loser, TV host, UN forces, welfare moms

Some of the examples on the list above are frequent enough to be considered lexicalized to some extent, but some of them, like *"motor-voter" denial, skinhead brothers,* and *"St.Elsewhere" star* are clearly nonce-forms that have not yet, and probably never will become part of the listed vocabulary of the language. They are no more lexicalized and barely more likely to be entered on a list than synonymous syntactic constructions like *brothers who are skinheads* or *star of "St. Elsewhere".*

The freedom of English compounding is brought home by noticing that some of the compounds on this list can themselves be compounded. Headlines about an *alibi witness hunger strike,* or *Simpson trial welfare moms,* or *no-smoking sign environment rules* would by no means be unthinkable. The existence of four-part compounds in English makes it statistically unlikely that they are all listed. Supposing (extremely conservatively) that a thousand nouns can freely enter such compounds, the total number of the four-part ones will then be a trillion, which is, I suspect, more than the human brain can hold.

Now one might think that newspaper headline writers are pathological compound producers. But compound-noun productivity doubters need only take a look at the following sample of what is found on a one-page electronics store ad from the same Tribune issue (p. 26):

(7) 3-way tower speakers, 5-jack audio/video jack panel, 5-key direct access disc selection, 10-key direct-access track selection, 16-bit sound card, 20 track music calendar, 100-Watt remote control rack system, double-speed CD-ROM drive, hi fi 5-disc CD changer; time, program, and link edit

If these are lexicalized items, we English speakers must have some terrific vocabularies.

The definition of compounds as lexicalized concatenations fails in the other direction too, as pointed out by numerous authors on numerous occasions. Idioms and collocations are lexicalized but they are not morphological units and specifically not compounds. The lexicalization criterion probably gives poorer results as a litmus for compounds than no criterion at all. It fails to distinguish compounds from lexicalized phrases such as *European Widgeon* and the *Tower of Babel*, that, as far as I can see, don't belong in the same morphological category as *pintail* or *the Eiffel Tower* at all, even though they are equally fixed names for individual things. Similarly, the expressions *Sadock supporters* and *supporters of Sadock's ideas* are novel (indeed virtually unheard of) constructions despite the fact that one is a compound and the other is not.

2.5 Phonological Unity

As most writers on the subject have pointed out, noun-noun compounds of English, including novel ones, frequently have earlier stress than corresponding phrases would have: *pie pan, cake pan, focaccia pan, flan pan*, etc. all have primary stress on the first element. But this is not always the case. In the sub variety of compounds whose first element is a material noun, expressing, as an adjective might, the stuff of which something is made, the primary stress falls on the second element: *apple pie, steel rails*, etc. The same is true where the first element is a location specifying where the second element is found: *White house memorabilia, Chicago Tribune, playground antics*, etc. Compound adjectives consisting of noun and adjective have phrasal stress: *blood red, snow white, jet black*. There are probably other types of exceptions to the left-hand stress rule for compounds, but I won't pursue them. The point is that the stress-position criterion does not isolate exactly the set of morphological compounds, but a subset of them. In any case, there are certainly many languages in which there is no particular phonological characteristic of compounds that is not also a characteristic of phrases.

2.6 Syntactic Atomicity

It is ordinarily said that compounds are syntactically inviolate. If syntax includes coordination, however, this is false for English, cf. *time, program, and link edit* in the list of Tribune compounds given above. In English and most (or perhaps all) other Germanic languages, any element of certain kinds of compounds can be conjoined: *Chicago area math and science requirements, voter anger and outrage*.

Now it is certainly true that compounds in English exclude internal determiners, possessors, and so on. Even when a determiner is lexicalized as part of a name, it is not possible inside a compound. The definite article is ordinarily used with descriptive names like *The Liberty Bell*, but it disappears inside compounds: *The Chicago Tribune (*The) Liberty Bell Awards for Citizenship*. Note also the frequent numerical quantification of parts of compounds in English as we see in many of the examples on list

(6) above. The reason that these are allowable is apparently that—quite independently of the syntax, which allows similar structures, of course—numerals and nouns can themselves form compounds: *thousand legger, three masted*, etc.

A rather spectacular exception to the frequent, but not invariable tendency for syntactic processes not to operate within compounds is found in Fox, as pointed out in Bloomfield 1933:232 and discussed in detail in Dahlstrom forthcoming. In that language compound verbs are formed with a preverb and verb stem, the whole complex then bracketed by discontinuous inflectional prefix/suffix combinations. Astonishingly, the preverb and verb stem in such compounds can be interrupted by syntactic constituents. In the following example the underlined items are the discontinuous inflection indicating first person subject and third person object. The preverb with its part of the inflection is here separated from the verb, with its part of the inflectional material by an adverbial phrase.

(8) <u>neki:ši-</u>   te:pi   tasenwi   -kano:na:wa
     perf-   enough so.many.times   -speak.to1-/ind.ind

'I have spoken to him enough times.'

2.7 Morphological Unmarkedness

It is sometimes said that the elements of compounds are what could be called morphological stems that lack typical inflectional material that would be required of independent elements. (See Matthews 1974:189.) Contrarily, it is also sometimes claimed that the elements of compounds are free forms that can be used independently in syntax. Bloomfield (1933:227) says, "Compound words have two (or more) free forms among their immediate constituents." These two criteria are only the same if it happens to be the case that in a certain language stems are freely usable as words, in which case it will look as if the compounds consist of free forms. If on the other hand, stems require additions of some kinds to be used independently in syntax, then it will be possible to tell whether it is stems or free forms that are the elements of compounds in that language.

What we find is considerable variability. Some languages compound stems, some compound words, and some compound forms that are specific to compounds. In Greek, Hebrew, and German, parts of the compound can assume some special morphological shape not found elsewhere. For example, Greek has a special noun-form ending in -ó that is used as the first (non-head) member of a compound: *tíri* 'cheese', but *tiró-pita* 'cheese pie'. Similarly German has unique compounding forms like *Versicherungs-* 'insurance' that occur only in compounds, e.g., *Versicherungs-gesellschaft* 'insurance company'.

The compounding of full, inflected word forms is perhaps less common than other sorts, but it does occur. To take only one kind of example, the exocentric compounds of Romance languages like Spanish *toca discos* 'record player' have the morphology of an imperative verb followed by a plural noun. Note that the plurality of the noun is irrelevant to the number of the whole expression (*el toca discos* 'the record player', *los toca discos* 'the record players'). Inside the compound, each member bears the inflection of an independent word, but that inflection in no way functions syntactically[1].

I conclude that independent morphological facts cannot in general be used in the definition of compounds.

2.8 Multifunctionality of Compounds

Compounds, when they are present in a language, tend to be employed for a variety of syntactic, semantic, and lexical purposes. None of these purposes is the exclusive domain of compounds, of course, for, as we have seen, there are languages that lack them altogether. In a language without compounds, necessary functions of the language have to be handled by other means, syntactic or morphological.

As with other word-building processes, one of the common uses of compounding is to expand the vocabulary. It is quite reasonable for vocabulary-expansion to be one of the functions of compounding since this process is often a near-minimal compositional technique, combining by mere juxtaposition. Compounds are usually shorter than their free-word paraphrases and since there is a penalty to be paid for length of lexical items (Cf. Zipf 1949), it makes sense that the relatively compact forms we call compounds are so frequently used to make new lexical items.

In the semantic sphere, compounds frequently serve to express a variety of relations. Noun-noun compounds, for example, are often used to encode part-whole relations, material-entity relations, location-entity relations, modifier-modified relations, and purpose-instrument relations. But these same relations can also be expressed by purely syntactic means, so the semantic facts alone cannot be used as a test for compounding:

---

[1] I note in passing that this fact poses a problem for theories such as Anderson's (1992) in which inflection is defined as morphology that is relevant to syntax.

(9) Relation   Compound   Syntactic Alternative

part-whole	*mountain top*	*top of the mountain*
material-entity	*wood house*	*house made of wood*
location-entity	*city boy*	*boy from the city*
modification	*skinhead brothers*	*brothers who are skinheads*
purpose-instrument	*sound card*	*card for producing sound*
other relations	*welfare moms*	*moms on welfare*
	no smoking sign	*sign reading "no smoking"*
	alibi witness	*witness capable of providing an alibi*

(See Levi 1978 for a survey of the relations expressed in noun-noun compounds discussion.)

In some languages, though not normally in English, kinship and ownership relations are also expressible by compounding. These relations are ordinarily expressed in English only by syntactic means, namely the genitive construction: *Joel's son, Joel's house* (but also *the Smith mansion*).

When a noun is related to a verb, it is not uncommon for it to enter into compounds with what would otherwise be arguments or adjuncts of the verb. Most common, perhaps, are object-verb relations: *weight loss, superward loser, CD changer, United-Way donations*. The instrumental relation is also frequent, e.g., in *ten-key track selection*, both the object (*track*) and the instrument (*ten key(s)*) are expressed as parts of the compound.

In English, too, there are at least two importantly different kinds of noun-noun compounding. One is the so-called "root compound" exemplified by some of the items on list (6) (e.g., *welfare moms, hunger strike, rookie officer*.) The other is the so-called "synthetic compound" exemplified by *custody struggle, Duvalier plotters* and by *CD changer*, and *disc selection* on the second list (7). Both of these types are productive in English, but only in the synthetic type do the internal parts of the compound have clear semantico-syntactic effects, as pointed out in considerable literature on these forms in English, e.g., Roeper and Siegel 1978, Lieber 1992.

I don't want to leave the impression that such multifunctionality is the unique province of nominal compounding. Indeed, in those languages like French that lack productive noun-noun compounding, the various sorts of functions that are assumed by compounds in English and other languages are carried by the syntactic devices used for indicating possession. What else could they be carried by? We will see examples of this in the discussion of the Welsh genitive and the Hebrew construct state constructions below. In West Greenlandic (forgive me for bringing it up again) the derivational system is invoked for the productive expression of various kinds of relations and for the coining of new lexical items. Thus 'X-store' is often *X-irniarfik* where the derivational suffix means 'place where something is sold', e.g., *atuagaarniarfik* 'bookstore' from *atuagaq* 'book'. Indeed, derivational affixes are used to express the same range of relationships we find in (9) above:

(10)	Relation	Affix	Meaning
	part-whole	*-mineq*	'piece of __'
	material-entity	*-taq*	'the part of it made of __'
	location-entity	*-mioq*	'one who dwells in __'
	modification	*-araq*	'young __'
	purpose-instrument	*-niut*	'device for catching __'

3 A Comparison of Welsh and Hebrew

As a case in point, I'd like to make a brief comparison between Welsh and Hebrew, unrelated languages that display an eerie degree of typological similarity. Both languages present strikingly similar constructions for joining nominals as well, but, as I shall argue, while sharing much syntax, the Hebrew construction is a compound, and the otherwise similar Welsh one is not.

As to typological similarity, both languages are verb initial (if by Hebrew we mean Biblical Hebrew), are prepositional, and place their adjectives after the noun but numerals and articles before the noun. Both exhibit a moderate amount of flexion in the verb and have no inflectional distinctions of case in the nouns; both combine the preposition and pronominal object into a single word, and have clitic articles (definite only in both languages) preceding the noun. In both languages the initial consonant of a word varies depending on its environment[2] and in both languages, coincidentally, the feminine singular pronoun is [hi].

What interests me most in the present connection is the constructions that these two peas-in-a-pod languages present for the connection of two nominal expressions, which I will call, using traditional terminology, the Hebrew construct state and the Welsh genitive construction. In keeping with the general typological similarities between

---

[2]The mutation of an initial consonant is not found in Modern Hebrew.

these two languages, the two constructions under scrutiny present remarkably similar surfaces to our view. They have at least the following features in common:

3.1 Left Headedness

In both languages the productive pattern is a binary branching expression consisting of two nominal constituents with the head element on the left and the modifying element on the right: Hebrew: *delet* 'door', *bayit* 'house', *delet bayit* 'door of a house'; Welsh: *drws* 'door' *tŷ* 'house', *drws tŷ* 'door of a house'.

3.2 Iterativity

In both languages the non-head element can itself be a complex nominal, making the structure iterative and right branching: Heb.: *delet beyt David* 'door of the house of David', Welsh: *drws tŷ Dewi* 'door of the house of David'. Heb.: *delet beyt bney David* 'door of the house of the sons of David', Welsh: *drws tŷ plant Dewi* 'door the house of the children of David'.

3.3 Rightmost Definite N

In both Welsh and Hebrew, there is only one position for definitizing these complex constructions, and that position is before the last, or most subordinate, of the parts of the nominal expression, even where the apparently definitized noun is not logically definite: Heb.: *beyt sefer* 'school' (lit: 'house book'), *beyt ha-sefer* 'the school' (lit: 'house the-book'; Welsh: *côr plant* 'children's choir' (lit: 'choir children'), *côr y plant* 'the children's choir' (lit: 'choir (the children)'). In both Welsh and Hebrew, then, all referential elements of the complex nominal expression must be understood as definite or as indefinite depending on whether the last nominal in the sequence is definite or indefinite. To express something like 'a house of the man' or 'the house of a man' the construction we are considering here will not serve and a more elaborate structure is required.

In the case of an iterated construction of this type, there is still only room for one explicitly definite item in both languages: *delet beyt ha-Amerikani* 'the door of the house of the American' (lit.: 'door house the-American'); *drws tŷ y Sais* 'the door of the house of the Englishman' (lit.: 'door house the Englishman').

3.4 Multifunctionality

Borer 1988 cogently describes two different functions of the construct-state compounds in Hebrew. First, there is a lexicalized, semantically opaque type exemplified (in Modern Hebrew) by *gan yeladim* 'kindergarten' (from *gan* 'garden' and *yeladim* 'children'). Second, there is a productive type represented by *gan peyrot* 'fruit garden (*peyrot* 'fruit (plural)'). Both types demand a special form for all but the last of a sequence of nouns.[3] Both types also admit definitization of only the last noun and both types reject adjectives internal to the series of nouns. They are, in other words, not different constructions from a formal point of view.

As with the Hebrew construct state, the Welsh genitive construction has both productive, semantically transparent uses and more idiomatic ones. It is productively used for expressing possession, part-whole, and kinship relations. It is also employed quite frequently to express semantically idiosyncratic relations such as those found in English root compounds, which, as a matter of fact, they are frequently used to calque. A few examples from Gruffudd and Ioan 1971 ought to demonstrate this:

(11)   *lle tân* 'fireplace' (*lle* 'place', *tân* 'fire')
         siop lyfrau 'book shop' (*siop* 'shop', *llyfrau* 'books')
         siop grefftau 'craft shop' (*crefftau* 'crafts')
         clwb golff 'golf club'
         stondin bysgod 'fish stand'
         coes oen 'leg (*coes*) of lamb (*oen*) ' (or 'a leg of a lamb')
         oes y cerrig 'the stone (*cerrig* (PL) age (*oes*)'
         oes yr ia 'the (*yr*) ice (*ia*) age (*oes*)'
         ystafell wely 'bed (*gwely*) room (*ystafell*)'
         castell tywod 'sand (*tywod*) castle (*castell*)'

3.5 Modifiability

In both languages component nouns can be modified by an adjective or relative clause. Heb.: *miSpaxat ha-iS hagadol* 'family (*miSpaxa*) of the big (*gadol*) man (*iS*)' (Hetzron 1990:700); Welsh: *merch frenhines ddoeth* 'daughter (*merch*) of the wise (*doeth*) queen (*brenhines*)'. (See Rouveret 1990:39.)

---

[3]Borer calls the syntactically transparent examples "construct states" and the opaque ones "compounds", but this terminology is both non-traditional and misleading since both types are equally compounded and both types are formed in the same way with the special construct-state morphological form.

3.6 Conjoinability of Constituents

Elements of both the Hebrew construct state and the Welsh genitive construction may be conjoined:

(12) *Somer*   *batim*   *u-mexoniyot*
      guard   houses   and-cars

'one who guards houses and cars'

(13) *clwy*   *y*   *traed* *a'r*   *genau*
      disease   the   foot   and.the   mouth

'foot and mouth disease'

3.7 Verbal Nouns

Both languages allow a verbal noun to be the head of the construction under consideration with the dependent noun representing one of the arguments of the verb.   When the head-noun of a Hebrew construct state construction is a deverbal noun and precedes what would correspond to the object of the verb following it, the subject of the related clause may surface as the object of a preposition, namely the compound preposition *al yedey* 'at the hands of'.[4] (See Borer 1994 and Hazout 1995.) For example, related to the clause *Dan oxel et ha-tapuax* (Dan eats ACC the-apple) we find:

(14) *axilat ha-tapuax*   *al*   *yedey*   *Dan*
      eating the-apple   at   hands   Dan

'Dan's eating of the apple'

In Welsh the verbal noun is used, among other things, in the formation of periphrastic verb forms.   Thus alongside *Gwelodd Arwin gi* 'Arwin saw (*gwelodd*) a dog (*ci*) the colloquial language allows (or prefers) *Mae Arwin wedi gweld ci* 'Arwin saw a dog' (lit.: 'Arwin is (*mae*) after (*wedi*) seeing (*gweld*) a dog (*ci*)'). The verbal noun is also found as the object of prepositions like *cyn* 'before' or *am* 'to' as in *am yfed schnapps* (cf. Thorne 1993:379) 'to (*am*) drinking (*yfed*) schnapps'. In both cases, the relation between the verbal noun and its object is formally similar to that of a possessed noun and its possessor in the genitive structure.

---

[4]The complex preposition *al yedey* consists of the ordinary preposition *al* 'to, toward' and what is at least historically the construct-state of the dual *yadayim* 'hands'. The PP *al yedey Dan* is therefore bracketed (*al yedey*) *Dan* from a functional perspective, but *al* (*yedey Dan*) from a formal perspective.

This similarity is bolstered by what happens to pronouns. When a possessor is a pronoun it shows up as a clitic preceding the possessum, and may (under interesting conditions that need not concern us here) be reinforced by an independent pronoun following the possessum: *car Emrys* 'Emrys's car' ~ ei gar (ef) 'his car (him)'; The same is true of the object of a verbal noun. When pronominal it shows up as a clitic preceding the verbal noun, possibly doubled by a following independent pronoun: *Mae Arwin wedi ei weld (ef)* 'Arwin has seen him' Similarly in Hebrew, the functional object of a verbal noun can shows up as a possessive clitic: *axilato* 'eating it', compare *tmunato* 'his picture' (*tmuna*).

As in Hebrew, what corresponds to the subject of the similar clause appears here as the object of a preposition:

(15) *cyn*   *i*   *Nesta fwyta'r*   *afal*
       before   to   Nesta eat.the   apple

      'before Nesta eats the apple'

Despite their many similarities, it is clear that the noun-connecting constructions I have been discussing are really quite different. I will try to show that what is found in Hebrew is properly labeled a compound, whereas the otherwise similar Welsh construction is a purely syntactic joining. Here is some of the evidence that leads to that conclusion:

3.8 Special Morphology

As already mentioned, the nonfinal noun in Hebrew is in a special morphological form called the 'construct state', e.g., *miSpaxa* 'family' — *miSpaxat Kelly* 'the Kelly family'; *bayit* 'house' — *beyt David* 'the house of David'; *banim* 'sons' — *bney David* 'sons of David'. In the Welsh genitive construction the nouns appear in their ordinary free forms.

3.9 Modifiability of Nonfinal Nouns

In both languages a non-final nominal may also be modified, but here there is an important difference. In Welsh a nonfinal noun may be modified by an immediately following in adjective: *merch ddoeth y frenhines* 'the wise (*doeth*) daughter (*merch*) of the (*y*) queen (*brenhines*)', whereas this is not possible in Hebrew: **miSpaxat (family) ha-gdola (big) ha-iS (the-man)*. A modifier of a non-final noun is possible in Hebrew, but it cannot occur in the middle of the possessive construction and must be reserved to the end: *miSpaxat ha-iS ha-gdola* 'the big-F,SG (*gdola*) family-F,SG (*miSpaxa*) of the man-M,SG (*iS*)'. This suggests that the construct-state noun and what follows it are more tightly integrated in Hebrew than in Welsh. In Hebrew the sequence of nouns cannot be interrupted by other syntactic material[5] whereas in Welsh it can. The order of modifiers in Hebrew will be discussed in more detail below.

3.10 Conjoinability of Non-final Nouns

In Welsh it is possible to conjoin non-final nouns freely: *ci a chath y tŷ* 'the dog (*ci*) and (*a*) the cat (*cath*) of the (*y*) house (ty)'. This is not allowed in Hebrew, however. Instead of **beyt vedirat Dan*, for 'the house and apartment of Dan' the second conjunct follows as a possessed noun: *beyt Dan vedirato* 'the house of Dan and his apartment (*vedirato*)'.

3.11 Subjects of Verbal Nouns

In Hebrew, but not in Modern Welsh, a verbal noun may be the head in construction with the notional subject. Hebrew allows this with both intransitive verbal nouns, as in (16) and (perhaps surprisingly) with subjects of transitives, as in (17). Note that in the latter case, the object is treated identically to the object of a clause. (See Borer 1994 and Hazout 1995 for discussion.)

(16) *Sevet*   *axim*   *(yachad)*
      sitting   brothers   (together)

      '(a) sitting of brothers (together)'

(17) *axilat*   *Dan* *et*   *ha-tapuach*
      eating   Dan   ACC   the-apple

      'Dan's eating the apple'

The corresponding constructions are both ungrammatical in Modern Welsh where the subject of the verbal noun is never part of a genitive-like construction but rather shows up independently preceding it, either as the subject of an auxiliary in the periphrastic verb construction or as the object of the preposition *i* 'to'. This is true for both the transitive verbal noun, as shown in (15) above, as well as for the intransitive, as in (18):

---

[5]There is one puzzling exception, namely the possibility of numeral quantifiers preceding non-initial parts of a construct state construction. When the construction is definite, the numeral itself turns up in the construct state and the morphological integrity of the whole form is thus preserved. In *tmunat SloSet ha-anaSim* 'the picture of the three people' the construct state form of the numeral *SloSet* produces a form entirely in keeping with a single morphological structure. When the construction is indefinite, however, a non-construct state form of the numeral appears between the construct state head noun and the final noun: *tmunat SaloS anaSim* 'a picture of three people' (Borer 1994: 21).

(18)   *cyn*   *i*   *Nesta canu*
        before   to   Nesta singing

        'before Nesta sings'

(19)   **cyn canu Nesta*

In Middle Welsh this sort of construction was possible with intransitive verbal nouns:

(20)   *gwedy*   *kychwyn*   *Bwrt*
        after   setting.out   Bwrt

        'after Bwrt set out'

The subjects of transitive verbal nouns could not be used in this way, however. (See Manning to appear for details.)

3.12 Existence of Other Compounds

Alongside of the Welsh construction under consideration, there are genuine compounds in Welsh that are clearly more tightly integrated morphologically than the genitive construction. Many of these are right-headed: *ffermdy* 'farm house'; *marchnerth* 'horse power (*march* 'horse'), etc. They also suffer phonological alterations that are different from those in the genitive construction. In *bracty* 'brewhouse' (from *brag* 'malt' and *tŷ* 'house') we find right-headedness and 'provection', a kind of consonantal assimilation otherwise found in derivational and inflectional morphology in Welsh. In the genitive construction, on the other hand, the only phonological alternation that is found is the soft mutation of initial consonants of words occurring after feminine singular nouns. Thus *pysgod* 'fish' is mutated after the feminine noun *stondin* 'stand': *stondin bysgod* 'fish stand', but not after the masculine noun *tŷ* 'house': *tŷ pysgod* 'fish house'. But feminine singular nouns also project soft mutation onto their following adjectives. Therefore, this particular phonological change is not indicative of morphologization.

In contrast to Welsh, there are no structures in Hebrew that are more clearly compounds than the construct-state forms we have been discussing.

4 A Sketch of a Treatment

In these two otherwise similar languages, two functionally and superficially similar constructions for joining nominals are different, I claim, in that one, the Hebrew construct-state construction, is an example of morphological compounding, whereas the other, the Welsh, is adequately described in the syntax alone. The similarities, I suggest, are appropriately handled by attributing to both the very same syntactic structure.

4.1 Syntax

Hebrew, Welsh, English, and a good many other languages present syntactic noun phrases that consist of a head nominal (N') and a determining NP, as set forth in the following rule. The head (N') is on the right in English, Eskimo, Japanese, etc., and on the left in Hebrew, Welsh, and other languages. The comma in this rule indicates the lack of ordering.

(21) NP → N', NP

In many languages there is a morphosyntactic fillip of some kind in (21): the determining NP may be marked in some way, either with a case feature (as in Latin, say), by an adposition, as in Japanese, or by means of a clitic genitive marker. In other languages the head N' may be marked, often with agreement features that reflect features inherent in the subordinate NP. (See Nichols 1986.) Some languages, Eskimo for example, mark both the head and the dependent.

Right-headed languages with (21) have NPs with the structure given in (22), and left-headed languages with (21) have that in (23):

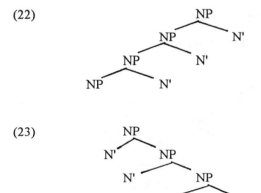

(22)

(23)

If a language with some version of rule (21) allows (or requires) NPs to be determined by an article that is in complimentary distribution with the determining NP, then in structures that can be iteratively characterized by this rule, no matter how big, there will be at most one article and it will be associated with the most subordinate NP. Articles, demonstratives, and numerals tend to initial position in an NP regardless of other features of the language. (See Greenberg 1966:86.) Now in a left-headed language with (21) and articles in initial position in NP, the article will turn up in penultimate position, as shown in (24).

(24)

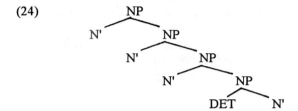

This is just what we find in Hebrew and Welsh:

(25)

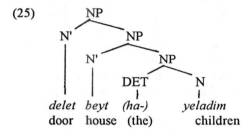

| delet | beyt | (ha-) | yeladim |
| door | house | (the) | children |

'the door of the children's house'

(26)

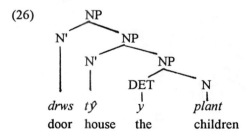

| drws | tŷ | y | plant |
| door | house | the | children |

'the door to the children's house'

4.2 Semantics

Languages that include a version of the schema (21) in their grammars and have determiners in NP are in a semantic bind: In any structure described by (21), there are two or more NPs in syntactic structure and each NP can correspond to a separate referential structure in the semantics; but only one NP, the most deeply embedded one, is capable of supporting an article and thus providing definiteness information. In *delet gan ha-yeladim* diagrammed in (25) there is reference to both a certain door, to a certain house, and to certain children. But there is only room for one determiner, as shown in the tree.

Without going into too much irrelevant detail, let us assume that the meanings of possessed NPs in natural languages are ordinarily arguments (ARG) containing two semantic quantifiers (QUANT) binding variables that are connected by a relational expression (R), as sketched in (27).

(27)   ARG = QUANT(x)[QUANT(y) R(x,y)]

The meaning of *the neighbor's dog* is then something along the lines of QUANT dog(x) (QUANT neighbor(y) (BELONG(x,y))).

But as observed, there are not enough syntactic DETs to fill in all the quantifiers demanded by the semantic form. The usual resolution to the problem of determiner deficiency is for the single syntactic determiner position to count as supplying to all the referentially required quantifiers. Thus *the neighbor's dog* is THE dog(x)(THE neighbor(y) (BELONG (x,y) or roughly 'the dog such that it belongs to the neighbor', or more colloquially, 'the dog of the neighbor' and *a neighbor's dog* would be equivalent to 'a dog of a neighbor'.

The semantic judgments can be subtle, but an old-fashioned argument still seems persuasive. If we assume, as seems reasonable, that the "definiteness effect" (Milsark 1977) in the existential *there* construction is a semantic phenomenon, then we have a test for semantic definiteness. The fact that *There's the dog's paw print on the rug* does not carry the existential sense (vs. *There's a dog's paw print on the rug*) convinces me that the spreading of the quantifier is what actually happens in English. (For a different view, see Woisetschlaeger 1983.) In other words, *the dog's paw print* contains two semantic definite quantifiers even though the syntax only officially indicates that *the dog* is definite. The same state of affairs holds for Welsh and Hebrew. Only one article is allowed but it renders the entire structure definite.

The definiteness of all parts is especially clear in Hebrew, as shown by Borer 1994, whose arguments I paraphrase here: Adjectives in Hebrew agree in definiteness with their heads. One says *mora tova* 'a good (*tova*) teacher (*mora*)' or *ha-mora ha-tova* 'the (*ha-*) good teacher' with two instances of the definite article. Only one article in the NP is ungrammatical: **ha-mora tova; *mora ha-tova.* Now as mentioned earlier, any of the nouns in a construct state NP can be modified by an adjective. Gender and number agreement between a noun and adjective in Hebrew can indicate explicitly which part of the structure is modified. In *ben mora* 'a son (*ben*) of a female teacher (*mora*)' one noun is masculine and one feminine. With a feminine adjective: *ben mora tova* the phrase can only mean 'a son of a good female teacher' and with a masculine adjective: *ben mora tov* it can only mean 'a good son of a female teacher'. Now when there is a definite article modifying the last noun in a construct state NP, it turns out that adjectives modifying any of the nouns have to be definite in form, clearly showing that the single article counts as more than one semantic quantifier:

(28) *ben*   *ha-mora*   *ha-tova*
   son (M) the-teacher (F) the-good (F)

   'the son of the good teacher'

(29) *ben*   *ha-mora*   *ha-tov*
   son (M) the-teacher (F) the-good (M)

   'the good son of the teacher'

(30) **ben ha-mora tova*

(31) **ben ha-mora tov*

4.3 Morphology

The general scheme for endocentric compounding in natural languages is (32), where X^0 is the class of stems and as before, the comma indicates lack of ordering. Compounds are often right headed but, pace Williams 1981, are frequently left headed as indeed they are in Hebrew.

(32) $X^0 = X^0, Y^0$

There are often language-particular specializations of (32). In Hebrew X and Y must be Ns, as we have seen, and the head element(s) must be in the particular morphological form called construct state. Thus the Hebrew rule is:

(33)   (Hebrew)

       N →   N[CS] N

This rule is iterative and produces right-branching compounds consisting of a series of nouns in the construct state followed by one in the absolute form.

(34)

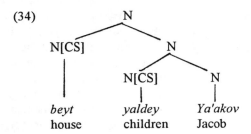

beyt	*yaldey*	*Ya'akov*
house	children	Jacob

'the house of the children of Jacob'

4.4 Simultaneous Representations

The essence of the Hebrew construct state construction is, I claim, that one and the same expression presents both the syntax of (21) and the compound morphology of (32). In other words, we can represent the example in (34) as simultaneously displaying both syntactic and morphological structure, as in (35):

(35)

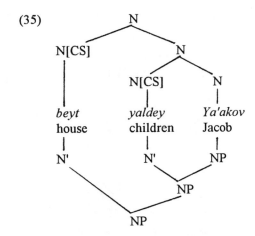

A number of the central properties of the construction are directly derivable from this simple claim. The single determiner and its position in the expression follow from the syntax for the reasons already mentioned. The semantic spreading of definiteness is also accounted for as explained above. From the morphology is derived the fact that modifiers inside the structure are disallowed since these morphological structures contain only nouns all but the last of which are in the construct-state form. Here I appeal to a principle that is well motivated in work on simultaneous analysis, namely the idea of a ranking of constraints. The syntax in (35) should admit an adjective immediately following *beyt* or *yaldey*, but the morphology does not admit it. Quite independently of the facts under consideration here, it has been shown several times (e.g., Sadock 1985, 1991, and Sadock and Schiller 1993) that morphological constraints are stronger than syntactic ones and that syntactic constraints are stronger than semantic ones. In case there is a conflict between two components, it is resolved in favor of the stronger one, in this case the morphology. Therefore, no adjectives inside the compound are possible.

While the morphology thus forbids internal modifiers, it does not prohibit modifiers outside of the morphological construction and the syntax of the construction clearly allows them. Thus example like *Somer mexoniyot gnuvot* 'guard (*Somer*) of stolen (*gnuvot*) cars (*mexoniyot*)' would have the structure (36) where the adjective is analyzed as modifying a noun in the syntax but is not part of the morphological structure at all.

(36)

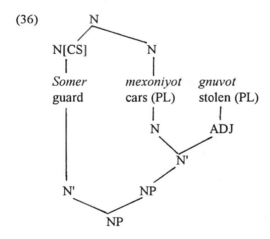

But we have also seen that non-final nouns in these constructions can also be modified, as in *Somer mexoniyot tov* 'a good (*tov*) guard

(*Somer*) of cars (*mexoniyot*)'. In such a case, the surface order of words cannot reflect the constituency of the phrase *Somer tov* 'good guard' because of the overriding influence of the morphology. But the relative order of the noun and adjective imposed by the syntax can be maintained, so the adjective comes right after the compound. The example is analyzed as follows:

(37)

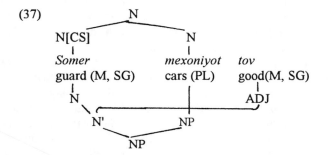

Welsh, as I have argued, has no independently constraining morphology on top of its syntax and therefore Welsh freely allows the modifiers of any of the nouns in a genitive construction *in situ*.

The possibility of coordination is explained in the same way. Assuming that coordination is a syntactic matter, viz. the joining of phrases, of the same type, it is the syntactic structure of the construct-state form that sanctions them. The first of the conjuncts will also participate in the morphological structure as in the following diagram:

(38)

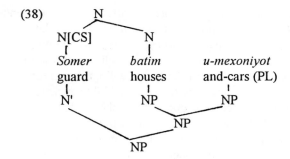

The non-conjoinability of non-final nouns in Hebrew follows from the fact that there is no room for conjunction within the morphological form.[6] Once again, Welsh, lacking a morphological structure for its genitive structures allows conjunction within them.

5 Conclusions

I have obviously not given a complete account of the constructions considered here. In particular, the interesting and intricate properties of verbal nouns have not been covered and much more would have to be said to do so. Delving into this area would take us far from the topic that I mainly intended to address and I will, therefore, with some sense of shame, duck the responsibility of treating them entirely.

An important feature of the Hebrew construct state was brought to my attention by Hagit Borer in a question following my talk. According to what I have said, syntactic constituency should not play a role in distributing adjectives, but syntactic order should. Thus this treatment seems to imply clearly that modifiers will occur following the construct structure in the order in which they would appear in syntax — adjectives that modify the first noun coming first, those that modify the second noun coming second, and so on.

Unfortunately, this prediction is quite wrong. As Borer (1994:18) has already shown, the order of modifiers is, in fact, the mirror image of the order of the elements they modify. Here is one of her examples:

(39)   *tmunat*   *ha-more*   *ha-ca'ir*   *ha-marshima*
       picture (F)   the-teacher (M)   the-young(M)   the-impressive(F)

       'the impressive picture of the young teacher'

It is my strong suspicion that close attention to the independent influence of semantic form will provide a natural account of the order of adjectives, but once again, such a study is beyond the aims and goals of this paper. For the time being, then, I will just have to live with the incorrect prediction of my analysis, reveling in the fact that linguistics is indeed an empirical science whose hypotheses are directly falsifiable by facts.

Despite these inadequacies, I hope to have shown that some of the most basic properties of Hebrew and Welsh noun phrases can be handled quite simply and straightforwardly in terms of two independent dimensions of analysis, one syntactic and one morphological. The account of the similarities and differences between these two languages cannot, I think, be

---

[6]Somehow or another there is room for conjunction in indubitable compounds of English as shown by some of the examples in (7) above. I do not know what this difference between English and Hebrew should be attributed to.

recapitulated as elegantly in any system of grammar that fails to grant the same degree of autonomy to both components. Chomsky wrote in *Syntactic Structures* (Chomsky 1957:42n) that the point of analyzing language in terms of levels of representation is " ... to rebuild the vast complexity of the actual language more elegantly and systematically by extracting the contribution to this complexity of several linguistics levels, each of which is simple itself." This is what I hope to have done in my description of Welsh genitives and Hebrew construct states, albeit in a limited way and in a rather different fashion from what Chomsky had in mind in 1957.

References

Anderson, Stephen R. 1992. *A-Morphous Morphology*. Cambridge, U.K.: Cambridge University Press,

Bloomfield, Leonard. 1933. *Language*. New York: Holt, Rinehart and Winston. Reprinted: 1984, University of Chicago Press, Chicago.

Bogoras, Waldemar. 1922. Chukchee. In Franz Boas, *Handbook of American Indian Languages, Part 2*, 631–903, Washington: Government Printing Office.

Borer, Hagit. 1988. On the Morphological Parallelism Between Compounds and Constructs. In Geert Booij and Jaap van Marle, eds., *Yearbook of Morphology*. Dordrecht, Netherlands: Foris.

Borer, Hagit. 1994. Deconstructing the Construct. Unpublished ms. University of Massachusetts, Amherst.

Chomsky, Noam. 1957. *Syntactic Structures*. The Hague: Mouton.

Dahlstrom Amy. forthcoming. *Morphology and Syntax of the Fox (Mesquakie) Language*. Ms., University of Chicago.

Frachtenberg, Leo J. 1922. Coos. In Franz Boas, *Handbook of American Indian Languages, Part 2*, 297–430. Washington: Government Printing Office.

Greenberg, Joseph H. 1966. Some Universals of Grammar with Particular Reference to the Order of Meaningful Elements. In Joseph Greenberg, ed., *Universals of Language, Second Edition*, 73–113. Cambridge: MIT Press.

Gruffudd, Heini and Elwyn Ioan. 1971. *Welsh is Fun!*. Talybont, Wales: Y Lolfa.

Hazout, Ilan. 1995. Action Nominalizations and the Lexicalist Hypothesis. *Natural Language and Linguistic Theory 13*, 355–404.

Hetzron, Robert. 1990. Hebrew. In Bernard Comrie, ed., *The World's Major Languages*, 686–704. New York: Oxford University Press,.

Hudak, Thomas John. 1990. Thai. In Bernard Comrie, ed., *The World's Major Languages*, 757–76. New York: Oxford University Press.

Levi, Judith N. 1978. *The Syntax and Semantics of Complex Nominals*. New York: Academic Press.

Lieber, Rochelle. 1992. *Deconstructing Morphology: Word Formation in Syntactic Theory*. Chicago: University of Chicago Press.

Manning, H. Paul. to appear. Fluid Intransitivity in Middle Welsh: Gradience, Typology and 'Unaccusativity'. *Lingua 97*.

Matthews, P.H. 1974. *Morphology: An Introduction to the Theory of Word Structure*. Cambridge: Cambridge University Press.

Milsark, Gary. 1977. Toward an Explanation of Certain Peculiarities of the Existential Construction in English. *Linguistic Analysis 3*, 1–29.

Nguyen, Din-Hoa. 1990. Vietnamese. In Bernard Comrie, ed., *The World's Major Languages*, 777–96. New York: Oxford University Press.

Nichols, Johanna. 1986. Head-marking and Dependent-marking Grammar. *Language 62*, 56–119.

Pawley, Andrew. 1980. On Meeting a Language that Defies Description in Ordinary Terms. Paper prepared for the Kivung Congress of the Linguistic Society of Papua New Guinea, Lae, Papua New Guinea.

Roeper, T. and M. Siegel. 1978. A Lexical Transformation for Verbal Compounds. *Linguistic Inquiry 9*, 148–73.

Rouveret, Alain. 1990. X-Bar Theory, Minimality, and Barrierhood in Welsh. In Randall Hendrick, ed., *Syntax and Semantics Volume 23: The Syntax of the Modern Celtic Languages*, 27–80. New York: Academic Press.

Sadock, Jerrold M. 1985. Autolexical Syntax: A Theory of Noun Incorporation and Similar Phenomena. *Natural Language and Lingusitic Theory 3*, 379–440.

Sadock, Jerrold M. 1991. *Autolexical Syntax: A Theory of Parallel Grammatical Representations*. Chicago: University of Chicago Press.

Sadock, Jerrold M. and Eric Schiller. 1993. The Generalized Interface Principle., *Papers from the 29th Annual Meeting, Chicago Linguistic Society*, 391–402. Department of Linguistics, University of Chicago.

Sapir, Edward. 1911. The Problem of Noun Incorporation in American Languages. *American Anthropologist 13*, 250–82.

Sapir, Edward. 1921. (1949.) *Language: An Introduction to the Study of Speech*. New York: Harcourt, Brace, and World.

Spencer, Andrew. 1991. *Morphological Theory*. Oxford: Blackwell.

Thorne, David A. 1993. *A Comprehensive Welsh Grammar*. Oxford: Blackwell.

Wheatley, Julian K. 1990. Burmese. In Bernard Comrie, ed., *The World's Major Languages*, 834–54. New York: Oxford University Press.

Williams, Edwin. 1981. On the Notions 'Lexically Related' and 'Head of a Word'. *Linguistic Inquiry 12*, 245–74.

Woisetschlaeger, Erich. 1983. On the Question of Definiteness in 'An Old Man's Book'. *Linguistic Inquiry 14*, 137–54.

Zipf, George K. 1949. *Human Behavior and the Principle of Least Effort*. Cambridge, MA: Addison-Wesley.

Comments on the Paper by Sadock

Mark C. Baker

Rather than offering a detailed, point-by-point commentary on Sadock's paper, I will try to engage his top-level claim: that compounding is an autonomous part of the grammar.[1] It naturally follows from this claim that the basic properties of compounding in a given language are not predictable from other features of the language, in particular from properties of its syntax. To support his view, Sadock gives some reasons to be pessimistic about a program that attempts to reduce compounding to syntactic principles (basically the program of Sproat (1985) and Lieber (1993)). In response, I will present some reasons to be optimistic toward such a program of research. By taking this approach, I will instantly skip over much that is interesting and valuable in Sadock's empirical observations, as well as much that is right-headed and elegant in his analytic approach, in order to discuss at length those few abstruse points on which I disagree with him (or at least am not yet convinced). While this kind of approach helps to give academic discourse its rather peculiar flavor, it makes a kind of twisted sense, inasmuch as when one disagrees with someone it takes many words to explain why, whereas agreeing with someone is much easier. Indeed, it is so easy that we usually do not take the trouble to do it.

Specifically, my comments fall into three parts. First, I review those principles of syntax which have heretofore been applied to compounding with some success, to see how they fare in the light of Sadock's discussion. Second, I bring up a small difference between the syntaxes of Celtic and Semitic languages that may be related to the putatively primitive difference in compounding that Sadock discusses. Finally, I briefly examine a syntactically homogenous group of languages with which I am familiar (roughly, the "polysynthetic" ones), to show that these languages do in fact have the

[1] I wish to thank Nigel Duffield and the participants at the Davis workshop on morphology for their help and comments on this paper, and particularly Steve Lapointe who organized that workshop. My research on polysynthetic languages which underlies section 2.2 was supported by the Social Sciences and Humanities Research Council of Canada, grant 410-90-0308, and by the FCAR of Quebec, grant 91-ER-0578.

same compounding possibilities to a substantial extent. Together, these facts suggest that the prospects for reducing compounding to other aspects of the grammar are not as bleak as Sadock suggests.

1. Syntactic Principles and Compounding Structure

At the beginning of his article Sadock mentions that in certain "ultra-modern" theories, "words tend to be constructed according to the parameterized principles of syntax." He then comments that the results of this approach seem to him "at best artificial, and at worst, an importation into syntax of linguistic principles that do not belong there with attendant complications that are artifacts of the failure to recognize the independence of morphology." In response, I will briefly review the history of how this "ultra-modern" approach developed, by surveying the (largely familiar) results of what one might call the "New England" school of compounding (because virtually all of the work took place at the University of Massachusetts-Amherst, MIT, and the University of New Hampshire). While the final results of a syntactic approach to morphology sometimes look baroque and artificial, much of this negative reaction may disappear when one sees how the claims developed step by step. Indeed, somewhat ironically, I believe that the case for syntactic principles governing morphological objects is actually *strongest* in the area of compounding.

Virtually all generative work on compounding traces back to the rich and seminal article Roeper and Siegel 1978. Putting the matter somewhat anachronistically, one of the basic points of this article is that something very much like theta-role assignment takes place in many English compounds. For example, the verb assigns a patient/theme role to its syntactic object in (1a), and the derived noun assigns the same thematic role to its complement in (1b). Strikingly, the same relationship seems to hold between the two parts of the compound in (1c).

(1) a. John drives a truck.
     b. John is a driver of trucks.
     c. John is a truck-driver.

Triplets like (1) can be created quite freely and productively in English. Thus, it seems that theta role assignment can happen in a compound as well as in the syntax in English.

One of the fundamental principles of most theories of syntax is what Chomsky (1981) called the Theta Criterion: the idea that there must be a one-to-one correspondence between the obligatory arguments of a word and the phrases in syntactic construction with that word. Crudely speaking, an intransitive verb must have no object, a transitive verb must have exactly one object, a ditransitive verb must have two objects, and so on. The Theta Criterion thus rules out examples like (2), in which a single argument of the verb (its patient) is expressed by two distinct NPs.[2]

(2)   *John drives a truck a 14-wheeler.

Interestingly, examples like (3) are also ungrammatical, in which the patient argument is expressed once inside the compound and once outside the compound.

(3)   *?John is a truck-driver of 14-wheelers.

A unified explanation of (2) and (3) becomes possible if one says that the Theta Criterion applies not just in the syntax, where phrases are constructed, but governs the construction of compound structures as well.

Another important syntactic distinction is the distinction between internal and external arguments, introduced by Williams (1981). Abstracting away from different versions of the distinction, the basic observation is that the designated external argument of a head is expressed by an NP that cannot be inside the smallest syntactic constituent containing that head. For example, the patient of the verb in (4) is its internal argument and can be inside VP, while the agent is its external argument and must be outside VP.

(4)   The shark [$_{VP}$ ate a man].

This same distinction is relevant to compounding: the internal argument of the head can appear inside the compound, but the external argument cannot:

(5)   a.   We must put a stop to man-eating (by sharks).
        b.   *We must put a stop to shark-eating (of men).

---

[2]More precisely, this sentence is completely ungrammatical on a neutral intonation comparable to the one that would be used in saying *John gave a man a cookie*. It is acceptable only with a heavy pause between *a truck* and *a 14-wheeler*, in which case the second NP is an afterthought or an adjunct in apposition to the true object.

Shark-eating is only natural on the reading in which sharks are being eaten, i.e., where *shark* is the internal (patient) argument of the head. Indeed, agents cannot appear in compounds even if the verb is intransitive and has no internal argument (Selkirk 1982):

(6)   **a.**   *Girl-swimming (is restricted at this pool).
         b.   *Kid-eating (makes a big mess).

Interestingly, judgments reverse in compounds where the head is a deverbal adjective, rather than a deverbal noun:

(7)   **a.**   That man looks shark-eaten.
         b.   *It looks man-eaten by a shark.

Here the nonhead noun in the compound must be understood as the agent of eating, not the theme. However, this apparent reversal is entirely expected given that themes are external arguments of adjectives and agents are internal arguments (or perhaps adjuncts) of adjectives in the syntax:

(8)   That man looks [$_{AP}$ eaten by a shark].

Thus, the external/internal argument distinction is relevant to compound construction in much the same way as it is in syntax. This observation is implicit in the way Roeper and Siegel 1978 used subcategorization frames, and is posited explicitly in Selkirk's (1982) Subject Condition.

     Another fact about English compounds discovered by Selkirk (1982) is that there is generally no compound that can be formed starting from a verb that has two obligatory internal arguments. Thus, one has (9a), but both (9b) and (9c) are bad:

(9)   **a.**   the putting of boots on the table
         b.   *boot-putting on the table
         c.   *table-putting of boots

Selkirk observes that there is a parallel between (9) and the syntactic fact that both the theme and the goal of a verb like *put* must appear in the smallest VP projection of the verb. Thus, one has the following pattern for VP-fronting:

(10)   John said that he would put the boots on the table, and ...

    a.   ... [$_{VP}$ put the boots on the table] he did.

    b.   *... [$_{VP}$ put the boots] he did on the table.

    c.   *... [$_{VP}$ put on the table] he did the boots.

To capture this generalization, she proposes the following condition, which is explicitly stated to hold of both phrasal syntax and "word syntax."

(11)   *The First Order Projection Condition (FPOC)*

    All non-subject arguments of a lexical category X must be satisfied within the first order projection of X.

    The *first order projection* of a category X^n is the category X^m that immediately dominates X^n in syntactic representation (i.e., in either S-syntactic of W-syntactic structure).

Subsequently, Sproat (1985) showed that this condition can be subsumed under the Projection Principle of Chomsky 1981, which says that the basic subcategorization properties of words must be met at every relevant level of representation. This explains the ungrammaticality of (9b) and (9c), as long as compounding counts as a "relevant level."

    Lieber (1983) shows that some of the severe restrictions on the presence and interpretation of prepositions and verbs in English compounding (stipulated in Selkirk 1982) can be derived from a very similar idea: verbs and prepositions differ from nouns and adjectives in that they typically require complements. The need to satisfy this requirement thus restricts the ways prepositions and verbs can be used in compounds.

    More controversial but very intriguing is Sproat's (1985) suggestion that the Case Filter of Chomsky 1981 also applies inside compounds. This suggestion covers a gap in the explanation of Selkirk's observation that there is no synthetic compound of triadic verbs like *put* or *give*. The FOPC would be satisfied if both arguments of the verb root were expressed in a ternary branching N-N-N compound. Nevertheless, this is **impossible**:

(12)   a.   *table-boot-putting

     b.   *child-candy-giving

Sproat suggests that these examples are ruled out by Case theory: both nouns need abstract Case, but the verb (or the noun derived from it) can Case-mark only one of them. In syntax, the Case marking problem is solved by including a preposition such as *in* or *to*, but it is independently known that such prepositions cannot occur in compounds. Sproat's suggestion also explains why the theme role of unaccusative (nonagentive) verbs cannot be expressed inside a compound:

(13)　　a.　*angel-existing
　　　　b.　*weather-changing
　　　　c.　*leaf-falling

Selkirk (1982) rules these examples out on a par with those in (6), but this explanation does not go through if one takes seriously the fact that the theme argument of these predicates is actually an *internal* argument (Burzio 1986). However, it is well-known that unaccusative predicates differ from transitive ones in that they cannot assign Case to their internal arguments. Thus, one can say that the examples in (13) also violate the Case Filter.

　　　　Another important feature of syntax is the so-called directionality parameters, which distinguish (in the simplest case) head-initial languages like French from head-final languages like Japanese. Clearly, some kind of directionality parameter is also at work in the area of endocentric compounds, determining whether in a given language the head precedes or follows the nonhead. Lieber (1993) explores the idea that the same headedness parameter governs both domains. Indeed, once one takes into account the fact that, internal to the syntax, different relationships can be subject to different ordering principles, it seems that the order in compounds generally recapitulates the order of comparable syntactic constructions. For example, adjectival modifiers in English precede head nouns both in the syntax and in compounding: compare the phrase *the black bird* with the compound *blackbird*. As Sadock points out, Hebrew is a more uniformly head-initial language, with nouns preceding adjectival modifiers. Predictably, Hebrew compounds are head-initial as well:

(14)　　a.　*be^{y}t sefer*
　　　　　　house-book
　　　　　　'school'

　　　　b.　*gan yeladim*
　　　　　　garden-children
　　　　　　'kindergarten'

On the other hand, Dutch is basically a head-final language, and Lieber shows that its compounds are also uniformly head-final: (15a) shows this for a modifier-modifiee relationship, and (15b) for a head-argument relationship.

(15)   a.   *diep-zee*
            deep-sea

       b.   *schoen-maker*
            shoe-maker

Of course there is one glaring exception to Lieber's generalization that will be immediately obvious to anyone who can read this paper: heads precede their theta-marked complements in English syntax but follow them in English compounding. Thus, one has [$_{VP}$ wash dishes] but [$_N$ dish-washer] and [$_N$ dish-washing]. However, this counterexample may not be as damaging as it seems. First, head-initial compounds do seem to be the norm in other VO languages. (16) gives examples from four such languages.[3]

(16)   a.   *lava-platos*   SPANISH
            wash-dishes

            'sink'

       b.   *m-pala-matabwa*   CHICHEWA (Sproat 1985:225)
            CL-scrape-wood

            'carpenter'

       c.   *pamatid-uhaw*   TAGALOG (Lieber 1993:46-47)
            cutter-thirst

            'thirst quencher'

---

[3] Abbreviations that are used in the glosses in this article are: 1, first person; 3, third person; AGR, agreement; APPL, applicative; ASP, aspect; CAUS, causative; CL, classifier; F, feminine; FU, future; HAB, habitual; IMP, imperative; M, masculine; N, neuter; NOM, nominalizer; O, object; PL, plural; PUNC, punctual; SUF, nominal suffix; S, subject; SG, singular.

d.   *potx'-o' txitam*   JACALTEC (Spencer 1991:349)

kill-NOM-pig

'pig-killing'

Second, it is well-known that English has undergone a significant change in word order; it used to have essentially the same syntactic word order as Dutch. Thus, it is reasonable to say that English is a marked case in view of its peculiar history: the order in phrases has switched, but the order in compounds has not (yet??) switched. Confirmation of this is the fact, reported by Clark, et al. 1986, that children learning English actually make mistakes in the order of their compounds: they produce examples like *pull-wagon* (or *puller-wagon*, or *pull-wagoner*) in place of the expected *wagon-puller*. If then we can put cases like this aside, it may be that the same directionality parameters hold for both syntax and compounding after all.

For the most part, this survey has concentrated on basic principles of phrase structure, theta-role assignment, and Case assignment. Some work has also looked at possible uses of more distinctively Chomskyan principles within the morphology as well, although this work must be considered more speculative. For example, Lieber (1993) claims that movement takes place in English synthetic compounds, as the specific mechanism for deriving the marked order in examples like *dishwasher*. English compounds are base generated with the order *washer-dish* (compare (16)), but the non-head *dish* incorporates into the head *washer* in the sense of Baker 1988.

(17)   [$_N$ dish$_i$-washer t$_i$]

Similarly, Sproat (1985) considers using Chomsky's Binding theory to account for the distribution and interpretation of compounds using the anaphorlike element *self* (e.g., *self-destruction, self-admirer*), and there are possible applications of control theory as well (cf. Di Sciullo and Williams 1987). Alternatively, one might hold that principles of movement, binding, and control have no application within compounds, but for a rather trivial reason: these principles hold of full phrases rather than of heads of phrases. It is not yet clear which of these approaches is closer to the truth.

To conclude this survey, we can ask what proportion of the principles of syntax seem to have value when applied to compounding? The answer seems to be a fairly high percentage. Conversely, we can ask what proportion of the basic facts of compounding can be accounted for by syntactic principles? Again, the answer seems to be a rather high proportion—at least for synthetic compounds in English. This then underlies the evolution in the so-called "New England School" from a strictly lexicalist position in the early 1970's, in which morphology was a separate module, to the "syntax of words" view of Selkirk and Williams in the early 1980's, in which morphology is a separate module but a kind of "syntax" of its own, using several of the same principles, to the Sproat-Lieber view of the late 1980's and early 1990's that compounding can be explained purely in terms of syntax. One may want to stop short of the strong Sproat-Lieber claim, but unless this body of work is fundamentally on the wrong track it seems too strong to say that compounding is completely autonomous from syntax. Rather, one wants a substantially unified theory of compounding and phrasal construction, although perhaps with some difference in levels of construction which second-order differences between the two can be attributed to.

Has Sadock shown that this syntax-oriented line of research is on the wrong track? Not as far as I can see. For the most part, he has not engaged it directly, choosing (legitimately) to keep his discussion mostly at a more general level. There is something of a challenge to Lieber's (1993) claim that the directionality of compounding is predictable in his observation that Hebrew and Welsh have the same basic syntax and word order, but do not have the same kinds of compounding. Hebrew has left-headed compounds, as predicted by Lieber. Welsh, on the other hand, has some right-headed compounds; Sadock gives the following examples:

(18)   a.   *fferm-dy*   farm-house
       b.   *march-nerth*   horse-power
       c.   *brac-ty*   brew-house

However, this pattern is not productive. Moreover, other Celtic languages such as Irish do have left-headed N-N compounds, as expected (Duffield, personal communication). Some examples are:

(19)   a.   *mac tíre*   son-country   'wolf'
       b.   *mac léinn*   son-learning   'student'
       c.   *sagart paróiste*   priest-parish   'parish priest'

These compounds are not always easy to distinguish from construct-state genitival constructions, but in some instances it is possible to do so by the position of adjectives and determiners, and by the presence or absence of initial consonant mutation.

(20)   a.   *an   sagart   paróiste   mór*   (compound)
              the   priest   parish   good

              'the good parish priest'

        b.   *sagart   mór   an   pharóiste*   (construct)
              priest   good the   parish

              'the parish's good priest'

Irish does have a few apparent right-headed compounds, such as *aerphort* 'airport'. However, it is clear where this came from. Similarly, it is possible that the Welsh examples in (18) are nativized borrowings from English, which Welsh has been in intense contact with for centuries.[4] Thus, there seems to be at least as much positive material as negative material here for the compounding-as-syntax program, at least at the level of comparing Celtic to Semitic, if not in comparing Welsh to Hebrew.

The other challenge to the syntactic approach that one can read into Sadock's paper is that it is not adequately general, but rather has artificially isolated a subpart of the data for scrutiny.[5] There may be some truth in this charge, inasmuch as the successes of the New England school of compounding are clearest in the domain of synthetic (deverbal) compounds in English. It has much less of interest to say about root compounds (such as simple N-N compounds), and has not yet had substantial successes beyond Western Indo-European languages—domains that Sadock is clearly concerned with. However, I am not convinced that there is reason to be differentially skeptical about the New England school in these respects. Other than perhaps predicting the position of the head (as already discussed), it is not clear that there is anything interesting to say about the structure or interpretation of root compounds: the structure is often very simple, and the semantic interpretation is quite unconstrained, as Sadock discusses (see his (9)). Even so, I am not convinced that the division between root and synthetic compounds is

---

[4]However, this may be too simple. Greg Stump pointed out to me at the conference that Breton also has some old right-headed compounds, although that is not the current productive pattern. This is true even though Breton has been in less contact with English than Welsh has. Thus, a study of compounding and NP structure in older varieties of Celtic might be instructive for the points at issue here. Nigel Duffield (personal communication) notes that many compounds involving adjectives are right-headed in Irish, and conjectures that there may be a syntactic explanation for this fact.

[5]This concern was raised explicitly in the open discussion at the conference.

as sharp as it is sometimes presented as being. Thus, consider the examples in (21).

(21)   a.   the leg of the piano

           b.   ??the piano's leg

           c.   the piano-leg

           d.   ??the piano-leg of the Steinway baby grand

(21a) shows a likely case of a noun that takes an argument even though it is not derived from a verb. The awkwardness of (21b) suggests that this argument is an internal argument, rather than an external one. (21c) is then an example of a productive whole-part N-N compound. This is a root compound in the sense that both members are simple nouns, but it is like a synthetic compound in that the head seems to assign a thematic role to the nonhead. Finally, the awkwardness of (21d) shows that something like the Theta Criterion applies to guarantee the uniqueness of the assigned theta-role (compare (3)). This then is a case where the basic ideas of the New England school can be generalized across the root-synthetic divide (see also Lieber 1983 for relevant discussion).

As for crosslinguistic/typological issues, it is striking how little compounding has been investigated in this way from any theoretical perspective, as far as I know. Thus, the empirical groundwork for making and defending interesting claims in this area—positive or negative—simply has not been laid yet. From what I know, there are some reasons to be optimistic that the New England approach to synthetic compounding will generalize to other languages (see (16) above, for example, for references to brief discussions of Chichewa, Tagalog, and Jacaltec).[6] However, I freely admit that I do not know very much in this area. Perhaps one important result of Sadock's paper will be to inspire new work in this domain.

2. Compounding and Syntactic Typology

Let us take up now this issue of crosslinguistic comparison in a somewhat broader context. One of the points that Sadock makes early in his paper is that there are no known predictive or causal connections between the syntax of a language and what kinds of compounding it has, if any. He takes this to be evidence that compounding is autonomous from other

---

[6]See also Li 1990a for an important first attempt to address issues of V-V compounding (which is quite common cross-linguistically) within the general assumptions of the New England school.

aspects of grammar, in particular syntax. However, there is another possible explanation: it could be that we do not yet know what properties of a language to attend to in creating the right syntactic typology. As our syntactic typologies deepen and improve, it may be that true correlations with compounding will emerge. I will consider two cases in point. First, I consider a more syntactic approach to the differences between Celtic and Semitic, which constitute Sadock's most extended illustration of his thesis. Second, I consider a partial answer to the question of why Eskimo does not have compounding while typologically similar Chukchee does.

2.1 The Comparison Between Celtic and Semitic[7]

Sadock's argument in favor of autonomous compounding from Celtic and Semitic is simple in its structure. Its first premise is that Hebrew and Welsh have similar VSO, head-initial syntaxes. The second premise is that Hebrew has left-headed N-N compounds, while Welsh does not. Thus, he concludes that the nature of compounding in a language cannot be predicted from its syntactic properties.

In fact, both premises are open to question. I showed above that Irish at least does have left-headed N-N compounds, more or less like Hebrew, although it takes some care to distinguish them from construct state constructions. Thus, at least at a broad level the possibilities in Semitic languages and Celtic ones are more or less the same. It is possible that further investigation into Welsh will reveal that such compounds exist in it too (see, for example, Spencer 1991:345, group C).

Here, however, I want to focus on the first premise: that Welsh and Hebrew have essentially the same syntax. In fact, this is not entirely true. While Welsh is a VSO language, Modern Hebrew has become predominantly an SVO language. Thus, (22) shows the standard word order.

(22)   *Eliseva   ra'ata   'et   ha-kof.*
       Elyseva   saw   ACC   the-monkey

(Here there is a slight but possibly important equivocation in Sadock's paper: in the syntactic typology he has Biblical Hebrew in mind, but the

---

[7] I want to give special thanks to Nigel Duffield for his help with this section; indeed, basically the whole line of argument is his (unless it is wrong of course, in which case I must have misunderstood him). Readers interested in more details and background on these issues should see Duffield 1995 and references cited there for extensive discussion.

subtle judgments on construct states and compounds come from Modern Hebrew, particularly the work of Hagit Borer.) In current Principles and Parameters-style theories of word order, this means that the verb raises out of VP to some inflectional category in both Welsh and Hebrew, but the subject NP raises (overtly) to the specifier of that inflectional category in Hebrew only. This is represented schematically in (23).

(23)

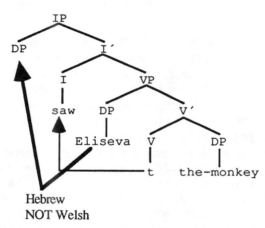

Hebrew
NOT Welsh

Does this minor syntactic difference have any impact on Sadock's argument about compounding? Perhaps. One of the key differences between Hebrew Construct State Constructions and their Welsh analogs is that modifiers of the head noun can come between the two nouns in Welsh but not in Hebrew:

(24)   a.   *beyt*   *ha-mora*   *ha-yafe*   HEBREW
            house(M)   the-teacher(F)   the-beautiful(M)

       'the beautiful house of the teacher'

       b.   *merch*   *ddoeth*   *y*   *frenhines*   WELSH
            daughter   wise   the   queen

       'the wise daughter of the queen'

Sadock interprets this as showing that the Hebrew N-N sequences count as uninterruptable morphological units—compounds—whereas the Welsh ones do not. However, a purely syntactic explanation of this fact may be available. The standard analysis of the NSO order found in nominals in Hebrew and other languages is to say that the head N raises into an initial determiner position, much as the V raises to an inflectional position in (23). This explains in a different way the fact that one cannot have an overt determiner associated with the head noun in a construct state construction, as discussed by Sadock. Suppose then the examples in (24) actually have a slightly elaborated version of this structure, as shown in (25).

(25)

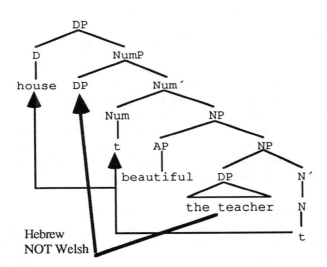

There the adjectival phrase is left-adjoined to the basic NP projection, as is standardly assumed. In addition, there is an "extra" functional category (called Number Phrase, following recent proposals by Elizabeth Ritter and others) between the determiner position and the core NP. Now the word order difference between Hebrew and the Celtic languages shown in (24) follows on purely syntactic grounds if we say that the genitive NP (the subject of NP) raises to the specifier of Number Phrase—and hence past the adjective—in Hebrew but not in Welsh. This is parallel to the fact that subjects move to a higher position in clauses in Hebrew than in Welsh. In this way, a connection can be drawn between the syntactic fact in (22) and the putatively morphological fact in (24).

Of course the basic syntactic analysis assumed here is more compli-cated than the one Sadock assumes. The existence of these functional categories in particular needs much more justification than I can give here. Moreover, some kind of cross-categorial harmony principle is needed to make it nonaccidental that the same NP movements happen (or do not happen) in both NPs and clauses. However, this syntactic approach has one large dividend. It easily accounts for a peculiar fact about Hebrew that Sadock leaves as an unsolved problem: the fact that when both NPs in a Hebrew Construct State Construction are modified, they appear in reverse, nested order, rather than in the same order as the nouns they modify.

(26)   *tmunat*   *ha-more*   *ha-ca'ir*   *ha-marshima*
       picture(F)   the-teacher(M)   the-young(M)   the-impressive(F)

       'the impressive picture of the young teacher'

As pointed out by Hagit Borer in discussion at the conference, this order is exactly what one would expect given an analysis like (25): the genitive noun phrase moves over the adjectival modifier of the head noun as a unit, carrying its own modifier with it. On the other hand, it takes special techniques to derive this word order in Sadock's autolexical approach. The tentative moral, then, is that there may be purely syntactic solutions to some of the phenomena that Sadock attributes to an autonomous morphology together with crossmodular constraints.

2.2 Compounding in Polysynthetic Languages

Finally, let us consider another kind of evidence for my suggestion that one does not see a connection between syntactic typology and compounding because we do not yet have the right syntactic typology, not because compounding is truly autonomous from syntax. If this suggestion is true, then stronger and more substantive correlations between syntax and compounding might emerge if one abandoned wide-scale typology, and restricted one's attention to a carefully chosen, medium-sized sample of languages. The advantage of this is that it then becomes feasible to show in some detail that the syntax of the languages in the sample is indeed the same in relevant ways, and to develop a reasonable level of understanding of the forces at work in shaping that syntax. The prediction is that such a class of languages should be observably similar in their compounding possibilities.

It so happens that I have recently completed a study of such a sample of languages (see Baker 1996). I refer to the relevant set of languages as "polysynthetic languages," although I mean by this only a subset of those languages traditionally known by that label. Specifically, the following seven languages or language families were investigated: Northern Iroquoian, Caddoan, Tanoan, Nahuatlan, Gunwinjguan, Chukchee/Koryak/Alutor, and Ainu. These languages were picked on the grounds that they are all the languages that are known to have discourse-relevant noun incorporation in the sense of Mithun 1984. Upon investigation, these languages also turn out to have many other (morpho)syntactic properties in common:[8]

(27) *Selected properties of polysynthetic languages*
   a. obligatory object agreement
   b. extensive pro-drop
   c. free word order
   d. no morphologically simple NP anaphor
   e. no nonreferential quantifiers (such as 'everyone', 'nobody')
   f. obligatory *wh*-movement
   g. agreement on nouns with the referent of the noun
   h. no true determiners
   i. agreement on nouns with the possessor (if applicable)
   j. argument structure restrictions on morphological causatives
   k. no morphologically simple adpositions
   l. complement clauses only if somehow nominalized
   m. no infinitival verbs; no obligatory control

Moreover, Baker 1996 claims that these properties and others can be derived directly or indirectly from the following simple condition:

(28) *The Polysynthesis Parameter*
      Every argument of a lexical item X must be coindexed with a morpheme in the word containing X.

This then seems to be a set of languages that are deeply similar in their syntax, even though they are historically unrelated and are separated geographically.

---

[8]See Baker 1996 for extensive discussion, as well as some nontrivial clarifications and caveats. In particular, Ainu does not have properties (c), (f), and (j), perhaps as a result of its intensive contact with Japanese.

The next question, then, is: Do these polysynthetic languages have the same compounding patterns? The answer seems to be Yes, to a large extent.

First of all, the polysynthetic languages all have noun-verb compounds in which the result is a verb. Simple examples include:

(29)   a   *ni-quin-xōchi-tēmo-lia*   NAHUATL
          1SGS-3PLO-flower-seek-APPL/PR

'I seek flowers for them'

     b. *bandi-marne-ganj-ginje-ng*   MAYALI
          3PLS/3PLO-APPL-meat-cook-PA/PUNC

'they cooked meat for them'

     c. *wa'-ke-nakt-a-hninu-'*   MOHAWK
          PA-1SGS-bed-Ø-buy-PUNC

'I bought a bed.'

This is not surprising in itself, since the languages were chosen for having that very feature in the first place. However, matters get more interesting when one tries to extend the domain of inquiry. In several years of looking, I have not been able to find any language that has the 13 properties listed in (27) and yet lacks N-V compounding. Languages I have checked include Greenlandic, Alambak, Yimas, Lakhota, Chichewa, Slave, Mojave, Tzotzil, Mapuche, Quechua, and Choctaw. These all differ from the above pattern in at least four other features. Very tentatively, it seems that no language has this constellation of properties and yet fails to have N-V compounding (i.e., noun incorporation).

The more detailed properties of the N-V compounds are also quite consistent across the polysynthetic languages. Thus, in every polysynthetic language compounding has the following three properties: (i) Only bare noun roots are incorporated, stripped of their inflectional affixes. (ii) The N root is (nearly) adjacent to the verb root; in particular, it comes inside of the verb's inflectional morphemes. (iii) The N root precedes the V root, rather than the other way around. Properties (i) and (ii) can be seen more clearly by comparing the Mohawk example (29c) with its unincorporated version in (30), where the normal inflections of nouns and verbs are evident.

(30)   *Wa'-k-hninu-'*   *ne   ka-nakt-a'*.
         PA-1SGS-buy-PUNC   NE   NSG-bed-SUF

         'I bought a bed.'

These three properties are not universally true of noun-verb compounding. For example, the noun root comes outside of verbal inflection in some Athapaskan and Mayan languages, whereas the V root precedes the N root in Oceanic languages, among others (see, e.g., Mithun 1984). However, these properties do consistently hold of the polysynthetic languages.

    These properties can be explained in a nonmodular approach, if one makes the following five assumptions, each of which has substantial independent motivation in the recent literature. (i) The noun and verb are combined by movement in the syntax in these languages (Baker 1988), a movement that is triggered by the need to satisfy the Polysynthesis Parameter in (28) (Baker 1996). (ii) The V and its inflectional morphemes are also combined by movement in the syntax (see Koopman 1984, Travis 1984, Pollock 1989, and many others). (iii) The verb together with its direct object NP forms the smallest syntactic constituent. (iv) Movement is cyclic, proceeding from most deeply embedded constituents outward. (v) Movement processes always adjoin material to the left of the landing site (Kayne 1995). On these assumptions, a simple example of noun incorporation in Mohawk has the following analysis:

(31)   *ra-'wáhr-a-k-s-kwe'*   MOHAWK
         MSGS-meat-Ø-eat-HAB-PA

         'he used to eat meat'

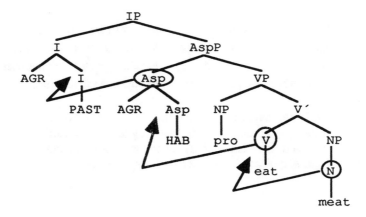

The fact that noun-verb compounds exist at all is a consequence of the requirement in (28). The fact that the noun-verb compound appears to be right-headed follows from the fact that adjoined material typically appears on the left, as can be seen from the fact that *wh*-movement is generally leftward, and clitics precede their hosts in Romance languages. The fact that the noun root appears inside the inflectional morphemes follows from the general architecture of the clause, together with the fact that combination must take place in a stepwise, cyclic fashion. Finally, only a bare noun can be incorporated because nouns (like verbs) become inflected by moving through functional categories. Once a head moves through a functional category, moving it back into a lexical category (such as verb) constitutes a kind of improper movement (Li 1990b)—although on this point the theoretical underpinnings are not well understood. Details aside, it seems that the existence and internal structure of these compounds is in fact influenced by many factors that have a much broader domain than compounding itself.

The empirical situation regarding verb-verb compounding in polysynthetic languages is somewhat more complicated. Roughly half of the polysynthetic languages have a limited number of V-V compounds (specifically Nahuatl, Tanoan, and Chukchee), and vestiges are found in others (e.g., the Gunwinjguan languages). Other polysynthetic languages have little or no such compounding (Mohawk, Ainu, Wichita). Furthermore, the kind of V-V compounds that is found in polysynthetic languages is significantly different from the kind found in languages in which V-V compounding is more prominent, such as Chinese, Igbo, Alamblak, and Yimas. In these "standard" V-V compounding languages, the two verb roots typically refer to actions that happen simultaneously or in a sequence, often a causal sequence. The following Chinese examples are fairly typical (Li 1990a):

(32) *xia-shu*   play-lose   'to play (a game) and lose (it)'
      bei-hui   memorize-know   'to learn (a poem) by memorizing'
      qi-lei   ride-be.tired   'to ride (a horse) to exhaustion'
      gai-liang   change-be.good   'to improve (something)'

This kind of compounding is not found in any polysynthetic language. Those that have V-V compounding have it with only a limited number of second verbs, and there is generally a head-argument relationship between the two verbs. A typical example is (33) from Nahuatl.

(33)   *Ni-c-chĭhua-z-nequi*
         1SGS-3SGO-make-FU-want

         'I want to make it.'

In fact, **these combinations have very much the same** properties as N-V compounds: an argument relationship holds between the elements, the head follows its argument, the nonhead is incorporated without its usual inflections, and the nonhead appears inside the inflections associated with the head verb. Thus, the same assumptions in (i)-(v) in the previous paragraph carry over to this case as well, with V(P) in place of N(P).

Why is V-V compounding less usual than N-V compounding in these languages? There seem to be at least three factors, each of which can plausibly be explained on general principles. First, the set of verbs that select for a VP argument across languages is generally much smaller than the set of verbs that select for a NP argument: one simply cannot do as many things to an event as to a thing. This is why in the polysynthetic languages the second verb of the V-V compound is drawn from a relatively small (often closed) class. Second, there are argument structure restrictions that follow from the fact that all arguments of both verbs must be morphologically expressed in the final word complex (see (28)). To make a long story short, this means roughly that either the matrix verb or the embedded verb must be intransitive (see Baker 1996 for details). Third, there is an important difference between VP complements and NP complements with respect to the Polysynthesis Parameter. Nominals in general have two ways of satisfying this condition: their heads can incorporate, or they can trigger agreement on the verb. VPs, however, often cannot trigger agreement, because they do not bear the relevant features of person, number and gender. As a result, they *must* incorporate. A consequence of this is that a VP-selecting verb such as 'cause' or 'go in order to' in (for example) Mohawk will *always* be in a complex word with another verb. In fact, all the polysynthetic languages have complex verbs comparable to (33) in Nahuatl, but the second verbal element is often classified as a derivational suffix, rather than as a root involved in compounding, because it never appears without a preceding verb root. (34) is a causative example in Mohawk.

(34)   *Ra-wis-a-hri-ht-s-kwe'*.
         MSGS-ice-Ø-break-CAUS-HAB-PA

         'He used to break the ice.'

Nahuatl is different from Mohawk in that verbal constructions can be nominalized by use of the demonstrative particle *in*. The resulting nominalizations then have third person singular neuter features, and hence can trigger agreement, as in (35).

(35)   *Ni-c-nequi*   *(in)*   *ni-c-chīhua-z.*
       1SGS-3SGO-want   IN   1SGS-3SGO-make-FU

       'I want to make it.'

Verb incorporation is therefore optional in Nahuatl, and when it occurs the result is analyzed as compounding. Thus, both the similarities and the differences between N-V and V-V compounding in the polysynthetic languages have a plausible syntactic account.

These remarks point to another respect in which compounding may not be an autonomous "module" in the polysynthetic languages. I have said that the argument noun or verb comes before the head verb in both N-V and V-V compounds in these languages, because of the properties of syntactic adjunction (Kayne 1995). However, the incorporated verb also comes before the argument-taking causative morpheme or purposive morpheme in Mohawk, even though these are generally considered derivational affixes. Furthermore, I have assumed that the verb in these languages also combines with (e.g.) tense and aspect morphology by moving into functional categories in the syntax (see (31)). Again the moved element (the verb) comes before the landing-site element (the tense or aspect), in accordance with the same principle of adjunction. Indeed, (34) shows all these ordering relationships in a single example from Mohawk: *hri* follows *wis* in a "compound", *ht* follows this in a derived stem, and *s* and *kwe'* follow this in an inflected word. However, a single syntactic principle accounts for morpheme ordering across these three traditionally different domains of morphology. Again, compounding does not act like it is autonomous.

Looking at the data, it appears that one should also have a principled explanation for why a language that is polysynthetic in my sense could not have Chinese-style sequential or resultative V-V compounds. This does not follow from simple morphological complexity: Yimas and other New Guinean languages are polysynthetic in the informal sense, but do have this kind of V-V compounding (Foley 1991). It is clear that the Polysynthesis Parameter will not *cause* this kind of V-V compounding, the way it does N-V compounding. It may even inhibit such compounding to the extent that all of the arguments of both verbs in the compound must be able to be agreed with. For example, it might not be possible for two transitive verbs to combine, where each verb takes distinct NPs as arguments, simply because there would not be enough kinds of agreement to express all the various NP arguments. However, this is not sufficient to rule out V-V compounds where both Vs are intransitive, or where the same NPs count as arguments of both verbs. Why such V-V compounds are impossible in polysynthetic languages thus remains as a topic for future research.

Finally, completing the survey of basic compounding types, it seems that the polysynthetic languages all have rather ordinary endocentric N-N compounds. Such compounding uncontraversially exists in Nahuatl, Mayali, Wichita, Kiowa, and Chukchee. Some examples are:

(36)					
	a.	*ä-cal-li*	water-house-SUF	'boat'	NAHUATL
	b.	*gun-dulk-dad*	IV-tree-leg	'root'	MAYALI
	c.	*pəlvəntə-qlaul*	iron-man	'blacksmith'	CHUKCHEE
	d.	*hǫ́:-tʰǫ̀:*	metal-club	'axe'	KIOWA

For Ainu, the fairly brief description in Shibatani 1990 does not discuss the matter one way or another. N-N compounding is not very salient in the Iroquoian languages, and is not mentioned in most grammars (which are understandably preoccupied with verbs). However it does exist; (37) gives two examples.

(37)   a.   *ká-tshe-'*   *k-áhi-'*   MOHAWK
                 NSG-bottle-SUF NSG-fruit-SUF

                 'bottle fruit' (i.e., pear)

        b.   *kwéskwes*   *o-'wáhr-u*
                 pig   NSG-meat-SUF

                 'pig meat' (i.e., pork)

The internal workings of N-N compounding are also reasonably consistent across the languages: it is usually endocentric, the order is always modifier before head, and it is usually uninflected stems that are combined. (Mohawk, however, is an exception to this last generalization; the examples in (37) are clearly instances of word-word compounding, rather than stem-stem compounding.[9]) Again, I have no particular insight into how this kind of compounding is related to other properties of the grammar of these languages; there is no obvious connection with the theoretical statement in (28), for example. However, we do find what appears to be a rather robust typological correlation between properties of the syntax and properties of compounding that seems worthy of further investigation.

The results of this survey thus show that when we restrict ourselves to a typological category that is relatively fine-grained and undergirded with some theoretical understanding, the languages within that category turn out to be quite consistent in their compounding properties. At two or three points in his paper, Sadock raises the question of why the Eskimo languages do not have compounding, whereas Chukchee does. We now have the beginnings of a possible answer: while Chukchee and Eskimo are similar in traditional, coarse-grained typological terms, Chukchee (arguably) counts as "polysynthetic" in the more refined sense of Baker 1996, whereas Eskimo (arguably) does not.[10] Given this, the fact that Chukchee has the kinds of compounds it does looks like it is predictable. The job will be complete when (and if) we figure out exactly where Eskimo fits into the true syntactic typology, together with how the defining principles of that type impinge on the domain of compounding.

It is impossible to tell at this point whether this strategy of using a more fine-grained and sophisticated typology to look for correlations between morphology and syntax will prove fruitful beyond the very restricted sample considered here. Since the strategy works for the polysynthetic languages, since there are relevant syntactic differences between Hebrew and Welsh after all, and since syntactic principles seem to go so far in analyzing synthetic compounds in English, I am inclined to be optimistic. But perhaps the real moral of this interchange is that we really do

---

[9]No doubt this is another reason why the existence of N-N compounding in the Iroquoian languages has gone largely unrecognized. However, the order between the elements in (37) is fixed, and the parts cannot be separated from each other as is otherwise possible for modifiers in this highly nonconfigurational language. Note also that (37a) is not entirely transparent semantically.

[10]This is far from certain, however. At the workshop I had opportunity to discuss with Jerrold Sadock the putative syntactic differences between Greenlandic and the languages that are polysynthetic in the sense defined in Baker 1996. The result of this discussion was that it may be possible to subsume Greenlandic to the polysynthetic class after all. This would be a welcome result from the point of view of syntactic typology, but it would reduce the chances of explaining the compounding differences between Chukchee and Greenlandic in syntactic terms. This is a topic for future research.

not yet have enough good typological and crosslinguistic research on compounding to ground either optimism or pessimism. Hopefully, Sadock's paper will call needed attention to this issue, and help motivate us to do this important work.

References

Baker, Mark. 1988. *Incorporation: A Theory of Grammatical Function Changing*. Chicago: University of Chicago Press.

Baker, Mark. 1996. *The Polysynthesis Parameter*. New York: Oxford University Press.

Burzio, Luigi. 1986. *Italian Syntax: A Government-Binding Approach*. Dordrecht: Reidel.

Chomsky, Noam. 1981. *Lectures on Government and Binding*. Dordrecht: Foris.

Clark, Eve, B. Hecht, and R. Mulford. 1986. Coining Complex Compounds in English: Affixes and Word Order in Acquisition. *Linguistics* 24:7–29.

Di Sciullo, Anna Maria and Edwin Williams. 1987. *On the Definition Of Word*. Cambridge, Mass.: MIT Press.

Duffield, Nigel. 1995. Particles and Projections in Irish Syntax. Dordrecht: Kluwer.

Foley, William. 1991. *The Yimas Language of New Guinea*. Stanford, Calif.: Stanford University Press.

Kayne, Richard. 1995. *The Antisymmetry of Syntax*. Cambridge, Mass.: MIT Press.

Koopman, Hilda. 1984. *The Syntax of Verbs*. Dordrecht: Foris.

Li, Yafei. 1990a. On V-V Compounds in Chinese. *Natural Language and Linguistic Theory* 8:177–208.

Li, Yafei. 1990b. X^0-binding and Verb Incorporation. *Linguistic Inquiry* 21:399–426.

Lieber, Rocelle. 1983. Argument Linking and Compounding in English. *Linguistic Inquiry* 14:251–286.

Lieber, Rochelle. 1993. *Deconstructing Morphology*. Chicago: University of Chicago Press.

Mithun, Marianne. 1984. The Evolution of Noun Incorporation. *Language* 60:847-893.

Pollock, Jean-Yves. 1989. Verb Movement, Universal Grammar, and the Structure of IP. *Linguistic Inquiry* 20:365-424.

Roeper, Tom and M.E.A. Siegel. 1978. A Lexical Transformation for Verbal Compounds. *Linguistic Inquiry* 9:199-260.

Selkirk, Elisabeth. 1982. *The Syntax of Words*. Cambridge, Mass.: MIT Press.

Shibatani, Masayoshi. 1990. *The Languages of Japan*. Cambridge: Cambridge University Press.

Spencer, Andrew. 1991. *Morphological Theory*. Oxford: Basil Blackwell.

Sproat, Richard. 1985. *On Deriving the Lexicon*. Doctoral dissertation, MIT.

Travis, Lisa. 1984. *Parameters and Effects of Word Order Variation*. Doctoral dissertation, MIT.

Williams, Edwin. 1981. Argument Structure and Morphology. *The Linguistic Review* 1:81–114.

Discussion of the Papers by Sadock and Baker

Perlmutter: I have a methodological comment on Mark's first set of arguments. Let's take the very first one. You're arguing that syntactic principles apply in compounding, and so you say, "Well, have theta-role assignment in *John is a truck driver*, in the same way as *John drives trucks*." Now obviously from that one example we can't conclude anything. In a sense this is very much like the discussion that we had this morning with respect to Patrick Farrell's comments on Shelly Lieber's paper. What you would need to show that would be to look through compounds somewhat extensively and show that you in fact have the same thing going on and you have the same class of examples, and they do not conflict. And the same for the others. So at the end when you conclude that all of this is the same syntactic principles, it seems somewhat empty without that demonstration.

Baker: So you have concerns about whether the data that this is based on is real?

Perlmutter: I have concerns about whether, if you look systematically at compounds, and then systematically at clauses—I mean obviously they do parallel in an enormous range of cases. The question is, does it hold all the way through, along the lines that we had [in] the discussion this morning? So I mean it's hard to tell at the end where you say "Summary" whether that is a result or simply your initial premise.

Carstairs-McCarthy: Just a point about English compounds and things that I don't think are compounds, but I think it has wider ramifications, perhaps. It's a bee I've had in my bonnet for quite a while. Whenever anybody sees a N-N collocation, they say "Compound," and I think that's true of Jerry's paper as well, and I went through the printed version writing "Not compound" against various things like *wood house, skinhead brothers, welfare moms* which to me are N-bars, N´s in which the first element is itself an N´. And you can tell the first element is an N´ because you can have a larger N´ there, like, *straight line relationship* on a graph—*straight line* is presumably an N´, and it's modifying an N to give you a bigger N´. Or *local body elections, hard-boiled egg salad, Saturday night fever*, and so on; they are all things that are clearly not compounds, so far as I can see. An advantage to saying these are not compounds is that we might be able to resurrect for English the No-Phrase Constraint. Now you immediately say, "Ah-hah, the No-Phrase Constraint is a counterexample itself because *no phrase* is itself a phrase, but my story on that is that *no phrase* is being mentioned rather than used there, just as when one says, "the novel *War and Peace* by Tolstoy," the phrase *war and peace* is being mentioned rather than used.

The wider question, then, is whether perhaps we are oversimplifying in talking about compounds or not compounds—are there subtleties being missed here, subtleties that would take in these N´-N collocations in English?

Sadock: Right, the first N in many of these, in fact in some of the examples I have in the written version of the paper, actually includes a modifier in a number of cases. So I have some dozen or so examples from [the] stereo store's ad, where the thing starts out with a numeral: *five speaker system, hundred watt stereo*, etc., but it doesn't seem to me that the freedom of modification is as great in those as it is with N´s in general. Maybe I'm wrong, but ... *hundred speaker system* sounds great, but *good speaker system* where *good* is supposed to modify *speaker* sounds just terrible to me. So, there are much more limited possibilities. I think you're right though, Andrew, that this is something like a "super-duper" compound that is maybe characteristic of English, and especially American English. But I don't think it therefore doesn't participate in some kind of morphological constraints that we also find operating in other compounds. So we don't say * *five speakers system* for the same reason that we don't get a plural in indubitable root compounds, I would think. But it's a good point that very well deserves more thinking.

Noyer: I just have a small point for Mark, which is that in these N-N compounds in Irish, the righthand member is genitive. I don't know whether Nigel said that. Typically there's not case assignment in compounds ...

Borer: That doesn't happen in Hebrew, because there's no case marking, but in Arabic there's genitive. But it's a good question why you can have genitive.

Sadock: I have an answer for that. It's because there's an NP there in the position that gets genitive case in any language that combines NPs in that case.

Baker: Sproat also says that the Case Filter applies in NPs. I don't know if you'd expect genitive necessarily, there's some questions about that.

Janda: I wanted to sandwich in a comment which supports Andrew on the one hand and David on the other. This is about the data. I think, Jerry, that we talked earlier about a parallelism between Adj's and Ns [that] supports the syntactic analysis rather than a compounding one. So you get these enormously long things like *US Department of Fish and Wildlife Southern Region Grand Canyon Branch Office* , where you've got a PP inside. On our plane we were given something that said *TWA Important Notice*, and it wasn't a notice that was important to TWA, it was for the passengers ...

On David's point, consider *John is a landscape artist* vs. **John arts/artists landscape(s)*—[here] syntax and compounding aren't parallel. If you pick different examples, you get different results, so you really do have to look at a huge amount of data. So, there's compounding, and then there's compounding ...

The other thing that would relate to this involves subjectival arguments, like *shark-eating*. It's hard to prove that you don't have some kind of ergative, such as with a *by*-phrase; so we find *doctor-testing of products; our products are doctor-tested*. I think these are a problem for interpretion. I myself think *a shark-eaten man* is much worse than *shark-eating of men* ...

Baker: ... Your points came through very quickly, so I'll drop the two in the middle which I missed. But there is the methodological question about Perlmutter's kinds of example too. Those all have a certain character to them that touches on something we said before. This literature is saying that there is this very productive vein of English compounding where you can make up new compounds easily that everyone understands immediately, and so on. And then there are some other things which don't have such stable and consistent properties. But if they're the kind of examples that are saying, "There are things in addition to what this theory is accounting for," that's not really an objection, I don't think. That's saying that we need to supplement our theory, there's another chapter to be had ... I'm saying that you find one coherent batch of stuff, and you say something about it. Maybe this is saying that morphology isn't monolithic, meaning that a single kind of theory is going to work for everything that could be called a word, but nobody here believes that, at least nobody here participating in this form of discussion. So, I'm not trying to hide from the data, I'm just trying to make progress on one piece of it at a time.

Identity Avoidance in Phonology and Morphology

Moira Yip

Many languages avoid sequences of homophonous elements, be they phonemes or morphemes. It is argued that a single principle underlies all such cases of avoidance, and that this principle can interact with the rest of the grammar resulting in the omission of one morpheme, or forcing a choice between different syntactic outputs. This paper is formulated within Optimality Theory, and makes three main points.[1] First, at least some inputs to the Optimality Grammar must be abstract morphological specifications like PLURAL. They are phonologically incomplete outputs of the morpho-syntax. Second, morpheme realization results from an attempt to meet output targets in the form of constraints: REPEAT, σ_2 =a; PL=s, and so on. Such morphemes do not have underlying forms in the familiar sense (cf Hammond 1995, Russell 1995). Third, the target constraints may be out-ranked by phonological constraints of various kinds, particularly constraints against the repetition of elements, here called the OCP. The elements may be phonological (feature, segment) or morphological (affix, stem). These findings support the view of Pierrehumbert (1993a) that identity has broad cognitive roots. Section 1 gives some background on the handling of morphological data in OT. Section 2 discusses identity avoidance in morphology and sets out the basic proposal. Section 3 discusses cases of adjacent homophonous morphemes in Mandarin, English, and Classical Greek. Section 4 looks at homophonous morphemes on adjacent words (but which are not themselves string-adjacent) in English and Hindi. Section 5 looks at reduplication in Javanese, and argues that echo-words result from the tension between a requirement that *penalizes* a sequence of two identical stems, OCP(Stem), and one that *requires* two identical stems, REPEAT(Stem).

This work took place over some time, and resulted in two papers: the

---

[1] This paper has benefited greatly from comments from audiences at this conference. and at the Conference on Features in Optimality Theory at the University of Arizona in April 1995, from the participants in the seminar on Constraints in OT at UC Irvine, and the workshop on Theoretical East Asian Linguistics, UC Irvine, and from a number of individuals, including Diane Brentari, Andrew Carstairs-McCarthy, Larry Hyman, Sharon Inkelas, John McCarthy, Orhan Orgun, David Perlmutter and Jerry Sadock. Special thanks to Steven LaPointe, Diane Brentari, Patrick Farrell and the rest of the Davis morphology community for making the conference and this volume possible.

present work, and a detailed exploration of reduplication and identity-avoidance in Javanese, Yip (forthcoming). The early sections form the necessary background to both papers, and are largely identical; the data and analyses in each paper are different, although complementary.

1. Morphology in Optimality Theory

Optimality Theory (Prince and Smolensky 1993, McCarthy and Prince 1993a, and a host of others) as currently conceived is a theory of not only phonology but also many aspects of morphology. It includes mechanisms for controlling the size and content of reduplicative morphemes, constraints responsible for the precise placement of affixes, constraints that explain the choice among allomorphs, and constraints that pick the right member of a suppletive set. The essence of Optimality Theory is that it is an output-based grammar in which all possible outputs for some input are assessed by a universal set of ranked and violable output constraints. Only the ranking is language specific. The optimal candidate is evaluated as follows. All outputs which violate the highest ranked constraint are thrown out, and those remaining are evaluated by the next highest ranked constraint. This procedure continues until only a single candidate survives. In the event of a tie at any point in the procedure, the tying candidates are passed on down to the next constraint, which decides matters. Let us see how a selection of morphological phenomena is handled in Optimality Theory.

1.1 Reduplication

McCarthy and Prince 1993a, 1994 lay out an approach to reduplication in which an abstract input morpheme, RED, passes through GEN and results in a set of output candidates in which RED is realized as a full or partial copy of the base. The choice among these candidates is governed by a set of constraints that determine the size of the reduplicant (such as RED=σ), and its content, controlled by a set of constraints that enforce identity between base and RED, and prefer maximal copying. If RED=σ is ranked above MAX(imality), the reduplicant will be monosyllabic (e.g. Ilokano *bas-basa, da-da.it*). If MAX is the higher-ranked of the two, reduplication will be total. (e.g. Yoruba *agba-agba, oru-oru*) These constraints can also interact with syllable structure constraints. For example, if NOCODA dominates MAX, the reduplicant will be coda-less (e.g. Balangao: *tagta-tagtag, tayna-taynan*).

1.2 Affix placement

A family of Alignment constraints (McCarthy and Prince 1993b) aligns the edges of prosodic and morphological categories with themselves and with each other. A purely phonological alignment phenomenon would be the placement of feet at the ends of prosodic words: ALIGN-LEFT: (PrWd, Foot) (e.g.

English *(Táta)ma(góuchi)*, * *Ta(táma)(góuchi))*. A purely morphological example would be the placement of an affix at the beginning of a stem: ALIGN-LEFT(Affix, Stem) (Tagalog prefix *ag-*). A morphology/phonology interface example would place a foot at the end of a root, ALIGN-RIGHT (Root, Foot) as in Indonesian *bi(cará)-kan* (Cohn and McCarthy 1994)

Particularly striking results come in the treatment of affixes that vacillate between prefixation and infixation as a consequence of the interaction between these alignment constraints and syllable structure constraints. For example, in Tagalog the prefix *um-* of *um-aral* is placed in position by a constraint ALIGN-LEFT (*um-*, stem), but this constraint is dominated by NO-CODA. The result is to force infixation of *um-* before C-initial roots, such as *gr-um-adwet*, since the prefixed form *um-gradwet would have an extra coda.[2] Zoll (1994) has used a similar approach to explain the behavior of morphemes that surface as floating features at varying positions in the root, like Chaha imperative palatalization; in some cases these moveable affixes may surface as independent segments as well, like Yawelmani suffixal glottalization.

1.3 Allomorphy

Carstairs (1990) discusses several cases in which allomorph choice is phonologically conditioned. This section and the next one summarize the treatement of such facts within OT. Mester (1994) proposes that a prosodic selection process in the lexicon can pick one allomorph from a set of alternatives by looking at which would form the optimal output with respect to a set of constraints. He studies Latin perfect stems, which can be formed by attachment of either *-u-* or *-s-*. The default choice is attachment of *-u*, e.g. *mon-u-i:*, but in stems with final heavy syllables, *-s* is used instead: e.g. *auk-s-i:* **aug-u-i:*. He suggests that this can be understood as the avoidance of an output in which a single light syllable, *.u.*, cannot be incorporated into a foot because it is 'trapped' between two heavy syllables (one from the root, and one from the final suffix); here I mark foot boundaries with [ ]:

(1)   **aug u i:*   cf   *auk si:*
           [ō] ŏ [ō]   [ō] [ō]

The prosodic selection process thus picks *auk-si:* from a set of alternative outputs {*aug-u-i:, auk-s-i:*} for the input /auk-PERF-i:/.

1.4 Suppletion

Tranel (1994) examines French determiners, where the feminine 1-sg-

---

[2] The root codas survive because PARSE dominates NOCODA. Note that ALIGN-ag >> NOCODA >> ALIGN-um, since *ag-* is always prefixed even if it results in NO-CODA violations.

poss *ma* is replaced by the masculine *mon* before vowel-initial feminine nouns, and the masculine *ce* 'this' is replaced by the feminine *cet* before vowel-initial masculine nouns.[3,4] Standard accounts simply stipulate this distribution, but Tranel's insight is that both suppletions supply an onset for the following syllable, and are thus phonologically driven. He suggests that a suppletion set is judged against constraints that require gender agreement, and onset satisfaction, and that no one form is basic. Gender agreement can be over-ridden by the need for an onset: ONSET >> GENDER. The result will be, correctly, that the grammar will pick the C-final candidate before a V-initial noun, irrespective of gender.

(2)

1-SG-POSS arme$_F$	ONSET	GENDER
a. ☞ mon$_M$ arme$_F$		*
b. ma$_F$ arme$_F$	*!	
c. ce$_M$ abbé$_M$	*!	
d. ☞ cet$_F$ abbé$_M$		*

These results make it hard to identify a clear dividing line between morphology and phonology. What is more, they go much further to blur the distinction than does the interleaving of phonology and morphology found in lexical phonology. In lexical phonology, each component has its own character: the entities are different, and the rules are different. In Optimality Theory, this is not necessarily the case. Alignment is the most striking example. Alignment appears to play a role in pure morphology, in pure phonology, and at the interface.

In this paper, I want to focus on another area in which phonology and morphology appear to overlap, the area of identity avoidance. It is a commonplace in phonology that sequences of adjacent identical elements are avoided, and this is enshrined as the Obligatory Contour Principle, or OCP (Leben 1973, McCarthy 1986, Yip 1988, Odden 1988, Myers 1993, Pierrehumbert 1993a, and others). What has received less attention in OT are superficially similar cases in morphology (but see Golston 1994, 1995), although the generative literature includes many such cases. See for example Sadock 1972, Menn and MacWhinney 1984, Hyman and Mchombo 1992, and particularly Stemberger 1981.

---

[3] *cet* and *cette* are orthographically distinct, but both are phonetically [sɛt]. I follow Tranel in assuming that both are feminine, and the orthography is irrelevant.

[4] Perlmutter (this volume) independently reaches very similar conclusions.

2. Identity Avoidance in Morphology

Avoidance of identity in morphology takes several forms. I will divide them into four categories.

(3)   a. The same morpheme cannot appear twice in the same word
        b. Different but homophonous morphemes cannot appear adjacent in the same word, or otherwise adjacent in the sentence
        c. Homophonous morphemes cannot appear on adjacent words
        d. The output of reduplication cannot be total identity

The first type is rare, perhaps non-existent, but it is not clear that the morpho-phonology underlies this: in most cases it seems likely that syntactic and morpho-syntactic principles will achieve this end without identity avoidance being involved at all. [5]

The second type is quite common; the references cited above include numerous examples. A familiar and typical example is the English possessive plural: *cats's, cats'*. Further examples discussed in this paper include Mandarin perfective *le* and Currently Relevant State *le* (Chao 1968, Li and Thompson 1981), Classical Greek determiners (Golston 1994) and Mandarin third person pronoun *ta* (Yeh 1994). A common response in these cases is blocking, as in Chichewa. Another strategy, the one chosen in the examples discussed in this paper, is omission of one morpheme, with the remaining one carrying the semantics of both. This phenomenon is called haplology, and will be discussed in section 3.

The third type involves identical morphemes attached to adjacent words, but where the morphemes themselves are not string adjacent. Since the presence of a morpheme on one word does not satisfy the requirements of the second word, omission of a morpheme is rarely the preferred strategy for resolving the situation; instead we are more likely to see syntactic movement, replacement by an alternative morpheme, or simple blocking. Cases of this kind include English *-ing* (see Ross 1972, Milsark 1988, and, for a different view, Pullum and Zwicky (1991)), and Hindi *-ko* Dative and Accusative markers (Mohanan 1992). In the Hindi example, sequences of two NP's, each marked by the suffix *-ko*, are avoided. These cases are discussed in section 4.

The fourth type are usually called "echo words": reduplication accompanied by a small change such that the two halves are not quite identical. English *table-shmable* is an example of an echo-word, and they are found in many

---

[5] But see Hyman and Mchombo (1992) on Chichewa, where two instances of the applicative morpheme with different semantic roles are acceptable within the same word, so long as they are not adjacent. I assume that the syntax allows this because one morpheme can be used for several semantic roles.

languages including Turkish, Bengali, Chinese, and a host of others. See Yip 1992 for many examples. I will propose that echo-words result from a tension between two constraints, one requiring repetition (reduplication) and one banning repetition (the OCP). The primary case discussed here is Javanese, in section 5. A much fuller discussion of echo-words can be found in Yip (forthcoming).

2.1 A Summary of the Proposal

The central theme of this paper is the avoidance of complete identity. In phonology the OCP has been the usual way of addressing such issues, and in morphology Menn and MacWhinney (1984) propose the Repeated Morph Constraint (RMC). Both principles rule out sequences of phonologically identical elements; even the RMC does not rule out sequences of phonologically distinct morphemes. The clear similarity between these two constraints suggests that both phonology and morphology are subject to a single general principle that avoids repetition. This principle may even have quite general cognitive roots, as proposed by Pierrehumbert (1993a). I shall continue to use the term OCP for this principle without intending some sort of sovereignty for phonology over a morphological domain. In Yip (forthcoming) I adopt a different term, *REPEAT, which has its origins in the RMC, and in a suggestion of Diane Brentari (this volume). In the rest of the paper I will continue to use constraints of the OCP family, as defined sweepingly below.[6]

(4)   OCP: Output must not contain two identical elements

Like many constraints, this is subject to adjacency effects, and it may also be judged gradiently at a featural level. The consequence is that violations will be more serious the nearer two things are, and the more similar they are (Pierrehumbert 1993a). In most of this paper these subtleties will play no role.

The model I am proposing has two main parts. I outline the proposal below; further details will become clear during the body of the paper. First, there is a set of UG constraints, including:

(5)   OCP: Output must not contain two identical elements
         MORPHDIS: "Distinct instances of morphemes have distinct contents, tokenwise"
         REPEAT: Output must contain two identical elements

---

[6] OCP was the term used in the first draft of the paper, and the oral version. I am thus retaining it here in line with the editors' stated policy. In any case the difference between OCP and *REPEAT is terminological, not substantive.

The OCP constraint blocks complete repetition.[7] The second constraint, MORPHDIS: "Distinct instances of morphemes have distinct contents, tokenwise", is drawn from McCarthy and Prince (1995:67). They find the need for a constraint that is violated any time a segment does double duty to fulfil more than one morphological role. If this constraint dominates the OCP, sequences of homophonous morphemes cannot be avoided by haplology. If the ranking is reversed, however, we will observe haplology: to avoid repetition, one set of segments is recruited to do the work of two morphemes:

(6)   OCP >> MORPHDIS   haplology
        MORPHDIS >> OCP   no haplology

The REPEAT constraint forces reduplication by self-compounding. Instead of supposing that there is an affix, RED, which must be filled, it assumes that the input has only a morphological annotation such as "PLURAL", and the grammar includes a constraint REPEAT$_{Plural}$ which must be satisfied for all plural inputs. This can be combined if necessary with constraints governing the size of the reduplicant: I will have nothing to say about this latter point.

If OCP >> REPEAT, we derive the echo-word pattern: reduplication that falls just short of complete identity. This proposal explain why echo-words seem to be most common in the case of word reduplication, where the reduplication would otherwise be total: in the case of partial reduplication, the OCP is satisfied anyway by the failure to copy the entire base. The ranking REPEAT >> OCP will mask the effects of the OCP completely, giving total reduplication.

Summarizing, the tension between the first and last constraints gives rise to the following partial typology:

(7)   REPEAT >> OCP   true reduplication
        OCP   >> REPEAT   echo words: change in one half

REPEAT bears obvious similarities to various constraints proposed in the OT literature on reduplication, particularly McCarthy and Prince (1993, 1994, 1995). It does much of the work of two constraints in their 1995 paper, IDENT-BR, and MAX-BR. For the purposes of this paper, it is sufficient to merge these two into the single REPEAT.

The second part of the proposal is as follows:

---

[7] I will assume that *REPEAT assesses complete morphological entities, such as stems, but an alternative is to assess all identity as the aggregate of individual identities between pairs of segments.

(8)   a. Inputs consist of morphologically annotated roots, rather than roots
       with phonologically specified affixes: /kæt$_{PL}$ /, not /kæt-s/, and
       /udan$_{HAB-REP}$/ not /udan-RED/.
       b. These are realized in order to satisfy specific output constraints

Within OT, this is very similar to proposals of Hammond (1995) and Russell
(1995). It is also what seems to be assumed by Mester (1994). Philosophically,
it has much in common with the proposals of Anderson (1992). The primary
advantage of this proposal in the present context is that it allows for the absence
of an affix precisely when some other affix or the root itself is able to satisfy the
output constraint in question. The discussion of English in the next section will
illustrate this point, and it will play an important role in Javanese.

3. Avoidance of adjacent homophonous morphemes
3.1 English 's

The best known case of haplology comes from English. The plural /s/
and the possessive /s/ cannot co-occur, although adding possessive /s/ to an
irregular plural is fine, and so is adding it to a singular ending in /s/, or even a
singular ending in /sɪs/.

(9)   *Singular*   *Plural*   *Poss. Sg.*   *Poss. Pl.*
       child   children   child's   children's
       mouse   mice   mouse's   ?mice's
       cat   cats   cat's   cats'   *cats's
       Katz   Katzes   Katz's   Katzes' *Katzes's
       coreopsis   coreopsis's

Compare especially *Katz's* vs *cats's*; *coreopsis's* vs. *Katzes's*. I must emphasize
that like all the cases examined in this paper the illicit sequences are ruled out by
some principle that disallows *phonological* identity; the sequence of a plural
morpheme followed by a possessive morpheme is fine if the two are
phonologically distinct, as in *oxen's*.

       Two strategies are used to avoid /s-s/. One strategy is haplology: the
omission of a morpheme, as in the possessive plural *cats'*. The other is insertion
of a buffer vowel, as in the simple possessive *Katz's*, *Kat*[sɪz] (and between all
stridents and suffixal -*s*).

       Optimality Theory, as an output-based grammar, is well-suited to
capturing Stemberger's (1981) insight that this and other cases of haplology do
not appear to involve deletion so much as a failure to insert a superfluous
morpheme if a homophonous morpheme is already in the right position. Thus if
the plural /s/ is present, a plural possessive can satisfy the need to end all

possessives in /s/ without adding a second /s/. This explanation, though, does not extend to the vowel-insertion between a root /s/ and a suffix /s/, and thus no unified explanation is possible. Within Optimality Theory, we can provide a single straightforward account.

I will now offer an explicit Optimality Theory analysis of the core aspects of identity avoidance, using this as my first example. Suppose, following Myers (1993), that the OCP is a constraint that can be ranked with respect to the other constraints of the grammar. Further suppose that the OCP is a sort of meta-constraint (Pierrehumbert 1993b) which can be instantiated with different arguments, and includes at least the following family;

(10)   OCP (feature)   OCP (segment)
        OCP (affix)   OCP (stem)

Consider a case in which insertion is the preferred remediation strategy. The OCP must then dominate some sort of constraint against epenthesis which, following Prince and Smolensky 1993, I will call FILL. Also high-ranked will be the output constraints that require some morphological category to be phonologically instantiated in a particular way:

(11)   English 's:
        a. PLURAL: Plurals must consist of a stem plus an -s affix.
        b. POSS: Possessives must consist of a phrase plus an -s affix.
        c. OCP (s): OCP (feature), where feature=[strident]
        d. FILL: Don't insert
        e. MORPHDIS: "Distinct instances of morphemes have distinct contents, tokenwise"

        PLURAL, POSS, OCP (s) >> FILL, MORPHDIS
        (Epenthesis as last resort)

In the tableau below, the possessive plural *cats'* with only one *s* wins because the candidate with two *s*'s violates OCP (s), and the candidate with epenthesis violates FILL. Crucially, the single *s* satisfies the PLURAL and POSS constraints; the winning candidate violates MORPHDIS, which must thus be low-ranked.

(12)

cat$_{\text{PLPOSS}}$	PL=s	Poss=s	OCP (s)	FILL	MORPHDIS
cat$_{\text{PLPOSS}}$-s-s			*!		
☞ cat$_{\text{PLPOSS}}$-s					*
cat$_{\text{PLPOSS}}$-s-I-s				*!	

In the possessive of *Katz's*, the affix must be retained to satisfy Poss. FILL is thus violated in order to satisfy the higher-ranked OCP (s).

(13)

Katz$_{\text{POSS}}$	PL=s	Poss=s	OCP (s)	FILL	MORPHDIS
Katz$_{\text{POSS}}$-s			*!		
Katz$_{\text{POSS}}$		*!			
☞ Katz$_{\text{POSS}}$-I-s				*	

These tableaux demonstrate that the omission of one affix after the possessive plural of *cat* versus the epenthesis into the simple possessive of *Katz* follow from the dominance of OCP (s), and of the output requirement that the plural and the possessive must end in an *'s* morpheme. This output requirement blocks deletion of a lone plural or possessive morpheme, and OCP (s) forces use of the fall-back strategy, epenthesis. Two *'s* affixes will never be optimal, because they will always violate either OCP (s), if adjacent, or FILL, if separated by an epenthetic vowel, and there is always available a candidate with only one affix that violates neither. This analysis thus allows us to link the morphological "haplology" of the plural and possessive morphemes with the phonological epenthesis of the English Plural Rule by assuming that OCP (s) plays a role in both "components".[8]

Note that in an interestingly similar case, Hungarian (Carstairs 1990:17) replaces the usual -*(a)sz* suffix of the 2nd singular indefinite present indicative with -*ol* after sibilants and affricates. Here the OCP(s) apparently selects between two allomorphs, choosing -*ol* to avoid a sequence of two stridents.

---

[8] The epenthesis depends crucially on the OCP, but the haplology in fact does not. The haplology could also follow instead from some notion of economy or faithfulness that penalizes insertion of [s], and from viewing the plural and possessive as output constraints that can be jointly satisfied by a single *'s*. However, the haplologized forms are certainly *consistent* with the OCP ranking necessary for the epenthetic cases.

English demonstrates the advantages of assuming that affixes are not present underlyingly, but are a response to satisfying an output constraint. In the next section we will see a similar case involving a verbal affix and a sentential affix which are presumably not juxtaposed until the syntax, and where the same avoidance of repetition is found.

3.2 Mandarin *le*

It is well known that Mandarin Chinese has a process of haplology that reduces expected adjacent instances of *le* to a single *le*. There are two different kinds of *le*. One is a verbal suffix, and marks perfective aspect. This is illustrated below.

(14) Perfective Aspect

    a. *Huo mie-le*
       fire went-out-PF
       The fire went out.

    b. *Wo wang-le   ta-de   dizhi*
       I   forget-PF 3sg-GEN address
       I forgot his/her address

    c. *Ta jintian mai-le hen duo shu*
       3sg today buy-PF very many book
       He/she bought a lot of books today

The other is a sentence-final particle, and conveys a subtle sense of change-of-state, relevance to discourse, and other things. For details see Chao (1968) and Li and Thompson (1981).

(15) Currently Relevant State (Li and Thompson)

    a. *Xia-ge   yue   wo jiu zai Riben le*
       next-CL month I   then at Japan CRS
       Next month I'll be in Japan.

    b. *Nei tian ta chu-qu mai dongxi le*
       that day 3sg exit-go buy thing CRS
       That day she went out shopping

If the semantics demand it, a sentence can carry both *le*'s at once, as shown below:

(16) Both - Non-adjacent
>   a. *Wo he-le   san bei kafei   le*
>   I   drink-PF three cup coffee CRS
>   I drank three cups of coffee

>   b. *Feiji   chu-le maobing le*
>   Airplane exit-PF trouble CRS
>   The airplane has developed some trouble

However, if the verb is intransitive and therefore sentence-final, so that both *le*'s would end up adjacent, only one occurs, and the resulting sentence is three ways ambiguous.

(17) *Both - Adjacent
>   a. **Huo mei-le le*
>   *Huo mei-le*
>   The fire went out (PF) (yesterday)
>   The fire has gone out (CRS) (already)
>   The fire went out, and that's what I'm telling you (PF/CRS)

>   a. *Bing dou hua   le (*le)*
>   ice   all melted PF/CRS
>   The ice all melted.

This is also true if the verb ends up sentence final because the object has been preposed, showing that it is surface adjacency that matters, not underlying adjacency, and also that trace does not interrupt the adjacency of the two instances of *le*.

(18)   *Wo yijing ba [nei san bei kafei]ᵢ dou he   le tᵢ (*le)*
>   I   already BA [those three cup coffee]ᵢ all drink PF tᵢ CRS
>   I already drank those three cups of coffee (that you left me).

Other sequences of homophonous *le* are also pretty bad; most informants reject sentences like the following, where the first *le* of the intensifying suffix *-jile* is arguably not the perfective.

(19) ?* *Ta yijing shuo "Hao jile" le*
>   He already said "Good-INT" CRS
>   He already said "Wonderful!"

Sequences of other reduced affixes followed by *le* are acceptable. The following examples show *de le, ge le*, showing that this is not a constraint on two Cə unstressed syllables.

(20) a. *Wo he-le   wo-de le*
　　　　I   drink-PF mine CRS
　　　　I drank mine.

　　　b. *Wo mai-le   nei-ge   le*
　　　　I   buy-PF   that one CRS
　　　　I bought that one.

Stemberger points out, though, that two instances of *de*, one a nominalizer and one showing modification, are out:

(21) *hou de*   'thick thing'
　　　shu de yanse   'the book's color'
　　　hou de (*de) yanse   'the thick thing's color'

Inspection of these data yields the following observations:

(22)　　●Phonological identity is needed : *de de* or *le le*. This is confirmed by the fact that in Cantonese, where the perfective and currently-relevant-state affixes are not homophonous, the combination is fine.
　　　　● The phonological identity targets the whole morpheme, not its component segments. This distinction could not be discerned in the case of English /s/, where the morpheme consisted of a single segment.
　　　　● Morphological identity is not involved (they are different morphemes), and indeed morphological information may not be needed either, given data like (19) which suggests that any two *le* are unacceptable.

　　　A very similar approach to that taken for English *-s* will work for Mandarin *le*. Again the crucial idea is that the output constraint and the OCP both dominate the MORPHDIS constraint, so that omission is a way to resolve OCP violations, and the remaining *le* satisfies the output-based morphological constraint.

(23) Mandarin *le*:
　　　　a. PERF: The Perfect verb must end in *le*.
　　　　b. CRS: Currently Relevant State utterances must end in *le*.
　　　　c. OCP (*le*): OCP (affix), where affix = *le*
　　　　d. MORPHDIS: "Distinct instances of morphemes have distinct

contents, tokenwise"

(24)　　PERF, CRS , OCP (*le*) >> MORPHDIS

(25)

mie_{PF/CRS}	Perf, CRS	OCP(*le*)	MORPHDIS
mie_{PF/CRS}	*!		
mie_{PF/CRS} -le-le		*!	
☞ mie_{PF/CRS}-le			*

3.3 Mandarin ta haplology

I now move to a case that involves not affixes, but pronouns, and ones that are not obviously clitics. Adjacent instances of the third person pronoun *ta* are avoided, but only when they are co-referential, as shown by the following data: (Yeh 1994)

(26) *Wo wen ta$_i$ ta$_j$ mingtian lai   bu lai*
　　I   ask he$_i$ he$_j$ tomorrow come not come
　　I asked him$_i$ whether he$_j$ would come tomorrow

(27) **Wo wen ta$_i$ ta$_i$ mingtian lai   bu lai*
　　I   ask he$_i$ he$_i$ tomorrow come not come
　　I asked him$_i$ whether he$_i$ would come tomorrow

(28) *Wo wen ta$_i$ $\emptyset_{i/*j}$ mingtian lai   bu lai*
　　I   ask he$_i$ he$_{i/*j}$ tomorrow come not come
　　I asked him$_i$ whether he$_{i/*j}$ would come tomorrow

We must distinguish between the obligatory deletion for at least some speakers in the case of adjacent *ta*, and the optional deletion in the case of a full NP antecedent seen below:[9]

---

[9] Yeh's data do not seem to hold in all dialects. Yeh has other cases, all involving unstressed function words. Somewhat suprisingly, although she claims that phonological phrasing is the domain of this process these deletions/omissions are apparently not blocked by pause.

(29) *Wo wen Lao Wang, ta/∅ mingtian lai bu lai*
    I   ask Lao Wang$_i$ he$_i$ tomorrow come not come
  I asked Lao Wang$_i$ whether he$_i$ would come tomorrow

The following observations hold true; for deletion of *ta:*

(30)   • Phonological identity is necessary but not sufficient
            • Referential identity is necessary but not sufficient
            • If vacuous application is invoked here, it is of a very unusual kind.
Insertion of an item into a syntactic position must depend on the absence of an identical item from another syntactic position, in a different clause.

Golston (1995) proposes an Optimality Theory model of the interaction between syntax, morphology and phonology in which the syntax and/or morphology provide multiple possible outputs, and phonological constraints may decide among them. Syntactic constraints outrank phonological constraints, so the phonology may not force the selection of a syntactically deviant output, but if more than one syntactic output is possible, the phonological constraint may decide the winner. Applying this model to Mandarin *ta*, note that the syntax clearly provides two choices in the case of adjacent co-referential NP's as shown by the two options in (29): either both NP's may surface, or the second may be lost. Now consider the case when both NP;s are *ta;* the syntax will produce both ...*ta ta*... and *ta t$_i$...* . The OCP will then decide matters, picking the single *ta*. It is the referential identity that allows the syntax to produce two candidates in the first place, but it is the phonology that narrows down the options in the case of homophonous *ta* sequences.

3.4 Classical Greek Articles [10]
Golston (1994, 1995) shows that Classical Greek texts never use sequences of two homophonous articles. Such sequences can arise with center-embedded genitive NP's. The genitive articles are shown below:

(31)   a. Fem Gen Sg.   *tées*
        b. Masc Gen Sg   *tóu*
          Neut Gen Sg
        c. Fem Gen Pl   *tóon*
          Masc Gen Pl
          Neut Gen Pl

---

[10] This section has been added since the conference; it appeared in the appendix to my handout, but not in the draft paper.

A typical center-embedded structure in which two articles (non-homophonous) end up adjacent is shown below:

(32) *[tées [tóon himatí-oon] ergasí-as]*
$\quad$ the$_{f.g.s}$ the $_{n.g.p.}$ clothing $_{n.g.p.}$ production$_{f.d.}$
$\quad$ 'of the production of clothing'

The syntax also allows for extraposition of the embedded NP, like the next example:

(33) $\quad$ *[[h-ee tólm-a] [t-óon leg-ónt-oon]]*
$\quad\quad$ the$_{f.n}$ courage$_{f.n.}$ the $_{m.g.p.}$ speak-ing$_{m.g.p.}$
$\quad\quad$ 'the courage of those speaking'

If the two articles are homophonous, the equivalent center-embedded phrase is unacceptable, but an extraposed version is fine:

(34) a. $\quad$ *[[tées arkh-ées] [tées pól-eoos]]*
$\quad\quad\quad$ the$_{f.g.s}$ dominion $_{f.g.}$ the $_{f.g.s.}$ city $_{f.g.}$
$\quad\quad\quad$ 'of the dominion of the city'
$\quad$ b. * $\quad$ *[[tées [tées pól-eoos] arkh-ées]]*

The prohibition is morpheme specific, since phonologically identical sequences involving a deictic, not an article, are fine:

(35) $\quad$ *toútou tóu érgou*
$\quad\quad$ this$_{n.g.}$ the$_{n.g.}$ job

My analysis draws again on Golston's proposals. The syntax makes available both center-embedded and extraposed versions, and the phonology forces the choice of the extraposed version exactly when the center-embedded candidate would violate the OCP.

$\quad\quad$ The four cases in this section all involve the avoidance of sequences of adjacent phonologically identical morphemes. The situation is resolved in one of two ways. First, we see omission of one morpheme, where the surviving morpheme does the job of both (*'s, le*). This is attributed to the OCP outranking MORPHDIS, and thus allowing haplology. Second, we see the choice of an alternative syntactic output which either lacks the offending morpheme (*ta*) or moves it away *(Greek articles)*. Here the OCP chooses between two options made freely available by the syntax.

4. Avoidance of non-adjacent homophonous morphemes

4.1 English- *ing*

We move now into a different domain, where the banned sequences involve identical morphemes attached to adjacent words, but where the morphemes themselves are not adjacent. For my first case I turn to English. Sequences of words ending in -*ing* are disliked in English, as pointed out by Ross (1972). For a different view, see Pullum and Zwicky (1991). A recent treatment of this well-known phenomenon is found in Milsark (1988), who proposes (36):

(36)   The Doubl-*ing* Filter
        At PF, mark as ill-formed any sentence containing contiguous -*ing*-affixed words.

This accounts for the data below:

(37)   a. * John was starting reading the book
        b. * John was keeping reading the book

Sequences of -*ing* that do not involve the same morpheme are fine:

(38)   Good choirs sing ringing choruses all day long.

Milsark argues that "-*ing* is a single lexical element free in category", and given this the constraint bans morphological identity. It is apparently blocked by empty elements with Case features, as pointed out by Jaeggli 1980. This explains why Gen subjects block the filter from taking effect, and (39b) is fine.

(39)   a. John enjoyed Bill's reading the book.
        b. John was enjoying [PRO]$_{GEN}$ reading the book.

Summarizing our observations:
(40)   • Morpheme identity, as well as phonological identity, is involved.
        • Certainly needs morphological information (to allow for the acceptability of (39), even if we do not accept Milsark's view that all -*ing* are a single morpheme with multiple interpretations.
        • Needs syntactic information, because empty categories can block.
        • Adjacency defined at word-level, not string adjacent.
        •Avoidance mechanism not clear, but it is not omission/deletion of one element, as shown by the ungrammaticality of (42).

(41)   **John was starting reading the book
        **John was starting reading the book

Notice that the reason that omission is not an option for this type of case is obvious. There is no sense in which the presence of -*ing* on one word renders unnecessary the addition of -*ing* to the next word.[11]

Within Optimality Theory, the -*ing* affix presents a new problem. It is fairly clear that we need a constraint OCP(ing), and presumably one requiring that PROG=*ing*. What is new here is that resolution is not possible: neither omission of -*ing* or movement of the offending word are possible strategies. Instead, speakers avoid such utterances altogether. It seems then that there is no optimal output at all, and yet in Optimality Theory there is always an optimal output, no matter how bad. P&S handle this situation by assuming that one candidate is the so-called Null Parse, in which the input morphemes are not parsed at all. If this output is picked as optimal by the grammar, then there is no phonetic output. This situation arises in languages if Parse is outranked by other powerful constraints that rule out all candidates with parsed material.

With this as background, I offer the following analysis of English -*ing*. A similar approach could be used form other cases of blocking, such as Chichewa. Suppose that OCP(*ing*) and a requirement that the progressive be marked with *ing* are both equally high ranked.

(42)   PROG=*ing*: The progressive must surface marked by *ing*
        OCP(*ing*): OCP (affix), affix = *ing*
        REALIZE-Verb: Verbs must not be deleted   (arguably a syntactic constraint).

Then we not only rule out sequences of V-*ing*, by the OCP, but also any attempts to improve things by omitting *ing*, because then we will violate the PROG= *ing* constraint. The best choice will thus be the fourth candidate, the Null Parse; angled brackets indicate unrealized material:

(43)

	PROG=*ing*	OCP (*ing*)	REALIZE-Verb
a. V*ing* V*ing*		*!	
b. V*ing* V	*!		
c. V V	**!		
☞ d. <V> <V>			**

---

[11] Junko Itô (p.c.) points out that *John was starting to read the book* could be the surface realization of *John was starting reading the book*. I will not pursue this idea here.

We must also assume that if neither verb is parsed, the sentence itself does not surface. The impossibility of improving things by movement presumably results from the dominance of whatever syntactic constraints block all possible movements of V-*ing*.

4.2 Hindi Case Endings

My next example comes from Hindi, and is another instance of homophonous affixes on adjacent words being unacceptable. The facts are quite complex, and apply to sequences of -*ko* (Dat, Acc) or -*se* (Inst), and some others. I will give data for -*ko* only. (T. Mohanan 1992) : [12] The dative and accusative suffixes are both -*ko*, and sequences of *N-ko N-ko* are considered strange.

(44)   ??   *raam-ko baccõ-ko samhaalna paḍaa*
               Ramm-D children-A take care-NF fall-PERF
               Ram had to take care of the children

If they are separated by another word, the sentence is acceptable, as shown below. In fact, extraposition of the accusative noun *bacco-ko* in (35) yields an acceptable sentence, and is one strategy for producing a well-formed version.

(45)   *raam-ko kal   baccõ-ko samhaalna paḍaa*
               Ramm-D yesterday children-A take care-NF fall-PERF
               Ram had to take care of the children yesterday

Another remedial strategy is to leave the accusative unmarked; this leaves it non-specific, but if the context allows this may not matter.

The prohibition on *N-ko N-ko* holds only if both NP's are arguments. Homophonous non-argument case-endings such as -*ko* (at) may co-occur with argument ones:

(46)   *raam-ko raat-ko ravii   milaa*
               Ram-D night-at Ravi-Nmeet-PERF
               Ram met Ravi at night

It is also clear that the relevant identity here is not abstract case identity, but requires that the cases be realized by phonologically identical elements. After pronouns, the Dative has two options for some speakers, -*ko* or -*e* . The -*e* Dative can freely co-occur with a -*ko* Accusative, as the contrast below shows:

---

[12] I am indebted to Utpal Lahiri for help with these data.

(47) a. ??   *ham-ko   bacce-ko samhaalna   paḍaa*
             we-D   child-A   take case-NF fall-PERF
             We had to take care of the child

b.   *ham-e   bacce-ko samhaalna   paḍaa*
             we-D   child-A   take case-NF fall-PERF
             We had to take care of the child

Mohanan also points out that the prohibition only holds if the two morphemes are in adjacent phonological words—simply marking the heads of adjacent NP's is not enough to cause a problem.

(48)   *raam-ko apnii bahin-ke baccõ-ko   samhaalna   paḍaa*
             Ramm-D self's sister-G children-A take care-NF fall-PERF
             Ram had to take care of his sister's children

Furthermore, they must be in the same phonological phrase: the effect is blocked by the re-phrasing that accompanies an intervening pause.

(49)   *raam-ko [PAUSE] baccõ-ko   samhaalna   paḍaa*
             Ramm-D   children-A take care-NF fall-PERF
             Ram [pause] had to take care of the children

These facts converge on the conclusion that:
- Identity calculation is phonological, not morphological
- It appears to need syntactic and morphological information as well.
- Resolution is by omission of *-ko* or movement

An Optimality Theory account must deal with the fact that there are three resolution strategies: The first is omission of the accusative suffix. To derive this we need

(50)   DAT *(ko)*: The dative must be marked by *-ko*, or *-e* for pronouns.
        ACC *(ko)*: The accusative must be marked by *-ko*.
        OCP(*ko*): OCP(affix): Affix = $ko_{Acc/Dat}$

Crucially, the constraint covering the accusative *-ko* that may be omitted is dominated by the OCP: DAT *(ko)*, OCP(*ko*) >> ACC-*ko*

(51)

N_D N_A	DAT (ko)	OCP (ko)	ACC (ko)
N_D-ko N_A-ko		*!	
☞N_D-ko N_A			*
N_D N_A-ko	*!		
N_D N_A	*!		

The second strategy is limited to pronouns, and chooses the alternative suffix *e*. This is achieved by adding a candidate with *e* to the set, Pronoun$_D$-*e* N_A-*ko*. This candidate satisfies all four constraints, and is thus optimal.

The third strategy is movement; usually only fairly heavy NP's are extraposed, but a light -*ko* NP may be extraposed to avoid an OCP(*ko*) violation. So we need:

(52)   OCP (*ko*) >> *Extrapose Light NP

Obviously a serious account of this latter strategy depends on our understanding of the nature of the syntactic/prosodic constraints limiting extraposition to heavy phrases. The most appealing accounts, such as Zec and Inkelas (1990) and Truckenbrodt (1995), suggest that extraposed phrases are intonational phrases (IP's), and that IP's are subject to a minimum size requirement, Min IP. In that case (48) can be re-stated as (49):

(53) OCP (*ko*) >> Min IP

Whether this account holds up to a more detailed investigation of Hindi extraposition and intonation must be left for further research.

The two cases in this section have looked at more distant adjacency effects.(See also Sadock (1972) on Danish *som*.) Not surprisingly, these are less common than effects on adjacent identical sequences, and also seem to be less strong. The offending sequences are often deviant rather than absolutely impossible. In phonology, Pierrehumbert 1993a points out the same gradient weakening effect of distance on the OCP, and links it to more general cognitive phenomena.

5. Echo-word Formation

The third type of identity avoidance to be discussed here involves reduplication. Since reduplication apparently strives to achieve identity, it is intriguing to find it apparently shunning total identity: instead, the echo-word outputs I will examine show *almost* perfect identity, but with a single flaw.

Many languages have reduplicative processes that replace one portion of the reduplicant with fixed segmental material. English *table-shmable* is an example of such a process: see Yip (1992) for a range of cases. The segmental material is sometimes arguably the default segment of the language, as argued by McCarthy and Prince for Akan, and Yip for Chaoyang (1993). In other cases, however this is not so: no-one has argued that /ʃ, m / are the default consonants of English. A striking characteristic of many such word formation processes is that if the input contains segments identical to the fixed replacement ones, so that the expected output would mimic total reduplication, the process either does not apply at all, or a different set of replacement segments is used. For example, the Tengxian dialect of Chinese (Deng 1995) reduplicates adjectives, replacing the rhyme of the first half by [ɐŋ]:

(54)	*dun*	*dɐŋ dun*	'short
	lɛŋ	*lɐŋ lɛŋ*	'cold'
	kou	*kɐŋ kou*	'tall'

This system is very productive, applying to more than 200 adjectives. Systematically, adjectives whose rhyme is [ɐŋ] or [aŋ] fail to undergo this process, instead using one of several alternatives available in the language: /nɐŋ/ does not yield *nɐŋ nɐŋ, but rather [nɐŋ hɐŋ tʃɛŋ].

A second example is drawn from Turkish, which reduplicates the first CV of the adjective to form an emphatic form. This CV addition is followed by a coda consonant from the set /p,s,m,r/, subject to the constraint that this consonant cannot be identical or too similar to any consonant of the base. For details, see Dobrovolsky (1987), Demircan (1987). [13]

(55) a.	*kap-kara*	'jet black'	*ap-ačik*	'wide open'
	cep-cevre	'very much around'	*sap-sari*	'fully yellow'
b.	*sim-siki*	'extremely tight'	*bem-beyaz*	'snow white'
	göm-gök	'sky-blue'	*bum-burusuk*	
c.	*kas-kati*	'extremely hard'	*bes-belli*	'unmistakably obvious'
d.	*ter-temiz*	'spotless'	*sir-siklam*	'wet through'
	tor-top	'fully round'		

The precise choice of consonant depends on a number of factors, and there is some degree of freedom, but the avoidance of repetition is a major consideration.

---

[13] Thanks to Orhan Orgun for help with this section.

Closer consonants, and coda consonants, exert more influence than do more distant ones, in line with the view of identity avoidance put forward in Pierrehumbert (1993a).

This echo-word type of reduplication accompanied by melody replacement shows a clear tension between a desire for repetition, which can be seen as the need to satisfy a constraint REPEAT, and avoidance of repetition, or a satisfaction of the OCP. The OCP is higher ranked, ruling out total reduplication, but REPEAT plays a central role in ensuring that the overall system is still one of reduplication, with only a minimal difference between base and reduplicant. In the next section I will discuss one complex case of this type, Javanese, in more detail, showing how this tension is played out. Javanese avoids repetition of two kinds: repetition of the entire stem, and repetition of the vowel [a]. It also has two output constraints, REPEAT, and a requirement that the second syllable have the vowel [a]. These interact in interesting ways, as we see in the next section.

5.1 Javanese

Javanese has a pattern of reduplication that is usually referred to as Habitual Repetitive, shortened to Hab-rep. It applies to verbs, adjectives, and even nouns. The whole stem is reduplicated, and then the vowel in the last syllable of the first half is replaced by [a]. Most roots are bi-syllabic, so usually the second syllable has the vowel [a]. However, if the stem is longer or shorter it becomes clear that the locus of [a] is consistently the final syllable of the first half. Some typical data is given below; all examples are given in phonemic transcription unless allophonic details become relevant. [14]

(56) **Normal pattern of Habitual-Repetitive (Hab-reps) Reduplication**

eliŋ	*elaŋ-eliŋ*	'remember'
tuku	*tuka-tuku*	'buy'
ele?	*ela?-ele?*	'bad'
bul	*bal-bul*	'puff'

In most cases, it is not possible to tell whether reduplication here is prefixing or suffixing in nature, a point made independently by McCarthy and Prince (1995). This suggests that it is not a type of affixation at all, but rather compounding of the stem with itself, with both halves of equal status. The reduplication is accomplished in response to the constraint REPEAT(Stem), which rules out any output without a reduplicated stem. See Yip (forthcoming) for

---

[14] Javanese has six vowel phonemes, /i,u,e,o,a,ə/. For a full treatment of the phonology of Javanese vowels see Dudas (1968), Yallup (1982). The data here is drawn from Dudas (1968), Kenstowicz (1986), and Horne (1964). For more detailed discussion of Hab-rep reduplication, see Yip (forthcoming).

arguments that reduplication is output-based. In addition to the reduplication itself, Hab-reps consistently use /a/ in the second syllable. This introduced [a] would traditionally be analyzed as an affix that forms part of the Hab-rep morphology. I will argue that its appearance is instead the result of an output constraint requiring the vowel of the appropriate syllable to be [a]. I formulate this constraint below:

(57) σ_2=a: The final syllable of the first half of Hab-reps must have an [a] nucleus

With these basics in hand, we can return to the OCP. The interest of the Javanese Hab-reps lies in their diverse mechanisms for avoiding identity of various kinds. First, the output may never have both halves completely identical to each other. The constraint in (58) achieves this immediately if the input ends in any vowel other than /a/, but what if it ends in /a/? The data are given below:

(58)   udan   udan-uden   'rain'   *udan-udan
         kumat   kumat-kumet   'have a relapse'   *kumat-kumat
         edan   edan-eden   'crazy'   *edan-edan
         tak   tak-tek   'tap'   *tak-tak

Simple satisfaction of σ_2=a would result in perfect total reduplication. Instead, the vowel of the second half dissimilates to [e]. The following constraint embodies the avoidance of total identity typical of Hab-reps; I should emphasize that other forms of reduplication in the language do allow complete reduplication , such as abat-abat 'century, PL'.

(59) OCP (Stem): Hab-reps must not consist of two identical stems.

These two constraints are both surface true and undominated. Between them they select udan-uden as the optimal candidate as shown below:

(60)

/udan/	σ_2=a	OCP(stem)
☞ a. udan-uden		
b. udan-udan		*!
c. uden-udan	*!	

The simplest argument in favor of treating [a] as the response to an output constraint, rather than as an affix, is based on the fact that identity violations can never be resolved by changing this introduced [a]. The dissimilation site is always the *other* /a/. If /a/ were an affix, it would be necessarily to somehow stipulate the choice of target, but the output-based analysis immediately explains the immunity of the introduced /a/ to change.

A different kind of identity avoidance is found if the input has /a/ in the first syllable. From what we have seen so far, we would expect to find outputs in which the first half has /a/ in both syllables, so that /lali/ would have a Hab-rep *lala-lali*, but instead we observe dissimilation of the root /a/ to [o]:

(61)
lali	*lola-lali*	'forget'	**lala-lali*
adus	*odas-adus*	'bathe'	**adas-adus*
melaku	*meloka-melaku*	'walk'	**meloka-melaku*

Following the same analytical approach used above, I formulate the following constraint:

(62)   *OCP (a): Sequences of /a/ are not allowed.

Note that the constraint does not apply across stem boundaries, since *lola-lali* is well-formed. The domain of this constraint is the stem, with the introduced [a] analyzed as part of the stem, confirming our earlier claim that it is not an affix. Note also that Kenstowicz (1986) has shown that Javanese roots with two identical vowels must have a single vowel melody occupying two nuclear slots. The argument rests on the fact that allophonic rules show their effects on both root vowels, even if only one of the vowels is in the proper context. Kenstowicz (1986) argues that this behavior is to be expected if these roots have one melody linked to both nuclei. This representation in turn follows if Javanese obeys the OCP as an MSC on the vowel tier. The OCP(a) constraint can now be seen as a specific instance of a more general constraint OCP(seg) found throughout Javanese vowel phonology.

Following precisely parallel arguments to those we used for a>e, we may understand why it is the root /a/, not the introduced [a], that changes to [o]. The following tableau demonstrates this point: candidate (b), in which the introduced /a/ has changed to [o], violates σ_2=a, and is thus eliminated.

(63)

/lali/	σ_2=a	OCP(a)
☞ a. lola-lali		
b. lalo-lali	*!	
c. lala-lali		*!

The ranking of OCP(a) >> FAITHFULNESS is validated by the following tableau:

(64)

/lali-lali/	OCP(a)	FAITHFULNESS
☞ a. lola-lali		*
b. lala-lali	*!	

We have now seen two types of dissimilation that conspire to remove identity violations. I leave for further research the question of why one chooses [e] while the other chooses [o] as their output vowel.

In the previous section I proposed that echo-word reduplication is a response to a contraint REPEAT. This means that there is a tension between a requirement that *penalizes* a sequence of two identical stems, OCP(Stem), and one that *requires* two identical stems, REPEAT(Stem). The two constraints are given here for comparison.

(65)   REPEAT (Stem) : Hab-Reps must consist of two identical stems.
(66)   OCP (Stem):   Hab-reps must not consist of two identical stems.

It is the former that produces the effect of total reduplication, but this is then minimally destroyed by the latter. The constraint REPEAT(Stem) plays a crucial role in ensuring that the dissimilations we observe are indeed minimal: a single vowel changes, just enough to satisfy OCP(Stem). [15] The following tableau demonstrates how this works; candidate (b), with two vowel changes, has two violations of REPEAT(Stem), and loses to candidate (a), which has only one violation.

(67)

udan$_{HAB-REP}$	OCP(Stem)	REPEAT(Stem)
☞ a. udan-uden		*
b. udan-iden		**!
c. udan-udan	*!	

---

[15] One unexplained issue is why in the second half only the vowel /a/ ever dissimilates. /udan/ could surface as *udan-ıdan* and satisfy OCP(Stem), and yet such changes are never found.

For a discussion of how to handle language-specific and morpheme-specific constraints in OT, see Yip (forthcoming).

I have argued that two aspects of Hab-Reps are best handled by output constraints. Firstly, the introduced [a] is present in response to the constraint σ_2=a. Secondly, the reduplication itself, and the dissimilations that accompany it, are the result of a set of contradictory output constraints OCP(Stem), OCP(a), vs. REPEAT(Stem). The Javanese data argue for two conclusions. First, at least some morphology must be handled by output constraints, and the inputs (if any: see Russell 1995) have morphological features, such as the information that something is a Hab-Rep, but not necessarily concrete morphemes, like /a/, or even abstract ones, like RED. Second, conditions that enforce identity, and avoid identity, can make reference to phonological objects, like the vowel /a/, or morphological entities, like Stem.

6. Conclusions

I have argued that avoidance of identity is found in many areas of morphology, not just in phonology, and that these phenomena should be given a unified treatment in terms of a family of OCP constraints. This constraint would appear to be part of a more general cognitive pattern, as argued by Pierrehumbert (1993a), suggesting that the nomenclature OCP is inappropriate, and should be replaced by something more general like *REPEAT. See Yip (forthcoming) for such an approach, prompted in part by the comments of Brentari and others at this conference.

The theme of this conference is the relationship of morphology to other components of the grammar, and I will end by tackling this issue with respect to phonology and morphology. The most important generalization to emerge from the facts examined here is almost trivially obvious:

(68)   The identity avoidance is fundamentally phonological in nature

That is, the starting point for all the cases discussed here is an abhorrence of phonological identity of some kind. This may not be a sufficient reason for avoiding identity, but it is always a necessary one. I conclude that we are dealing here with a phonological phenomenon, but it may or may not *also* be a morphological phenomenon. In other words, we must ask if we can distinguish clearly whether a sharp line can be drawn between the two components as far as their treatment of identity avoidance is concerned?

There are, as we have seen, many kinds of non-phonological information needed for the identity calculation. If we try to draw a firm boundary between phonology and morphology, we do not necessarily deny the possibility that morphological information can be used by phonology, or that morphology can use information from phonology. Such a division does however have two implications:

(69)   a. Information transfer between the two components should be constrained in certain ways

b. Each component should have its own grammar, principles of well-formedness, etc.

If neither of these is true, then calling either phonology or morphology "components" is meaningless, merely a descriptive convenience. If only one is true, this is, in my view, sufficient to consider the two components distinct.

The first criterion, restricted information flow, does not block information transfer, but requires that it be somehow limited to certain channels or directions. Morphological information is well-known to be available to phonology in multitudinous ways. Cyclic phenomena, lexically restricted rules, and the whole edifice of lexical phonology, make this point quite clear. It is also true that phonological information plays a role in morphology, as shown by the work of Carstairs, and the recent work of Mester and Tranel discussed above. Information flow, then, must be two-way. It might still be possible to constrain the *type* of information flow, but it is not clear to me at present that this is the case. For example, the phonological information needed by morphology must include syllabic information (French, Turkana *-isi/-u*), metrical information (Latin, Italian *fin-/finisc-*), and segmental information (Hungarian *-ol/-(a)sz*; English *-ion, -ition, -ion*). The type of morphological information needed by phonology must include structural information (root, prefix, suffix, headedness of compounds (Malayalam: Mohanan 1982)), construction- specific information (Habitual Repetitives in Javanese), vocabulary-type (Germanic vs. Graeco-Roman in English, Yamato vs. Sino-Japanese, etc), and categorical information (English extrametricality in noun stress vs. verb stress).

The second criterion, separate grammars, is also unclear. In Optimality Theory, Alignment theory supposes a single set of constraints whose arguments can be morphological or phonological (especially prosodic) entities. And in the phenomena discussed in this paper the OCP appears to take as its arguments phonological, syllabic, morphological or word-sized units. At the very least, then, there is an overlap between the two components in the form of a shared set of rules, principles or constraints.

It looks, then, as though neither of the criteria in (61) can be satisfied, and we may have to conclude that phonology and morphology blur into each other too much for us to consider them as discrete formal components. This does not of course change the fact that both sets of phenomena form worthy objects of study, nor that the terms remain useful as rough labels for domains of study. Rather it reinforces what linguists have always known: phonologists and morphologists have a lot to learn from each other's domains, and the boundary line between them is not sharply defined.

References

Anderson, Stephen. 1992. *A-morphous Morphology*. Cambridge University Press.

Brentari, Diane. 1995. Comments on the Paper by Yip. (this volume).

Carstairs, Andrew. 1990. Phonologically Conditioned Suppletion. In W. Dressler, H. Luschützky, O. Pfeiffer, and J. Rennison, eds., *Contemporary Morphology*, 35–40. Mouton de Gruyter, Berlin, New York.

Chao, Yuen-Ren. 1968. *A Grammar of Spoken Chinese*. Berkeley: University of California Press.

Cohn, Abigail, and John McCarthy. 1994. Alignment and Parallelism in Indonesian Phonology. Ms, Cornell and UMass.

Demircan, Ömer. 1987. Emphatic reduplications in Turkish. H. Boeschoten and L. Verhoeven, ed., Studies in Modern Turkish: *Proceedings of the 3rd Conference on Turkish*, 24–41. Tilburg University Press.

Deng, Yurong. 1995. The reduplication of monosyllabic adjectives in Tengxian dialect. (In Chinese). *Fangyan* 33–46.

Dobrovolsky, M. 1987. Why CVC in Turkish Reduplication. In P. Liliw and M. Saari, eds., *The Nordic Languages and Modern Linguistics 6* , 131–146. Helsinki.

Dudas, Karen. 1968. *The Phonology and Morphology of Modern Javanese* Ph D Dissertation, U. of Illinois.

Golston, Chris. 1994. The Syntax-Phonology Interface in Optimality Theory. Paper presented at *WCCFL* XIII, Berkeley

Golston, Chris. 1995. Syntax Outranks Phonology : Evidence from Ancient Greek. *Phonology* 12:343–368.

Hammond, Michael. 1995. There is no lexicon. Ms, U of Arizona, Tucson.

Horne, Elinor. 1964. *Javanese-English Dictionary*. Yale University Press.

Hyman, Larry, and Sam Mchombo. 1992. Morphotactic constraints in the Chichewa verb stem. In L. Buszard-Welcher, L.Wee and W. Weigel, eds., *Proceedings of the 18th Annual Meeting of the Berkeley Linguistics Society* : 350–364 Berkeley Linguistic Society, Berkeley.

Jaeggli, O. 1980. Remarks on *To* Contraction. *Linguistic Inquiry* 11:239–245.

Kenstowicz, Michael. 1986. Multiple Linking in Javanese. *NELS 16*

Leben, Will. 1973. *Suprasegmental phonology*. Doctoral dissertation, MIT.

Li, Sandra and C. Thompson .1981. *Mandarin Chinese: A Functional Reference Grammar*. Berkeley: U. of California Press.

McCarthy, John. 1986. OCP Effects: Gemination and antigemination. *Linguistic Inquiry* 17: 207–263.

McCarthy, John & Alan Prince. 1993a. Prosodic Morphology I: Constraint Interaction and Satisfaction. To appear, MIT Press. Technical Report #3, Rutgers University Center for Cognitive Science.

McCarthy, John & Alan Prince. 1993b. Generalized Alignment. In Geert Booij & Jaap van Marle (eds.), *Yearbook of Morphology 1993*, 79–153. Dordrecht: Kluwer. Technical Report #7, Rutgers University Center for Cognitive Science, 1993. ROA-7.

McCarthy, John & Alan Prince. 1994. The Emergence of the Unmarked: Optimality in Prosodic Morphology. In Merce` Gonza`lez (ed.), *Proceedings of the North-East Linguistics Society 24*, 333–379. Amherst, MA: Graduate Linguistic Student Association.. ROA-13.

McCarthy, John and Alan Prince. 1995. Faithfulness and Reduplicative Identity. In J. Beckman, L.W.Dickey, S.Urbanczyk eds. *Papers in Optimality Theory. UMOP* 18:249–384.

Menn, Lise and Brian MacWhinney. 1984. The Repeated Morph Constraint. *Language*: 60: 519–541

Mester, Rolf-Armin. 1994. The Quantitative Trochee in Latin. *Natural Language and Linguistic Theory*.12.1: 1–62

Milsark, Gary. 1988. Singl-ing. *Linguistic Inquiry* 19.4: 611–634

Mohanan, Tara. 1992. Case OCP: A Constraint on Word Order in Hindi. Ms, National University of Singapore.

Myers, Scott. 1993. OCP Effects in Optimality Theory. Ms., University of Texas, Austin. ROA-6.

Odden, David. 1988. AntiAntigemination and the OCP. *Linguistic Inquiry* 19: 451–75.

Perlmutter, David. 1995. A grammar can explain allomorphy. This volume.

Pierrehumbert, Janet. 1993a. Dissimilarity in the Arabic Verbal Roots. In Amy Schafer, ed.,*Proceedings of NELS 23*, 367–381. Amherst, MA: Graduate Linguistics Student Association.

Pierrehumbert, Janet. 1993b. Alignment and Prosodic Heads. ESCOL 1993. 268–286.

Prince, Alan and Paul Smolensky. 1993. Optimality theory: constraint interaction in generative grammar. To appear, MIT Press. TR-2, Rutgers University Cognitive Science Center.

Pullum, Geoff and Arnold Zwicky. 1991. A misconceived approach to morphology. *Proceedings of WCCFL 10*. 387–398.

Ross, John Robert. 1972. Doubl-ing . *Linguistic Inquiry* 3: 61–86

Russell, Kevin. 1995. Morphemes and Candidates in Optimality Theory. Ms, U. of Manitoba.

Sadock, Jerrold. 1972. A conspiracy in Danish relative clause formation. In P. Peranteau, J. Levi, G. Phares eds., *The Chicago Which Hunt: Papers from the Relative Clause Festival*. A Paravolume to Papers from the

Eighth Regional Meeting of the Chicago Linguistic Society: 59–62.

Stemberger, Joseph. 1981. Morphological Haplology. *Language*. 57.4:791–817.

Tranel, Bernard. 1994. French Liaison and Elision Revisited: a unified account with Optimality Theory. Ms, UC Irvine.

Truckenbrodt, Hubert. 1995. A prosodic constraint on extraposition and the syntax-phonology mapping. Talk given at *WCCFL* 14, University of California.

Yallup, Colin. 1982. Phonology of Javanese Vowels. In A. Halim, L. Carrington, and S. Wurm, eds., *Papers from the Third International Conference on Austronesian Linguistics, 299–319.* Canberra, Australian National University.

Yeh, Ling-hsia. 1994. Haplology in Mandarin. Ms., UMass Amherst

Yip, Moira. 1988. The Obligatory Contour Principle and phonological rules: A loss of identity. *Linguistic Inquiry* 19, 65–100.

Yip, Moira. 1992. Reduplication with fixed melodic material. In K. Broderick, ed., *Proceedings of NELS 22* Amherst, Ma: Graduate Linguistics Association. 459–476.

Yip, Moira. 1993. The interaction of ALIGN, PARSE-PLACE, and ECHO in reduplication. Talk given at ROW-I, Rutgers University. Available on the Rutgers Optimality Archive.

Yip. Moira. (forthcoming). Repetition and its avoidance: the case of Javanese. To appear in K. Suzuki and D. Elzinga, eds., *Arizona Phonology Conference 4: Features in Optimality Theory.* U. of Arizona, Coyote Papers. Tucson.

Zec, D. and S. Inkelas. 1990. Prosody constrained syntax. In S. Inkelas and D. Zec, eds. The Phonology-Syntax Connection., 365–378. Chicago: Univesrity of Chicago Press.

Zoll, Cheryl. 1994. Anchors away: a unified treatment of latent segments and floating features. Ms., University of California, Berkeley.

Comments on the Paper by Yip

DIANE BRENTARI

1 Introduction

My comments on Moira Yip's paper will address three main points.[1]
The first concerns whether using Optimality Theory (OT) offers advantages
over a derivational account of morphological haplology. I will conclude
that it does. The second point concerns the ways in which Yip has extended
the notion of the Obligatory Contour Principle (OCP). Should we employ
the OCP to account for identity avoidance when the units are not purely
phonological, when they are larger than a single segment, or when they are
non adjacent in a strict sense (e.g., the *-ing* case in English)? My third
point will address the way in which morphological constraints are expressed
and combined with phonological constraints in Yip's constraint tableaux to
account for identity avoidance. For our purposes, I will define the type of
identity avoidance which involves morphology or "morphological
haplology" as that set of operations which produces surface alternations in
order to avoid adjacent morphemes with identical phonological shapes.

2 OT and Identity Avoidance

With respect to the use of OT to account for identity avoidance, I think
the OT account of the haplology facts has several advantages over a
derivational account, and raises one challenge for OT as well. By using the
constraints *REPEAT[2] and MORPHDIS, we will see that OT economizes and
systematizes phenomena that appear to be due to disparate causes if one uses
a derivational account. The advantages of OT are only partially due to the
constraint tableaux; a formalism that allows representations to play a greater
role in expressing phonological operations is equally responsible for making
possible a more explanatory account of haplology. These developments
began with autosegmental phonology (Goldsmith 1976) and were continued
with developments in the use of the syllable and higher order prosodic
structure to explain phonological phenomena (McCarthy 1979, Prince 1983,
Itô 1986, McCarthy & Prince 1986). The OCP itself illustrates this
because it is a structural condition that is active at the level of
autosegmental tiers as well as at the level of whole segments (Odden 1986,
McCarthy 1986, Yip 1988). The challenge to OT is to address the set of

---

[1] Since Yip substantively revised and added to the paper presented at the
conference, I have responded to the version submitted to the volume.

[2] I will address my reasons for calling the OCP *REPEAT in §2.

questions surrounding constraints which refer to the phonological shapes of particular morphemes and their integration into constraint tableaux.

The problem of haplology and identity avoidance was given attention by Stemberger (1981) and by Ross (1972) using a derivational account and serially applied rules; there are insights from these works that are relevant here. Stemberger and Yip both correctly point out that in order to account for even the canonical cases of haplology involving a single segment (e.g., the case of POSS-*s* and the PL-*s* in English), a derivational approach must appeal to vacuous or semi-vacuous rule application, which is problematic.

There are two examples of haplology from Choctaw from Stemberger 1981, which illustrate the advantages of an OT account of haplology. Following analyses by Lombardi and McCarthy (1991) and Nicklas (1974), some basic facts about Choctaw are as follows. Choctaw has iambic foot structure, with Light-Heavy (L-H), Light-Light (L-L), Heavy (H), or Light (L) expansions; because of its lack of participation in a number of morphological processes, the entire final syllable is sometimes considered extraprosodic in predicates (i.e., verbs and some adjectives). There are no word-internal "super-heavy" syllables CV:C; in rare cases they may occur word-finally, and the final C is considered extraprosodic. Hiatus is tolerated only at the prefix+stem boundary, not at the stem+suffix boundary. There are no clusters allowed in syllable codas.

The first example comes from causative constructions in Choctaw, and it shows how phonological constraints unrelated to the OCP or identity avoidance can conspire to achieve something that looks like haplology, but which doesn't involve suppression of material due to identity avoidance, per se. This type of causative suffixation adds -C*i* to a verb stem, geminating the preceding consonant as in (1a); shortening the stem vowel preceding the geminate when it is long is also a result as in (1b); however, when the root already ends in a geminate, the result is not a triple consonant (1c-d); furthermore, forms ending in a vowel are reported not to take this suffix (1e) (data from Stemberger 1981). Stemberger treats this case as one of normal affixation involving lack of addition, considering it to be a marginal case of haplology. I would argue that this is a case of maximum constraint satisfaction of purely phonological constraints on syllable structure and on metrical structure, and it should not be described as haplology at all.

(1)   a. *akam-* 'close', caus. *akammi* 'close (something)
       b. *kaso:f-* 'clean', caus. *kasoffi* 'make clean'
       c. *koĉĉ-go* out of', caus. *koĉĉi* 'take out of' (**koĉĉĉi*)
       d. *fokk-* 'be inside of', caus. *fokki* 'put inside of' (**fokkki*)
       e. *lakna-* 'yellow', caus. *laknai* (**lakknai, *laknnai*)

An OT account using metrical and syllabic constraints is sufficient to account for the forms in (1). Hiatus is prohibited by the constraint ONS, which requires syllables to have an onset. The constraint CODACON disallows complex codas, where "complex" is defined as having two slots on the timing tier; geminates (C_aC_a), consonant clusters (C_aC_b), or the second half of a long vowel plus a consonant (VC) are thereby disallowed in codas, except in word-final position, where the final segment is extraprosodic. Superheavy syllables are allowed word-finally by a combination of two constraints—NONFINALITY and ALIGN (affix to foot, leftmost), which can result in an extraprosodic elements at the right word edge, in the form of consonants or whole syllables. The Foot Structure is captured by the constraints FTBIN and IAMBIC. MAX and DEP (proposed in McCarthy and Prince 1995) capture "correspondences" or identity relations between the input and output forms. MAX (formerly PARSE) insures that all material in the input has a correspondent in the output; that is, don't delete anything from the input. DEP (formerly FILL) insures that all material in the output has a correspondent in the input; that is, don't add anything to the form that isn't in the input. These constraints are listed in (2); the tableaux containing only the relevant constraints for *fokk-i, kasof-fi* , and *lakna* are given in (3). Notice that none of the constraints in (2) involve morphology in any way.

(2) Principle prosodic constraints of Choctaw
       ONS: all syllables require an onset
       CODACON: no complex codas. *CV: C, *CVCC
       IAMBIC: L, H, L-L, or L-H expansions are okay
       NONFINALITY: no prosodic head of prosodic word is final
       ALIGN: Affix to foot, leftmost
       MAX: Every element in S_1 has a correspondent in S_2.
       DEP(C): Every consonant in S_2 has a correspondent in S_1.

(3) Tableau of *fokki, kasoffi,* and *lakna*

fokk-Ci	CODACON	ONS	DEP(C)	MAX
☞ fokki				*
fokkki	*!			
fokkCi	*!		*	

kaso:f-Ci	CODACON	ONS	DEP(C)	MAX
☞kasoffi				
kaso:ffi	*!			
kaso:fCi	*!		*	

lakna-Ci	CODACON	ONS	DEP(C)	MAX
laknai		*		
laknaCi			*	
laknnai	*			
☞ Ø				

Akam-Ci (1a) undergoes affixation straightforwardly, resulting in *akammi; kaso:f-Ci* (1b)/(3b) geminates the stem final consonant and shortens the stem vowel, since otherwise CODACON would be violated, resulting in *kasoffi. Fokk-Ci* (1d)/(3a) does not geminate the stem-final C —not because of identity avoidance, but because it would create a complex coda and violate CODACON if a CCC cluster were created—so the final C-slot is not realized, thereby violating lower ranked MAX, resulting in *fokki.* Finally, there are no outputs of vowel-final stems+causative suffix that are structurally well-formed with respect to the top three ranked constraints, such as *lakna- Ci* (1e); therefore, the result is the null set, and no stem form having this structure is realized with this causative suffix. We must conclude on the basis of these forms that CODACON and ONS are high-ranking constraints in Choctaw, the violation of which is fatal. We can also conclude that between MAX and DEP, DEP is the higher ranked constraint; otherwise we might expect lakna-Ci to surface, where C might be a filler consonant of some type.[3] Recall that DEP requires that all information in the output have a correspondent in the input. I have specified the particular DEP constraint needed for Choctaw as DEP(C), because the forms in the next section clearly require epenthetic vowels. This apparent case of haplology requires no special identity avoidance constraint, and it can be accounted for by constraints that exist independently in the language.

The second Choctaw case comes from forms translated as "instantaneous" or "h-grade" adjectives; the forms surface with an [h] after the penultimate vowel (Stemberger 1981, Nicklas 1974). If two consonants follow this vowel, a (short) copy of the vowel is placed after the infixed /h/; but when the first of two consonants following the penultimate vowel is already /h/, no additional /h/ is added (4). This case cannot be explained without some type of identity avoidance constraint, and therefore is a true case of morphological haplology.

---

[3] Another logical possibility is that there are no appropriate filler consonants for this purpose in the language.

(4)　　a. *cito* 'big', inst. *cih[o]to*
　　　　b. *lakna* ' yellow' inst. *lah[a]kna*
　　　　c. *toh[o]bi* ' white, inst. *toh[o]bi (*toh[o]h[o]bi, *tohhbi)*
　　　　d. *coh[o]mi* ' almost', inst. *coh[o]mi (*cohohomi, *cohhmi)*

The short echo vowel in (4b) might be seen as a strategy to satisfy *CODACON (no complex codas); the insertion of a 'filler' vowel is allowed due to fact that the DEP constraint applies only to consonants—DEP(C). Upon investigating the forms in Stemberger (1981) further, it appears that an echo vowel appears after all instances of [h].[4] The single surface /h/ in (4c-d) clearly has two sources—from the base and from the affix, and, crucially, we cannot explain the deletion of one of them without some type of identity avoidance mechanism, like that proposed by Moira Yip in her paper. Without it, we cannot explain why *tohobi* is the preferred output form over *tohohobi,,* a form which does not violate any of the constraints in (2). At this point we also introduce another constraint proposed by McCarthy and Prince (1995)—MORPHDIS (Morpheme Disjointedness): "distinct instances of morphemes have distinct contents, tokenwise," also used by Yip. This constraint discriminates against all types of haplology. In Choctaw h-grade forms, MORPHDIS must be ranked below the identity avoidance constraint, which Yip calls *REPEAT (Yip, in press)

(5)Tableau for *tohobi*

toh-h-bi	*REPEAT	*CODACON	MORPHDIS	DEP(C)	MAX
☞tohobi			*		*
tohhbi	!*	*			
tohohobi	!*				

To summarize this section, I have given additional support for Moira Yip's use of an OT analysis for identity avoidance, showing that OT discriminates between cases that require a haplology account, which is equated with the use of an explicit *REPEAT constraint, and those that can be explained on the basis of independently motivated phonological constraints. The causative suffix in Choctaw can be accounted for by

---

[4] The form in (4c) is a different surface form than that cited in Stemberger (1981). He cites the surface form of the stem as *tohbi* and the h-grade form as *tohobi*. After consulting a linguist who has worked with a Choctaw informant (George Aaron Broadbent, p.c.) it appears that an echo vowel is inserted after all 'h's', not just those of the h-grade forms. Given these new facts, the form reported by Stemberger as the stem form is in error; the stem surfaces as *tohobi*, as does the instaneous adjectival form. The two surface forms are identical.

constraint satisfaction without a constraint for identity avoidance; the h-grade suffix requires an identity avoidance constraint and shows how haplology results from an *REPEAT >> MORPHDIS constraint ranking, rather than the ranking, MORPHDIS >> *REPEAT, which results in morphological disjointedness.

3 The OCP and Identity Avoidance

Yip argues that the identity avoidance phenomena we have seen can, at least in spirit, be considered extensions of the OCP. Originally proposed in Leben 1973 (6), the OCP has been the subject of heated debate, especially in the late eighties (McCarthy 1986, Odden 1986, 1988, Yip 1988). The main points of controversy concern the degree to which the OCP is universal as a phonological principle, and the extent to which it can be extended beyond its original formulation in the purely phonological component of the grammar. Many of the specific questions addressed in attempts to expand the range of the OCP concern the meaning of the terms "identical" and "adjacent," given the possibilities presented in autosegmental phonology and feature geometry. Work for and against expanding the coverage of the OCP has also addressed whether its use outside the domain of the single morpheme increases or decreases its force as an agent of predictability in phonology, and whether the idiosyncratic restrictions that must be placed on the OCP in certain morphophonological circumstances sufficiently weaken it so as to make it less than a universal principle (Odden 1986, 1988).

(6) The Obligatory Contour Principle (Leben 1973)
Adjacent identical tones are banned from the lexical representation of a morpheme.

Before getting into the identity avoidance cases, I would like to make one clarifying remark about interpretations of the OCP. If we look at Leben's formulation, we see that the OCP can potentially perform two grammatical functions. One is at the level of inputs, and here the OCP is a principle requiring economy of phonological representations. It says, in essence, that when two elements have identical specifications and need not be separated for morphological or lexically contrastive purposes, they must not be separate. Another function that the OCP performs operates at the level of outputs, and underscores the terms "obligatory" and "contour" in the OCP's name: "The OCP enforces alternating patterns, and the quintessential example of an alternating pattern is the perfect grid." (Yip 1988). This captures the fact that alternation is preferred in the speech stream—between C's and V's, between heavy and light syllables, etc. The effects we see in haplology are those that effect output forms, rather than input structure, since we can assume that the morphological component of the grammar (if there is one) would prefer each morpheme to have a distinct shape, following MORPHDIS.

I would like to make a proposal to formulate "identity avoidance" within an OT framework as a family of constraints, similar to MAX , ALIGN, DEP ; it could be abbreviated IDAVOID, or *REPEAT. The OCP, roughly as formulated in Leben (1973) could be seen as the canonical case of *REPEAT in the phonological component; that is, tier adjacent, morpheme internal *REPEAT. The OCP could be further specified even in phonology, as Yip and Pierrehumbert (1993) argue, with respect to whether all tiers—or a specific tier or set of tiers—are subject to *REPEAT under specific phonological conditions. This would in fact provide a way to account for the language specificity of *REPEAT in some cases, while recognizing its status as a universal constraint on underlying representations. *REPEAT could be specified as a relation between two phonological constituents (e.g., *REPEAT(V)/PrWd -a), or between a phonological and a morphological or syntactic constituent. The *REPEAT statements for the cases presented are given in (7).

(7) Examples of two-part *REPEAT relational statements

*REPEAT(seg)/NP	-s
*REPEAT(-σ)/VP	-ing
*REPEAT(-σ)/VP	-ko
*REPEAT(−σ)/VP/S	-le
*REPEAT(-σ)/NP	-de
*REPEAT(V)/PrWd	-a

One generalization we can make on the basis of the cases in Yip's paper is that identity avoidance is more strongly in force in the same syntactic domain. This is supported by examples from English (8) and from German (9), where sentences containing two phonologically identical elements are tolerated only if the elements are in different syntactic constituents.

(8) English: one stem [s], one NP suffix -s , one auxiliary -s
   a.   Davis's is great. -> Davis's's great.
        (Context: Talk about the weather in different parts of the US.)
   b.   The Prince's is coming -> The Prince's's coming.
        (Context: a motorcade of cars is making its way down a street, and the Prince's car just came into view.)

(9) German: one prepositional -auf, -an attached to a particle da, and one separable prefix auf-, an-
   a.   . . .   Er pabt darauf auf. (verb: aufpassen 'to pay attention to')
        (Eng: He paid attention to that.)
   b.   . . .   Sie lehnt daran an. (verb: anlehnen 'lean against')
        (Eng.: She leaned against it.)

    c. . . . Der Teig sitzt darauf auf (verb: aufsitzen 'to rest on')
        (Eng.: The dough is resting/sitting over there/on that place.)
    d. (from Golston, 1994) . . . die, dei dei Blumen gekauft haben'
        (Eng, "those who have bought the flowers")

The specific *REPEAT would replace OCP in the tableaux in Yip's paper. An additional benefit of these specific statements is that they would draw the discussion of the OCP away from any particular formulation of it, and place it in the realm where it can be discussed as a constellation of language-particular effects, all of which share the idea that there is a strong pressure to avoid adjacent phonological material in a limited range of language-particular ways.

One important similarity between the OCP as a principle constraining surface forms and *REPEAT is the variety of ways languages have of avoiding such constraint violations, which can be generally characterized as movement, change, deletion, and epenthesis. I will briefly review such cases, presented in Yip 1988. Degemination is a form of deletion of one of the identical elements; this familiar strategy is employed in Seri, where the second of two glottal stops in a syllable is deleted (10). In Berber an OCP violation resulting from two adjacent coronals causes total assimilation (11). A rule in Japanese that adds a [+voice] feature to the first consonant of the second half of compound is blocked (a type of dissimilation); otherwise, the rule would create an OCP violation (12).

(10a) Degemination (Deletion) in Seri
        ʔa-a:ʔ-sanx -> *ʔaa:sanx* 'who was carried
        ʔi-ʔ-a:ʔ-kasni > *ʔiʔa:kasni* 'my being bitten'

(10b)

```
On Nu Co      On Nu Co
 |     |  |     |
 C     C -> C
 |     |  |        ø
 ʔ     ʔ  ʔ
```

(11a) Total Assimilation in Berber
        t-dlu -> *dlu* 'she covered'
        t-dfəs -> *ddfəs* 'she folded'
        ad-t-ru -> *attru* 'she will cry'
        ad-t-fa-m -> *attfam* 'you(pl.) will yawn'

(11b)

```
    [+cor]      [+cor]
      |           |
      C     +     C
      |           |
   [αvoice]    [αvoice]
```

(12a) Dissimilation in Japanese
    iro-kami -> irogami 'colored paper'
    maki-sushi ->makizushi 'rolled sushi'
    *kami-kaze -> *kamigaze* 'divine wind'
    *siro-tabi -> *sirodabi* 'white tabi'

(12b)   * C   C
              | |
        [αvoice] [αvoice]

(13) Movement-away (Stress Clash Resolution)
    a. English
        i. Dundée mármalade -> Dùndee mármalade
        ii. achromátic léns -> àchromatic léns
    b. Italian (dialectal)
        i. *metá tórta -> mèta tórta*
        ii. *cittá spórca -> cítta spórca*

Epenthesis and movement-away are strategies for the resolution of *REPEAT violations employed by languages to resolve purely phonological OCP violations as well as violations of *REPEAT involving morphological haplology Epenthesis occurs in the English case of PL-s and POSS-s haplology. Movement-away is used to resolve OCP violations, as in stress-clash resolution in English and in a dialect of Italian (13), as well as in the resolution of *REPEAT violations. When the syntax provides us with a well-formed extraposed option and a well-formed center-embedded option, the phonology will decide (Golston, 1994). Sometimes, alternates offered by allomorphs already existing in the language can provide an option for resolution of constraint violations—in French (Tranel 1994), in Latin (Mester1994), and in Estonian (Kager 1995). The choice of allomorph in these cases is motivated by constraints on foot or syllable structure; however, in Italian, there is an example that cannot be explained without a *REPEAT constraint; it is motivated by no otherwise existing phonological constraint (14).

(14) Chosen Allomorph motivated by *REPEAT (Italian)

preposition+MPL article before C-initial nouns	before V-initial nouns
dei cani 'of the dogs'	*degli amici* 'of the friends'
dei professori 'of the professors'	*degli artisti* 'of the artists'
dei ripasti 'of the meals'	*degli arbori* 'of the trees'
**dei dei* 'of the gods'	*degli dei* 'of the gods'

The contracted preposition+article plural masculine form of the partitive construction is *dei* before consonant-initial words (except when the consonant(s) are an s-cluster or an 's') and *degli* before vowel-initial words; however, when this construction appears before the word *dei* 'gods' the surface form is *degli dei* 'of the gods', rather than the expected **dei dei*, which would create a case of identical adjacent forms. We can conclude from these examples that the strategies employed to resolve OCP violations and *REPEAT violations are wide-ranging, and that the strategies of conflict resolution are sufficiently similar to warrant placing the OCP and haplology under the single family of constraints *REPEAT.

4 The integration of phonological constraints with other types of constraints in constraint tableaux

The final point I wish to address in this comment is the challenge of finding a principled way of integrating purely phonological constraints with those that refer to specific morphemes of a particular phonological shape, such as POSS(s) and PL(s) in English, and DAT(ko) and ACC(ko) in Hindi. Whatever is the correct formulation of morphological structure, we can minimally assume that there is a L-specific hierarchical arrangement of morphological features that must be taken into account when phonological tableaux include morphological constraints, which can be thought of as PARSE^{morpheme} constraints. It appears that Yip has ranked PARSE^{morpheme} constraints, such as those for -*s* in English and -*ko* in Hindi, according to a principle, which says that the closer to the stem a morpheme is, the more likely for it to be realized, and the further away from the stem it is, the more likely it is to be deleted. In the English case, the plural morpheme is more tightly bound to the noun stem and the clitic is more promiscuous (Sadock 1991), and, therefore, mobile or even—according to the tacit assumption stated above—expendable. By analogy, because datives are thought to bear a tighter relation to the stem than do accusatives, we can perhaps assume that it is the accusative whose phonological shape is deleted in Hindi *ko*- haplology. In sum, how do we know which of the two phonological realizations of the two identically expressed morphemes survives? McCarthy and Prince (1995) address this question in their analysis of reduplication in Chumash, and place the responsibility on the GEN function. "The relevant condition on GEN must therefore compare morphological structure with its expression in phonological structure, banning certain kinds of mismatches." (McCarthy and Prince 1995:322). Illicit mismatches might be those, for example, which involve different ranking M(orphological)-Scope and P(honological)-Scope of affixes. For example, in the case of reduplication, McCarthy and Prince (1995) propose that GEN would not present us a form with the morphemes in all possible orders, with all possible scope possibilities. In a form, such as *siksikuk* (from RED+*s*+*ikuk* or possibly *s*+RED+*iksuk* in Chumash, the question is whether the first [s] or the second [s] is the expression of the prefix.

McCarthy and Prince suggest that only forms with the structure RED-prefix-stem are possible outputs of GEN, and therefore, the first [s] must be an expression of reduplicative identity, not the expression of the prefix. This is the flip-side to the problem that haplology presents to us. In the haplology cases, we have two morphemes and one surface expression; in cases, such as in the Chumash reduplication case just mentioned, we have one morpheme and two surface expressions. Both require integration of external morphological information in constraint tableaux. In the specific cases discussed in Yip's paper, it is plausible to assume that knowing which of two PARSE^{morpheme} constraints will have the higher ranking will depend upon a hierarchy of morphological features or considerations of scope and the order of morphemes, but this topic is beyond the scope of these comments.

5. Conclusion

Yip's analysis of haplology has put in sharp relief the types of tensions that languages express, both between components and within a single component of a L-particular grammar. First, by employing MORPHDIS and *REPEAT, we can capture the morphological component's requirement that each morpheme have its own phonological expression, yet by ranking *REPEAT above MORPHDIS, we see how haplology can result. A ranking of *REPEAT above MORPHDIS expresses the tension between the aims of the morphological component and that of the phonological component; that is, each morpheme should have its own phonological shape, but that identical, adjacent shapes are problematic. Second, we can see that a language might have a REPEAT constraint (as a reduplicative morpheme) and a *REPEAT constraint requiring that the reduplicant be almost-but-not-exactly identical, as is true in the case of Javanese habitual/repetitives. These pairs of constraints expresses the tension between the requirement of reduplicants to copy the base—to have base/reduplicant identity—and the use of *REPEAT to keep them from having complete identity. These more global mismatches are lost in a model in which each operation applies serially to achieve the correct output.

References

Goldsmith, John. 1976. *Autosegmental Phonology*. Doctoral dissertation, MIT . (1979 Garland Press)

Golston, Chris. In press. Syntax Outranks Phonology: Evidence from Ancient Greek. ms. Heinrich Heine Universität, Düsseldorf. To appear in *Phonology 12*.

Inkelas, Sharon, and Orgun, Orhan. this volume. Level (Non)ordering in Recursive Morphology: Evidence from Turkish.

Itô, Junko. 1986. *Syllabic Theory in Prosodic Phonology*. Doctoral dissertation, University of Massachusetts.

Kager, René. 1995. On Affix Allomorphy and Syllable Counting. Paper presented at the Interfaces in Phonology conference, Berlin.

Leben, William. 1973. *Suprasegmental Phonology.* Doctoral dissertation, MIT .

Lombardi, Linda, & John McCarthy. 1991. Prosodic Circumscription in Choctaw Morphology. *Phonology* 8, 37-72

Nicklas, Thurston. 1974. *The Elements of Choctaw.* Doctoral dissertation, University of Michigan .

McCarthy, John. 1979. Formal problems in Semitic phonology and morphology. Doctoral dissertation, MIT .

McCarthy, John. 1986. OCP effects: Gemination and antigemination. *Linguistic Inquiry* 17, 207-63

McCarthy, John, and Alan Prince. 1986. *Prosodic Morphology I.* ms. University of Massachusetts and Rutgers University.

McCarthy, John, and Alan Prince. 1993. *Prosodic Morphology II.* ms. University of Massachusetts and Rutgers University.

McCarthy, John, and Alan Prince. 1995. Faithfulness and Reduplicative Identity. In Jill Beckman, Laura Walsh Dickey, and Suzanne Urbanczyk, eds., *Papers in Optimality Theory*, 249-384. Amherst, MA: Graduate Linguistic Student Association.

Mester, Rolf-Armin. 1994. The Quantitave Trochee in Latin. *Natural Language and Linguistic Theory* 12.1, 1-62.

Odden, David. 1986. On the Role of the Obligatory Contour Principle in Phonological Theory. *Language* 62, 353-83.

Odden, David. 1988. Anti Antigemination and the OCP. *Linguistic Inquiry 19,* 451-75.

Pierrehumbert, Janet. 1993. Dissimilarity in the Arabic Verbal Roots. In Amy Schafter, ed., *Proceedings of NELS 23*, 367-31.

Prince, Alan. 1983. Relating to the Grid. *Linguistic Inquiry 14,* 19-100.

Prince, Alan, and Paul Smolensky. 1993. *Optimality Theory: Constraint Interaction in Generative Grammar.* To be published by MIT Press.

Ross, John. 1972. Doubl-ing. *Linguistic Inquiry* 3, 61-86.

Sadock Jerrold. 1991. *Autolexical syntax.* Chicago: University of Chicago Press.

Stemberger, Joseph Paul. 1981. Morphological Haplology. *Language* 57, 791-817.

Tranel, Bernard. 1994. French Liaison and Elision Revisited: A Unified Eccount with Optimality Theory. ms. UC Irvine.

Yip, Moira. 1988. The Obligatory Contour Principle and Phonological rules: A Loss of Identity. *Linguistic Inquiry 19,* 65-100.

Yip, Moira. In press. Repetition and its Avoidance: The Case of Javanese. To appear in K. Suzuki and D. Elzinga, eds., *Arizona Phonology Conference 4: Features in Optimality Theory.* U of Arizona, Coyote Papers. Tucson.

Discussion of the Papers by Yip and Brentari

Noyer: I have a number of things to say. First of all … I think there's a lot of literature by Zwicky and his collaborators on this topic of -*s*, and there's a dissertation by Philip Miller, in which there's a chapter in which he discusses a number of cases of French cacophony rules. So you can't say [French example with * *de de*]—this is famously impossible. You can't say * *Personne ne n'a rien vu.* And so, he talks about a number of these cases in a kind of edge feature approach, but I thought those were very interesting.

I think a lot of work is being done in your proposal by the expression of constraints, so that they are allowed to refer to the same morpheme, but two different morphological requirements. Specifically, you have PLURAL or POSSESSIVE [that] can be -*s*, and something wins as long as it's got an -*s*. If it's PLURAL or POSSESSIVE or both, it's got to have an -*s*. So what that means is, -*s* suffices to discharge the need of those values to be expressed, so to speak. Now, that's kind of interesting—that's I think where part of the explanatory action resides here, it's that the constraint is formulated exactly that way.

The other thing I want to mention is I'm sort of curious about whether these cases of haplology—is it really identity? Because Miller talks about these cases where you can't get the French enclitic -*ci* and you can't get * -*ci* -*ci* , so for example, you can't say * 'this church of that village' -*ci* -*ci*, but you can't get * 'this church of that village' -*ci* -*la* either, and there, they're not phonologically identical. So this kind of brings up the question of Pierrehumbert's remark, "How close do they have to be before you start not wanting them together."

Yip: * -*ci* -*la* seems fairly clear. That would not succumb to this kind of explanation.

…

Perlmutter: Moira's paper brought up so many interesting cases, but I think hidden in the background there lurks a monster to whose presence I would like to call attention. What Optimality Theory enables you to do very nicely is to say, "OK, in this situation how do these various constraints conspire to yield the optimal output in every case?" But the monster is, How do we distinguish those cases where you get something from those cases where there's no output whatsoever? So a long time ago, a quarter of a century now, I did some work on Spanish clitics, and I had a lot of syntactic constructions which would yield a clitic sequence *se se*, with a repetition, and what I showed there I think, there are just no outputs. It's not that they accommodate to something, but no output at all will work. And I posited an inviolate or exceptionless output constraint for that. Now the question is, How can we distinguish those cases where we get some output from those cases where there's no output?

Yip: Yes, it's a big question, because the claim of Optimality Theory is that there is always some optimal candidate—it doesn't mean it's good, it doesn't mean it's perfect—but there's always something that's better than everything else. It's a claim of the theory. And so, this is a real problem. There is a technical proposal that addresses this, which says that one of the candidates in this infinite candidate set is something called the 'null parse', where nothing in the input is parsed, and that if you set up your constraint ranking, in certain circumstances, the null parse is the best you can do, and that's your zero output. So there's a technical way around it, but I think the more interesting question is, the very spirit of Optimality Theory suggests there should always be some sort of output, and I don't consider this a very satisfactory solution. I don't have a solution for that.

Perlmutter: It seems to me, one way of doing it is simply to say that certain constraints are inviolate, and that will do it, and this doesn't provide an explanation; it's a stipulation, but it gets you the facts.

Yip: Yes. I mean, I address this stuff a little bit in the stuff on double *-ing* which I didn't actually talk about for time reasons, but there just isn't any very good way of saying this double *-ing* can't be in sentences. There's nothing that people are totally happy with, and it's not clear that you're not free just to leave the *-ing* off something—that's not a way out. Well, unless you consider the infinitive to be what you get when you leave *-ing* off something, but then the semantics are a little different, so ?? *I was starting reading the book* which is weird vs. *I was starting to read the book*, they don't mean quite the same thing, and * *I'm starting read the book* is not a possible sentence of English. I suggest that dropping the *-ing* isn't going to obey all the strategies. There just doesn't seem to be any very good way to do it. You can't extrapose it— * *I started the book reading*, it's quite clear that you can't fix it up very easily, and in OT you sort of always expect that you could.

Inkelas: I'd like to expand on a couple of points that Rolf made. The first has to do with the constraints [PLURAL=s and POSS=s] ... What this bundle of constraints is essentially saying is that a word that has both PLURAL and POSSESSIVE features has to have -*s* in it. It seems to me that that's equivalent to a portmanteau analysis, where we're saying that there's one formative, -*s*, which corresponds to both these features. Now we know independently that we need to have a theory of blocking which says that a portmanteau morpheme will block the occurrence of the two separate morphemes which together would express the same features, or correspond to the same features, that the portmanteau does. Given that, I wonder if the OCP is necessary here at all.

Yip: ... As far as the plural possessive cases go, just in OT terms, the analysis that's behind [(12),(13)] that I didn't make as explicit as I might have done because of time is that those -*s*'s are being inserted by GEN. Phonological material is being inserted by GEN. That means that any phonological insertion incurs a cost because it's a Faithfulness violation; some action has taken place—well, maybe we shouldn't call GEN action. But anyway, there is a difference between the input which has no phonological material and the three candidate outputs in [(12)] which have phonological material. Now the less phonological material you put in, the less cost you incur. In other words, it's cheaper to put in one -*s* than two. So the candidate with one -*s* is better than the candidate with two -*s*'s quite apart from the OCP, just because it's the minimal action you can take in order to satisfy these constraints. And the same is true in the case of the Mandarin.

Inkelas: I think that the insight really isn't dependent on the realizational approach that you're assuming here. You could do it just as well with morphemes—I think Rolf has a paper on this where he proposes an economy constraint that says, "Have as few affixes as you can get away with."

Noyer: But really, what this says is, "If I'm PLURAL, I need to have an -*s* hanging on my right." "OK, if I'm a POSSESSIVE, I need to have an -*s* hanging on the right, and it can be the same -*s*." So, that's really how you're getting away with this, which is really what you're saying. It's like saying, well, -*s* does double duty.

Yip: Absolutely. I agree entirely. This is a particular instantiation of that familiar insight in OT.

Baker: Yeah, I have a comment on the Hindi example … it may raise some interesting questions about the interpretation of how this all fits with the syntax as well. So, you talk about [the fact] that you avoid the *-ko* that's DATIVE and the *-ko* that's ACCUSATIVE next to each other in the sentence. But it seems to me that those aren't entirely different *-ko*'s. They're probably somewhat different, but they must be at least historically related, and probably synchronically related, too. You see this pattern happening in a wide variety of languages, that the DATIVE marker gets brought over to the ACCUSATIVE, especially when it's animate and definite. That brings up the whole relationship between case marking and aspect that we talked about yesterday with Hagit, that maybe there's some kind of delimiter of the event or the endpoint of the event [that] gets that *-ko*—it's always the Goal-like thing if there's one there. If there is not one there, then certain kinds of Themes can play that same aspectual sort of syntactic role. I don't think that will get all of the texture of the facts that you give, but I think it's probably an important piece of what's underlying there, and it would have some explanatory advantage in that in the pure OCP version. You could have ranked the *-ko* to spell out ACCUSATIVE above the spell out (for) DATIVE, and I suspect that never happens in this kind of case.

Yip: That's absolutely correct …

Sells: I just wanted to continue Mark's point. I think the point about the two *-ko*'s being quite similar is a good point, but I worry about the interaction of this with syntax, in particular, the ranking you have in the tableau in [(51)]. If you think about how you get out of it, namely by having an unmarked ACCUSATIVE, we can think of that as basically incorporating the object into the verb, in some sense of incorporation, in the way that was talked about yesterday. Now that couldn't possibly happen with the DATIVE; the DATIVE here is a dative subject of the whole construction. So independently, it is possible for ACCUSATIVEs to appear without *-ko*, but not DATIVEs to appear without *-ko* … This is a statement of the fact, but it's not the thing in the grammar that you write. So the question is what is this tableau doing.

Yip: It's entirely stipulative. OK; this is my ignorance. Mohanan and my informant, neither of them made it clear to me that the *-ko* in ACCUSATIVEs can be dropped under other circumstances. In fact on the contrary, Lahiri's judgments on these was that dropping the *-ko* on the ACCUSATIVE was really a desperation [effort] that he really didn't like, but it was the only way out of the pickle. So if the facts are as you explained them, then that point is completely being missed here, and this is not a satisfactory answer. Maybe there are dialect differences in this respect in how free one is to drop these -*ko*'s.

Sells: Until you said you could drop the -*ko*, I would have thought that this was actually a case like the one David was talking about, where for cases like [(44)], that's the only way you can say it, but nobody wants to say it that way.

Yip: Well, that's my impression from my informant, that this is very much like double -*ing* in English, that's why these have double question marks by them instead of asterisks. People say them because it's the only way, I mean really the only way to say it, but unlike double -*ing* there are a few things you can do to try to fix it up.

Aronoff: A very general point. I remember that when I first read the first Prosodic Morphology manuscripts, I said, "This is very interesting, but it's not morphology." Basically, what you're dealing with here is realization, what a morphologist calls realization, and that's where the phonology hits the morphology. So, we expect this. And in fact, what you've shown is that where syntax hits phonology you get the same fact—in other words, where syntactic realization hits phonology. And that of course makes perfect sense because realization is phonology. So I don't think you've made your major point at all, because what you've demonstrated is something that we have accepted from the beginning.

Yip: Well, it wasn't my major point in the sense that it's something that bothers me or I think is earth-shaking. It also seems very normal and natural to me. So I guess it's a misunderstanding of what I would have thought morphologists would like to consider morphology. I would have thought morphologists would have thought some of this was morphology—

Aronoff: It's part of morphology, but it's the realizational part of morphology, which is the part of morphology which interacts with the phonology by definition ...

Yip: There's no suggestion intended that every aspect of morphology can be suddenly somehow dealt with in OT. The suggestion was that there were some aspects of morphology that seemed to overlap so much with phonology, to obey a similar set of principles, and that they were more interestingly viewed as being like this.

Impoverishment Theory and Morphosyntactic Markedness

ROLF NOYER

Theories of morphology differ in the means by which they account for morphological neutralization.[1] One means of deriving neutralization is through underspecification of affixes (or, of rules introducing affixes). This paper discusses a second means of expressing neutralization, namely Impoverishment (Bonet 1991, Noyer 1992, Halle & Marantz 1993, 1994, Harris 1994, Calabrese 1994). Whereas underspecification is a modification of the content of morphological signals such as affixes, Impoverishment is a simplification operation on information in the morphosyntactic positions corresponding to these signals. In this sense, Impoverishment shares important properties with Rules of Referral (Zwicky 1985, Stump 1993). Essentially, Rules of Referral are feature-changing readjustments, potentially interspersed with rules of exponence, whereas Impoverishments are normally assumed, following Bonet (1991), to be feature-deleting and to precede all spell-out rules.

I show here that feature-deleting Impoverishments are insufficiently expressive to explain neutralizations, and I propose instead that Impoverishment may effectively have feature-changing capability, but crucially is limited to moving from more marked to less marked representations, thus differing importantly from Rules of Referral. If the present proposal is correct, the space of possible grammars available to the language learner is more restricted than on Stump's (1993) theory, a desirable and important result. In this sense, the present paper hopes to contribute to the line of research begun by Carstairs (1983, 1987), that is, to provide a substantive theory of possible morphological syncretisms in natural language.

Sections 1–5 set out the assumptions of the morphological model I will employ, introduce what I will call "the paucity of marked values problem," and compare Impoverishment with Rules of Referral. In sections 6–8 I discuss the interactions of three neutralizations in the verbal

---

[1]Many ideas presented here emerged in discussion with Morris Halle, Alec Marantz, and Mark Johnson. In addition, I would like to thank audiences at Yale University and the University of Düsseldorf for helpful comments.

morphology of Nimboran (Inkelas 1993). In section 9, I show that the syntagmatic use of Impoverishment obviates the need for arbitrary position classes based solely on disjunctivity of morphemes.

1   Underspecification of Signals

All theories of morphology make use of underspecification in some form or another to express certain neutralizations. Consider for example the various forms of the Romanian adjective (Farkas 1990, Lumsden 1992):

(1)   Romanian adjectival desinences

	SG	PL
MASC	-Ø	-i
NEUT		
FEM	-ă	-e

As seen in the table above, the masculine and neuter are syncretized in the singular, whereas the neuter and feminine are syncretized in the plural. In analyzing these facts, Lumsden (1992) draws on the important Jakobsonian contrast between morphosyntactic *positions* and the morphological *signals* which occupy or realize these positions. He suggests that neutralizations such as those in the Romanian declension are neutralizations of the signals and not of the morphosyntactic positions, which are fully specified.

We might then ascribe the following content to the signals in (1).[2]

(2)   -i   [+pl +masc]
      -e   [+pl]
      -ă   [-pl +fem]
      -Ø   Elsewhere

The paradigm cells in (1) represent the range of syntactically generable feature combinations. At S-structure — after the application of agreement rules — the morphological signals in (2) compete for insertion for fully-specified positions. Only affixes consistent with the fully specified underlying position may be inserted. Beyond this, priority is given to more fully specified affixes following the principle of descending specificity (Panini; cf. the Elsewhere Condition of Kiparsky 1973).[3]

---

[2]The following diverges from the account given in Lumsden 1992 in certain details. See Farkas & Zec 1993 for further discussion.

[3]In the event that two affixes are compatible but neither's structural description is fully contained in the other's, a feature hierarchy must be consulted to determine which affix has priority (Noyer 1992, Lumsden 1992).

An important assumption underlying this view, which underlies all work now called Distributed Morphology (Halle & Marantz 1993), is that the morphological signals are provided (inserted) after syntactic rules have applied. In this sense, this model resembles other realizational theories of morphology, including Matthews 1972, Anderson 1982 and following work, and Zwicky 1985. In a rule-based realizational framework, the idea that affixes are underspecified amounts simply to the possibility that the structural description of realization rules will not exhaustively detail the environment in which the rule may apply.

2 The Paucity of Marked Values Problem

In contrast to realizational theories, affix-based lexicalist theories of morphology such as Lieber 1980, Williams 1981, and DiSciullo & Williams 1987 assume that word formation applies presyntactically.   In accordance with the Lexical Integrity Hypothesis, it is assumed that syntax is permitted to see only those properties of a word which are represented in its complex symbol (feature matrix). As a result, the complex symbol must contain all the syntactically relevant information. Problems arise for this approach when percolation of values from the affixes, along with redundancy rules supplying unmarked values, does not provide enough values to ensure the correct distribution of forms in sentences. We may call this the *paucity of marked values problem.*

Consider again for example the Romanian adjectival desinences in (2). The elsewhere affix percolates no features, so any form created with -Ø in the lexicon should (incorrectly) be able to agree with any noun, as long as feature compatibility (Unification) is the only condition on licensing of such forms. In the present case, one might attribute content to the -Ø, excluding it from all but the [−pl −fem] cases. But such a strategy is useless in detailing the heterogeneous distribution of true elsewhere affixes such as the German weak adjectival -*en* (Zwicky 1985, Carstairs-McCarthy 1992:209–210), or the Ugaritic prefix *y-* (Noyer 1992). The only option for a lexicalist account in such cases is to abandon the notion of elsewhere and to set up a variety of accidentally homophonous lexical items.

To avoid the use of accidental homophony, it might be proposed that the most specific form must be used where two lexical forms are compatible (cf. Inkelas 1993:567, Andrews 1990). But the question here is: compatible for what? If the lexical items themselves project the space of syntactic possibilities, there can be no space of possibilities autonomous from the resources of the lexicon.   As soon as positions or situations autonomous from those created by lexical resources are invoked, we are already dealing with some variant of a realizational theory, since the question is what form will be realized (or inserted) in a given autonomously generated situation.

3   Impoverishments and Rules of Referral

To avoid the paucity of marked values problem, I will assume here a realizational model like that of Halle & Marantz 1993, concentrating on the question of what operations might apply to (abstract) morphemes prior to spell-out. Such operations will manipulate only morphosyntactic features: phonological material is unavailable until spell-out.

To my knowledge, operations of this kind were first proposed in Zwicky 1985 under the heading *rules of referral* and were developed further in Stump 1993.[4]   A Rule of Referral, according to Zwicky (1985:372), stipulates "that certain combinations of features have the same realization as certain others."

Rules of Referral correspond roughly to what Bonet (1991) termed *morphological impoverishment*.   There are two important differences between Zwicky's Referrals and Bonet's Impoverishments. First, Referrals amount to feature changing operations while Impoverishments are typically feature-deleting operations.   Second, Referrals may be interspersed with rules of exponence.   Impoverishments on the other hand are assumed to apply in a block before any spell-out takes place.

For example, Zwicky (1985:378) proposes a Rule of Referral to account for the syncretism of nominative and accusative nominal ("nounal") desinences in German, such as in *klein-es*   (nom/acc sg neut 'small'). The proposed rule and its interpretation are as follows:

(3)   In the context of [CAT:Nounal], [Case: acc] has the same realization as [Case: nom].

The feature-changing nature of (3) is made clear by the fact that the rule effects a feature substitution (Zwicky 1985:378).   Thus (3) is equivalent to:

(4)   [acc] $\rightarrow$ [nom] / [Nounal ___]

However, the accusative and nominative are not always syncretized. Specifically, the two cases are distinguished in the masculine singular, hence: *klein-er* [masc nom sg strong] vs. *klein-en* [masc acc sg strong], and *klein-e* [masc nom sg weak] vs. *klein-en* [masc acc sg weak].   For this reason, Zwicky crucially orders rule (3) after the realization rules

---

[4]The idea that certain paradigm positions have the same realization as others has been explored in some detail by other authors, in particular Carstairs (1987) and Wurzel (1988).   In these works, syncretisms are normally expressed by *static equations* which assert the identity of two positions, e.g. cell A = cell B.

introducing the accusative affixes. A fragment of the proposed rule system is shown below (notation altered):

(5)   a.   [acc masc sg] → *en*   ≈ Zwicky's rule (1´)
      b.   [weak dir] → *e*   ≈ Zwicky's rule (2´)
      c.   [acc] → [nom]   ≈ Zwicky's rule (10)

The affixes of e.g., *klein-en* [masc acc sg strong] and *klein-e* [masc acc sg weak], are introduced by rules (5a) and (5b) respectively, before the syncretism (5c) takes place.

Bonet (1991), investigating the realization of clitics in Romance and elsewhere, also proposes adjustments of morphosyntactic representations prior to realization. For example, Bonet observes that in Warlpiri there is a specific form of the reflexive only for the 1st person singular. In all other persons and numbers, a default reflexive is used. To obtain this distribution, she proposes that the values [1 pl] are deleted from a 1st person plural reflexive:

(6)   [1 pl] → ∅ / [reflexive]

The morphological readjustment rule (6) Impoverishes a [1 pl] reflexive morpheme, making the insertion of the specific [1 refl] clitic impossible. This exemplifies the general pattern: Impoverishment *deletes* certain values and bleeds a later insertion process.

4   Representations and Expressiveness

So far, the achievements of Impoverishment (and, by implication, of Referral) seem rather unimpressive, limited to the omission of one or two cases of accidental homophony from the vocabulary list. We might liken such cases to what Steriade (1995) has called "opportunistic" or unmotivated underspecification.

Moreover, in many cases, an enriched theory of representations (i.e., morphological features) allows for syncretisms to be expressed by the vocabulary items themselves. The grammar of Warlpiri will need no Impoverishment rule (6), if the distribution of the first person singular reflexive clitic could be obtained *representationally* by specifying it as [-pl]. On the other hand, if bivalent features are not admitted (Stump 1993), the class of phenomena that cannot be treated representationally expands.

But Zwicky (1985) and Stump (1993) both argue that representational solutions are inadequate for a second reason, namely that although they are capable of generating the correct word forms, they fail to capture a broad pattern of neutralization, and hence are not explanatorily adequate. More concretely, for the analysis of Romanian given in (2), one must conclude that the only reason there are no specifically neuter adjectives or determiners is because there happen to be no vocabulary items which express [+neut] forms. In other words, the generalization is ascribed to a conspiracy of the lexicon. The point becomes more pressing the more extensive the conspiracy happens to be.

On the other hand, Rules of Referral and Impoverishment are both capable of expressing the relevant generalizations. Specifically with regard to Romanian, we have recourse to the following Impoverishment rule:

(7)   [−masc −fem] → ∅ / [Adjective ___]

This rule asserts, effectively, "there are no specifically neuter adjectives." But there is in fact no reason that (7) must apply. It could equally well be understood as a static redundancy rule over vocabulary items (cf. Jackendoff 1975). What (7) in fact captures is not only that there are no neuter adjective signals, but moreover *that there could not be any* and that this proposition is part of speakers' knowledge of Romanian.

Because rules like (7) play no active role in morphology, the more interesting scenarios arise when representational solutions are inadequate, and a rule of Impoverishment or Referral does some crucial work in the grammar. Sections 6–7 provide a striking example of this from Nimboran.

Because all Impoverishments precede spell-out — by hypothesis — and are limited to feature-deletion operations, it is clear that Impoverishment is less expressive than Referral. Put differently, Referral can express any syncretism which Impoverishment can but not vice versa. Formally speaking there is nothing to prevent Referral from converting any morphosyntactic representation into any other. As Carstairs-McCarthy (1992:203) puts it, "if unconstrained, the mechanism is suspiciously powerful." The possibility of extrinsic ordering of Referrals within the realizational rule block adds further possibilities.

On these grounds alone we should be prepared to reject Referral in favor of Impoverishment, provided it can be shown that Impoverishment accounts for all the systematic inflectional syncretisms in natural language. This is the question I pose here. Anticipating the conclusion, the answer I provide is that feature-deleting Impoverishment is not in fact powerful enough: there appear to be cases where conversion of one category to another is unavoidable. However, it may be possible to constrain Rules of Referral to moving from more marked to less marked representations, thereby cutting in half the hypothesis space of the learner. This will be accomplished here formally by allowing unmarked values to be reinserted by independently needed persistent redundancy rules after Impoverishments delete marked values: [mF] → ∅ → [uF]. The net effect is a conversion of [mF] → [uF]. Conversion of [uF] → [mF] will however be strictly unavailable. Thus we predict an important correlation between markedness relations — whether universal or learned — and grammars of neutralization.

5 The Morphological Category Alphabet

One important use of Impoverishment, discussed in Noyer 1992, is to provide the formal expression of the alphabet of morphological categories in a language. The following is a simple example.

Classical Arabic has no 1st person dual, although 1st person dual verbs might conceivably be formed by affixation of ʔ- [+1] and -ā [+dual] to a verb in the so-called prefix conjugation:

(8)　a.　*ʔ–aktub–ā　　　　'we (dual) write'
　　　b.　ʔ-aktub　　　　　'I write'
　　　c.　t-aktub-ā　　　　'you (dual) write'　　　(Arabic)

The South Arabian languages Mehri and Soqotri in fact do precisely this (Johnstone 1987, Bittner 1918), although in most respects their verbal affixes are roughly isomorphic to those of classical Arabic:

(9)　a.　ə-rəkz-ō　　　　'we (dual) straighten'
　　　b.　ə-rūkəz　　　　'I straighten'
　　　c.　tə-rəkz-ō　　　　'you (dual) straighten'　　(Mehri)

The difference between Mehri/Soqotri and Arabic is simply that Arabic has rule (10) and Mehri and Soqotri do not:

(10)　[dual] → ∅ / [1]

Because (10) is not in force, Mehri and Soqotri have innovated 1st dual pronouns as well. Unless the restriction (10) is assumed as a default during acquisition, there is no explanation for why speakers of Arabic failed for many centuries to innovate a category which the affixal resources could readily produce. Cases like these, which are not rare, call into question theories in which the space of paradigmatic possibilities is generated solely by the set of affixes (signals), as suggested by Wunderlich & Fabri (1993).

Rules such as (10) must also be directional. Directional rules (Gazdar et. al. 1985:28-29) are superior to a system of static filters or feature-value cooccurrence restrictions like *[+1 dual] because filters do not predict what substitution speakers will make. More precisely, the question is why expression of duality is sacrificed in favor of person and not vice versa. Every theory of morphology must somehow address this issue.[5]

To summarize, only generalized and directional rules of neutralization correctly derive the morphosyntactic category alphabet. Impoverishments then have a triple function in the theory of grammar: (1) to express the set of morphological categories; (2) to derive what form is substituted in a formally possible but excluded category; and (3) to express systematic syncretisms within the inflectional morphology of a language.

6 Three Neutralizations in Nimboran

A compelling case for Impoverishment comes from the verbal morphology of Nimboran (New Guinea: Anceaux 1965), analyzed in some detail in a lexicalist framework by Inkelas (1993). For reasons of space, I will restrict attention here to three neutralizations: (a) the neutralization of [dual:plural] in the 2nd person, (b) the neutralization of [masc:nonmasc] in the 3rd person plural, and (c) the leveling of [singular:dual:plural] to [unmarked:plural] in the context of certain morphemes.

Consider first the subject agreement affixes for person and number:

(11)   Subject Agreement Affixes of Nimboran

	SINGULAR [+sg −pl]	DUAL [−sg −pl]	PLURAL [−sg +pl]
1	... *u*	*k* ... *u*	^{i}... *u*
12	*maN* . . . *ám*	*k* ... *ám*	
2	... *e*	*k* ... *e*	
3 MASC	... *am*	*k* ... *am*	^{i}... *am*
3 FEM/INAN	... *um*	*k* ... *um*	

---

[5]The directionality of such rules might arise from generalized feature hierarchies determining which values "want" to be expressed most (cf. Zwicky 1977). But such preferences are not likely to be universal; for example, Harris (1994:327) shows that Latin American Spanish neutralizes the opposition between 2nd and 3rd person in the plural for "every syntactically second person plural item." Person here is neutralized in the context of number, violating any universals about a hierarchy of preferences. On the other hand, as Prince & Smolensky (1993) have shown, the fact that a given contraint is violated does not mean that the constraint is not present. In other work, Noyer 1993, I have derived the directional effects of Impoverishment through constraints on the output of syntax, but will not explore this issue further here.

I am denoting by [^{i}] an autosegmental entity whose effect is to induce a palatalization of nearby segments. The affixes designated above appear discontiguously in a complete verbal form, although their precise positions will not concern us here. For concreteness, let us assume that the three Nimboran genders are represented by the following features:

(12) Nimboran Gender Features

	±masc	±anim
MASCULINE	+	+
FEMININE	–	+
NEUTER	–	–

Of particular interest to the present discussion is the distribution of the number affixes [^{i}] vs. *k* and the gender affixes *um* vs. *am*.

Consider first the number affixes. Affix *k* appears in the dual forms of all arguments and in the plural of the [+2] (i.e., 2nd person or 1st inclusive) arguments. Affix [^{i}] occurs in the remaining plural arguments. It should be clear by now that, aside from accidental homophony, there are two ways of accounting for this distribution, one representational (13) and the other by means of Impoverishment (14a) and the signals in (14b):

(13) [^{i}]   [+pl –2]
       k   [–sg]

(14) a.   [+pl] → $\emptyset$ / [+2 –sg __]
      b.   [^{i}]   [+pl]
            k   [–sg]

Exactly similar considerations apply to the distribution of *am* vs. *um*. In the representational analysis in (15), the affix *um* appears to be restricted to [–masc] arguments in the nonplural; *am* can then be treated as the default realization of 3rd person:

(15)   *um*   [–masc –pl]
       am   Elsewhere

The Impoverishment analysis (16) on the other hand will derive the restriction of *um* to the nonplural arguments by deleting the distinction [±masc] in the plural:

(16) a. $[\alpha \text{ masc}] \rightarrow \varnothing$ / [+pl −sg __]
    b. *um*   [−masc]
       am   Elsewhere

The representational analyses seem much simpler for both cases, but in fact become problematic in the face of the more complex data that follows.

The distribution of affixes and of verb root allomorphs shifts dramatically when certain particles, the plural object morpheme *dar*, or the durative affix <u>*tam*</u> appear in the verb root (underlining denotes that the affix triggers an ablaut of following affixes). Consider first the root allomorphs.

As shown by Inkelas, the Nimboran verb root exhibits an allomorphy which is conditioned by the number of the verbal subject:

(17) a. *ŋedúo–d–u*
      draw[A]–FU–1   'I will draw (here)'

    b. *ŋedóu–k–d–u*
      draw[B]–NONSG–FU–1   'We (excl, dual) will draw (here)'

    c. *ŋedói– ⁱ –d–u*
      draw [C]–PL–FU–1   'We (excl, plur) will draw (here)'

Inkelas labels these allomorphs {A, B, C}. Examples are repeated below:

(18) Nimboran root allomorphs

root	B	A	C
'draw'	*ŋedóu*	*ŋedúo*	*ŋedói*
'pull out'	*betáo*	*betuá*	*betaói*
'water'	*sáoŋ*	*suáŋ*	*saóiŋ*
'flee'	*krí*	*krí*	*krɨ*
'say to'	*u*	*u*	*i*

The B allomorph appears to be the underlying form; the C allomorph is ablauted and the A allomorph shows metathesis of the final syllable nucleus if complex. As shown in (17) normally the A allomorph appears with singular subjects, the B allomorph with dual subjects and the C allomorph with plural subjects. To derive these effects I will simply assume that morphophonological stem formation rules of metathesis and ablaut are sensitive to the values [+sg] and [+pl] respectively (19).

(19) a. [+sg] ↔ metathesis rule
      b. [+pl] ↔ ablaut rule   (informal implications)

Note in (18) that the underlying form of the stem appears in the dual since neither allomorphy rule in (19) applies.

In the special environment associated with the durative and certain other particles, the distribution of root allomorphs shifts:

(20) Roots allomorphs in normal and special environment

subject number	normally	special case
SINGULAR	A	B
DUAL	B	C
PLURAL	C	C

The following examples illustrate the shift for the "special case" (durative):

(21) a. ŋgedóu–_tam–t–u_
          draw[B]–DUR–PR–1   'I am drawing'

      b. ŋgedói– ^{i} – _tam–t–u_
          draw[C]–PL–DUR–PR–1   'We (excl, dual/plur) are drawing'

The first peculiarity of the special case is that the B allomorph now appears in the singular as in (21a). Inkelas observes that the B allomorph also appears in verb forms which appear to be passive. Given the heterogeneous distribution of the B allomorph, the B allomorph must be the elsewhere allomorph, as already suggested by the phonology of the stem forms.

A second peculiarity of the special case is that the distinction between dual and plural number is neutralized, as shown by (21b). In both duals and plurals the C allomorph — restricted to [+pl] in the normal case — appears.

7 Impoverishment Analysis of Nimboran

I propose here to derive this shift by the following Impoverishment rules, which are triggered by features residing in the durative, plural object, and certain other particles:

(22) a. [–pl] → ∅
      b. [α sg] → ∅

The deletion of [–pl] has the effect of neutralizing the contrast between the dual category and the plural category. But to ensure that duals in fact become featurally equivalent to plurals, it is necessary that once the marked value [−pl] is deleted from a dual argument, the value [+pl] is automatically inserted by a persistent redundancy rule (23):

(23)   [−sg] → [+pl]

The proposed redundancy rule expresses the universal markedness of [−pl] in the context [−sg] (the combination of which gives rise to dual). In the unmarked case a language will distinguish only two numbers, as predicted by (23). I return in section 10 to a discussion of the use of redundancy rules of this sort.

The Impoverishment of a category labeled "dual" is then as follows:

(24)   [−sg −pl]   underlying: dual label
       [−sg]   Special Impoverishment (22a)
       [−sg +pl]   Redundancy Rule: [−sg] → [+pl]
       [+pl]   Special Impoverishment (22b)

The effects of Special Impoverishment on the representation of underlying positions in Nimboran are illustrated below:

(25)   The Effects of Special Number Impoverishment

		normal case			special environment		
		±sg	±pl		±sg	±pl	
SINGULAR	A	+	−		Ø	Ø	B
DUAL	B	−	−	→	Ø	+	C
PLURAL	C	−	+		Ø	+	C

The distribution of root allomorphs is now accounted for. Specifically, the metathesized A allomorph is conditioned by the value [+sg], which is deleted by Special Impoverishment (22b). Similarly, the dual is converted to the plural by the combined force of Special Impoverishment (22a) and the Redundancy Rule (23) supplying [+pl] to [−sg] arguments. The ablauted C allomorph therefore appears in both the dual and the plural. Affix *k* [−sg] never appears in the special environment since it will be inserted only if [−sg] is present (cf. 21b). Special Impoverishment (22b) deletes all values for [α sg], bleeding the insertion of *k* [−sg] in all instances.

Turning now to the pattern of agreement affixes in the special case, we find a change in the distribution of both the number *and* the gender affixes.

Specifically, [^{i}] now appears in the 2nd person forms, although normally it does not:

(26) ŋgedói– ^{i} –_tam_ –t–e
      draw [C]–PLUR–DUR–PR–2

      'You (dual, plural) are drawing'

This shows that the representational analysis for the distribution of [^{i}] (13) cannot be correct. Recall that on this analysis [^{i}] is specifically restricted to [–2] contexts, which would exclude it from ever occurring in a form such as (26). Consider however the Impoverishment analysis:

(27) [+pl] → Ø / [+2 –sg __]

The inclusion of [–sg] in the structural description of (27) ensures that Plural Impoverishment applies only when the distinction [±sg] is present.[6] In virtue of Special Impoverishment (22b), all values for [±sg] are deleted in the special case environments. Consequently neither the [+sg] root allomorph A nor _k_ [–sg] ever appear in this environment. In addition, Special Impoverishment (22b) will prevent Plural Impoverishment (27) from applying (a bleeding relation). When Plural Impoverishment does not apply, nothing prevents [^{i}] [+pl] from being inserted in the second person. This accounts for the anomalous appearance of this affix in (26).

Exactly parallel results hold for the gender affixes — an important fact not discussed by Inkelas. The following example shows that _um_ appears in the plural in the special environment, although normally it is restricted from the plural:

---

[6]It should be noted that the Elsewhere Condition prevents the persistent Redundancy Rule (23) from 're-inserting' [+pl] where Plural Impoverishment (14a = 27) deletes this value. These two rules are disjunctive since one inserts a value which the other deletes: Plural Impoverishment is more specific and therefore takes precedence. An important implication of this is that marked values can be deleted (rather than replaced by unmarked values) only if unmarked values are also deleted. There are therefore three scenarios:

(i)   [mF] → [ØF] → [uF]   Deletion plus insertion of unmarked value
      [αF] → [ØF]   Deletion of both marked and unmarked values
      [uF] → [ØF]   Deletion of only unmarked value

(28)   ŋgedoi-^{i} -*tam*-*t*-*um*   → *ŋgedóitiemtým*
         draw[C]–PL–DUR–PR–3.NONMASC

'They (dual or pl, fem or inan) are drawing'   (Anceaux 1965:234)

Again this shows that the representational solution (15), restricting *um* to specifically [–pl –masc] contexts, cannot be correct. In (28) *um* must appear in the plural, and will do so because the deletion of [±sg] by Special Impoverishment (22b) bleeds the application of Gender Impoverishment (16a) in the special environments.   The [–masc] *um* affix appears automatically when not prevented from doing so by Gender Impoverishment, yielding such forms as (28).

8   Lexicalist Analysis of Nimboran

Let us now compare the analysis offered here to that of Inkelas 1993. Inkelas proposes that what I have called the special environment arises whenever durative *tam*, plural object *dar*, and certain other particles block the appearance of the number affixes *k* or Ø 'singular.' This occurs because these affixes all happen to occupy the same level in word formation, and no two affixes can attach at the same level.

She analyzes *k* as 'Dual' or '2.–sg' (effectively, as an accidental homophony), and [^{i}] as '–Sg.'   To obtain the shift in pattern of root allomorphs, Inkelas proposes that the root must agree precisely in number and person features with the affixes, which comprise a constituent she names "Modifier."

Inkelas' analysis relies on the following featural representations of the root allomorphs:

(29)   A =   [Sg]
         C =   [–Sg]
         B =   [Du] or [ØF] or [2.–Sg]

Since by hypothesis in the special environment *k* 'Dual' or '2.–sg' cannot attach, the only way to express nonsingulars is by attaching [^{i}] [–Sg]. This means that both Duals and Plurals will have C roots, since C is the only root which can agree with [–Sg]:

(30)   4

Root	Modifier	ŋgedói- [i]– tam–t–u
g	g	draw[C]–PL–DUR–PR–1
C	i	'We (excl, dual/plur) are drawing'
[–Sg]	[–Sg]	

Similarly, since Ø [+sg] is blocked from attaching in the special environment, the only way to express singular is to leave out number entirely. Accordingly, the B affix in its [ØF] form must be chosen to agree with a modifier unmarked for number:

(31)   4

Root	Modifier	ŋgedóu–tam–t–u
g	g	draw[B]–DUR–PR–1
B	no affix	'I am drawing'
[ØF]	[ØF]	

A serious objection arises to this alternative however. Although Inkelas acknowledges that the B allomorph is the elsewhere or unmarked allomorph, her analysis takes no account of this observation, since it is crucially necessary to assume that the B allomorph is *triply accidentally homophonous* between a featurally unmarked [ØF] case and forms with 'Dual' and '2.–Sg' specifications. The fact that *k* is also (accidentally) homophonous between 'Dual' and '2.–Sg' is treated as a further accident, although surely the recurrence of 'Dual' and '2.–Sg' in both cases demands some more systematic explanation. This is a clear example of the paucity of marked values problem: the B allomorph is evidently the elsewhere allomorph, yet it "requires" certain marked values in order to agree with the Modifier, given Inkelas' assumptions.

A second problem relates to the distribution of gender affixes. Inkelas proposes that it is positional blocking of *k* and Ø by durative, plural object, and other particles that leads to the skewing of number allomorphy in the roots. The anomalous appearance of [[i]] in the 2nd person is a consequence of the fact that *k* '2.–Sg' is prevented from appearing, allowing the less specified [[i]] '–Sg' to attach. But no such account can be given for the redistribution of gender affixes, which is totally unexpected. First, the gender affixes are realized peripherally at the very end of the Modifier constituent far away from the number affixes' position, so positional blocking cannot be in any way responsible. Second, neither *am* nor *um* is blocked in the special environment; rather, it is their distribution that shifts.

Third, the expansion of *um* to the plural cannot be a consequence of the failure of *k* to appear in the dual, since these facts are totally unconnected.

The Impoverishment analysis, on the other hand, although somewhat complicated, derives the redistribution in a straightforward way, without appeal to accidental homophony, while still capturing the systematicity of the neutralizations. Effectively, it has been proposed that the special environments are characterized by a neutralization of number features: the opposition [singular:dual:plural] is leveled to the opposition [unmarked: plural] as exhibited most obviously in the distribution of root allomorphs. Impoverishment rules which derive the neutralization of the distinction [dual:plural] in the [+2] arguments and the neutralization of gender in the [plural] arguments cannot apply if the opposition [dual:plural] is not in force. The neutralizations effected by these Impoverishment rules therefore also cease to be in force and the environments of insertion for [^{i}] [+pl] and *um* [−masc] expand automatically. It is especially noteworthy that a distinction in gender [masc:nomasc] that is not present in the "normal environment" *emerges* in the plural in the "special environment."

Unlike neutralizations that are best captured by underspecification of morphological signals, Impoverishments apply generally and — in the cases of greatest interest — affect the distribution of affixes or stem allomorphs across-the-board. Nimboran provides ample evidence for such general shifts. Specifically, we have seen it is not simply the case that in a certain special environment certain distinctions are neutralized. Rather, the entire pattern of affix and allomorph distribution changes. To derive this effect, it was proposed that one Impoverishment rule can bleed another, allowing the emergence of otherwise unexpected forms (such as 26 and 28) in specific circumstances.

9 Syntagmatic Impoverishment and Position Class

Recall that Inkelas proposes to account for the neutralization of number in the Nimboran special environment by positional blocking. The affixes such as durative *tam* which induce the special environment block the appearance of the number affixes *k* and $\emptyset$ by occupying the lexical level where the number affixes must attach. Specifically, the affixes in question have the following representations:

(32)   a.   Durative   [tam [ ]$_B$]$_D$
        b.   Dual or 2.–Sg   [k [ ]$_B$]$_C$
        c.   Sg   [$\emptyset$ [ ]$_B$]$_C$

All three affixes must attach to a base of level B. They are all in consequence disjunctive.

The Impoverishment analysis given in section 7 would appear to treat as accidental the fact that the affix realizing 'durative,' for example, appears near or perhaps in the same position as the number affixes which it appears to block. This is in fact not so, as I now detail.

The Impoverishment analysis assumes that a durative morpheme triggers the special Impoverishment rules which bleed the insertion of k. It is not necessary on this view for k and durative _tam_ to occupy the same position or lexical level. In fact, it is more natural to assume that they do not, since k realizes a number morpheme and durative _tam_ does not.

The lexicalist analysis of Inkelas 1993 has recourse neither to Impoverishment nor to Referral. In consequence the only means by which affix disjunctions can be obtained is by making the two affixes in question occupy the same position or level. In this way, Inkelas' account is in fact a translation of structuralist position class accounts into the levels of attachment formalism of Lexical Phonology and Morphology (Kiparsky 1982). Disjunctivity is in this model the only diagnostic for strict position class. But if Impoverishments can apply syntagmatically, that is, if a morpheme is able to delete part or all of the content of another morpheme, then disjunctivity and position need not be intrinsically connected.

Suppose morpheme A has content $[\alpha F]$ and B has content $[\beta G]$. If only A appears when both might logically be expected, then on a position class analysis both must occupy the same level. But in a theory with Impoverishment, this need not be so. Instead, $[\alpha F]$ might trigger Impoverishment of $[\beta G]$. But $[\beta G]$ and $[\alpha F]$ do not have to occupy the same syntagmatic position; they may be in an appropriate local relation, sisterhood being unquestionably local enough:

(33) $[\beta G] \rightarrow \varnothing \ / \ 2$

$\underline{\hspace{2em}}$ $[\alpha F]$

In such cases the *illusion* of position class arises where in fact the disjunctivity is deletion under adjacency.

Precisely this situation is found in Nimboran. Restricting attention to positions 0-3, Inkelas proposes the following distribution of affixes:

(34)

0	1	2	3
root	PlSubj [^{i}]	DuSubj k	MObj *rar*
		SgSubj $\varnothing$	Particles (vary)
		Pl Obj *dar*	
		------------ Durative _tam_ ---------------	

Because the positions occupied by affixes — positions motivated solely on the grounds of disjunctivity — are not correlated in any obvious way with the content of the affixes which occupy the positions, Inkelas presents Nimboran as important evidence against the view that word formation is a syntactic process manipulating abstract morphemes. But given the possibility of syntagmatic Impoverishment, the motivation for these arbitrary position classes evaporates. Instead, it is possible to align the affixes according to their content as follows:

(35) Root ∧ SubjNumber ∧ Obj/Particle ∧ Durative . . .

Because their syntactic function is unalike, the subject number affixes and the object affixes need not and should not occupy the same position. Disjunctions between them must be accomplished by syntagmatic Impoverishment.

The disjunction of PlObj *dar* and DuSubj *k* for example, need no longer be ascribed to competition for attachment at a certain level. Rather it is accomplished by the Special Impoverishment rules operating under sisterhood:

(36) $[-\text{pl}] \rightarrow \emptyset$ / 3
$$\underline{\quad\quad} \quad [+\text{pl}]$$

(37) $[\alpha \text{ sg}] \rightarrow \emptyset$ / 3
$$\underline{\quad\quad} \quad [+\text{pl}]$$

(38) ROOT - [−sg −pl] − [+pl] − [−masc]   Abstract morphology
   ROOT - [+pl] − [+pl] − [−masc]   Impoverishments
   ngedoi –   *i*   -*dar*   −*um*   spell-out, ablaut
   draw[C]– PL –   PL– NONMASC

   'They (nonmasc) draw them (pl) here'   (Anceaux 1965: 218)

As shown in (38), if the targeted (subject agreement) morpheme happens to be dual, i.e., [−pl −sg], the persistent universal redundancy rule supplies [+pl] to the Impoverished morpheme. This then triggers insertion of [^{i}] rather than of *k* when the object is plural. The appearance of [−masc] *um* in the plural under such circumstances shows that in all respects the appearance of *dar* 'plural object' is associated with the shift in affix distributions discussed earlier.

The remaining disjunctions can be captured by other syntagmatic Impoverishments. I conclude that Nimboran verbal morphology is not a counterexample to abstract (syntactic) word formation.   More generally, I see no reason to retain the structuralist assumption that disjunction implies position class — or lexical level in present-day terms.   The existence of syntagmatic Impoverishment opens up the possibility that a great many apparently arbitrary position class systems are amenable to a more principled account in terms of affix alignment by content, as predicted by theories incorporating the notion of abstract morpheme.

10   Redundancy Rules and Impoverishment

The persistent redundancy rule [−sg] → [+pl] introduced in the analysis of Nimboran complicates the idea that Impoverishment is limited to feature-deletion.   Recall that duals were converted to plurals by allowing Impoverishment to delete [−pl], with the Redundancy Rule then inserting [+pl]. The net result is in fact a feature-changing operation:

(39)   [−sg −pl] → [−sg] → [−sg +pl]

It might therefore be objected that Impoverishment-plus-Insertion is in fact equally expressive as feature-changing Referral.   But there is still an important distinction, namely, that the only values which may be inserted by persistent redundancy rules are in fact unmarked values.   Hence Impoverishment-plus-Insertion will always move from a more marked to a less marked state. Referral is indifferent to markedness, and could equally convert plurals to duals or dual to plurals.   Plurals could never be converted to duals by Impoverishment but could be by Referral.[7] Moreover, the redundancy rule inserting the unmarked value is independently necessary to express markedness relations in the grammar. Acquisition of a Referral then requires only the observation of neutralization of contrast; principles of universal (or, perhaps, language-specific) markedness dictate what consequences such a neutralization will have.[8]

To summarize, while Bonet (1991) originally proposed that Impoverishment is in all cases a feature-deleting operation, subsequent work

---

[7]Calabrese (1994) explores a similar idea in a paper on the historical morphology of the Italian and Sardinian clitic systems.   His proposal differs crucially from the one here in that it dispenses with many cases of underspecification in the representation of vocabulary items.

[8]Noyer (1992:275 ff) discusses a similar case from Nunggubuyu (Heath 1984). In this language, duals and trials are normally marked for masculine or feminine gender, but when in object function, duals and trials neutralize with generic nonsingulars and are marked with a special so-called "plural" gender. Like the Nimboran case, this presents a case of moving to a less marked category, since the special plural gender is the default gender for nonsingular objects.

has also invoked feature-insertions, which give rise to a net effect of feature-changing in some circumstances (Noyer 1992, Calabrese 1994). However, if it is assumed that feature insertions occur only through the operation of persistent redundancy rules, the expectation is that marked values may change to unmarked, but never vice versa. An important prediction is that wherever discordant agreement arises, the target of agreement should always be a less marked category than the trigger (or antecedent) of agreement. I leave this question open to future research.

11   Some Outstanding Cases and Outlook

For reasons of space I am unable to discuss the great variety of neutralizations cited in the literature on Rules of Referral, particularly in Stump 1993. An examination of these shows that many, such as the Russian animate accusative, are amenable to reanalysis as neutralizations into less marked representation, although not obviously so. For the sake of completeness, I will list here some remaining cases which may provide evidence for markedness reversals in Impoverishment.

(40)   a.   ablative $\rightarrow$ genitive   (Vedic, Stump 1993:455-56)
      b.   3rd person $\rightarrow$ 1st person   (Vedic, Stump 1993:465-66)
      c.   1st sg future $\rightarrow$ subjunctive   (Latin, Carstairs 1987)

The question of whether the generalized syncretisms of natural language morphology conform to the restrictions I have outlined here is undoubtedly an empirical matter. I leave these remaining cases for future research. It is of course always possible to retreat to feature-changing rules, thereby expanding the space of possible grammars available to learners. If this is so, then the differences between Impoverishment as proposed here and Referral as proposed by Stump become less significant. But my hope remains that continued and careful examination of such cases will show that neutralizations are in fact universally feature-erasing operations, validating the original insight of Bonet 1991. An important consequence of this view may be that Impoverishment rules can be reformulated as choices among universal constraints on the output of syntax rather than as specific rules, a line of research begun in Noyer 1992, 1993, and Calabrese 1994.

References

Anceaux, J.C. 1965.   *The Nimboran Language: Phonology and Morphology.* 's Gravenhage: Martinus Nijhoff.

Anderson, Stephen. 1982. Where's Morphology? *Linguistic Inquiry* 13:571-612.

Andrews, Avery D. 1990. Unification and Morphological Blocking. *Natural Language and Linguistic Theory* 8:4:507-558.

Bittner, M. 1918. Charakteristik der Sprache der Insel Soqotra. *Akademie der Wissenschaft, Wien. Anzeiger.* Philosophisch-historische Klasse, Jahrg. 55:48-83.

Bonet, Eulàlia. 1991. *Morphology after Syntax: Pronominal Clitics in Romance.* Doctoral dissertation, MIT.

Calabrese, Andrea. 1994. Syncretism Phenomena in the Clitic Systems of Italian and Sardinian Dialects and the Notion of Morphological Change. *Proceedings of the North East Linguistics Society 25*, vol. 2, 151–174. Graduate Student Linguistics Association, University of Massachusetts, Amherst.

Carstairs, Andrew. 1983. Paradigm Economy. *Journal of Linguistics* 19:115-28.

Carstairs, Andrew. 1987. *Allomorphy in Inflexion.* London: Croom Helm.

Carstairs-McCarthy, Andrew. 1992. *Current Morphology.* New York: Routledge.

Di Sciullo, Anna Maria, and Edwin Williams. 1987. *On the Definition of Word.* Cambridge, Mass.:MIT Press.

Farkas, Donca 1990. Two Cases of Underspecification in Morphology. *Linguistic Inquiry* 21:4: 539-550.

Farkas, Donca and Draga Zec. 1993. Agreement and Pronominal Reference. Ms., University of California, Santa Cruz, and Cornell University.

Gazdar, Gerald, Ewan Klein, Geoff Pullum, and Ivan Sag. 1985. *Generalized Phrase Structure Grammar.* Cambridge, Mass.: Harvard University Press.

Halle, Morris & Alec Marantz. 1993. Distributed Morphology and the Pieces of Inflection. In Kenneth Hale and Stephen Jay Keyser, eds., *The View from Building 20*, 111–176. Cambridge, Mass.:MIT Press.

Halle, Morris & Alec Marantz. 1994. Some Key Features of Distributed Morphology. In Andrew Carnie and Heidi Harley, eds., *MITWPL 21*, pp. 275-288. Cambridge, Mass.: MIT Working Papers in Linguistics.

Harris, James. 1994. The Syntax-Phonology Mapping in Catalan and Spanish Clitics. In Andrew Carnie and Heidi Harley, eds., *MITWPL 21*, 321-353. Cambridge, Mass.: MIT Working Papers in Linguistics.

Heath, Jeffrey. 1984. *Functional Grammar of Nunggubuyu.* Canberra: Australian Institute of Aboriginal Studies.

Inkelas, Sharon. 1993. Nimboran Position Class Morphology. *Natural Language and Linguistic Theory* 11:559-624.

Jackendoff, Ray. 1975. Morphological and Semantic Regularities in the Lexicon. *Language* 51: 639-71.

Johnstone, T. 1987. *Mehri Lexicon and Word List.* Compiled by G.R. Smith. The School of Oriental and African Studies, London.

Kiparsky, Paul. 1973. The Elsewhere Condition. In Stephen Anderson and Paul Kiparsky, eds., *A Festschrift for Morris Halle*, 93-106. New York: Holt, Rinehart and Winston.

Kiparsky, Paul. 1982. Lexical Phonology and Morphology. In I. S. Yang, ed., *Linguistics in the Morning Calm*, 3–91. Seoul: Hanshin.

Lieber, Rochelle. 1980. *The Organization of the Lexicon*. Doctoral dissertation, MIT.

Lumsden, John. 1992. Underspecification in Grammatical and Natural Gender. *Linguistic Inquiry* 23:3:469-486.

Matthews, P.H. 1972. *Inflectional Morphology*. Cambridge: Cambridge University Press.

Noyer, Rolf. 1992. *Features, Positions and Affixes in Autonomous Morphological Structure*. Doctoral dissertation, MIT.

Noyer, Rolf. 1993. Optimal Words: Towards a Declarative Theory of Word Formation. Paper presented at Rutgers Optimality Workshop-1. Ms., Princeton University.

Prince, Alan & Paul Smolensky. 1993. *Optimality Theory: Constraint Interaction in Generative Grammar*. Rutgers University Center for Cognitive Science Technical Report #2, Rutgers, New Jersey.

Steriade, Donca. 1995. Underspecification and Markedness. In John Goldsmith, ed. *Handbook of Phonological Theory*, 114-174. Cambridge, Mass.:Basil Blackwell.

Stump, Greg. 1993. *On Rules of Referral*. Language 69:3:449-479.

Williams, Edwin. 1981. On the Notions 'Lexically Related' and 'Head of a Word.' *Linguistic Inquiry* 12:245-274.

Wunderlich, Dieter & Ray Fabri. 1993. Minimalist Morphology. Ms., Universität Düsseldorf.

Wurzel, Wolfgang. 1988. *Inflectional Morphology and Naturalness*. Dordrecht: Kluwer.

Zwicky, Arnold. 1977. Hierarchies of Person. *Papers from the Thirteenth Regional Meeting of the Chicago Linguistics Society*, 714–733. Chicago Linguistics Society, University of Chicago.

Zwicky, Arnold. 1985. How to Describe Inflection. *Proceedings of the Berkeley Linguistics Society 11*, 372-386. Berkeley, Calif.

Comments on the Paper by Noyer

Andrew Carstairs-McCarthy

Noyer proposes that inflectional neutralization or syncretism is usually best accounted for in terms of the mechanism of Impoverishment, supplemented by persistent redundancy rules which can introduce only unmarked values.[1] I will argue that the Impoverishment approach to neutralization is less restrictive than it seems at first sight, and that some neutralizations can be more naturally accounted for in terms of an approach to affixal meaning which invokes characteristics of lexical semantics. There is space here to do no more than sketch the outlines of such an approach, but I hope to persuade readers that it is a worthwhile line of inquiry.

1 The Unrestrictiveness of Noyer's Approach

Impoverishment involves a rule which deletes a morphosyntactic feature from a morphosyntactic representation in some context, either on the basis of its value (plus or minus) (e.g. $+F \rightarrow \emptyset$) or absolutely, irrespective of value (e.g. $\alpha F \rightarrow \emptyset$). Noyer's Impoverishment rules (14a) and (16a) for Nimboran, reproduced here as (1) and (2), illustrate these two situations.

(1) $[+pl] \rightarrow \emptyset / [+2 \ -sg \ \_\_]$
(2) $[\alpha \ masc] \rightarrow \emptyset / [+pl \ -sg \ \_\_]$

What is important for present purposes is the kind of thing which can count as an environment for such a rule. In (1) and (2) the environment consists of a set of features which are not syntagmatically structured with respect to the deleted features. But syntagmatically structured environments for Impoverishment are allowed by Noyer, and indeed are presented as an improvement over Inkelas's (1993) position-class analysis for handling certain apparent positional blockings in Nimboran. Noyer illustrates the general format of such a rule at (3) (his (33)):

(3) $[\beta G] \rightarrow \emptyset /$
$\_\_ \ [\alpha F]$

The trouble with such rules, irrespective of their possible usefulness in Nimboran, is that they will in general allow things to happen that we

---

[1] I am grateful to Rolf Noyer for discussion of earlier versions of this article. Faults that remain are my responsibility.

almost certainly do not want. One of the earliest of recent proposals about constraining neutralization was my suggestion that, except under narrow conditions, the triggering environment for homonymy must be realized simultaneously with the neutralized features (Carstairs 1984, 1987, Carstairs & Stemberger 1988). If this is broadly correct, homonymies should be more common in patterns of morphological expression which are cumulative (like case-number inflection in Latin) than in patterns of expression which are agglutinative (like case-number inflection in Turkish). And that seems to be true. Moreover, one can find a rationale for this in language acquisition, in that cumulative honomonymies reduce the learning burden whereas agglutinative homonymies increase it. Yet syntagmatic Impoverishment makes it easy to express homonymies of the undesirable kind. Let me illustrate this with some data from Pseudo-Turkish:

(4)

	Singular	Plural
Nominative	*ev* 'house'	*ev-ler*
Accusative	*ev-i*	*ev-ler-i*
Genitive	*ev-in*	*ev-ler-in*
Dative (or Allative)	*ev-e*	*ev-ler-e*
Locative	*ev-de*	*ev-ler-de*
Ablative	*ev-den*	*ev-ler-de*

Pseudo-Turkish differs from real Turkish in showing a neutralization of the ablative and locative contrast in the plural; the ablative plural form in real Turkish is *evlerden*. From the purely morphosyntactic point of view, such a neutralization is in no way out of the ordinary. It recalls the well-known dative-ablative plural neutralization in Latin, and it complies with the usual expectation that neutralizations should take place in marked contexts (such as plural) rather than in the corresponding unmarked contexts (such as singular). Nevertheless, Pseudo-Turkish is not an actual language, and I have suggested that it may be an impossible language, or at any rate a highly implausible one, because its agglutinative structure renders the homonymy "bad". But in Noyer's framework it is easily describable in terms of a syntagmatic Impoverishment rule as at (6a), assuming a feature structure for the three local cases as at (5) and a plausible-looking persistent redundancy rule as at (6b):

(5)

		[locative]	[to]	[from]
Dative	*e*	+	+	−
Locative	*de*	+	−	−
Ablative	*den*	+	−	+

(6)   a.   Ablative Impoverishment: $[+\text{from}] \rightarrow \emptyset /$

$$[+\text{pl}] \underline{\quad}$$

   b.   Redundancy rule: $[+\text{locative}] \rightarrow [-\text{from}]$

So syntagmatic Impoverishment, even if it does what we want in Nimboran, needs restraining. The question is: how? I offer no answer here, but it is a question which must have high priority for anyone exploring Noyer's framework.[2]

The Pseudo-Turkish example seems to suggest that Noyer's framework is in one respect not restrictive enough. But, quite apart from the question of whether it is restrictive enough in general, it is certainly not restrictive in relation to the first two of the Nimboran neutralizations which Noyer discusses. Within his framework, Noyer can certainly describe the two affixal neutralizations illustrated in his table (11): dual-plural in the 2nd person, and masculine-nonmasculine in the 3rd person plural. In the terminology of referral, it looks as if the plural is referred to the dual while the nonmasculine is referred to the masculine. The trouble is that, as I shall show, one can easily envisage a Pseudo-Nimboran in which the referrals go in the opposite direction but which is just as easily describable in Noyer's framework. The relevant Pseudo-Nimboran data are set out here:

(7)		singular	dual	plural
		$[+\text{sg} -\text{pl}]$	$[-\text{sg} -\text{pl}]$	$[-\text{sg} +\text{pl}]$
1		... *u*	*k* ... *u*	*i* ... *u*
1 2		*maN* ... *ám*	*i* ... *ám*	*i* ... *ám*
2		... *e*	*i* ... *e*	*i* ... *e*
3m		... *am*	*k* ... *am*	*i* ... *um*
3fem, inan		... *um*	*k* ... *um*	*i* ... *um*

The actual Nimboran dual-plural homonymy is analyzed by Noyer in terms of an Impoverishment rule at his (14a), with the meanings of the vocabulary items [*i*] and *k* as given at his (14b). But even without changing Noyer's feature analysis for Nimboran number, one can get the corresponding Pseudo-Nimboran homonymy by means of the Impoverishment at (8a) and the assumptions about meaning in (8b):

---

[2]To a careful reader it may seem that the gender neutralization in the 3rd person plural in Nimboran, illustrated at Noyer's (11), illustrates just the sort of neutralization which occurs in Pseudo-Turkish and which I claim should not occur in natural languages. I will return to that issue in section 3.

(8)   a. $[-pl] \rightarrow \emptyset$ / $[+2\ -sg \ \_\_\ ]$

        b. $[^i]$ $[-sg]$

             k $[-sg\ -pl]$

Readers are reminded that in Noyer's framework there is nothing wrong with deleting a minus-valued feature; examples in his paper are at (7), (22a) and (36).

The actual Nimboran gender homonymy in the 3rd person plural is analyzed by Noyer in terms of an Impoverishment rule at his (16a), with the meanings of the vocabulary items *um* and *am* as given at (16b). But even without changing Noyer's feature analysis for Nimboran gender, one can get the corresponding Pseudo-Nimboran homonymy with just the same Impoverishment rule, restated at (9a), and a difference only in the meanings assigned to the vocabulary items at (9b):

(9)   a. $[\alpha\ masc] \rightarrow \emptyset$ / $[+pl\ -sg \ \_\_\ ]$

        b.   *am* $[+masc]$

             um   Elsewhere

Whether Pseudo-Nimboran should be regarded as a possible language is a moot point. I see no obvious objection to it, unlike Pseudo-Turkish. But the ease with which we can describe the neutralisations of both languages, Nimboran and Pseudo-Nimboran, in Noyer's Impoverishment framework throws into doubt his claim that the framework is intrinsically restrictive. Noyer certainly limits both what Impoverishment can do (as its name implies, it can only delete, not add, morphosyntactic feature specifications) and what persistent redundancy rules can do (they can insert only unmarked values); but discipline sags, so to speak, when it comes to the variety of morphosyntactic features and values which are allowed to appear in affixal meanings.

Noyer discusses a third Nimboran neutralization, a more complex one involving stem forms as well as affixes. I will return to that briefly in section 5.

2 A Lexical Semantic Approach to Neutralization

Let us now consider the light which lexical semantics may shed on morphological neutralization, so that we can compare it with Noyer's approach. This may seem an odd suggestion. Lexical semantics may be relevant to derivational morphology (you will probably say), but it has little to contribute to inflectional morphology. Arriving at a satisfactory definition, even at an unsophisticated pretheoretical level, for everyday words like *red*, *bachelor* and *penguin* is notoriously difficult, so it is not surprising that the treatment of lexical semantics within linguistic theory is so controversial. By contrast, for many inflectional affixes, the meaning (or morphosyntactic content) seems quite clearcut and easy to pin down, at least pretheoretically; it is just the formal analysis that we argue about. So why should morphologists seek enlightenment in such an unpromising quarter?

One reason is the parallel behavior of lexical items and inflectional affixes from the point of view of synonymy avoidance or the Principle of Contrast (Carstairs-McCarthy 1994; cf. Clark 1993). In Carstairs-McCarthy 1994 I observed that lexical items had two semantic characteristics which they seem to share with inflectional affixes, if we construe inflection class identification as potentially part of the "meaning", or information content, of an affix. Firstly, lexical items do not have meanings containing mutually incompatible disjuncts; for example, there are words in English such as *banana* meaning BANANA, *apple* meaning APPLE, and *peach* meaning PEACH, but there is no word meaning APPLE OR BANANA. Secondly, a lexical item cannot contain in its meaning the complementary negation of another item in the same domain; for example, there is no word meaning FRUIT, NOT APPLE, i.e., any fruit which is not an apple.

Both these claims will strike many readers as contentious. What about *citrus fruit*, which seems to mean ORANGE OR LEMON OR GRAPEFRUIT OR ...? What about *illegal* and *Gentile*, which seem to mean NOT LEGAL and NOT JEWISH respectively? Yet both can be adequately defended.[3] For present purposes, I ask readers to suspend their disbelief; what I want to explore here is not the lexical semantic justification of the two claims, but rather their possible morphological implications.

The first claim refers to mutually incompatible disjuncts. What about disjuncts which are mutually compatible? These certainly are allowed within the meanings of lexical items; that is, meanings can contain X OR Y in the sense of X AND/OR Y, provided that X and Y are such that X AND Y is not contradictory. An example is the verb *climb*, discussed by Jackendoff (1985). He analyzes its meaning as containing "preference features" (P-features) UPWARD and CLAMBERING, which are disjunct but mutually compatible. In some contexts both P-features may be satisfied, as in (10a) below; in others only one is satisfied, as in (10b) and (10c); in yet others neither may be satisfied, as in (10d).

---

[3]*Citrus fruit* means not a random disjunction of fruits but a class of fruits with certain shared characteristics. So-called complementary antonyms such as *legal* and *illegal* are complementary only for pragmatic reasons; from the point of view of lexical semantic theory all such antonymy must be analysed as gradable, as is shown by the frequency and acceptability of usages such as *Murder is more illegal than theft*. And the same applies to *Gentile* and *Jewish*, as is shown by usages such as *It wasn't a particularly Jewish occasion*.

(10)   a.   The boy climbed up the tree.
        b.   The boy climbed down the tree.
        c.   The snake climbed up the tree.
        d.   *The snake climbed down the tree.

It is only (10d), where both UPWARD and CLAMBERING are excluded, which is semantically illformed. The meaning of *climb* can thus be represented roughly as GO, UPWARD OR CLAMBERING, where OR stands for inclusive rather than exclusive disjunction. Similarly, the meaning of *crown* can be analyzed in part as HEADGEAR, WITH POINTS AROUND RIM OR EMBLEM OF OFFICE OF MONARCH OR VICTOR. A prototypical crown, one may say, is one which satisfies both of the disjuncts, like the crown worn by a British monarch at the coronation ceremony; however, a crown may lack the first disjunct, like the olive-leaf crown worn by victors in the original Olympic Games, or the second, like the paper crowns found inside Christmas crackers.

    There is a further, more exotic, fact about lexical semantics which I will claim to be relevant. It is possible for a language to have two entirely disjoint lexicons, one of which is used in special circumstances such as when speaking in the presence of people related to oneself by marriage in certain ways. This phenomenon has been nicknamed "mother-in-law language". In the North Queensland language Dyirbal the "ordinary" lexicon, known as Guwal, contains about four times as many lexical stems as the "special" lexicon, Dyalnguy (Dixon 1971, 1972). To some extent this disparity is compensated for in Dyalnguy by increased use of derivatives and by periphrasis, but there are still much neutralization in Dyalnguy in that many groups of distinct Guwal terms will normally be rendered by a single Dyalnguy term; for example, Guwal *nudin* 'cut deeply' and *gunban* 'cut less deeply' are both normally rendered in Dyalnguy by *dyalnggan* 'cut'. The fact that this Dyalnguy term bears no particular resemblance to either of the corresponding Guwal terms is absolutely typical; the Dyalnguy vocabulary really is distinct from Guwal, not just a subset of Guwal in which each term has a wider denotation than usual.

    Let us now explore further the idea that the meanings of inflectional affixes obey the same rules as the meanings of lexical items. The facts which we have just observed about lexical items—I ask the reader to continue regarding them as facts for the purpose of this discussion—will lead us to expect that inflectional affixes will have the following four characteristics:

A.   Inflectional affixes should not have meanings containing incompatible disjuncts, such as [... past OR future ...], [... ablative OR locative ...], where the disjuncts are morphosyntactic properties belonging to the same category (in the terminology of Matthews 1991), or competing values for one morphosyntactic feature (in the terminology of Zwicky 1985).

B.   Inflectional affixes should not have meanings containing negations, such as [... NOT past ...], [... NOT masculine ...].

C.   Inflectional affixes may have meanings containing compatible disjuncts, such as [... past OR definite, ...], [... masculine OR plural ...], where the disjuncts are properties belonging to intersecting categories. (Compare Jackendoff on *climb*.)

D.   The distinction in normal contexts between two or more affixes with distinct but related meanings may be neutralized in some special context, namely one where the normal affixal vocabulary is replaced by a special vocabulary such that corresponding items in the two vocabularies have no particular resemblance in shape. An affix appearing in a neutralizing context will therefore differ from any of the affixes which realize the same meanings in normal contexts. (Compare Dyirbal.)

Two questions now face us. Firstly, how well are these expectations (let's call them "Axioms A–D") borne out by the evidence? Secondly, what are their implications for the extent and nature of the restrictions which linguistic theory can place on inflectional homonymy? The first of these questions will occupy us in the next section. The second question is large, and an answer which is both brief and complete is impossible. Three things stand out, however. First, Axiom B bans meanings such as [–sg] or [–2], and so outlaws (for example) Noyer's account of the two affixal neutralizations in Nimboran. I will therefore show presently that, at least for the first of these, an alternative account is available, consistent with Axioms A–D. Secondly, Axiom C permits affixal meanings of a kind which Noyer does not in practice posit, namely ones containing disjunctions. On the face of it, this means that Axioms A–D are weaker than Noyer's framework in this respect. Is such weakening really necessary? Thirdly, Axioms A–D suggest that inflectional homonymy can arise for at least two quite different reasons: because of special inflectional vocabularies, analogous to Dyalnguy in Dyirbal, or because of ambiguity due to disjunctions within affixal meanings (as we will see shortly). This contrasts with Noyer's view of inflectional homonymy as a phenomenon whose interesting aspects mostly arise through Impoverishment.

3 Illustrations of the Lexical Semantic Approach

If we continue to assume that Pseudo-Turkish as presented in (4) is a 'bad' language, we will naturally hope that it is not easily describable in terms of Axioms A–D. And this hope turns out to be justified. The axioms do not allow for an analysis of the Pseudo-Turkish neutralization in terms of Impoverishment and so in effect force us to seek what Noyer would call a "representational" analysis, that is an analysis under which it arises not through referral or Impoverishment but directly from the meanings of the affixes concerned. On the other hand, the axioms allow us to posit representations containing disjunctions. Let us take as our starting-point the feature analysis of *e*, *de* and *den* proposed at (5), when we were considering a Noyerian analysis of the facts in terms of Impoverishment. To ensure that *den* never appears in the plural, two representational analyses for *de* and *den* suggest themselves, as in (11):

(11) a. *den* [+locative, –to, +from, –plural]
          de   [+locative, –to]
      b. *de*   [+locative, –to, –from OR +plural]
          den [+locative, –to]

In (11a) the Panini Principle ensures that *de* is excluded from the ablative singular cell but appears in all three other [+locative, –to] cells. In (11b) it is *den* which has "elsewhere" status, confined to the ablative singular ([+from, –pl]); the disjunction in the meaning of *de* is consistent with Axiom C because [–from] and [+pl] are compatible. But both (11a) and (11b) are inconsistent with the ban on negatively defined meanings at Axiom B, since both of them contain [–to] and either [–from] or [–plural]. The features [±to] and [±from] are devices which allow us to treat the case-pairs locative-ablative ad locative-dative as two-member subcategories within the whole six-member category of case in Turkish. One might consider replacing them with some other features for which precisely the relevant case-pairs would share a plus rather than a minus value; but since the sole motivation for such features would be a desire to reconcile Pseudo-Turkish with Axiom B, the reconciliation would be transparently ad hoc.

There is a wider issue here. The assumption that the category of case has subcategories based on the sharing of values for features such as [direct], [object], [oblique] or [governed] has a respectable history in generative morphology, extending from Bierwisch 1967 through Williams 1981 to current work. Such subcategories seem tailor-made to make sense of at least some morphological neutralizations, and sometimes they may have genuine syntactic or semantic motivation. But one must avoid being seduced by generative grammar's love-affair with binary features (Jakobson's dubious legacy) into recognizing case groupings which are easily expressible in binary terms but for which there is no motivation apart from the very neutralizations which they are meant to explain. Axiom B, with its lexical semantic motivation, in effect requires that the morphosyntactic meanings which inflections are allowed to express must be singulary, or privative, rather than binary. This in turn implies that, unless there is clear evidence to the contrary, any morphosyntactic category containing three or more members will have a flat structure, with all its constituent properties ranged on a par; for, without any automatic requirement to analyze the category in terms of binary features, there will be no automatic partitioning of the category into subcategories on the basis of shared feature values. And this flattening of the internal structure of categories has desirable empirical consequences in relation to Pseudo-Turkish. There can be no privative case property to play the role of [+locative, –to] in (11)—the role of grouping the locative and ablative together while excluding the dative and all other Pseudo-Turkish cases. Also, there is no possibility of describing the meaning of *de* in terms of a disjunction such as [locative OR ablative], because as privative cases [locative] and [ablative] are incompatible. It follows that, with Axioms A–D, there can be no way of describing Pseudo-Turkish short of positing two affixes *de* with the distinct meanings [locative] and [ablative plural], in which case the homonymy is treated as accidental.

At this point, it may seem that I have thrown out the baby with the bathwater. Granted, the Pseudo-Turkish homonymy may seem implausible, so that it is advantageous for morphological theory to ban it. But surely we do want case neutralizations to be allowed sometimes, as in the cliché example of the dative-ablative plural neutralization in Latin. How can this be possible, unless we posit just the sort of case-pair grouping which I rejected as arbitrary for Pseudo-Turkish? The answer lies in Axiom D, which allows neutralizations in the expression of even incompatible meanings in "special contexts". What "special" means here will need to be made more precise, otherwise there is a risk that Axiom D could freely be invoked to permit neutralizations of unwelcome kinds. However, there is a difference between Latin and (Pseudo-)Turkish which ensures that in Latin the vocabulary of case affixes used in the plural must be "special" in the sense of being entirely distinct from the vocabulary used in the singular. This difference is the cumulation of case with number, which Latin has but Turkish lacks. It is easy to demonstrate that consistent case-number cumulation requires an affixal vocabulary for case in the plural which is distinct from the vocabulary used in the singular. Suppose that for some case the same affix is used in both the singular and plural. It must either cooccur with an identifiable plural affix or not. If it does, then case and number are not cumulated, which is inconsistent with our assumption that cumulation is consistent. If it does not, then number is simply not expressed at all in this case, which is again inconsistent with our assumption of consistent cumulation. So the plural in Latin constitutes a context which can justifiably be called "special" for case purposes, because it requires an entirely distinct case vocabulary. The neutralization of dative and ablative plural in Latin, despite the incompatibility of [dative] and [ablative] as privative case meanings, is therefore allowed under Axiom D.

The restriction of syncretisms to contexts where exponence is cumulative, in Matthews' terms, constituted the most robust evidence for my Systematic Homonymy Claim in 1987. It looks now as if cumulation may really be only an incidental factor, in that it can make for 'specialness' of the relevant kind but is perhaps not the only thing which can do so. The possibility that Axioms A–D may usefully legitimize some syncretisms which would be problematic for the Systematic Homonymy Claim remains to be explored in detail, though we will find an example in the next section. In Pseudo-Turkish, however, because there is no case-number cumulation, there is nothing in the inflectional pattern itself which imposes a "special" vocabulary for case in the plural, so Axiom D is not automatically brought into play to 'save' the locative-ablative homonymy.[4]

But are Axioms A–D compatible with the affixal neutralizations in Nimboran? Let us consider first the gender neutralization in the 3rd person plural, where *am* replaces the expected *um*. Gender is not cumulated with number in these Nimboran examples, so there is no obvious motivation for a Dyirbal-style "special context" neutralization. We must therefore seek a representational analysis. Noyer's own representational analysis at his (15) gives [−masc −pl] as the meaning of *um*, with *am* as the elsewhere alternant. That analysis is inconsistent with Axiom B. But an alternative is available:

(12)   *am*   [3, masc OR pl]
         um   [3]

---

[4]The alert reader may see a deficiency in Axiom D, in that there is nothing in it which will ensure that the dative-ablative homonymy in Latin will apply in all inflection classes, irrespective of the actual suffix used (*i:s* or *ibus*). The Systematic Homonymy Claim suffers from the same deficiency; we can describe the actual Latin situation in terms of it, but we could equally well describe a Pseudo-Latin situation where the homonymy appears in only the 1st, 2nd and 3rd declensions, not the 4th and 5th. A relevant issue here will be whether parallel domains of Guwal and Dyalnguy vocabulary (say, verbs for going and verbs for carrying, or age-sex terminology for different species of animal) show similar patterns of neutralization in Dyalnguy. I will not embark on that issue here.

Since [masc] and [pl] are compatible, the disjunction here is allowed by Axioms A and C. If we were to treat *am* as the "elsewhere" form, we would have to assign to *um* a meaning containing the disjunction [sg OR dual], which is not allowed because [sg] and [dual] are incompatible specifications for number.

An interesting aspect of this neutralization is that the absence of gender-number cumulation makes it problematic for my Systematic Homonymy Claim, just like the Pseudo-Turkish locative-ablative neutralization, yet it is compatible with the Axioms A–D, unlike Pseudo-Turkish. So the fact that the lexical semantic axioms permit this Nimboran homonymy while still forbidding the Pseudo-Turkish one provides an element of confirmation that they are a genuine theoretical improvement.

The other affixal neutralization, that involving *k* and [^{i}] as exponents of dual and plural, is more problematic. I will return to it in section 5.

4 A Hungarian Case Study

The forms at (13) of the Hungarian verb *vár* 'wait' illustrate a neutralization common to all Hungarian verbs which provides a useful basis on which to compare Noyer's and my approaches:

(13)

INDICATIVE

	PRESENT		PAST	
	Indefinite	Definite	Indefinite	Definite
1Sg	*vár-ok*	*vár-om*	***vár-t-am***	***vár-t-am***
3Pl	*vár-nak*	*vár-ják*	*vár-t-ak*	*vár-t-ák*

	CONDITIONAL		SUBJUNCTIVE	
	Indefinite	Definite	Indefinite	Definite
1Sg	*vár-né-k*	*vár-ná-m*	*vár-j-ak*	*vár-j-am*
3Pl	*vár-ná-nak*	*vár-ná-k*	*vár-j-anak*	*vár-j-ák*

In every tense and mood, Hungarian has two sets of person-number forms, or two "screeves", labelled respectively "indefinite" and "definite".[5] The definite screeve is used when there is a definite 3rd person direct object, whether overt or implied; the indefinite screeve is used otherwise, i.e. where either there is no object or the object is indefinite or non-3rd-person. But the 1st person singular indefinite and definite forms are syncretized in the past indicative screeves. 1st singular indefinite forms nearly always end in

---

[5] I borrow from Aronson 1982 the term "screeve" to mean "set of verb-forms differing in respect of person and number but identical as regards all other morphosyntactic properties such as tense, mood, aspect and voice".

k; only in the past indicative does this form end in *m*, making it 'look' definite.

I have included 3rd person plural forms in (13) because they suggest a motivation for this syncretism. Suppose that the 1st singular indefinite past form ended in the usual *k* rather than *m*, so as to be *vártak* rather than *vártam*. Then it would be identical with the 3rd plural form of the same screeve. But that would violate a generalization characteristic of all Hungarian verb forms (what Wurzel (1984) would call a "system-defining structural property"): all six person-number forms in any one screeve are distinct. Our business, however, is not with why the syncretism occurs but with how it should be described.

The actual Hungarian pattern at (13) does not constitute the only way in which tense could condition a neutralization of definiteness among 1st person singular forms. I set out schematically at (14) the four logical possibilities, of which (14a) corresponds to actual Hungarian:

(14) a.

	Indef	Def
Present	*k*	*m*
Past	*m*	*m*

b.

	Indef	Def
Present	*k*	*m*
Past	*k*	*k*

c.

	Indef	Def
Present	*m*	*m*
Past	*k*	*m*

d.

	Indef	Def
Present	*k*	*k*
Past	*k*	*m*

It will be desirable if as many as possible of the three Pseudo-Hungarian patterns at (14b–d) are excluded by our theory. I will argue that Noyer's approach does not do so well in this respect as Axioms A–D, supplemented by Axiom E below:

E. An affix cannot have a meaning which contains the least marked property within a morphosyntactic category.[6]

Axiom E is the morphosyntactic analog of the fact that (for example) in the English lexicon, where arguably the semantic property FEMALE is marked in relation to MALE, there is no word for a specifically male actor or a specifically male secretary, although there is a derived word for a specifically

---

[6]At first sight Axiom E may seem incompatible with (12) above, where [masculine] and [3] are mentioned in the meanings of *um* and *am*. But [3] could without damage be omitted there, so that we would rely on the Panini Principle to ensure that these affixes not appear in 1st and 2nd person contexts; and [masculine] is arguably a marked gender in Nimboran, with feminines and inanimates grouped together in the unmarked gender.

female actor (*actress*). (There are of course words for a specifically male sibling and child, namely *brother* and *son*, for example; but these are suppletive rather than affixally derived.) In relation to Hungarian, Axiom E has the important effect of barring meanings which contain [singular], [indefinite] or [present], since these are all unmarked in relation to [plural], [definite] and [past] respectively. (The relatively unmarked status of indefinite forms is shown by the fact that they are the only forms available to intransitive verbs and that they are used even with definite objects when these are 1st or 2nd person.) But let us first consider how Impoverishment fares in relation to (Pseudo-)Hungarian.

An Impoverishment analysis for actual Hungarian, as shown at (13) and (14a), is offered at (15), where (15a) states the Impoverishment rule and (15b) states appropriate meanings for the affixes *k* and *m*:

(15) a. [−definite] → Ø / [+1 −pl +past __]
      b. *k*   [+1 −pl −definite]
          m   [+1 −pl]

But it is easy to construct Impoverishment analyses for the three Pseudo-Hungarians too. For (14b), (14c) and (14d) respectively, the appropriate rules and affixal meanings are as stated in (16), (17) and (18):

(16) a. [+definite] → Ø / [+1 −pl +past __]
      b. *m*   [+1 −pl +definite]
          k   [+1 −pl]
(17) a. [−definite] → Ø / [+1 −pl −past −condit −subjunc __]
      b. *k*   [+1 −pl −definite]
          m   [+1 −pl]
(18) a. [+definite] → Ø / [+1 −pl −past −condit −subjunc __]
      b. *m*   [+1 −pl +definite]
          k   [+1 −pl]

So Noyer's approach does not appear to discriminate between real Hungarian and the three Pseudo-Hungarians in which the definiteness contrast is neutralized in other ways.

Let us now consider a lexical semantic approach. Axiom B prevents us from assigning to affixes meanings containing minus values, and Axiom E prevents us from assigning to them the meanings [singular], [indefinite] or [present]. Obeying these constraints, we can construct a representational analysis for actual Hungarian as follows:

(19)   *m*   [1 (definite OR past)]
       k   [1]

The disjunction is consistent with Axioms A and C because a verb form can be both definite and past. The meanings of both *m* and *k* lack any mention of number, but there is no risk that they will appear as interlopers in plural contexts because the 1st person *plural* suffix, lexically specified as such, will take precedence there by the Panini Principle.

If we look just at the data at (13) and (14), it may seem that we can also construct an analysis for the Pseudo-Hungarian of (14d), like this:

(20)   *m*   [1 definite (past OR conditional OR subjunctive)]
       k   [1]

The trouble with this is that, as (13) shows, the property [past] is relevant only to indicative verb-forms, so the disjunction in (20) should probably not be regarded as compatible with Axioms A and C.

Difficulties of a different kind arise with Pseudo-Hungarians (14b) and (14c). As the reader can check, there is no way of contriving representational analyses for these without violating either Axiom B (banning minus values) or Axiom E (banning least marked properties). So the lexical semantic approach has the desirable characteristic that, of the four possible definiteness neutralizations considered, only the one which actually occurs in Hungarian is expressible in it.

5   Are Rules of Referral Still Needed?

One of Noyer's concerns is to minimize or remove entirely the need to invoke "rules of referral" of the kind discussed by Zwicky (1985) and Stump (1993). I suspect that such rules will still be needed, for example to account for the Latin future-subjunctive syncretism in the 1st person singular which Noyer mentions at his (40c). I suspect that they may also apply in two Nimboran neutralizations for which I have not offered any lexical semantic analysis: plural-dual in the 2nd person and (affecting stems as well as affixes) in certain special contexts. This certainly looks like a defect of my approach by comparison with Noyer's handling in terms of Impoverishment. But in the spirit of the lexical semantic approach which I have been exploring, it is worth considering whether there are any instances outside the area of affixal meaning where a word-form looks as if it ought to mean something other than what it does—where, in other words, the expression of one meaning could be said to be "referred" to a form more appropriate for another. If so, it will not be too surprising or discouraging to find that rules of referral play a role in affixal semantics also.

Instances of the relevant kind do indeed exist. They are instances of the "X-in-form-but-Y-in-meaning" phenomenon, as found in pluralia tantum in many languages (nouns which are idiosynratically plural in form but singular in meaning) and deponent verbs in Latin and Greek (passive or middle in form but active in meaning). One fact about this phenomenon is that the referral generally seems to be from a less to a more marked property; we do not find verbs which are active in form but passive in meaning, for example. There is an intriguing correspondence here with the problematic Nimboran neutralizations. The neutralized forms in the 2nd person "look" dual rather than plural, while in the special contexts it is the singular which "looks" dual, with plural-looking forms occupying the whole dual-plural territory. So in both these instances, as well as in the Latin subjunctive-future syncretism, a case can be made for saying that a less marked property is referred for realizational purposes to a more marked one. If this turns out to be how things are generally, the phenomenon of referral may indeed be satisfyingly constrained, but paradoxically in a fashion directly opposed to the spirit of Noyer's analysis of it in terms of Impoverishment.

References

Aronson, Howard. 1982. *Georgian: A Reading Grammar*. Columbus, Ohio: Slavica.

Bierwisch, Manfred. 1967. Syntactic Features in Morphology: General Problems of the So-Called Pronominal Inflection in German. In *To Honor Roman Jakobson*, 241–270. The Hague: Mouton.

Carstairs, Andrew. 1984. Outlines of a Constraint on Syncretism. *Folia Linguistica* 18:73–85.

Carstairs, Andrew. 1987. *Allomorphy in Inflexion*. London: Croom Helm.

Carstairs-McCarthy, Andrew. 1994. Inflection Classes, Gender and the Principle of Contrast. *Language* 70:737–788.

Carstairs, Andrew and Joseph P. Stemberger. 1988. A Processing Constraint on Inflectional Homonymy. *Linguistics* 26:601–617.

Clark, Eve. 1993. *The Lexicon in Acquisition*. Cambridge: CUP.

Dixon, R.M.W. 1971. A Method of Semantic Description. In Danny D. Steinberg and Leon A. Jakobovits, eds., *Semantics: An Interdisciplinary Reader in Philosophy, Linguistics and Psychology*, 436–471. Cambridge: CUP.

Dixon, R.M.W. 1972. *The Dyirbal Language of North Queensland*. Cambridge: CUP.

Inkelas, Sharon. 1993. Nimboran Position Class Morphology. *Natural Language and Linguistic Theory* 11:559–624.

Jackendoff, Ray. 1985. Multiple Subcategorization and the θ-Criterion: The Case of *Climb*. *Natural Language and Linguistic Theory* 3:271–295.

Matthews, P.H. 1991. *Morphology*. (2nd edition.) Cambridge: CUP.

Stump, Gregory T. 1993. On Rules of Referral. *Language* 69:449–479.

Williams, Edwin. 1981. On the Notions "Lexically Related" and "Head of a Word". *Linguistic Inquiry* 12:245–274.

Wurzel, Wolfgang Ullrich. 1984. *Flexionsmorphologie und Natürlichkeit*. Berlin: Akademie-Verlag.

Zwicky, Arnold. 1985. How to Describe Inflection. *Berkeley Linguistic Society Papers* 11.372–386.

Discussion of the Papers by Noyer and Carstairs-McCarthy

Lapointe: I have a number of comments and questions; I'll try to reduce them to a few. One of the morals I came away with after reading the circulated versions of your two papers was this: if you add the notion of more marked and less marked to the Referral system, you end up saying very similar things to the Impoverishment system.

Noyer: Right, I think they're quite the same; that's the leading insight.

Lapointe: I wanted to underscore that because I didn't think that it had come out. The second thing I came away with was that in order to decide whether the generalization about moving from more marked to less marked is correct what we probably really need to do first is to decide on what the markedness for morphosyntactic features is. Because I got the sense that in the case of different languages in the same morphosyntactic domain you were giving feature analyses which split the values in different way ...

Noyer: I have a remark to make about that. I think that this is just a misunderstanding, because to say that 'plus' is marked and 'minus' is unmarked, is first of all to misunderstand what markedness is. I mean, it's not the 'plus' or the 'minus'. Secondly, it's contextualized. So [+singular] is perhaps the unmarked or [+plural] might be marked, but [–plural] is marked in the context of [–singular]; if you're nonsingular, you're likely to be plural. So, I think that markedness is a sort of evaluative rule system on top of the representation. It's not just that you look at the representation and then say, "Ah-hah, this is marked." So, you have to give a system of redundancy rules, or a system that gives you what's marked and what isn't.

Lapointe: Fair enough; the point's well taken, but I think your last remark was the one that I was trying to make as well, and that is that we have to decide on exactly what we are taking as the marked and unmarked first.

But I had a question for Andrew, and that had to do with your [Axiom] E. I saw this in the circulated paper, and immediately wondered how one describes the pedestrian case of the English present tense, because under the usual Elsewhere sort of story that would pop into one's mind, you'd say, "The third person singular is marked with -*s* and everything else is the stem form." But given the rest of your assumptions here, and [Axiom] E, I think what you'd have to say is something like, "The first singular and the second singular and the plurals are marked by the stem form, and then the -*s* is the Elsewhere case." No?

Carstairs-McCarthy: No, I think there are genuine problems for Axiom E, but this is not one of them, because people tend to say that the -*s* ending is third person singular simple present. Well, my answer is that it's not simple present; what it is is habitual or future—because when do you use that -*s*? *He comes to Davis every year* or *He comes tomorrow; we're going to meet him at the airport.* That is, apart from verbs like *know*, certain verbs of intellectual activity: *knowing, seeing, believing* that sort of thing, where it is true that in contemporary English you have to use the present. But my story about that would be on the lines of saying, "Well, -*s* is a disjunction of relatively marked morphosyntactic situations, namely habitual or future, and it crops up in the third person—well, I don't have anything very good to say about that. Why doesn't it crop up everywhere as it does in many dialects, of course where the -*s* is regularized throughout. You could say, "Well, third person is the least marked context and in Jakobsonian terms, the least marked context is the one where you expect most distinctions to be made ... so it's perhaps the context where you expect the most aspectual and tense distinctions to be made."

Noyer: That is Impoverishment, what you just said. It's saying that tense distinctions are obliterated except in the third person, right, and you get -*s* there because that's the only place where tense is left.

Carstairs-McCarthy: All right, OK. Well, you know I'm not against Impoverishment generally. I think what I was tackling in this paper was the view that Impoverishment made important, correct claims about the class of possible languages, which I think we agree now it doesn't succeed in doing.

Noyer: Weakly generable languages.

Carstairs-McCarthy: Weakly generable, OK. For me, weakly generable languages are what matter.
[Laughter]

Janda: I'd like to ask a question of both speakers. You seem to know lots of things about what's a generalization and what's not, and when to avoid homophony, and I'd like to ask about how you know that.

Noyer: I *don't* know. [Laughter]

Janda: Your paper depends on it, so let me ask you ...   I think what you'd say is that you lose a generalization if you impose constraints on how you put features together, just so as not to happen to have a certain thing. Now, I'd like to know how you know that. Do Romanian speakers remark to each other, "No, we can't say such a thing"? ...

Noyer: You're right. This depends on the assumption that part of explanatory adequacy is to express the theoretical impossibility of a certain distinction, irrespective of the presence of signals to express that. Now, I don't know, Donka, where are you? What do you think? Can I make up a Romanian adjective and say, "Well, this happens to be the NEUTER form here for this neologism"?

Donka Farkas: Well, in principle, you might try to make it up, but the fact of the language is that you never do.

Janda: But do people notice that they don't have an ending?

Farkas: I think what people notice is what is actually relevant to the real domain, there are three classes of nouns, as opposed to two classes of adjectives and determiners.

Janda: But speakers usually don't know about these classes, right? I mean, the grammarians are the ones who make lists of classes.

Farkas: But what you know that speakers know is how they use these nouns, and they use them differently. So, that's how we know that speakers know something. If you ask the speaker of Romanian whether the word for 'sound' is MASCULINE, FEMINE, or NEUTER, what the speaker will do is think, "*zgomot/zgomote*—ah! it changes, it's a NEUTER noun."

Noyer: The Impoverishment theory defines what the classes are. It's saying exactly what Donka is saying. It's saying that in this particular morphosyntactic context this distinction doesn't exist, this category is not there.

Farkas: But the further point is that the speaker will treat the word 'chair' differently from a MASCULINE even in the SINGULAR and differently from a FEMININE even in the PLURAL in certain cases. That would show that there is a three-way categorization in nouns.

...

Stump: [At the end of Noyer's paper], you list [in (40)] some remaining cases you hope to look at in future research. I actually have a [(40d)] that I would like to have you add there. This is actually yet another syncretism from Romanian, and I'm bringing it up because it embodies what I think are going to be the two big problems that you're going to run into with the Impoverishment approach to syncretism.

In Romanian, there are four main conjugations, and in all but the first, there's a regular syncretism in the present tense of the first person singular and the third person plural. Now that would make you want to hope to be able to say that either the first person singular or the third person plural is the unmarked person number combination in Romanian. Now I agree with Steve that we do have to have explicit criteria for deciding what counts as the least marked, but I really think that in Romanian you're going to find that third person singular is the least marked person/number combination. If you have impersonal verbs in Romanian, they always default to third person singular agreement. So here you seemingly have a case where you have two categories standing in a syncretic relationship, in which neither is less marked than the other; the least marked person/number combination is yet something else. That's the first problem.

The second problem, exemplified by the same referral, is this. In some paradigms, it's clearly the third plural form that's taking after the first singular. You know that this happens in the paradigm of the verb 'to talk', because you get a singular stem form showing up in all the singular forms, and it shows up where else? In the third person plural. In the paradigm of the verb 'to be' on the other hand, you have just the reverse situation. That is, you have a special plural stem form that shows up in all the plural stem forms—where else? First person singular. In other words, it's a good example of what I in my *Language* paper call a bidirectional referral; in other words the referral goes one way in one set of forms and the other way in a complementary set of forms. Again, that seems to me incompatible with the Impoverishment approach that you're proposing here. Again, I would add that on as a [(40d)]—something to look at.

Noyer: Well, yeah, certainly there are going to be other cases I'm going to have to look at, but in the written version I talked about Old Icelandic, which appears to be a case of precisely this sort. My position here, I can always concede, but before doing that, I'd just like to remark that exactly as Andrew said, I'm not claiming that the signal that you get is going to be naively correlated with such and such. So it looks like third person is becoming first singular—that depends on the assumption of what you see in first singular is representationally first singular. So, really what the Impoverishment theory claims is that there's two things going on. There's the changes in the position, and then there's the representation; together they give the distribution. Now, when it looks like this is becoming that, it might be this is becoming that, but it might be this is becoming something else, and the representations are together collaborating to give that distribution. That was how I tried to do the Old Icelandic. Now that may or may not work, and that may or may not be motivated, but it's certainly something I can try in this instance.

Aronoff: [In the Romanian case,] in the PLURAL, the FEMININE PLURAL seems a little odd. It strikes me that one way of looking at this is, well, what Donka said, "It switches, so it must be NEUTER." I think that's why in some sense it's the FEMININE—in effect it's that switching, and none of these theories can really express that. In other words, this is something whose realization goes across categories, and it seems to me that all of these frameworks are missing that functional aspect of it. But it's the fact that it switches that allows this particular third form to persist in some way.

Carstairs-McCarthy: I do have something to say about Romanian gender in my *Language* article, but it's perhaps slightly off your point. The point is that even though there are as it were more genders than are strictly necessary in Romanian, so as to give everything work to do, still there is only one gender which is the Elsewhere gender in singular and plural respectively.

Noyer: I guess my response to that is that if Romanian didn't look like this, then we would just call it another name. So if the extra gender had some other distribution, we wouldn't be talking about functionality, so I guess my position would be that this is an accident. If it worked differently, we'd call it some sort of allomorphy. Oh, and by the way, I think that pseudo-Nimboran looks like a fine language, and I don't know about anybody else, but I don't see why we shouldn't allow it to come up.

Interfaces: Explanation of Allomorphy and the Architecture of Grammars

DAVID M. PERLMUTTER

1. Goals

What is the range of possible interactions among the components of a grammar? This paper addresses this question by examining one type of "C/V-sensitive allomorphy" (conditioned by whether some segment external to the allomorph is a consonant or vowel).[1] Our first goal is to show that it is possible to explain why such allomorphy exists and why it has the properties it does. Optimality Theory makes it possible to achieve this

---

[1] This is a revised and expanded version of the paper presented at the conference. §7 was not presented there, but was developed in response to comments by the conference participants, to whom I am grateful.

At the conference I became aware of Tranel 1994, whose analysis is very close to that developed here. Tranel considers French elision and liaison to be a phonological problem and shows the data can be accounted for with the constraint ranking: ONSET >> GENDER >> AIF ("Avoid Integrating Floaters"). He then shows that the same devices can account for the allomorphy analyzed here. The present paper begins with the morphological problem of allomorphy and then shows that the devices that solve it can account for the phenomena analyzed phonologically in terms of elision and liaison. The key elements shared by both analyses are Optimality Theoretic constraint ranking and ONSET. There are also differences. Tranel derives alternants phonologically from a single underlying form with a latent vowel or consonant, while this paper regards alternating forms as distinct in the lexicon. This paper uses NO-CODA, while Tranel's (1994) AIF constraint is uniquely for latent segments; he adopts NO-CODA in Tranel 1995c. Tranel does not deal with the consequences for syntax and the architecture of grammars discussed in §§7-8. Despite these differences between the two papers, the domains of data and solutions are very close. Together they show what neither shows alone: regardless of whether these phenomena are analyzed as phonological or morphological, the relevant generalizations are captured in a grammar with Optimality Theoretic constraint ranking in which ONSET outranks the device that usually ensures Concord in gender.

I have benefited from discussions of these matters with Farrell Ackerman, Chris Barker, Sean Erwin, Patrick Farrell, Gilles Fauconnier, Sharon Inkelas, John Moore, Irina Nikolaeva, Orhan Orgun, Karin Pizer, Maria Polinsky, Sanford Schane, Bernard Tranel, and Moira Yip. Farrell Ackerman, Chris Barker, Diane Brentari, Sean Erwin, Steven Lapointe, John Moore, Orhan Orgun, and Karin Pizer gave me helpful comments on earlier drafts of manuscript fragments. I am also indebted to Françoise Santore, Karin Pizer, Gilles Fauconnier, and Pascal Beausoleil for native judgments on some of the French data, and to Patrick Farrell and Svetlana Vasina for invaluable cyberhelp. Responsibility for errors and inadequacies is mine alone.

without rules of allomorphy because the allomorphs' distribution follows from independently needed constraints if they are ranked and violable. Allomorph selection is then one aspect of optimal output selection in the phonological component. This reveals the allomorphs to be multiple inputs to the phonological component. Most interestingly, French allows violations of NP-internal Concord in order to satisfy ONSET, a phonological constraint. But such interaction is not possible under current conceptions of grammatical architecture, which do not allow phonology to influence syntax. We explore the consequences of this result for the architecture of grammars.

The key syntactic phenomenon in this paper is French NP-internal Concord, illustrated in (1-2):

	Masculine		*Feminine*	
(1)	a. *ce choix*	'this choice'	b. *cette voix*	'this voice'
(2)	a. *mon choix*	'my choice'	b. *ma voix*	'my voice'

In (1a) and (2a), the demonstrative *ce* and the possessive adjective *mon* are masculine in agreement with the masculine head *choix*. In (1b) and (2b), on the other hand, the demonstrative and possessive adjective have the feminine forms *cette* and *ma*, respectively, in agreement with the feminine head *voix*.

To account for such data, syntactic theories have incorporated rules of NP-internal Concord. If we define the notion "Concord set" as in (3), we can state Concord for French informally as in (4).

(3)   A *Concord set* consists of a head noun and its adjectival modifiers.[2]

(4)   *Concord:* No two members of a Concord set can have distinct gender or number feature values.

Most current syntactic theories formalize Concord with some kind of feature-checking device that ensures that the relevant feature values on the head noun and its adjectival modifiers do not clash.

2. Four Cases of C/V-Sensitive Allomorphy in French

2.1. The Demonstrative

The allomorphs of the French demonstrative - *ce* and *CET*[3] - have the distribution in (5-6):

---

[2]In French this class (henceforth "adjectivals") includes articles, demonstratives, possessives, certain quantifiers, and locative determiners (cf. §2.4), as well as ordinary adjectives.

[3]Orthographically distinct feminine *cette* and masculine *cet* are phonologically identical. Throughout this paper I use the masculine spelling in capital letters to indicate such forms, e.g. *CET, BEL, NOUVEL, VIEIL.*

(5)   *Feminine*   *Masculine*
Pre-C   *cette voix* 'this voice'   *ce choix* 'this voice'
Pre-V   *cette épée* 'this sword'   *cet été*   'this summer'

The feminine form is always *CET*. For the masculine, *ce* is used before a consonant and *CET* before a vowel. (6) shows that what is relevant is whether the *immediately following word* begins with a vowel or consonant.

(6) a. cet homme 'this man'   b. *ce jeune homme* 'this young man'

Vowel-initial masculine *homme* /ɔm/ determines the allomorph *CET*, but if it is preceded by a consonant-initial word (e.g. *jeune*), the allomorph *ce* is used, as in *ce jeune homme*.

Traditional analyses of this distribution state the form of the feminine demonstrative, as in (7), accounting for the distribution of forms with a masculine head with rules of allomorphy, as in (8):

(7) Feminine demonstrative: *CET*
(8) Masculine demonstrative: *ce* before a C, *CET* before a V

A rule of allomorphy like (8), however, leaves important questions unanswered:

(9)   a.   Why does the masculine have allomorphy instead of the feminine?
      b.   Why is there allomorphy in this environment (pre-C vs. pre-V)?
      c.   Why is the pre-V masculine form the same as the feminine form?

These questions must be answered if the allomorphy is to be explained.

2.2. Possessive Adjectives

Possessive adjectives also display allomorphy, but in the feminine form rather than the masculine:

(10) *Feminine*   *Masculine*
Pre-C *ma voix*   'my voice'   *mon choix* 'my choice'
Pre-V *mon épée*   'my sword'   *mon été*   'my summer'
(11) *ma nouvelle épée* 'my new sword'

The masculine form of the first person singular possessive adjective is always *mon*. For the feminine, *ma* is used before a consonant and *mon* before a vowel. As with the demonstrative, what is relevant is whether the *immediately following word* begins with a vowel or a consonant. In (11), where the vowel-initial noun is preceded by a consonant-initial adjective, the feminine form is again *ma*. The second person singular *(ta/ton)* and third person singular *(sa/son)* possessive adjectives have the same distribution.

A grammar of French thus needs rules like those stated informally in (12-13):

(12) Masc. poss. adjs.: *mon* (1st Sg.), *ton* (2d Sg.), *son* (3d Sg.)
(13) The feminine possessive adjectives have two allomorphs:
      a. *ma* (1st Sg.), *ta* (2d Sg.), and *sa* (3d Sg.) before a consonant
      b. *mon* (1st Sg.), *ton* (2d Sg.), and *son* (3d Sg.) before a vowel

A grammar with such rules of allomorphy leaves important questions unanswered:

(14)   a. Why does the feminine have allomorphy rather than the masculine?
       b. Why does the allomorphy occur in the environment where it does (pre-C vs. pre-V)?
       c. Why are the pre-C feminine allomorphs the same as the masculine forms?

2.3. Prenominal Adjectives

Attributive adjectives in French generally follow the head noun. Certain adjectives can precede the head, however, and a few of these display allomorphy sensitive to pre-C vs. pre-V environments.

(15)	*Feminine*	*Masculine*
Pre-C	*une belle voix*	*un beau choix*
	'a beautiful voice'	'a beautiful choice'
Pre-V	*une belle épée*	*un bel été*
	'a beautiful sword'	'a beautiful summer'
(16)	*un bel homme*	*un beau jeune homme*
	'a good-looking man'	'a good-looking young man'

The feminine form is always *BEL*. The masculine displays *beau* before a consonant, but *BEL* before a word beginning with a vowel, as illustrated in (16). Like *beau/BEL* 'beautiful' are *nouveau/NOUVEL* 'new', *vieux/VIEIL* 'old', *fou/FOL* 'crazy', *mou/MOL* 'soft, half-hearted', and a few others.[4]

In addition to listing the feminine adjective forms *BEL, NOUVEL, VIEIL*, etc., a grammar of French needs a rule of allomorphy like (17):

(17)   The masculine form is *beau, nouveau*, etc. before a consonant, *BEL, NOUVEL*, etc. before a vowel.

---

[4]Tranel (1992) argues that *bon/bonne* 'good' and *sot/sotte* 'silly' are in this class.

Rules like (17) again fail to answer the questions in (9), leaving the allomorphy unexplained.

2.4. Locative Determiners

Certain geographical names usually require a definite article, but have a locative form that replaces it and displays allomorphy sensitive to the contrast between pre-C and pre-V environments. I call these "locative determiners."[5]

(18)	*Feminine*	*Masculine*
a. Pre-C	en France	au Japon
	en Suède	au Mexique
	en Grèce	au Portugal
	en Terre-Neuve	au Manitoba
	en Colombie-Britannique	au Québec
b. Pre-V	en Italie	en Ontario
	en Espagne	en Alberta
	en Algérie	en Irak
	en Allemagne	en Israël

With a feminine head, the locative is *en*. With a masculine head, there is allomorphy: *au* before a consonant and *en* before a vowel. A grammar of French thus needs (19) to state the feminine form, and rules of allomorphy like those in (20) to account for the masculine forms:

(19) Feminine form: *en*

(20) The masculine form is *au* before a consonant, *en* before a vowel.

These rules fail to answer the questions in (9), leaving the allomorphy in (18) unexplained.

3. Summary of Allomorphy and Key Generalizations

3.1. Summary of Allomorphy

The four cases of allomorphy in §2 are summarized in (21).

---

[5]The generative literature on these forms includes Cornulier 1972, Zwicky 1987 (which characterizes the semantic differences between them and the locative preposition *à*), Miller 1992: 279, and Miller, Pullum, and Zwicky 1992, which analyzes them as a case of phonologically conditioned allomorphy (which can be explained under the analysis developed below). Miller, Pullum, and Zwicky also point out the distribution of *du* and *de* (in pre-C environments) and *d* (in pre-V environments), which would also be explained by the analysis developed below.

(21)	*Feminine*	*Masculine*
Demonstrative	*CET*	*ce* before C
		CET before V
Possessive Adj.	*ma/ta/sa* before C	*mon/ton/son*
	mon/ton/son before V	
Prenominal Adj.	*BEL*	*beau* before C
		BEL before V
Loc. Determiner	*en*	*au* before C
		en before V

This summary reveals two generalizations that require explanation.

(22) *Generalization 1:* Each case of allomorphy is sensitive to the same environments: pre-C vs. pre-V.

(23) *Generalization 2:* In each case of allomorphy, one allomorph is the same as the other gender's form.

3.2. Where Does Allomorphy Occur?

The cases where allomorphy does and does not occur are distributed as follows:

(24)	*Feminine*	*Masculine*
Demonstrative	No	Yes
Possessive Adjective	Yes	No
Prenominal Adjective	No	Yes
Locative Determiner	No	Yes

This reveals further generalizations to be explained.

(25) *Generalization 3:* Where there is no allomorphy, there is a C-final form.[6]

(26) *Generalization 4:* Where there is allomorphy, (i) there is a V-final form, and (ii) a C-final form is used as allomorph in a pre-V environment.

3.3. "Basic" vs. "Special" Forms

We now take a new step in analysis:

(27) a. The form that occurs in pre-C environments is the "basic" form.

  b. The form that occurs in pre-V environments is a "special" form.

---

[6]The forms *mon/ton/son* have the distribution of C-final forms. What is crucial, as will be seen below, is the fact that they provide the following syllable with an onset, e.g. *[mõ.ne.pe]* 'my sword'. These forms are discusssed in §6.2.

This division of the allomorphs into "basic" and "special" allows us to see their distribution in a new way:

(28) *Generalization 5:* All and only V-final "basic" forms have a "special" allomorph.

(29) *Generalization 6:* The "special" allomorph is always C-final.

(30) *Generalization 7:* The "special" allomorph is always the same as the other gender's form.

(31) *Generalization 8:* The "special" allomorph occurs always and only in pre-V environments.

These generalizations can be seen clearly in (32):

(32)	*Feminine*	*Masculine*
Demonstrative	Basic: *CET*	Basic: *ce* before C Special: *CET* before V
Possessive Adj.	Basic: *ma/ta/sa* before C Special: *mon/ton/son* before V	Basic: *mon/ton/son*
Prenominal Adj.	Basic: *BEL*	Basic: *beau* before C Special: *BEL* before V
Loc. Determiner	Basic: *en*	Basic: *au* before C Special: *en* before V

3.4 Syntactically vs. Phonologically Determined Forms

The division of allomorphs into "basic" and "special" enables us to see that the distribution of forms in pre-C and pre-V environments is governed by different considerations:

(33) *Pre-C*	*Feminine*	*Masculine*
Demonstrative	CET	ce
Possessive Adjective	ma/ta/sa	mon/ton/son
Prenominal Adjective	BEL	beau
Locative Determiner	en	au
(34) *Pre-V*	*Feminine*	*Masculine*
Demonstrative	CET	CET
Possessive Adjective	mon/ton/son	mon/ton/son
Prenominal Adjective	BEL	BEL
Locative Determiner	en	en

This reveals two further generalizations that need explanation:

(35) *Generalization 9:* Only pre-C environments allow forms *contrasting for gender* .

(36) *Generalization 10:* Pre-V environments have whichever form in (33) ends in a consonant.

These generalizations reveal very clearly the error embodied in the analysis in (21), which (i) treats each case of allomorphy separately and (ii) treats the two allomorphs as being on a par in each case. The distribution of forms in pre-C and pre-V environments is due to different principles:

(37) a. The forms in pre-C environments are *syntactically determined*.
      b. The forms in pre-V environments are *phonologically determined*.

Thus, they must result from different devices:

(38) a. The pre-C forms in (33) are due to Concord.
      b. The pre-V forms in (34) are *determined by the phonological environment*.

The question is how to incorporate these generalizations into a grammar.

4. An Explanation

4.1. Why C-final Allomorphs in Pre-V Environments?

Accounting for the "basic" forms in (33) is not problematic; standard approaches to agreement will handle them straightforwardly. The interesting cases are the "special" allomorphs in (34), which have the following properties:

(39)   a. They occur in pre-V environments.
          b. They have C-final forms.
          c. They replace V-final forms.

The first problem is to explain these properties. The second is to make them follow from the grammar.

To address the first problem, one must ask why a C-final form is used instead of a V-final form in pre-V environments. The relevant forms and environments are characterized in terms of a phonological contrast (V vs. C). The explanation is rooted in the cross-linguistic preference for syllables with an onset over V-initial syllables. Since the final consonant of a C-final form will be syllabified as onset of the following syllable in a pre-V environment, a "special" C-final allomorph in a pre-V environment ensures that the following syllable will have an onset, which it would lack if a V-final allomorph were used.

How is a grammar to capture this intuition? Optimality Theory (Prince and Smolensky 1993, McCarthy and Prince 1993) has proposed a universal constraint, ONSET, that requires a syllable to have an onset. This constraint plays a key role in the solution proposed in §4.3.

4.2. Special Allomorphs' Phonological Shape Explained

The most striking fact about the "special" allomorphs is their phonological shape:

(40) The "special" allomorph always has the same phonological shape as the opposite gender's form.

This generalization holds systematically for all cases of allomorphy discussed here: demonstratives, possessive adjectives, prenominal adjectives, and locative determiners. Why does it hold?

The first step is to realize that the "facts" of allomorphy in §2 incorporate an implicit analysis under which the demonstrative (for example) has three forms: the two masculine allomorphs *ce* and *CET*, and the feminine *CET*. *Ce* and the masculine *CET* would be marked [–Fem] in the lexicon, and the feminine *CET* [+Fem]. Under this analysis, we are faced with the problem of explaining the homophony of the masculine pre-V form *CET* and the feminine *CET*.

But suppose there are not three forms but two: a masculine form *ce* and a feminine form *CET*, and that the feminine form *CET* is used with a masculine head in pre-V environments. If there are only two forms, what appeared to be homophony under the standard analysis is merely an artifact of analyzing masculine *CET* as an allomorph of the masculine *ce*, instead of analyzing it as an instance of the feminine *CET*. Under this analysis, there is no accidental homophony; if there are only two forms, what appeared to be accidental homophony is explained.

Why is the feminine *CET* used with a masculine head in pre-V environments? If the V-final form *ce* were used, the following syllable would lack an onset, violating the ONSET constraint:

(41) ONSET: A well-formed syllable has an onset.

The key idea is that in pre-V environments, C-final forms are used for phonological reasons: to satisfy ONSET. Where the C-final form bears the opposite gender features, Concord is violated.

Why have scholars assumed analyses with accidental homophony, such as those exemplified by the rules of allomorphy (8), (13), (17), and (20)? These analyses seem to be motivated by the widespread assumption that modifiers agree with their heads in gender *in all cases*.[7] Under the analysis proposed here, however, examples such as *cet été* and *cet homme* in (5-6) have the feminine form *CET* although the head noun is masculine (a Concord violation) because masculine *ce* would yield **ce été* and **ce homme* (ONSET violations). In pre-C environments, however, ONSET is

---

[7]Such agreement, of course, is the usual case cross-linguistically; French is unusual in sacrificing Concord to ONSET.

satisfied, so Concord holds (cf. (33)). Thus, the forms in pre-C environments are syntactically determined.

The same analysis, *mutatis mutandis*, extends to the possessive adjectives, prenominal adjectives, and locative determiners. In each case, the opposite gender's form is used in pre-V environments to satisfy ONSET. This explains the phonological shape of the form used in pre-V environments.

4.3. A Solution without Allomorphy

How does the grammar allow Concord violations? A solution comes from the key idea of Optimality Theory: linguistic constraints are violable and ranked; lower-ranked constraints are regularly and predictably violated when necessary to ensure satisfaction of a higher-ranked constraint. We can account for Concord violations in pre-V environments by specifying that ONSET outranks Concord:

(42) ONSET >> Concord

Concord will be violated just in case such a violation is needed to ensure that ONSET is satisfied. In pre-V environments, a V-final form violates ONSET, while a C-final form does not. Thus, although they violate Concord, C-final modifiers such as those in *CET homme* 'this man' and *mon épée* 'my sword' are chosen over the alternatives **ce homme* and **ma épée*, which violate the higher-ranked constraint ONSET. In pre-V environments, Concord is regularly and predictably violated to satisfy ONSET. In pre-C environments, however, the following syllable has an onset, so ONSET is satisfied. Thus, Concord is respected as well. That is why the forms in pre-C environments are syntactically determined.

This solution automatically accounts for the fact that where a form is syntactically determined, it is determined by the gender of the *head noun*, but where it is phonologically determined, it is determined by the *following word*:

(43)	a.	*cet homme*	'this man'
	b.	*ce jeune homme*	'this young man'
(44)	a.	*ce bel homme*	'this good-looking man'
	b.	*ce beau jeune homme*	'this good-looking young man'

CET is used in the pre-V environment of (43a); in the pre-C environments of (43b) and (44), *ce* is required by the masculine head *homme*. Similarly, *BEL* is used in the pre-V environment of (44a), and *beau* in the pre-C environment of (44b).

Our solution also accounts for pre-pausal environments, which pattern with pre-C environments:

(45) *Cet homme est beau.* 'This man is good-looking.'

Since ONSET cannot be violated in pre-pausal environments, Concord must be satisfied and the masculine form *beau* is used.

Under this solution, there is no allomorphy. What initially appeared to be allomorphy is the use of one gender's form instead of the other's to avoid ONSET violations. This simplifies both the lexicon and the grammar. The lexicon is simplified because it does not need to list two different allomorphs in each case of apparent allomorphy; it suffices for each lexical entry to list one form for each gender:

(46) | | Masculine | Feminine |
|---|---|---|
| Demonstrative | œ | CET |
| Possessive Adjective | mon/ton/son[8] | ma/ta/sa |
| Prenominal Adjective | beau | BEL |
| Locative Determiner | au | en |

The grammar is simplified because the rules of allomorphy in (8), (13), (17), and (20) are not needed; the distribution of what appeared to be allomorphs is accounted for by the ranking in (42) of two independently needed constraints.

4.4. The Generalizations Explained

This solution not only results in a simpler lexicon and grammar, it also explains why the generalizations in the data hold. The fact that the apparent allomorphy is motivated by the need to avoid ONSET violations explains generalizations 1, 3, 4, 5, 6, 8, 9, and 10 in §3. The fact that the "special" allomorph is simply the other gender's form explains generalization 2/7.

Most importantly, this solution explains why there appears to be allomorphy in the first place. Together with the independently needed lexical entries, the constraint ranking in (42) automatically predicts in what environments a non-agreeing form will be used, yielding allomorphy effects. A grammar that eliminates allomorphy is not only simpler, it achieves genuine explanation of the phenomenon itself.

In sum, a grammar that states rules of allomorphy fails to explain:

(47)   a.   Why there is allomorphy
       b.   Why the allomorphy occurs in the environments it does
       c.   Why the allomorphs have the phonological shape they do

---

[8]The lexical entries for these forms are refined in (62) in §6.2 below.

It can explain none of these things because what a grammar stipulates it cannot explain. By contrast, the grammar proposed here explains all three with the constraint ranking in (42).

4.5. On Rules of Referral

"Rules of referral" (Zwicky 1985a, 1985b, 1987) provide an account of generalizations like 2/7 in §3, stating that one bundle of morphosyntactic features is realized in the same way as another. Rules of referral, however, are just a subclass of rules of allomorphy; our arguments against rules of allomorphy are also arguments against rules of referral. Explanation comes from eliminating such rules entirely.

Zwicky (1987) states rules of referral for the definite article, demonstratives, possessive adjectives, and locative determiners in French, all of which have the same environment: "when a V-initial word follows." He attempts to generalize them into a single rule (1987: 223), but Miller (1992: 278–279) points out that this attempt fails because in pre-V environments, the feminine possessives have the masculine form, while the masculine demonstratives and locative determiners have the feminine forms.[9] This brings out the fact that rules of referral are *directional*: we would need one rule to say that certain masculines have the same realization as the corresponding feminines, and another to "refer" certain feminines to the corresponding masculines. A single rule of referral cannot generalize over all cases with C/V-sensitive allomorphy in French. Thus, rules of referral fare no better than other rules of allomorphy in capturing the French generalizations.

4.6. Independent Evidence for the Role of ONSET: Words Beginning in Aspirate *h*

Independent evidence for the role of ONSET comes from so-called "aspirate *h*" (*h aspiré*), which has no phonetic realization. The V-final form occurs before aspirate-*h* words, although they begin with a vowel phonetically.

(48)	Correct form	Gloss		Incorrect form
Demonstrative	*ce héros*	'this hero'		**cet héros*
Possessive Adj.	*ma Hongrie*	'my Hungary'		**mon Hongrie*
Prenominal Adj.	*un beau héros*	'a good-looking hero'		**un bel héros*
Loc. Determiner	*au Honduras*	'in Honduras'		**en Honduras*

A number of solutions to the problem of aspirate *h* have been offered in French phonology. Tranel (1995a) reviews this literature and concludes

---

[9]In addition, the definite article has a third form in pre-V environments that is distinct from both genders' pre-C forms (cf. (65) below). Miller also points out that Zwicky's rules incorrectly yield *à* + *l* instead of *en* for the place names in (18b).

that the best account is provided by the "syllable-island hypothesis," under which a preceding consonant cannot serve as onset of a syllable beginning in aspirate *h* (Tranel 1992),[10] i.e., words beginning in aspirate *h* systematically violate ONSET. The fact that before aspirate *h* the C-final forms are *not* used accords with our hypothesis that the appearance of the C-final forms in pre-V environments is due to ONSET.

5. The Interface between the Lexicon and the Phonological Component

5.1. Multiple Inputs: The Status of Suppletive Allomorphs

The key idea of Optimality Theory is that the ranked constraints determine the optimal output from a set of *candidate outputs*. From a given input, a function, GEN, generates the candidate set, which is essentially the set of all outputs generable from that input by some possible natural language grammar. The *de facto* candidate set is reduced to more manageable proportions by faithfulness constraints, which require that a form be faithful to input. Where other constraints outrank faithfulness constraints, outputs differing from inputs in specific ways are well-formed.

Under our analysis, in cases of suppletion *more than one form* serves as input to GEN. Let us call the set of inputs to GEN the "input set." From each member of the input set, GEN generates a set of candidate forms. If there are multiple inputs, the candidate set will be the union of the candidate sets generated by GEN from each member of the input set. Each member of the input set is then a target of faithfulness. Informally we speak of a given allomorph violating some constraint. This means that those candidate outputs generated by GEN from that input and faithful to it in relevant respects violate the constraint.

5.2. A Consequence for the Phonology-Morphology Interface

A standard view of the phonology-morphology interface is that in each environment, rules of allomorphy select a single allomorph that serves as input to the phonology. This view is stated clearly by Zwicky (1985b: 432): "inflectional allomorphy rules (as a set) are distinct from, and precede, phonological rules of all types." Anderson (1988: 150) states that "current research assumes a distinction between rules of 'phonology' and rules of

---

[10]Tranel (1994) formalizes this in terms of alignment, using the constraint "ALIGN-LEFT" to designate the requirement that the left edges of word and syllable coincide. The idea is that when a word "borrows" a consonant from the preceding word to satisfy ONSET in the initial syllable, the ranking ONSET>>ALIGN-LEFT holds because left edges of syllable and word do not coincide. This is what happens in most cases. Tranel claims that aspirate-h words are exceptional in imposing the reverse ranking ALIGN-LEFT>>ONSET, i.e. they systematically violate ONSET in order to satisfy ALIGN-LEFT.

'allomorphy' virtually without comment." Eliminating rules of allomorphy and having ONSET do their work means that (at least in this case) allomorph selection occurs in the phonological component. Since ONSET rejects candidates faithful to one allomorph in favor of those faithful to the other, both allomorphs must be in the input set from which GEN generates the set of candidate outputs. Allomorph selection is thus not a separate phenomenon, but results from the phonological constraints' selecting the optimal output from the candidates generated by GEN.[11]

5.3. Lexical Sourcing

Whether the input set has one member or more than one is determined by the lexicon:

(49)   *Lexical Sourcing:* The input set is supplied by the lexicon.

In some cases the lexicon supplies more than one input. For example, the adjective that means "beautiful" has a single lexical entry with a semantic representation and morphosyntactic features. But two forms, each with its own gender feature and phonological shape, constitute the input set:[12]

(50) *bo* [–Fem]; *BEL* [+Fem]

5.4. Some Consequences of Lexical Sourcing

Lexical Sourcing predicts that *ceteris paribus* constraint violations will be found in French where the lexicon provides no input that does *not* violate them.[13] The correctness of this prediction can be seen in the cases below, where no lexical form is available to satisfy ONSET.

5.4.1. Case One: V-Final Prenominal Adjectives

The prenominal adjectives *beau/BEL, nouveau/NOUVEL, vieux/VIEIL,* and a few others have distinct masculine and feminine forms, the masculine ending in a vowel and the feminine in a consonant. Lexical Sourcing correctly predicts that ONSET violations will be found where the lexicon provides only one form of an adjective and it is V-final:

(51)   *un vrai ami*   'a true friend'
(52)   *un joli enfant*   'a pretty child'

---

[11]Future research will determine the extent to which this is true of phonologically conditioned allomorphy cross-linguistically. It seems to hold for C/V-sensitive allomorphy universally (Perlmutter, in preparation).

[12]Space limitations prevent analysis of the plural here.

[13]All other things would *not* be equal if ONSET outranked relevant faithfulness constraints. Then French would require an epenthetic consonant in the environments discussed below where ONSET violations occur.

ONSET does not characterize (51-52) as ungrammatical *because there is no alternative form that does not violate ONSET*. Compare these with:

(53)   a. *un bel enfant*   'a beautiful child'
         b. **un beau enfant*

The contrast between (52) and *(53b) results from the interaction of the ranked constraints with the fact that the lexicon happens to have two alternative forms of *beau/BEL* but only one form of *joli*. Under the grammar proposed here, the ungrammaticality of *(53b) follows from the availability of (53a), while the grammaticality of (51-52) follows from the absence of C-final alternatives.

5.4.2. Case Two: Locative Prepositions

The locative determiners in §2.4 have both C-final and V-final forms whose distribution is determined by the ranked constraints in (42). However, the French lexicon provides only one form of other locative prepositions. If it is V-final, ONSET violations are predicted to occur before a V-initial word, and they do:

(54)   a. *à Amiens* 'in Amiens'
         b. *à Arles* 'in Arles'

Such ONSET violations qualify as grammatical because the lexicon provides no violation-free alternatives.

5.4.3. Case Three: The French Lexicon

The French lexicon contains many words in which some syllable lacks an onset, including vowel-initial words and words such as *Noël* 'Christmas', *haïr* 'to hate', *naïf* 'naïve', etc. Such ONSET violations support Lexical Sourcing: where the lexicon provides no alternative, they qualify as grammatical.

6. Evidence for NO-CODA

6.1. Some Further Alternations in Prenominal Adjectives

Some prenominal adjectives display alternations different from those discussed in §2.3.[14]

---

[14]To make the relevant alternations more perspicuous, these forms are cited in transcription rather than in standard French orthography.

		Masculine		*Feminine*	
(55)	a.	*grãt ɔm*	'great man'	*grãd arme*	'large army'
	b.	*grã prɔblem*	'big problem'	*grãd fot*	'big mistake'
(56)	a.	*foz ami*	'false friend (M)'	*fos ami*	'false friend (F)'
	b.	*fo pa*	'faux pas'	*fos pat*	'faux paw'

There are several related differences between adjectives of this type and the prenominal adjectives discussed in §2.3. These adjectives display three forms: one feminine and two masculine. They have two C-final forms which contrast in gender. Further, there are no cases where one gender's form is found with a head noun of the opposite gender. How are these alternations to be accounted for?[15]

The fact that forms of the appropriate gender are always used with these adjectives is accounted for by Concord. Here there is a C-final form of each gender, so Concord never needs to be sacrificed to ONSET satisfaction. Thus *grãd ɔm*, which violates Concord, will be ruled out in favor of *grãt ɔm*, which satisfies Concord as well as ONSET.

Here we must account for the alternations between distinct masculine forms. C-final forms are used in pre-V environments, which is accounted for by ONSET. To account for the V-final forms in pre-C environments, we invoke the Optimality Theory constraint NO-CODA:

(57) NO-CODA: A well-formed syllable has no coda.

Forms like *grãt problem* and *foz pa* violate NO-CODA, while the corresponding forms with *grã* and *fo* do not. The alternations in (55-56) thus provide evidence for NO-CODA in French.

But what prevents use of masculine adjectives with feminine heads, e.g. *grã fot* and *fo pat*, which obey NO-CODA but are ungrammatical? *Grãd fot* and *fos pat* violate NO-CODA but are grammatical because *grãd* and *fos* are feminine forms. Here Concord must be satisfied rather than NO-CODA. The constraint ranking in (58) accounts for this:

(58) Concord >> NO-CODA

To satisfy Concord, NO-CODA can be violated.

Combining (58) with (42), we have the constraint ranking:

(59) ONSET >> Concord >> NO-CODA

---

[15]There are two straightforward arguments against a phonological account of these alternations. First, the environment cannot be stated in phonological terms. Second, the putative phonological effects are not uniform: in (55) the feminine ends in a voiced consonant and the masculine in a voiceless one; in (56) the reverse holds. A phonological rule would not account for both alternations.

This constraint ranking accounts for all the data presented so far. Lexical Sourcing supplies three forms of certain adjectives as inputs, and the constraint ranking in (59) determines well-formedness.

Cross-linguistically it is common for alternants whose distribution is determined by ONSET and NO-CODA (henceforth the "margin constraints") to be alike except for one (or several) segment(s) at the relevant edge. With a convention of Lexical Collapsing for such pairs with the same morphosyntactic features, lexical entries can be simplified so that the entries of *grand* and *faux* in (55-56) are:

(60) *grã(t)* [–Fem]; *grãd* [+Fem]

(61) *fo(z)* [–Fem]; *fos* [+Fem]

6.2. Some Further Prenominal Forms

With Lexical Collapsing, the forms of *mon/ton/son* and of the locative determiner *en* discussed in §2 and those of the indefinite article can be listed lexically as:[16]

(62) *mõ(n)/tõ(n)/sõ(n)* [–Fem]; *ma/ta/sa* [+Fem]

(63) *ã(n)*

(64) Indefinite article: *ɛ̃(n)* [–Fem]; *yn* [+Fem]

The C-final forms occur in pre-V environments - an ONSET effect. V-final forms occur in pre-C environments - a NO-CODA effect. Concord is violated to satisfy ONSET but not to satisfy NO-CODA, an effect due to the constraint ranking in (59).

The singular definite article has three forms:

(65) Definite Article: *lə* [–Fem]; *la* [+Fem]; *l*

Lə and *la* satisfy Concord. Where they would violate ONSET, gender-neutral *l* occurs, as predicted by the constraint ranking in (59). The distribution of the forms of the definite article is thus accounted for without any new devices, and without an elision rule or the equivalent stated in terms of "latent" vowels.[17]

---

[16]Here I assume that nasalized vowels are represented as such underlyingly, following Tranel (1981). The arguments of this paper would not be affected if they were represented as sequences of a vowel plus nasal consonant (*mo(n)*, *to(n)*, etc.). The representations in (62) correctly predict that *mõ* and *mõn* occur in pre-C and pre-V environments, respectively.

[17]Schane's (1968) elision rule was followed by accounts that make the vowels in the definite article "latent," as in the literature summarized by Tranel (1995a, 1995b). There are arguments in the literature that the distribution of these (and other) allomorphs cannot be accounted for phonologically (Kaye and Morin 1978, Zwicky 1987, Miller 1992, and others). Nonetheless, latent vowels are posited in papers as recent as Tranel (1994).

The possessive adjectives in (62) modify a singular head. Their plurals have two allomorphs, both with suppletive stems (*me, te, se*). One allomorph has the regular plural suffix *-z*:

(66) me, me+z; te, te+z; se, se+z

The forms in (67) have similar representations:

(67)   Definite Plural   *le, le+z*
           Indefinite Plural   *de, de+z*
           Demonstrative Plural *se, se+z*

If the input set includes both the suffixed and unsuffixed form in each case,[18] the margin constraints will account for their distribution.[19]

Our account of all the data relies on the lexical entries, Lexical Sourcing, and the constraints and their ranking in (59). These devices supplant the phonological rules of elision and liaison and/or the latent segments used in earlier analyses (cf. §6.4 below).

6.3. Further Evidence for Ranking NO-CODA below Concord

Additional evidence for the ranking in (59) comes from the cases discussed in §§2-4. As summarized in (33), C-final forms that violate NO-CODA occur in pre-C environments if needed to satisfy Concord. This follows from ranking Concord above NO-CODA in (59).

6.4. The Role of the Margin Constraints in Elision and Liaison

The final consonant of certain French prenominal adjectives and other words is realized before a vowel but not before a consonant:

(68) *petit enfant*   'small child'   [pətitãfã]
(69) *petit garçon*   'little boy'   [pətigarsõ]

Such consonants, called "latent" in the literature, exhibit liaison in pre-V environments (68), and elision in pre-C environments (69). Latent consonants contrast with "fixed" consonants (always realized):

(70) *net effet*   'clear effect'   [nɛtefɛ]
(71) *net contraste*   'clear contrast' [nɛtkõtrast]

Petit is typical of words with a latent final consonant.

These phenomena pose two problems that have been central to French phonology: how to account for (i) the contrast between fixed and latent consonants, and (ii) the distribution of latent consonants. There is

---

[18]The inclusion of both suffixed and unsuffixed forms in the input set is not restricted to the forms in (66-67), but is far more general in French (Perlmutter, in preparation).

[19]The margin constraints account for C/V-sensitive allomorphy cross-linguistically, including cases like the indefinite article in English (Perlmutter, in preparation).

also a morphological problem: how to account for the contrast between masculine and feminine forms where they differ. Each new development in phonological theory has brought new solutions which use whatever new devices phonological theory makes available to give latent and fixed consonants different representations.[20] All these solutions share the twin assumptions that (i) the problem is phonological, and (ii) the right phonological representations for latent consonants will solve it.

The devices we have used to account for the distribution of the suppletive adjectival allomorphs will account for the distribution of the putative latent consonants without positing latent consonants at all. What has been assumed to be a phonological problem has two aspects - morphological and phonological. To solve the morphological problem for adjectives analyzed as having latent consonants, the grammar must provide distinct stems for the masculine and feminine.[21] The masculine stems can be collapsed by Lexical Collapsing:

(72) [–Fem]: *peti(t)*
(73) [+Fem]: *petit*

An adjective like *net* has only one stem.

The ranking in (59) accounts for the stems' distribution. With a masculine head, the C-final stem appears when needed to satisfy ONSET, but not when it would violate NO-CODA, in which case the V-final stem appears. With a feminine head, the feminine (C-final) stem always appears because Concord outranks NO-CODA. If latent consonants do not exist, the problem of how to represent them phonologically disappears. The contrast between adjectives ending in fixed and latent consonants reduces to that between adjectives with one stem and those with two.[22] This analysis accounts for the data without any exotic grammatical devices. Most of the work done by special representations for latent consonants is done by the margin constraints. Eliminating latent consonants makes possible a welcome reduction in the class of representations needed by phonological theory.

---

[20]Tranel (1995a, 1995b) provides excellent reviews of this literature.

[21]Masculine and feminine stems are not phonologically predictable (Gaatone 1978). However, a morphological device is available that makes it unnecessary to list both stems as such in the lexicon. This analysis is developed in Perlmutter, in preparation.

[22]Our solution has some points in common with the suppletion analyses of Gaatone (1978), Long (1978), and Klausenburger (1981). Not accounted for here are (i) the dislocation construction mentioned by Morin and Kaye (1982) and used by Tranel (1992) to argue against a suppletion analysis of elision and liaison, and (ii) the different behavior of masculine and feminine forms of adjectives like *petit* with respect to vowel laxing in Canadian French (Walker 1980, Klausenburger 1981, Tranel 1993). These matters must be left for future research (Perlmutter, in preparation).

7. A Consequence for Syntactic Representations: The Feature Clash Problem

7.1. Gender Features and Syntactic vs. Phonological Environments

7.1.1. The Need for Gender Features

Those French adjectives with distinct masculine and feminine forms must have gender features for two reasons. First, within the NP, attributive adjectives agree with the head noun in gender:

(74)   a.   *cette belle fille* 'this good-looking girl'
        b. **ce beau fille*
(75)   a.   *ce beau garçon* 'this good-looking boy'
        b. **cette belle garçon*

Thus, *ce* and *beau* are [–Fem], *CET* and *BEL* [+Fem]. Second, they must have gender features to account for agreement in predicate position:

(76)   a.   *Ce garçon est beau.*   'This boy is good-looking.'
        b. *Cette fille est belle.*   'This girl is good-looking.'

7.1.2. The Distinctness of Syntactic and Phonological Environments

Two things affect the distribution of masculine and feminine adjectival forms in the NP. When syntactically conditioned, as in (74-75), it is determined by the gender of the *head noun*; when phonologically conditioned, it is determined by the *following word*.

(77)   a.   cet ancien professeur 'this former teacher'
        b.   ce jeune professeur 'this young teacher'

Ce is conditioned by the head noun in (75a) and (77b). *CET* is conditioned by the head noun in (74a) and (76b), but by the following vowel in (77a).

7.2. The Feature Clash Problem

A key consequence of our results is that modifiers violate Concord in structures like (78), where they are needed to prevent ONSET violations.

(78)   a.   *cet*   *homme*   'this man'
          [+Fem]   [–Fem]
      b.   *mon*   *épée*   'my sword'
          [–Fem]   [+Fem]

In these structures a modifier's morphosyntactic features clash with those of the head. To account for agreement, syntactic theories have introduced devices to ensure that features of the head and modifier do *not* clash. How can a grammar allow structures like these while ruling out those where feature clash causes ungrammaticality?

7.3. Attempts to Avoid Feature Clash

The feature clash problem arises with the features [+Fem] and [-Fem]. Can it be avoided by using different features that allow examples like (78) without feature clash? We consider four proposals. Two try to use features that directly state the environments in which allomorphs can appear. Three attempt to avoid feature clash by leaving unspecified the allomorphs whose features would clash.

7.3.1. Solutions A and B: Features Combining Syntactic and Phonological Environments

Solution A is based on the observation that the forms that cause feature clash have two functions: to satisfy Concord in pre-C environments and to prevent ONSET violations in pre-V ones. Instead of the morphosyntactic features [+Fem] or [–Fem], these forms could have a feature that directly encodes these environments. For C-final feminine forms like *CET* and *BEL*, this feature could be:[23]

$$(79) \qquad \underline{\quad\quad} \quad \left\{ \begin{array}{c} \text{[+Fem]} \\ \text{V} \end{array} \right\}$$

Ce and *beau* would have conjunctive feature specifications:

$$(80) \qquad \underline{\quad\quad} \quad \left\{ \begin{array}{c} \text{[–Fem]} \\ \text{C} \end{array} \right\}$$

(79) encodes the occurrence of *CET* and *BEL* before a feminine or a vowel, and (80) that of *ce* and *beau* before a C-initial masculine. For the possessives *mon/ton/son* and *ma/ta/sa*, the features would be like (79) and (80), respectively, but with [+Fem] and [–Fem] reversed.

Solution A overlooks the fact that the conditioning factor in pre-V and pre-C environments is different: in pre-V environments, it is the initial segment of the *next word,* in pre-C environments, the gender of the *head noun,* as seen in (43-44) and (77). A feature like (79) cannot combine gender and a vowel as conditioning factors because they are properties of different constituents.

Solution B would give *ce* and *beau* the feature in (80), but would leave *CET* and *BEL* unspecified, relying on some version of Panini's Specificity Principle to ensure use of the more specified allomorph where its conditions are satisfied. (80) requires that the constituent conditioning allomorphy be both C-initial and [–Fem]. The C-initial constituent is the

---

[23](79) was proposed by Richard Janda in his commentary on this paper at the conference.

next word. But then (80) would not account for two kinds of cases where the next word is not marked for gender: (i) where the next word is an adjective unmarked for gender (as in (81a)), and (ii) where it is not an adjective or noun (as in (81b)):

(81)   a. *cet aimable homme*   'this nice man'
         b. *ce très aimable homme* 'this very nice man'

Neither *aimable* (which occurs with both masculine and feminine heads) nor the adverb *très* bears gender features. Giving them gender features would needlessly require two lexical entries for each.

Solutions A and B have another fatal flaw. Their features combining syntactic and phonological environments cannot account for the agreement of predicate adjectives, as in (76), which requires the standard gender features [+Fem]/[−Fem]. (79) and (80) would therefore be *additional* features—a needless complication of the feature inventory and of individual lexical entries.

Solutions A and B fail because they attempt to encode syntactic and phonological environments in the same features. In addition, some of the arguments in §§7.4-7.5 against other proposals also argue against Solutions A and B.

7.3.2. Solution C: Separate Gender and Phonological Subcategorization Features

Solution C differs from A and B in positing distinct environmental and gender features. It attempts to avoid feature clash by leaving unspecified the gender features that would cause clash, positing gender features in pre-C but not in pre-V environments.[24] Thus, *CET* and *BEL* would be unspecified, while *ce* and *beau* would have two features:

(82) [−Fem]
(83) [__C]

(82) is a gender feature and (83) a phonological subcategorization feature encoding the restriction to pre-C environments. Since CET and BEL would have neither feature, Solution C also relies on Panini's Specificity Principle to ensure use of the more specified allomorph (*ce, beau,* etc.) where its conditions are satisfied. The possessive pronous *ma, ta,* and *sa* would have feature (83) and the gender feature [+Fem], since they modify feminine heads in pre-C environments.

There are arguments against both key elements of Solution C. The arguments against phonological subcategorization features are given in §7.4, those against non-specification of gender in §7.5.

---

[24]Solution C was suggested by Cleo Condoravdi.

7.3.3. Solution D: ONSET and Gender Markedness

Solution D differs from A, B, and C in eschewing features encoding allomorphs' phonological environments. It adopts our claim that ONSET is what ensures C-final forms in pre-V environments. However, Solution D avoids our conclusion that ONSET outranks Concord by marking for gender only the V-final form occurring in pre-C environments; the C-final form would bear no gender feature.[25] Thus *ce* and *beau* would be marked [–Fem] and *ma*, *ta*, and *sa* [+Fem], but *CET*, *BEL*, *mon*, *ton*, and *son* would not be marked for gender. Consequently, all and only the modifiers with gender features would agree in gender with their heads; feature clash would be eliminated. Like Solution C, Solution D needs the Specificity Principle, which requires the most narrowly specified allomorph in each case, to exclude unspecified allomorphs from environments where allomorphs marked for gender can occur. The arguments against Solution D are given in §7.5.

7.4. Arguments against Encoding Environments in Features

7.4.1. Argument One: Redundancy of Features Encoding Pre-C Environments

Solutions A, B, and C all posit features restricting V-final allomorphs to pre-C environments, but this is predictable from their phonological shape. Encoding V-final shape as a feature posits an otherwise unnecessary feature and needlessly complicates lexical items. This argument still holds if one posits a rule predicting features like (83) from phonological shape. Both the feature and the rule predicting it would be needless complications of the grammar. Under our solution, none of these devices are necessary because the restriction of V-final allomorphs to pre-C environments follows from ONSET outranking Concord.

7.4.2. Argument Two: Predictability of Feature Clash Environments

Feature clash occurs only in pre-V environments - a phonological generalization that the attempts to eliminate feature clash from morphosyntactic representations fail to explain. Ranking ONSET above Concord explains it because with this ranking Concord can be violated only to prevent ONSET violations, which are possible only in pre-V environments.

7.4.3. Argument Three: Environment Features' Obliviousness to Syllable Well-Formedness

To encode allomorphs' distribution in terms of phonological subcategorization features is to ignore *why* they have this distribution: to

---

[25]Solution D was suggested by Gregory Stump.

improve syllable well-formedness by avoiding ONSET violations. Our account captures this directly.

7.5. Arguments against Partial Specification of Gender

Leaving the C-final member of each allomorph pair unspecified for gender initially seems to be an easy way to avoid feature clash. However, there are clear arguments against it. Two arguments focus on the fact that this proposal is just a device to encode phonological information. Two others show that it fails to specify features needed for NPs' interpretation. The final argument shows that the features this proposal leaves unspecified must be specified if certain NPs are to be characterized as ill-formed.

7.5.1. Argument One: The Phonological Predictability of Gender Specification

Solutions C and D mark one allomorph in each pair for gender, leaving the other unspecified. But which allomorph is marked for gender is predictable: it is always the V-final allomorph. Solutions C and D do not take advantage of this predictability, nor do they explain it.

Positing a lexical rule to predict markedness of gender features from phonological shape would be no better. Under our analysis, the phonological conditioning of allomorphs' distribution follows directly from their phonological shape without recourse to a feature whose sole function is to encode it.

7.5.2. Argument Two: Gender Specification and Phonological Environment

By attempting to account for allomorphs' distribution in terms of gender markedness, Solutions C and D treat that distribution as arbitrary. In particular, there is no explanation of why forms unmarked for gender supplant forms marked for gender always and only in pre-V environments. Under Solution D this is due to the accident that V-final forms are marked for gender and C-final forms are not. Under Solution C this is due to the same accident, and to the accident that all and only forms marked for gender have the feature [___C]. Neither solution provides an explanation.

Our analysis, however, claims that the allomorphs' distribution in pre-V environments has nothing to do with gender marking. The forms Solutions C and D analyze as unmarked for gender are all C-final; they occur in pre-V environments to avoid ONSET violations. Their distribution is explained in terms of syllable well-formedness.

7.5.3. Argument Three: Gender in NPs with an Unspecified Head

Some nouns, e.g. *AMI*,[26] can refer to a human of either gender and are compatible with adjectivals of either gender:

(84)   a. *un AMI danois*   'a Danish (male) friend'
         b. *une AMI danoise*   'a Danish (female) friend'

We could posit two nouns *AMI* identical phonologically, semantically, and syntactically in all respects other than gender, but contrasting in gender features. But this posits two lexical entries where only one is needed, needlessly duplicating their shared information. Instead we posit a single lexical entry unspecified for gender, thereby accounting for its compatibility with adjectivals of both genders.

Yet (84a-b) are interpreted as gender-specific. This is because the adjectivals *un* and *danois* in (84a) are marked [–Fem], *une* and *danoise* in (84b) [+Fem]. Given Concord, the only possible interpretation for each NP is the one that accords with the adjectivals' gender feature values.[27]
C-final adjectivals must be specified for gender because they impose an interpretation on the NP:

(85)   a. *mon CHER AMI*   'my dear (male) friend'
         b. *ma CHER AMI*   'my dear (female) friend'

Both *CHER* and *AMI* are unspecified for gender. Yet the meanings of (85a-b) are gender-specific. With *mon* marked [–Fem], (85a) is accounted for in the same way as (84a). If *mon* were unspecified for gender, as Solutions C and D claim, some additional stipulation would be needed to account for this.

7.5.4. Argument Four: Gender in Plural NPs with an Unspecified Head

Plural forms provide a similar argument for specifiying the gender of C-final adjectivals:[28]

---

[26]French orthography distinguishes masculine and feminine forms of *AMI, CHER*, etc., but the spoken language does not. As before, I use the masculine spelling in capital letters to represent the gender-neutral form of the spoken language.

[27]Such cases of Concord with an unspecified head are the reason for the formulation of Concord in (4), as opposed to the usual formulation which claims that modifiers agree with the head noun.

[28]Under our account of plurals, both the suffixed and the unsuffixed form are included in the input set; the margin constraints govern their distribution. The ranking of the margin constraints and the constraint that ensures Concord in number follows from universal principles without language-particular stipulation (Perlmutter, in preparation). Space limitations prevent discussion here.

(86)   a. *mes nouveaux* [nuvoz] *AMI* 'my new friends'
        b. *mes nouvelles* [nuvɛlz] *AMI* 'my new (female) friends'

The plural suffix *-z* satisfies ONSET. As elsewhere in the plural, masculine forms can have gender-neutral reference. The key example is (86b). Both *mes* and *AMI* are unspecified for gender. Under Solutions C and D, so is *NOUVEL*. Then why does (86b) have an exclusively feminine interpretation? Under our analysis this follows from the [+Fem] specification of *NOUVEL*.

7.5.5. Argument Five: How Can Unspecified Features Clash?

Concord is generally violated if a head has modifiers whose gender or number feature values clash. Thus, interchanging *danois* and *danoise* in (84) would be ungrammatical. Now consider:

(87)   a. *mon nouveau camarade de chambre* 'my new (male) roommate'
        b. *ma nouvelle camarade de chambre* 'my new (female) roommate'
        c. **mon NOUVEL camarade de chambre*

If *mon* and *NOUVEL* are both unspecified for gender, why is *(87c) ungrammatical? As (87a-b) show, *camarade* is unspecified for gender. Where is the feature clash in (87c)? Under our analysis, ungrammaticality results from feature clash: *mon* is [–Fem] and *NOUVEL* is [+Fem]. In claiming that *mon* and *NOUVEL* have no gender features, Solutions C and D have no non-*ad hoc* way to account for this.

7.5.6. The Evidence for Specification of Gender Features

Two kinds of arguments have been given against the attempt to avoid feature clash in representations by leaving the C-final allomorph unspecified for gender. The first two bring out the fact that this is just a way to encode phonological information; it leaves unexplained the relation between underspecification and (i) the forms' phonological shape and (ii) the environments in which they appear. The last three arguments show that these forms must be specified for gender to account both for the interpretation and the well- or ill-formedness of NPs in which they occur.[29]

---

[29]These arguments bring out the contrast between forms used to satisfy ONSET in pre-V environments and the syntactically conditioned forms used in pre-C environments. The phonologically conditioned forms do not impose their gender on their NPs (*mon AMI* 'my friend' is gender-neutral) and they do not clash with modifiers of the opposite gender (*mon NOUVEL AMI* 'my new (male) friend' is well-formed). These forms contrast with (85a) and (87c). Solutions C and D might claim that the C-final allomorphs are unmarked for gender in pre-V environments and marked in pre-C environments, but that would make it necessary to posit homophonous forms with different gender markings as distinct lexical entries, needlessly complicating the lexicon. For a theory that predicts the contrasts pointed out in this footnote, see Perlmutter (in preparation).

If our goal is only to get a grammar that works, none of these arguments need present an overwhelming obstacle. Encoding phonological shape and environments as features does not prevent a grammar from working; it only obscures the true generalizations. The conclusions of Arguments Three through Five can be avoided by claiming that *camarade*, *AMI*, and all the nouns that accept modifiers of either gender are in each case two distinct lexical items, one marked for each gender. This would needlessly complicate the lexicon, duplicating the semantic, syntactic, and phonological information shared by each pair. If underspecification is ever possible in grammars, why would French grammar not use it here? Recognizing underspecification for head nouns like *AMI* and *camarade* leads to the conclusion that the C-final adjectival forms *are* specified for gender.

7.6. Conclusions

These attempts to contrive features that yield clash-free representations were motivated by the desire to preserve current syntactic theories that characterize as ungrammatical any NP with a Concord violation. Though intended to rescue Concord, these proposals paradoxically render it unable to account for data like (85-87), which any theory of Concord must handle.

Concord can be maintained without the devices of Solutions A-D. The analysis proposed here does this by allowing Concord violations just in case they are needed to prevent ONSET violations. The syntactic component consequently does not need to be modified. The constraint ranking in (59) allows these syntactic violations because they prevent ONSET violations, preserving syllable well-formedness. This raises questions about how the components of a grammar interact.

8. Consequences for the Architecture of Grammars

8.1. Allomorphy in the Phonological Component

One of our major results is that C/V-sensitive allomorphy results from independently needed syllable well-formedness constraints. As was pointed out in §5.2, this means that allomorph selection occurs in the phonological component. This contrasts with the standard view that allomorphy is accounted for by rules that are distinct from, and precede, the phonology.

8.2. The Syntax-Phonology Interface in the Input-Output Model of Modular Grammars

Key assumptions of generative grammatical theory since its origins have been:

(88)   a.   Grammars are modular, with separate syntactic, phonological, etc. components.

b. The output of one component serves as input to another.

Under this conception of the architecture of grammars, the problem for interface theory is:

(89) *Interface Theory:* For a given component A, which other component's output does A take as input, and which other component takes A's output as its own input?

In accordance with this view, theories of the syntax-phonology interface since the beginnings of generative grammar have claimed the input-output relation between syntax and phonology to be that in (90), which makes the claim in (91).

(90) Syntax $\Rightarrow$ Phonology
(91) Syntax "feeds" phonology, but the reverse is impossible.

This claim has remained constant from the *Aspects* theory of Chomsky 1965 to the Minimalist Program of Chomsky 1995, and has been adopted in other theorists' theories of grammar. With the one-way arrow between syntax and phonology in (90), there is no way for anything in the phonological component to influence syntactic well-formedness. The impossibility of such influence has been elevated to the level of a principle—the Principle of Phonology-Free Syntax ("PPFS")—by Pullum and Zwicky, who have defended it against contrary analyses in a series of publications.[30] Studies of the syntax-phonology interface (e.g., Zwicky and Kaisse 1987, Inkelas and Zec 1990) generally address the question of how syntax influences phonology—not the reverse. Chen's (1990) title "What must phonology know about syntax?" is the question asked; the reverse question

---

[30]Cf. Pullum and Zwicky 1988, Zwicky and Pullum 1986, Miller, Pullum, and Zwicky 1992, and references cited there. Miller, Pullum, and Zwicky (1992: 320) state the PPFS as follows: "Syntactic rules cannot be subject to phonological conditions or constraints." Some of the phenomena analyzed here have been claimed to violate the PPFS, e.g. by Plank (1984), who claims that in pre-V environments, French possessive adjectives *disagree* with their heads "even though this requires a somewhat unusual complication of the rules of agreement" (p. 336). Zwicky (1985b, 1987) develops alternative accounts of some of these phenomena based on rules of referral (cf. §4.5). The analysis presented here differs from such previous attempts in two ways. First, it accounts for a wider range of data (presented in §2 and §6). Second, it does so without any new rules or constraints (exploiting independently needed phonological constraints), introducing only the constraint ranking in (59). It is this use of independently needed constraints and the ranking in (59) that achieves explanation. Interestingly, this analysis does not bear on the PPFS as formulated by Miller, Pullum, and Zwicky because a constraint ranking is not a syntactic rule or constraint. However, the contrast between French and other languages that rank Concord above ONSET does bear on Pullum and Zwicky's (1988: 278) essential claim that "if there are systematic phonological influences on syntactic phenomena at all, they do not vary idiosyncratically from language to language." See Perlmutter (in preparation) for discussion.

is not.[31] The architecture of grammars has been designed so that syntax can influence phonology, but not the reverse.

Our explanation of French allomorphy, however, crucially relies on ONSET, a phonological constraint, overriding Concord, a syntactic constraint. Whether Concord must be enforced in a given case depends on whether ONSET would be violated in the phonological component. How is this possible, given (90)?

8.3. Problems for Constraint-Based Theories of Grammar

Constraint-based theories of grammar have taken over the modular architecture of derivational theories. Our results pose a problem for such theories: How can a syntactic constraint such as Concord be ranked between two phonological constraints, as in (59)? This raises a more general question:

(92) *Cross-modular ranking:* Which constraints can be ranked relative to which other constraints? Are cross-modular rankings possible?

If cross-modular rankings like that in (59) are allowed, are there any limits on which constraints can be ranked relative to each other? If not, this would vastly increase the class of possible grammars.

Another problem posed by our results concerns the characterization of well-formedness. Modular theories have generally assumed:

(93) *Modular well-formedness:* A sentence is well-formed just in case it is characterized as well-formed by each component of the grammar.

The ranking in (59) makes it impossible to determine well-formedness locally in each component, for feature clash is allowed in the syntactic component only if ONSET would otherwise be violated in the phonological component.

8.4. Where Things Stand

Our analysis of C/V-sensitive allomorphy in French has made the essential problems clear:

(94) a. How can a grammar allow the allomorphs that violate Concord in pre-V environments?
  b. How can a grammar enforce Concord in pre-C environments?

The problem is to accomplish both tasks simultaneously. Our major result has been to show that the constraint ranking in (59) does this. In so doing, it explains the allomorphy: why it exists and why the allomorphs have the

---

[31]An exception is Zec and Inkelas 1990, which proposes a constraint-based theory with bidirectional influence, but where all phonological influence on syntax is mediated by prosodic structure, excluding segmental information.

distribution and phonological shape that they do. This sets a standard for alternative analyses to equal or surpass.

The most obvious implementation of (59), however, comes at the cost of being inconsistent with the architecture of grammars on which the last three decades of theory construction in linguistics have been based. Cross-modular constraint ranking has (at least) two undesirable consequences: it vastly increases the class of grammars and makes it impossible to determine well-formedness locally in each component. The problem is how to achieve the explanation that (59) achieves without these undesirable consequences.[32] This must be left for future research.

9. Conclusions

The first focus of this paper has been to show that it is possible to explain why allomorphy exists and why it has the properties it does. Optimality Theory makes this possible because the allomorphs' distribution follows from independently needed constraints if they are ranked and violable. The margin constraints ONSET and NO-CODA play a key role in explaining the suppletive allomorphy analyzed here. They also account for the alternations traditionally analyzed phonologically in terms of elision and liaison. Both sets of data can therefore be analyzed as allomorphy. In each case the lexicon provides the input set, which may have more than one member. Allomorph selection is consequently just one aspect of optimal output selection in the phonological component.

Our explanation of the allomorphy rests on the ability of ONSET to outrank Concord. This raises an important issue: can a phonological constraint such as ONSET outrank a syntactic constraint such as Concord? The architecture of grammars has been designed so as to make the syntactic component impervious to phonological influence. To accommodate our result, something must be changed. Future research will determine what.

References

Anderson, Stephen R. 1988. Morphological Theory. In Frederick J. Newmeyer, ed., *Linguistics: The Cambridge Survey*, Vol. 1, 146-191. Cambridge and New York: Cambridge University Press.

Chen, Matthew. 1990. What Must Phonology Know about Syntax? In Sharon Inkelas and Draga Zec, eds., *The Phonology-Syntax Connection*, Chicago and London: University of Chicago Press.

Chomsky, Noam. 1965. *Aspects of the Theory of Syntax*. Cambridge, Mass. and London: MIT Press.

---

[32]A proposal that achieves this is developed in Perlmutter, in preparation.

Chomsky, Noam. 1995. *The Minimalist Program*. Cambridge, Mass. and London: MIT Press.

Cornulier, Benoît de. 1972. A Peeking Rule in French. *Linguistic Inquiry* 3: 226-227.

Gaatone, David. 1978. Forme soujacente unique ou liste d'allomorphes? (A propos des consonnes de liaison en français). *Linguistics* 214: 33-54.

Inkelas, Sharon and Draga Zec. 1990. *The Phonology-Syntax Connection*. Chicago and London: University of Chicago Press.

Kaye, Jonathan D. and Yves-Charles Morin. 1978. Il n'y a pas de règles de troncation, voyons! In Wolfgang U. Dressler and Wolfgang Meid, eds., *Proceedings of the Twelfth International Congress of Linguists*, 788-792. Innsbruck: IBS.

Klausenburger, Jürgen. 1981. Liaison in Canadian French Revisited. *Lingvisticæ Investigationes* 5: 405-410.

Long, Mark. 1978. Discussion of Klausenburger's paper. *Studies in French Linguistics* 1: 21-26.

McCarthy, John J. and Alan Prince. 1993. *Prosodic Morphology I: Constraint Interaction and Satisfaction*. Ms., University of Massachusetts, Amherst and Rutgers University.

Miller, Philip H. 1992. *Clitics and Constituents in Phrase Structure Grammar*. New York: Garland Publishing.

Miller, Philip H., Geoffrey K. Pullum, and Arnold M. Zwicky. 1992. Le Principe d'inaccessibilité de la phonologie par la syntaxe: Trois contre-exemples apparents en français. *Lingvisticæ Investigationes* 16: 317-343.

Morin, Yves-Charles and Jonathan D. Kaye. 1982. The Syntactic Bases for French Liaison. *Journal of Linguistics* 18: 291-330.

Perlmutter, David M. In preparation. *The Emergence of Morphology*.

Plank, Frans. 1984. Romance Disagreements: Phonology Interfering with Syntax. *Journal of Linguistics* 20: 329-350.

Prince, Alan and Paul Smolensky. 1993. *Optimality Theory: Constraint Interaction in Generative Grammar*. Ms., Rutgers University and University of Colorado, Boulder.

Pullum, Geoffrey K. and Arnold M. Zwicky. 1988. The Syntax-Phonology Interface. In Frederick J. Newmeyer, ed., *Linguistics: The Cambridge Survey*, Vol. 1, 255-280. Cambridge and New York: Cambridge University Press.

Schane, Sanford A. 1968. *French Phonology and Morphology*. Cambridge, Mass. and London: MIT Press.

Tranel, Bernard. 1981. *Concreteness in Generative Phonology: Evidence from French*. Berkeley, Los Angeles, and London: University of California Press.

Tranel, Bernard. 1992. On Suppletion and French Liaison. In Paul Hirschbühler and Konrad Koerner, eds., *Romance Languages and Modern Linguistic Theory*, 269-308. Amsterdam and Philadelphia: John Benjamins Publishing Co.

Tranel, Bernard. 1993. Moraic Theory and French Liaison. In William J. Ashby, Marianne Mithun, Giorgio Perissinoto, and Eduardo Raposo, eds., *Linguistic Perspectives on the Romance Languages*, 97-112. Amsterdam and Philadelphia: John Benjamins Publishing Co.

Tranel, Bernard. 1994. French Liaison and Elision Revisited: A Unified Account within Optimality Theory. *Linguistic Symposium on Romance Languages* 24.

Tranel, Bernard. 1995a. Current Issues in French Phonology: Liaison and Position Theories. In John Goldsmith, ed., *Handbook of Phonological Theory*, Oxford: Basil Blackwell.

Tranel, Bernard. 1995b. French Final Consonants and Nonlinear Phonology. *Lingua* 95: 131-167.

Tranel, Bernard. 1995c. Exceptionality in Optimality Theory and Final Consonants in French. *Linguistic Symposium on Romance Languages* 25.

Walker, Douglas C. 1980. Liaison and Rule Ordering in Canadian French Phonology. *Lingvisticæ Investigationes* 4: 217-222.

Zec, Draga and Sharon Inkelas. 1990. Prosodically Constrained Syntax. In Sharon Inkelas and Draga Zec, eds., *The Phonology-Syntax Connection*, Chicago and London: University of Chicago Press.

Zwicky, Arnold M. 1985a. How to Describe Inflection. *Berkeley Linguistics Society* 11: 372-386.

Zwicky, Arnold M. 1985b. Rules of Allomorphy and Syntax-Phonology Interactions. *Journal of Linguistics* 21: 431-436.

Zwicky, Arnold M. 1987. French Prepositions: No Peeking. *Phonology Yearbook* 4: 211-227.

Zwicky, Arnold M. and Ellen M. Kaisse, eds. 1987. Syntactic Conditions on Phonological Rules. *Phonology Yearbook* 4: 3-263.

Zwicky, Arnold M. and Geoffrey K. Pullum. 1986. The Principle of Phonology-Free Syntax: Introductory Remarks. *Ohio State University Working Papers in Linguistics* 32: 63-91.

Comments on the Paper by Perlmutter

RICHARD D. JANDA

1. Introduction and Overview

The present discussion shares with other commentaries in this volume a title of the form "Comments on the Paper by ...".[1] But, at the workshop for which the papers collected here were prepared, this commentary—like a number of others—had a very different title, one more indicative of its content. So as to illustrate some of the problems which plague recent Optimality-Theoretic claims that the use of certain apparently wrong-gendered forms in French follows from the lower ranking of a syntactic constraint of gender agreement (variously called GENDER or Concord) vis-à-vis a phonological constraint (ONSET) favoring C[onsonant]-initial syllables, this discussion originally had a highly iconic, if somewhat *recherché*, French title. That title was (now in slightly revised form, with M[asculine] or F[eminine] assigned to each relevant word in the gloss), namely, *Un franc/*franche entretien, m'amie: maint Franc/*Franque entretien*([t]) '*un/*une amie'*, meaning 'A (M) frank (M/*F) discussion (M), my (F) dear (F): many a (M) Frank (M/*F) maintains *un/*une amie* [as the form for] 'a (M?/F??) friend (F)'.'

Here, consider first the fact that a V[owel]-initial M noun like *entretien* must be immediately preceded by the V-final M adjective *franc* = [fʁɑ̃] —rather than by the suppletive alternant C-final F *franche* = [fʁɑ̃š]—in the N[oun]P[hrase] *un* [fʁɑ̃] *entretien*. This situation (cf. Morin 1992, Lamarche 1996, Mascaró 1996) shows that gender disagreement for the sake of onset presence (and hiatus avoidance) does not hold generally in French, but is instead at most a minor pattern. Related, but revealing in a different way, is what happens when an NP consisting of a M DET[erminer] (like *maint*) plus a noun like the one that means 'Frank, Frankish person' is followed by a V-

[1] For helpful comments and/or for other aid of various sorts, I am grateful to G. Ansart, F. Anthomé, M. Aronoff, J. Auger, D. Augier, F. Barral, D. Brentari, A. Carstairs-McCarthy, M. Clayton, C. Condoravdi, K. de Jong, L. Dekydtspotter, R. Desrochers, D. Dinnsen, L. Dobrin, T. Ernst, C. Étienne, P. Farrell, A. Gaëlle, M. Gilbert, J. Goldsmith, J. Good, L. Hyman, F. I., B. Joseph, K. Kazazis, S. Kim, J. Lamarche, L. McNair-Dupree, F. & P. Meadows, J. Merceron, J.-P. Montanay, S. Mufwene, B. Need, M. Noske, J. Ntihirageza, S. Pargman, D. Perlmutter, N. Poincaré, J. Sadock, P. Sells, A. Spencer, G. Stump, B. Tranel, A. Valdman, B. Vance, and M. Yip. None of these people agree with everything in this commentary, and only a few agree with most of it. But they have collectively helped me reach a point where the evidence here may eventually lead some of them to reconsider their views.

initial verb-form (like *entretient*). The head noun here must be invariant V-final M *Franc* = [fʁɑ̃] (which never surfaces with a final [k]), again rather than its suppletive alternant, C-final F *Franque* = [fʁɑ̃k]—even though, in a uniformly F NP like *mainte Franque*, the final /k/ of *Franque* manifestly undergoes ONSET-satisfying (re)syllabification with a following V-initial verb like *entretient*, yielding [mɛ̃t. fʁɑ̃.k ɑ̃.tʁə.tjɛ̃(.t)] (where periods divide syllables). Clearly, the French "linking phenomena" referred to as *liaison* do not reduce to matters of (re)syllabification (cf. Booij 1986, Encrevé 1988, Klein 1995); instead, they also depend partly on morphological issues of gender and/or its realization (cf., e.g., Morin 1986, Desrochers 1994).

This conclusion is strengthened further when we realize that the precursor of modern *mo.n a.mie* 'my (M?/F??) friend (F)' was *m'a.mi.e* (now an archaism meaning 'my dear, my sweetheart'), where the elided POSS[essive] DET *m'*, from former *ma*, alerts us to the fact that an onset was already present in such combinations (with hiatus resolved via deletion, rather than (re-) syllabification). Hence the ousting of *m'* by *mon*—a form which first occurred only with M nouns but later became the POSS DET before V-initial F nouns—was not historically motivated by considerations of syllable structure, and so the latter need not be its current synchronic motivation, either.

Clinching evidence that what is going on here is at least partly morphological in nature, rather than exclusively phonological, comes from the fact that, over a substantial checkerboard-like area stretching across northern France and some parts of francophone Canada (cf. Péronnet 1989 and her references), the indefinite article has come to have a single form—quite often M-looking *un*—before both M and F V-initial nouns, and for reasons totally unrelated to syllable structure. This widespread characteristic of non-standard French appears to reflect the influence of regional varieties where constructions like *u.n* (M?/F??) *a.mie* (F) arose independently in broadly scattered locations—and, in this respect, it is crucial that the competition between *un* and *une* which was resolved by the victory of one form or the other—quite often the first—was not decided by reference to onsets or other parts of syllable structure. After all, both *un* and *une* allow resyllabification of a final /n/ with a following V-initial element in their NP. Rather, there simply exists a trend toward neutralization of overt expression for the M/F distinction in DETs preceding V-initial words. Hence it is not surprising that, for both non-standard and regional varieties of French, this neutralization survives robustly in DET forms (like *mon* and *un*) but is recessive (in both types and tokens) for the small set of adjectives that in the standard dialect show such surface-homophonous M/F forms as *bel(le)* in, respectively, M vs. F NPs like 'an attractive uncle' *un bel oncle* vs. *une belle onde* 'an attractive wave'.

Lastly, even if—contrary to fact—the use of apparently wrong-gendered DET-forms like *mon* before V-initial F words did occur primarily due to

syllable-structural (onset-based) factors, rather than equally due to morphological ones, this would still not allow the conclusion that the distribution
of C-final vs. V-final forms within French lexemes is a purely phonological
matter. In the sample utterance above, this caveat (well-known since long
before Selkirk 1972) is suggested by the parentheses around the phonetic [t]
in the first element of the phrase *entretien*([t]) *'un amie'*, which reflect the
fact that this 3SG verb-form's final consonant may be pronounced (and resyllabified with a following V-initial word) in formal but never informal style
(cf. Tranel 1981:225). I.e., the overall complex of French liaison phenomena would still have to be analyzed in partly non-phonological terms involving stylistic and other sociolinguistic information even if the data did not do
what they actually do—which is to reflect additional conditioning of a morphosyntactic nature that involves (i) not only gender but also number, and
(ii) categories like DET as well as the relation between syntactic and phonological phrases. This has been discussed by, e.g., Booij and de Jong 1987.

In short, there does seem to be a need for *un franc/*franche entretien*,
m'amie 'a frank discussion, my dear', as shown by the fact that *maint Franc
/*Franque entretien*([t]) *'un/*une amie'*—'many a Frank [≈ French speaker]
maintains *'un/*une amie'*.' There is simply no way for an analysis of Modern French to succeed if its explanation for seeming gender-clash in phrases
like *mon* (M?/F??) *âme* (F) 'my soul' depends crucially on a modular account
that—whether or not it invokes Optimality Theory—stakes everything on a
purely syntactic generalization of M/F agreement being overridden by a purely phonological one requiring the presence of an onset. This is because, as
has been argued by earlier writers, the data at issue here (which involve liaison in that they concern C-final vs. V-final forms of lexemes) simply do
not reduce to the facts of (re)syllabification (frequently called *enchaînement*),
from which they are distinct both in principle and in practice. And the data
additionally reflect idiosyncratic morphosyntactic considerations which make
French liaison as a whole notoriously non-autonomous and non-modular.

In this sense, Optimality-Theoretic (OT) accounts like Perlmutter's
represent a demonstrably retrograde trend vis-à-vis much of the large body of
previous generative work on the V-final vs. C-final alternants involved in
French liaison. Even the claim that NPs such as *mon âme* involve a wrong-
gendered DET (and thus violate a syntactic constraint) cannot yet be considered as well-supported—especially since Perlmutter's invariant [-Fem]*mon
AMI*[0Fem] needs an ad-hoc extra device invoking phonology (?!; see his
footnote 29) to block the incorrect prediction that a string like [mõ.n a.mi]
can be interpreted only as a M NP, despite unanimity in the literature that a
homophonous string such as *mon amie* exists and is a F NP. In this case,
an alternative option dismissed by Perlmutter but needing further discussion
is that the above notion of neutralization in gender-marking before V-initial

words may be reflected in a non-clashing, Ø gender-value for a POSS DET—as in [0Fem]*MON amie*[+Fem]; this has been advocated by Lamarche 1996.

And another (not necessarily incompatible) option remains available because Perlmutter gives little more than a footnoted promissory note as an argument against the common generative practice (cf. Tranel 1994a) of positing non-homophonous remote representations for surface-homophonous C-final adjectives like *petit* vs. *petite* in phrases such as *le.* [p(ə.)ti.t] *ours* vs. *la.* [p(ə.)ti.t]<*e*> *ours*<*e*> 'the little bear (M vs. F.)'. (Here, angled-bracketed elements like <*e*>'s are purely orthographic, in the Canadian and northern French dialects at issue, and parentheses flank schwas often omitted in connected speech). Thus, if phonetic homophony between M *petit* and F *petite* can arise despite their having phonologically quite distinct representations, then parity of reasoning would seem both to allow and to require the conclusion that there are two forms M *bel* and F *belle* which (for Québec and northern France) are homophonous but have phonologically distinct underlying forms. In that case, there is no violation of gender agreement to be found here, and so no outranking of a syntactic constraint by a phonological one.

This conclusion is confirmed by the results of a questionnaire given to 16 native French speakers so as to distinguish the issues of gender, (re-) syllabification, and competing C-final vs. V-final forms for certain lexemes (= liaison). Assigned the task of judging possibilities for a DET-form separated from a V-initial adjective or noun by a C-initial parenthetical expression that prevents simple resyllabification (or hiatus), speakers massively prefer a C-final variant whose terminal consonant remains in a syllable coda, as in *cet/*ce—comment dirait-on—incroyable exploit* 'this (M)—how would one say (≈ should I say)—incredible (M?/Ø??) exploit (M)'. *Cet* here cannot be a F form: it fails to favor ONSET and so as a disagreeing F would be less optimal than *ce*. But a real F *cette* parenthetically divided from a C-initial F adjective, as in *cette—comment dirait-on—merveilleuse performance* 'this— ... —marvelous performance', is readily accepted; cf. Janda (in preparation).

French speakers, it would seem, have spoken: the particular subdomain of liaison which involves competing C-final vs. V-final suppletive forms of lexemes (as part of Perlmutter's "allomorphy") does not reduce to syllabification, nor does it seem to involve wrong-gendered forms, and so any attempt to reach overarching conclusions concerning grammatical architecture based on the assumption of contrary premises is beside the point.

In what follows, I review the part of Perlmutter's analysis shared by Tranel's 1994b, 1996 treatment, mention a number of historical precedents, and list its innovative aspects before surveying convergences between such an approach and my own perspective on these issues. I then devote the rest of the discussion to general areas of divergence between the latter two sorts of approaches, concentrating on the implications of variation and change.

2. OT Liaison Summarized; Converging Other Views

As Perlmutter's first footnote acknowledges, his independently arrived at attempt to provide a unified account for French phrases like *mon* (M?/F??) *âme* (F) 'my soul (F)' and *un* (M) *bel* (F?/M??) *oncle* (M) 'an attractive uncle (M)' represents the second such proposal within OT, coming over a year after the basically identical analysis of these forms in Tranel 1994b (revised by Tranel 1995 before appearing as Tranel 1996). In fact, though, these two versions—each a treatment where a phonological constraint forcing a syllable to have an onset outranks a syntactic constraint requiring gender agreement—were both anticipated over 400 years ago by Claude de Sainliens, a Huguenot refugee in England from 1564 to at least 1597 who anglicized his name and wrote lengthy notes on French grammar as part of a bilingual pedagogical work published as Hol(l)yband 1576/1609/1953.

Holyband first noted (p. 192, in spelling and punctuation which are here only slightly modernized): "*bel* ... is alwaies put before words beginning with a vowel, as *un bel arbre* 'a faire tree' ...[,] but ... *beau* ... cometh alwaies before a consonant, as *beau filz* '... faire child'." He then stated (p. 194) that "*mon, ma, ton, ta, son, sa* ... are of like nature as *bel* ... and *beau*: to avoide the gaping [= hiatus] which should follow, we say ... *mon âme* 'my soule' ...[; that is,] if the substantive beginneth by a vowell, although it be of the feminine gender, we joyne unto it these masculines ... *mon, ton, son*." Clearly, hiatus avoidance via (re)syllabification was treated by Holyband as motivating the choice of a C-final variant for either of two different prenominal modifiers when it precedes a V-initial word, despite the fact that this often entails a mismatch in gender. Nearly three centuries later, in Diez 1869:II.112/1882:483, the founder of modern Romance linguistics gave such phenomena perhaps their aptest characterization when, in reference to the French use of apparently M *mon* before a V-initial F noun, he called this "the most extreme sacrifice which form could offer to euphony" (my translation—RDJ). Sometimes, an echo can take 100 years; cf. Perlmutter's footnote 7: "French is unusual in sacrificing Concord to ONSET".

By way of comparison, it should be noted that, nearly half a century before Holyband, an even earlier description of *mon* as M in its use before F nouns was given by Giles Du Wés (yet another French emigré to England) in ca. 1532/1972:E.ii.[recto]. Much later, such a labeling was discussed as a distinct possibility by the influential French grammarian Claude Favre de Vaugelas in 1647/1934:351-352. But Vaugelas first mentioned a view—essentially that of Lamarche 1996 (cf. above), and close to the present writer's position—in which there is simply no gender contrast in most French DETs before a V-initial noun (or ADJ[ective](P), as well): "[As for] *mon* ..., *ton*, and *son* ...[, s]ome believe they are of common gender, serving always for the M and sometimes for the F (i.e., for all F words starting with a vowel ..., though ... we say endearingly *m'amie* ...)" (my translations—RDJ). He went on: "Others maintain that these ... [POSS] pronouns are always M but that ...[, so as to avoid] cacophony, one does not fail to link them with F words beginning with a vowel—in the same way, they say, as the Spaniards use the M article *el* before a F word beginning with a vowel, saying *el alma* ['the soul'] and not [*]*la alma*". Vaugelas himself abstained on this issue: "In whatever fashion it may be done, it suffices to know that it is done thus, and it matters ... not at all that it be in one way rather than the other".

Unlike Vaugelas, we cannot abstain. For our present purposes, one crucial question at issue is precisely: what gender should be attributed to, e.g., *mon* in *mon* (M?/F??) *âme* (F) 'my soul (F)'—M, F, or neither (i.e., Ø [zero])? Since at the current juncture we are concerned with points of convergence, we might ask whether there can be anything shared by (i) the OT approach of Tranel 1994b, 1996 and Perlmutter—which treats this *mon* as a disagreeing M form required by a purely phonological (re)syllabification constraint that outranks syntactic agreement—and (ii) the diametrically opposed orientation of this critique, which analyzes such a *mon* as a non-disagreeing but special non-M form conditioned by factors whose nature is morphosyntactic or even lexical, as well as partly phonological (and segmental, as well as syllabic)? It turns out that there are a number of significant issues on which the two perspectives are in agreement: e.g., as to the conclusion that paired surface-forms like *mon/ma* and *beau/bel(le)* are each realizations of a pair of underlying forms that are suppletively related as variants of a lexeme (i.e., an overall lexical form). To determine the full range of convergences between a syllable-structural, gender-clashing OT treatment and the current alternative, though, we first need to summarize the former's essentials.

Recent OT studies on the suppletive aspect of Modern French liaison (word-final C/Ø alternations)—most notably those of Tranel 1994b, 1996 and Perlmutter—are oriented around one particularly central conclusion. To repeat: in the large and productive class of cases where there seems to be a wrong-gendered DET, as in *ton âme exquise* 'your [≈ thy] (M?/F??) exquisite (F) soul (F)' vs. *ta grande âme* 'your (F) great (F) soul (F)' vs. *ton gran*[t] *âne* 'your (M) great (M) donkey (M)', this situation is attributed to the higher ranking of a purely phonological ONSET constraint over a purely syntactic (or at least totally non-phonological) constraint of GENDER (i.e., Concord): ONSET >> GENDER. Thus, the violation of ONSET found in gender-agreeing but ungrammatical *[+Fem]ta. âm<e>[+Fem] (where [+Fem] = F) is more serious than the violation of GENDER in disagreeing but still grammatical [-Fem]*to.n âm<e>*[+Fem] (where [-Fem] = M)—because, in the latter, the underlying final /n/ of *ton* can be (re)syllabified so as to satisfy ONSET and thereby yield the optimal form. There exists no C-final [+Fem] allomorph of 'your (informal)' whose employment in this particular context would allow us to avoid a violation of either ONSET or GENDER—but contrast, e.g., [+Fem]*ta*. [+Fem]*gra<n>.d<e>* *âm<e>*[+Fem] (as above) and [+Fem]*ta*. *gra<nd>.-mèr<e>*[+Fem] 'your grandmother', both of which obey both constraints because V-final [+Fem] *ta* precedes a C-initial [+Fem] substantive.

At the cost of a (large, open-ended) class of syntactic GENDER-violations which are viewed as tolerable due to the concomitant satisfaction of higher-ranked phonological ONSET, this OT treatment claims to avoid three aspects of what Perlmutter calls the "traditional" account and its reliance on "allomorphy" in the sense of 'multiple underlying variants for a single gender' (though the two genders together still need two underlying stems, so that "allomorphy" within one lexeme is not really eliminated). This traditional, morphological analysis views French 'his, her, its, one's' as being realized before a V-initial noun by either *son*[+Fem] or *son*[-Fem], respectively, depending on whether that noun is itself [+Fem] or [-Fem] (whereby a C-initial noun is also preceded by *son*[-Fem] if M, but by *sa*[+Fem] if F).

Three negative traits of the traditional view are, says Perlmutter: (i) accidental (and total) homophony between, e.g., *son*[+Fem] and *son*[-Fem]; (ii) failure to predict that this homophony should occur only before V-initial words, and (iii) inability to explain why, in this environment, the two homophones are C-final (cf. *so.*[n] *a.mi* 'his ... friend (M)' and *so.*[n] *a.mi<e>* 'his ... friend (F)'). It is such negatives that the two OT analyses seek to avoid by invoking (re)syllabification via ONSET and by ranking the latter constraint higher than GENDER (Concord), in order to get by with a single form *son*—which is analyzed as invariantly [-Fem] because of its similarity to indisputably [-Fem] *son* in, e.g., *son chat* 'his ... cat (M)'. This is the first major part of the OT analysis under consideration in this commentary.

The second major part of the OT account at issue involves the claim that there is in French just one underlying form and one gender-value, not only for each of above *mon* 'my', *ton* 'your (informal)', and *son* 'his/her/its/one's'—spelled invariantly *mon, ton, son*, respectively, and all invariantly [-Fem]—but also for the further DET [+Fem][sɛt] 'this, that' (spelled either *cet* or *cette*), as well as for five prenominal adjectives. The latter all have V-final forms when they are M and precede a C-initial word: viz., *beau* 'attractive', *nouveau* 'new', *fou* 'crazy', *mou* 'soft', and *vieux* 'old'. But all have corresponding variants that occur before a V-initial and/or F word; the latter ADJ-forms (viewed by OT as invariantly F) are, respectively: [+Fem][bɛl] (spelled either *bel* or *belle*), [+Fem][nuvɛl] (spelled *nouvel* or *nouvelle*), [+Fem][fɔl] (spelled *fol* or *folle*), [+Fem][mɔl] (spelled *mol* or *molle*), and [+Fem][vjɛj] (spelled *vieil* or *vieille*). These F variants are all invariantly C-final, phonologically, but they are orthographically C-final before M V-initial words, and orthographically Ce-final before all F ones. Clearly, these F C-final ADJ-forms all contrast in gender with M C-final *mon, son, ton*.

Given that the OT approach in question treats the five French forms just listed as [+Fem] in all contexts, even M ones, it analyzes all the representative NPs in the next sentence as involving a wrong-gendered prenominal modifier. The still-optimal status of the latter is again attributed to the fact that phonological ONSET is ranked higher than syntactic GENDER: cf., e.g., [-Fem]*mo.n arm<e>*[+Fem] 'my weapon', [+Fem]*ce.t ar<t>*[-Fem] 'this art', [-Fem]*ce.* [+Fem]*be.l <h>om<me>*[-Fem] 'this attractive man', as well as [-Fem]*ce.* [+Fem]*fo.l ex.ploi<t>*[-Fem] 'this crazy exploit', and, finally, [-Fem]*ce.* [+Fem]*vie.il* = [vjɛ.j] *ân<e>*[-Fem] 'this old donkey'.

While Tranel 1994b, 1996 does not do so, Perlmutter takes the additional step of claiming that, for what he calls (revising an analysis by Miller et al. 1992) the "LOC[ative] DET", it is the ranking ONSET >> GENDER which predicts the occurrence of *en*, not *au*, before M V-initial non-urban toponymic nouns. I.e., he treats *en* before place names (though it virtually never occurs with cities) as an ONSET-governed port(e)manteau which combines a preposition with a covert (Ø) F article in exactly the same way that *au* combines *à* with a M article—as in [+Fem]*e.n I.ra<n>*[-Fem] 'in Iran' vs. [-Fem]*au. Li.ba<n>*[-Fem] 'in (the) Lebanon'. Here, the assignment of [+Fem] to *en* in all cases rests on the fact that *en* is the exceptionless "LOC DET" with F place-names; cf. [+Fem]*e<n>. Sy.ri<e>*[+Fem] 'in Syria'.

The third major part of Perlmutter's OT approach to French liaison extends the analysis from radically suppletive cases like *cet(te)/ce* to regular word-final C/Ø alternations like those for 'small': cf. C-final (and resyllabified) F *pe.ti.*[t]*<e> âm<e>* 'little soul' and pre-V M *pe.ti.*[t] *ân<e>* 'little donkey' vs. V-final pre-pausal M *pe.ti<t>*. While Tranel follows the dominant generative practice of positing one root with a constant phonemic melody for both M and F forms of such ADJs, Perlmutter adopts a solution involving partial suppletion, thereby essentially conceding the correctness of the arguments advanced in favor of such an approach much earlier by Klausenburger 1984 (and previous works cited there), Tranel 1981, and others.

Thus, Perlmutter recognizes one underlying form for the F of 'small', /pətit/, and provisionally two forms for the M—/pətit/ and /pəti/—regarding which he says that "pairs with the same morphosyntactic features ... can be collapsed by Lexical Collapsing" (a mechanism which is not discussed further), as /pəti(t)/. In order for the V-final M form /pəti/ to be the preferred variant prepausally and before a C-initial word (where a C-final form cannot be resyllabified), the OT constraint NO-CODA must be invoked, and ranked below GENDER (a.k.a. Concord). Regarding the fact that [+Fem]/pətit/ and [-Fem]/pəti(t)/ share everything but the parentheses in the latter, Perlmutter's footnote 21 issues a vague promissory note stating that "a morphological device is available that makes it unnecessary to list both stems in the lexicon ...[; t]his analysis is developed in Perlmutter (in preparation)".

The fourth and final major part of Perlmutter's OT analysis (not included explicitly in Tranel 1994b, 1996) is related to that just mentioned, since both interact to at least some extent with a tacit principle whereby apparently accidental homophony between identical forms differing only in inflectional features is to be avoided at any cost. Perlmutter ascribes to speakers of French, at any rate, an extremely virulent (call it *genderalized*) case of what is in effect *homophonophobia*. The need to invoke ONSET in order to rationalize the feature clash created by interpreting, e.g., *mon* as invariantly [-Fem] even before, say, [+Fem]*âme* 'soul' is motivated by the desire to avoid both (i) homophony (of *mon*[+Fem] with *mon*[-Fem]) and (ii) rules of allomorphy (such as 'my (F)' = *mon* /__#V, *ma* / elsewhere). But the reduction of the Ns *ami* 'friend (M)' and *amie* 'friend (F)' (both pronounced [ami], in northern France and Québec) to "a single lexical entry unspecified for gender", [0Fem]*AMI,* is due purely to homophony avoidance. I.e. (cf. §7.5.3), to "posit two nouns *AMI* ... contrasting in gender features ... [alone is to] posit ... two lexical entries where only one is needed, needlessly duplicating their shared information"; identical reasoning is applied to *cher* 'dear (M)' and *chère* 'dear (F)', yielding a single genderless ADJ [0Fem]*CHER*; cf. also the DET [0Fem]*l'* 'the' (plus abovementioned [+Fem]*CET* = *cet(te)*, etc.).

This rather extensive summary of Tranel's and Perlmutter's sequential OT proposals regarding ONSET-satisfying GENDER-violations in French suppletive (and other) liaison allows us to arrive rather quickly at a short summary of the points where there is convergence between Perlmutter's analysis and certain non-OT (or at least not-yet OT) accounts for the same phenomena. First, the ONSET >> GENDER approach is strikingly close to the similar-minded 16th-century analyses of Du Wés and Holyband, as well as to the 17th-century views cited by Vaugelas and the 19th-century ones of Diez (see above). Second, surely all modern linguists would endorse the claim that, at least part of the time, many aspects of both suppletive and other French liaison have at least something to do with the matching of C-final forms with following V-initial words, and of V-final forms with following C-initial words or with pauses—i.e., with an irreducible if not constant minimum of syllable-related information, and so with one prosodic-phonological factor.

The fact that, third, such at least partly syllabic conditioning interacts in parallel ways with the variants of a quite large range of lexemes—e.g., *mon/ton/son*, *cet(te)*, *bel(le)*, *fol(le)*, and *vieil(le)*, to name just a selection of suppletive forms—should compel virtually unanimous agreement on the point that a grammar must provide some way to indicate that the shared conditions across the various forms may at least be related to one another, if not forming a single set. As above, however, there is room for considerable disagreement as to the best method for expressing such shared similarities in a grammar. The invocation of a single OT constraint—ONSET—in the selection of a variant from a lexeme's "suppletion set" (in Tranel's analysis) or in Perlmutter's equivalent mechanism of "lexical sourcing" is certainly a plausible option for capturing the relevant generalization, but it is to be preferred only if purely phonological considerations of syllable structure do not need to be simultaneously supplemented by morphosyntactic information.

On the other hand, if it is indeed the case that lexical identity as well as morphological features and/or syntactic phrasing must play a crucial role in determining where C-final vs. V-final forms of a lexeme occur, then redundancy-stating generalizations of some sort may be the preferred option. Since Natural Generative Phonology's first use of *via rules* in Vennemann 1972, several variously named but surprisingly uniform versions of lexical redundancy "rules" have been exploited, especially by process morphologists with a Word-and-Paradigm-leaning orientation (like Aronoff 1976ff., Anderson 1982ff., or Janda and Joseph 1992); cf. most recently the application of Zwicky's 1994 *meta-generalizations* by Stump (in this volume).

Since many such morphologists envision a grammatical organization where phonological processes may become morphological rules while remaining embedded in a network of (other) phonological generalizations, they tend to presuppose a model in which rules (or constraints) are formally or functionally divided into types which may be interspersed with one another, rather than compartmentalized in uniform components or modules. This thus leads to a fourth point of convergence—one in which the OT approach to liaison of Tranel and Perlmutter represents a move toward the earlier position of, e.g., Anderson 1975, who explicitly argued for possible interactions among rules of different (e.g., phonetic vs. morphological) types.

A final—fifth—convergence along similar lines arises from the fact that many historical linguists have viewed the operation of both synchrony and diachrony as the interaction of vectors representing forces of qualitatively different types, and so in that sense very similar to Tranel's and Perlmutter's suggestion that the range of facts in Modern French liaison arise from constraint interaction involving phonology and syntax. E.g., Malkiel 1981: 91 explicitly states that the forces active in "internal processes of language change ... fundamentally ... fall into three categories: increase of economy, sharpening of clarity ...[, and] enhancement of expressivity".

From this perspective, however, one would expect that work in OT would much more often invoke sociolinguistic and even pragmatic-functional constraints, since these can sometimes simultaneously explain disparate sets of phenomena in much the same way as output-oriented syllable-structural generalizations can predict the existence of conspiracies among (former) generative-phonological rules. For example, in the description of Montréal French, one could establish distinct (sets of) constraints as proposed explanations for two very different changes respectively favoring the innovative diphthong [wa] over [wɛ] and the innovative *r*-sounds [ʀ]/[ʁ] over [r]. But in fact these both reflect the influence of Québec-City and, in turn, European French (cf. Walker 1984), and a sociolinguistic constraint(-family) of the type "EMULATE (the pronunciation of the prestigious people to the east along the water)" would be able to achieve a double coup with one blow.

This mention of sociolinguistic variation in French phonology leads naturally to a discussion of the ways in which Perlmutter's idealized presentation of suppletive and other liaison diverges from the reality of numerous ONSET-violating phenomena of a relevant sort in both European and Canadian varieties of the language. It can thus provide a transition from a focus on points of convergence to one on areas of divergence between Tranel's and Perlmutter's ONSET >> GENDER OT approach and competing proposals.

3. OT Liaison Blocked; Merits of Diverging Views

As will be seen shortly, if a strength hierarchy is set up for the evidence brought to bear on French suppletive liaison by each of the categories treated in Perlmutter's paper, this yields a ranking as follows. The probative value of DET POSSs like *mon* is rock-solid, that of DEM[onstrative] *cet-(te)* much less robust, and that of special ADJs like *bel(le)* very shaky, while the alleged "LOC DET" *en* turns out to show, if anything, that French P[repositional]Ps with initial elements introducing a place name—whether these involve a preposition alone or combine a preposition with a DET—do not in the general case obey ONSET. Before turning to the facts, though, it is important to review why this kind of reduction in the evidence is so serious.

Perlmutter's "Interfaces: Explanation of Allomorphy and the Architecture of Grammars" [hereafter usually "IEAAG"] strongly emphasizes the alleged consistency and unity of both (i) suppletive liaison and (ii) gender-clash across the mostly multiple members in four different lexical categories of morphosyntactic elements in French. It does so because this is one of the best ways to show that a wide variety of surface-phenomena actually arise from the interfacing of two simple generalizations in distinct grammatical modules—these being in the current case, as we have seen, phonological ONSET and syntactic GENDER/Concord. It is the contention of this commentary, however, that a full consideration of the relevant evidence (and of the existing literature) reveals French liaison to be limited to an extremely circumscribed set of elements and environments, and so not reducible to the effects of OT's ONSET constraint or any purely phonological generalization.

Rather, a complete account of French word-final C/Ø alternations also must make crucial reference to syntactic information, and to morphological categories that include gender. In this sense, the facts at issue here turn out to involve, not the interfacing of pure modules (since gender plays a role in both Concord and liaison), but rather a constellation of patterns each of whose generalizations itself brings together heterogeneous information of diverse grammatical types: phonological, syntactic, morphological, and lexical. Each intersection between two such smaller units of diverse information within a pattern can be said to involve an internal, mini-interface: an *interfacet*—or, more felicitously, an *intraface*.

Combining phonological and morphosyntactic conditioning within a single generalization may at first appear inconsistent with the "Principle of Phonology-Free Syntax" defended by Zwicky 1989 but challenged by Perlmutter, yet the phenomena in question here clearly are not essentially syntactic but morphological and lexical in nature. Hence they instead support Zwicky's 1989 advocacy of idiom- and construction-based approaches to grammar. Ironically, then, in its opposition to the non-constructional modularity of both Perlmutter and Chomsky 1995:170, the present commentary reveals those two orientations to be closer together than IEAAG implies.

Consider, e.g., the support for idiom/construction approaches provided by the difference in synchronic regularity and historical persistence shown by French *mon/ton/son* vs. *bel(le)*, *fol(le)*, *vieil(le)*, etc. A consultation of the dialectological literature (especially the focused survey in Morin 1986) reveals that a C-final suppletive variant like *mon* (or a skeletally parallel cognate form) tends to be maintained as a M/F liaison form for the POSS DET in most varieties of French (e.g., normative or colloquial, urban or rural, regional-standard or patois). But many regional dialects in Belgium and northern France no longer have suppletive M C-final forms for some or all of the ADJs in question. E.g., in the Picard of Gondecourt (near Lille; cf. Cochet 1933:33-34), 'old (F)' is invariant C-final *viel*, but 'old (M)' is regularly V-final *viu*, even before V-initial *áab* 'tree (M)' (since *viel*, the liaison variant that formerly preceded such M nouns, now survives only in fixed expressions like *viel om* 'geezer, old man (M)'). The ADJ 'soft (M)', on the other hand, is invariant *mol*. Tranel 1981:271-272 cites similar cases in the Walloon of Roux as proof of "the relatively unstable status of adjective liaison" (both suppletive and otherwise), as directly opposed to the robust nature of gender-marking final consonantism in F forms like *vieille*.

Such evidence shows that, if French liaison is indeed just OT's ONSET (perhaps plus NO-CODA), then—in some dialects not really so far from the standard variety—this constraint nonetheless continues to outrank GENDER only for some DETs, not (any longer) for suppletive ADJs. More importantly for our present purposes, comments on non-dialectal French by Dauzat 1950:187-188, Price 1971:112, and Grevisse 1986:60-62 (in the edition substantially revised by Goose) all stress the fact that "*le peuple*" 'the common people' tend not to use suppletive C-final ADJs before M V-initial forms, but instead hiatus-creating V-final variants, as in *un beau edifice* 'an attractive building' or *un vieux homme* 'an old man'—the latter a classic of relaxed speech (while *vieil* often forms with its noun a sort of fixed expression). Phrases like *un fol enfant* 'a crazy child' or *un mol oreiller* 'a soft pillow', on the other hand, "tend to go out of use ... [due to their] adjectives being hardly ever used before a substantive" (Dauzat 1950). Grevisse 1986 labels this usage as familiar to novelists, who attribute phrases like *le vieux* [vjø] *oeuf* 'the old egg' to their characters so as to create natural dialogue.

In past centuries, moreover, the pre-V use of V-final forms for suppletive ADJs was common in writing even outside of fictional conversation, so that Grevisse and Dauzat are able to cite numerous examples like *un beau idéal* 'a beautiful ideal' or *un vieux ami* 'an old friend' from a roster of authors including Chénier, Hugo, La Fontaine, Molière, Montesquieu, Rousseau, Stendhal, and Voltaire. Indeed, Vaugelas 1647/1934:377-378 admitted that both *vieux* and *vieil* were common before M V-initial words, though he still maintained that the latter "is much better" in that context. This historical fact points to what must be a central concern of any attempt to determine the status of liaison with suppletive C-final ADJ forms in current normative French: the influence of grammarians and the French Academy. I.e., while IEAAG implies that the use of a disagreeing suppletive form like *vieil* before, e.g., *homme* is due to the ranking ONSET >> GENDER and so reflects the great naturalness of a hiatus-avoiding constraint, the evidence of French usage since the 16th century is that it is mainly grammarians who have seen the direct contact of vowels across a word boundary as a major problem.

But how difficult can hiatus be for speakers of a language in which 'John has had (= gotten) a loon' is *Jean a eu un huard*? In Québécois, this has a six-V sequence: [žã. ɑ. y. œ̃. y.aʁ]. Relevant here is Kroch's 1976 suggestion that the dominant classes in society keep their linguistic distance from other groups either by soft-pedaling their degree of participation in natural phonetic processes engaged in by the latter or by cultivating their own less natural changes. In France, such activities seem to have been combined via the maintenance of suppletive C-final forms like *vieil*. In any case, the data of both current and older usage show that the phenomena which IEAAG wishes to treat as elegant and modularly simple are actually rather marked. The moral: an account based on data that have no grounding in present variation or in past developments is an analysis with no future. Thus, dialectal and social variation(s) in French jointly suggest that it is misguided to treat alternations like *beau* (M) vs. *bel* (F?/M??) as purely phonologically-conditioned, rather than as the morpholexical residue of former sound-changes.

A parallel example involving external sandhi in a Romance language is provided by the above case of Spanish *el alma* 'the soul', etc., where the evolution leading to the existence of F nouns preceded by seemingly M *el* has been seen as likewise supporting the invocation of ONSET constraints (cf. Mascaró 1996). However, the course of this development was as follows (cf. Malkiel 1981:101-102, Posner 1985:441-446). The Vulgar Latin DEM *illa* (F) originally underwent syllable-structurally conditioned processes reducing it to V-final *<il>la* in pre-C position but to C-final *ill<a>* in pre-V position, presumably reflecting the purely phonological constraint ONSET. Since the later development of (F) *ill > ell > el* intersected with the change of (M) *ille > ill > ell > el*, Spanish eventually ended up with *el* as a uniform definite DET before both F and M V-initial words. Later, though, so many morphosyntactic and lexical conditions accreted onto to this "feminine" *el* that they gradually reduced the scope of its general phonological conditions.

Thus, whereas this *el* (rather than *la*) in F NPs first occurred before a word starting with (i) any vowel, this V subsequently had to be (ii) *a*, then (iii) stressed *á*, next (iv) stressed *á* in a noun, later (v) stressed *á* in a noun other than the name of a person, city, or letter, and finally (vi) stressed *á* in a noun other than the name of a person, city, or letter or any of certain idiosyncratic lexical items. It is even known that a single grammarian (the influential Venezuelan Andrés Bello [1781-1865]) was primarily responsible for the form of the current standard norm! At present, two paths of radical development seem to be taking place with Spanish "feminine" *el*. For some speakers, it is coming to be viewed as completely idiosyncratic, occuring only before (vii.a) a small, closed set of arbitrary lexical items that all happen to be Ns starting with stressed *á* (cf. Posner 1985). For other speakers, though (at least in Spain), *el* still accompanies (vii.b) most F Ns beginning with stressed *á* (like *alma*), but these words have been reanalyzed as having the peculiar morphosyntactic property of *lateral hermaphroditism* (cf. Janda and Varela-García 1991). That is, these *á*-initial Ns take M agreement to the left (whereby *el* may immediately precede, e.g., a M C-initial ADJ) but F agreement to the right—hence *el cristalino agua esa* 'the (M) crystalline (M) water (F?/M+F??) that (F)' = 'that crystal-clear water'. The Vulgar Latin starting-point here was indeed ONSET-satisfying (re)syllabification, but the mid- and end-points all crucially involve morphosyntax and the lexicon, with some arbitrary phonological baggage left behind. In other words, this is not the clean interface of two grammatical modules but, like French suppletive liaison, a pattern (idiom/construction) built from disparate intrafaces.

And, even when patterns of this sort maintain their syllable-structural aspect more strongly, there can still be further phonological conditioning that is arbitrary, along with lexical restrictions. Thus, Perlmutter mentions English *an* (vs. *a*) as parallel to French *mon/ton/son*, etc., but the former is associated with a situation of inverse *h-aspiré* (≈ of *h-inaspiré*) that the latter lacks completely. I.e., in present-day English, there are many speakers for whom the /h/-initial word *historical* is unique in being preceded by *an*, not *a*. With only one ADJ conditioning this use of a variant for one DET, this is surely the ultimate in innovative lexical conditioning of a once purely ON-

SET-related C/Ø alternation. Moreover, the fact that *historical* is C-initial means that the *n* of *an* cannot here resyllabify, and so violates NO-CODA.

As is evident from relics like the song line "*Mine eyes (have seen the glory ...)*", DET-final *n*/Ø alternations dependent on a V-/C-initial following word were likewise once characteristic of English *mine* (vs. *my*) and *thine* (vs. *thy*). Yet these suppletive variants soon were severely reduced in scope or lost from normal speech. The form *thine* was lost along with its entire lexeme, while *mine* disappeared from all contexts other than predicate position (where it not only violated NO-CODA but also displayed its dependence on syntactic conditioning). Even before these events, however, there was a time during 16th-century Early Modern English when the C-final POSS-DET variant *mine* was regularly used not only before V-initial forms, but also before words whose initial /h/ was fully pronounced, as in *mine heart* (cf. Barber 1976:207)—in which case its *n*, too, could not resyllabify and so violated NO-CODA. In short, even to hint at a claim that word-final C/Ø alternations always remain dependent on junctural syllable-structure, especially a millennium after they arose phonologically, is to venture into a *mine*-field.

There are thus excellent precedents for believing that, during the centuries of liaison which have passed since French word-final consonants first began to be omitted in pre-C contexts after ca. 1250, this originally ONSET-conditioned phonological process has had more than ample time to become heavily morphosyntacticized and lexicalized. Such a reanalysis can explain how a C-final ADJ-form like *vieil*, though it is normatively used before V-initial M words, can there have come to possess a marked and even doomed status in non-standard French (and to have been abandoned as a pre-M form in many northern dialects)—but without this having had any consequences for *mon, son, ton*. After all, morphologization of a formerly phonological alternation (like German umlaut) may involve its being reanalyzed as conditioned by a disjunction containing numerous independent elements—any of which may then be lost or modified without consequences for the remainder. And so it seems to be in French for the independence of, e.g., *vieil* vs. *mon*.

We are then led to ask whether the contemporary liaison-behavior of the C-final DEM-form *cet*, which in normative French precedes V-initial M words, shows any trends toward variation or change bearing on Perlmutter's claim that NPs like *cet homme* 'that man (M)' contain a disagreeing [+Fem] form *cet* that is identical to F *cette*. Again, the answer is positive, but the mechanism involved is quite different from that seen with ADJs; cf. Bauche 1951:89-90 and Steinmeyer 1979:34-36 on Continental French and Daveluy 1988 on Canadian French. While many non-standard and regional varieties of the language avoid possible gender-clash in an ADJ like *vieil* by replacing it with M *vieux* in M pre-V contexts (despite the resulting hiatus), the relevant innovation for *cet* involves its being replaced—along with M *ce*—by what is effectively a blend of *cet* and *ce*: viz., *ç't(e)* = [st(ə)], whose schwa turns up in pre-C contexts but suffers elision before V-initial words. Thus, the M DEM-forms of Popular French are exemplified by NPs like *ç'te gars-la* 'that guy (there)' and *ç't'homme-ci* 'this man (here)'. At the same time, the speech varieties at issue replace normatively invariant (and gender-agreeing) F *cette* with *ç'tt(e)*, which also represents two forms—pre-C *ç'tte* and pre-V *ç'tt'*-—that are homophonous with the contextually corresponding M forms (and, in popular orthography, often spelled identically with them): hence *ç'tte femme-là* 'that woman (there)' and *ç'tt'heure-ci* 'this hour (here)'.

These DEM forms originated in the 17th century, when the root vowel of both *cet* and *cette* was a schwa that was often syncopated in connected speech—to the point where the writer Thomas Corneille 1687/1936:II.747 could state that, in "familar discourse", it would be a "vicious affectation" not to say "*st homme, ste femme*". The use of *ç'te* and not *ce* before C-initial M nouns, though, seems to be a much more recent and radical innovation, since it has had the effect of eliminating overt gender-contrasts from the SG DEM-forms of Popular French, which for Perlmutter thus have to be [0Fem] and so can never show gender clash. Admittedly, the distribution of the two context-determined variants of *ç't(t)(e)*—[stə] and [st]—gives the impression of being phonologically conditioned (by ONSET), but the impossibility of any gender clash involving Popular French SG DEM-forms makes them irrelevant for the debate over whether apparently wrong-gendered forms exist and are required by the higher ranking of ONSET over GENDER in OT. And many regional dialects have a unique C-final pre-V DEM-form that does not overtly distinguish gender and so cannot clash (cf. Price 1969:491).

But this does not mean that the *ç't(t)(e)* forms are not relevant for any issues which arise in the analysis of normative French, even if they belong to a different grammar from normative *cet* or *ce*. For one thing, they are by no means uncommon. In France, e.g., *ç't(t)(e)* forms are heard often enough at home, in the street, or at work to be adopted in the slice-of-life dialogue-style of writers like Queneau or San Antonio; indeed, their frequency is sufficient to win them a place in a textbook for foreigners like Burke 1988:33-37 (even in pattern drills!). For Québec, Daveluy 1988 found that, even in interview style, the variant *ç't(t)'* occurred more than twice as often as did *cet(te)* before V-initial words in NPs ending with the DEM particle -*là* 'there'.

In addition, the generalization of *ç't(t)'* and the concomitant loss of gender-clashing *cet* before M V-initial words resembles the abovementioned replacement of *vieil* by *vieux* in also occuring without visible repercussions for *mon, ton, son*. Most crucially, the fact that the /t/ of the *ç't(t)e* which replaces M *ce* clearly derives from *cet(te)* (rather than from *ce*) suggests that, pace Perlmutter, normative *cet(te)* (once also colloquial, before the 17th century) is not invariantly F. This is because, in the history of French, analog-ical extensions more often involve generalizations from M or gender-neutral stems to F forms than vice versa. Consequently, normative *cet(te)* would appear to be either a single [0Fem] default-form (as proposed by Lamarche 1996) or else a homophonous pair consisting of two distinct forms, F *cette* and M *cet*, as suggested by some of the answers given to the present author in response to the abovementioned questionnaire. E.g., 9 of the 16 speakers had more positive acceptability-judgments for a phrase with Perlmutter's putatively F disagreeing *cet*, like *cet—comment dirait-on—incroyable exploit* 'this—how would one say —incredible exploit (M)', than for one with clearly F agreeing *cette*, like *cette—comment dirait-on—incroyable performance* 'this—how would one say—incredible performance (F)', though both were dominantly judged acceptable or better; cf. Janda (in preparation). In addition, treating *cet* as M in the former phrase accords better with the standard view (cf. Bernstein 1993) that Romance D[ET]Ps are headed by DET.

4. Coda: Homophony—but No ONSET—in Liaison

Given the lack of support for OT-based ONSET >> GENDER analyses that is provided by the variation- and change-laden form *cet(te)/ç't(t)(e)*, we are left with the putative LOC DET *en* as the only remaining candidate for a F C-final form which could strongly complement the claim that French POSS DETs like *mon* exhibit phonologically dictated violations of GENDER. Yet the evidence available to bolster the claim that *en* is F and stands in a suppletive relationship with a V-final variant (M *au*) turns out to be the least solid of all. The ultimate collapse of the argument based on this form constitutes a significant development because it eliminates the main point criticized by Perlmutter in Zwicky's 1985 rule-of-referral analysis as it applies to French final C/Ø alternations: that one such rule each is needed for M and F C-final forms. But this problem disappears if the only well-supported apparent gender-mimatches involve POSS DET forms that are M, like *mon*.

Recall that Perlmutter treats the LOC elements *en* and *au* when used with country names as being the two gender-bearing variants (*en*[+Fem] and *au*[-Fem]) of a single "LOC DET" lexeme (thus considerably extending Miller et al.'s 1992 view of these forms as port(e)manteau-like realizations of preposition + DET), and so he analyzes PPs like [+Fem]*e.n I.ra<n>*[-Fem] 'in Iran (M)' as ONSET-satisfying violations of GENDER/Concord. Here, first off, it is surprising that an approach which rejects the positing of homophonous entities like *mon*[-Fem] and *mon*[+Fem]—since they share extensive morphosyntactic and semantic information—should contemplate positing any abstract lexeme implying the existence of large numbers of homophonous LOC elements: e.g., not only *en*[+Fem]1 as well as *en*[+Fem]2 and *en*[+Fem]3, but also *au*[-Fem]1 as well as *au*[-Fem]2 and *au*[-Fem]3. Yet this is precisely what follows from Perlmutter's assumption that the "LOC

DET" {*en*[+Fem], *au*[-Fem]} is a single lexical item, since the same logic that motivates this multipartite entity leads to the creation of other lexemes consisting either of the identical variants or of overlapping sets of variants.

After all, *au*—being the coalescence of *à* 'to, at, in' with *le* 'the (M SG)'—alternates not only with *en*, as in *au. Ma.roc* 'in/to Morocco (M)' vs. *e.n Al.gé.ri<e>* 'in/to Algeria (F)', but also with *à la* 'to the (F SG)' and *à l'* 'to the (M/F SG)'. Thus, e.g., cf. *ses références au. Ma.roc, à. la./*e<n>. Tu.ni.si<e>, à. l'/*e.n Al.gé.ri<e> e<t>. à. l'/*e.n I.ra<n>* 'his references to Morocco, to Tunisia, to Algeria, and to Iran'; this motivates another abstract lexeme "*À* DET" {*à la*[+Fem], *à l'*[0Fem], *au*[-Fem], ...}, though here only *au* is maximally port(e)manteau-like. And the different semantics at play when *en* and *au* precede temporal expressions would also lead us to have a "TEMP[oral]DET" {*en*[+Fem], *au*[-Fem]} whose two different realizations appear in *au. pri<n>.te<mps>* 'in spring (M)', *en. se.main<e>* 'during the week (F)', and *e.n é.té* 'in summer (M)'. Add to this both Perlmutter's urban LOC preposition *à* (involving only {*à*[0Fem]}; cf. *à. Arl<es >*'in Arles') and the preposition *en* (involving only {*en*[0Fem]}) that means '(traveling) by (means of)', as in *e.n au.to, e<n>. voi.tur<e>* 'by car (F)' or *e<n>. traî.neau* 'by sled (M)', and we end up with three homophones for each of *à*, *au*, and *en*. The members in each such triple nearly all share important lexical-categorial, morphosyntactic, or semantic information at the same time as their gender varies. If genderal homophony is bad, such a trend is pessimal.

At this point, one option is to adopt the above notion of redundancy-stating meta-generalizations—like the *meta-templates* of Janda and Joseph 1992—so that the identity of the shared properties common to two or more homophonous elements can be expressed even when such entities appear in different parts of a grammar (e.g., in distinct lexical entries). Otherwise, though, we are forced to drop the view that French has any abstract gender-bearing "LOC DETs". Instead, we are led to adopt an idiom/construction approach that treats the PPs at issue as falling into patterns which, although they have certain overall semantic and/or syntactic characteristics, all draw from a unique set of prepositions and of DETs as their lexical items—whereby only the DETs have gender, not the prepositions. In that case, however, gender clash and Perlmutter's device of "lexical sourcing" become irrelevant for PPs like *en Israël* 'in Israel (M)' vs. *au Liban* 'in (the) Lebanon (M)'.

Indeed, there are strong reasons to conclude that no DET at all is present in *en Israël* or the like, and hence no gender in any element other than their Ns. E.g., usage in normative French is such that *Israël* and the names of certain other countries never take an article in any normal context, and *en* is at any rate known to be a preposition that tends to occur without a DET, especially a definite F SG one (cf. Grevisse 1986:924, 1528f.). Historically, too, it can be shown that *en* + place-name once normally occurred without an article; more tellingly, it turns out that the diachronic source for phrases with *au* + place-name was *en* + *le* + place-name, and that *en* + *le* underwent the series of developments *en-le* > *enl* > *el* > *eu* > *ou*, whose last stage was reinterpreted as being equivalent to *au* from *a* + *le* (cf. Rickard 1974:74).

Given the further problems for liaison-as-ONSET posed by LOC PPs like *à Elbe* 'in Elba (F)' vs. *en Irlande* 'in Ireland (F)', or the data in Morin and Kaye 1982 and later works by Tranel (see Perlmutter's footnote 22), homophony of M and F *mon* seems like a small price to pay, *mon ami(e)*!

References

Andersen, Henning, ed. 1986. *Sandhi Phenomena in the Languages of Europe.* Berlin: Mouton de Gruyter.

Anderson, Stephen. 1975. On the Interaction of Phonological Rules of Various Types. *Journal of Linguistics* 11, 39-62.

Anderson, Stephen. 1982. Where's Morphology? *LI* 13, 571-612.

Aronoff, Mark. 1976. *Word Formation in Generative Grammar.* Cambridge: MIT Press.

Barber, Charles. 1976. *Early Modern English.* London: André Deutsch.

Bauche, Henri. 1951. *Le langage populaire ....* Paris: Payot (new, 4th ed.).

Bernstein, Judy. 1993. *Topics in the Syntax of Nominal Structure Across Romance.* Doctoral dissertation, City University of New York.

Booij, Geert. 1986. Two Cases of External Sandhi in French: Enchaînement and Liaison. In Andersen, ed., 93-103.

Booij, Geert and Daan de Jong. 1987. The Domain of Liaison: Theories and Data. *Linguistics* 25 [291], 1005-1025.

Burke, David. 1988. *Street French ....* New York: Wiley.

Chomsky, Noam. 1995. *The Minimalist Program.* Cambridge: MIT Press.

Cochet, É. 1933. *Le patois de Gondecourt (Nord) ....* Paris: Droz.

Corneille, Thomas. 1687/1936. Notes. In Thomas Corneille, ed., *Remarques sur la langue françoise de ... Vaugelas ..., I-II.* Paris: Girard, and in Jeanne Streicher, ed., *Commentaires sur les Remarques ....* Paris: Droz.

Dauzat, Albert. 1950. *Phonétique et grammaire historiques de la langue française.* Paris: Larousse.

Daveluy, Michelle. 1988. L'alternance entre les déterminants démonstratifs .... In Julie Auger, ed., *Actes du colloque "Tendances actuelles de la recherche ...",* 121-142. Québec City: CIRB (Centre International ...).

Desrochers, Richard. 1994. Les liaisons dangereuses: Le statut équivoque des erreurs de liaison. *Lingvisticae Investigationes* 18, 243-284.

Diez, Friedrich. 1869/1882. *Grammatik der romanischen Sprachen, 1. Theil.* Bonn: Weber [Flittner], 1869 (3rd ed.), repaginated in 1882 (5th ed.).

Du Wés, Giles. ca. 1532/1972. *An Introductorie for to Lerne ... French Trewly.* London: Godfray; Menston: Scholar Press (facsimile).

Encrevé, Pierre. 1988. *La liaison avec et sans enchaînement: Phonologie tri-dimensionelle et usages du francais.* Paris: Seuil.

Grevisse, Maurice. 1986. *Le bon usage: Grammaire française.* Paris: Éditions Duculot (12th ed., recast by André Goose; 1st ed. 1936).

Hol(l)yband, Claudius. 1576/1609/1953. *The French Littleton.* London: Vautroullier (1st ed., misdated 1566); Field, 1609 (2nd ed.); Cambridge: Cambridge University Press (M. Byrne, ed.; facsimile of 2nd ed.).

Janda, Richard. In preparation. An—Parenthetically Speaking—Other Argument Against French Liaison as Syllabification.

Janda, Richard and Brian Joseph. 1992. Meta-Templates and the Underlying (Dis-)Unity of Sanskrit Reduplication. In Germán Westphal et al., eds., *Proceedings of the 8th Eastern States Conference on Linguistics (1991)*, 160-173. Columbus: Ohio State University.

Janda, Richard and Fabiola Varela-García. 1991. On Lateral Hermaphroditism and Other Variation in Spanish 'Feminine' *el.* In Lise Dobrin et al., eds., *Papers from the 27th Regional Meeting of the Chicago Linguistic Society, Part 1*, 276-290. Chicago: Chicago Linguistic Society.

Klausenburger, Jürgen. 1984. *French Liaison and Linguistic Theory.* Stuttgart: Steiner.

Klein, Ewan. 1995. Alignment Constraints in French. *Phonology at Santa Cruz* 4, 13-20.

Kroch, Anthony. 1976. Toward a Theory of Social Dialect Variation. *Language in Society* 7, 17-36.

Lamarche, Jacques. 1996. Gender Agreement and Suppletion in French. In Karen Zagona, ed., *Grammatical Theory and Romance Languages*, 145-157. Amsterdam: Benjamins.

Malkiel, Yakov. 1981. Hypercharacterization of Pronominal Gender in Romance. In T. Hope, ed., *Language, Style, and Meaning: Essays in Memory of Stephen Ullmann*, 91-107. Leeds: Leeds University Press.

Mascaró, Joan. 1996. External Allomorphy and Contractions in Romance. *Probus* 8, 181-205.

Miller, Philip, Geoffrey Pullum, and Arnold Zwicky. 1992. Le principe d'inaccesibilité de la phonologie par la syntaxe: Trois contre-exemples apparents en français. *Lingvisticae Investigationes* 16, 317-343.

Morin, Yves-Charles. 1986. On the Morphologization of Word-Final Consonant Deletion in French. In Andersen, ed., 167-210.

Morin, Yves-Charles. 1992. Un cas méconnu de la déclinaison de l'adjectif français: Les formes de liaison de l'adjectif antéposé. In André Clas, ed., *Le mot, les mots, les bons mots ...: Hommage à Igor A. Mel'cuk ...*, 235-250. Montréal: Presses de l'Université de Montréal.

Morin, Yves-Charles and Jonathan Kaye. 1982. The Syntactic Bases for French Liaison. *Journal of Linguistics* 18, 291-330.

Perlmutter, David. 1996. Interfaces: Explanation of Allomorphy and the Architecture of Grammars. In this volume. [Abbreviated "IEAAG".]

Perlmutter, David. In preparation. The Emergence of Morphology.

Péronnet, Louise. 1989. La question du genre dans le parler acadien.... In Raymond Mougeon and Édouard Beniak, eds., *Le français canadien parlé hors Québec* ..., 213-226. Québec City: Presses de l'Université Laval.

Posner, Rebecca. 1985. Non-Agreement on Romance Disagreements. *Journal of Linguistics* 21, 437-451.

Price, Glanville. 1969. La transformation du système français des démonstratifs. *Zeitschrift für romanische Philologie* 85, 489-505.

Price, Granville. 1971. *The French Language: Present and Past.* London: Grant and Cutler.

Rickard, Peter. 1974. *History of the French Language.* London: Hutchinson.

Selkirk, Elisabeth. 1972. *The Phrase Phonology of English and French.* Doctoral dissertation, MIT.

Steinmeyer, Georg. 1979. *Historische[s]... français avancé.* Geneva: Droz.

Stump, Gregory. 1996. Comments on ... Inkelas and Orgun. In this volume.

Tranel, Bernard. 1981. *Concreteness in Generative Phonology: Evidence from French.* Berkeley: University of California Press.

Tranel, Bernard. 1994a. Current Issues in French Phonology. In John Goldsmith, ed., *Handbook of Phonolog[y]...*, 798-816. Oxford: Blackwell.

Tranel, Bernard. 1994b. French Liaison and Elision Revisited: A Unified Account Within Optimality Theory. Paper given at 24th Linguistic Symposium on Romance Languages; Los Angeles; March 10-13.

Tranel, Bernard. 1995. Exceptionality in Optimality Theory and Final Consonants in French. In Karen Zagona, ed., *Grammatical Theory and Romance Languages* ..., 275-291. Amsterdam: Benjamins.

Tranel, Bernard. 1996. French Liaison and Elision Revisited: A Unified Account Within Optimality Theory. In Claudia Parodi et al., eds., *Aspects of Romance Linguistics* .... Washington: Georgetown University Press.

Vaugelas, Claude Favre de. 1647/1934. *Remarques sur la langue françoise.* Paris: Camusat and Petit; Paris: Droz (facsimile; Jeanne Streicher, ed.).

Vennemann, Theo. 1972. Rule Inversion. *Lingua* 29, 209-242.

Walker, Douglas. 1984. *The Pronunciation of Canadian French.* Ottawa: University of Ottawa Press.

Zwicky, Arnold. 1985. Rules of Allomorphy and Syntax-Phonology Interactions. *Journal of Linguistics* 21, 431-436.

Zwicky, Arnold. 1989. Idioms and Constructions. In Joyce Powers and Kenneth de Jong, eds., *Proceedings of the 5th Eastern States Conference on Linguistics (1988)*, 547-558. Columbus: Ohio State University.

Zwicky, Arnold. 1994. Morphological Metageneralizations .... Paper given at the Kentucky Foreign Language Conference; Louisville; April.

Level (Non)Ordering in Recursive Morphology: Evidence from Turkish

SHARON INKELAS & C. ORHAN ORGUN

1. Introduction

In this paper we consider a number of different morphological constructions in Turkish, a language with recursive morphology in which constructions are segregated into different phonological levels. An examination of the interactions among the various constructions considered leads to the conclusion that there is no benefit to be gained in Turkish from the standard assumption that phonological levels are ordered. Instead we advocate a theory in which level nonordering is the expected case.

2. Level ordering: the standard view

The claim in classical level-ordering theory (Kiparsky 1982a,b; Mohanan 1982, 1986) is that every form, derived or underived, is subjected to every level of phonology and morphology as it passes through the lexical component of the grammar. Mohanan invokes a factory metaphor in which lexical levels correspond to rooms filled with workers performing phonological and morphological operations (Mohanan 1986:47):

(1)   There is a conveyor belt that runs from the entry gate to the exit gate passing through each of these rooms. This means that every word that leaves the factory came in through the entry gate and passed through every one of these rooms.

The hypothesis that every form undergoes every level is not dependent on the (serial) factory metaphor, however; a theory such as that of Selkirk (1982), Cohn (1989), Inkelas (1990, 1993a,b), or Orgun (1994, 1995a,b), in which lexical levels are defined as hierarchically related constituent types, is capable of incorporating the same fundamental principle. This goal lies behind Inkelas's (1990) proposal to extend into lexical structure Selkirk's Strict Layer Hypothesis, developed originally for postlexical prosodic constituent structure (Selkirk 1984:26):

(2)   Strict Layer Hypothesis: "a category of level i in the hierarchy immediately dominates a (sequence of) categories of level i-1"

Languages with multiple levels which have been analyzed in some detail within the level ordering framework include Malayalam (4 levels) (Mohanan 1982, 1986), English (2 to 4 levels) (Kiparsky 1982a,b, 1985; Mohanan 1982, 1986; Halle and Mohanan 1985; Borowsky 1986), Tamil (2 levels) (Christdas 1988), Sekani (4 or 5 levels) (Hargus 1985, 1988), Kashaya (5 levels) (Buckley 1994b), Manam (4 levels) (Buckley 1994a), and Turkish (4 levels) (Inkelas and Orgun 1995).

3. Deviations from the standard

The standard model has witnessed two phenomena requiring major deviations from the strict ordering assumptions of (1) and (2). One is LEVEL ECONOMY, in which not all levels are activated in the derivation of a given word. The other is THE LOOP, in which levels are activated in an order contrary to that expected from their stated ordering in the grammar.

3.1. Level Economy

Various studies have found evidence that not all forms are subject to the phonology of all levels in the system. For example, in other work on Turkish (Orgun and Inkelas 1992, Inkelas and Orgun 1995) we have argued that the phonology of a given suffixation level in Turkish is imposed only on those stems which are subject to the morphology of that level. One example from these studies involves a disyllabic minimal size condition on Turkish words, first observed by Itô and Hankamer (1989). As demonstrated in Inkelas and Orgun (1995), this condition causes the ungrammaticality, for some speakers, of monosyllabic stems containing level 2 or level 3 suffixes (3a,b); however, nonderived monosyllabic stems are judged grammatical by the same speakers (3c). In the following example, subscripts indicate relevant phonological level:[1]

---

[1]The following abbreviations are used in this paper: 1 = first person, 2 = second person, 3 = third person, abl = ablative, agt = agentive, adj = adjectivizer, caus = causative, cop = copula, dat = dative, dim = diminutive, evid = evidential, fut = future, gen = genitive, impf = imperfective, inf = infinitive, interr = interrogative, loc = locative, n = noun, neg = negative, O = object, pass = passive, pl = plural, poss = possessive, prog = progressive, psr = possessive, rel = relativizer, sg = singular, vbl = verbalizer. Turkish examples are given in standard phonemic transcription; the symbol "i" represents IPA [ɯ], the high back unrounded vowel, and uppercase letters represent archiphonemes whose feature values are determined by context. Vowel length is marked with a colon, while vowel doubling indicates heterosyllabicity.

(3)   Disyllabic size condition
   a.   *ye-n_2 'eat-PASS'   violated at level 2

        *fa:-m_3 'note 'fa'-1SG.POSS'   violated at level 3

   b.   ye-n_2-ir_2 'eat-PASS-IMPF'   satisfied at level 2

        fa-mɨz_3 'note 'fa'-1PL.POSS'   satisfied at level 3

   c.   yen$_\omega$ 'defeat'   not imposed at word level

        ham$_\omega$ 'unripe'   not imposed at word level

These facts follow if the disyllabic size condition is imposed only at levels 2 and 3, which monomorphemic forms "skip" by virtue of containing no suffixes from those levels.

An alternative to Level Economy might be to assume that all forms are subject to the phonology of all levels, as indicated in (4), regardless of whether or not they undergo morphology there, but that the Strict Cycle Condition (SCC) (e.g. Mascaró 1976; Kiparsky 1982a,b, 1993) blocks the disyllabic condition from applying at levels 2 and 3:

(4)   [[[[[[ham]$_1$]$_2$]$_3$]$_4$]$_5$]$_\omega$

However, this alternative proves unworkable; as Inkelas and Orgun (1995) point out, the disyllabic minimum meets none of the usual criteria of the SCC (e.g., it is not structure-changing and neutralizes no lexical contrasts).[2] Furthermore, Orgun and Inkelas (1992) have shown that there is another, bimoraic minimal size condition in Turkish to which even roots are subject; Mester (1994) and Prince and Smolensky (1993) discuss a similar situation in Latin. It is therefore clearly not the case that nonderived forms are immune to minimal size conditions in general.

Buckley (1994a) has also found Level Economy effects in Manam, for which he proposes four lexical levels (root, prefix, suffix, and clitic). According to Buckley, the facts of Manam show that "...a form is not subjected to the constraints of a level if no morphological operation at that level applies." Finally, Inkelas (1993b), in a study of affix ordering in Nimboran, demonstrates that certain suffixes cause entire levels or sequences of levels to be skipped, another instance of Level Economy.[3]

---

[2] However, Itô (1990) does invoke the SCC to account for a related phenomenon in Japanese, where nonderived words evade the bimoraic word minimum. See Kiparsky (1993) for a related approach.

[3] A similar proposal is made by Kaisse (1986) for Turkish; see fn. 17 and §8.4.

3.2. The loop

A second deviation from the strict ordering predictions of the factory metaphor (1) or Strict Layer Hypothesis (2) is the existence of loops, i.e. cases where the output of some phonological level serves as input to another level which is extrinsically ordered first.

The most famous example of the loop is Mohanan's (1982, 1986) analysis of two types of compounding in Malayalam, which Mohanan locates on lexical levels 2 and 3, respectively. The fact that either type of compounding can feed the other necessitates a loop. Mohanan's proposal has been the target of numerous attempts to avoid the loop by appealing, for example, to prosodic constituency (Sproat 1986, Inkelas 1990) or semantics (Christdas 1986); some of these analyses have been rebutted by Mohanan (1995). Other, less controversial cases of the loop include those of Hargus (1985, 1988) for Sekani, Szpyra (1989) for Polish (though see Inkelas 1994b), and Hualde (1988, 1989) for Basque.[4] Here we briefly illustrate the cases from Sekani and Basque, each of which has properties for which the theory we develop on the basis of Turkish will prove relevant.

3.2.1. Sekani

Hargus (1985, 1988) argues for the loop in Sekani on the basis of the application of a rule of Continuant Voicing in complex morphological structures. As Hargus demonstrates, the initial continuant of a morpheme which is the right branch of a morphological construction undergoes voicing at level 1. In (5a), the second element of a compound undergoes the alternation. The data given here are from Hargus 1988 (pp. 228-239).

(5)   a. Type 1 compounding: voicing of initial fricative of right member
       [tsà? yhè̵]₁   'beaver trap'
          ↓
       [y]

---

[4]Another case of the loop, rather dubious in our opinion, is the proposal by Mohanan (1982, 1986) and Halle and Mohanan (1986) that English requires a loop between level 2 (affixation) and level 3 (compounding). However, this claim is based on a single rule and makes the incorrect prediction that compounds should be able to undergo all phonology which the authors locate on level 2, including nasal assimilation, velar softening, and other rules that in fact never apply across the internal boundary of compounds. For a reanalysis without the loop, see Inkelas 1990.

    b. Type 2 compounding: no voicing
       [łès -sə̀s]5   'flour skin = sack of flour'
         ↓
       *[z]

    c. Possessed type 2 compounds: voicing
       [ma [xès sə̀s]5]1   '3sPSR egg skin = his scrotum'
         ↓
       [gh]

In (5b) we see a different type of compound (type 2) which resists Continuant Voicing. It is apparently not predictable from the identity of the morphemes involved which type of compound will result; thus two different morphological constructions are required (see Rice 1989 for a discussion of semantic differences between the two analogous types of compounds in Slave). Hargus (1988) proposes that type 2 compounding takes place on level 5, the other level of nominal morphology in Sekani and a level on which Continuant Voicing is inapplicable.[5]

    The paradox for this analysis is illustrated by the data in (c), where it can be seen that type 2 compounds *are* subject to Continuant Voicing when combined with a possessive prefix. Because possessive morphology and Continuant Voicing both take place on level 1, Hargus (1988) proposes a loop from level 5 back to level 1. This is a novel kind of loop, as pointed out by Christdas (1986), in that it connects two nonadjacent levels.

3.2.2. Basque

    Hualde (1988, 1989) discusses an unusual type of looping which occurs in certain dialects of Basque. According to Hualde, vowel raising in these dialects applies at stratum 1 but not at stratum 2. However, clitics, added at a later (syntactic) stratum, trigger the rule, suggesting that vowel raising applies to the output of cliticization as well. To account for this, Hualde proposes a loop from the cliticization level back to level 1 for the purpose of re-applying level 1 phonology.[6] This loop differs from the

---

[5]Hargus (1985), operating with only four levels, locates type 2 compounding on level 4.

[6]Bonet (1993) proposes an alternative analysis in which vowel raising applies post-lexically to strings dominated by X^0 nodes. The affixes that trigger the rule fall under the X^0 node; clitics incorporate into such nodes by virtue of head-to-head movement (p. 253) in PF. Compounds, by contrast, consist of multiple BP ("Bila Phrase") nodes under another BP node, and therefore do not meet the description of the raising rule. Bonet's proposal has something in common with the reanalyses of Malayalam by Sproat (1986) and Inkelas (1990); assigning each word or phrase two different constituent structures, one for use by morphology and syntax and the other for use by the phonology, weakens expectations of correlation between morphological and phonological

others in the literature because its effects are purely phonological. The output of cliticization can undergo the phonology but not the suffixation or compounding operations of the lexical levels.

4. Cophonologies: an alternative view

In this paper we adopt an approach to level stratification which differs from the standard model, arguing on the basis of evidence from Turkish for abandoning the assumption of fixed ordering among levels. Instead, we propose that each morphological construction, e.g. an individual affix, a compounding rule, a rule of nickname formation, and so on, has its own associated phonology; we call each such phonological mapping a "cophonology", following Inkelas, Orgun and Zoll (1994).

(6) "Cophonology": the phonological mapping associated with a given morphological construction

In this approach, the term "level" lacks formal status, though it is still useful as a descriptor of the set of all morphological constructions associated with a given cophonology.

An important aspect of this proposal is that all phonological alternations are handled by cophonologies, including not only regular alternations that apply to all morphological constructions but also "minor" ones which may be associated with only one morphological construction. Thus, while cophonologies are specific to certain morphological constructions, the phonological alternations occuring within each cophonology are blind to morphological information. Our approach thus differs in this respect from previous implementations of level ordering, in which phonological rules can be directly sensitive to morpheme identity.

5. Level economy and the loop as consequences of the new approach

Under the proposed approach, in which cophonologies are associated with particular morphological constructions, both of the deviations from standard level ordering theory that we observed above now follow as natural consequences, rather than being embarrassments. If, as we are assuming, cophonologies are associated with morphological constructions, it follows, first of all, that a word containing many such constructions will be subject to more applications of phonology than a word

---

levels, reducing the need for the loop to get the phonology to come out right. The question is to what extent morphologically-based and phonologically-based constituent structure can diverge.

containing few constructions. This is Level Economy: forms are subject to all and only the cophonologies of the constructions which comprise them.

As we have seen, this expectation is borne out in Manam (Buckley 1994a) and Turkish (Inkelas and Orgun 1995), in which a word has as many "levels", or cophonology types, represented in it as the morphology warrants—but no more.[7] The following examples are from Turkish:[8]

(7)

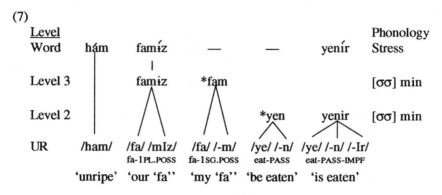

Level						Phonology
Word	hám	famíz	—	—	yenír	Stress
Level 3		famɨz	*fam			[σσ] min
Level 2				*yen	yenir	[σσ] min
UR	/ham/	/fa/ /mIz/	/fa/ /-m/	/ye/ /-n/	/ye/ /-n/ /-Ir/	
		fa-1PL.POSS	fa-1SG.POSS	eat-PASS	eat-PASS-IMPF	
	'unripe'	'our 'fa''	'my 'fa''	'be eaten'	'is eaten'	

The second consequence of the new conception of cophonologies is the loop. In the cophonology view, "looping" is the situation in which two morphological constructions associated with the same cophonology are separated, in a given word, by a third construction associated with a different cophonology. Recall that on our view, level (or cophonology type) is not a formal construct; nothing requires all morphological constructions associated with the same cophonology to cluster in the same area of a word. Cophonologies apply in the order in which their affiliated morphological constructions happen to appear in a word; thus looping is a perfectly natural and expected effect.

The approach advocated here provides a natural account of the relatively standard loop phenomena found in Sekani as well as of the more exotic case of Basque. In each case, some but not all morphological constructions are associated with a given cophonology In the rough Sekani

---

[7]Interestingly, in both Manam and Turkish, there is an obligatory root cycle, though for ease of exposition this is not represented in the Turkish example in (7) (see Inkelas and Orgun (1995) for extensive discussion). It is thus not the case that phonology is triggered only by those morphological constructions creating complex forms. Inkelas and Orgun (1995) suggest that the root cycle is functionally motivated by the need to implement morpheme structure constraints, which seem to thrive in at least some languages. The word cycle is another potentially obligatory cycle with a functional motivation.

[8]See Orgun (1994, 1995a,b) for a discussion of the significance of the flat structure accorded to *yenir.*

constructions below, both Type 1 and Type 2 compounding concatenate two input forms whose phonological strings are referred to as "Q" and "P", respectively; the cophonology of Type 1, but not Type 2, compounding imposes Continuant Voicing on string P.

(8)   **Type 1 compounding:**

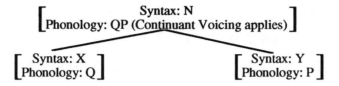

$$\left[\begin{array}{c} \text{Syntax: N} \\ \text{Phonology: QP (Continuant Voicing applies)} \end{array}\right]$$

$$\left[\begin{array}{c} \text{Syntax: X} \\ \text{Phonology: Q} \end{array}\right] \qquad \left[\begin{array}{c} \text{Syntax: Y} \\ \text{Phonology: P} \end{array}\right]$$

Type 2 compounding:

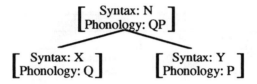

$$\left[\begin{array}{c} \text{Syntax: N} \\ \text{Phonology: QP} \end{array}\right]$$

$$\left[\begin{array}{c} \text{Syntax: X} \\ \text{Phonology: Q} \end{array}\right] \qquad \left[\begin{array}{c} \text{Syntax: Y} \\ \text{Phonology: P} \end{array}\right]$$

In the case of Sekani, the cophonology analysis is essentially equivalent to the loop proposed by Hargus (with the possible advantage that in the cophonology framework there is no false expectation that levels connected via the loop should be "adjacent"). However, the cophonology analysis arguably provides a superior account of Basque. While under Hualde's account it was unexplained why clitics would not be subject to stratum 1 and 2 morphology as a result of looping back to stratum 1, on our account that is to be expected: clitics and "stratum 1" stems happen to be associated with the same cophonology, but the morphology ensures that cliticization will never be input to affixation.

6. Recursive morphology and level (non)ordering in Turkish

In this section we will make a detailed case for the proposed cophonology approach on the basis of a fragment of Turkish,[9] examining in depth the interactions among a number of different morphological

---

[9]Data reflect the speech of the alphabetically second author, a native speaker of the standard Istanbul dialect.

constructions. These interactions provide strong support for the hypothesis that "levels", or cophonology types, are not extrinsically ordered.

Our starting point is an existing proposal for a partial segregation of Turkish suffixes into levels, based both on their phonology and also on morphological evidence adduced by Orgun (1995a,b). According to Inkelas and Orgun (1995), the Turkish lexicon includes the levels, i.e. cophonologies with associated morphological constructions, in (9).[10] (We will not attempt to defend these levels here, as we have defended them elsewhere; the focus of the present work is on other morphological constructions which we have not previously analyzed in this context.)

(9)

Level:	1	2	3	4	5
Morphology	root	passive aspect relative negative	plural possessive	case	tense agreement interrogative
Phonology	[μμ]				
		[σσ]			
			intervocalic velar deletion		

A fairly long word exhibiting affixes from all five levels is given below. (Note that not all suffixes have been assigned a level. This is because we have not yet found positive evidence for their membership in any particular level.) In this particular word, affixes occur in the order one would expect given the chart in (9):

(10)   [[[[[[[[[[[[čekoslovakya]₁ li] laš] tir]₂ ama] yaǰak]₂ lar]₃ ...
        Czechoslovakia-from-become-CAUS-unable-FUT-PL- ...

        ... imiz]₃ dan]₄ mi]₅ ydi]₅ niz]₅
        ... 1PL-ABL-INTERR-past-2PL

'Were you one of those whom we are not going to be able to turn into Czechoslovakians?'

Of course, as noted earlier, not all words contain suffixes from all levels:

---

[10]Inkelas and Orgun (1995) actually posit only four levels, failing to distinguish 4 and 5. Kaisse (1985, 1986), Hameed (1985), and Barker (1989) define other levels on the basis of stress patterns; later in the paper we give our reasons for not assuming their level distinctions.

(11) a. [[[[ev]₁ ler]₃ im]₃ de]₄
      house-PL-1SG.POSS-LOC   'at my houses'
   b. [[[söyle]₁ di 5] m]₅
      say-past-1SG   'I said'
   c. [ič]₁
      drink   'drink!'

Because Turkish has a lot of recursive morphology, it should come as no great surprise that the neat level ordering suggested by the chart in (9) is illusory. Although the focus of our paper is not on suffix ordering per se, mainly because we still have only fragmentary information as to which suffixes belong to which levels, we would like to introduce just a few examples to illustrate the potential for non-ordering among suffixational levels. The data in (12) highlight the behavior of the suffix -ki. All of the examples in (12) are consistent with an analysis in which -ki belongs to level 4 or 5; (13) suggests that -ki attaches specifically at level 4, as it can occur inside a level 4 suffix.[11]

(12) a. šimdi-ki (L)   1-*ki*
      now-ki
      'the one that's current'
   b. <ihtiyarin bahšiš> al-ir-ken-ki <durumu> (L)   1-2-?-*ki*
      <the old man's tip> take-IMPF-while-ki <attitude>
      'the old man's attitude while taking tips'
   c. ev-in-de-ki (U)   1-4-4-*ki*
      house-GEN-LOC-ki
      'those in his house'
   d. kutu-da-ki-y-miš (H)   1-4-*ki*-?-5
      box-LOC-ki-COP-EVID
      'it's allegedly the one in the box'
   e. arkadaš-lar-iniz-in-ki (L)   1-3-3-4-*ki*
      friend-PL-2SG.POSS-GEN-ki
      'the one belonging to your friends'

---

[11]"L" indicates that the data was taken from Lewis 1967:69-70, 251; "U" stands for Underhill 1976:209-212; "S" for Swift 1963:139, and "H" for Hankamer 1986:43, 49.

(13)   a.   baba-si-nin-ki-ni (L)   1-3-4-*ki*-4
            father-POSS-GEN-ki-ACC
            'that of his father (accusative)'
       b.   on-un-ki-nden (U)   1-4-*ki*-4
            3SG-GEN-ki-ABL
            'that which is his (ablative)'
       c.   köše-de-ki-nin-ki (S)   1-4-*ki*-4-*ki*
            corner-LOC-ki-GEN-ki
            'the one which belongs to the one that is in the corner'

The data in (14), however, show that -*ki* can occur *inside* level 3 suffixes. The fact that -*ki* occurs outside level 4 but inside level 3 points incontrovertibly to a loop, i.e. to level nonordering.

(14)   a.   kardeš-ler-iniz-in-ki-ler-den (L)   1-3-3-4-*ki*-3-4
            sibling-PL-2PL.POSS-GEN-ki-PL-ABL
            'those of your brothers (ablative)'
       b.   köy-de-ki-ler (U)   1-4-*ki*-3
            village-LOC-ki-PL
            'the ones in that village'
       c.   čöp-lük-ler-imiz-de-ki-ler-den-mi-y-di (H)   1-?-3-3-4-*ki*-3-5-?-5
            trash-for-PL-1PL.POSS-LOC-ki-PL-ABL-INTERR-COP-past
            'was it from those that were in our garbage dumps?'

According to Hankamer (1986:44), the potential for recursion around -*ki* is quite high. Clearly, -*ki* words provide evidence minimally for recursion between levels 3 and 4.

7. Morphological constructions and cophonologies in Turkish

We will appeal to two other productive morphological constructions to make the definitive case for level nonordering in Turkish. These are the following:

(15)   a. Sezer stems (a certain (open) class of mostly place names)
       b. Compounding

The relevant phonological evidence consists of productive stress alternations, transparently diagnostic of level in these cases. There is a large literature on Turkish stress, including Lees 1961; Swift 1963; Lewis

1967; Foster 1970; Dobrovolsky 1976, 1986; Lightner 1978; Underhill 1976; Sezer 1981; Kardestuncer 1982; Poser 1984; Hameed 1985; Kaisse 1985, 1986, 1993; Hammond 1986; Halle and Vergnaud 1987; Barker 1989; Kiparsky 1991; Idsardi 1992; Inkelas, Orgun and Zoll 1994; Inkelas 1994a; and Hayes 1995. In this paper we will be assuming the particular analysis of Inkelas (1994a).

7.1. The "basic" pattern: Final stress

As is well-known, the basic stress pattern in Turkish is final. As exemplified in (16), final stress is assigned to monomorphemic as well as to suffixed words, regardless of the number of suffixes, as long as no morpheme in the words bears exceptional lexical stress.

(16) Final stress: words containing only "neutral" morphemes
    elmá, elma-lár, elma-lar-dán   'apple(-PL(-ABL))'
    kitáp, kitab-ím, kitab-ım-á   'book(-1SG.POSS(-DAT))'
    gél, gel-eǰék, gel-eǰek-lér   'come(-FUT(-PL))'
    tekmé, tekme-lé, tekme-le-dí   'kick(-VBL(-past))'

Because Final stress is clearly assigned noncyclically to words, we assume that it is handled by the cophonology of the Word construction:[12]

(17) Word construction: $\begin{bmatrix} \text{Syntax: Word} \\ \text{Cophonology: Final stress} \end{bmatrix}$

As demonstrated in the extensive literature on Turkish, a number of morphemes, roots as well as suffixes, perturb this final stress pattern.

(18)   a. Example of a stressed root:
      pénalti-da   'penalty-LOC' (cf. patlıǰan-dá 'eggplant-LOC')
    b. Example of a pre-stressing suffix:
      tekmelé-me   'kick-NEG'   (cf. tekmele-dí 'kick-past')
    c. Example of a stressed suffix:
      yap-íyor   'do-PROG'   (cf. yap-aǰák 'do-FUT')

We follow Inkelas (1994a) in attributing this phenomenon to lexically specified stress feet on the morphemes in question; in words containing

---

[12]By "Word" we mean whatever syntactic specification uniquely identifies syntactic terminals. In some theories this would be X^0.

one or more such morphemes, the stress of the leftmost surfaces. Thus words which have prespecified stress in the input to the Word cophonology override the Final stress pattern.[13]

7.2. Sezer stems

We now turn to those constructions exhibiting the "Sezer" stress pattern, named after Engin Sezer, who discovered it (Sezer 1981). Stems exhibiting the Sezer stress pattern—hereafter "Sezer stems", include most place names, both Turkish and foreign, as well as most foreign personal names used in Turkish.[14] They display the following unique stress pattern, analyzed in metrical theory by a number of authors (see especially Sezer 1981; Kaisse 1985, 1986, 1993; Inkelas 1994a; and Hayes 1995).

(19) "Sezer" stress pattern: if the antepenultimate syllable is heavy [i.e. closed or containing a long vowel] *and* the penultimate syllable is light, stress the antepenultimate syllable; otherwise, stress the penultimate syllable (Sezer 1981)

The pattern is illustrated in (20) on monomorphemic Sezer stems, grouped according to the weight of their antepenultimate and penultimate syllables. Note that the Sezer pattern is imposed on names from other languages even when the stress in the source language is on a different syllable, as in, for example, *ayzınhó:ver* (from *Éisenhower*), *arkánsas* (from *Árkansas*) and *santamoníka* (from *Santa Mónica*). Periods indicate syllable boundaries; closed syllables and those containing long vowels are heavy.

(20) ...H H́ σ   an.tál.ya, ay.zın.hó:.ver, ar.kán.sas

   ...H́ L σ   án.ka.ra, ka.li.fór.ni.ya, mér.ji.mek, ból.va.din, mén.te.še

---

[13]Kaisse (1985, 1986) and Hameed (1986) offer a level-ordering treatment of some of these facts, proposing that prestressing suffixes are attached at a level following that in which neutral suffixes are attached and word stress is assigned. As Kaisse notes, however, such accounts fail to explain why prestressing suffixes (such as the negative (18b)) can be followed in the same word by neutral suffixes. Of course, this is no problem if, as advocated in this paper, levels are unordered. In any case, however, such accounts fail to extend to initially stressed disyllabic suffixes, such as the future ((18c)). Inkelas (1994a) offers a number of arguments in favor of a prespecification account of all suffix-specific stress and against a grammatical account; we find there to be no need to use levels, i.e. cophonologies, to account for the different stress behaviors of Turkish suffixes.

[14]Contrary to some past claims (e.g. Halle and Vergnaud 1987:53, Barker 1989), it cannot be said that loanwords predominantly take Sezer stress. Although a few appear to (e.g. *mása* 'table', *lokánta* 'restaurant'), most do not (e.g. *televizyón* 'television', *kompütür* 'computer', *vités* (< Fr. *vitesse*) '(transmission) gear', *pikáp* 'pick-up', *tinér* '(paint) thinner').

...L H́ σ   e.dír.ne, va.sínk.ton, ha.li.kár.nas, mon.tá:.na, ka.díl.lak

...L Ĺ σ   a.dá.na, pa.pa.do.pú.los, o.ré.gon, san.ta.mo.ní.ka

The Sezer stress pattern is productive, as revealed by its applicability to derived stems. As shown in (21), derived words which do not normally exhibit Sezer stress do shift to the Sezer pattern when used as place names (Sezer 1981:67; Inkelas, Orgun and Zoll 1994):

(21)

	Suffixed word Final stress		as place name Sezer stress
H H σ	kuzgun-ǰúk	'raven-DIM'	> kuzgúnǰuk
H L σ	sirke-ǰí	'vinegar-AGT (=vinegar seller)'	> sírkeǰi
L H σ	kavak-lí	'poplar-with'	> kaváklɨ
L L σ	bak-aǰák	'look-FUT (=s/he will look)'	> bakáǰak

Based on these data, we may posit a morphological construction along the following lines:

(22)

place/foreign name construction: $\begin{bmatrix} \text{Semantics: place/foreign name} \\ \text{Syntax: proper noun} \\ \text{Cophonology: Sezer stress} \end{bmatrix}$

Like prestressed morphemes, Sezer stems retain their stress when suffixed with neutral suffixes,[15] as shown in (23a); the Sezer pattern is itself overridden by prestressed morphemes, as shown in the monomorphemic and derived place names in (23b) and (23c), respectively.

(23)   a. istánbul, istánbul-da   'Istanbul(-LOC)'
           (cf. patlɨ̆ján, patlɨ̆jan-dá   'eggplant(-LOC)')
       b. üskǘdar   (place name)
           (not *ǘsküdar, with Sezer stress)
       c. čam-lí-ǰa   (place name,
           (not *čámlɨ̆ǰa, with Sezer stress)   lit. 'pine-with-sort of')

---

[15]As Kaisse (1985) notes, monosyllabic place names do not retain stress when suffixed (*Ván*, *Van-dán*, etc.). See Kaisse 1985, Barker 1989, and Inkelas 1994a for analyses.

Following Inkelas (1994a), we take this as evidence that, like the Final stress pattern, the Sezer pattern is overridden by preexisting stress.

A complication to the analysis is posed by the data in (24). Here we find place names which lack fixed nonfinal stress, whether of the prespecified kind or of the Sezer kind. These place names take the Final stress pattern, as can be clearly seen from the fact that their stress "migrates" onto suffixes:

(24)   a. Monomorphemic place name with Final pattern[16]
       anadolú, anadolu-dán   'Anadolu (-ABL)'
       anadolu-lu-lar-í   'Anadolu-one from-PL-ACC'
     b. Complex place names with Final pattern
       söyle-méz,   'Söylemez [wait-NEG.IMPF] (-ABL)'
          söyle-mez-dén
       išik-lár, 'Işıklar [light-PL] (-DAT)'
          išik-lar-á
       kork-maz-lár,   'Korkmazlar [fear-NEG.IMPF-PL] (-LOC)'
          kork-maz-lar-dá

Because these place names do not have fixed stress, it would be unreasonable to attribute their behavior to a prespecified stress foot. Our proposal is that there are two different place name constructions (25), one associated with a Sezer stress-imposing cophonology and another whose cophonology does not impose stress. The forms in (24) belong to the latter.

(25)

Sezer place name construction:
$$\left[\begin{array}{c} \text{Semantics: place/foreign name} \\ \text{Syntax: proper noun} \\ \text{Cophonology: Sezer pattern} \end{array} \right]$$

NonSezer place name construction:
$$\left[\begin{array}{c} \text{Semantics: place name} \\ \text{Syntax: proper noun} \\ \text{Cophonology: stress-neutral} \end{array} \right]$$

NonSezer place names receive their stress from the Word cophonology, as in the following illustration of the derivation of the place name in (24b):

---

[16]So far this is the only monomorphemic form with this pattern that we have found.

(26)

Construction		Cophonology
Word:	söyleméz	Final stress
NonSezer place name:	söylemez	Stress-neutral
UR	/söyle/ /mEz/	

Note that a consequence of adopting these two constructions for place names is that the analysis of the data in (23) is now underdetermined. We do not know if these prestressed place names are formed by the Sezer place name construction or by the nonSezer place name construction. In either case, their underlying stress would prevail.

7.3. Compounds

There are two ways of forming compounds in Turkish: either straight concatenation, as shown in (27a), or by attaching a third person possessive suffix to the second constituent, as in (27b) (the "Izafet" construction; see e.g. Lewis 1967). The following examples are taken from Swift 1963 and Lewis 1967; "+" indicates compound juncture:

(27) a. čengél+köy   'Çengel-village'
          orhán+bey   'Orhan-Mr. (=Mr. Orhan)'
          báš+bak-an   'head-look-REL (= prime minister)'

          süt+beyaz   'milk-white'
      b. bebék-hasta:ne-si   'baby-hospital-POSS'
          čojúk+kitab-i   'child-book-POSS'
          ye-mék+oda-si   'eat-INF-room-POSS (= dining room)'
          yíl+baš-i   'year-head-POSS (= New Year)'

The stress patterns of these two compound types are identical: stress always goes on the first constituent of compounds headed by nouns, normally on the final syllable, unless the first constituent independently takes nonfinal stress (28a-c). The second constituent is stressless, even if it otherwise has idiosyncratic stress (c-d):

(28) a. bébek+hasta:ne-si   'Bebek (place name)-hospital-POSS'
      b. tarhána+čorba-si   'dried yogurt-soup-POSS'
      c. meksíka+fasulye-si   'Mexico-beans-POSS (= Mexican
          (cf. fasúlye)   jumping beans)'
      d. pašá+mandira   'pasha-farm'
          (cf. mándira)

If the second constituent of the compound is a predicate of which the first constituent is an argument, however, then the compound stress pattern seen above does not apply. Instead, the compound is stressed as a regular word would be (see (29b), where final stress "migrates" off the last compound in (a) onto a neutral suffix). Examples are taken from Swift 1963:

(29) a. el-i+ačík   'hand-POSS-open (= generous)'
         baš-i+bozúk   'head-POSS-spoiled (= civilian)'
         haǰi+yat-máz   'pilgrim-lie down-NEG.IMPF (= toy
                                     which remains upright)'
         hünkʸar+been-dí   'sultan-like-past (= eggplant dish)'
      b. [hünkʸar+been-di]-ler-dén 'eggplant dish-PL-ABL'

In order to account for the two different stress patterns found in compounds, we will have to make the same move we made with place names and assume two types of compound constructions. The first (which generalizes over both Izafet and non-Izafet compounds) assigns stress to the first constituent, whereas the second (which, as far as we know, pertains only to non-Izafet compounds) assigns no stress at all. As indicated below, both constructions concatenate the phonological strings of two input forms. In the first construction, stress is assigned to the first such string; in the second construction, where the first input element is constrained to be an argument of the second, no stress is assigned by the relevant cophonology.

(30) Stressed compounds:

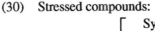

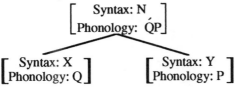

Unstressed compounds:

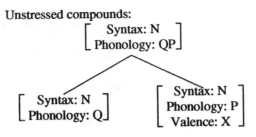

Like the nonSezer place names, unstressed compounds receive their stress from the Word cophonology:

(31)

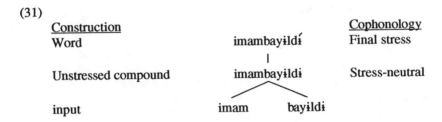

Construction		Cophonology
Word	imambayïldí	Final stress
Unstressed compound	imambayïldï	Stress-neutral
input	imam bayïldï	

8. Relationships among the constructions

We now turn to an examination of the morphological relationship between suffixes, Sezer place names, and compound constructions. Discovering what morphological interactions are possible will tell us the relative "order" in which the various cophonologies can apply.

8.1. Sezer stems and suffix levels

The expectation of classical level-ordered morphology and phonology is that place name level will be ordered in a fixed manner with respect to the four suffix levels of the grammar.

It is well-known that suffixes can occur outside of Sezer place names; in fact, Kaisse (1985, 1986) proposes that Sezer stress is assigned to place names on level 1 and that suffixation occurs later on levels 2 and 3:[17]

---

[17]Kaisse also makes the innovative claim that roots not destined to be place names simply skip level 1, proceeding directly to level 2 for potential suffixation and stress assignment. This proposal is the earliest version of Level Economy that we are aware of. Although we depart from Kaisse's analysis in many particulars, we share her basic insight that stems skip levels at which they are not derived.

(32)

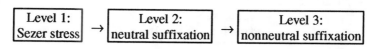

Stems derived and stressed at the Sezer level block the assignment of Final stress at the Word level, as shown in (33); bracketed strings are Sezer stems:

(33) a. [adána]ѕ-mi
       'Adana-INTERR'
     b. [ánkara]ѕ-li-las-tir-di
       'Ankara-of-become-CAUS-past
       (=caused to become ones from Ankara)'

These facts follow from a generalization we have already made, namely that stress which is present in the input to a cophonology prevails over the stress that would otherwise be assigned by that cophonology. In case of more than one input stress, the leftmost prevails. In (34), the output of the Sezer cophonology is input to level 5 suffixation and then to the Word level:

(34)

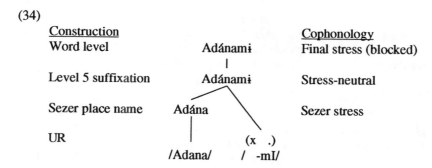

What complicates the general picture portrayed by Kaisse (1985, 1986) is the fact that a number of suffixes can also occur *inside* Sezer stems—such that it cannot be the case that suffixation levels are strictly ordered to follow the Sezer stem level. We have found, so far, five suffixes which can be clearly shown to occur both inside and outside of Sezer stems.

In (35), we show that a level 2 suffix, the future aspect marker -*EcEk*, is able to occur both inside (a) and outside (b) a Sezer stem (enclosed in brackets). *-EcEk* is a neutral suffix; the fact that it is stressed in (a) shows it is inside the Sezer stem and receives the stress of the Sezer pattern. (Note that when the same string is *not* used as a place name, the expected final stress pattern emerges.) That the future suffix is unstressed in final position in (b) follows from the fact that *Adana*, the place name at the base of this verb, is a Sezer stem and takes Sezer stress. As we know, Sezer stress overrides Final stress.

(35) a. [bak-áǰak]S   cf. bak-aǰák
         'Bakacak (place name)'   'look-FUT'
      b. [adána]S-li-laš-aǰak   cf. anadolu-lu-laš-aǰák
         'Adana-from-become-FUT'   'Anadolu-from-become-FUT'

In (36), we show that a level 5 suffix, the past tense marker *-DI*, can also occur either inside (a) or outside (b) a Sezer stem (note: *-DI* is prestressing when it attaches to nouns):

(36) a. [beén-di-k]S   cf. been-di-k
         'Beğendik (place name)   'like-past-1PL'
      b. [beén-di-k]S-ti   cf. mühendís-ti
         'Beğendik-past'   'engineer-past'

Example (37) shows three other suffixes which are able to occur either inside or outside a Sezer place name. Although our independent tests for levelhood have not yet enabled us to identify the level of these suffixes, we note that they are clearly not members of the Sezer level, since when they are in final position in a word whose other morphemes are all stress-neutral, the observed stress pattern is not the Sezer one.

(37) a. Sezer stem containing diminutive suffix *-CUk*
            [kuzgún-ǰuk]S   cf. kuzgun-ǰúk
            'Kuzguncuk (place name)'   'raven-DIM'
         Diminutive suffix outside Sezer stem
            [ménteše]S-ǰik   cf. menteše-ǰík
            'Menteşe (place name)-DIM'   'hinge-DIM'
      b. Sezer stem containing *-lI* 'with'
            [kandíl-li]S   cf. kandil-lí
            'Kandilli (place name)'   'oil lamp-with'

-*ll* outside Sezer stem

[ménteše]_S-li   cf.   menteše-lí

'someone from Menteşe'   'hinge-with'

c. Sezer stem containing prestressing -*CE* (meaning 'sort of' or 'in the manner of'; on place names, -*CE* means 'language of')

[yarím-ǰa]_S   cf.   yarím-ǰa

'Yarimca (place name)'   'half-sort of'

-*CE* outside of Sezer stem

[istánbul]_S-ǰa   cf.   Anadolú-ǰa

'Istanbul-language'   'Anadolu-language'

It is clear that under any hypothesis of a fixed ordering among Sezer and suffixation levels, looping would be required. Loops clearly exist between the Sezer level and levels 2 and 5 (38); we suspect that loops exist as well with the levels of the as yet imperfectly understood suffixes discussed above.

(38)

However, a Mohanan-style loop analysis, in which all forms pass through all levels at least once, would still require some explanation for why Sezer stress isn't assigned to all forms containing neutral morphemes, regardless of whether or not those forms actually constitute place names.

A more reasonable proposal, which overcomes this problem, would simply be to say that the Sezer stress level is simply intrinsically unordered with respect to the other levels. The actual "order" in which Sezer and suffix-specific cophonologies apply in any given word follows intrinsically from the order in which the morphological constructions combine—an order itself governed by the syntax and semantics of the word, rather than by any extrinsic statements about the ordering of constructions and their cophonologies. Illustrations are provided below:

(39)

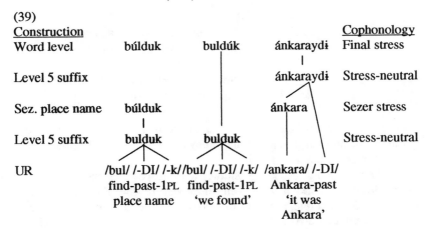

Construction				Cophonology
Word level	búlduk	buldúk	ánkaraydɨ	Final stress
Level 5 suffix			ánkaraydɨ	Stress-neutral
Sez. place name	búlduk		ánkara	Sezer stress
Level 5 suffix	bulduk	bulduk		Stress-neutral
UR	/bul/ /-DI/ /-k/	/bul/ /-DI/ /-k/	/ankara/ /-DI/	
	find-past-1PL	find-past-1PL	Ankara-past	
	place name	'we found'	'it was Ankara'	

8.2. Compounding and suffix levels

We now turn to the interaction between compounding and suffixation. As shown in (40)-(42), we have found that three individual suffixes, as well as all of the case and possessive endings,[18] can occur either inside compounds (the (a) examples) or outside them (the (b) examples). In (40), a level 5 suffix occurs both inside and outside compounds (bracketed and labeled with "C"); (41) and (42) show the same behavior for level 4 and level 3 suffixes, respectively.

(40) Past tense suffix -DI (level 5)

    a. [imam+bayɨl-dɨ́]ᴄ   'imam-faint-past (= eggplant dish)'

        [kap-tɨ+kač-tɨ́]ᴄ   'grab-past-run off-past (= pickup truck)'

    b. [orhán+bey]ᴄ-di   'Orhan-Mr.-past (=it was Mr. Orhan)'

        [báš+bak-an]ᴄ-dɨ   'head-look-REL-past (=it was the prime minister)'

(41) Case endings (level 4)

    a. [gün-é+bak-an]ᴄ   'sun-DAT-look-REL (= sunflower)'

        [unút-ma+ben-i]ᴄ   'forget-NEG-1SG (= forget-me-not)-ACC'

    b. [báš+bak-an]ᴄ-ɨ   'head-look-REL (=prime minister)-ACC'

        [ortá+okul]ᴄ-a   'middle-school-DAT'

---

[18]The third person plural possessive suffix -lEr is a possible exception to this generalization; with respect to both affix ordering and stress, the third person plural behaves differently from the other possessives. See Lewis (1967) for exemplification.

(42)   Possessive suffixes (level 3)
  a. [el-i+ač-ík]_C 'hand-his-open-ADJ (= generous)'
    [baš-i+boz-úk]_C 'head-3.POSS-break down-ADJ
           (= civilian)'
  b. [ön+söz]_C-ümüz 'front-word (=foreword)-1PL.POSS'
    [ortá-okul]_C-um 'middle-school-1SG.POSS'

The finding that suffixation can occur inside or outside of compounding parallels our observations about the interaction between suffixation and the Sezer stem construction.

  The ordering of compounding with respect to the rest of the morphology in Turkish has been discussed in the literature. Barker (1989:11), for example, proposes that compounding takes place on its own level, ordered after affixation (his Level I corresponds to our levels 1-5):

(43)   Barker 1989:

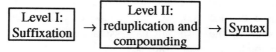

Hameed (1985) proposes two levels for compounding. Level II is the component of semantically and phonologically somewhat irregular compounds, while more productive compounding takes place at Level III:

(44)   Hameed 1985:

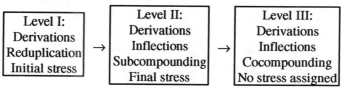

But both Barker and Hameed overlook the fact that compounds are all subject to suffixation that on their accounts would have to be accomplished on earlier levels. Hameed assigns stress-neutral suffixes (e.g. case) to Level II; Barker assigns all suffixes to Level I. The fact that compounds can occur inside stress-neutral suffixes is a problem for both accounts.

  One possibility might be to say that compounding can take place "at any level". But since we are defining levels in phonological terms, and since compounds do have a distinctive phonology, this would make little sense. There *is* a compounding construction with its own unique phonology—i.e. a level; it is simply not extrinsically ordered with respect at least to suffixational levels 3, 4 and 5, as the following example of several complex words illustrates for level 4:

(45)

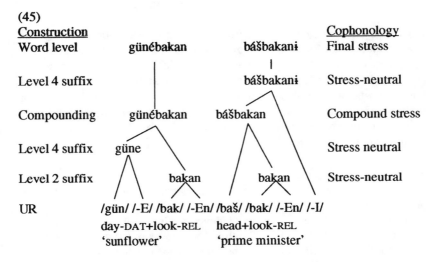

Construction			Cophonology
Word level	günébakan	bášbakanɨ	Final stress
Level 4 suffix		bášbakanɨ	Stress-neutral
Compounding	günébakan	bášbakan	Compound stress
Level 4 suffix	güne		Stress neutral
Level 2 suffix		bakan	bakan	Stress-neutral
UR	/gün/ /-E/ /bak/ /-En/	/baš/ /bak/ /-En/ /-I/	
	day-DAT+look-REL	head+look-REL	
	'sunflower'	'prime minister'	

It seems clear that there is nothing to be gained in stipulating any particular ordering relationship between the level of compounding and the levels of suffixation.

8.3. Compounding and Sezer stems

Now that we have determined that both Sezer stem and compounding constructions are intrinsically unordered with respect to (at least some of) the suffixational levels, it is logical to ask the question of whether Sezer stem and compounding constructions are ordered with respect to one another. Unfortunately, the fact that each type of construction possesses its own unique stress pattern makes this question difficult to answer. It is certainly true that place names can contain stressed compound (46a) and that compounds can contain Sezer stems (b):

(46)   a.   Stressed compounds (bracketed) inside place names:

       [[saím+bey]_C-li]_S   'Saimbeyli [Saim-Mr.-with]'

       [[áy+do:-muš]_C]_S   'Aydoğmuş [moon-rise-EVID]'

b. Sezer stems (bracketed) inside compounds

[[yürék+[sela:nik]$_S$]$_C$ 'heart-Salonika (=coward)'
                                (cf. selá:nik 'Salonika')

[[kandíl-li]$_S$+cadde-si]$_C$ 'Kandilli [oil lamp-with]-street-POSS
                                (=Kandilli street)'

Before we can conclude from this data that there is a "loop" between the Compounding and Sezer levels, however, recall that in addition to stressed compounds and Sezer place names, Turkish also has unstressed compounds and nonSezer place names. Unfortunately, we have no way of knowing whether the place names in (46a) are formed with the Sezer or the nonSezer construction; likewise, we have no way of knowing for sure whether the compounds in (46b) are formed with the stressed or unstressed compounding construction.

8.4. Summary

We have shown that there is no evidence to support any extrinsic ordering between the Sezer level, affix levels, and compounding, and we have shown that there is positive evidence against any extrinsic ordering between Sezer stems and suffixation, on the one hand, and between compounding and suffixation, on the other hand. Further, we have shown that even among suffixational levels there is at least a limited amount of recursion; we suspect that more will be found as we investigate more data.

Our conclusion is that the Turkish lexical component consists of a collection of constructions—suffixes, place names, compounding—and that these combine freely, subject to various syntactic, semantic, and morphological restrictions. Fixed temporal or hierarchical phonological level ordering is not one of those restrictions.

A similar conclusion was foreshadowed by Kaisse (1985), who proposed that nonfinal stress is assigned on stratum 1. Because only place names (and some adverbs) display this pattern, Kaisse proposed that all other forms simply skip stratum 1 and go directly to stratum 2. Here we are taking Kaisse's proposal to its logical conclusion: forms exhibit only the phonology of those morphological constructions they are composed of. Of course, for the model of lexical phonology Kaisse was assuming (namely Kiparsky 1982a,b; Mohanan 1982, 1986), this conclusion was an embarrassment. For the proposed cophonology approach, it is entirely natural, even a virtue. Level ordering is not something which is extrinsically imposed on the cophonologies of a language, to be circumvented only at great expense through devices such as the loop.

Rather, order of application of cophonologies of different sorts follows purely from the intrinsic ordering of the related morphology.

9. Implications

In this section we discuss implications of level nonordering and Level Economy beyond the mere coverage of the Turkish data discussed.

9.1. Morpheme-specific phonology

First, once the idea of "level" is implemented in the form of cophonologies that are part of individual morphological constructions, it becomes clear that there is no formal difference between phonological alternations that affect only one morpheme and those that affect a larger set of morphemes. All lexical phonological alternations are encoded in the same way, in the form of cophonologies.

In contrast, past work in Lexical Phonology assumed that, in addition to the phonological alternations common to all morphemes in a given level, there could also be alternations that were specific to only certain morphemes. For example, Barker (1989) handles place name stress in Turkish by assuming that a particular stress rule, applying within level 1 of the phonology, targets just those stems marked diacritically as [+odd].

One implication of our methodology is that there will almost surely be more distinct cophonologies than there have been levels in past level ordering theory. For example, we posit a separate level for place names in Turkish, whereas Barker (1989) does not. This fact does not, however, mean that our theory is less restrictive, or that it is somehow proliferating levels in an uncontrolled way. It simply means that we are holding our theory responsible for *all* phonology that is sensitive to morphological information, rather than setting aside certain effects in favor of building a theory around those judged in some manner to be more general.

9.2. Phonology-morphology clustering

A second implication of associating cophonologies with individual morphological constructions is that there is no longer an automatic expectation that those morphemes inducing identical phonological alternations will cluster together in words in which they co-occur. It is possible to *stipulate* such a correlation, on a language-specific (and level-specific) basis. In fact, Orgun (1995a,b) shows that such a correlation must be assumed for certain suffixational levels even in Turkish to account for aspects of the phenomenon of suspended affixation (see also Lewis 1967, Inkelas and Orgun 1995). But nothing makes such a stipulation automatic.

This may seem like a drawback to our model, weakening its predictive power with respect to that of past theories, in which a tight correlation between morphological and phonological level was definitional. However, evidence from languages like Basque suggests that the generalization about phonological and morphological level clustering that such theories intended to capture is simply not true to begin with. In Basque, both early derivational morphology and clitics trigger the same phonological alternations, which forced Hualde (1988, 1989) to posit a loop providing for phonological but *not* morphological recursion. On our model there is no need for a loop per se; it is simply a coincidence that the cophonologies of clitics and derivational affixes happen to share a rule of vowel raising. As our model has no expectation that those morphemes triggering vowel raising should appear contiguously in words in which they co-occur, the Basque facts present no paradox at all. Similarly, the fact that in Turkish, suffixational levels, nonSezer place names and compounds which are predicates all have stress-neutral cophonologies does not commit us to the claim that these constructions cluster together morphologically to the exclusion of other constructions whose associated cophonologies do assign stress. This is fortunate, since the claim would be false.

9.3. The Stratum Domain Hypothesis

A related implication involves the Stratum Domain Hypothesis (SDH) (Mohanan 1982, 1986; see also Halle and Mohanan 1985:86). In initial studies of level ordering, when it appeared that levels could be extrinsically ordered (modulo the loop), it also appeared that the phonological makeup of the levels was constrained in a principled way: if a given alternation applied at more than one level, then the levels must be consecutive. (An even stronger hypothesis was proposed by Kiparsky (1984); the Strong Domain Hypothesis requires each rule to apply from the very earliest level.)

Once one gives up the universal hypothesis that all levels are ordered, however, the status of (either version of) the SDH becomes unclear. Insofar as the SDH captured real generalizations, this might be seen as a loss. However, it is probably impossible to draw conclusions either way at present, for the reason that, because of the way levels have been defined in past analyses, a significant amount of data potentially bearing on the validity of the SDH, namely construction-specific phonology not general throughout the level, has been set aside. Consider, for example, the hypothetical case in which one suffix at level 1 and another at level 3 both trigger the same rule R. In past approaches, R would not be part of the packet of phonological rules defining either level; rather, it would be treated as a minor rule marked to apply just to thes two individual suffixes. The SDH would therefore not have scope over R. But in our approach, R would be part of the cophonologies associated with the two suffixes; if the SDH is imported into our theory, it should hold over R as well as over the more widely distributed phonological rules. The point is that if past theories had had to account for the same data that we hold our cophonologies accountable for, the SDH might never have been proposed in the first place. We simply do not know, and this makes it difficult to evaluate the consequences of our abandonment of the SDH.

We do have some speculation to offer, however, and this is that one possible source for SDH effects—namely contiguity of ordered levels in which a given phonological alternation takes place—might be that the SDH is a historical artifact of the interaction between grammaticalization and the loss or gain of phonological alternations over time (see Zec (1993) for related discussion). It may be that affixes originating in the same historical era are ordered close to each other in the word and display a set of phonological alternations which differs in some but not all respects from those of affixes added to the language at earlier or later stages. We have no data at present to back this up, but see it as a promising idea to pursue.

9.4. "Serialism" and recursive levels

Finally, the conclusion that levels may be extrinsically unordered has implications for theories that crucially assume a serial model of level ordering. For example, McCarthy and Prince (1993) and McCarthy (1993) (in work otherwise advocating nonserial analyses) are explicit as to the serial nature of the three ordered levels they assume in their Optimality-theoretic (Prince and Smolensky 1993) analysis of Axininca Campa. According to the standard model of level ordering assumed by McCarthy and Prince, the amount of serialism introduced in this manner is necessarily limited by the fixed number of levels in the system, and thus may not represent a serious threat to the (cognitive, computational, or other) concerns which motivate nonserialism elsewhere. Clearly, however, if levels are unordered and are recursive as we have suggested on the basis of Turkish, then the serialism associated with level ordering can in no sense be said to be limited. Theories that strive to limit serialism will be in trouble if they continue to assume that level ordering is serial.

However, Orgun (1994, 1995a,b) has argued for an alternative, nonderivational implementation of level ordering ("Monotonic Cyclicity") according to which the finding of infinitely recursive levels poses no problem for attempts to limit serialism. According to Monotonic Cyclicity (which we have implicitly been assuming an informal version of in this paper), the relationship among levels in phonology is equivalent to that among, for example, bar levels in syntax (or morphology). Orgun's proposal is couched within a sign-based theory related to Head-Driven Phrase Structure Grammar (e.g. Pollard and Sag 1987, 1994) and Construction Grammar (e.g. Fillmore, Kay and O'Connor 1988, Fillmore and Kay (in progress)). Although we cannot go into the details here, it is important to note that there is at least one theory of level ordering for which our discovery of unlimited looping poses no cognitive or computational problems—at least none greater than those already generated by recursive syntactic systems.

10. Conclusions

The theory of level ordering has not previously come to terms with agglutinative languages with productive recursive morphology. It should come as no surprise that the hypothesis of a small number of levels organized into a fixed, nonrecursive ordering is too rigid for such systems. We have argued that it is inappropriate for Turkish, in which a number of morphological constructions associated with different cophonologies occur in whatever order that the word-internal syntax and semantics motivate. Extrinsic level ordering is not enforced in the lexical phonology of Turkish.

References

Barker, Christopher. 1989. Extrametricality, the Cycle, and Turkish Word Stress. In Junko Itô and Jeff Runner (eds.), *Phonology at Santa Cruz*. 1-33. UC Santa Cruz: Syntax Research Center.

Bonet, Eulalia. 1993. Vowel Assimilation in Baztan and Levels in Phonology. In J. Hualde and J. de Urbina (eds.), *Generative Studies in Basque Linguistics*. 243-261. Amsterdam Studies In The Theory And History Of Linguistics Science, Series IV: Current Issues In Linguistic Theory. Amsterdam: John Benjamins.

Borowsky, Toni. 1986. *Topics in the Lexical Phonology of English.* Doctoral dissertation, University of Massachusetts.

Buckley, Eugene L. 1994a. Manam Stress and Optimality. Unpublished manuscript, University of Pennsylvania.

Buckley, Eugene L. 1994b. *Theoretical Aspects of Kashaya Phonology and Morphology*. CSLI dissertation series. Stanford: CSLI Publications.

Christdas, Prathima. 1986. On Constraining the Power of Lexical Phonology. In Joyce McDonough and Bernadette Plunkett (eds.), *Proceedings of NELS 17*. 122-146. Amherst, MA: GLSA.

Christdas, Prathima. 1988. *The Phonology and Morphology of Tamil.* Doctoral dissertation, Cornell University.

Cohn, Abigail. 1989. Stress in Indonesian and Bracketing Paradoxes. *Natural Language and Linguistic Theory* 7. 167-216.

Dobrovolsky, Michael. 1976. Is Turkish an Agglutinative Language? *Montreal Working Papers in Linguistics* 6. 87-101.

Dobrovolsky, Michael. 1986. Stress and Vowel Harmony Domains in Turkish. In Vassiliki Nikiforidou et al. (eds.), *Proceedings of the Twelfth Annual Meeting of the Berkeley Linguistics Society.* 61-71. Berkeley, CA: Berkeley Linguistics Society.

Fillmore, Charles and Paul Kay. in progress. Construction Grammar. UC Berkeley manuscript.

Fillmore, Charles, Paul Kay and Mary Catherine O'Connor. 1988. Regularity and Idiomaticity in Grammatical Constructions. *Language* 64. 501-538.

Foster, Joseph F. 1970. *On Some Phonological rules of Turkish.* Doctoral dissertation, University of Illinois.

Halle, Morris and K. P. Mohanan. 1985. Segmental Phonology of Modern English. *Linguistic Inquiry* 16. 57-116.

Halle, Morris and Jean-Roger Vergnaud. 1987. *An Essay on Stress.* Cambridge, MA: MIT Press.

Hameed, Jumah. 1985. Lexical Phonology and Morphology of Modern Standard Turkish. *Cahiers linguistiques d'Ottawa* 14. 71-95.

Hammond, Michael. 1986. The Obligatory-Branching Parameter in Metrical Theory. *Natural Language and Linguistic Theory* 4. 185-228.

Hankamer, Jorge. 1986. Finite State Morphology and Left to Right Phonology. In M. Dalrymple et al. (eds.), *Proceedings of the Fifth West Coast Conference on Formal Linguistics.* 40-52. Stanford: Stanford Linguistics Association.

Hargus, Sharon. 1985. *The Lexical Phonology of Sekani.* Doctoral dissertation, University of California, Los Angeles.

Hargus, Sharon. 1988. *The Lexical Phonology of Sekani.* Outstanding Dissertations in Linguistics series. New York: Garland Publishing Co.

Hayes, Bruce. 1995. *Metrical Theory: Principles and Case Studies.* Chicago: University of Chicago Press.

Hualde, José. 1988. *A Lexical Phonology of Basque.* Doctoral dissertation, University of Southern California.

Hualde, José. 1989. The Strict Cycle Condition and Noncyclic Rules. *Linguistic Inquiry* 20. 675-680.

Idsardi, William. 1992. *The Computation of Prosody.* Doctoral dissertation, Massachusetts Institute of Technology.

Inkelas, Sharon. 1990. *Prosodic Constituency in the Lexicon*. Outstanding Dissertations in Linguistics series. New York: Garland Publishing Co.

Inkelas, Sharon. 1993a. Deriving Cyclicity. In Sharon Hargus and Ellen Kaisse (eds.), *Phonetics and Phonology 4: Studies in Lexical Phonology*. 75-110. San Diego: Academic Press.

Inkelas, Sharon. 1993b. Nimboran Position Class Morphology. *Natural Language and Linguistic Theory* 11. 559-624.

Inkelas, Sharon. 1994a. Exceptional Stress-Attracting Suffixes in Turkish: Representations vs. the Grammar. To appear in René Kager (ed.), *Prosodic Morphology*. Mouton.

Inkelas, Sharon. 1994b. Review of Jolanta Szypra (1989), *The Phonology-Morphology Interface: Cycles, Levels and Words. Phonology* 11:341-353.

Inkelas, Sharon and Cemil Orhan Orgun. 1995. Level Ordering and Economy in the Lexical Phonology of Turkish. *Language* 71.763-793.

Inkelas, Sharon, Cemil Orhan Orgun and Cheryl Zoll. 1994. Subregularities as Cogrammars: the Theoretical status of Nonproductive Patterns in Grammar. Unpublished manuscript. University of California, Berkeley.

Itô, Junko. 1990. Prosodic Minimality in Japanese. In Michael Ziolkowski, Manuela Noske et al. (eds.), *Papers from the Twenty-Sixth Regional Meeting of the Chicago Linguistics Society. Volume 2: the Parasession on the Syllable in Phonetics and Phonology*. 213-39. Chicago: Chicago Linguistics Society.

Itô, Junko and Jorge Hankamer. 1989. Notes on Monosyllabism in Turkish. In Junko Itô and Jeff Runner (eds.), *Phonology at Santa Cruz 1*. 61-69. Santa Cruz: University of California, Santa Cruz Syntax Research Center.

Kaisse, Ellen. 1985. Some Theoretical Consequences of Stress Rules in Turkish. In William Eilfort, Paul Kroeber et al. (eds.), *Papers from the General Session of the Twenty-First Regional Meeting of the Chicago Linguistics Society*. 199-209. Chicago: Chicago Linguistics Society.

Kaisse, Ellen. 1986. Towards a Lexical Phonology of Turkish. In Michael Brame, Helen Contreras et al. (eds.), *A Festschrift for Sol Saporta*. 231-39. Seattle: Noit Amrofer.

Kaisse, Ellen. 1993. Theoretical Aspects of Non-Final Stress in Turkish. Talk given at the Linguistic Institute, Ohio State University.

Kardestuncer, A. 1982. A Three-Boundary System for Turkish. *Linguistic Analysis* 10. 75-117.

Kiparsky, Paul. 1982a. From Cyclic to Lexical Phonology. In Harry van der Hulst and Norval Smith (eds.), *The Structure of Phonological Representations, Part I*. 131-75. Dordrecht: Foris.

Kiparsky, Paul. 1982b. Lexical Morphology and Phonology. In I.-S. Yang (ed.), *Linguistics in the Morning Calm.* 3-91. Linguistics Society of Korea. Seoul: Hanshin.

Kiparsky, Paul. 1984. On the Lexical Phonology of Icelandic. In Claes-Christian Elert, Iréne Johansson et al. (eds.), *Nordic Prosody II: Papers from a Symposium.* 135-62. Umeå: University of Umeå.

Kiparsky, Paul. 1991. Catalexis. Unpublished manuscript. Stanford University and Wissenschaftskolleg zu Berlin,

Kiparsky, Paul. 1993. Blocking in Non-Derived Environments. In Sharon Hargus and Ellen Kaisse (eds.), *Phonetics and Phonology 4: Studies in Lexical Phonology.* 277-313. San Diego: Academic Press.

Lees, Robert. 1961. *The Phonology of Modern Standard Turkish.* Indiana University Publications Uralic and Altaic Series. 6. Bloomington: Indiana University Publications.

Lewis, Geoffrey. 1967. *Turkish Grammar.* Oxford: Oxford University Press.

Lightner, Theodore M. 1978. The Main Stress Rule in Turkish. In Mohammad Ali Jazayery, Edgar Polomé et al. (eds.), *Linguistic and literary studies in honor of Archibald Hill.* 267-70. The Hague: Mouton.

Mascaró, Joan. 1976. *Catalan Phonology and the Phonological Cycle.* Bloomington: Indiana University Linguistics Club.

McCarthy, John. 1993. The Parallel Advantage. Paper presented at the Rutgers Optimality Workshop 1.

McCarthy, John and Alan Prince. 1993. Prosodic Morphology I: Constraint Interaction and Satisfaction. To be published by MIT Press.

Mester, Armin. 1994. The Quantitative Trochee in Latin. *Natural Language and Linguistic Theory* 12. 1-61.

Mohanan, K. P. 1982. *Lexical Phonology.* Doctoral dissertation, Massachusetts Institute of Technology.

Mohanan, K. P. 1986. *Lexical Phonology.* Dordrecht: Kluwer.

Mohanan, K. P. 1995. The Organization of the Grammar. In John Goldsmith (ed.), *The Handbook of Phonological Theory.* 24-69. Cambridge, MA: Blackwell Publishers.

Orgun, Cemil Orhan. 1994. Monotonic Cyclicity and Optimality Theory. In Mercè Gonzàlez (ed.), *Proceedings of the Northeastern Linguistic Society 24.* 461-74.

Orgun, Cemil Orhan. 1995a. Flat vs. Branching Morphological Structures: the Case of Suspended Affixation. In Jocelyn Ahlers, Leela Bilmes et al. *Proceedings of the Berkeley Linguistic Society 21.* Berkeley, CA: Berkeley Linguistics Society.

Orgun, Cemil Orhan. 1995b. Suspended Affixation: a New Look at the Phonology-Morphology Interface. In Manfred Bierwisch (ed.), *Proceedings of the Conference on Interfaces in Phonology.*

Orgun, Cemil Orhan and Sharon Inkelas. 1992. Turkish Prosodic Minimality. Sixth International Conference on Turkish Linguistics. Anadolu University,

Pollard, Carl and Ivan Sag. 1987. *Information-Based Syntax and Semantics: Volume 1, Fundamentals.* CSLI Lecture Note Series, no. 13. Stanford, CA: CSLI Publications.

Pollard, Carl and Ivan Sag. 1994. *Head-Driven Phrase Structure Grammar.* Chicago: CSLI Publications and University of Chicago Press.

Poser, William J. 1984. *The Phonetics and Phonology of Tone and Intonation in Japanese.* Doctoral dissertation, Massachusetts Institute of Technology.

Prince, Alan and Paul Smolensky 1993. Optimality Theory: Constraint Interaction In Generative Grammar. To be published by MIT Press.

Rice, Keren. 1989. *A Grammar of Slave.* Berlin: Mouton de Gruyter.

Selkirk, Elisabeth. 1982. *The Syntax Of Words.* Cambridge, MA: MIT Press.

Selkirk, Elisabeth. 1984. *Phonology and Syntax.* Cambridge, MA: MIT Press.

Sezer, Engin. 1981. On Non-Final Stress in Turkish. *Journal of Turkish Studies* 5. 61-69.

Sproat, Richard. 1986. Malayalam Compounding: a Non-Stratum Ordered Account. in *Proceedings of the fifth West Coast Conference on Formal Linguistics.* Stanford: Stanford Lingusitics Association.

Swift, Lloyd B. 1963. *A Reference Grammar of Modern Turkish.* Indiana University Publications Uralic and Altaic Series. 19. Bloomington: Indiana University Publications.

Szpyra, Jolanta. 1989. *The Phonology-Morphology Interface: Cycles, Levels and Words.* London: Routledge.

Underhill, Robert. 1976. *Turkish Grammar.* Cambridge, MA: MIT Press.

Zec, Draga. 1993. Rule Domains and Phonological Change. In Sharon Hargus and Ellen Kaisse (eds.), *Phonetics and Phonology 4: Studies in Lexical Phonology.* 365-405. San Diego: Academic Press.

Comments on the Paper by Inkelas & Orgun

GREGORY T. STUMP

1. Introduction

I am in complete agreement with Inkelas & Orgun's main conclusion that morphological constructions associated with the same cophonology needn't exhibit a single, fixed ordering with respect to constructions associated with some distinct cophonology; this general conclusion is strongly supported by the widespread incidence of "loop" effects and of bracketing paradoxes of the *ungrammaticality* type.   I shall therefore concentrate my attention on the framework in which Inkelas & Orgun arrive at this conclusion.   In particular, I wish to contrast the assumptions underlying this framework with those underlying the alternative framework set forth in Stump 1995; throughout, I shall refer to Inkelas & Orgun's approach as the CONSTRUCTION-AND-COPHONOLOGY (CC) approach and that of Stump 1995 as the RULE-AND-METAGENERALIZATION (RM) approach (a label whose significance will be clarified below).   My point is to show that the assumptions on which the CC approach rests include two distinctions which have no place in the RM approach, and that these two distinctions are dispensable; once these two distinctions are abandoned, the Turkish data discussed by Inkelas & Orgun take on a rather different character, as I shall show.

2. Constructions and the Lexicon

A first difference between the CC and RM approaches is (1). ·

(1)   CC approach: Affixes are listed lexically.
       RM approach: An affix is a marking stipulated in the definition of the
                     morphological rule determining some class of stems or
                     words.

Thus, the CC approach presupposes a fundamental distinction between concatenative and nonconcatenative morphology; the RM approach, by contrast, presumes no such distinction. The dispute over the validity of this distinction is, of course, a long-standing one among contemporary morphologists, but the question takes on particular salience in the context of the CC approach. Inkelas & Orgun assume that a language's grammar includes specifications of its various morphological constructions; for instance, the Turkish place-name construction has the specification in (2).

(2) place/foreign name construction: $\begin{bmatrix} \text{Semantics: place/foreign name} \\ \text{Syntax: proper noun} \\ \text{Phonology: Sezer stress} \end{bmatrix}$

Likewise, each affix in the language is associated with a specification of this sort. What is unclear, however, is how the construction specified for a particular affix differs from that affix's lexical entry under the CC approach. If it doesn't differ, then the construction specified for an affix makes its lexical listing redundant. On the other hand, if an affix's lexical listing is *identified with* the specification of its construction, then an unmotivated asymmetry emerges: constructions associated with affixes are specified in the lexicon, while constructions such as (2) are specified somewhere else. Neither difficulty arises if one simply dispenses with the assumption that affixes have lexical entries. One could, of course, maintain that the construction specified for a particular affix and that affix's lexical entry comprise distinct bodies of information; but it is not clear what sort of evidence could be claimed to motivate the assumption that the grammar encodes these two bodies of information separately rather than together.

3. Cophonologies and Metageneralizations

A second difference between the CC and RM approaches relates to the distinction between cophonologies and morphological metageneralizations. Here some background is necessary. The notion of MORPHOLOGICAL METAGENERALIZATIONS was first proposed by Zwicky 1994 and is elaborated on by Stump 1995. Simply put, a morphological metageneralization is a generalization about the classes of forms determined by two or more rules of morphology. Suppose, for example, that English has the derivational rules in (3):

(3) Morphological rules:
   a. Where X is the stem of a verbal lexeme L, the stem of L's IBLE derivative is X*ible*.
   b. Where X is the stem of an adjectival lexeme L, the stem of L's ITY derivative is X*ity*.
   c. Where X is the stem of a verbal lexeme L, the stem of L's ABLE derivative is X*able*.

The generalization that rules (3.a,b) are associated with trisyllabic laxing (*div*[I]*s-ible*, *div*[I]*n-ity*) while rule (3.c) is not (*div*[ay]*d-able*) is then expressible as the metageneralization in (4).

(4)   Metageneralization:
      In (3.a,b) [etc., though not (3.c)], suffixation has trisyllabic laxing as
      a concomitant.

In what follows, it will be useful to have a more succinct notation for
morphological rules and metageneralizations. I shall therefore use the
format in (5) for the formulation of morphological rules:

(5)   Format for morphological rules: $MLR_n(X) \Rightarrow Y$

The double-shafted-arrow notation in (5) is to be interpreted as follows:
When rule MLR_n takes stem X as its argument, the corresponding value is
the result of subjecting Y to all operative metageneralizations (if any). In
this notation, the rules in (3) might be formulated roughly as in (6);
correspondingly, metageneralization (4) can now be restated as in (7).

(6)   Morphological rules (3.a-c) reformulated:
      a. $MLR_a(X) \Rightarrow Xible$
      b. $MLR_b(X) \Rightarrow Xity$
      c. $MLR_c(X) \Rightarrow Xable$

(7)   Metageneralization (4) reformulated:
      Where *n* is a or b [etc., but not c], the value of $MLR_n(X)$ has
      trisyllabic laxing.

In this example, the metageneralization serves a purpose very much like that
of a construction's cophonology under the CC approach: it captures a
morphophonological generalization without presuming a system of
extrinsically ordered levels. Thus, one might assume that the morphological
metageneralizations of the RM approach are the equivalent of cophonologies
in the CC approach. There are, however, two clear differences between
them.
      The first of these is the difference in (8):

(8)   RM approach: By definition, metageneralizations generalize over the
                   classes of forms determined by two or more
                   morphological rules.
      CC approach: The cophonology of a given morphological
                   construction needn't be shared by any other
                   morphological construction.

Thus, a central assumption in Inkelas & Orgun's analysis of Turkish is that the distinctive stress pattern associated with the Sezer-stem construction constitutes the cophonology of that construction, even though no other construction shares that cophonology. Under the RM approach, by contrast, the Sezer stress-pattern must be directly assigned by the rule of Sezer-stem formation.

Given that neither the specification of a construction's morphology nor the specification of its cophonology has to express a broader generalization under the CC approach, the question arises of how to distinguish a construction's morphology from its cophonology. Inkelas & Orgun do not discuss this question in detail. They do, however, assume that except in cases of lexically prespecified stress, all Turkish stress patterns are determined by the cophonologies of the relevant morphological constructions. The tacit presumption, apparently, is that except in cases of lexically prespecified stress, a particular stress pattern can never be the morphological mark of a construction in the way that an affix might be; that is, Inkelas & Orgun seem to assume a significant distinction between the kinds of markings that may constitute a construction's morphology and the kinds that may be introduced by its cophonology.

In the RM approach, however, no parallel distinction is assumed to exist between rules of morphology and morphological metageneralizations; in particular, a stress pattern restricted to the class of forms defined by a single rule is assumed to be stipulated by the rule itself. Thus, a second difference between cophonologies and metageneralizations is the one in (9):

(9)   CC approach: Except in cases of lexically prespecified stress, a construction's stress pattern is always determined by its cophonology.

        RM approach: By definition, metageneralizations determine stress patterns only when a generalization over two or more rules is involved.

Thus, the division of labor between morphological rules and metageneralizations under the RM approach doesn't coincide with the division of labor between a construction's morphology and its cophonology under the CC approach. The difference, in effect, is that cophonologies are meant to do two things, while metageneralizations are meant to do only one: a metageneralization expresses a generalization over the classes of forms determined by two or more morphological rules, period; cophonologies express this same sort of generalization, but also serve to support a consistent theoretical segregation of stress markings from affixal markings, even in those cases in which a stress pattern is restricted to a single construction.

The segregation of a construction's affixal morphology from its stress pattern is important for Inkelas & Orgun's argument. Because they define a level as a class of constructions having the same cophonology, it is, on the one hand, important that a construction's affixal marking be separate from its cophonology---otherwise, every affix would constitute its own level. On the other hand, it is also important that stress be cophonological even in constructions having unique stress patterns. Were this not the case, neither the Sezer-stem construction nor the stressed compound construction would clearly constitute its own level, and for this reason, the two constructions would fail to counterexemplify level ordering in many of the instances which Inkelas & Orgun cite as counterexamples. My question, though, is whether there are any *independent* reasons for requiring that a construction's stress pattern count as a part of its cophonology even when this pattern is unique to that construction; that is, aside from facilitating the argument against level ordering, why should a grammar enforce a distinction between a construction's morphology and its cophonology in instances in which neither is shared with any other construction? Languages draw upon a wide range of phonological devices for the direct marking of morphological distinctions, and stress is as available for this purpose as segmentable markings are; indeed, it is not at all unusual to find an affixal difference in one paradigm paralleled by an accentual difference in another paradigm.

Consider an example. In Sanskrit, C-stem nominals often exhibit two distinct oblique stems in their declensional paradigms---a so-called Middle stem appearing before case endings beginning with consonants and a Weakest stem appearing before endings beginning with vowels. For instance, in the oblique paradigm of the perfect active participle TASTHIVANS in Table 1, the Middle stem is *tasthivát-* while the Weakest stem *tasthús-*. In this instance (as in many others), the morphological markings distinguishing the two oblique stems are affixal: the Middle stem carries the suffix *-vat* while the Weakest stem has the suffix *-us*. In the inflection of present active participles, however, the oblique stems are distinguished accentually: thus, in the oblique paradigm of the present active participle ADANT in Table 2, the Middle stem is *adát-* while the Weakest stem is *adat-*. I know of no compelling reason to assume that the accentual difference between the oblique stems in ADANT's paradigm is any less of a morphological mark of the Middle/Weakest distinction than the affixal difference between the oblique stems in TASTHIVANS' paradigm.

	SINGULAR	DUAL	PLURAL
INSTR	tasthús-ā	tasthivád-bhyām	tasthivád-bhis
DAT	tasthús-e	tasthivád-bhyām	tasthivád-bhyas
ABL	tasthús-as	tasthivád-bhyām	tasthivád-bhyas
GEN	tasthús-as	tasthús-os	tasthús-ām
LOC	tasthús-i	tasthús-os	tasthivát-su

TABLE 1. Oblique forms of the Sanskrit perfect active participle TASTHIVANS 'having stood' [Middle stem: *tasthivát-*, Weakest stem: *tasthús-*] (Whitney 1889:§461)

	SINGULAR	DUAL	PLURAL
INSTR	adat-ā́	adád-bhyām	adád-bhis
DAT	adat-é	adád-bhyām	adád-bhyas
ABL	adat-ás	adád-bhyām	adád-bhyas
GEN	adat-ás	adat-ós	adat-ā́m
LOC	adat-í	adat-ós	adát-su

TABLE 2. Oblique forms of the Sanskrit present active participle ADANT 'eating' [Middle stem: *adát-*, Weakest stem: *adat-*] (Whitney 1889:§447)

To summarize, the CC approach rests on the assumption of two distinctions whose motivation is unclear: first, some of the markings associated with a morphological construction are assumed to have lexical listings while others are not; second, certain kinds of markings are assumed to count as part of a construction's morphology while certain other kinds are assumed to be necessarily cophonological. (It's possible that these two distinctions are assumed to be coextensive; that is, the assumption may be that only lexically listed elements may function as the overt marks of a construction's morphology, and that overt nonlexical markings must be introduced cophonologically. Inkelas & Orgun don't address this question, however.) In any event, neither distinction is drawn under the RM approach.

In view of these differences, the Turkish stress patterns discussed by

Inkelas & Orgun take on a somewhat different character under the assumptions of the RM approach. Thus, consider some details of an alternative to their analysis afforded by this approach.

4. Turkish Stress under the RM Approach

In this analysis, no affix is listed in the lexicon; rather, affixes are introduced by rules such as those in (10.a-c). Rules introducing stressed suffixes, such as those in (10.b), are subject to the metageneralization in (11.a), which guarantees suffixal stress in instances in which the stem itself is unstressed. Similarly, rules introducing "prestressing" suffixes, such as those in (10.c), are subject to metageneralization (11.b), which guarantees stem-final stress in instances in which the stem is otherwise unstressed. This same metageneralization also determines the value of the rule of stem-to-word conversion in (10.d), guaranteeing final stress in any otherwise unstressed stem that is to be used as a word in syntax. The class of "polymorphemic" Sezer stems---those deriving from ordinary stems---is defined by the rule in (10.e); note that in the formulation of this rule, the Sezer stress-pattern is accorded precisely the same status as the affixal markings in rules (10.a-c). As for "monomorphemic" Sezer stems---those not deriving from anything, such as *Ánkara*---my assumption is that they are listed in the lexicon, stress pattern and all. The relation of monomorphemic Sezer stems to rule (10.e) is the same as the relation of *retribution* and *conflagration* to the English rule of *-ion* suffixation: they fit the morphological pattern defined by the rule except that there is no source (**retribute*, **conflagrate*) for their derivation. In cases such as these, one can assume---following Bochner (1992:75ff)---that underived forms which fit the pattern defined by a morphological rule are easier to learn than---and are therefore preferred to---fully arbitrary underived forms. The class of stressed compounds is defined by the rule in (10.f); metageneralization (11.b) guarantees that a compound in this class has stress on its first member, for which stem-final stress is the default.

(10) Morphological rules:
   a. Neutral suffixes:
      $MLR_1(X) \Rightarrow XlAr$ (e.g., stem *elma* → stem *elma-lar* 'apple-PL')
      $MLR_2(X) \Rightarrow XAjAk$ (e.g., stem *gel* → stem *gel-ejek* 'come-FUT')
      $MLR_3(X) \Rightarrow XA$ (e.g., stem *adam* → stem *adam-a* 'man-DAT')
      [etc.]
   b. Stressed suffixes:
      $MLR_4(X) \Rightarrow XIyor$ (e.g., stem *yap* → stem *yap-íyor* 'do-PROG')
      $MLR_5(X) \Rightarrow XArAk$ (e.g., stem *gid* → stem *gid-érek* 'go-by')

$MLR_6(X) \Rightarrow XInjA$ (e.g., stem *gel* → stem *gel-ínje* 'go-when')
[etc.]

c. "Prestressing" suffixes:

$MLR_7(X) \Rightarrow XmA$

(e.g., stem *tekmele* → stem *tekmelé-me* 'kick-NEG')

$MLR_8(X) \Rightarrow XmI$

(e.g., stem *araba* → stem *arabá-mɨ* 'car-INTERR')

$MLR_9(X) \Rightarrow XjA$ (e.g., stem *güzel* → stem *güzél-je* 'nice-ly')
[etc.]

d. Stem-to-word conversion:

Where $X \in$ {stems}, $MLR_{10}(X) \Rightarrow X, \in$ {words}

(e.g., stem *elma-lar* → word *elma-lár* 'apple-PL';

stem *gel-ejek* → word *gel-ejék* 'come-FUT')

e. Sezer stems:

$MLR_{11}(X) \Rightarrow X'$, where X' is like X except that it exhibits the Sezer stress-pattern.

(e.g., stem *kuzgun-juk* 'raven-DIM' → stem *Kuzgúnjuk*;

stem *sirke-ji* 'vinegar-AGT' → stem *Sírkeji*)

f. Stressed compounds:

$MLR_{12}(X,Y) \Rightarrow XY'$, where Y' is like Y except that it is stressless.

(e.g., stem *Orhan* + stem *bey* → stem *Orhán-bey* 'Mr. Orhan';

stem *paša* + stem *mándɨra* → stem *Pašá-mandɨra* 'pasha-farm')

(11) Morphological metageneralizations:

a. Where X is an unstressed stem, the value of $MLR_n(X)$ has suffix-initial stress. ($n = 4, 5, 6$ [and others])

b. Where X is an unstressed stem, the value of $MLR_n(X...)$ has stem-final stress on X. ($n = 7, 8, 9, 10, 12$ [and others])

This analysis has numerous advantages. Note first that the metageneralizations in (11) afford three sorts of improvements over Inkelas & Orgun's analysis. First, whereas Inkelas & Orgun treat word-final stress (e.g., *yap-tɨ* 'do-PAST') and stem-final stress before a "prestressing" suffix (e.g., *yáp-ɨn* 'do-2.PL.IPV') as independent phenomena, metageneralization (11.b) treats them as instances of a single, unified pattern. Second, Inkelas & Orgun must appeal to the "input wins" principle in (12) in order to account for the absence of final stress in cases such as those in (13.a), for the absence of presuffixal stress in cases such as those in (13.b), and for the absence of suffixal stress in cases such as (13.c); in particular, this principle must be called upon to erase lexically prespecified stresses in cases of the latter two sorts. But the formulation of the metageneralizations in (11) makes it possible to dispense with the "input wins" principle; as they are treated in the present analysis, cases such as (13.b,c) do not involve the erasure of lexically prespecified stresses. Third, the fact that all prestressing suffixes induce the same pattern of prestressing (situating stress on the immediately preceding syllable and not, say, on the second preceding syllable) is portrayed as a coincidence of lexical stipulation in Inkelas & Orgun's account; in the analysis proposed here, by contrast, the missing generalization is captured in the rule system, by means of metageneralization (11.b). By the same token, the fact that all stressed suffixes exhibit initial (rather than final) stress---again a coincidence in Inkelas & Orgun's account---is captured in the rule system by metageneralization (11.a) under the analysis proposed here.

(12) "[S]tress which is present in the input to a cophonology prevails over the stress that would otherwise be assigned by that cophonology." (Inkelas & Orgun, §8.1.1)

(13) a. Sezer stem + neutral suffix: *Ánkara-dan* 'Ankara-ABL'
          "Prestressing" suffix + neutral suffix: *gít-me-meli* 'go-NEG-NECESS'
          Stressed suffix + neutral suffix: *gel-íyor-du* 'come-PROG-PAST'
      b. Sezer stem + "prestressing" suffix: *Ánkara-mɨ* 'Ankara-INTERR'
          Stressed suffix + "prestressing" suffix:
                          gel-íyor-mu 'come-PROG-INTERR'
      c. "Prestressing" suffix + stressed suffix: *gél-me-inǰe* 'come-NEG-ADV'

A more general theoretical advantage of this analysis is that it doesn't presuppose either of the unmotivated distinctions discussed earlier: that is, it presupposes neither that affixes are listed in the lexicon nor that certain kinds of overt markings---in particular, stress markings---are excluded in principle from serving as a construction's identifying morphology.

5. The RM Approach and the Level-Nonordering Argument

In Inkelas & Orgun's analysis, the distinctive stress pattern of Sezer stems is assumed to be assigned by the cophonology of the Sezer-stem construction, which is therefore taken to be devoid of overt morphological marking. In the foregoing analysis, by contrast, this special stress pattern *is* the overt morphological marking introduced by the rule defining the class of Sezer stems; no metageneralization is needed here because the Sezer stress-pattern is unique to the class of stems defined by this rule.

Once this sort of analysis is assumed, the evidence which Inkelas &

Orgun cite in favor of their conclusion of level nonordering doesn't always clearly support this conclusion. They define a level as a class of constructions having the same cophonology; but because their notion of cophonology loses its theoretical integrity under the assumptions of the RM approach, so therefore does this conception of level. Suppose, though, that one redefined LEVEL as a class of morphological rules subject to the same metageneralizations. With this new definition, some of the Turkish examples that Inkelas & Orgun cite as evidence against level ordering no longer work. For instance, given that the diminutivizing rule of *-CIk* suffixation is stress-neutral, it's not clear that it is subject to any metageneralization, and if it isn't, then it belongs to the same level as the Sezer-stem rule (10.e) (which is likewise not subject to any metageneralization). For this reason, the fact that the *-CIk* suffix can appear either inside or outside of a Sezer stem (as in (14)) doesn't clearly constitute evidence against level ordering. Nevertheless, the fact that the prestressing *-CA* suffix can appear either inside or outside of a Sezer stem (as in (15)) would still count as evidence against level ordering, since the rule of *-CA* suffixation, being subject to metageneralization (11.b), would still belong to a different level from the Sezer-stem rule.

(14) a. *-CIk* suffix inside Sezer stem: [*Kuzgún-juk*]

                     (cf. *kuzgun-júk* 'raven-DIM')

    b. *-CIk* suffix outside Sezer stem: [*Adána*]-*jɨk* 'Adana-DIM'

(15) a. *-CA* suffix inside Sezer stem: [*Yarɨm-ja*]

                     (cf. *yarɨm-ja* 'half-sort of')

    b. *-CA* suffix outside Sezer stem: [*Istánbul*]-*ja* 'Istanbul language'

Similarly, because the stressed compound rule (10.f) is subject to metageneralization (11.b), the fact that a stressed compound can appear either inside or outside of the neutral dative suffix *-A* would likewise still count as evidence against level ordering.

(16) a. *-A* suffix inside stressed compound:

           [*gün-é+bak-an*] 'sun-DAT+look-REL (= sunflower)'

    b. *-A* suffix outside stressed compound:

           [*ortá+okul*]-*a* 'middle school-DAT'

6. Metageneralizations and Stem Choice

    In the foregoing discussion, all of my examples of metageneralizations serve to capture a morphophonological generalization across two or more rules. Before leaving the topic of metageneralizations, however, I should emphasize that they can also be assumed to capture purely morphological generalizations---in particular, generalizations about stem choice. Thus, consider again the Sanskrit facts in Tables 1 and 2, recalling that in a Sanskrit C-stem nominal's oblique paradigm, the Weakest stem appears before vowel-initial suffixes, and the Middle stem is used preconsonantally. To capture this fact, I assume that the Sanskrit rules of case suffixation are all subject to the metageneralization in (17):

(17) Metageneralization:
Where L is a C-stem nominal lexeme, X is L's Middle stem, Y is L's Weakest stem, and MLR $\in$ {case suffixation rules}:
if MLR(X) $\Rightarrow$ X[+syll]..., then stem Y supplants stem X in the value assigned to MLR(X).

Thus, suppose that the morphological rules introducing the locative singular and plural suffixes are as in (18); suppose, too, that the default stem to which these rules apply is a nominal lexeme's Middle stem.

(18) a. $\mathrm{MLR}_{\mathrm{I,[CASE:loc,\ NUM:sg]}}(X) \Rightarrow Xi$
      b. $\mathrm{MLR}_{\mathrm{I,[CASE:loc,\ NUM:pl]}}(X) \Rightarrow Xsu$

On these assumptions, the locative plural form of TASTHIVANS is---by default---built upon its Middle stem, as in (19.a); but by virtue of metageneralization (17), the corresponding locative singular form is instead built upon the Weakest stem, as in (19.b).

(19) a. The value of $\mathrm{MLR}_{\mathrm{[CASE:loc,\ NUM:pl]}}(tasthivát\text{-})$ is *tasthivát-su*.
                                                                    [by (18.b)]
      b. The value of $\mathrm{MLR}_{\mathrm{[CASE:loc,\ NUM:sg]}}(tasthivát\text{-})$ is *tasthús-i*.
                                                                    [by (17), (18.a)]

Metageneralizations similar to (17) might be assumed to account for a wide range of syntagmatically conditioned stem alternations, including, for example, the alternation of *perceiv-/percept-* in English. Inkelas & Orgun don't address the issue of stem choice; but to the extent that they assume that stem choice must be effected by means other than a construction's cophonology, this assumption would constitute another fundamental difference between the CC and RM approaches, as in (20).

(20) CC approach: ?Stem choice is never effected by a construction's cophonology.

RM approach: Stem choice may be effected by a morphological metageneralization.

7. A Final Remark Concerning Affix Position Classes

In concluding, I wish to contrast Inkelas & Orgun's notion of level with that of Inkelas 1993. In the latter paper, Inkelas proposes a level-ordering approach to the problem of affix position classes; in this approach, affixes belonging to the same position class are analyzed as belonging to the same level, so that the ordering of affix positions is simply the manifestation of a stipulated ordering of levels. The fact that this approach presumes an ordering of levels does not, of course, make it incompatible with Inkelas & Orgun's conclusions, since they do not exclude the possibility that some or all levels might be ordered as a matter of language-specific stipulation. Nevertheless, the notion of level as position class is not directly compatible with the cophonological conception of level proposed by Inkelas & Orgun, since affixes belonging to distinct position classes don't necessarily exhibit distinct cophonologies. One can reconcile the two conceptions of level by assuming that the existence of a cophonological difference between two affixes is a sufficient condition but not a necessary one for their assignment to distinct levels. It's not clear, however, that this reconciliation should be pursued, since the device of level ordering is unable to account for the full range of position-class phenomena. For instance, languages sometimes exhibit the phenomenon of reversible affix positions (Stump 1993:164ff)--- positions which appear in one order in one class of words, but in the opposite order in a complementary class of words. Thus, in relative past tense verb forms in Fula, there are four suffix position classes: class I contains affixes expressing tense and voice; class II contains a preterite marker; class III contains subject agreement affixes; and class IV contains object agreement affixes. The sequence of these suffix positions varies according to a verb's agreement features: while the default ordering is I - II - III - IV, verbs having both first-person singular subject agreement and either second-person singular or third-person singular (class 1) object agreement instead exhibit the ordering I - II - IV - III. Cases such as this one show that the ordering of affix positions in a word's morphology may vary according to that word's morphosyntactic feature content. I know of no straightforward way of accounting for this fact under the level-ordering approach; indeed, this is one of the sorts of evidence which unequivocally motivates the very different approach to position classes set forth in Stump 1992, 1993.

References

Bochner, Harry. 1993. *Simplicity in Generative Morphology*. Berlin & New York: Mouton de Gruyter.

Inkelas, Sharon. 1993. Nimboran Position Class Morphology. *Natural Language and Linguistic Theory* 11, 559-624.

Stump, Gregory T. 1992. On the Theoretical Status of Position Class Restrictions on Inflectional Affixes. In Geert Booij and Jaap van Marle, eds., *Yearbook of Morphology 1991*, 211-241. Dordrecht: Kluwer.

Stump, Gregory T. 1993. Position Classes and Morphological Theory. In Geert Booij and Jaap van Marle, eds., *Yearbook of Morphology 1992*, 129--180. Dordrecht: Kluwer,

Stump, Gregory T. 1995. Stem Formation, Stem Indexing, and Stem Choice. Ms., University of Kentucky.

Whitney, William Dwight. 1889. *Sanskrit Grammar* [2nd edition]. Cambridge, MA: Harvard University Press.

Zwicky, Arnold M. 1994. Morphological Metageneralizations: Morphology, Phonology, and Morphonology. Paper presented at the Kentucky Foreign Language Conference, University of Kentucky, April 1994.

Discussion of the Papers by Inkelas/Orgun and Stump

Brentari: I wanted to ask Sharon and Orhan about learnability and predictions that we might make with respect to the cophonology approach that you're proposing. There are lots of different places where a child, in the abstract, might find it difficult to learn a language conceived in the way that you conceive of a cophonology. It could be due to the sheer quantity of cophonologies that a language might have, or it might have to do with the variation within a language of the different cophonologies that exist, or it could be related to the complexity in a single cophonology. And I wondered if you had any speculation about what might make a language harder to learn if you conceive of morphology in this way.

Inkelas: I don't have too much to say about learnability. I guess my response would be that presumably it's the number and type of alternations that would make a language easier or harder to learn. Nothing we say is affecting that. Cophonologies are a pretty concrete way, I think, of handling the alternations that have to be learned somehow.

Orgun: According to the model we have, what the child has to learn is each morpheme and the phonological alternations that go with each morpheme. And although we have used level as a certain … mechanism, it's not necessary to come up with these level generalizations in order to produce the right language. So it seems to me that if anything it would make it easier to learn a language in which the only levels that are represented with the words are those that correspond to the morphological constructions that are represented in a word. And although we haven't talked about that, there is something that could follow from learnability issues, which is one question that we've been asked in the past: "Well, you are proposing cophonologies. How come you never have a language in which one cophonology just concatenates and the other cophonology assigns a Chinese tone system or something?" This sort of thing, presumably you could say it's lots of history or something to do with learnability.

Noyer: I want to defend Sharon and Orhan a little bit. I think the idea of encoding certain prespecifications in the representation makes certain claims about what's possible and what isn't. So Bill Idsardi spent a lot of time looking at prespecification, trying to develop a theory about what kinds of lexical specifications you might have in morphemes to override the general systematic properties of the stress system. So, in Russian you get certain stems marked with certain kinds of accentual properties, and then there's the general system of stress that applies on top of that. I think that insofar as there's a line to be drawn, really the question is what's being predicted. I'm a little concerned about the metageneralization approach because my concern is that these are plain language descriptions of the facts, and what more is being accomplished than a plain language description of the facts? That's my concern about the metageneralization approach.

...

Will Leben :   I wanted to ask Sharon and Orhan if they think that to some extent they're taking exceptions and making them the rule. I guess I want to be reassured that [for] the original kinds of cases where Lexical Phonology seemed to work, all the explanatory power that seemed to come with that can be preserved with these cophonologies. So the kind of cases I had in mind are just the early things; for example Paul Kiparsky showed, that you can get *teeth marks* but not * *claws marks*, or *mice-infested* but not * *rats-infested*—there are just certain correlations that went along with positing levels as such. Or you have the negative prefixes *in-* vs. *un-* and *non-*, and there's just a certain very dramatic coherence from knowing whether one of those prefixes was level 1 or 2. You could automatically predict facts about syllabification, nasal assimilation, and stress, and so on, and not just for those prefixes, but actually for whole classes of morphemes. Is that now kind of accidental under your cophonology approach? Are you still able to predict that things will fall together?

Inkelas: Well, we don't predict it; we make it possible to describe such cases. One possibility that Greg raised that we haven't talked about would be—say we have a bunch of affixes with the same cophonology. We haven't talked about it, but it would be possible to extract out that commonality, and say that there was this cophonology that they all subscribe to. That would certainly be a possible elaboration of what we're saying. As far as ordering facts, if it turned out that suffixes with one cophonology were always ordered inside of suffixes that had another, supposing that were true, it's also possible to capture that by placing restrictions on the order in which the morphological constructions can combine. Certainly languages need those kinds of relations all the time, whether it's for level ordering or for arbitrary affix ordering. But we haven't tried to do that for cases like English because our methodology requires us to go and look at not only the existing analyses that have generalizations about certain phonological alternations that apply within a level, but also all of the morpheme specific phonology, and we just haven't had the time to do that yet. So we don't know if we would actually want to analyze English the way it's been analyzed in the past or not.

Yip: I have a question for Sharon and Orhan, and it's really the same point that's come up in several other ways. And actually Orhan you sort of raised it yourself just now. If each affix has its own cophonology, then each affix can have an entirely different phonology, isn't that correct? So you might expect to find languages in which that's the case, and such languages are rare, perhaps unknown, so the theory must have some way of stating that the grammar is simpler if there is considerable overlap across these various cophonologies, surely. You just don't find languages in which one suffix does front harmony, a different one does ATR harmony, another assigns high tone. That's not the way things are.

Orgun: There are several things to say. One way in which you can do these things would be if there is a cophonology that every form has to undergo. We've assumed in this paper that the word level is segmental phonology. And every other cophonology would be subject to the condition that whatever structure they create will have to be something that the word cophonology will accept. It seems to me that it's probably enough to rule out the kind of language with Chinese tones in one cophonology and vowel harmony in another. Other than that, I don't think one wants to force the cophonologies ... [to] have to be similar to one another. After all, you do have languages like let's say Arabic where one cophonology would have to do the interdigitation, another would have to do simple concatenation, another would have to do infixation. The things these cophonologies do are pretty different from one another, and what is similar is the kinds of outputs that these cophonologies create. I think that that's the kind of thing we don't have a problem with, since the outputs are subject to the conditions that they will be accepted by the word-level cophonology. Otherwise you wouldn't posit those structures to begin with.

Inkelas: Also, we assume that a lot of morphology arises through grammaticalization at different periods of time, and since it's the same language, we assume that a language won't simply change into Chinese and then back into Hebrew, and so on, as things are being grammaticalized, so due to that there will be a similarity across constructions anyway. So we don't know to what extent we actually have to enforce that formally.

Orgun: It seems to me that this kind of story will also account for some cases where morphological constructions with similar cophonologies tend to cluster together in a word, but not perfectly. That's probably partly due to the fact that maybe the [words] that have similar cophonologies presumably get morphologized at essentially the same time period when the phrasal phonology was similar. That's probably part of the reason why cophonologies tend to cluster together within words.

Carstairs-McCarthy: A point to Greg, really. Greg criticized Orhan and Sharon on the ground that they impose a distinction between two kinds of what he calls morpholexical rules, namely the affixing ones and the nonaffixing ones. I in the past sympathized with something like Greg's current position, but I'm sort of coming round to a view that affixal morphology really is rather different from nonaffixal, simply because the whole Paradigm Economy phenomenon seems to effect or interact with affixation [different] from how it interacts with nonaffixal morphology. I don't know if you or the other speakers have any comment on that. That would suggest that it would be really rather important to look at closely related languages which differ in that one of them has a lot of plain concatenative affixal morphology and the other doesn't, for whatever historical reason, such as Estonian and Finnish.

Stump: I think it's an important open question; I don't think the last word is in. I don't think we should take it for granted, though, that affixes are listed in the lexicon or not. You know it may be that there is some fundamental morphological distinction between concatenative and nonconcatenative morphology, but even then the question is, "Is that a difference in whether or not the thing is lexically listed?" That's not necessarily self-evident.

Spencer: A comment for Orhan and Sharon. Concerning this question about learnability and also clustering of phonological phenomena in cophonologies, Pullum and Zwicky some while ago suggested that there's such a thing as "expressive" morphology, which is different from the rest of morphology, and what they were talking about to a large extent I think was the phonological effects of things like diminutives and that kind of business. It strikes me that you might want to say that there are clues of that sort, semantic clues in the case of expressive morphology, to guide a child to think, "Well, yeah, if we're going to have diminutives and that sort of thing, then maybe we're going to have one type of phonological effect, distinct from what you would get for just ordinary morphology." Likewise, children might be able to spot that loan words which don't quite fit the basic phonotactics of roots might undergo different sorts of phonology from the native vocabulary, and so on. Do you have any views on that?

Inkelas: Well, it sounds like a plausible way to think about acquiring these things, if certain constructions are inherently more likely to have unique cophonologies than others ...

Janda: In defining what a cophonology is, as opposed to a comorphology—which is what I think Greg is saying (the marking of categories by some deformation of the stem ...) —you'd want to constrain it. There was a workshop in September-October, 1994, where Kiparsky finally defined what phonology and morphology are. Raj Singh had organized a workshop on morphophonology where people had to draw lines, and Paul said, "If something affects more than one segment, it's morphology ." [Laughter]

  [So, regarding] *thought*, he said (roughly), "No, I give up; I throw in the towel. That's not a rule, that's stem manipulation." This is in the direction of what Greg was saying also ... So, have you thought about defining phenomena on locality principles, or the number of segments affected; otherwise, someone could ask, "Where's the line between cophonology and comorphology?"

Orgun: We haven't, but I'll tell you why we haven't. First, I think what we call a "cophonology" is more similar to an MLR than a metageneralization. Given that, what we want to capture in a cophonology, or rather in constructions, is basically everything that you don't want to list as a separate allomorph, but everything that you want your constructions to derive. So these questions about what's phonology and what's morphology aren't really the questions you can ask. For us, everything phonological that the construction is responsible for is going to the phonology or the morphophonology or whatever you want to call it. So these questions about what Kiparsky is or is not willing to call morphology, for us, it's a question of, "What alternations do you want your constructions to be able to handle, and which one's do you not want to handle." So I guess we make the same distinction, but we don't call it phonology vs. morphology. And the answer is, No, we haven't talked about this, but that's probably because everyone has talked about this, and haven't found the answer.

Inkelas: But whatever answer they find, we'll have to accommodate it.

Isomorphism and Monotonicity: Or the Disease Model of Morphology[1]

MARK ARONOFF

I entered graduate school twenty-five years ago, and in 1970 a conference of this sort would have been unthinkable. There were fewer than a dozen people in generative linguistics who had enough to say about morphology to warrant spending an entire weekend arguing about it. And if some of the papers I have heard this weekend are on target, 25 years from now, such a conference will be equally unthinkable. You won't have any morphologists to kick around anymore. Savor the moment.

More seriously, I am here to try to tie everything together. A colleague of mine asked me what I was going to talk about at this conference, and when I described my role, he said, "Ah, you are to be the elder statesman." Statesman, I hope; elder or elderly, I hope not. So, first of all, I am not going to include all the papers and responses in my remarks. In fact, I will try to mention as few of them as I can directly.

Let me start with some comments on methodology. At this meeting, we have seen two strikingly different ways of approaching morphology. The first strategy has been to use the tools that one has— those developed in the study mostly of syntax and phonology. From a practical point of view, this is eminently sensible, very American. But it has two serious flaws that I would just like to point out very briefly. First, as Stephen Anderson has noted in several places (Anderson 1992, 1993), and as in fact Andrew Spencer reminds me I also have emphasized recently (Aronoff 1994), there is what we call the "drunk under the lamppost problem". So, if we only look where the light is, we're limiting our search to what we already know, and this may prevent us from actually discovering the truth.

The second problem with this use-the-tools-that-you-already-have approach is less frequently remarked on, and hence more important, and that is what I call the Kripkean problem, which is that we call many notions syntactic or phonological because they were developed in the study of syntax or phonology, and not necessarily because they have any inherent ties to that phenomenological domain, in the physicist's sense of *phenomenology*,

---

[1] In this work, I am more indebted than usual to other people; first, to Steve Lapointe, who organized the conference—a weekend in morphological paradise; and second, the Bhavani Saravanan, with whom I have happily talked about Tamil morphology for several years. The data is hers and the analysis comes out of these conversations.

and not the philosopher's sense. For example, the notion of thematic role—I think it's a very dramatic example—lies very clearly within the field of conceptual semantics. Yet, because it was developed by syntacticians, and because it has been used by syntacticians for so long, it has become somehow syntacticized. Even the most autonomous of syntacticians will trade in thematic structures, though they are always careful to say "theta" rather than "thematic", and they don't worry about this miscegenation of levels or components. I think that similar things can happen for example with optimality theory, where there's nothing about optimality as a formalism that has anything to do with phonology, and yet, because it was developed for the study of phonology, we tend to think that it's phonology. And so when we find this miscegenation with morphology, well, that's just a caveat.

The other strategy that we have seen at this conference is almost the opposite, and that is to look precisely for those things in morphology that other subdisciplines don't seem to cover properly. This has been my own method for many years, and its flaws are also very well known. The major flaw of course is that it is somehow perverse— we have all these tools, so why not use them? I won't respond to that. In the end, I think that the choice between methodologies is almost purely aesthetic. As my mother used to say, "Whatever turns you on." I will always rankle when someone triumphantly announces that their theory of syntax or phonology can account for 90% of morphology. Other people will always wonder why I am so worried about that last 10%. I also believe quite strongly that we need both kinds of people, what the biologists call the lumpers and the splitters (though I can't help but note that the most avid of lumpers are equally avid splitters when it comes to the relation between language and general cognition).

So much for methodology. My remaining remarks will be thematic, though in a different sense from that of thematic role. When I read all of the papers and the responses, I noticed a common thread which runs through most of them, which is the question of isomorphism, so that's what I would like to talk about. This is a very old problem in linguistics, dating back at least to Jakobson's time. For Jakobson, isomorphism was a key to unlocking the inner structure of language. But for Jakobson, isomorphism was tied to the "substance" of language. So, for example, along with Russian psychologists like Luria, Jakobson was very interested in synesthesia, which they regarded as a key to the inner structure of the senses. Similarly, Jakobson would have said that the connection between vowel height and the expression of size tells about the essence of humanity. But this is in a way that no longer resonates for us, because he was interested in substance, in the inner substance of human nature. We're more interested in the more purely formal or structural aspects of language or human nature. Substantive universals have held very little charm for us since at least the days of *Aspects*.

Most recently, isomorphism has been important in the study of autonomy, and the idea has been that to the extent that two systems seem to be isomorphic or not, then we can see them as related or not. The classic example of this is the argument over the autonomy of syntax from semantics—this is Chomsky's work from the mid seventies (Chomsky 1977). He argued that to the extent that syntactic structures are not isomorphic with semantic structures, syntax can be said to be autonomous. The connection between morphology and isomorphism or nonisomorphism is at first glance parallel to that of syntax. So, to the extent that morphology is not isomorphic with syntax or semantics or phonology, we can say that it is autonomous. This has been a major theme of much work in pure morphology over the last decade, including most of my own.

But, there is in fact a deeper connection here between morphology and nonisomorphism, and that is that morphology is inherently unnatural. It's a disease, a pathology of language. This fact is demonstrated very simply by the fact that there are languages, though not very many, that manage without it—you don't need morphology— and by the perhaps more widely recognized fact that some languages like West Greenlandic or Navajo have morphology much worse than others do. I think it's clear that the notion of morphologization or grammaticalization is rooted in this disease view of morphology as being inherently unnatural, as is also Sapir's view of language, read *morphology*, as a collective art. Morphology, or grammar, is to a great extent not isomorphic, that's what makes it morphology, or as Saussure would have said, arbitrary. It seems to me that the connection between morphology and unnaturalism is dramatically illustrated in the study of juncture, which is what I'm going to talk about. Since Sapir, who attributed this observation to Bloomfield, linguists have felt that there should be an intimate tie between the closeness of the phonological juncture and the hierarchical standing of the constituents whose boundaries that juncture marks: juncture should increase monotonically with the hierarchy of syntactic constituents. One could argue from the punctuation system of the Hebrew Bible that the Masoretes believed this (Aronoff 1985, Dresher 1994), and the American structuralists certainly operated as if it were true (Hockett 1950).

If juncture strength truly does increase monotonically with constituent structure, then phonological structure is syntactic structure, in some real sense, and morphology can be dispensed with. But, the problem, as some of us have emphasized for many years, is that very often that is not true. Levels are not always ordered nor are they paralleled by constituent strength. A language may apparently have n sets of structural types, where n ranges quite widely—and if you want to see a large n, see Stanley's work on Navajo juncture, which involved twelve juncture types (Stanley 1973). This is interestingly parallel to the number of inflectional classes that a language can have, which varies for nominals from one, which is of course the minimum, to about 25 in some Arapeshan dialects (Foley 1986,

Aronoff 1994, Dobrin 1995). The point is that a language in its natural state, a non-diseased language, will show isomorphism between juncture and syntactic structure. This is demonstrated by the fact that we can order junctures monotonically in terms of their strength, and furthermore, we can even give them names, like "morpheme boundary" and "word boundary". But that is only true of untainted languages. My observation, which is only about diseased languages, that is to say most languages, is that this order is not usually isomorphic with syntactic structure. So, not all morphological boundaries occur where they should from a syntactic point of view.

I will very quickly go through some data from Tamil that demonstrate this. The basic observation is that you can see two types of junctures in Tamil words—I am using the term "juncture" just to be as atheoretical as I can—which are revealed in facts about voicing. In the close juncture, you get voicing across the juncture, which is what you find within morphemes: voiced stops appear more or less intervocalically, and the only way you can get voiceless stops intervocalically is if they are geminated. Voiceless stops also appear morpheme-initially. Tamil inflectional morphology follows this pattern. Like all Dravidian languages, Tamil inflection is entirely suffixal. A typical suffix is given in (1):

(1) vaaɹ   'live'   + -kɛ   -->
     vaaɹgɛ   'live long' (blessing)
     jɛɹid   'write'   + -kɛ   -->
     jɛɹidigɛ   '(please) write'
     kɔrid   'consider'   + -kɛ   -->
     kɔridigɛ   'consider this'

In 1, we have an inflectional suffix, -kɛ, which is an imperative or hortative. The initial stop of this particular -kɛ suffix voices—you can see it after a retroflex, and you can see that after a stem-final d you get the voiced stop with an epenthetic vowel inserted. The inflectional suffix in (2), which is the plural marker in nouns, also shows voicing:

(2) aaɳ   'man'   + -kɔl   -->
     aaɳgɔl   'men'
     tuɳı   'cloth'   + -kɔl   -->
     tuɳıgɔl   'cloths'

The inflectional suffixes, so far as I can tell, all have weak juncture. Many derivational suffixes show this same weak juncture, as shown in (3) and (4):

(3) sɛj   'do'   +-tı   -->
     sɛjdı   'news'

mərə	'forget'	+tɪ	-->
mərədɪ	'forgetfulness'		
pəgʊ	'divide'	+tɪ	-->
pəgʊdɪ	'division'		

(4)
pəɳ		+pɨ	-->
pəɳbɨ	'good manners'		
an		+pɨ	-->
anbɨ	'affection'		

But some derivational suffixes, instead of being voiced at the juncture, are in fact voiceless. So you get [k] and [t] suffix-initially in (5) and (6):

(5)
vaaɹ	'live'	+kɛ	-->
vaaɹkɛ	'life'		
vaɨ	'slip'	+kɛ	-->
vaɨkkɛ	'bald'		

(6)
vaaɹ	'live'	+tɨ	-->
vaaɹtɨ	a greeting		
kərɪd	'consider'	+tɨ	-->
kərɪttɨ	'opinion'		
jɛrɪd	'write'	+tɨ	-->
jɛrɪttɨ	'written work/script'		

Note that the suffix in (5) is phonologically identical to the suffix in 1, but shows no voicing, so that the two form a minimal pair of sorts. Note also that voiceless stops appear geminated intervocalically; when the stem ends in a sonorant rather than a vowel, there is no gemination, which is most likely attributed to the phonology of codas: the combination of the sonorant and the geminate would produce an overlong coda.

The contrast in the language between the two sets of derivational suffixes, those like the ones in (3) and (4) which show a weak juncture and those like the ones in (5) and (6) which show a stronger juncture, is not echoed semantically or syntactically: both sets pattern alike in that domain. Stepping back a little bit, since derivation is syntactically internal to inflection, what we expect from syntax, in the absence of morphological disease, is that all derivational suffixes will show a weak boundary and inflectional suffixes a stronger boundary. Such would be the case in a healthy language. In fact, most inflectional suffixes in the language show the weak boundary and the derivational suffixes are divided. That is why we say that the situation is pathological. Morphology destroys the isomorphism between syntax and phonology that we expect to find in a healthy language.

You might be tempted to say to yourself, "Well, maybe our syntax is wrong." So maybe syntactically in Tamil, for whatever reasons, the derivational system operates *outside* the inflectional system, and so therefore we would expect a stronger juncture with derivational suffixes than we do with inflectional suffixes. But the two in (3) and (4) show the weak juncture at the boundary, which means that the problem is not a syntactic one. Indeed, just as in English, some derivational suffixes are variable, with some words in that suffix showing voicing and others not, as in (7):

(7)   pəɳ   +-paari   -->   pəɳbaari   'culture'
         jɛɛr   +-paari   -->   jɛɛrpaari   'arrangement'

I will now turn to compounds, which pattern as we expect. Externally, in relation to inflection, compounds pattern normally: compounds whose members are both otherwise free show a strong juncture—as opposed, incidentally, to the weak juncture in inflection. I should note in passing that this statistically altogether normal pattern of compounds showing a strong juncture regardless of the juncture shown in inflection is a puzzle for syntactically based theories of juncture. Internally, looking only at compounds, there is a difference between free and bound stems. The stem in (8) is bound and does not occur freely by itself in the language.[2] With such bound stems you get voicing, as (8) shows:

(8)   maa   'mango'   +-kaa   'vegetable'   -->
         maaŋgaa   'unripe mango'
         maa   'mango'   +-mərəm   'tree'   -->
         maamərəm   'mango tree'
         maa   'mango'   +-jɛlɛ   'leaf'   -->
         maavɛlɛ   'mango leaf'

When you look at free stems, you get the voiceless stop showing up inside compounds. So because you can say vaaɹɛɛ all by itself to say 'banana plant', then in vaaɹɛkka (which literally means 'banana vegetable', because the unripe fruit is used as a vegetable), the suffix is voiceless -*kka* in contrast to the -*ga* in the word for 'mango' in (8) (*maaŋgaa*). There is also no linking consonant of the sort that is found with the *maa* compounds in (8). Compounds with *vaaɹɛ* exactly parallel to those in (8) are shown in (9), and they show strong rather than weak juncture:

(9)   vaaɹɛ   'banana'   +-pəɹəm   -->
         vaaɹɛppaɹam   'banana fruit'

---

[2] The [n] in *maaŋgaa* 'mango' is one of these empty linking morphs that one finds in classical Greek compounds and Germanic compounds.

vaaɹɛ   'banana'   +-jɛlɛ   'leaf'   -->
vaaɹɛjɛlɛ   'banana leaf'

The pattern shown in (9) is normal in the language. Most compounds are formed on free stems and show strong juncture. What's most important about the contrast between (8) and (9) is that it too is normal, but cross-linguistically. We expect to get closer juncture when there is a bound stem because the structural syntactic and semantic connection there is closer and because the stem doesn't occur by itself; it only shows up in these lexicalized forms. Whereas with stems which are not inherently bound, we expect to find the more open juncture.

Why is this important? It's important because this normal case shows you that there is in fact a hierarchy of juncture strengths. We can order juncture strengths in terms of the phonological connection between the elements. The strength of the junctures is monotonic in some sense, but the function from juncture strengths to syntactic constituency is not monotonic. So we know what it means to increase juncture strength. We can perhaps even measure that. But, if you map that index of juncture strength against syntactic structure it goes up and down. That's what morphology is; it's an unnatural mapping between components.

References

Anderson, Stephen R. 1992. *A-Morphous Morphology*. Cambridge: Cambridge University Press.

Anderson, Stephen R. 1993. Wackernagel's Revenge: Clitics, Morphology, and the Syntax of Second Position. *Language* 69: 68-98.

Aronoff, Mark. 1985. Orthography and Linguistic Theory: The Syntactic Basis of Masoretic Hebrew Punctuation. *Language* 61:28-72.

Aronoff, Mark. 1994. *Morphology by Itself: Stems and Inflectional Classes*. Cambridge, Mass.: MIT Press.

Chomsky, Noam. 1977. *Essays on Form and Interpretation*. Amsterdam: Elsevier North-Holland.

Dobrin, Lise. 1995. Theoretical Consequences of Literal Alliterative Concord. In *Papers from the 31st Regional Meeting, Chicago Linguistic Society*, 127-42. Chicago Linguistic Society, University of Chicago.

Dresher, B. Elan. 1994. The Prosodic Basis of the Tiberian Hebrew System of Accents. *Language* 70:1-52.

Foley, William A. 1986. *The Papuan Languages of New Guinea*. Cambridge: Cambridge University Press.

Hockett, Charles F. 1950. Peiping Morphophonemics. *Language* 26: 63-85 (Reprinted in Martin Joos, ed., *Readings in Linguistics I*, 315-28. Chicago: University of Chicago Press).

Stanley, Richard S. 1973. Boundaries in Phonology. In Stephen R. Anderson and Paul Kiparsky, eds., *A Festschrift for Morris Halle*, 321-47. New York: Holt, Rinehart, and Winston.

Some Remarks on the Morphology-Syntax Interface

Steven G. Lapointe

As part of our advertising for the conference, we sent out notices to various local media organizations, including the *Davis Enterprise*, which characterized the conference in the following way: "Linguistics Program at UC Davis is hosting a conference on morphology (syntax), beginning today and running ..." Now you all may think of this as a typo, because you know what the name of the conference ended up being, but since the *Davis Enterprise* is the source of all knowledge and wisdom around here, I'm afraid the phonologists present are out of luck. The *Enterprise* says it's syntax, so that's that.

Unfortunately, I didn't have a chance before the conference to dig out a neat set of morphosyntactic facts to build a moral around. I think that's OK, though, since I view my job at this point as bringing back into the foreground a number of issues that we were discussing, and in some cases tiptoeing around, back during the sessions on Friday, issues which we might have, if not forgotten, at least pushed further back into our little gray cells. What I want to do is to talk about two broad issues related to the question of interpenetrability of morphology and syntax, one having to do with head movement, the other having to do with compounds.

Turning to issues relating to head movement then, as I understand it—and to say that I understand it may be stretching things a bit—the main idea behind head movement through functional categories was that it was supposed to capture a number of facts simultaneously, at least some of which are the ones in (1).

(1) a. Assignment of case to NPs
     b. Scope properties of functional elements
     c. Joining of inflectional morphemes with their morphosyntactic hosts
     c.´ Order of inflectional morphemes with respect to their hosts

I've undoubtedly left some things out here, and that can also be a point of further discussion.

The original idea was that we could not only account for the joining of morphemes in inflectional head positions with their morphosyntactic bases, but we could actually account for the order of those morphemes with respect to their hosts. As has been noted, I believe, in at least one paper and perhaps several at this conference, a number of people have backed off from this stronger claim, which I have listed as (1c´). I bring it and (1c) up here for the purpose of underscoring some of the issues again. As Peggy Speas has noted in a number of works (Speas 1991a, 1991b), and as I believe that Mark Baker mentioned in his talk, head movement alone doesn't give the order of morphemes. All it does is move a lexical head and adjoin it to a morpheme in a higher functional head position, as in (2).

(2)

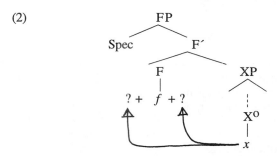

In fact, in one of Peggy's articles the concession is made that not all of the inflectional material should be generated in syntax via head movement, and the conclusion is that some sort of checking theory can be used only to constrain, but not completely determine, morphological order. Such a conclusion seems quite compatible with the arguments that Hagit made in her paper, and also in other of her recent work (e.g., Borer 1991), that syntactic categories have to be kept separate from morphological categories, so that it makes sense even within a Principles and Parameters setting to talk about X^0 words in the syntax, but something else—call them 'W words' or some such—in the morphology. In addition, in the same works Hagit has argued that UTAH, the Uniformity of Theta Assignment Hypothesis, or the Universal Alignment Hypothesis, cannot be taken as the driving force behind NPs having to appear in particular positions in D-structure.

Now, if we put these points together—the ones that Hagit has been making and the one that Peggy has made in her earlier work—it seems to me, at any rate, that much of the motivation for head movement has disappeared. If UTAH doesn't enforce where NPs are in D-structure, then it would seem that they could just as easily appear in their surface positions to start out with and could receive case by some means other than through interacting with functional nodes. That would leave just the scopal properties of functional elements in (1) that would need to be dealt with. Now, we could pull back a bit from what I just said and instead say something like the following: "There's still some purely syntactic motivation for head movement through functional categories, so long as we also recognize that there's something else that has to be doing the actual work of getting the morphemes to occur where they need to occur."

Presumably, that something else is the "disease" of morphology. That in turn leads to the question of how to actually carry out the realization of inflectional morphemes. Distributed Morphology is an answer that Halle and Marantz and Rolf and others have given to this question, but as this question appears to be separate from the details of the syntactic considerations involved, it seems to me that one could at least in principle wed a realizational sort of morphology onto a reduced head movement sort of syntax.

Before I move on to talk a little bit about compounding, I want to make two small side comments, lest any of the presenters from the syntax and morphology sessions on Friday feel that I have failed to abuse them sufficiently. First, in the case of the *-ize* affixation facts that Shelly and Patrick discussed, if we set aside what I think are Patrick's reasonable comments about possible analyses that Hale and Keyser could present for the case that Shelly suggested they would have problems with, and if we accept the UTAH for the sake of the present argument, then I think that Hale and Keyser are OK for the two cases that Shelly mentioned. All they have to assume is that *-ize* actually has two different lexical meanings, since under UTAH that means that they ought to have two different deep structures. Under those assumptions, then, we could maintain both of these derivations that Shelly gives in her (10) and (14) simultaneously.

(3) (= Lieber's (10))

(4) (= Lieber's (14))

Now, Hale and Keyser probably wouldn't be inclined to accept the assumptions I've just suggested, but my point is, if they did, they would be partly ceding the argument to Shelly that there are in fact multiple, distinguishable lexical meanings for *-ize*.

Second, I also wanted to repeat, again for purposes of highlighting it, a point that David made about Peter's paper, which some of us pursued rather inconclusively at dinner, which I wanted to throw back out on the table for other people to think about again. If basically the only languages that have the Philippine style voice marking systems are the Philippine languages, do we really want to say that they form a separate type, parallel to nominative-accusative languages and ergative-absolutive languages? If it's true that the only languages with this kind of voice marking system are the Philippine languages, and this is I think an open empirical question at the moment, then we probably wouldn't want to say that they are a separate type from the other two, but then the question arises as to how to tie them together with the other kinds of systems. That's where the discussion at dinner ended completely inconclusively. It's likely that part of the answer has something to do with the fact that these languages are verb initial, but that can't be all there is to it, since there are plenty of well-known verb initial languages that have, as it were, well-behaved case and voice systems, so the question remains, What else is going on here? We couldn't figure it out; if anybody else has any suggestions, that's certainly grist for the proverbial mill.

Now, going on to compounding. Contrary to what Mark Baker was suggesting in his comments, it's not entirely clear to me that a large percentage of the properties of compounds in English can be handled syntactically. In the case of synthetic compounds in English, most researchers who have written on this topic have simply assumed that the Theta-role assignment, or whatever corresponds to that in one's favorite theory, works in an exactly parallel fashion — modulo the issue of directionality — in VPs, when a V assigns a thematic role to its direct object NP, and in synthetic compounds, when the V inside the second element assigns the thematic role to the first element, as sketched in (5).

(5) a. V   NP

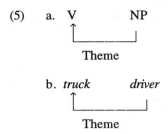

Theme

b. *truck*   *driver*

Theme

It's not entirely clear that those two processes are the same. Minimally, the entities that are being linked to the predicate-argument structure are vastly different, as Jerry pointed out in his talk. So, in the case of Theta-role assignment in the syntax, the Theta-role assignee is a full NP which comes with all of its attendant function words, modifiers, and relative clauses, and whatever else we can pack into a NP. In compounds, the theta-role assignee is a single N with none of the rest of that stuff. Further, as Jerry also pointed out, the N inside of compounds is typically bleached of all meanings except, in some sense, the basic meaning of the N. In particular, it typically is bleached of meanings having to do with number and definiteness and so on, whereas these semantic notions are all expressed or are at least expressible in NPs. Indeed, given these distinctions, we might be led to think that syntactic Theta-assignment is carried out by whatever mechanism is responsible for linking NPs to lexical predicate-argument structures in one's favored framework, whereas in compounds, some different mechanism is involved, say one which, intuitively, "plugs" one of the arguments of the second element in the compound with the first item in the compound.

Exactly how one implements this V argument plugging varies from theory to theory. One way we could think of this is to say that the variables in the predicate-argument structures for the items end up getting identified, so that whatever quantifier actually binds, in this case, the second argument of the V, it will automatically bind the argument for the leftmost element, as suggested in (6).

(6) $truck\,'(w)$ & $drive\,'(x, y)$ $\longrightarrow$ $truck\,'(y)$ & $drive\,'(x, y)$

Actually, I don't care about these details here; all I am trying to do is to point out that it is possible to formulate a mechanism that manipulates argument structures which is distinct from Theta-role assignment in the syntax and can be exploited in accounting for the properties of synthetic compounds. Also, I should note that nothing that I've said answers the question of why it's the second of the V's arguments that gets plugged in these sorts of cases, but there are ways of accounting for this fact in a framework which separates out the two kinds of linkages.

A related point about synthetic compounds that I wanted to mention is this. People who are inclined to use head movement in accounting for the properties of synthetic compounds could well respond by saying, "Well, look Steve, the reason why full NPs in the syntax can have number and definiteness and the like expressed in them is that they contain functional phrases for those notions, whereas the Ns in compounds don't, and that's why we simply don't find those notions present in the semantics of compounds." It would be perfectly OK, I think, to say that, but it would also effectively be admitting that there is in fact a difference between the morphology and the syntax in the generation of these forms.

The final point that I want to make about compounds concerns the relations between modifiers and head Ns in syntactic phrases vs. compounds. If we look at that relation in the syntax, particularly in English, I don't think it is clear that the correlations are all that straightforward. There are modifiers of various categories—APs, PPs, CPs—none of which are NPs. Now, while the AP modifiers in the syntax typically occur to the left of the head N, the others *must* occur to the right, and even certain kinds of predicative APs can appear to the right, in familiar looking sets of data like those in (7).

(7) a.   the linguists [at the conference]
     b.   the linguists [who fell asleep at the conference]
     c.   the linguists [overly proud of their accomplishments at the
          conference]

However, in the N-N compounds, which are the major culprits here, the non-head, modifying element is a N, a nominal element, and it appears exclusively on the left. Several people, including Shelly in her book (Lieber 1992), have offered accounts in terms of syntactic mechanisms to try to unify the properties of the modifiers in NPs and the properties of modifiers in N-N compounds. It's not clear to me that any of these approaches have been completely successful, in part because, as I suggested earlier, the elements involved in compounds are different from the elements occurring in full NPs, and so they have rather different properties. So, it's not obvious that one can claim so freely that properties of compounds are largely attributable to the action of syntactic mechanisms. Of course, I'm saying all this so that we can talk more about it, and I am hoping that these comments will engage further debate on these issues.

References

Borer, Hagit. 1991. The Causative-Inchoative Alternation: A Case Study in Parallel Morphology. *The Linguistic Review* 8:119–158.

Lieber, Rochelle. 1992. *Deconstructing Morphology: Word Formation in Syntactic Theory.* Chicago: University of Chicago Press.

Speas, Margaret. 1991a. Functional Heads and the Mirror Principle. *Lingua* 84:181–214.

Speas, Margaret. 1991b. Functional Heads and Inflectional Morphemes. *The Linguistic Review* 8:389–417.

General Discussion

Carstairs-McCarthy: I wanted to pick up Mark's point about morphology being a disease. It seems to me that if one has a certain assumption about what language is for—that language is for efficient communication of information, requests, instructions, etc.— this is true. On the other hand, if you think language is a device for making sure that the noises we make contrast, well, morphology may not be a disease; it may be one way of ensuring contrast. There are languages which take, you could argue, a rather banal and utilitarian approach to the task of ensuring contrast, or avoiding synonymy, and that is by assigning meanings which are utilitarian ones out there—they're meanings like "tree" and "run" and so on—and they just compose these syntactically, and there you have contrast achieved, and at the same time communication facilitated. But, one could envisage a language which operated totally at the opposite extreme, and this has actually occurred to me [as] what Derek Bickerton envisages in his novel about dolphins. He suggests that dolphin language is a kind of glass-bead game, that essentially these highly intelligent creatures are just creating art most of the time; it's ephemeral art, of course, because it's just sound, unrecorded. And you could see some kinds of morphology as a sort of synonymy avoidance which is more in the direction of art—it doesn't do any good, for the purposes of communication, but it does ensure contrast.

Yip: I detect a certain value judgment here between the banal languages and the artistic ones. It's slightly worrying. [Laughter]

Lapointe: So where does English fall?

Carstairs-McCarthy: Oh, it's fairly utilitarian—

Lapointe: Yes, I think so.

...

Sadock: I'd also like to jump to the defense of languages suffering from galloping morphitis, such as the one that I've been studying for a long time. I agree with Mark Baker that there really is a stable type, that involves not just the morphology alone, but ramifications throughout the

426

grammar of the language. And the Eskimo languages, for example, show absolutely no sign of changing in this regard. They're identical [in] their general grammatical form, even though they've been separated for 2500 years. All that ever happens is they disappear all of a sudden, altogether, but they never sort of collapse, and I don't think they could. I think there's something about the entire build of the language, the way its morphology fits its syntax and semantics, that produces a quite stable type.

Baker: Just a footnote: Mohawk, too, is disappearing, and it's under pressure from English. There are loanword nouns in Mohawk, but there's not a single loanword verb, as far as I can tell, and you can imagine why. I'm sure it's not completely immune from language death things, but there's very little interference, because it's such a different system.

Aronoff: Well, it's very difficult to borrow verbs in any language. A colleague of mine did statistical studies on that, and across a wide variety of languages, borrowing verbs is just really rough.

Carstairs McCarthy: Well, it's interesting, [in] Turkish they borrow verbs, but they do it by having a little auxiliary, or whatever.

Perlmutter: What they're borrowing, they're making it into a noun.

Carstairs-McCarthy: They're making it into a sort of nominal, yeah.

Janda: I have a question ... Since we're cognitive scientists (since we're linguists), if morphology is a disease, then it must be a mental disease, and then what morphologists are is the R.D. Laing of the psychiatric world: we believe these people [with morphology] are not sick, and everyone else actually is—

Sadock: Thought should be incarcerated. [Laughter]

Janda: Yes, but we think we should get all these people on our couch. So, Mark, I would like to know what these languages [without morphology] are. Are you buying Mark Baker's line and saying that compounding doesn't count as morphology? I don't know of any languages that have neither affixation nor compounding.

Aronoff: Yes, I am buying that compounding is not morphology.

...

Sells: I wanted to pick up on this idea of stability or non-stability. Whenever I've said what I said about the Philippine languages, one obvious reaction is, "Well, it's something about what else is going on in these languages that makes them be that way." I tend to think it's the other way. There are various things that one can see in the Philippine languages that I think sort of conspire to show things the way they are. So, the key thing about the voice system basically is that when the agent is not the subject, it's still a direct argument rather than an oblique, and in general, for either the nominative-accusative or ergative-absolutive systems when the thing that isn't the unmarked subject isn't the subject, it's not an oblique, and in fact, there is no real notion of unmarked subject, at least in the morphological sense. They're verb-initial, that seems to be something to do with it, and then there's also this idea that the overt nominative that you see is not actually the subject itself. When you move off the Philippines, then that clustering begins to break down. But I think it's sort of mutually self-supporting, but it's not that as soon as you break any one of those pieces, the others automatically all fall away, but they do tend to fall away. So, for example, if you go to Indonesian, which is SVO, then the voice system basically reduces to a two-way voice system, but you still can see vestiges of the actor being a direct argument when it's not the subject. At least in Malay, I think in Indonesian, too, that sort of *by*-phrase marker is *oleh* with a noun phrase, and when the passive agent is marked with that as a prepositional phrase, it can basically float around in the clause. On the other hand, you can just have the actor bare, in which case it must appear right adjacent to the verb, and I suspect in that case it's still a direct argument. And if you look at Chamorro, for example, in Chung's analysis, the language is underlyingly VOS, and to get the right order for the subject, she lowers the subject from a final high SPEC position back down into the clause, which I take as kind of what I was saying—that really the overt subject you see is actually an adjunct, and that its subject properties are defined independently of its surface position. So, I think that is a different system. I think that it's a mistake to try and fold it into one of the other two systems, but what you want to explain is how there is a clustering of properties that goes with that. I can assert that one is there, but I don't know how to explain that clustering. And then, once that breaks down, it's like these other cases of breakdown that we've been hearing about, that somehow we start losing one of the pieces, and then the whole sort of house of cards falls down, and you fall back to either a nominative-accusative or an ergative-absolutive system. For whatever reason, those are much more prevalent cross-linguistically, and presumably more stable. So I think for the point that you made about how those languages fit in, that that's the view that I would take. I certainly don't have a problem with saying that right now, they're the only languages in the world that have those particular properties.

Baker: Well, maybe I can bring something up for a general topic of discussion. It will be biased [by] my own interests, believe it or not, a little bit. One of the things that Steve pointed out in his remarks was the whole topic about head movement and the correlation between case assignments, scope of functional projections, inflection joining to heads. The strongest claim you could get is the order of inflectional morphemes, but you don't seem to get that exactly right, so you need to put in some caveats or some extra stuff. You get some morphology there, some disease, I think, on almost anyone's view. The thing that I'm intrigued about is—well, here's my impression about morpheme order, and I would be happy for it to be corrected by other people here, and I would be happy to drive out more work on this kind of question. My impression is that morpheme order is—I don't know, some of you were giving statistics before—but it's 80% predictable or 85% predictable from the syntax. Some pretty high percentage, but a long way from 100%, so, the 10% that Mark cares about is there too. So I think you want a system that will get you the order of morphemes predictable from the syntax in many situations, but you want to be able to tinker with it a bit to get the facts that you see. And what kind of theory will allow you to do that? To stir things up a little bit, I can see Distributed Morphology, that's the kind of facts that it's apparently engineered to explain. If you take things that look in many cases the same, such as Chomsky's Checking Theory, Hagit's Parallel Morphology, maybe Jerry's autolexical syntax, if you get something that has enough power to get that extra 10% that you need, you're in danger of losing your 80%. What do we do about that?

Janda: There's always a dichotomy here between people who are interested in realization and those who are not. I can reveal that someone here said to me today, "Yesterday was much more interesting than the day before, because we got into realization." I think, Mark, you're [not] talking about order of realization, but in fact, whether you get all suffixes or all prefixes, or something like *non-unfriendlinesses* in English, where you'd be going back and forth, and so can't predict the ordering at all, given the syntax.

Baker: Suffixes and prefixes?

Janda: You can predict the order of addition of these things, yes, but not whether the language will have all suffixes or all prefixes, or alternate in placing them.

Baker: I think in the polysynthetic languages, you can, and maybe I've been more influenced by this idea than I should have been—

Janda: In certain languages, you certainly can, but as a general proposition?

Baker: Well, here I will give the impression that I got lying on my couch, in the Center for Advanced Studies in the Behavioral Sciences, not doing my work ... Anyway, the point is that I picked out these polysynthetic languages because they all had noun incorporation, and then I studied their syntactic properties. And, three years later, I realized that they all had the same morpheme order—not quite, and Chukchee has some problems, but 90% have the same morpheme order, and that includes whether it's prefix—

Aronoff: What is the 10%?!

Janda: Where is the incorporated noun, on the left or the right of the verb?

Baker: The incorporated noun is always on the left of the verb root.

Aronoff: But where are the affixes?

Baker: It's subject agreement – object agreement – incorporated noun – verb – higher predicate things like causative, desiderative, etc., in order of their scope – aspect – tense.

Janda: And this is independent of the syntactic word-order?

Baker: Well, the syntactic word-order is free. They're non-configurational languages. And there are exceptions that you have to make. I have some data from Matthew Dryer, who collected a lot of this stuff. So, let's take the higher predicate affixes like causatives, desideratives, purposives like *go* and *come*, and so on. In my seven language families (it's a nice, small group; I can actually read the grammars of all those language families—Jerry keeps trying to make me expand it, but then I can't read all the grammars) if you look at those, they're always suffixes.

Now, suppose we try to look beyond that list of languages. You could say that morpheme order is predictable in this type, that's part of the parameter, that's a possibility that I would seriously consider. But suppose you look more broadly; what do you find? Well, I had lots of help from Matthew Dryer on this. He printed out his database on order, and you come out with the following. Desideratives are suffixes in 93% of the world's languages, something like that. Causatives are suffixes in 66% of the world's languages. So, [for] desideratives, the correlation is not [quite] perfect, we've got Mark Aronoff's whatever percent, but it's very good. [With] causatives, there seems to be something else going on. Now, you look at causatives, and they show up as prefixes in Southeast Asia, Papua New Guinea, a few places in Africa and Central America, you ask what else do these places have in common, and they're all places where you have—

Spencer: And in Chukchee, I'm afraid.

Baker: Chukchee, there it's a circumfix—

Spencer: Well, the basic thing is a prefix, and the suffix bit has other functions as well. So, the *real* causative morpheme is a prefix.

Baker: That's interesting ... But, anyway, I'm pontificating, so don't interrupt me with facts. [Laughter]
    The interesting thing that stands out to me is that Matthew Dryer's [data] collapses Southeast Asia and Australia, but in Australia, you don't have serial verb constructions, and it's always a suffix. In Papua New Guinea, you have rampant serial verb constructions, and it's a prefix. If you look in these serial compounding things, what you always see (I have no idea why) is that the order of morphemes in a complex verb mirrors the order you'd see in a serial verb construction. So that suggests to me that really the order is predictable for causatives. It is predictable from the syntax, but there are two syntaxes of causative. If you have serial verbs, anyway, there's a sort of serial structure, you know that independently. If you don't have serials, you use a complementation kind of structure, and you get the other order. If you look at any of these things, you find plenty of exceptions, but it seems to me like there's a big truth there in something like 95% of the cases.

Aronoff: Yeah, I just want to respond to this subject-prefix thing, very briefly, because there, of course, you have an interesting separate factor which has been worked on by lots of people, which is the fact, although we still don't know why, that suffixes are much more prevalent than prefixes, overwhelmingly, and that in fact, outside Athabaskan, you get very few exclusively prefixing languages. People have tied that to a sort of purely cognitive reason. Now, I don't know whether that's correct or not—

Baker: Right, but it shows up differently in the different factors, is what I think's important. So, again, here's more from Matthew Dryer's database. The tense-aspect things are suffixes 85% of the time, or some very high number. The agreements are suffixes 50% of the time, prefixes 50% of the time. There are other things one could tie this to, but one thing you can tie it to is the fact that [with] tense ... you'd really get some mileage out of saying those are functional categories, with scope properties that are definable the way Steve was alluding to, whereas agreements aren't.

Aronoff: You also get mileage out of Bybee-type accounts—

Baker: Oh, absolutely ... I think generativists need to pay more attention to those facts.

Aronoff: So maybe if we take all of those, if we take the pure processing stuff, and we take the syntax, and we take the pragmatic stuff and we stick them all together, we'll be able to account for 90% of the data, and the rest is—art.

Lapointe: I have a quick question ... how is it, having the tense and aspect markers as higher heads, going to get them as suffixes? I missed that.

Baker: The pitifully simple thing I said in my talk, which is not nearly as elegant as what everybody else said in their talks, [is] that the way that incorporation works—I'm not sure this fully works—but you throw out the morphological subcategorization frames. You make it impossible for a morpheme to say "I'm a prefix" or "I'm a suffix," and you say that when you do the incorporation, it always adjoins to the left. That gives you the order of noun incorporation, it gives you the order of causatives, it gives you the order of desideratives.

Borer: I wanted to relate to another aspect of what you said, and that's the redundancy aspects. So basically what you said is, suppose we assume that there was in fact a component of morphology that was doing a lot of this word-formation, then we seem to be missing on the 80% of what the syntax could do, and in fact that seems undesirable, in a sense that I agree with, in the sense that if the syntax can do so much, and then you just shift something to another component for the other 20%, then you seem to be missing some kind of a generalization—

Aronoff: That's only if you believe in reducing redundancy.

Borer: That's true. But that was something that Mark implied, namely that basically you would be failing to capture the fact that there is a correlation there between morphosyntax [and syntax]. In the way that I view morphology, it is not necessarily a problem, because I don't think that the syntax does your morphology for you, but I think the syntax can create environments for the application of morphological rules, but I think that the evidence for the existence of morphology is not whether or not the syntax could or could not get you something or another, but the existence of forms which have identical morphology but different syntax. So that way, you could say something like the morphology had gotten to apply to these forms, maybe as a result of syntactic input, maybe not. But morphologically, they're identical, and by morphology, I really just mean gluing together morphemes ... in a particular way, and the resulting properties would just follow from the fact that in some cases you do have a syntactic structure, and in some cases you don't. So, the fact that you *do* have a syntactic structure corresponding to some of these things is exactly built into the system, in the sense that when you do have it, the properties will be of a particular nature, and when you don't have it, they will be different—the syntactic properties, not the morphological ones.

Baker: Yeah, that aspect I fully agree with. It's sort of Mark Aronoff's point about juncture again, too, that you can get different syntaxes with the same morphology. That's a very important fact that your system is designed to capture. The thing that I had in mind is something more boring; maybe it's more prominent in Chomsky's Checking Theory, but if you make it so that the syntax builds you this abstract thing, and then you consult with the morphology to see how to pronounce it, you're in danger of losing the structure of the syntactic thing, once you start consulting the morphology. Here's the critical aspect of Distributed Morphology that comes up there—they don't replace it word by word, but they replace it morpheme by morpheme. That's what could protect the structure that you want to maintain.

Borer: Concerning theories like checking theories, and in general what would be my quibble [with] abstract representations, let's say abstract representations of morpheme in the syntax which you then spell out—I just think there are some pretty serious counterexamples to this, where it turns out that abstract representations, which are spelled out by means of particular forms, behave one way, and if they're spelled out by means of other forms, they behave completely differently. And so, it really seems like there might be something very concrete sitting there in the representation.

Noyer: What is your -EN? Is that phonologically concrete?

Borer: No, it's not phonologically concrete, but it's morphologically concrete.

Noyer: Well, that's the question. We're talking about phonological realization. I mean, your theory is an abstract morphology. It has a thing that's abstract.

Borer: There is a certain abstract feature to it, but I don't assume, for instance, that you can decompose every word, if it's not morphologically decomposable. So I'll give you a very specific example. Suppose you took in Hebrew borrowed forms from English, that do not have a verbal source, but which mean exactly the same as a derived nominal form from a verb plus a nominalizing suffix, they would behave differently, morphologically and syntactically differently, even though, if you try to decompose them, according to some kind of abstract representation— especially if you try to assume that words have some kind of conceptual structure that corresponds to some abstract nodes on the tree, then you would have to give the borrowed word for *transformation* and the native word for *transformation* exactly the same representation, but the one that is borrowed behaves very differently in terms of how the verbal properties do or do not come to be realized syntactically from the one that's native. So, that leads one to think that if you do decompose and if you do give abstract representations, they have to be at least sensitive to the existence of a distinct morpheme, even if the phonological representation of the morpheme may be more abstract in nature. In other words, -EN definitely has an abstract phonological representation, that's obvious, but as a morpheme, it's a unit which is independent just from its function as a passivizer ... There's not much else I can say.

Noyer: Well, I agree with what you're saying, it's just a question of whether they're abstract entities.

Borer: OK, that's why I said morphological and not phonological, and not semantic.

Sells: Mark said something like, "If you know you can get this stuff from the syntax, why don't you?" It seems to me in many languages the only evidence of what you would have in the syntax is from the morphology. But there are cases where the morphology works differently. So, in Japanese if you look at the suffixes that follow the verb, the suffix that marks whether you're being sort of plain, or polite, or super-polite, comes before the tense suffix. So you have the order verb stem, level of speech, and then tense. Adjectives in Japanese also take suffixes, and you get the other order, so you get adjective, tense, and then level. And, in Korean verbs, you get the opposite from the Japanese verbs, so in Korean verbs, like Japanese adjectives, you get verb, tense, speech level. There's no evidence that I've ever seen for any syntactic hierarchy of functional categories that anybody has ever shown for these languages. So, the only evidence you could have is from the order of morphemes, but the order of morphemes is precisely flipped in some cases. Andy has a paper, on similar cases with nominal morphology in various European languages, I think. And so, I just don't understand what it means to say "if you can get it from the syntax," because in many languages I don't see the evidence in the syntax.

Spencer: Picking up on the remark about nominal inflection. My feeling is that it is actually worse than that. It's actually a counterexample, and the argument is frighteningly simple. In a noun phrase—DP, whatever you want to call it—if you've got possessive agreement and case-marking, possessive agreement is internal to that syntagma—it's a relationship between the possessor and the possessed, and it's nothing to do with anything outside—whereas case-marking is to do with outside, whether you've got a verb [that] marks it, or a preposition mark[s] it. So, the only order that you can get [for] these morphemes, from the syntax, is first possessor and then case, which means that Finnish doesn't exist, and I don't see any way around that argument. That's just a footnote to Peter's remark.

The question I wanted to ask is one I've been wanting to ask for years and years, which is— [Laughter]

Sadock: Now's your chance—

Lapointe: Unburden yourself, please!

Spencer: I shouldn't have said that—

Janda: Lie down—

Sells:　　　What is the solution to that exercise on page 300? [More laughter]

Spencer:　　It was a misprint. I shouldn't have said that because if my question sounds really dumb, then I could have blamed it on jet lag. But the question is this: Suppose we all do agree on this 85%. What follows from this, given that we also agree that a hell of a lot of morphology comes from earlier syntax? And provided the syntax hasn't changed really radically, then of course you don't get the same kind of order. Except in the case of English synthetic compounding, and then in one or two other cases—Navajo presumably must have switched at some stage, given it's SOV, and the affixes are OSV—so why do we need to build this explanation into the architecture of grammar? And as a corollary of that, suppose formal semanticists came up with a theory of logical form, where they said, "Well, it's basically predicate calculus, and there's some parameters as to whether it's Polish [order], or not Polish order, and so forth ... and we can predict 85% of the syntax."

Borer:　　Actually, I'll make it even stronger. 85% of the sentences that people utter are subject-verb-object, and the rest of the 15% is what we've been doing, right? So, I mean 85% is very little. It's just above chance, as far as I'm concerned.

Carstairs-McCarthy:　　Worldwide?

Borer:　　No, I mean, in other languages it's verb-subject-object, but it doesn't matter. Most of the stuff around is straightforward, right? And the other 15% is why we say nothing is straightforward.

Baker:　　I sort of forgot what the question was that was burdening Andy so much—

Spencer:　　Well, if we agreed on this 85% isomorphism, why can't we just say, "Well, this is kind of uninteresting, it's really history.

Baker:　　Right. First of all, I'm not sure I'm convinced. I won't deny that there's a big interaction between history and morpheme order, but take the generalization I gave about the polysynthetic languages, in particular Mohawk. I don't know enough about historical linguistics to know about time frames, but this is typical—it's got a very rigid morpheme order and a very free word order, and it's been like that back to Proto-Iroquoian and

Proto-Macro-Siouan, and so on. What it was back in the dawn of time I don't know, but I'm not sure that that's what's determining the morpheme order in those cases, especially when you take the fact that the seven language families from around the world have the same morpheme order, although in Australia we know it came from verb-final languages, for example. Maybe that's what you'd expect for some of them, but not for others. Moving on to Peter's case about the politeness morphology and Andy's case about Finnish, there are a couple of things one could say, and this will raise Hagit's question, maybe. About the politeness morphology in Korean and Japanese, there are two things one could say: there's something about the syntax of politeness that I don't understand, but if I did, I could predict the morpheme order from it—since I know nothing about politeness, that's a logical possibility. The other thing, which is probably more likely, is that we're talking about something that's in the 10%, we're focusing on something that's in the 10% that I've conceded. We come to Finnish, and it's the same thing. I'm actually told that it's not clear that case is actually doing the same thing in all of those languages, when you look at things like conjunctions and scope. That would be in my view the best thing, where you get some interaction with some other syntactic stuff that's interesting. The only reason why it's the best view is because it does uncover those kinds of interactions. Or, it's in the 10%. And that then leaves Hagit's question about is 90% a big ratio or not a big ratio and how you interpret that. I don't know—

Aronoff: If I could just respond quickly to the Finnish example. [In] Dravidian, it turns out that postpositions have cases, and so what you get is many words where you have stem-case marker-postposition-case marker, with a different case marker, because the postposition demands a certain case marker of the noun, and it has its own case marker, because most of these postpositions were originally nominals to begin with. And so you can get some pretty weird orders out of that, and I know that in Finnish the boundary between case markers and postpositions is pretty fuzzy, so, that may buy you something.

...

Borer: Maybe I can give you a concrete example about the 90%, if that's what it is. Take something like LGB Binding Theory, or for that matter any of its precursors. And compare this with a binding theory that is purely thematically-based, that just says something like, "An agent will bind a patient, a patient will bind whatever." The only obstacle to the thematic based binding theory, and to any kind of binding theory that is based entirely on argument structure information and lexical entry, are cases of what used to be known as raising-to-object, what has become raising-to-object again recently. So, these are really the only cases that seem to be, at least in English, prima facie problematic to a completely thematic theory of binding. These are, by far, the minority of the cases; most of the cases are extremely well-behaved. And yet, the existence of these particular forms was sufficient, and I think rightly so, to say that the Binding Theory is something structural, and not something thematic, and here is the reason why it's got to be structural. So, 90%, in this case, in my opinion, is missing precisely the 10% that can shed light on whether it's this theory or that theory.

...

Noyer: I wanted to respond to Andy's remark about Finnish. I think I concur pretty much with Mark on this point. I'm rather concerned that we not naïvely apply labels such as "case" to different phenomena. Specifically what has been called "case" might arise in a number of constructions, as we know automatically, from the syntactic use of "case": a noun can pass the Case Filter in a number of ways. So morphologists, myself included, have a tendency to look at a grammar and take the labels that structuralists apply to phenomena very seriously. Then, we take another grammar, and we take another label, and we say, "Case in this language works like this, case in this language works like this, they don't work the same, therefore they can't be compatible, no theory can account for both of them." But that presupposes that they're both case. Now this is a big problem. In Finnish, and Finno-Ugric in general, I think what's going on is that sometimes what is called "case" is something internal, and sometimes it's something external, maybe assigned by a functional projection outside of the determiner phrase, or whatever. So, that's my first caveat.

My second caveat is that I'm very nervous about all of this discussion about 90% and 100%, because, after all, what is our project here? Is our project to write books that capture all the facts? Or is our project here to try to understand how children learn language? I hate to sound like I just got off the plane from Building 20, but this really is a concern that I have. I mean, what are we trying to find out? Are we trying to write a book that says, "OK, in this language I've got all this art"? OK, that might be interesting, but, what I want to know is what do children come into the world expecting to see, and how do they get to the final state, where they know that thing?

Sells: The answer might be art—

Lapointe: I'm not sure we can't do both—

Noyer: Well, OK, maybe so, but this question is like, "Who gets to claim the prize of having written the Book that's got all the facts in it?"

Sells: No one—

Borer: It's the right theory that explains 100% of the facts.

Spencer: What are the learnability problems in morphology, that are comparable to syntax? Where is the poverty of the stimulus problem in morphology?

Baker: I think in Mohawk, there is. I mean, if you look at any traditional structuralist grammar, I haven't seen one yet that fully predicts the order of morphemes. They don't give you all of the facts about when they all go together.

Perlmutter: To say something about the point Rolf is raising, the point of typology is to give us some idea of what is the class of possible human languages. If you want to conceive of it in psychological terms, as you're doing, then presumably the child is expecting that the language it encounters will be one from this class of possible human languages. Typology can tell us something about the extent of this class, thereby indirectly telling us something about the range that the child has to consider, or expect in those psychological terms.

Carstairs-McCarthy: I think there's an aspect of the 10% which people haven't talked about yet. We're talking as if the 10%, the oddities and so on, has to do with order and degree of fusion. But—surprise, surprise—I think there's something missed out there, which is the paradigmatic dimension. A feature of the 10% is that you have allomorphy, you have different forms which sort of do the same job, but they're distributed in some fashion or other. Well, now there is a question which arises: "Why doesn't the paradigmatic dimension loom so large with the 90%?" And, there's a sort of answer you could give, which is the 90% has to do with objects which have vast privileges of occurrence, and you couldn't possibly learn that we have object A and object B which kind of partition the space of occurrences, and in the 10% area you're dealing with objects which are bound, and which therefore have limited privileges of occurrence, and it's learnable that there should be this kind of allomorphy. Well, then the important question, it seems to me, is, "Does UG have anything to say about this part of it, the paradigmatic dimension?" It's possible it has nothing to say, and that this is an aspect of language which is just learned from the data. That seems to me one of the big questions about morphology: "Does UG have anything much to say about the paradigmatic dimension with regard to bound forms?" And that's not something which syntax has any parallel in.

Sadock: I think Mr. Spencer has put the red meat on the rug, and Hagit started to deal with it, but we really need to consider semantics ... Not only is a lot of morphology sort of redundantly specified in syntax, or vice-versa if you want to look at it that way, but then when you bring semantics into the picture, we've now got a 3-way turf war, a Balkan conflict on our hands. And, the way these turf wars always work in linguistics, is as follows. Hagit's example was a very good one. You say, "Well, you can deal with 90% of the cases, but there's this residue of 10% of the cases and you can't deal with them. *I* can deal with them, then the entire pie is mine. I own it all." But on the other side, you can only deal with 90% of the cases syntactically, and some cases remain intransigently, let us say, semantic. So, even in binding, we hear people say things like, "While walking home they stole my car," right? Then we say, "Well, you're not supposed to say that ... " But why *do* people say it? Because of the thematic properties of the sentence, and that's what allows us to say that sort of thing. We have to recognize that perhaps, as Mark very briefly mentioned, redundancy exists and isn't a bad thing. Maybe all three of the components that we're particularly interested in—syntax, morphology, and semantics—largely do everything. But—

Sells: (You just made some people on your left [some of the phonologists] really unhappy—)

Sadock: But the 10% lack of overlap is what indicates that there actually are three things. If there were complete overlap, there'd be only one thing.

...